Challenges for America
in the Middle East

To Laird Graeser, a very special friend!
R. W. M.

To my Berry students, who challenge and inspire
me every day.
K. L. T.

Challenges for America in the Middle East

Richard W. Mansbach
Iowa State University

Kirsten L. Taylor
Berry College

FOR INFORMATION:

CQ Press
An Imprint of SAGE Publications, Inc.
2455 Teller Road
Thousand Oaks, California 91320
E-mail: order@sagepub.com

SAGE Publications Ltd.
1 Oliver's Yard
55 City Road
London EC1Y 1SP
United Kingdom

SAGE Publications India Pvt. Ltd.
B 1/I 1 Mohan Cooperative Industrial Area
Mathura Road, New Delhi 110 044
India

SAGE Publications Asia-Pacific Pte. Ltd.
3 Church Street
#10-04 Samsung Hub
Singapore 049483

Acquisitions Editor: Michael Kerns
Development Editor: Elise Frasier
Editorial Assistant: Zachary Hoskins
Production Editor: Olivia Weber-Stenis
Copy Editor: Talia Greenberg
Typesetter: C&M Digitals (P) Ltd.
Proofreader: Theresa Kay
Indexer: Sheila Bodell
Cover Designer: Janet Kiesel
Marketing Manager: Amy Whitaker

Printed in the United States of America.

Library of Congress Cataloging-in-Publication Data

Names: Mansbach, Richard W. | Taylor, Kirsten L.

Title: Challenges for America in the Middle East / by Richard W. Mansbach, Kirsten L. Taylor.

Description: Thousand Oaks, California : SAGE Reference/CQ Press, 2016. | Includes bibliographical references and index.

Identifiers: LCCN 2015042982 | ISBN 9781506308227 (pbk. : alk. paper)

Subjects: LCSH: Middle East—Foreign relations—United States. | United States—Foreign relations—Middle East. | Islamic fundamentalism. | Terrorism—Religious aspects—Islam. | Terrorism—Prevention—Government policy—United States. | Arab Spring, 2010- | Arab-Israeli conflict. | Islam and politics—Middle East. | Shiites—Political activity—Middle East.

Classification: LCC DS63.2.U5 C435 2016 | DDC 327.73056—dc23 LC record available at http://lccn.loc.gov/2015042982

This book is printed on acid-free paper.

SFI Certified Sourcing
www.sfiprogram.org
SFI-00453

16 17 18 19 20 10 9 8 7 6 5 4 3 2 1

Brief Contents

PART IV: THE SHIA CRESCENT   229

Detailed Contents

1 | Sources of American Foreign Policy   1

2 | Competing Currents in U.S. Foreign Policy   29

PART I: ARAB SPRING OR ARAB WINTER? 57

3 | America and the Arab Middle East before the Arab Spring   60

15 | Conclusion: America and the Complex Middle East 285

List of Tables, Figures, and Maps

TABLES

FIGURES

MAPS

1

Sources of American Foreign Policy

Israeli prime minister Benjamin Netanyahu and U.S. president Barack Obama discuss the Palestinian peace process

Reuters/Kevin Lamarque

The Middle East often seems like a "special case" to students of foreign policy in the United States: especially troubled, especially hard to understand, especially enmeshed in a set of seemingly unique and intractable political, social, and economic issues. While that is in some ways true, it is also possible—and we think quite useful—to approach policy toward the region and the issues it faces the same way we would begin to understand policy toward any other region or set of issues. Such an approach allows us to view challenges in the region as normal problems of foreign policy. Even the most intractable problems have potential solutions, and our ability to manage these challenges is limited by the same factors that constrain U.S. foreign policy in other regions and issues. Our first chapter lays out a framework that articulates the key influences on U.S. foreign-policy formulation and implementation, regardless of issue area. Specific sources of foreign policy relevant to key challenges in the Middle East are discussed in the opening chapter of each of the book's four parts—the Arab Spring (chapter 3), radical Islam (chapter 6), Israel and Palestine (chapter 9), and the Shia Crescent (chapter 12). Readers will see these sources at work in the successive chapters that explain the historical development of the challenge and present-day dynamics and U.S. foreign-policy efforts. As we examine the key factors influencing how the United States formulates and implements its foreign policy toward the region, you will discover that these factors are the same ones that influence America's policy toward other regions. We begin by discussing how the foreign and domestic arenas have become intermingled in a globalized world and then examine the several sources of foreign policy.

THE LINKAGE OF DOMESTIC AND FOREIGN POLICIES

Recent decades have witnessed growing links between domestic and foreign policies. Indeed, President Barack Obama came to office in 2008 promising a foreign policy based on domestic values. However, globalization has been a long process, and the mixing of the two arenas is not entirely new. America's domestic policies were profoundly affected by wars in Korea and Vietnam, and more recently in Afghanistan and Iraq. International organizations such as the World Trade Organization and the North American Free Trade Association have a direct impact on America's domestic economy. Conversely, domestic policies on trade, taxation, economic investment, and even civil rights have had a significant impact overseas. Indeed, it is frequently the case that issues that arise in a domestic context have consequences overseas. Thus, the appearance of a fourteen-minute film trailer posted in July 2012 on YouTube, featuring a blasphemous treatment of the Prophet Muhammad, produced rage throughout the Islamic world after it appeared on Egyptian television.

More recently, the Republican-controlled Congress tried to force President Obama to declare additional sanctions against Iran even while negotiations with that country regarding its nuclear aspirations were continuing, and John Boehner, then the Republican Speaker of the House of Representatives, invited Israeli prime minister Benjamin Netanyahu to address Congress about the dangers posed by Iran and Islamic terrorists, issues that Republicans believed the president did not take sufficiently seriously. The president, who did not get on well with Netanyahu, with whom he disagreed strongly on several issues—including Iran—was not consulted, and he declared he would not see the Israeli leader when he came to Washington. Netanyahu then authorized expansion of West Bank settlements, which Obama opposed. Obama regarded Boehner as exceeding his role as House Speaker and intruding on the president's leading role in foreign affairs. He also viewed Netanyahu's acceptance and the actions of Israeli ambassador Ron Dermer as gratuitous interference in America's domestic affairs. And after the March 2015 framework agreement with Iran, the Senate, led by Bob Corker (R-TN), chair of the Foreign Relations Committee, sought to force the president to obtain its approval for any final agreement. Obama agreed to allow Congress to reject an agreement, but its vote could be vetoed by the president.

All states are subject to external influences, and their external environment is in turn affected by domestic events, as the cases above involving countries in the Middle East and the United States illustrate. Foreign policy is the point at which influences arising in the global system cross into the domestic arena and domestic politics is transformed into external behavior. The traditional view was that America like other states is sovereign and, as such, controls its boundaries and territory, is subject to no higher external authority, and is the legal equal of other states. This perspective assumes that sovereign states have a clear and unitary national interest and that their governments interact directly with one another and with international organizations. It also assumes that publics and domestic interest groups in different societies do not interact directly with those in other societies. Instead, they present their views to their own governments, which then represent them in relations with other governments. Figure 1.1 illustrates this traditional perspective in which interstate politics remains distinct from domestic politics.

The traditional model is inadequate to describe the full range of factors shaping foreign policy, and events in the Middle East—especially in recent years—have sharpened our awareness of its limits. We have seen the emergence of powerful nonstate actors that pose transnational threats and also those that challenge the sovereignty and security of existing states in the region, like Israel or Syria. In the Arab Spring, we have observed popular movements overturn regimes that we once thought were so deeply entrenched that they were resistant to revolution, and we have seen many of those same populations rise up in protest against U.S. policies in the region. Indeed, in this region, the domestic and foreign arenas have become so blended that they are impossible to disentangle. In the words of former secretary of state Hillary Rodham Clinton,

FIGURE 1.1   Model of State-Centric World

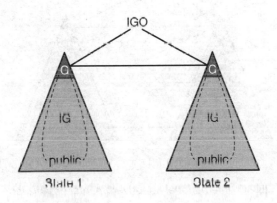

G	*government*
IGO	*intergovernmental organization*
———	*classical interstate politics*
------	*domestic politics*
IG	*interest groups*

Source: Adapted from Robert O. Keohane and Joseph S. Nye Jr., "Transnational Relations and World Politics: An Introduction," *International Organization* (Summer 1971), 332–334.

[I]ncreasing global interconnectedness now necessitates reaching beyond governments to citizens directly and broadening the U.S. foreign-policy portfolio to include issues once confined to the domestic sphere, such as economic and environmental regulation, drugs and disease, organized crime, and world hunger. As those issues spill across borders, the domestic agencies addressing them must now do more of their work overseas, operating out of embassies and consulates.[1]

Figure 1.2 presents a picture of a world in which external and domestic factors interact directly. The domestic pyramid of policy formation is penetrated at several levels, and links among governments and domestic groups are multiplied to reflect the complex exchanges that occur. Thus, there is interaction among interest groups at home and abroad and governments, among interest groups in different states, and among interest groups and both international organizations and nongovernmental organizations.

Israel poses an especially complicated problem for America in that every challenge the United States faces in the Middle East is in some fashion made more difficult by American support for that country—for

FIGURE 1.2 Model of Transnational World

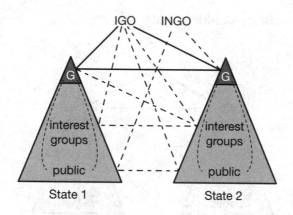

INGO   *international nongovernmental organization*

———   *classic interstate links*

------   *domestic links*

– – –·   *transnational links*

IGO   *intergovernmental organization*

G   *government*

Source: Adapted from Robert O. Keohane and Joseph S. Nye Jr., "Transnational Relations and World Politics: An Introduction," *International Organization* (Summer 1971), 332–334.

FIGURE 1.3 Communications Model of Israeli Recognition, 1948

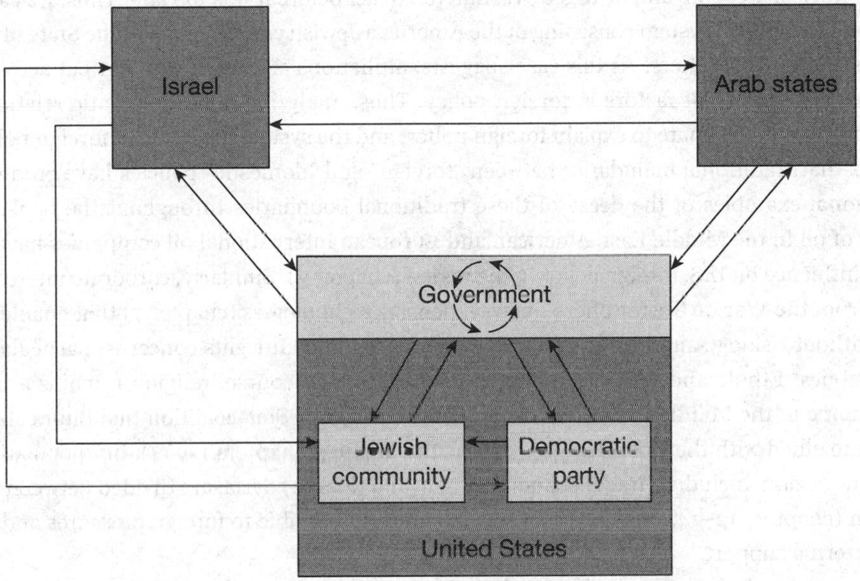

Source: Raymond F. Hopkins and Richard W. Mansbach, *Structure and Process in International Politics* (New York: Harper & Row, 1973), 135.

which there is a vocal domestic constituency—and the resentment that support generates within states in the region, including those on which the United States has long relied for oil to fuel its economy. Some of this complexity was reflected by American recognition of the State of Israel. Israel declared its statehood in 1948, a presidential election year in America. Both candidates had to take a position on the question of whether to recognize Israel, but it was especially important that Harry Truman, the incumbent Democrat, adopt a favorable attitude toward the new state because he sought Jewish political and financial support in key states like New York. For President Truman, Israelis constituted a significant constituency because of their links with America's Jewish community. Truman adopted a pro-Israeli policy, despite objections from the Departments of Defense and State, which feared that recognition of Israel would alienate oil-rich Arab states. Figure 1.3 represents schematically the links among groups in 1948 that interacted in relation to the question of recognizing Israel. Arrows represent the flow of communications among key actors. To understand Truman's decision, we would have to describe communications between him and other government officials, between the government and groups like the Jewish community and the Democratic Party, and between the U.S. government and those of other countries.

   A similar link between the domestic and external arenas involving the Middle East was evident during the 2012 U.S. presidential election. In a televised debate on October 16, 2012, President Obama and Republican candidate Mitt Romney vigorously disputed the origins of the assault on the U.S. consulate in Benghazi that climaxed with the death of America's ambassador. Earlier in the campaign, Governor

Romney had visited Israel, where he had sought to depict Obama as hostile to Israel and weak toward Iran. Injecting himself into the campaign, Israeli prime minister Benjamin Netanyahu thereafter gave a speech at the United Nations in which he declared that Iran was approaching the point where it could produce a nuclear weapon, and he urged Washington to act before it was too late. Thus, we can describe an issue-based political system consisting of the American Jewish community and the State of Israel that cuts across national frontiers. As this case suggests, affiliations and identities that cut across national boundaries are important factors in foreign policy. Thus, analyzing only diplomatic relations among governments is not adequate to explain foreign policy, and the systematic study of foreign policy entails awareness that traditional boundaries between "foreign" and "domestic" policies have eroded. We will see additional examples of the decay of these traditional boundaries throughout the book. Since the discovery of oil in the Middle East, American and European international oil companies have exerted a powerful influence on U.S. foreign policy in the region (chapter 3). Similarly, corporate interests seeking to profit from the War on Terror offered new, expensive technologies (chapter 7) that enabled America to fight without risking American lives but that also raised human-rights concerns, particularly among foreign publics. Ethnic and religious identities matter, too. Of course, religion remains a profoundly powerful force in the Middle East, where Iran leads an informal Shia coalition that Sunni states, many of which are allied with the United States, view as threatening (chapters 13–14). But populations of key states in the region, including Iraq, Lebanon, Yemen, and (less so) Syria, are divided between Sunni and Shia Islam (chapters 12–14), making their regimes more susceptible to foreign pressures and in greater need of external support.

Moreover, globalization has facilitated the movement of persons, things, and ideas across national boundaries, making those boundaries more porous. Even a superpower like America is "penetrated" by flows of illegal migrants, illegal drugs, and subversive ideas. For its part, Washington employs a variety of tools to penetrate foreign societies—propaganda favoring democracy and human rights in countries like China and Russia, illicit assistance to opposition groups in hostile states like Iran, foreign aid to friendly governments, and financial and political support for American corporations like Boeing. We will see evidence of these flows throughout our study of the U.S. foreign policy of the Middle East. The massive flow of people from conflict in Syria, for example, has spread instability across porous borders to Lebanon, Turkey, and Jordan from the region into Europe. These same porous boundaries also enable the Islamic State (ISIS) to recruit from abroad, allow Hamas to smuggle weapons into Gaza, empower Iran to traffick arms to Hezbollah, and facilitate the spread of radical Islam.

SOURCES OF U.S. FOREIGN POLICY

Let us now examine the major sources of influence on U.S. foreign policy. We shall discuss five categories of factors that influence American policy-making: external, governmental, societal, role, and individual.[2] The degree to which these affect foreign policy varies by country, and any assumption that the United States can have a single, coherent "Middle East policy" is necessarily faulty owing to the substantial political, social, and economic diversity across the region. For example, the United States is a large, democratic country with a high level of economic development. As such, it has a large government with numerous foreign-policy agencies and bureaucracies, as well as innumerable and active societal pressure groups. And, increasingly, interest groups at home and abroad are linked transnationally. External factors, while important in shaping U.S. foreign policy, are likely to have a greater impact on small countries like Tunisia, Bahrain, or Jordan because they are more dependent on trade and allies for economic and military security. Societal factors are likely to have less of an impact on countries like Egypt and Syria, which have authoritarian governments that limit the freedom of social groups, unlike the United States, which is an open society governed by democratic norms and the rule of law. In addition, in large countries like America, the impact of particular individuals like the president, while substantial, is likely to be constrained by the host of bureaucratic and social actors competing to have their views taken into account. In the chapters that follow, you will see how each of these factors (many of which are internal to the United States) shapes U.S. foreign policies in the Middle East.

External Factors

Globalization itself, as perhaps the leading external constraint on foreign policy because interdependence dilutes American sovereignty, makes the United States increasingly vulnerable to the actions of other countries and, as the opening paragraphs of this chapter reflect, makes those countries vulnerable to American policies. Globalization also is a key source for the disappearing distinction between domestic and foreign policy. President Obama explicitly recognized growing global interdependence when, upon entering office, he spoke of the need for multilateral cooperation to tackle "common problems." Thus, globalization and the interdependence of the U.S. economy with economies worldwide were largely responsible for the rapid spread globally of America's subprime mortgage crisis in 2007–2008, and Obama declared that restoring U.S. influence abroad required reinvigorating the economy at home. In a word, American economic recession became a global contagion.

The porosity of its borders makes the United States vulnerable to flows of people, things, and ideas from abroad—for instance, cyberattacks, extremist political views, drugs, diseases, terrorists, and any interruptions in patterns of trade. One such vulnerability became apparent after 9/11 as U.S. officials came to understand how al-Qaeda operatives used *hawula*—a traditional way of moving money across borders that relies upon networks of trusted individuals instead of banks or other officially monitored mechanisms—to finance their operations in the United States and Europe. America's longtime reliance on imported oil offers an illustration of the vulnerabilities produced by interruptions in trade patterns. Dramatic changes in the price or supply of oil fuel growth—or produce recession, as did supply shocks in 1973 and 1979.

Other external factors of great significance are the distributions of resources and attitudes in the global system. America's own resources—economic, military, political, and social—are part of the country's domestic environment, but the *distribution* of such factors elsewhere are external and must be considered by decision-makers in Washington. American decision-makers must ask what U.S. capabilities are *relative* to those of potential friends and foes rather than what is the *absolute* level of American capabilities. Thus, American military and economic capabilities have declined significantly since the end of the Cold War in relative terms, though not in absolute terms.

Although some observers conclude that "America will never again experience the global dominance it enjoyed in the 17 years between the Soviet Union's collapse in 1991 and the financial crisis of 2008,"[3] this does not imply that America is in the midst of absolute decline. As political scientist Joseph Nye observes, "The word 'decline' mixes up two different dimensions: absolute decline, in the sense of decay, and relative decline in which the power resources of other states grow or are used more effectively." This leads Nye to conclude, "A smart-power narrative for the twenty-first century is not about maximizing power or preserving hegemony. It is about finding ways to combine resources in successful strategies in the new context of power diffusion and 'the rise of the rest.'"[4] Nye also reminds us of the interdependence of domestic and foreign policy in arguing that challenges to U.S. strength include remedying the American economy, ending the political stalemate between Republicans and Democrats, and reforming immigration policy to encourage the inflow of talented individuals from overseas.

In addition, Americans have become increasingly preoccupied with domestic issues, which they believe should take precedence over involvement abroad—particularly in the Middle East, where policy solutions seem so far beyond American control. Nevertheless, it is not that the United States has less absolute military or economic capability—"hard power"—than it did in the 1990s, but rather that other countries such as China and India have significantly increased their own military and economic capabilities. The United States remains the world's only "superpower," but new centers of military and economic power have emerged in the global system. With less relative power, it becomes more challenging politically for the United States to intervene in faraway places like Libya, Iraq, or Syria, where clear national interests do not appear to be at stake.

The distribution of political views and ideologies is equally important. If emerging centers of military and economic power are American allies and friends, the relative decline in U.S. resources matters far less than if those new centers are American enemies or potential enemies. The fact that Great Britain, France, and Israel have nuclear weapons does not concern Washington because they have been allies for many years. Indeed, as U.S. allies they enhance America's military reach and capability. By contrast, the growth in China's nuclear capability, the acquisition of nuclear weapons by North Korea, and the possibility of Iran acquiring them pose serious problems for American national security because those countries are rivals and possibly enemies of the United States.

The importance of attitudes becomes apparent in other ways as well in the Middle East. The wars in Afghanistan and Iraq and the Great Recession at home sapped American global influence, especially its reputation, or "soft power"—a fact reflected in the hostile attitudes of growing numbers of Muslims toward the United States. Indeed, one reason why President Obama in June 2009 spoke in Cairo of "a new beginning" was that American popularity among Muslims globally had fallen precipitously owing to wars in Iraq and Afghanistan, tensions with Iran, and U.S. support for Israel. According to the White House press secretary, Egypt had been selected as the site for the speech because it "is a country that in many ways represents the heart of the Arab world, and I think will be a trip, an opportunity for the President to address and discuss our relationship with the Muslim world."[5]

Geographic location is also an external factor of importance, though perhaps less so now than in past decades. Historically, the United States has enjoyed the protection of two great oceans, the Atlantic and the Pacific, which also serve as highways for trade with Europe and Asia, respectively. In addition, America's northern and southern neighbors, Canada and Mexico, are relatively weak countries militarily and are in the main close political and economic partners of the United States. Geographic location remains an important factor in the Middle East. Contrast the security historically afforded the United States by geography with the insecurity of a country like Israel, whose dangerous neighborhood includes

MAP 1.1   Israel and Neighboring States

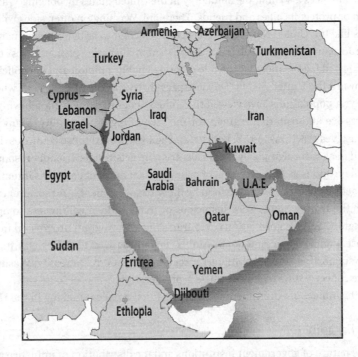

adversaries such as Iran, Syria, the Palestinians, and terrorist groups such as Hezbollah in Lebanon to the north and Hamas in the Gaza Strip to the southwest. It is hardly surprising that Israel, surrounded by foes and with a relatively small population and territory (both societal factors), is preoccupied with military security and has both literally and figuratively sought "to wall itself" off. Other countries in the region also face increased vulnerabilities by virtue of their neighboring other unstable states, as Turkey, Lebanon, Jordan, and Iraq do owing to their proximity to Syria.

At the same time, globalization has, however, also reduced the overall impact of geography. Notwithstanding the protection of the oceans, America is vulnerable to intercontinental ballistic missiles (ICBMs) as well as terrorists and cyberattacks. It is dependent on raw materials located thousands of miles from its shores. Economic and financial interdependence, the growth of global markets, and the growing role of technology in the movement of funds globally make Americans vulnerable to economic decisions or difficulties in all corners of the world, but especially in the Middle East, where much of the world's energy is produced and where terrorism and insurgency threaten to spread political and economic instability.

Other external factors also affect policy decisions. As noted above, alignments and alliances such as the North Atlantic Treaty Organization (NATO) and the less formal U.S. alliance with Saudi Arabia, combined with the strong political, economic, and social ties among the members of such alliances, enhance overall U.S. capabilities and facilitate the projection of U.S. power around the world. The security relationship with Saudi Arabia was critical, for example, to the U.S. effort to support anti-Soviet *mujahideen* forces in Afghanistan in the 1980s and to conduct the Persian Gulf War to oust Iraqi forces from Kuwait in 1991. On the other hand, alliances also limit the autonomy of the United States by obliging Washington to act in certain ways to aid or protect its allies and friends. Therefore, Washington often sides with its ally Israel in diplomatic forums like the United Nations and has been reluctant to criticize the human-rights abuses of allied regimes like Jordan and Hosni Mubarak's Egypt, thereby alienating peoples across the Middle East.

A final set of external factors includes the role of foreign public opinion and the policies and actions of other countries toward the United States. This is especially true in the Middle East, where in places like Egypt, Iraq, and Syria populations have viewed the United States negatively for allowing—if not outright supporting—oppressive authoritarian regimes for the sake of regional stability. Many policies of other countries are themselves reactions to U.S. policies and actions toward those countries. Indeed, reciprocity explains a good deal of foreign policy. As a rule, friendly acts trigger friendly responses, and hostile acts produce hostile responses. One problem, of course, is that another country's intention is not always clear, and that its actions may be misunderstood by those in government. And so, after decades of hostile relations, many in the United States were suspicious of Iran's sudden willingness to open communications with Washington. And, as negotiations over Iran's nuclear program progressed in 2015, U.S. allies in the region, most notably Israel and Saudi Arabia, feared the United States was turning away from them and directly supporting Iran's ambitions for regional hegemony. In reality, Washington was—and remains—far more concerned with limiting nuclear proliferation.

Let us turn to the impact of governmental factors on foreign policy–making in the United States.

Governmental Factors

Such factors as the nature of government institutions and the distribution of influence among them; the means by which personnel are selected, recruited, and promoted; the bureaucratic and societal interests that are their constituents; and the degree to which government institutions are accessible to societal concerns are all relevant to American foreign policy. The size of government bureaucracies matters as well. Thus, the larger and more complex such bureaucracies are, the more information they can absorb and the greater attention they can pay to problems. On the other hand, as bureaucracies grow larger, more individuals must approve decisions; "red tape" increases; and, in general, it takes longer to make policy decisions. The following are key governmental factors that influence U.S. policy-making, regardless of issue or region, although we offer examples of their role in the formulation of U.S. policy toward the Middle East.

Separation of Powers Among the constitutional factors that influence U.S. foreign policy–making is "separation of powers" among the branches of government—executive, legislative, and judicial. The authors of the Constitution intended this by distributing authority among the branches of government and constructing a system of checks and balances to prevent any branch from accumulating too much power. The separation ensures that there will be a fragmentation of decision-making authority in American policy-making.

Constitutionally, the president is "Commander in Chief of the Army and Navy of the United States, and of the Militia of the several States," and has responsibility for overseeing the major foreign-policy bureaucracies—the Departments of State and Defense; the Central Intelligence Agency (CIA); and the National Security Council (consisting of the vice president, the secretary of state, the secretary of the Treasury, the secretary of defense, and the national security advisor), which serves to coordinate foreign-policy planning for the president. Other agencies with both domestic and foreign-policy responsibilities include the Treasury; the Bureau of the Budget; the Office of National Drug Control Policy; the Federal Bureau of Investigation (FBI); the Bureau of Alcohol, Tobacco, Firearms, and Explosives; and the Departments of Homeland Security, Agriculture, Justice, and Commerce. Some of these agencies have grown more important in recent decades. For example, the Treasury and Commerce Departments and the Office of the U.S. Trade Representative have expanding responsibilities in an era of economic globalization, and the intelligence agencies, along with Homeland Security, have a special role in combating terrorist threats.

These agencies frequently have overlapping responsibilities—for example, the State Department and the National Security Council—and may compete with one another for primacy in particular issue areas. Indeed, the position of national director of intelligence was established in 2004 with an eye toward coordinating intelligence activities following intelligence failures regarding 9/11 and Iraqi president Saddam Hussein's alleged program for developing weapons of mass destruction (WMD). Nevertheless, coordinating the activities of powerful intelligence agencies such as the CIA, the Defense Intelligence Agency, the National Security Agency, the Department of Homeland Security, the FBI, and the State Department's Bureau of Intelligence and Research remains a daunting task.

Presidents share their role in making foreign policy with Congress. Article II, Section 2, of the Constitution states: "He shall have Power, by and with the Advice and Consent of the Senate, to make Treaties, provided two thirds of the Senators present concur; and he shall nominate, and by and with the Advice and Consent of the Senate, shall appoint Ambassadors, other public Ministers and Consuls. . . . " Moreover, Congress is vested with responsibility to "provide for the common Defense," "raise and support armies," and declare war.

On some occasions presidents have asked for and received resolutions from Congress short of declarations of war, while on others they have used NATO and UN resolutions as the bases for committing troops to combat. The presidency affords considerable latitude in foreign affairs and, despite the constitutional requirement that only Congress can declare war, the presidential prerogative to commit U.S. combat forces overseas has grown dramatically since President Franklin D. Roosevelt had to cope with an Isolationist Congress before World War II. There were no official declarations of war for conflicts in Korea (1950–1953), the Dominican Republic (1965), Vietnam (1965–1973), the Persian Gulf (1990–1991), Somalia (1992–1993), Bosnia (1992–1995), Kosovo (1999), Afghanistan (2001–2014), Iraq (2003–2011), and Libya (2011). To rein in presidential power to go to war, Congress passed the War Powers Resolution in 1973, by which Congress must approve troop commitments in conflicts lasting over sixty days. Nevertheless, in 2014, when President Obama decided to launch air strikes in Iraq against ISIS, he welcomed congressional approval but declared that he could do so regardless owing to his power as commander in chief, as we see in chapter 14. When he then decided to expand the strikes to Syria, he also invoked Congress's 2001 Authorization for the Use of Military Force against terrorists and its 2002 Authorization of Military Force against Iraq as providing him authority to go forward. Thereafter, however, he decided to seek congressional authorization for his military campaign against ISIS while limiting it to three years, ruling out ground combat, and rescinding the 2002 authorization.

Congress retains the power of the purse—the authority to levy taxes and determine public expenditures without which foreign and security policies could not be implemented. A host of committees and subcommittees in the Senate and House of Representatives deal with foreign-policy legislation, among which the most important are the Senate Foreign Relations, Homeland Security, and Armed Services Committees, and the House Foreign Affairs, Armed Services, Homeland Security, and Intelligence Committees and Select Committee on Intelligence. These committees and their subcommittees are managed by powerful chairs, can hold hearings on foreign policy, and play a role in determining budget appropriations. But the power of the purse is a blunt instrument, and Congress rarely uses it if a president argues that national security is at risk.

If either house of Congress is dominated by a different political party than the president's, there will almost certainly be partisan disagreements. Thus, although congressional Democrats initially supported President George W. Bush's decision to invade Iraq, they repeatedly sought to limit the president's freedom of action once it appeared that the war would continue after the fall of Saddam Hussein.

Although congressional influence on foreign policy fluctuates, that influence rarely sways the executive branch on major issues. Congressional weakness in formulating foreign policy partly reflects lack of information and the exigencies of time, especially if situations require prompt action. Although some members of Congress, notably committee chairs who have served on key committees for long periods of time, come to be foreign-policy experts, most lack the expertise or time to learn much about foreign policy. America's intervention in Iraq provoked little congressional opposition until public frustration with the war led to Democratic control of the House and Senate in 2006. Congress has also asserted itself periodically during the Obama years on matters such as the New START Treaty with Russia, especially after Republicans took control of the House of Representatives in 2010. Nevertheless, congressional criticisms of presidential decisions failed to alter significantly Obama's cautious approach to foreign policy.

Although the judicial branch is less frequently involved in foreign policy than are the executive or legislative branches, it too has from time to time an important input, especially in adjudicating disagreements between the president and Congress. In general, the Supreme Court has supported the president's prerogatives as commander in chief. One analysis reviewed 347 cases dealing with foreign policy that the Supreme Court decided between 1789 and 1996 and concluded that it had ruled in favor of the executive branch in over two-thirds of these: "The executive branch was more likely to emerge victorious when the case involved the President's constitutional powers, the supremacy of federal over state law, and when the case involved foreign actors."[6] Nevertheless, the Court has not been reluctant to overrule the executive branch in cases involving foreign policy if they touch on civil rights, as discussed in chapter 7. For example, in *Hamdi v. Rumsfeld* (2004) the Court ruled that, while the government could detain those judged to be "enemy combatants" indefinitely, it could not deprive an American citizen of the right of habeas corpus and, therefore, had to allow Yaser Esam Hamdi (a U.S. citizen captured in Afghanistan in 2001) the right to challenge his detention and status as an enemy combatant in an American court.

Policy Incrementalism Conflict among different branches of government constitutes only one of the impediments to foreign-policy consensus in America. The executive branch consists of a host of agencies and departments that define the national interest from their own perspective. The Department of Homeland Security that we shall discuss in chapter 7, for example, is comprised of twenty-two different agencies involved in one way or another with protecting the nation's borders. One consequence of the need to gain agreement among the branches of government and, even more, among the bureaucracies that constitute the foreign-policy community is that it impedes making bold policies that diverge in clear fashion from past policies or that change in a significant way America's orientation to the world. Instead, foreign policy–making tends to be pragmatic and incremental, a style of decision-making that Roger Hilsman, director of the State Department's Bureau of Intelligence and Research during the Kennedy administration, described:

> [I]t is an uneasy . . . compromise among competing goals. . . . A government does not decide to inaugurate the nuclear age, but only to try to build an atomic bomb before its enemy does. . . . Rather than through grand decision on grand alternatives, policy changes seem to come through a series of slight modifications of existing policy, with new policy emerging slowly and haltingly by small and usually tentative steps, a process of trial and error in which policy zigs and zags, reverses itself, and then moves forward.[7]

Most American foreign policy consists of routine procedures in maintaining relations with other countries and of bureaucratic competition in pursuit of institutional goals. With imperfect information and inability to foresee accurately the consequences of their decisions, leaders tend to proceed cautiously. Radical shifts in policy are also inhibited by the numerous cross-pressures to which policy-makers are subject, failure to reach consensus in the face of different interests, and different perceptions. All of this fosters minimal decisions even on important issues. Thus, the process by which American troop strength in Vietnam grew from 760 in 1959 to over 536,000 in 1968 was a gradual one, consisting of numerous discrete decisions in response to specific events that led to modest troop increases without any single decision to intervene massively. The U.S. intervention in Iraq to counter ISIS, discussed in chapter 14, also exhibited incrementalism, owing in large part to conflicting views about the appropriate level of U.S. involvement in that effort. And so in 2014 U.S. officials conducted surveillance and offered military support to the Kurds and Iraqi government, incrementally increased U.S. forces in Iraq, and then escalated to air strikes against ISIS targets. In 2015 the United States stepped up support for Kurdish forces fighting ISIS and intensified air strikes against ISIS-controlled oil fields and infrastructure in an effort to cut off the group's key source of revenue. As we shall see, policy-makers are bound by their own roles, the push and pull of parochial interest groups, and competition among bureaucracies—the topic to which we now turn.

Bureaucratic Competition Incrementalism presupposes the existence of a government that consists of "a conglomerate of semi-feudal, loosely allied organizations, each with a substantial life of its own."[8] Although presidents are in charge of the executive branch, they cannot always bend foreign-policy bureaucracies to do their bidding. They need the bureaucracies to collect, process, and interpret information, as well as to allocate resources and responsibilities for performing important tasks. Whether the information they provide is slanted to support a particular policy is often difficult to ascertain, and whether they implement policy in the manner leaders wish may be impossible to determine. Large foreign-policy organizations like the Departments of State and Defense have their own "culture" based on collective memories, routines, and sources of information, and perpetuated by recruitment of similarly minded employees. We see evidence of these routines in many of the issues examined throughout the book.

Bureaucracies devise standard operating procedures for dealing with routine issues. Such procedures are especially helpful in dealing with recurring problems because most high-ranking policy-makers have neither the time nor expertise to do so. On such issues, low-echelon bureaucrats can act within policy guidelines set by political leaders. But routine decisions can have serious consequences. Americans with passports can routinely leave the country, but in an age of global terrorism those seeking to fly to Turkey may actually be extremists who seek to join terrorist groups and use their passports to return home and commit terrorist acts. Presidents can alter standard operating procedures, priorities, and institutional perspectives, but such change is usually a complex undertaking, and presidents need several years before they understand how to run the executive branch.

American leaders rarely have the time, information, or expertise to supervise the implementation of policy. At best they may concentrate on those aspects of immediate importance to them, ignoring other issues. President Obama was intimately involved in the three-month review of the Afghanistan war leading to a decision to add 30,000 U.S. troops in the 2009 "surge" discussed in chapter 6. He spent so much time on the issue, including eleven hours on the day after Thanksgiving, that he joked, "I've got more deeply in the weeds than a president should, and now you guys need to solve this."[9] Presidents who expect to give orders and have them carried out as they desire will be disappointed. Thus, President Truman said of his successor: "He'll sit here and he'll say, 'Do this! Do that!' *And nothing will happen.* Poor Ike—it won't be a bit like the Army. He'll find it very frustrating."[10]

The existence of large bureaucracies encourages competition. Much of foreign policy is the product of interaction among members of government and nongovernmental organizations and groups. The belief that "rational" decisions are based on "national interest" is remote from reality. Instead, much of foreign policy is the outcome of politicized bureaucratic processes involving competition and bargaining in which the outcome depends as much on the relative power of the participants as on the wisdom of their arguments. The budgetary process is often an important battleground for competing interests. Some argue that bureaucratic rivalry can be reduced through reorganization, but as one observer put it: "The 'best' organization is that which distributes power and responsibility in such a fashion as to facilitate the policies you favor."[11]

Bureaucratic competition is especially common in situations when time is available for debate and decisions may lead to the distribution or redistribution of resources among bureaucracies. The Defense Department may argue for a larger share of the overall budget, declaring that military threats from overseas are increasing and therefore more important than concerns about the economy, the environment, or other issues. Rivalry is also common among the U.S. Army, Navy, Air Force, and Marines for a larger share of the defense budget, each arguing that its role is more valuable for national defense than the others, and that it ought to have control over key missions or technologies like the drone program discussed in chapter 7. Sometimes a decision may be aimed at protecting bureaucratic interests by following "accepted practice." Thus, the military services may agree to maintain an existing distribution of funds in order not to "rock the boat."

Bureaucratic competition encourages the formation of coalitions across organization boundaries. Thus, the Defense Department may ally with members of Congress who favor high defense spending, especially from districts or states with substantial employment in defense industries, as well as with those industries. In return, defense-related industries may provide campaign contributions to those who favor defense spending. This coalition became known as the "military-industrial complex."

Small Groups Unlike day-to-day issues that engage large foreign-policy bureaucracies, international crises—high-threat issues that arise unexpectedly and necessitate rapid decisions—require that decisions be made by small groups of top-level U.S. leaders. Most famously, in the 1962 Cuban missile crisis, President John Kennedy bypassed the ordinary mechanisms of policy formation and set up a small group of about fifteen trusted advisors, which came to be known as the "Ex Comm" (the Executive Committee of the National Security Council). The need for secrecy, speed, imagination, and consensus limits the size of decision-making groups during crises.

Small-group decision-making differs from that of large organizations in several ways. First, the parochial interests of the group members' bureaucratic organizations (in which the individuals occupy high places) tend to be subordinated to the purposes of the ad hoc group, which is under pressure to behave cooperatively and expeditiously. The shortage of time in which to make decisions and the threatening nature of the situation generate stress. Although individuals tend to perform less effectively under intense stress, moderate stress may increase productivity and efficiency, heighten morale, and enhance problem-solving abilities in small groups. Moderate stress may also reduce selfish behavior and increase group cohesion. Under time pressure, groups are more able to reach agreement quickly. Such cooperation may facilitate decisions but may also lead to bad ones, especially if no one offers divergent views. Attorney General Robert Kennedy argued that if his brother, President Kennedy, and his advisors had been forced to make a decision during the missile crisis twenty-four hours before they did, they would have chosen to initiate an air strike against Soviet bases in Cuba rather than impose a naval blockade, with very dangerous consequences.

In conditions of stress and limited time, the members of small groups tend to rely on their own memories of past events, drawing simplified comparisons and analogies between the present and the past. President Truman's determination that the invasion of South Korea in 1950 not be "another Munich" and Robert Kennedy's concern lest his brother be viewed as "another Tojo" (Japan's prime minister who gave the order for the surprise attack on Pearl Harbor on December 7, 1941) suggest that simple analogies may prove potent in the decisions of small groups. Except in crises, foreign-policy decision-making is more open to public view in democracies like America than in countries with authoritarian regimes that can determine foreign policy without consulting citizens.

Even in ordinary circumstances, group decision-making dynamics can profoundly shape policies. Subtle and not-so-subtle group pressures can cause individuals to self-censor alternative perspectives and internalize the views of the group. *Groupthink*, a term coined by psychologist Irving Janis, describes the "deterioration of mental efficiency, reality testing and moral judgment that results from in-group pressures."[12] Political scientist Dina Badie argues that after 9/11 "stress, promotional leadership and intergroup conflict conduced groupthink" within the U.S. foreign-policy establishment "as members of the core [decision-making] group were under pressure to produce effective policy in response to the attacks."[13] These pressures, which included illusions of unanimity within the group, direct pressures on dissenters to conform with emerging group views, and self-censorship, influenced how decision-makers interpreted and evaluated incoming information and selected among policy responses. From this perspective, decision-making pathologies led U.S. officials to revise their threat assessment of Saddam Hussein, no longer viewing him as an isolated case of a "troubling dictator" and instead associating Iraq with the threat of terrorism and incorporating it into the War on Terror.

Regime Type The type of government or regime is seen by many observers as a crucial factor in foreign policy. Thus, according to "democratic peace theory," democracies do not go to war with one another. America is a democracy, and although democracy has many virtues, some critics argue that foreign-policy decision-making is not among them. In an oft-recited passage, French political thinker Alexis de Tocqueville, writing early in the nineteenth century, declared: "Foreign policy does not require the use of the good qualities peculiar to democracy but does demand the cultivation of almost those which it lacks," and "a democracy finds it difficult to coordinate the details of a great undertaking and to fix on some plan and carry it through with determination in spite of obstacles. It has little capacity for combining its measures in secret and waiting patiently for the result."[14] Even earlier, then New York assemblyman Alexander Hamilton declared during the Constitutional Convention in 1787 that "the people" are "turbulent and changing" and "seldom judge or determine right."[15] The journalist Walter Lippmann echoed de Tocqueville in arguing that democracy places checks on government leaders, notably by public opinion, and inhibits them from adopting foreign policies they believe to be necessary but unpopular: "The devitalization of the governing power is the malady of democratic states," and "It can be deadly to the very survival of the state as a free society, if, when the great and hard issues of war and peace, of security and solvency, of revolution and order are up for decision, the executive and judicial departments, with their civil servants and technicians, have lost their power to decide."[16] Lippmann's pessimistic analysis suggests that the role of public opinion in shaping decisions in democratic societies is the source of democracy's "devitalization."

Societal Factors

Societal factors also have a great impact on U.S. foreign policy in the Middle East. Societal factors reflect America's political culture: the pattern of beliefs, identities, and values held by members of society. American history, myth, education, language, experience, and ideology all affect national identity and common goals. American politicians routinely try to appeal to values such as democracy, individual liberty, equality of opportunity, the virtues of capitalism, separation of church and state, and entrepreneurial initiative. Many Americans value the separation of church and state and women's rights, in contrast to several Islamic societies. Public opinion broadly reflects America's political culture, and the nature of its impact on foreign policy is highly contested.

Public Opinion Observers differ about what the "public" is and whose views matter. Public opinion exists even though it only episodically affects policy directly and is difficult to identify or even measure.

The public's "mood" fluctuates, as does its attention to foreign affairs. Relatively few people are well informed about foreign policy or have more than superficial views about it, and much of the time the public is divided in its views and unable to articulate those views clearly.

Although public opinion is diffuse, however, there are social elites or "opinion leaders" who can guide the public in certain directions. Religious leaders assume positions that can influence their flocks, the mass media popularize some policies and criticize others, and educators have an impact in shaping the beliefs of their students. Business and labor leaders like other socioeconomic elites frequently help shape the views of those whom they represent. Politicians persistently seek to persuade partisan followers of the virtues of particular courses of action. Congressional hearings on foreign policy routinely feature opinion leaders with different views testifying about policies that they support or oppose.

How significant is public opinion? The impact of public opinion in bringing to an end America's war in Korea in the 1950s, for example, or its intervention in Vietnam in the 1970s or more recently in Iraq and Afghanistan lend credence to the claims of de Tocqueville and Lippmann. In addition, the American public was aroused in 1992 by television images of the effects of famine and violence in Somalia, and in 2001 by television coverage of al-Qaeda's attack on New York's Twin Towers. In 2014 grisly images of Americans being decapitated by ISIS in Syria rapidly transformed public opinion. Initially averse to intervention following wars in Iraq and Afghanistan, after the beheadings the U.S. public supported attacking ISIS in Iraq and Syria.

Typically, in crises the U.S. public rallies around its leaders, especially if Washington makes an effort to mobilize public support for American commitments overseas. As foreign threats loom, congressional efforts to oversee executive actions tend to lessen. Thus, the events of 9/11 united Americans, and Congress quickly authorized President Bush to use force "against those nations, organizations, or persons, he determines planned, authorized, committed, or aided the terrorist attacks," and public opinion willingly accepted the resulting American intervention in Afghanistan and the effort to capture Usama bin Laden. In September 2014 Congress quickly gave approval to President Obama's request for authorization to train and arm Syrian rebels in the face of ISIS, with majorities of "hawks" in both parties supporting the request. Both events reinforced, at least temporarily, the role of the president as the principal architect of foreign policy. However, presidents often have to "oversell" what they are trying to accomplish, such as "leading the free world" or "making the world safe for democracy."

Overselling, however, makes it difficult for leaders to change course. Once an adversary has been demonized and depersonalized, and once blood and treasure have been expended, it is difficult to back away from those commitments without facing an angry electorate. Thus, political scientist Gabriel Almond described the public's mood as prone to "dangerous overreactions,"[17] and diplomat George Kennan compared the public to a dinosaur in the sense that "you practically have to whack his tail off to make him aware that his interests are being disturbed; but once he grasps this, he lays about him such blind determination that he not only destroys his adversary but largely wrecks his native habitat."[18]

Nevertheless, we should not overestimate the impact of public opinion on policy. First, relatively few Americans pay much attention to foreign affairs except when sensational events occur like the 9/11 terrorist attacks discussed in chapter 6. In 2012 only 12 percent of the U.S. electorate regarded foreign policy among their top three concerns, only 15 percent regarded defense as one of their three main concerns,[19] and in a national exit poll only 5 percent regarded foreign policy as the major issue in the 2012 elections.[20] Indeed, some analysts argue that, far from influencing leaders, leaders have the capability to shape public opinion in most cases. Thus, the Florentine political philosopher Niccolò Machiavelli cynically declared that "men are so simple and so ready to obey present necessities that one who deceives will always find those who allow themselves to be deceived."[21] This reflects an elitist model in which leaders can shape and manipulate public opinion and use the media to do so.

Others, however, including Thomas Jefferson, accept a pluralist model and view public opinion as shaping the view of foreign-policy elites. Thus, political scientist William Caspary concluded that "American public opinion is characterized by a *strong* and *stable* 'permissive mood' toward international involvements."[22] Almond perhaps best captures the role of the American public in foreign policy when he writes that "the function of the public in a democratic policy-making process is to set certain policy criteria in the form of widely held values and expectations, leaving to those who have a positive and informed interest the actual formation of policy."[23]

Thus, what is perceived as public opinion may actually reflect the views of relatively small but highly vocal minorities, and, although few Americans have consistent views of foreign policy, those who do pay attention may feel intensely about particular issues. Public opinion can flow into the foreign-policy process through various channels—elections, mass media, political parties, Congress, and interest groups. Although most of the public is not organized and only a small proportion is attentive to foreign-policy issues, vocal minorities are frequently associated with interest groups that use political and economic influence to shape foreign policy and frequently contribute financially to the campaigns of politicians whose views they support. The American Israel Public Affairs Committee, considered in chapter 9, provides one such example. American political parties are especially important in this respect because they combine interests of many stripes into broad coalitions.

Interest Groups Major socioeconomic groups in America enjoy access to the government arena and can exercise indirect or even direct influence on decisions. Such groups represent ethnic and religious communities (e.g., African-American, Jewish, Islamic, Arab-American, Cuban-American, and Mexican-American), labor and business, veterans, farmers, and women, among others. Some have broad agendas, but many are single-issue groups that focus solely on what they regard as most important—for example, environmental causes, human-rights violations, defense, Israel, and so forth. The influence of such groups varies depending on a group's ability to gain access to and lobby policy-makers, its capacity to provide campaign contributions and deliver votes, and its overall public support. As a result, decisions with foreign-policy consequences are frequently made to satisfy domestic constituencies rather than deliberately to shape the external environment.

George Kennan recalled that his first lesson on becoming a diplomat was that "one of the most consistent and incurable traits of American statesmanship" was "its neurotic self-consciousness and introversion, the tendency to make statements and take actions with regard not to their effect on the international scene to which they are ostensibly addressed but rather to their effects on those echelons of American opinion, congressional opinion first and foremost, to which the respective statesmen are anxious to appeal."[24] Political scientist Robert Putnam makes a similar point when he writes of "two-level games": "At the national level, domestic groups pursue their interests by pressuring the government to adopt favorable policies and politicians seek power by constructing coalitions among those groups. At the international level, national governments seek to maximize their own ability to satisfy domestic pressures, while minimizing the adverse consequences of foreign developments."[25] We see U.S. foreign policy–makers attempting such two-level games across the Middle East as they try to craft policies to satisfy domestic interests and foreign partners in managing challenges like the Israeli–Palestinian conflict, Iranian nuclear proliferation, the spread of ISIS, and the stalled Arab Spring in Egypt, Libya, and elsewhere in the region.

Indeed, sometimes Washington tries to modify or oppose the efforts of domestic interest groups to act in ways that policy-makers believe will alienate other countries. Thus, Armenian-Americans in California have repeatedly sought to persuade Congress to declare the murderous actions of Ottoman Turkey in 1915 as "genocide," and every year on April 24 that community reiterates its demands publicly. For its part, the Turkish government vociferously denies that what happened constituted genocide and warns America that a congressional resolution that labels the event genocidal would greatly harm relations between two countries that have enjoyed a long history of friendship. Repeatedly, U.S. presidents have sought to prevent congressional action, but in 2007 and 2010 the House Foreign Affairs Committee passed nonbinding resolutions over the objections of Presidents George W. Bush and Obama, respectively. During the 2008 presidential campaign, Obama had promised to declare the events of 1915 a genocide, thereby illustrating the link between the foreign and domestic arenas, but altered his position after his election. In response, in 2007 and again in 2010 Turkey recalled its ambassador to Washington "for consultations" in protest. Although the resolution failed to gain congressional approval on those occasions, a similar bill was referred to committee in March 2012 and again in 2015.

Individuals rarely have an impact on legislators or bureaucrats through letters or visits because, without the aid of interest groups or political parties, most lack sufficient organization or resources. There are, of course, exceptions to this. For example, the billionaire casino owner Sheldon Adelson contributed roughly $100 million to Mitt Romney's 2012 presidential campaign because he believed that Republicans are more likely than Democrats to support Israel's security. Others include Charles and David Koch, owners of the conglomerate Koch Industries, who "have funded opposition campaigns against so many Obama Administration policies—from health-care reform to the economic-stimulus program—that, in political circles, their ideological network is known as the Kochtopus."[26]

Members of Congress, however, are seldom swayed by the opinions of those who have no direct interest in the foreign-policy issue being discussed. Thus, the influence of interest groups frequently involves economic issues and is exercised by professional lobbyists (often former politicians or bureaucrats who have friends in Washington). Interest groups are likely to exercise greater influence on issues that affect them directly. Labor unions, for instance, are likely to enjoy access to political allies on issues that involve the outsourcing of American jobs to other countries. Sometimes informal coalitions develop between interest groups and congressional committees or executive agencies responsible for selected areas of policy.

If government and society constitute complex systems, individuals are the parts of those systems. The following sections examine the impact of individuals in formulating and implementing foreign policy. The first describes the impact of the roles of officeholders and policy-makers, and the second deals

KEY DOCUMENT

S.RES.399—Affirmation of the United States Record on the Armenian Genocide Resolution (Introduced in Senate—IS)

112th CONGRESS

2d Session

S. RES. 399

IN THE SENATE OF THE UNITED STATES

March 19, 2012

RESOLUTION

Calling upon the President to ensure that the foreign policy of the United States reflects appropriate understanding and sensitivity concerning issues related to human rights, crimes against humanity, ethnic cleansing, and genocide documented in the United States record relating to the Armenian Genocide, and for other purposes. . . .

FINDINGS

Sec. 2. The Senate finds the following:

(1) The Armenian Genocide was conceived and carried out by the Ottoman Empire from 1915 to 1923, resulting in the deportation of nearly 2,000,000 Armenians, of whom 1,500,000 men, women, and children were killed, 500,000 survivors were expelled from their homes, and the elimination of the over 2,500-year presence of Armenians in their historic homeland.

(2) On May 24, 1915, the Allied Powers of England, France, and Russia, jointly issued a statement explicitly charging for the first time ever another government of committing 'a crime against humanity'. . . .

(7) The Armenian Genocide and these domestic judicial failures are documented with overwhelming evidence in the national archives of Austria, France, Germany, Great Britain, Russia, the United States, the Vatican and many other countries, and this vast body of evidence attests to the same facts, the same events, and the same consequences. . . .

(15) As displayed in the United States Holocaust Memorial Museum, Adolf Hitler, on ordering his military commanders to attack Poland without provocation in 1939, dismissed objections by saying '[w]ho, after all, speaks today of the annihilation of the Armenians?' and thus set the stage for the Holocaust. . . .[27]

with the characteristics of individuals that are unique to them. The roles of policy-makers comprise the demands that their positions place on their actions. A role constitutes a piece of a larger organization and intervenes between that organization and an individual's personal preferences and perceptions.

Role Factors

A role is a set of socially prescribed behaviors associated with individuals occupying similar official positions in a political system that encourages them to view foreign-policy issues in similar ways. The individual's role entails a set of responsibilities and tasks associated with the organization in which she is involved. As a rule, those with similar roles confront their tasks in similar ways, using the organization's standard operating procedures. Thus, American diplomats and military officers, however different in personal attributes, occupy similar roles in the government and will handle routine and repetitive tasks in similar ways that have in the past proved efficient and effective.

Role can be defined as the interaction of individual officeholders' interpretation of what is expected of them, their actual behavior, and the expectations of those who are responsible for their recruitment or career advancement. When individuals assume new positions their knowledge of role norms is based on the behavior of previous occupants of those positions as well as legal statutes, job descriptions, organizational charts, and peer groups. Thus, those who are promoted to the rank of U.S. Army generals will likely behave like their predecessors and act in ways expected by the higher officers who promoted them.

A role, therefore, is partly shaped by what superiors expect. Individuals who wish to retain their positions or advance in their careers try to behave in ways that they think are expected of them and meet the obligations to the organization of which they are members rather than following personal convictions. In this sense, an individual's role involves a commitment to serve the interests of that individual's institutional home. From a role perspective, where individuals "stand depends upon where they sit." Military officers are expected to support increased budgets for defense and improvements in the status of the military profession in society. Those who behaved otherwise would find it difficult to advance in their profession. The highly competitive promotion systems in organizations like the Departments of State and Defense and the CIA tend to limit creativity and encourage conformity. Since a key factor in promotions are the efficiency reports written by superiors, career aspirations can deter the forthright expression of views on foreign policy that differ from the views of supervisors. It would have been a courageous foreign-service officer who publicly took issue with the Bush administration's intervention in Iraq in 2003 or would have expressed doubt about whether Saddam Hussein was seeking weapons of mass destruction at that time.

The obligations of role occupants to superiors shape their perceptions of foreign-policy issues. A member of Congress is likely to take positions that conform to the interests of constituents—those who elect him to office rather than to the interests of the country as a whole. Thus, members of Congress see no conflict between seeking to close down military bases to reduce the budget while opposing closing bases in their districts. Institutional loyalty also narrows the frame of reference for interpreting information and, not surprisingly, stimulates rivalries among executive organizations.

Role prescriptions can be passed on to individuals in various ways, but primarily through socialization and recruitment. Government bureaucracies tend to recruit individuals with beliefs and backgrounds similar to those of the existing elite. Role prescriptions are thus perpetuated by self-selection. Those who are recruited and able to gain promotion have usually been able to internalize role prescriptions—that is, to adopt them as personal role conceptions. As such, prescriptions are generally resistant to change.

If a position occupied by an individual is new, that individual may enjoy greater latitude in defining her role. George Washington set significant precedents as America's first president. Thus, his interpretation of the constitutional requirement (Article II, Section 3) that the president "shall from time to time give to Congress Information of the State of the Union" led him to deliver the first State of the Nation address to Congress on January 8, 1790. After he delivered a second State of the Nation address the following year, he established a precedent that later presidents would follow in reporting to Congress either in a speech or, beginning with Thomas Jefferson, in a formal written letter. In 1913 President Woodrow Wilson reverted to speaking annually before a joint session of Congress. Until recent decades, presidents sometimes spoke directly to Congress and sometimes followed Jefferson's example. Washington's original precedent has dominated recent decades, however, owing to the unique opportunity offered presidents in advocating policies in an annual televised speech with officials from all three branches of government in attendance.

As time passes, role norms become set; precedents grow; and expectations become more widely shared and deeply anchored. It is thus difficult for officeholders, even presidents, to impose their personalities on or remold well-established roles. For that reason even high officials find themselves with few alternatives even if a particular policy violates their personal principles. Whether individuals can modify role norms depends upon the strength of role prescriptions, the force of their personality, and the uniqueness of the problems they confront. Robert McNamara's career as secretary of defense for Presidents John Kennedy and Lyndon Johnson illustrates how such factors can enlarge a role. Between 1961 and 1968 McNamara gradually expanded his role vis-à-vis Congress and the military services, reviewing the programs of the Defense Department and introducing novel cost-effectiveness techniques that helped him to evaluate them comparatively: "McNamara innovated both in the types of decisions that he did make and in the manner in which he made and carried them out. Both types of innovation stemmed from a conception McNamara had of his office—a conception unlike that of any of his predecessors."[28]

McNamara's career illustrated how role and personal characteristics combine in fostering the views and actions of policy-makers.

An individual like McNamara can rationalize a policy decision by referring to the demands of his role. Presidents do so as well, and overall Americans tend to accept a president's policy in foreign affairs more readily than in domestic affairs. In a 2002 speech delivered at West Point, President George W. Bush explained that after 9/11 his role demanded that he take extraordinary steps to meet his obligation to provide security for Americans:

> Homeland defense and missile defense are part of a stronger security, and they're essential priorities for America. Yet the war on terror will not be won on the defensive. We must take the battle to the enemy, disrupt his plans, and confront the worst threats before they emerge. In the world we have entered, the only path to safety is the path of action. And this nation will act.[29]

Unlike presidents, however, other role occupants have more limited scope for individual initiatives, and the role expectations of their organizations reflect more parochial interests. In sum: "Role, in and of itself, cannot explain the positions adopted by individuals; after all, the very notion of role implies a certain latitude over how to play the role," but "role occupiers do become predisposed to think in certain, bureaucratic, ways, and for a variety of psychological reasons they tend to adopt mind-sets compatible with those of their closest colleagues."[30] Thus, role only explains part of how individuals affect foreign policy. We have seen that in new or top-level political posts, individuals like McNamara may be able to take initiatives or follow their personal beliefs rather than the positions dictated by their roles. Let us now examine some of the individual traits that can have an impact on foreign-policy views.

Individual Factors

The nineteenth-century Scottish essayist and historian Thomas Carlyle attributed nearly all change and drama in history to the wills of great men. But history is the product of both people *and* their times. We can distinguish those characteristics of individual decision-makers and their behaviors—personality, experience, intellect, values, and political style—that make them unique.

Since decision-making is partly the product of environmental and psychological predispositions, the relevance of individual traits is significant. As we shall see in Part III, the mistrust between President Obama and Prime Minister Netanyahu complicated efforts to achieve peace in the Middle East. Observers regarded their relationship as so frayed that they predicted that U.S.–Israeli relations would be soured at least until America's 2016 presidential election. Throughout the text, we will see examples of how the personality traits, beliefs, experiences, leadership styles, and even health of key individuals shaped U.S. foreign policy in the Middle East.

 ## *KEY DOCUMENT*

Thomas Carlyle, "On Heroes, Hero-Worship, and the Heroic in History"[31]

We have undertaken to discourse here for a little on Great Men, their manner of appearance in our world's business, how they have shaped themselves in the world's history, what ideas men formed of them, what work they did;—on Heroes, namely, and on their reception and performance; what I call Hero-worship and the Heroic in human affairs. . . . Universal History, the history of what man has accomplished in this world, is at bottom the History of the Great Men who have worked here. They were the leaders of men, these great ones; the modelers, patterns, and in a wide sense creators, of whatsoever the general mass of men contrived to do or to attain: all things that we see standing accomplished in the world are properly the outer material result, the practical realization and embodiment, of Thoughts that dwelt in the Great Men sent into the world: the soul of the whole world's history, it may justly be considered, were the history of these.

Personality Among the most interesting individuals are those with personality variables that lead to aberrant behavior. Sometimes such behavior reflects an individual's unconscious attempt to cope with inner conflict or need—in political scientist Harold Lasswell's classic formulation, the displacement of private motives onto public objects.[32] Lasswell was concerned with what he called "social psychiatry," which he believed clarified the process of policy-making.[33]

Certain emotional issues tend to evoke aberrant behavior. For example, ego-defensive behavior occurs in agitation for or against communism, pacifism, birth control, and obscenity. Studies of prejudice suggest that certain individuals have greater needs than do others to defend their identities. Their behavior, often hostile, may compensate for unconscious needs and personality defects. Thus, historian Garry Wills describes how Richard Nixon acted during a press conference in 1962 after he had been defeated in California's election for governor as follows:

> Nixon entered, laboring unsuccessfully at the game smile of politicians who have submitted to the judgment of voters and now must accept it. But as he advanced to the podium, his eyes picked out this or that face in the press corps; and behind the faces—behind pens slanting in a hostile scrawl, mikes held up for every slip—he could see again the words they used against him, headlines, leads, last paragraphs all stored in his retentive memory bank, that library of grievances.[34]

When individual factors have an impact, studying leaders' life histories can help us to understand their adult behavior. Their relations with their parents, their education, and their socialization as children and adolescents may have created enduring frustrations or anxieties. An analysis of President Woodrow Wilson's behavior concluded that his unwillingness to compromise with political opponents and, therefore, his failure to get the Senate to agree to America's entry in the League of Nations were a consequence of his childhood competition with his strict Presbyterian father. The authors suggest that Wilson had repressed his rebellion against his father but unconsciously refused to submit to him. As a result, Wilson

> could brook no interference. *His* will must prevail if he wished it to. He bristled at the slightest challenge to his authority. Such a characteristic might well have represented a rebellion against the domination of his father, whose authority he had never dared openly to challenge. Throughout his life his relationship with others seemed shaped by an inner command never again to bend his will to another man's.[35]

Wilson, who set out to "make the world safe for democracy," has been described by political scientist John Stoessinger as "the classical crusader"—that is, an individual who "tends to sacrifice unwelcome facts on the altar of a fixed idea." Stoessinger contrasts crusaders, who are frequently moralists, with "pragmatists" like President Truman: "The pragmatist always tests his ideas against the facts of his experience. If the design does not hold up against the facts, the design will have to change."[36] According to

Bruce Bartlett, an advisor to President Ronald Reagan, President George W. Bush became a crusader during his presidency. Bush was "clear-eyed about Al Qaeda and the Islamic fundamentalist enemy," whom he understood "because he's just like them." Bush "truly believes he's on a mission from God. Absolute faith like that overwhelms a need for analysis."[37]

Individuals motivated by repressed hostility may also assume a posture of moral superiority toward those with whom they are in conflict, and this may lead to dangerous foreign-policy decisions. Those in the foreign-policy establishment with such attitudes may encourage ethnocentric behavior—that is, behavior reflecting suspicions of other societies and nations and showing little respect for them. Ethnocentrism produces hostility. For example, many Pakistanis, including those who do not hold radical Islamic views, believe that American leaders are ethnocentric, haughty, and disrespectful because Washington persists, as we see in Part II, in sending unmanned drones over their country to kill Islamic militants, thereby violating Pakistani sovereignty. Such personality factors contribute to an individual's beliefs.

Beliefs The beliefs of leaders and the strength with which those beliefs are held may have a significant impact on the way in which they deal with new information, including information that seems to contradict those beliefs. People usually have coherent attitudes toward and beliefs about the world that reflect their values and preferences. The stronger these attitudes and beliefs, the greater the contradictory evidence and information needed to alter them. When confronted with evidence that contradicts strong beliefs, policy-makers must alter their beliefs, deny the evidence, or rationalize it so that it no longer seems contradictory.

An analysis of Secretary of State John Foster Dulles by political scientist Ole Holsti concluded that he consistently explained changes in Soviet behavior during the Cold War, including conciliatory actions, in terms of hostility, weakness, or treachery, which eliminated the need for him to alter his beliefs in the face of new evidence. "Dulles selected two aspects of Marxist theory—materialism and atheism—for special emphasis," and "After pointing out that the free world had such high moral standards as to preclude the use of immoral methods, Dulles concluded that 'atheists can hardly be expected to conform to an ideal so high.'" Thus, "He attributed the characteristics of the Soviet leaders—insincerity, immorality, brutality, and deceitfulness—primarily to their atheism."[38] Dulles's experience in negotiating with Soviet leaders had contributed to his suspicions of their motives. As in the case of Dulles, people's experience can shape their beliefs and foreign-policy preferences.

Experience The experiences of policy-makers help them interpret the challenges they face. Different experiences are likely to endow officeholders with unique qualifications that may or may not be suitable for solving the problems at hand. George C. Marshall, who served as secretary of defense in 1950–1951, had been a five-star general of the army and chief of staff. More than any other U.S. secretary of defense, Marshall understood the difficulties confronting the military services. In addition, having also served as secretary of state, he was in a position to judge between the military services and the political objectives that they were supposed to serve.

In contrast to Marshall, Charles E. Wilson had been president of General Motors before becoming secretary of defense in 1953. His previous experience equipped him to cut military expenditures and design military plans that would enable the Eisenhower administration to maintain a balanced budget.

Wilson had little military training, and toward the end of the Eisenhower years, professional officers were complaining that American military forces had been permitted to grow obsolete. More recently, Ashton Carter replaced Chuck Hagel as secretary of defense, largely because Carter's wide experience in formulating defense policy made him more willing than Hagel to consider using force—a trait sought by many in Congress, especially Republicans.

Age is also an important aspect of experience. The events of the era in which individuals were socialized are likely to be reflected in the way in which they consider problems. Such individuals will have different points of reference and concerns from others of a different generation. Thus, policy-makers who were socialized shortly before and during World War II are more likely to be concerned about "appeasing" a foe than are those raised earlier, during World War I, or later, during the Vietnam War. The generations that came of age during the slaughter of World War I, the American defeat in Vietnam, or the frustrating wars in Afghanistan and Iraq are likely to be less concerned about appeasing other countries if such a policy would avoid war. The experiences of policy-makers also may also affect their leadership style—that is, how they approach making decisions.

Leadership Style Leadership style refers to the ways in which policy-makers reach decisions. President Dwight Eisenhower, who had served much of his adult life as a high-ranking army staff officer, expected as president to coordinate the work of others and consult widely with advisors and subordinates. Not only did Eisenhower solicit the advice of others and delegate authority to them, but he tried not to impose his views on them in order to achieve consensus. Although this approach minimized conflict among decision-makers, it also tended to blur the lines of responsibility and produce decisions at the "lowest common denominator."

President Bill Clinton was a "policy wonk" who took great pleasure in engaging subordinates and advisors in discussion and debate. That style is also characteristic to some extent of President Obama. He was less able than Eisenhower or George W. Bush to operate hierarchically, and less willing than Eisenhower or Bush to let others narrow the alternatives presented to them. Obama "had very little foreign policy experience" and "lacked any executive-management experience." Thus, he was "deliberative to a fault and an inveterate seeker of the middle ground" and was not "inclined to develop strong bonds with most of his cabinet members or to empower them or agency heads, which is essential in a sprawling U.S. government that is the world's largest and most complex organization."[39] Finally, his dependence on a small circle of advisors meant that the administration was overwhelmed by the multiple challenges to America during Obama's second term—confrontation with Russia over Ukraine, the Ebola epidemic, the Islamic State of Iraq and Syria, civil war in Syria, and Chinese truculence. According to a former U.S. diplomat, "Personal relationships are not his style," unlike Presidents Clinton and George W. Bush, who "yukked it up with everybody."[40] And former CIA director and defense secretary Leon Panetta criticized Obama for vacillation and lacking "fire": "Too often, in my view, the president relies on the logic of a law professor rather than the passion of a leader."[41]

In contrast to Obama, President Franklin D. Roosevelt, previously assistant secretary of the navy and governor of New York, encouraged his subordinates to compete with one another, making it necessary for him to serve as ultimate arbiter in the disputes that inevitably erupted. He let situations develop and crystalize, and "the competing forces had to vindicate themselves in the actual pull and tug of conflict; public opinion had to face the question, consider it, pronounce upon it—only then, at the long frazzled end, would the President's intuitions consolidate and precipitate a result." Roosevelt "organized—or disorganized—his system of command to insure that important decisions were passed on to the top."[42]

An interesting comparison of recent leadership styles is apparent when comparing Gen. David Petraeus and his ebullient predecessor, Leon Panetta, as director of the Central Intelligence Agency. Petraeus, a former four-star army general who was prominently involved in America's wars in Iraq and Afghanistan, had a quieter and less public demeanor than did Panetta, a former member of Congress with considerable political experience, who went on to become secretary of defense. According to a friend of Petraeus, "He thinks he has to be very discreet and let others in the government do the talking."[43] Fearful of leaks, Petraeus, unlike Panetta, gave few interviews and kept a low profile.

Finally, foreign-policy decision-making can also be affected by the physical and mental health of policy-makers.

Health Leaders are frequently old and less able to act with the vigor and dynamism that they had when they were younger. The strain of high public office in Washington is great. Both Eisenhower and Woodrow Wilson, for example, suffered serious illnesses while in office, which lessened their control over decisions. President Roosevelt was already ill when he met Soviet leader Joseph Stalin at Yalta in February 1945. He would die two months later, and some observers claim that Roosevelt was unfit to negotiate effectively with the Soviet dictator.

As the stress of making life-and-death decisions increases, mental illness may become a problem. James Forrestal, the first American secretary of defense, took his own life in 1949 by throwing himself from the sixteenth floor of the Bethesda Naval Hospital, where he was undergoing psychiatric treatment. "The most lasting tribute to James Forrestal," wrote his biographer, "would be a massive effort to reduce the incidence of physical and mental breakdown in political life."[44] Indeed, although America requires military officers in charge of nuclear weapons to undergo extensive psychological tests, it provides no such safeguards for the president, who would order their use in the event of war.

CONCLUSION: U.S. FOREIGN POLICY IN THE MIDDLE EAST

This chapter has examined several of the key sources of influence on the formulation and implementation of American foreign policy. Although there is a tendency to view the Middle East as "unique" or a "special case" with especially stubborn political, social, and economic challenges, U.S. foreign policies toward the region and the countries in it are shaped by the same kinds of factors that influence foreign policy elsewhere. We have seen how foreign and domestic policies have become increasingly entangled in recent decades. In a large democratic country like the United States, it is difficult to identify a unitary national interest that is the outcome of individual rationality. Instead, many government and societal groups as well as individuals define the national interest from their own perspective.

External factors like globalization and accompanying international and transnational interdependence have limited sovereign independence, and the relative distribution of power constrains what is possible while the distribution of attitudes shapes what is probable in U.S. foreign policy. A host of government characteristics such as separation of powers and the competitive views of government bureaucracies shape the way foreign policy is made and the outcomes of policy-making. Societal factors such as the lobbying of interest groups and public opinion also influence policy outcomes. The roles that individuals have in government and society influence their perceptions and their actions, as do individual characteristics such as a president's personality, beliefs, and health. In sum, American foreign policy is the outcome of a complex, continuous, and messy process in which alternatives are put forward by many individuals and interests and frequently are the outcome of domestic conflict and compromise rather than rational consensus.

The relative potency of these sources of influence varies over time and by issue, but recognizing that the same factors that operate elsewhere also shape U.S. foreign policy in the Middle East is an important insight. The next chapter examines how these influences have affected the contours of American foreign policy historically and the changing patterns in policy over time.

2

Competing Currents in U.S. Foreign Policy

Policy continuity under Obama

Paresh Nath 2013

This chapter continues our discussion of influences on American foreign policy, focusing on how these influences have produced competing orientations in the Middle East, but also in foreign policy generally. In what follows, we introduce competing currents, or dichotomies, that have been present in U.S. foreign policy since America's founding: the pursuit of interests versus values, isolationism versus internationalism, unilateralism versus multilateralism, and interventionism versus noninterventionism. Although the Middle East only came to have a permanent and central place in U.S. foreign policy in the early twentieth century, ever since American policies in the region have reflected these enduring tendencies. We see these currents at play as we examine the historical and present-day development of America's relations with regimes in the Middle East, efforts to combat radical Islam and seek peace in the Israeli–Palestinian conflict, and engagement with Shia and Sunni governments in the region, but the tension among these dichotomies is especially apparent in the policy options offered in each part's concluding chapter. As we shall see throughout the text, U.S. efforts to develop a coherent policy in the Middle East are constrained as much by the existence of competing orientations in America's own foreign-policy process as by the distinctive challenges inherent in the region.

Most casual observers of American foreign policy are aware of the existence of multiple policy orientations. The conventional narrative describes America as isolationist until World War II, after which it accepted the mantle of global leadership and became permanently engaged in global life, including in the Middle East. The narrative becomes more complicated in the twenty-first century after 9/11—when U.S. engagement in the region increased dramatically—depicting U.S. foreign policy as unilateralist and interventionist under President George W. Bush and increasingly multilateralist under President Barack Obama. The reality, though, is more complicated. Multilateralism was never completely abandoned under Bush, and unilateralism did not disappear during the Obama years. Thus, Obama shocked many who expected him to be a norm-driven multilateralist when in receiving the 2009 Nobel Peace Prize he reminded the world of the role U.S. military power had played, emphasizing that "the world must remember that it was not simply international institutions—not just treaties and declarations—that brought stability to a post–World War II world," and "the plain fact is this: The United States of America has helped underwrite global security for more than six decades with the blood of our citizens and the strength of our arms."[1]

Employing power to pursue U.S. interests *and* values is described as "multilateralism with teeth"[2] and was a frequent theme under Obama, just as in many earlier administrations. Foreign policy is an area where presidents have considerable latitude, but they are not free of constraints. Their policies are

Timeline

1700

1775–1783 American Revolution

1800

1812 War of 1812

1823 Monroe Doctrine

1844–1848 Mexican–American War

1845 Annexation of Texas

1848 Addition of California, Arizona, and New Mexico

1898 Spanish–American War, annexation of Hawaii, and acquisition of the Philippines and Puerto Rico

the products of competing interests that seek a variety of goals and also competing values. Many public and private actors are involved in this process, as we saw in chapter 1. While these actors may share fundamental ideals like democracy and individualism, they may disagree on how to pursue such values. Moreover, interests are frequently incompatible, and policies are often compromises that achieve minimal common interests. In sum, America is not a rational, unified actor coherently acting in the "national interest." Nonetheless, as we shall see, there are some patterns that have emerged in foreign policy toward the Middle East and elsewhere over the course of American history. In various eras, U.S. leaders have placed more or less relative emphasis on values and interests in their conduct of foreign policy. At the same time, America's relationship with the rest of the world has involved isolationism and internationalism, unilateralism and multilateralism, and interventionism and noninterventionism. Students of U.S. history readily cite the interwar period as isolationist, or the Cold War period as interventionist, and America's post-9/11 policy as interventionist *and* unilateral. As we shall see, however, no era has been immune to debates about America's place in the world. This chapter is the most historical and general in the book, and the account will emphasize symbolic events and actors that highlight enduring tendencies and tensions in U.S. foreign policy. As you read further in the book, you will see how these tendencies have shaped American engagement in the Middle East—including, for example, unilateralism and interventionism in conducting the War on Terror and intervention and nonintervention in the Arab Spring.

COMPETING CURRENTS

American foreign policy is often described in dichotomies: pursuit of values *versus* interests, isolationism *versus* internationalism, unilateralism *versus* multilateralism, and interventionism *versus* noninterventionism. These contrasts are often false, especially in the Middle East. In every era several perspectives coexist and compete for influence, even though one may dominate. Foreign policy has *always* been

1900

1904 Roosevelt Corollary extends the Monroe Doctrine

1917–1918 U.S. and World War I

1941–1945 U.S. and World War II

1947 Truman Doctrine

1950–1953 Korean War

1964–1975 Vietnam War

1991 First Persian Gulf War

1992 The Cold War ends

2000

September 2001 Al-Qaeda terrorist attacks in New York and Washington

2001–2014 Afghanistan war

March 2003 U.S.-led invasion of Iraq

2011 Withdrawal of U.S. forces from Iraq

a concern of U.S. leaders and a topic of debate, and whether leaders explicitly acknowledge it or not, through much of America's history, they have been guided by a reasonably consistent and coherent view of America's interests in foreign affairs. Such a structured worldview is called *grand strategy*. First popularized by British military strategist B. Liddell Hart in the mid-1900s, grand strategy initially involved synchronizing means and ends in the conduct of war.[3]

Contemporary grand strategy refers to a broad framework that structures a country's approach to foreign affairs. According to historian Paul Kennedy, it is "the capacity of the nation's leaders to bring together all the elements, both military and nonmilitary, for the preservation and enhancement of the nation's long-term"[4] interests, however defined. In this sense, it encompasses a coherent articulation of core interests, a clear understanding of key threats, and an awareness of resources and capabilities that can be mobilized to advance those interests. It represents the logic by which a government employs the tools of foreign policy to achieve the greatest advantage in its pursuit of core interests.[5] Grand strategy reveals the nexus of foreign and domestic politics because it "is precisely about the broader, often ignored, context of building and reinforcing the domestic political and economic foundations of American national power."[6] It guides leaders when they confront new challenges in foreign affairs and helps them use resources wisely, avoid overstretch, and maintain policy coherence across the range of foreign-policy issues. However, as we shall see here and again in later chapters, not all presidents have a grand strategy, and even when they do it may be insufficient to meet foreign-policy challenges.

Although for much of U.S. history there existed no such label to identify core interests or the strategies for accomplishing them, key foreign-policy initiatives reflected implicit grand strategies. We begin by examining the enduring tension that exists between considerations of interests and values in American foreign policy, and then turn to the competing currents of isolationism and internationalism, unilateralism and multilateralism, and interventionism and noninterventionism in the pursuit of interests and values.

Interests and Values

In explaining the shifts between the several dimensions of American foreign policy, it is important to recognize that decisions are *simultaneously* the outcome of considerations of interests *and* values. The former reflects the role played by concerns about America's security and preservation of its geopolitical interests, emphasizing power and expediency. The latter involves the maintenance and spread of American values—democracy, human rights, rule of law, free-market capitalism, and individualism. Those who describe themselves as "realists" believe that interests should dominate foreign policy, while "liberals" argue that pursuing values should take precedence. In fact, power and values are not antithetical. No policy is shaped that does not involve seeking security against foes and preserving America's ideals. The attraction of American values constitutes "soft power" because it influences others to accept American policies, while "hard power" such as military and economic capabilities is necessary to preserve those values and project them abroad.

Conflicts can arise, however, about which to emphasize, and successful foreign policies require a balance between the two that changes depending on circumstances. Efforts to export American values to countries with inimical beliefs are likely to meet with failure. Thus, despite America's overwhelming military superiority, efforts to negotiate with Iran about that country's nuclear aspirations were thwarted for many years by mutual suspicion arising in part from American secularism and Iranian Islamism. By contrast, notwithstanding the many differences between the United States and Israel, a shared belief in democracy constitutes a strong bond between the two countries.

Power and values are related in other ways. Insufficient power makes it dangerous to try to spread values abroad. During its formative years in the late eighteenth and early nineteenth centuries, America was weak militarily and dependent on European trade, and efforts to spread values would have endangered U.S. security and, therefore, also placed at risk the values it sought to preserve. By contrast, the effort to use power to impose American values on others as in Iraq after 2003 can appear as bullying and produce a backlash. Even more dangerous is when such efforts appear to threaten others' security. U.S. efforts to use financial and diplomatic power to support political opposition groups in countries like Iran and Syria and empower nongovernmental organizations have long been viewed as endangering the stability of the regimes in those countries. These same practices also produced a backlash among democratic opposition groups in the region for their inconsistency, as with U.S. support for strategically valuable but abusive regimes in Egypt and Saudi Arabia.

The changing balance between power and values will arise repeatedly as we examine American policies in later chapters. We will see that so often in the Middle East, U.S. policy is driven by interests, including maintaining access to oil, preventing the spread of hostile ideologies like Islamic extremism, and advancing long-held U.S. values like democracy promotion and human rights. It will also become apparent that it is frequently not possible to achieve all of these goals simultaneously. Throughout the text, we will see U.S. leaders struggle to balance interests and values in their relations with governments in the Arab world (Part I); their efforts to prevent the spread of Islamic extremism and protect American territory, people, and interests (Part II); their attempts to pursue peace in the Israeli–Palestinian conflict (Part III); and their relations with Shia and Sunni states in the Middle East (Part IV).

We will now examine the enduring tendencies in U.S. foreign policy, indicating where possible how these tendencies played out in American relations with actors in the Middle East.

Isolationism and Internationalism

One outcome of the interplay of interests and values is the choice between isolationism and internationalism—concepts used to describe U.S. disengagement or engagement in world affairs. Isolationism had deep roots in American foreign policy even before President George Washington advised Americans to avoid "entangling alliances." Isolationism gained widespread currency in the 1930s and came to be associated with avoiding "political and military commitments to or alliances with foreign powers, particularly those of Europe."[7] In fact, isolationism does not require that a state remain uninvolved in world affairs. Instead, an isolationist government is one that exercises restraint in its ambitions and maximizes its freedom of action. Such a policy is "based on the belief that most of what happens outside of America's borders poses no military threat to the country; the belief that America's military power, short of war, can accomplish little to shape that environment; and the belief that it is not worth the costs and risks of waging war to do so."[8] In U.S. foreign policy, isolationism refers to reliance on American power to ensure freedom of action, including an aversion to multilateral treaties or international organizations that may limit autonomy.[9]

Although its foreign policy has often been described as isolationist, America has never been completely disengaged from world affairs. "External assistance was essential to the birth of an independent United States; concerns about international commerce and foreign threats decisively influenced the form of government created in the Constitutional Convention of 1787. Foreign policy molded the political culture of new nation."[10] Complete isolation has never been an option, and America has always relied on international trade and a "complex web of international cultural connections."[11] The country's founders did not want to be cut off from the rest of the world, but instead sought to "safeguard the independence of a new and not yet powerful nation by avoiding, whenever possible, involvement in the military and political affairs of the major powers while, at the same time, expanding trade and commerce as a means of fostering national development."[12] Today's "neo-isolationists" regard themselves as conservatives who look to the example of the country's founders. In the Middle East, this means avoiding becoming embroiled in distant conflicts that have no (or limited) direct impact on America's vital interests.

Like isolationism, internationalism is often oversimplified, and is frequently used to describe "any U.S. involvement overseas, even if it is action undertaken unilaterally or in the narrow case of American national interest, simply because it is international in a geographic sense."[13] Other interest-based interpretations stress international involvement "as a means of realizing and protecting goals."[14] By contrast, still others insist that internationalism must also include efforts to promote cooperation, including establishing laws and institutions to achieve a more just and peaceful world—that is, values in addition to interests. In the Middle East, as elsewhere, internationalism requires engagement. American internationalists share "the vision of a peaceful world ordered by law"[15] and believe that U.S. involvement is necessary to create this world. America, they believe, should act as a leader in a partnership of democratic nations and that the national interest is best sought by cooperation within a larger community, a perspective incorporating both interests and values. Thus, internationalism can involve employing multilateral forums to pursue an Israeli–Palestinian peace, negotiating with Iran to limit its nuclear ambitions, and defining counterterrorism and detention policies that are consistent with international law.

Internationalism and isolationism are not incompatible. The emphasis may change, but even if one is dominant, elites debate the merits of both: "Isolationism and Internationalism have a somewhat symbiotic relationship and need to be understood as longstanding features of American politics beyond the typically accepted highpoint of the 'twenties and thirties.'"[16] We will see the interplay of these features repeatedly throughout the text.

Unilateralism and Multilateralism

The question about acting alone or cooperating with others in foreign policy has long been debated in America and plays out clearly in the formulation of U.S. foreign policies in the Middle East. *Uni*-lateralism involves "acting alone," while *multi*-lateralism involves working with others. Unilateralism is "a tendency to opt out of a multilateral framework (whether existing or proposed) or to act alone in addressing a particular global challenge rather than choosing to participation in collective action."[17] Multilateralism has several meanings. It may simply describe policy coordination among three or more states.[18] Sometimes there is an implication regarding the nature of such coordination: for example, the normative idea that coordination must be consistent with principles that "specify appropriate conduct for a class of action, without regard to the particularistic interests of the parties or the strategic exigencies that may exist in any specific occurrence." Multilateralism, then, is "a highly demanding institutional form"[19] that is achieved less frequently than bilateralism or unilateralism. Identifying policies as unilateral or multilateral is further complicated by the reality that, in actual practice, "there are many possible gradations between the two orientations and there may be complex situations where elements of unilateralism and multilateralism coexist."[20]

The first century of American foreign policy was characterized by unilateralism as leaders sought to remain aloof from European power politics. American leaders wished to craft policies to increase U.S. strength by encouraging trade and economic development, enlarging U.S. territory, and reducing foreign influence on the continent. Multilateralism is a more recent current in foreign policy. While there was support for involvement in multilateral institutions in the early twentieth century, U.S. leaders did not pursue a sustained policy of multilateralism until after World War II. As that war ended and the Cold War began, Washington helped establish several multilateral organizations like the UN and the Bretton Woods economic institutions to manage global politics and economics and to establish global rules that were compatible with U.S. interests and values. Although these institutions remain, U.S. influence in them has declined with the emergence of new states in Africa and Asia after decolonization. Today, Washington often turns to institutions where it has more influence as well as bilateral arrangements when these alternatives offer more favorable outcomes. And American leaders have always retained the right to act unilaterally when vital interests are at stake. The tendency to adopt multilateralism when it offers a favorable solution to challenges is an "instrumental" multilateralism that fits the narrower definition of multilateralism above.

Interventionism and Noninterventionism

Another enduring debate involves intervention—"unsolicited interference by one state in the affairs of another,"[21] often *military* intervention for humanitarian ends. In recent decades, the Middle East has been the focus of U.S. interventions. In practice, intervention can take the form of military, economic, and diplomatic interference for a variety of purposes, expedient and altruistic. Intervention rarely occurs for purely selfless motives, and on various occasions in U.S. history has involved adding territory or enhancing security. Nonintervention is the avoidance of "unsolicited" interference. Analysis of intervention-nonintervention is complicated by norms favoring intervention. In the eighteenth and nineteenth centuries, for example, intervention was permitted under international law and was even considered a sovereign *right* of states. For Europe's rulers, intervention sanctioned by the balance of power and Concert of Europe was considered a moral duty "to uphold their common culture and to protect the political status quo."[22] Today, the normative climate generally prohibits intervention except to rectify violations of international law or protect vital interests. America's position on the legality of intervention has generally been broad, accepting that states have a right to determine which interests are sufficiently vital to justify it. Even in eras when U.S. leaders have practiced nonintervention, they have retained the *right* to intervene when vital interests are at stake.

THE PAST: COMPETING CURRENTS IN HISTORICAL PERSPECTIVE

During much of its first century, America was a weak former colony, and its leaders were preoccupied with securing independence from the "Old World." When intervention occurred, its purpose was to consolidate control over territory or prevent European meddling. America avoided intervening to acquire

Canada because of the possibility of war with Britain. American leaders could not afford to emphasize values in their foreign policy, but had to secure U.S. interests. Unilateralism and later interventionism served as bases for a grand strategy to ensure independence and evict Europe's powers from the Americas. As America amassed economic and military power in the twentieth century, core interests expanded to include a variety of interests and values, and grand strategy became difficult to design. The early Cold War was a golden age of U.S. grand strategy defined by containing Soviet power. Multilateralism and interventionism were combined to achieve containment. America turned to international law and institutions to advance its interests and, although it practiced nonintervention in the Soviet sphere of influence, it repeatedly intervened in support of noncommunist governments outside that sphere. The strategic landscape changed dramatically with the collapse of the USSR, the emergence of nonstate terrorists, and transnational threats such as nuclear proliferation, financial crises, and climate change. These changes prompted a reevaluation of foreign-policy orientations, with significant implications for U.S. foreign policy in the Middle East.

Isolation or Unilateralism? The Foreign Policy of a Young Nation

There was an isolationist element in American politics in the colonial era and the early years of the new republic, and isolation has remained an enduring orientation in U.S. foreign policy ever since—even shaping policies toward the Middle East. The first colonists had left Europe to escape wars and religious intolerance, and "in venturing to the New World, they had accepted the prospect of a life of virtual isolation from the Old World."[23] But wanting and achieving isolation were very different objectives. Complete isolation was never possible, nor was it desirable. The dilemma for early Americans was how to maintain trade relationships without becoming dangerously entangled in European politics.

This dilemma persisted beyond the American Revolution, although tension remained between the desire to remain free of foreign entanglements and the need for foreign support to ensure the country's independence. Several events during George Washington's presidency (1789–1796) forced American leaders to consider carefully their place in the world. The Neutrality Proclamation (1793), declaring American neutrality in the war between France and Britain, and Washington's Farewell Address are often cited as the sources of American isolationism. But Washington was not an isolationist. Rather, he recognized that America was too weak to become embroiled in foreign conflicts, notably the wars France waged against other European powers following its revolution. The question hinged less on *whether* to ally and more on *with whom* to ally. Should America aid its fellow democracy, France, or assist its trading partner and the world's leading naval power, Britain, to combat the war waged by France's revolutionary government? Public opinion sided with France. Washington, however, refused to do so, fueling domestic debate. Federalists led by Alexander Hamilton sought to aid Britain. Democrat-Republicans, led by Thomas Jefferson, supported France in gratitude for French assistance to the colonies during the Revolutionary War. And Washington's predilection to remain neutral in Europe's conflicts did not prevent him from negotiating several treaties to ensure America's military security and economic prosperity, including the 1794 Jay Treaty with Britain that granted commercial rights to both countries and the 1795 Treaty of San Lorenzo with Spain that resolved their territorial disputes and gave American ships access to the Mississippi River.

During this era, American interest in the Mediterranean—including North Africa—focused on trade. Prior to independence, colonial merchant vessels received the protection of British treaties with the Barbary rulers of independent Morocco and the Ottoman regencies Algiers, Tunis, and Tripoli. That protection was revoked after independence, and the Barbary States targeted U.S. ships and captured their crews for ransom or the slave trade. In 1785 Algiers declared war on the United States and captured two ships and held their crews for ransom. It took ten years to negotiate an end to that crisis. In 1786, following the capture of a U.S. merchant ship by the sultan of Morocco two years prior, the United States negotiated a treaty with that kingdom. By 1801, when Thomas Jefferson became president, Washington had negotiated tribute treaties with all four of the Barbary States, promising to make annual payments in exchange for the safety of U.S. vessels. In the early years of the nineteenth century, Tripoli (1801–1805) and then Algiers (1815–1816) declared war on the United States for, respectively, late payments of tribute and dissatisfaction with previously negotiated tribute. Washington expanded its navy and won both Barbary Wars, thus refusing to continue payments of any kind. "Few events in the post-independence world had a more transformative impact on America than its war in the Middle East," argues Michael Oren. "A dire threat from the region prompted former colonies to coalesce and pool their resources, to create naval strength and project it far from America's shores."[24]

KEY DOCUMENT
Excerpt from George Washington's Farewell Address (1796)[25]

Upon retiring from public office, George Washington offered to "Friends and Fellow-Citizens" reflections on threats to the Union. Some, like those posed by political factions, were domestic but several were foreign. In articulating the risks of "foreign influence" and "permanent alliances," Washington encouraged his successors to craft foreign policies that were honorable and prudent—that were consistent with American values but that also would protect American interests: "The great rule of conduct for us in regard to foreign nations is in extending our commercial relations, to have with them as little political connection as possible. So far as we have already formed engagements, let them be fulfilled with perfect good faith. Here let us stop. Europe has a set of primary interests which to us have none; or a very remote relation. Hence she must be engaged in frequent controversies, the causes of which are essentially foreign to our concerns. . . . Our detached and distant situation invites and enables us to pursue a different course. . . . Why forgo the advantages of so peculiar a situation? . . . Why, by interweaving our destiny with that of any part of Europe, entangle our peace and prosperity in the toils of European ambition, rivalship, interest, humor or caprice? It is our true policy to steer clear of permanent alliances with any portion of the foreign world; so far, I mean, as we are now at liberty to do it."

MAP 2.1 Louisiana Purchase

By the 1820s American trade in the Mediterranean was flourishing and no longer a central concern of U.S. foreign-policy debates, which shifted focus to the Western Hemisphere. Although at times isolationism seemed to dominate in this era, internationalism never vanished. The first century or so of American foreign policy was a "regional era" in which leaders "sought to expand the country's borders, provide security to its peoples, and promote capitalism"[26] to enhance American security and power. Two events that illustrated the tension between isolationism and internationalism were the 1803 Louisiana Purchase and the 1823 Monroe Doctrine.

The Louisiana Purchase involved the purchase of 530 million acres of territory from Napoleon Bonaparte in 1803 for $15 million, doubling the size of the United States. The transaction had profound implications for American foreign policy. Sought by President Thomas Jefferson to safeguard U.S. control of the mouth of the Mississippi River, the purchase enjoyed wide public support while also igniting political controversy. There was a question of whether Jefferson was constitutionally authorized to make such a purchase. Equally important was the question of whether prior treaty obligations allowed Napoleon to sell the territory. There were also concerns about its impact on domestic politics, especially the citizenship of "foreigners" and the shifting political balance of power among American states after the addition of so many new citizens. Nevertheless, in providing control of the Mississippi River, the acquisition enhanced U.S. security, enabled westward expansion, provided commercial advantages, and marked the initial retreat of European powers from the Western Hemisphere while establishing a precedent for expansion into neighboring territories.

The tension between isolationism and internationalism again appeared in the Monroe Doctrine. In his annual message to Congress in December 1823, President James Monroe outlined two principles of U.S. policy relating to the emerging political order in the Americas—noncolonization and nonintervention. Regarding the former, the Monroe Doctrine is recalled for the warning that "the American continents, by the free and independent condition which they have assumed and maintain, are henceforth not to be considered as subjects for future colonization by any European power." But Monroe's address also affirmed that America would not intervene in the "internal affairs" of European powers, and declared that it "should consider any attempt on their part to extend their system to any portion of [the Western] hemisphere as dangerous to [American] peace and safety."[27] Some Europeans were outraged that Monroe would presume to issue such a statement, given America's military weakness. Austrian statesman Klemens von Metternich called it "a new act of revolt," and the Russian government regarded it with "only the profoundest contempt." Decades later Prussian chancellor Otto von Bismarck would call it "a species of arrogance peculiarly American and inexcusable."[28] Latin American leaders, many of whom perceived no threat from Europe, were more anxious about U.S. ambitions in the region. In fact, the doctrine had been suggested by British foreign minister George Canning and was premised on British naval power preventing Spain or France from regaining colonies in Latin America. In 1826 Canning famously declared, "I called the New World into existence to redress the balance of the Old."[29]

The doctrine's promise that America would not tolerate European interference in its hemisphere became a cornerstone of American foreign policy and has long been equated with isolationism. Better viewed as an example of unilateralism (or bilateralism), the Monroe Doctrine ushered in a new era in American foreign policy in which America was more engaged in hemispheric *and* world affairs. Indeed, one can see "Monroe thinking" in the many interventions that the United States undertook in the nineteenth and twentieth centuries.[30] Let us now examine the following era in American foreign policy, often described as isolationist but involving unilateralism and emerging interventionism.

Interventionism: America Expands, 1823–1914

For the rest of the nineteenth century and into the early twentieth century, isolationist sentiment remained strong in America and its leaders continued to avoid war with European powers. The era also featured a steady expansion of U.S. trade and interventionism. Attention was focused on westward expansion to curtail European influence on the continent. America expanded to include new territories that would eventually become states, beginning with Texas (annexed in 1845); then California, Arizona, and New Mexico (1848); then Alaska (1867) and Hawaii (1898). Washington also intervened aggressively in hemispheric affairs and added links with Asia, reflected in commercial treaties with China (1844) and Japan (1853). Following Spain's defeat in the Spanish–American War (1898), America also acquired the Philippines and Puerto Rico. Interventionism did not spread to the Middle East, where in 1833 the United States entered its first treaty of mutual recognition with an Arab state, the Sultanate of Oman. The era reflected competing isolationist, internationalist, and interventionist tendencies in the idea of Manifest Destiny that fueled westward expansion, growing interest in the stability of smaller countries in the Americas, and a global agenda to spread American values.

Manifest Destiny (1842–1848) By the logic of Manifest Destiny, the American people and institutions were uniquely virtuous and so Americans were obliged to "remake the world in their image."[31] In the Middle East an evangelical Protestant missionary movement that had begun in the 1820s had the support of millions of Americans. These missionaries believed "the destiny of America is inevitably bound up with the destiny of the world" and "America is only safe in the salvation of mankind."[32] Missionaries across the Middle East sought and received the protection of U.S. diplomats and warships against Muslim rulers hostile to their agenda.[33]

It was the idea, though, that America was divinely destined to expand and had a superior claim to the territory stretching to the Pacific and beyond that dominated American foreign policy during this period. To some extent interests also fueled the desire to spread westward. America's population was growing rapidly, and revolutions in communication and transportation technologies made it possible to absorb this growth. Americans also feared Europeans would expand into this "empty, unused"[34] land if they did not.

Manifest Destiny was nationalistic, idealistic, and entwined with concerns about national security. It was controversial, and political parties differed on the value of expanding, with Democrats viewing it as the "solution to the problems of modernization" and Whigs fearful that uncontrolled growth would create economic disparities and fuel internal conflict.[35]

Manifest Destiny was instrumental in President James Polk's reinterpretation of the Monroe Doctrine in 1845 and the Mexican–American War (1846–1848) that followed, America's first major occupation of foreign soil. Polk's desire to annex Texas, Mexican California, and the Oregon Territory played a central role in his presidential campaign. European efforts to thwart Polk prompted the new president to extend the Monroe Doctrine to prohibit European interference with American expansion.

When Polk's effort to purchase land in northern Mexico failed, he sent troops to the disputed U.S.–Texas border, triggering a controversial war. Although Polk had expected a brief war, it took a year for U.S. troops to occupy the territories he sought because Mexico, Secretary of State Daniel Webster argued, was an "ugly enemy": "She will not fight—and will not treat."[36] Mexico refused to negotiate and used guerrilla warfare to resist occupation. Finally, in 1848 by the Treaty of Guadalupe Hidalgo, Polk achieved his aims, including acquiring Texas. As a result, America increased its territory by one third, including most of Arizona, New Mexico, California, Colorado, Texas, Nevada, Utah, Kansas, Oklahoma, and Wyoming.

The war had consequences at home and abroad. The acquisition of new territories elevated the slavery issue on the national agenda and propelled the country toward civil war—a war that posed foreign-policy challenges for both North and South. Elsewhere in the Americas, governments grew fearful that the "colossus of the North" had greater ambitions. These fears seemed to be confirmed in the Spanish–American War (1898) and the construction of the Panama Canal. The administration of Theodore Roosevelt began two interventionist decades during which America acquired Puerto Rico, Guam, the Philippines, Hawaii, Samoa, and the Panama Canal Zone. This last was viewed as so important that America enabled Panama to become independent of Colombia and repeatedly intervened in countries near the canal to ensure political stability, including treaties with governments in the Americas securing the right to intervene.

Interventionism and the Roosevelt Corollary   Until the turn of the twentieth century, U.S. foreign policy could, with the exception of the Mexican–American War, be characterized by the effort to avoid foreign conflicts. Reluctance to become engaged in Europe's affairs began to recede with Theodore Roosevelt's presidency owing to new overseas interests after the Spanish–American War, as well as Roosevelt's desire to make the country more influential internationally and his belief that the United States should "accept responsibility for order and stability in its own region."[37]

The Roosevelt Corollary was formalized in 1904 after attempts by European governments to use naval power to collect debts owed them by Latin American countries. To end these efforts, Roosevelt extended the Monroe Doctrine, proclaiming a right to use military force in the Americas to keep Europeans out *and* (his corollary) the prerogative to intervene to restore stability in unstable countries in the Americas. He insisted that, when disputes arose between European powers and governments in the Western Hemisphere, the United States would intervene, adding,

> Chronic wrongdoing, or an impotence which results in a general loosening of the ties of civilized society, may in America, as elsewhere, ultimately require intervention by some civilized nation, and in the Western Hemisphere the adherence of the United States to the Monroe Doctrine may force the United States, however reluctantly, in flagrant cases of such wrongdoing or impotence, to the exercise of an international police power.[38]

His corollary served as justification for later interventions, often by "gunboat diplomacy," in Venezuela, Cuba, Nicaragua, Haiti, and the Dominican Republic. In 1931 Marine General Smedley Butler recalled,

> I helped make Mexico safe for American oil interests in 1914. I helped make Haiti and Cuba a decent place for the National City Bank boys to collect revenue in. I helped purify Nicaragua for the international banking house of Brown Brothers. . . . I brought light to the Dominican Republic for American sugar interests in 1916. I helped make Honduras "right" for American fruit companies in 1903. Looking back on it, I might have given Al Capone a few hints.[39]

While Roosevelt is remembered for his "big stick" diplomacy in the Americas and his imperialist views, he was also a strong internationalist who recognized "that the United States was affected by events around the globe and believed that it was in the country's best interest to work with other developed nations to maintain peace and stability."[40] He largely succeeded, although U.S. public opinion generally remained opposed (as in previous eras) to involvement in European disputes. Although Roosevelt recognized the limits posed by public opinion, he brought America into international institutions to help settle international disputes. In 1902 he called upon the Permanent Court of Arbitration at The Hague to hear a long-standing dispute between America and Mexico, the first taken to the body after its establishment in 1899. In 1904, at the request of the Inter-Parliamentary Union, he called for a second Hague conference to develop the laws of war. And the following year he offered his good offices to help end the 1905 Russo–Japanese War, for which he was awarded a Nobel Peace Prize. In 1906 he cosponsored the

Algeciras Conference to resolve disputes among European powers over their influence in Morocco. In the era that followed, the United States would emerge as a world power, with interests beyond the Western Hemisphere and Europe.

A Global Leader Emerges, 1914–1945

The early twentieth century again witnessed tensions among isolationism, unilateralism, and interventionism in U.S. policy. As in earlier eras, American policy was to avoid involvement in Europe's wars—that is, until those wars posed a clear threat to American interests. And, through much of this era, much of today's Middle East was under European administration and not a U.S. foreign-policy priority. As for great power politics, America only reluctantly entered World War I after Germany's adoption of unrestricted submarine warfare threatened U.S. commercial interests and risked American lives. Washington pursued a noninterventionist policy before World War II and only joined that conflict after Japan's attack on Pearl Harbor. American power and prestige grew after these conflicts, setting the stage for Washington to accept the mantle of global leadership.

World War I and Wilsonian Diplomacy, 1914–1920 In this era, the United States was only beginning to express an interest in the Middle East, with the discovery of oil in that region (chapter 3). For the most part, the United States was preoccupied with the conduct of World War I and the implementation of the peace that followed.

America reluctantly entered World War I, having demanded that the belligerents respect American rights as a neutral party. Noninvolvement in the Great War was a cornerstone of President Woodrow Wilson's foreign policy during his first term in office and aided his reelection in 1916, with Democrats campaigning on the slogan, "He kept us out of war!" The potential for conflict among America's diverse immigrant populations was only one reason for remaining neutral. Equally important was a desire to trade with both sides—a policy only a neutral government could follow. However, U.S. neutrality was undermined by the large loans it made to Britain and France.

As war raged, Americans debated their role in the world and how to promote U.S. interests and values. Conservative internationalists saw Germany's defeat as necessary for establishing a new international order based on law and collective security, whereas progressive internationalists argued for peace as necessary to advance domestic social and economic reform, including labor reform and women's rights. Isolationists advocated sticking to America's "long-standing tradition of noninvolvement as a way to safeguarding the nation's way of life."[41] Several factors persuaded Wilson to rethink his views by 1916. In 1915 Germany launched a submarine campaign that resulted in American deaths, notably the sinking of the British-registered *Lusitania*. In 1917, when Germany declared an official policy of unrestricted submarine warfare, the threat to U.S. vessels grew, and pressure to enter the war intensified. As German U-boats sank U.S. ships, Americans learned that Germany had offered Mexico an alliance and support for Mexican efforts to regain Texas, New Mexico, and Arizona. On April 2, 1917, Wilson asked Congress to declare war on Germany.

Woodrow Wilson is recalled for seeking a generous peace at the conclusion of World War I. An idealistic, liberal interventionist, Wilson represented America at the 1919 Versailles Peace Conference. His

Fourteen Points encapsulated his goals for a postwar world, including renunciation of secret treaties, free trade, independence and self-determination for subject peoples, and the creation of a League of Nations to preserve peace. Wilson's idealistic internationalist objectives were, however, largely thwarted by the opposition of British and French leaders who, in part, used the peace process to carve formerly Ottoman-ruled territories among themselves. Nevertheless, Wilson's proposal for a League of Nations based on collective security under which members would unite to repel aggression was incorporated into the Treaty of Versailles. A political battle ensued when the treaty was brought to the U.S. Senate for ratification.

Many observers interpret what happened as a battle between isolationists and internationalists, the former represented by Wilson and the latter by Henry Cabot Lodge, a Republican and Senate majority leader. There was a small bipartisan group of "irreconcilables" in the Senate, who were opposed to the treaty under any circumstances, though for different reasons. Some thought it protected liberal ideals insufficiently, while others viewed it as a threat to U.S. sovereignty and feared League membership might involve America in war without congressional approval. This group, comprised of only fourteen senators, received support from influential industrialists, including Andrew Mellon and Henry Clay Frick. Lodge was not himself an irreconcilable, but represented a larger group that was willing to consider ratification *if* reservations could be included that preserved the right of Congress to determine whether the country would go to war. Wilson refused to compromise, and the Senate failed to ratify the treaty by a vote of 38 in favor and 52 opposed.

Renewed isolationism is too simple an explanation for the Senate's refusal to ratify, but there was a turn inward in America after World War I. A number of policies reflected an "America-first" mentality, including new tariffs imposed on foreign goods to protect American manufacturers, and quotas on immigration. Following the Great Depression, the U.S. public became increasingly isolationist, opposing American involvement in conflicts in Europe and Asia (although seeking increased trade with Latin America).

American Isolationism in the 1930s Fueled by the Great Depression and the experience of World War I, including a belief that bankers and arms manufacturers had pushed America into war, U.S. public opinion and government policies became increasingly isolationist in the 1930s. Isolationists, much as in earlier eras, sought to avoid involvement in foreign conflicts and foreign entanglement more generally to preserve the country's freedom of action in foreign affairs. Isolationists were united in the belief that American "[p]articipation in war would weaken the United States and indeed place her survival as a free republic in jeopardy."[42] Otherwise, isolationists were a diverse lot. Some were conservatives who believed that war would lead to inflation and price and wage controls that would threaten the foundations of capitalism. Others were liberals who feared that war would bring Franklin Roosevelt's New Deal to an end and fuel "armament economics" that would threaten labor rights and civil liberties. Indeed, isolationists were powerful because they were diverse and faced no organized, consistent opposition from internationalists.

Isolationism led Congress in the 1930s to pass the Neutrality Acts, a series of laws intended to ensure America would remain neutral as conflicts developed in Europe and Asia. These acts prevented Americans from exporting arms and ammunition to countries at war and made it difficult for Washington to aid Britain and France to resist Nazi aggression. This era highlighted the challenges presidents may face in implementing foreign policy. President Franklin D. Roosevelt was an internationalist, but his actions were constrained by isolationist sentiment. FDR sought to help quarantine "the epidemic of world lawlessness." In 1940 he argued America could best defend its interests by supporting Britain because "the best immediate defense of the United States is the success of Great Britain in defending itself," which he justified both by America's "historic and current interest in the survival of democracy in the world as a whole" and "from a selfish point of view of American defense."[43]

Isolationists opposed policies that would, they argued, trigger war with Germany. All the while, there were influential internationalists fighting the isolationist current. Henry Luce, for example, the founder of *Time, Life,* and *Fortune* magazines and an influential voice for internationalism, argued that Americans "accept wholeheartedly our duty and our opportunity as the most powerful and vital nation in the world"[44] by supporting Britain and create a new world order based upon American principles. Those principles were encompassed in what Roosevelt called the "four freedoms"—freedom of speech, freedom of worship, freedom from want, and freedom from fear. Congress finally abandoned neutrality in March 1941 with the passage of the Lend-Lease Act allowing America to provide supplies to Germany's foes. Then, in August, Roosevelt and British prime minister Winston Churchill agreed to the Atlantic Charter, publicly demonstrating U.S. support for Britain and laying out an internationalist agenda for the postwar world—freer trade, self-determination, disarmament, and collective security. Nonetheless, isolationist sentiment remained strong, and only Japan's attack on December 7, 1941, convinced the public to enter World War II.

Instrumental Multilateralism: Containing Strategic Challenges

U.S. isolationism had ended by 1945. World War II had left power vacuums in Europe and Asia, and America emerged as a great power. We now explain the development of America's global interests and responsibilities in this era, and in later chapters you will see how this transformation played out in the Middle East, especially in shaping U.S. relations with Arab regimes (chapter 3), Israel (chapter 9), and Iran (chapter 12).

The Cold War America was the first nuclear power, and U.S. leaders viewed the Soviet Union as the greatest threat to the postwar era. In the Cold War, Washington pursued a grand strategy that included multilateralist, unilateralist, interventionist, and noninterventionist policies. On the one hand, this was an internationalist and multilateralist era of foreign policy in which U.S. leaders encouraged the development of global institutions founded on liberal democratic and economic principles, including the United Nations, an outgrowth of the Atlantic Charter; the Bretton Woods financial institutions; the Marshall Plan; and the North Atlantic Treaty Organization (NATO).

In other respects, however, America remained unilateral, even when dealing with multilateral institutions like the UN or NATO. America's European allies, for example, were repeatedly frustrated by the failure of American leaders to consult them on policies that had a direct bearing on NATO defense, as in the decision to remove U.S. missiles from Turkey as part of an agreement with Moscow to end the 1962 Cuban missile crisis. Simultaneously, U.S. policy balanced interventionism and noninterventionism with a tacit policy of noninterference in the Soviet bloc alongside interventionism to prevent the spread of Soviet influence into new areas, especially those in Washington's sphere of influence. In the Western Hemisphere unilateral policies were pursued under the Hemispheric Defense Doctrine, an extension of the Monroe Doctrine, that claimed Latin America as part of the "free world" and thus under U.S. protection. This doctrine justified military interventions and covert operations to support anticommunist forces in Guatemala and Brazil (1954), Cuba (1961), the Dominican Republic (1965), Chile (1973), and Nicaragua (1980s). In the Middle East, Washington intervened with diplomacy and foreign aid to support authoritarian regimes like those in Egypt, Saudi Arabia, and the shah's Iran to prevent the spread of communism, to maintain social and political stability necessary to protect the flow of oil to Western markets, and to ensure the security of Israel.

After the Cold War With the fall of the Berlin Wall in 1989, the reunification of Germany in 1990, and the collapse of the USSR in 1991, the world radically changed. Suddenly, U.S. leaders no longer had a clear adversary, and America's grand strategy of containment was no longer relevant. For a time, observers were optimistic that a new, peaceful world order would ensue—one in which liberal institutions could flourish and in which America would no longer have to invest heavily in military preparedness. With the "peace dividend" produced by the end of the Cold War, Washington would have additional resources to invest in economic and social development. Reality did not match expectations. New, unanticipated threats emerged—many of them centered on the Middle East, as we will see in later chapters—and there has been significant continuity across post–Cold War administrations in managing this new environment.

Postwar administrations sought to maintain U.S. leadership and assumed that other countries seek that leadership.[45] All the presidents in this era—George H. W. Bush (1989–1993), Bill Clinton (1993–2001), George W. Bush (2001–2009), and Barack Obama (2009–2017)—were internationalists in the limited sense of seeking a major role for America in the world. They have differed, however, about why such a role is necessary and the means to sustain it. None has been isolationist or exclusively unilateralist. As George W. Bush's first secretary of state, Colin Powell, observed in 2001, today "You can't be unilateralist. The world is too complicated."[46]

Since the end of the Cold War there remains an enduring commitment to preserving sovereignty and maximizing flexibility in foreign affairs as well as elements of unilateralism and multilateralism. As in the past, "America behaves unilaterally when it can, and it is always at moments of nationalist crisis that the impulse is strongest."[47] Even when it does work through multilateral institutions, we see an instrumental multilateralism that seeks to preserve flexibility, even as America engages the world. We do not see a coherent grand strategy such as containment, and there is no consistent sense of when to emphasize values over interests or which values and interests are worth fighting for. While observers have tried to find such strategies in the form of presidential "doctrines," none in fact has had a comprehensive view of America's role in the world and the appropriate instruments for preserving that role.

As president when the Cold War ended, George H. W. Bush devoted considerable attention to foreign affairs. He had extensive foreign-policy experience, having served as vice president under Ronald Reagan, ambassador to China and the UN, and CIA director. Perhaps owing to this experience he had a multilateral orientation that shaped his approach to the 1991 Persian Gulf War, the Middle East peace process, famine in Somalia, and the emerging conflict in Yugoslavia. In the Persian Gulf War, he organized a UN-backed international coalition of thirty-four countries to force Iraq's withdrawal from Kuwait. The coalition's victory ushered in, Bush declared, a New World Order, "where the rule of law, not the law of the jungle, governs the conduct of nations . . . an order in which a credible United Nations can use its peacekeeping role to fulfill the promise and vision of the UN's founders."[48] In other words, America ought to use its power to support universal values.

At the same time, however, U.S. intervention in Panama in 1989 to oust Manuel Noriega signaled that Bush was willing to act unilaterally on matters of vital interest. Noriega, the military dictator of Panama since 1983, had supported U.S. anticommunist policies in Central America, but he also had a long record of involvement in drug trafficking. In 1988 he was indicted by federal grand juries in Tampa and Miami on charges of drug smuggling and money laundering. The following year, he annulled a presidential election that would have brought the opposition to power. In December 1989, just a day after an off-duty U.S. Marine was killed by Panamanian soldiers, Bush authorized "Operation Just Cause" to overthrow Noriega. The president justified the invasion as necessary to combat drug trafficking, defend democracy in Panama, and protect the Panama Canal (permitted under the 1977 Torrijos-Carter Treaties). The operation was successful, and Noriega was tried and convicted by a U.S. court in 1992. However, the U.S. invasion had violated international law and was denounced by the OAS and the UN.

Bush's New World Order was never realized, and as the first fully post–Cold War president, Bill Clinton faced a changed strategic environment. America had become the world's sole superpower with the collapse of the USSR. In the absence of a major challenger, Washington seemed free to pursue its own global agenda, but there would be less public support for engagement in international institutions and overseas involvement than before. Thus, the Clinton administration faced greater domestic constraints than had previous administrations in pursuing foreign policy, especially after the Republicans gained a majority in the House of Representatives in 1994. Political foes like Sen. Jesse Helms (R-NC), chair of the Senate Foreign Relations Committee, opposed much of Clinton's international agenda, including the payment of UN dues and U.S. participation in global treaties like the Kyoto Protocol for reducing greenhouse gas emissions and the Rome Statute that created the International Criminal Court (ICC).

Clinton's strategic vision involved advancing both values and interests, although the emphasis changed during his two terms in office. During his first term, Clinton emphasized the spread of democracy. This emphasis encompassed four goals that Clinton believed would produce security and prosperity: (1) "strengthen the community of market democracies," (2) "foster and consolidate new democracies and market economies where possible," (3) "counter the aggression and support the liberalization of states hostile to democracy," and (4) "help democracy and market economies take root in regions of greatest humanitarian concern."[49] Clinton's first term emphasized economic issues and in some ways foreshadowed the policies of his successor, George W. Bush.

A competing "Clinton Doctrine" emerged during his second term, and it is for this that he will be remembered. In a reaction to admitted foreign-policy failures in Clinton's first term—notably, the 1994 Rwandan genocide—the Clinton Doctrine emphasized humanitarian intervention. This emphasis was shaped by recognition that U.S. citizens and interests faced a broad spectrum of threats including terrorism, ethnic unrest, and criminal violence, and that America had an interest in guaranteeing global stability and must maintain sufficient military force to operate against multiple adversaries simultaneously.[50] The crux of the doctrine was that Washington would intervene militarily, even without UN approval, to end human-rights abuses when it could do so at limited cost. According to one official, Clinton viewed "genocide as itself a national interest where we should act"[51]— a policy distinctive for the principle that intervention should serve moral ends.

Clinton was a multilateralist who valued international institutions and norms, and his policies were frequently unilateralist and interventionist as well. Clinton unilaterally removed U.S. troops deployed in Somalia to implement a UN humanitarian mission after the death of U.S. soldiers in the 1993 Battle of Mogadishu, and he refused to form a coalition to prevent genocide in Rwanda. The Clinton administration also witnessed interventions in Haiti (1994), Bosnia (1995), and Kosovo (1999). There were air strikes in Afghanistan and Sudan in 1998 in retaliation for the bombing of U.S. embassies in East Africa, and in Iraq in 1993 after an alleged assassination plot against former president George H. W. Bush and in 1996 in response to interference with aircraft patrolling no-fly zones. These actions were evidence of U.S. military power that no state or coalition of states could challenge. U.S. dominance was so great that French foreign minister Hubert Védrine argued the label *superpower* no longer did it justice. America had achieved the status of *hyperpower,* a unique degree of power in all categories, including "this domination of attitudes, concepts, language and modes of life."[52] This designation called attention to what France and others viewed as growing U.S. unilateralism.

THE PRESENT: THE IMPACT OF 9/11

The 9/11 terrorist attacks transformed U.S. policy, as discussed in chapter 7. The most notable shift was a resurgence of unilateralism that had direct implications for U.S. policy toward a number of countries in the Middle East.

The Unilateralist Turn

U.S. unilateralism after 9/11 was most clearly directed toward regimes in the Middle East or challenges arising in that region, and included articulation of a preemptive war doctrine, military intervention in Iraq without UN authorization, the creation of new and less formal mechanisms for countering WMD proliferation, the use of bilateral treaties to protect U.S. citizens from prosecution in the ICC, and the use of unmanned drones for targeted killing of suspected terrorists overseas. In an era in which enemies were often disparate and invisible, multilateralism was viewed as a luxury that America could not afford in dealing with threats requiring decisive action.

Effective multilateralism requires governments with different values and interests to agree on common objectives *and* appropriate means to achieve them. The process takes time and often leads to lowest-common-denominator policies. This is not to say that Washington abandoned multilateralism, but after 9/11 it used it selectively—especially in the security realm, where interests frequently trump ideals. The willingness of U.S. officials to practice interventionism was another trend, marked by wars in Afghanistan in 2001 and Iraq in 2003. More recently, there has been a reluctance to intervene in messy conflicts, notably Syria, as the American public grew weary of long and costly wars. When the United States did intervene in Syria beginning in 2014, it employed air strikes and not combat troops, and even in the immediate aftermath of ISIS-claimed terrorist attacks in Paris in 2015, Americans continued to oppose sending troops to fight in Iraq and Syria.[53] Republican George W. Bush and Democrat Barack Obama had contrasting worldviews, but there was considerable continuity in their foreign policies.

Early in the Bush administration foreign-policy leaders focused on state-based threats. Of key concern to Bush and his senior policy advisors were great powers China and Russia and rogue states Iraq, Iran, North Korea, and Libya. It was to deal with the latter that Bush pursued a more active missile-defense program (approved during the Clinton administration), a policy that heightened tension with Russia. Bush also rejected U.S. participation in several international treaties that he viewed as potentially harmful to U.S. political and economic interests, including the Rome Statute and the Kyoto Protocol. It appeared that under the younger Bush, America would emphasize disengagement. This trend continued with the December 2001 abrogation of the 1972 Anti-Ballistic Missile Treaty and the rejection in 2002 of a protocol to the Biological Weapons Convention.

But after 9/11 global terrorism became the highest priority, and the War on Terror (chapter 7) was framed as a struggle between good and evil. Interests and norms were integrated in the formulation of U.S. foreign policies that sought simultaneously to enhance security and spread liberal values. Thus, there was tension between supporting Arab dictators like Egypt's Hosni Mubarak, whose polices enhanced U.S. security, and opposing Egypt's popularly elected Islamic president, Mohamed Morsi. This War on Terror was not just between America and al-Qaeda but targeted worldwide terrorism. America, Bush argued, could not afford to be defensive, reacting to terrorist attacks, but had to prepare to attack preemptively.

Anticipatory defense meant military engagement. By October 2001 America had invaded Afghanistan in search of al-Qaeda leaders responsible for the attacks and to oust the Taliban regime that had given sanctuary to al-Qaeda. Iraq also became part of this strategy (chapter 13). Saddam Hussein, who remained in power in Iraq after his defeat in 1991, "embodied the convergence of Bush's three fears—terrorism, tyrants and technologies of mass destruction."[54] America could not wait, in the words of National Security Advisor Condoleezza Rice, "for the smoking gun to be a mushroom cloud."[55] Bush turned to the UN Security Council, seeking international support for intervention, but when that failed he crafted a "coalition of the willing" and invaded without UN approval. The fact that the Iraq war did not receive Security Council authorization reinforced perceptions of U.S. unilateralism and interventionism.

Democracy promotion was a second goal in Bush's strategy in the War on Terror, based on a belief that democracies do not go to war with one another. This gained greater prominence when formally articulated as the Bush Doctrine in his second inaugural address when he declared, "It is the policy of the United States to seek and support the growth of democratic movements and institutions in every nation and culture with the ultimate goal of ending tyranny in our world."[56] The Afghan and Iraq wars were not just about "regime change." They were also fought to establish stable democracies, a daunting goal, and both conflicts turned into costly protracted wars that were still continuing when Bush left office in 2009. Nonproliferation was a third, related, goal that ranked high on the post-9/11 security agenda. It reflected a disengagement from multilateral efforts like the Nuclear Nonproliferation Treaty and the Comprehensive Test Ban Treaty in favor of bilateral and informal arrangements like the Proliferation Security Initiative.

Bush also pursued an active foreign policy outside the security realm. In economic policy, his administration pursued free trade and investment, signing several free-trade agreements. Critics countered that the emphasis on bilateral agreements and trade ties undermined multilateral efforts organized by the World Trade Organization. Washington also substantially increased its foreign aid commitments, with significant support going to fight global disease. Taken in its entirety, this agenda was mixed. Except for security, there was no clear strategy. Even as the administration championed democratization as a goal, it cut funding for democracy promotion. And democratization conflicted with other goals, like fighting terrorism.

Thus, U.S. foreign policy during Bush's first term shifted toward disengagement except for the use of military force. Foreign policy reflected a dislike for international treaties and organizations that might limit freedom of action, growing reliance on military preemption to cope with security threats, and military intervention to spread democracy. This reorientation was described by some as the "Bush revolution," but was it really? We see considerable continuity in using of foreign policy to pursue historically American values[57] like liberty, democracy, free-market capitalism, and the belief in a unique responsibility to spread those values.

Bush was a Wilsonian (a staunch liberal interventionist) in his commitment to spread democracy, even by force. But Bush also represented an unapologetic return to the tradition of unilateralism. Unilateralism has never been repudiated by American leaders, who have consistently been willing to act on their own when they believed it was the best way to serve U.S. interests. Where the Bush administration's shift was distinct was the militant expansion of American power in reaction to security threats. Thus, the "Bush revolution" represented a shift in style, not substance, although the shift in style was dramatic.

Several factors contributed to this shift, beginning with the unprecedented gap in military power between America and other countries. The United States turned to unilateralism because, in the absence of other actors capable of challenging it militarily, it could do so. But while the global distribution of power partly explains American unilateralism and interventionism, it is not the only factor. One must also consider the president's personality. Bush came to office with little foreign-policy experience but with a Manichean worldview of good versus evil shaped by his religious faith. Perhaps because he had little foreign policy experience, he relied on key advisors. In his first term Bush had appointed a diverse foreign-policy team of staunch neoconservatives including Vice President Dick Cheney and internationalists such as Secretary of State Colin Powell and Richard Armitage and Richard N. Haass, senior officials in the State Department.

After 9/11, Bush embraced the views of the hard-line nationalists in his administration. The rally 'round the flag effect of 9/11 on public opinion, which saw a 35-percentage-point increase in the president's approval ratings,[58] provided him with leeway to pursue unilateralist and interventionist policies. But the internationalist camp, represented by National Security Advisor and later Secretary of State Condoleezza Rice and Secretary of Defense Robert Gates, gained influence in Bush's second term when it became necessary to underplay unilateralism and engage allies to make progress in nuclear proliferation and Middle East peace.[59]

Critics argued that the costs of this unilateralist and interventionist orientation were greater than the short-term advantages it produced. They claimed that it undermined U.S. legitimacy abroad, alienated allies, actually increased the threat of terrorism, and drove America into debt. Such critics were eager for a change of course with the election of Barack Obama in 2008, but they were frustrated when a decisive shift did not occur.

A Return to Multilateralism

On the campaign trail, then junior senator from Illinois Barack Obama called for a new "American moment" in which the United States would "provide global leadership grounded in the understanding that the world shares a common security and a common humanity":

> This century's threats are at least as dangerous as and in some ways more complex than those we have confronted in the past. They come from weapons that can kill on a mass scale and from global terrorists who respond to alienation or perceived injustice with murderous nihilism. They come from rogue states allied to terrorists and from rising powers that could challenge both America and the international foundation of liberal democracy. They come from weak states that cannot control their territory or provide for their people. And they come from a warming planet that will spur new diseases, spawn more devastating natural disasters, and catalyze deadly conflicts.[60]

Environmental issues aside, Obama's view of the threats facing America was not unlike that of his predecessor, but he had a different interpretation of how the world worked, emphasizing that threats had a transnational dimension and that the American military might have a role to play in managing some of them but was unsuited for managing others. This interpretation held the promise of a transformation in U.S. policies in the Middle East. On the campaign trail, Obama opposed the war in Iraq and promised to withdraw U.S. troops within sixteen months, but he also espoused sending additional troops to Afghanistan, a conflict he regarded as more important than Iraq. He supported more open, multilateral diplomacy, arguing that diplomacy was necessary to rally global support for U.S. policies. He fostered nuclear nonproliferation efforts; leadership in climate negotiations; direct engagement with foes like Iran, Venezuela, North Korea, and Myanmar; and obeying international law—a commitment that extended to human-rights treaties and closing the Guantánamo Bay detention camp in Cuba. These positions set him apart from his Republican opponent, Sen. John McCain (R-AZ), but he also argued that military intervention still had a role in U.S. policy.[61] In the words of a national security advisor, Obama's foreign-policy goals on entering office were to "Wind down these two wars [Iraq and Afghanistan], reestablish American standing and leadership in the world, and focus on a broader set of priorities, from Asia and the global economy to a nuclear-nonproliferation regime."[62]

Presidents, however, are rarely able to pursue the foreign-policy agenda they wish. Once in office they face unexpected challenges, have access to new information, and encounter constraints, both foreseen and unforeseen. Obama's supporters were eager to see his vision reflected in foreign policy to reverse what they saw as "cowboy" diplomacy. Obama's opponents, by contrast, believed his policies would erode U.S. influence and compromise American security. Both groups expected Obama to be a multilateralist who would reaffirm support for international law and institutions while disengaging from costly military ventures, reversing the unilateralism and interventionism that had characterized the Bush years. As it turned out, at least in his first term, Obama lacked a grand strategy. Americans got something different than what they had expected. As president, Obama turned out to be more pragmatic than ideological in both the formulation and implementation of foreign policy. This preference for what is practical has been especially apparent in U.S. policy toward the Middle East, as we shall see in our analysis of Obama administration policies toward the region in later chapters.

Retrospectively, it was premature for the Norwegian Nobel Committee to announce in 2009 that it would award the Nobel Peace Prize to President Barack Obama "for his extraordinary efforts to strengthen international diplomacy and cooperation between peoples." The committee noted that Obama had "as President created a new climate in international politics. Multilateral diplomacy has regained a central position, with emphasis on the role that the United Nations and other international institutions can play."[63] The award generated criticism at home and abroad. Former Polish president and 1983 Nobel Peace Prize recipient Lech Walesa summed up the controversy: "So soon? Too early. He has no contribution so far."[64] Obama was not the first American president to receive the prize, but he had been in office less than nine months, whereas past recipients Theodore Roosevelt, Woodrow Wilson, and Jimmy Carter were awarded the prize for actions while in office or after their presidency. Suggests one presidential historian, "The committee seems to have been saying, 'We had eight years without strong US leadership for peace and now we have someone who will put the country's energies behind Middle East talks and nuclear arms control.'"[65]

Obama was not a value-driven multilateralist but a practical leader who was realistic and cautious, evaluating policy options according to their likelihood of success. "In office Obama has been a progressive where possible but a pragmatist when necessary. And given the domestic and global situations he has faced, pragmatism has dominated."[66] His caution was related to a second factor—the number and complexity of global challenges that faced America as he took office. As later chapters demonstrate, much of the complexity of Obama's foreign-policy dilemmas stemmed from the linkages among issues. These dilemmas appeared across a range of issues and made it virtually impossible to shape a one-size-fits-all vision of foreign policy. A third factor that constrained Obama's efforts to pursue the visionary, multilateral foreign policy he had promised as a candidate was public and congressional suspicion of internationalism. The country was divided over core values, and while public opinion was broadly internationalist, there was vocal opposition from neoconservatives, new sovereignists, and others influential in the previous administration who continued to oppose deeper cooperation with international institutions or new treaty commitments in arms control, climate change, and human rights.

Budget constraints were another factor that yielded pragmatism in foreign affairs. Implementing grand strategy is expensive because it tends to lead to extensive commitments, as it did for Monroe, Truman, and George W. Bush. Thus, arguments about U.S. involvement abroad became almost inseparable from arguments about restoring fiscal discipline.

Obama's rhetoric reflected an ideological commitment to multilateralism. Addressing the UN General Assembly in 2009, he urged, "Those who used to chastise America for acting alone in the world cannot now stand by and wait for America to solve the world's problems alone. We have sought in word and deed a new era of engagement with the world, and now is the time for all of us to take our share of responsibility for a global response to global challenges."[67] And in his second inaugural address in 2013, he declared, "We will show the courage to try and resolve our differences with other nations peacefully—not because we are naïve about the dangers we face, but because engagement can more durably lift suspicion and fear. America will remain the anchor of strong alliances in every corner of the globe; and we will renew those institutions that extend our capacity to manage crisis abroad."[68]

Hybrid Multilateralism

Obama's multilateralism has been variously described as "hybrid multilateralism," "multilateralism with teeth," and "soft unilateralism." Depending on the issue, he has even been described as an outright unilateralist. Liberals who looked forward to an Obama revolution after his election found the president insufficiently multilateral, as did many citizens in other countries (Figure 2.1). During Obama's first term, America failed to adopt several high-profile multilateral treaties, including the Law of the Sea Treaty, the Comprehensive Test Ban Treaty, the Ottawa Convention (known as the Mine Ban Treaty), and the Rome Statute. After lengthy negotiations, Washington delayed action on an arms trade treaty in 2012, a decision that delighted opponents of the treaty such as Russia, China, and Indonesia, but vexed its supporters, who charged Obama with abdicating U.S. leadership in order not to threaten his reelection prospects. Key military decisions were also taken without consultation with allies, including Obama's 2009 decision to send additional troops to Afghanistan, the 2011 raid that killed Osama bin Laden, and the continued use of drones in Pakistan.

Even policies that seemed multilateral like the proposed Transatlantic Trade and Investment Partnership and the Trans-Pacific Partnership were criticized for their possible negative impact on global trade negotiations. On the other hand, relations with the UN improved during the Obama years, with a reversal of the Bush-era refusal to participate in the UN Human Rights Council and a willingness to seek Security Council approval for multilateral sanctions against North Korea and Iran for their proliferation efforts and for a NATO-led humanitarian mission in Libya. Obama also sought to improve U.S. standing in several regions, seeking a "reset" with Russia and a "pivot" to Asia in his first term, and during his second term a "pivot back" to Europe (owing to Russo–American confrontation in Ukraine), nuclear talks with Iran, and a resumption of the peace process between Israel and the Palestinians.

Although Obama argued that military intervention still had a place in American foreign policy, after lengthy wars in Afghanistan and Iraq, the president became wary of new foreign entanglements and armed intervention and only engaged in them with multilateral support. By some accounts, the guiding principle of Obama's foreign policy was restrained multilateralism, or "retrenchment," reducing U.S. commitments abroad while shifting some of the burden for global leadership onto American partners,[69] a tendency that reflects less overall public support for U.S. involvement overseas (Figure 2.2). As explained by then secretary of defense Gates in a speech at West Point, "Any future defense secretary who advises the president to again send a big American land army into Asia or into the Middle East or Africa should

FIGURE 2.1   How Much Does the United States Consider Your Country's Interests?

> *Survey question: "In making international policy decisions, to what extent do you think the United States takes into account the interests of countries like (survey country)—a great deal, a fair amount, not too much, or not at all?"*

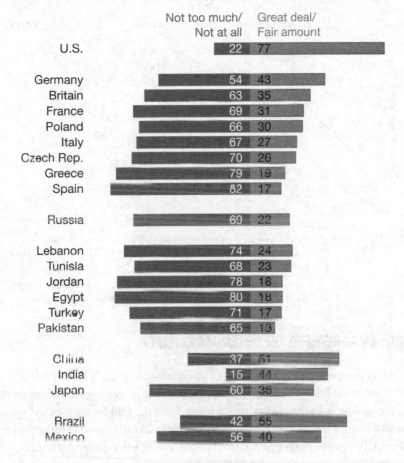

	Not too much/ Not at all	Great deal/ Fair amount
U.S.	22	77
Germany	54	43
Britain	63	35
France	69	31
Poland	66	30
Italy	67	27
Czech Rep.	70	26
Greece	79	19
Spain	82	17
Russia	69	22
Lebanon	74	24
Tunisia	68	23
Jordan	78	18
Egypt	80	18
Turkey	71	17
Pakistan	65	13
China	37	51
India	15	44
Japan	60	36
Brazil	42	55
Mexico	56	40

Source: "Views of the U.S. and American Foreign Policy," Pew Global Attitudes Project, June 13, 2012, http://www.pewglobal. org/2012/06/13/chapter-1-views-of-the-u-s-and-american-foreign-policy-4/

'have his head examined.'"[70] Thus Obama showed pragmatic caution in crises in Libya, Mali, Egypt, Syria, and Ukraine. Skeptics worry about the long-term implications of such a low-key policy: "Step back too far from big sticks, and when America speaks, it may not be heard."[71] Supporters, by contrast, argued that this kind of leadership is required in a complex, interconnected world.

FIGURE 2.2 Majority Says United States Should "Mind Its Own Business" Internationally

➤ *Graph shows percentage of respondents agreeing with the following statement: "The U.S. should mind its own business internationally and let other countries get along the best they can on their own."*

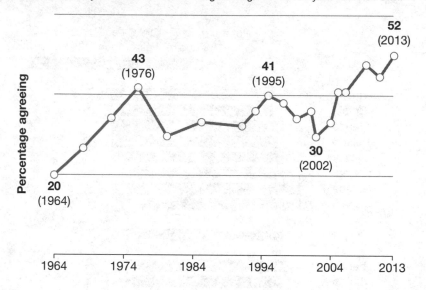

Source: "Majority Says U.S. Should 'Mind Its Own Business' Internationally," Pew Research Center, December 3, 2012, http://www.people-press.org/2013/12/03/public-sees-u-s-power-declining-as-support-for-global-engagement-slips/

CONCLUSION: ENGAGEMENT OR DISENGAGEMENT?

This examination of competing U.S. foreign-policy orientations imparts lessons for U.S. involvement in the global arena and in the Middle East specifically. Isolationism is no longer a real option in foreign policy, especially for dealing with the challenges emerging from the Middle East. Even "neo-isolationists" recognize America cannot completely retreat from the region. Washington is unlikely, for example, to end economic and diplomatic support for Israel or for friendly oil-producing states, or withdraw militarily from the Middle East. America will continue to maintain economic and military ties to the region and remain involved in international political organizations that operate there. Even the UN, with which Washington has had a troubled relationship in recent decades, is viewed by most Americans as playing a necessary role in Middle Eastern and in global affairs more generally.[72] The question becomes, *how engaged* will America be? American leaders have two possible options, both with historical roots.

The first entails greater engagement with the Middle East. It anticipates an expansion of the U.S. commitments to influence events there. As a "shaper," Washington would expand commitments to foster an international and regional order favorable to pursuing its interests, much as it did at the outbreak of the Cold War. Today's shapers tend to be liberal internationalists who seek to increase America's presence in international institutions and are willing to extend international legal commitments to ensure a more stable international environment that they see as beneficial to all countries. The advantage of engagement, shapers argue, is that America retains its global leadership.

Continuing security commitments, shapers contend, reduce conflict in key regions like the Middle East and constrain potential rivals, and alliances reduce the risk of involvement in unwanted conflicts by giving America greater influence over weaker partners. Continued U.S. engagement also maintains an open world economy and affords influence in economic negotiations that shape the global economy in ways that benefit U.S. interests and cooperate with others in managing global economic crises. Although one estimate in 2013 predicted that U.S. military expenditures in Afghanistan, Iraq, and Pakistan would ultimately cost over $4 trillion,[73] some argue that engagement is possible at a reasonable cost.[74]

The second option, disengagement or retrenchment, involves a retreat from commitments abroad. "Retrenchers" or "restrainers" seek a limited foreign policy in which an overextended, indebted America withdraws from all but vital foreign commitments. Restrainers are *not* isolationists who want to cut off ties to the outside world. Rather, they wish to align U.S. commitments with U.S. interests, resources, and public opinion.[75] They believe that by allowing other countries to take greater responsibility for their own security, America can focus on economic recovery and military reform. Restrainers come from a variety of traditions. Some are liberal multilateralists who emphasize nation-building at home as the way to restore American stature. Others represent a more conservative position associated with a sort of neo-isolationism that assumes the United States is sufficiently powerful that by disengaging from marginal commitments abroad it can insulate itself from dangerous overextension. Restrainers argue that current levels of engagement are too expensive in budget and manpower costs. American defense budgets are much higher than those of allies or adversaries, and the United States subsidizes its allies' security. Restrainers want allies and partners like Afghanistan to shoulder greater responsibility for their own security. They also argue that military involvement produces foreign enemies, while alliances risk trapping America in wars it does not seek.

Engagement, retrenchers claim, has harmed U.S. security: "It makes enemies almost as fast as it slays them, discourages allies from paying for their own defense, and convinces powerful states to band together and oppose Washington's plans, further raising the costs of carrying out its foreign policy."[76] Some retrenchers go further, arguing that engagement dilutes American sovereignty,[77] a belief apparent in America's rejection of numerous multilateral treaties. Hegemonic strategy in particular, reflected in seemingly endless wars in Afghanistan and Iraq, retrenchers claim, should give way to restraint: "This undisciplined, expensive, and bloody strategy has done untold harm to U.S. national security."[78]

The debate over how engaged the United States should be persists. In the chapters that follow, we examine how this debate affects a variety of issues and problems in the Middle East.

I

Arab Spring or Arab Winter?

Protesters in Cairo's Tahrir ("Martyr") Square during Egypt's revolution

America's relations with the Arab world (defined here as the members of the Arab League) that stretches from Morocco on the Atlantic Ocean to the Sultanate of Oman at the mouth of the Persian Gulf and the Comoro Islands off East Africa emphasized stability and expediency rather than values until the "Arab Spring." U.S. policy aimed to maintain secure sources of oil, support oil-rich friends in the Persian Gulf, limit Soviet influence in the region, contain aggressive foes like Saddam Hussein and Shia Iran, and ensure Israel's security. As the Arab Spring swept across the region in 2011, Washington came to believe that liberal values were the wave of the future. America supported democratic transitions both because they reflected U.S. ideals *and* would secure U.S. influence against anti-Americanism among democratic regimes angered by prior American support for hated dictators like Libya's Muammar Qaddafi, Syria's Bashar al-Assad, and Egypt's Hosni Mubarak.

A turning point in the spreading anti-government and pro-democratic protests that swept across North Africa and the Middle East in 2011 was a revolution in the most populous Arab country, Egypt, that led to the overthrow of President Mubarak, whose military-based authoritarian rule had lasted for thirty years. This event was the high point of what came to be called the "Arab Spring" and marked a moment when American policy in the region shifted from unquestioning support of Arab authoritarian leaders to a more nuanced policy of encouraging and supporting democratic reforms in much of the region. Mubarak's regime gave way to elections in which, as we shall see, an Islamist group, the Muslim Brotherhood, came to power with the Brotherhood's candidate, President Mohamed Morsi, at the country's helm in July 2012.

Only a year later, President Morsi had so alienated many Egyptians, especially those constituting the country's urban and secular middle class, that mass protests again erupted in Cairo's Tahrir

Timeline

1900–1959

1902 Saudis conquer much of southern Arabia

1909 British begin extracting oil in Iran

1916 Arab revolt against Ottoman Turkey begins

1916 British and French agree to partition the Middle East

1919 France claims Syria and Lebanon

April 1920 San Remo conference endorses British rule over Palestine and Iraq

1921 Feisal I proclaimed king of Iraq

1927 Huge oil fields discovered near Kirkuk, Iraq

1928 Muslim Brotherhood established in Egypt

1932 Saudi Arabia established; Iraq becomes independent

1943 Syria and Lebanon declare independence and the Arab League is established

1950 Saudi Arabia and Aramco agree to split oil profits

1951 America and Saudi Arabia sign a military treaty

1952 Nasser comes to power in Egypt

1954 Egypt bans the Muslim Brotherhood

1955 The Baghdad Pact is signed; Soviet arms sales to Egypt begin

1956 Nasser nationalizes the Suez Canal; British and French invade Egypt and unsuccessfully try to oust Nasser

July 1958 Iraqi monarchy overthrown; U.S. intervention in Lebanon

1960–2010

1960 OPEC founded

1966 Sayyad Qutb hanged in Egypt

1968 Saddam Hussein is put in charge of Iraq's internal security

1969 Muammar Qaddafi seizes power in Libya

1970 Anwar Sadat becomes Egypt's president

1970–1971 Hafez al-Assad assumes power in Syria; Soviet influence in Syria deepens

1972 Egypt expels Soviet military advisors

1979 Iran's Islamic Revolution

November 1979 The Iranian hostage crisis

December 1979 The Soviet Union invades Afghanistan

1981 Sadat assassinated: Hosni Mubarak becomes president of Egypt

1986 U.S. planes bomb Libya

1987 Zine El Abidine Ben Ali seizes power in Tunisia

September 1989 Qaddafi renounces terrorism

August 1990 Iraq invades Kuwait

1991–2002 Algerian civil war

January–February 1991 U.S.-led coalition expels Iraqis from Kuwait

December 2010 Mohamed Bouazizi, Tunisian street vendor, immolates himself

Square, as well as elsewhere throughout Egypt—only this time demanding that Morsi step down. In response to growing disorder around the country, Egypt's army demanded that Morsi meet the grievances of the protesters, and when he failed to do so the military once more intervened to replace him. Writing before his overthrow, Edward D. Mansfield and Jack Snyder had presciently noted that "there is a considerable risk of war in states that are starting to democratize and that lack the coherent political institutions needed to make democracy function, such as an effective state, the rule of law, organized parties that compete in fair elections, and professional news media. When these institutions are deformed or weak, politicians are better able to resort to nationalist or sectarian appeals, tarring their enemies of the nation, in order to prevail in electoral competition."[1] Thereafter, Egypt's army imposed an authoritarian regime that triggered an upsurge in terrorism in the country conducted by Islamic extremists.

2011–2012

January 2011 Tunisian dictator Zine El Abidine Ben Ali flees

February 2011 Egyptian president Hosni Mubarak steps down; an insurgency begins in Libya

March 2011 Uprising against President Bashar al-Assad begins in Daraa, Syria; Saudi troops enter Bahrain to put down rebellion; NATO warplanes bomb military targets in Libya

June 2011 Yemeni president Ali Abdullah Saleh is wounded in a bombing

August 2011 Former Egyptian president Hosni Mubarak is brought to trial

October 2011 Libyan dictator Muammar Qaddafi is killed

February 2012 President Saleh of Yemen officially resigns

April 2012 Thousands of Egyptians pack Cairo's Tahrir Square demanding a faster transfer of power

June 2012 Egypt's election commission decides that Muslim Brotherhood candidate Mohamed Morsi has won Egypt's presidential runoff

July 2012 Syrian government forces and anti-Assad insurgents begin fighting a battle to capture Syria's largest city, Aleppo

September 2012 U.S. ambassador to Libya Christopher Stevens is killed by terrorists in Benghazi

October 2012 Huge protests follow President Morsi's decree that no judicial body can dissolve the Constituent Assembly, which was drafting a new Egyptian constitution

December 2012 Egypt confirms that the controversial new constitution has been approved, and President Morsi signs the constitution into law

2013–2016

April 2013 Israel and the United States separately voice suspicion that the Syrian regime has used poison gas

May 2013 Deadly bombs explode in a Turkish border town, and Hezbollah fighters openly invade Syria

June 2013 Syrian army and Hezbollah capture the strategic town of Qusayr

July 2013 After millions of Egyptians protest in the streets, Gen. Abdul Fatah al-Sisi removes President Morsi and suspends the Egyptian constitution

August 2013 Syrian military kills 1,100 civilians with poison gas

September 2013 United States and Russia agree that Syria must surrender its chemical weapons

January 2014 The Geneva II Conference on Syria begins; Egypt adopts a new post-Morsi constitution

2014 Rival Libyan governments compete for power

October 2014 American bombing of Islamic State forces in Syria begins

September 2015 Russia begins bombing campaign in Syria

November 2015 Syrian peace talks begin in Vienna

January 2016 UN-brokered Syrian negotiations continue in Geneva

March 2016 Russia removes its forces from Syria

3

America and the Arab Middle East before the Arab Spring

Our initial chapter on the Arab Spring deals with the historical background of American foreign policy toward the Arab world. It opens with an examination of the sources of U.S. foreign policy toward the Arab states. It then examines the evolution of the Arab world from the end of Ottoman Turkey's dominance of the region in World War I. Central to this evolution was the role of oil, to which we then turn, which is followed by a discussion of U.S.–Soviet rivalry in the Middle East during the Cold War and the central role played by Egyptian president Gamal Abdel Nasser and Egypt in that competition. Egypt remains a focus in the next section, the origins of political Islam and especially the origins and evolution of the Muslim Brotherhood. The chapter concludes with a brief examination of the compatibility of political Islam and democracy.

MAP 3.1 The Present-Day Middle East and North Africa

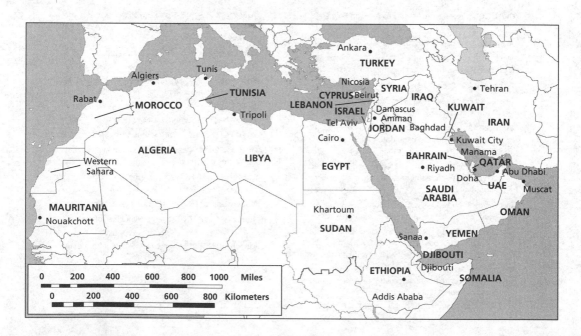

SOURCES OF AMERICAN POLICY TOWARD THE ARAB MIDDLE EAST

Until recently, American policy toward the Middle East has largely aimed to maintain stable and secure sources of oil and support oil-rich countries in the Persian Gulf like Saudi Arabia and Kuwait; minimize Soviet influence in the region (until the end of the Cold War); isolate and contain aggressive regional foes such as Iraq under Saddam Hussein and Iran after the overthrow of its shah; and provide security for its regional ally, Israel. In pursuing these objectives, American policy toward the Arab world has been influenced by a variety of factors and groups.

External factors have been among the most prominent reasons for U.S. interest in the region. Owing to its strategic location, the Arab Middle East has been a focus of American foreign policy for decades. The region is strategically valuable for many reasons. Among them: Egypt as a bridge between Europe and Africa and the site of the Suez Canal, which links the Mediterranean Sea and Indian Ocean; the region's oil resources, especially around the Persian Gulf; the presence of American foes such as the Soviet Union during the Cold War and contemporary Iran; American friendship with Israel; the spread of Islamic extremism; and the political volatility of the region and the many wars fought there.

The centrality of U.S. security concerns has made selected government agencies including the National Security Council, the Department of Defense, the Department of Energy, and the State Department principal players in making foreign policy toward the Arab world. At least since the United States emerged as a global superpower during World War II, American presidents have inevitably played a direct and ongoing role in shaping policy toward the region. As we shall see, several issues raised by the Arab Spring have divided American decision-makers.

American military leaders, for example, were reluctant to get involved in Libya's insurrection against Col. Muammar Qaddafi's regime. They were even more reluctant to intervene in Syria's civil war lest U.S. forces get mired in a prolonged and unwinnable conflict. By contrast, congressional leaders such as Sens. John McCain (R-AZ) and Lindsey Graham (R-SC) pressed for greater involvement, while Secretary of State Hillary Rodham Clinton advocated a no-fly zone over Libya and, along with former president Bill Clinton, pressed for a more activist policy in Syria. After the government of Syria's Bashar al-Assad used chemical weapons in defiance of President Barack Obama's warning that such action would prove a "red line," the president sought congressional approval for his action. Both Republicans and Democrats in Congress were divided on the issue. Within the administration, Secretary of State John Kerry and Secretary of Defense Chuck Hagel strongly advocated using force, while Gen. Martin E. Dempsey, chief of the Joint Chiefs of Staff—who had previously pointed to the risks of U.S. intervention in Syria—was willing to support but not enthusiastic about the president's decision. Alluding to American experience in Iraq and Afghanistan, Dempsey cautioned, "We have learned from the past 10 years. . . . that it is not enough to simply alter the balance of power without careful consideration of what is necessary in order to preserve a functioning state."[2]

As this suggests, individual factors are important here. The attitudes of Presidents Woodrow Wilson and Franklin D. Roosevelt toward the Middle East were influenced by their opposition to European imperialism, and President George H. W. Bush's close personal relationship with Saudi leaders helped Washington involve Saudi Arabia in the 1991 conflict with Iraq. More recently, President Obama's preference in Libya, in the words of one of his advisors, to lead "from behind"[3] and let America's European

TABLE 3.1   Arab League Members

Algeria	Morocco
Bahrain	Oman
Comoros	Palestine
Djibouti	Qatar
Egypt	Saudi Arabia
Iraq	Somalia
Jordan	Sudan
Kuwait	Syria (suspended in 2011)
Lebanon	Tunisia
Libya	United Arab Emirates
Mauritania	Yemen

allies get out in front, as well as his reluctance to get deeply involved in Syria, reflect "lessons" the president believed he had learned from America's wars in Iraq and Afghanistan. Instinctively cautious and averse to "isms," his definition of leadership, according to one observer, "comes from two unspoken beliefs: that the relative power of the U.S. is declining as rivals like China rise, and that the U.S. is reviled in many parts of the world." Thus, pursuing American ideals "requires stealth and modesty as well as military strength."[4]

Overall, societal factors have played a role in U.S. policy toward the Arab world, but not uniformly across issues. Major American oil companies such as ExxonMobil, ConocoPhillips, and Chevron lobby effectively when policies toward the Arab world affect their interests. And in the case of civil strife in Libya and Syria, President Obama was sensitive to the popular opposition of a war-weary public to getting bogged down in new conflicts even while America was preparing to remove its forces from Afghanistan.

Ethnic interest groups matter as well: for example, pro-Israel groups exercise influence when policy affects Israel. The Arab-American population in the United States, though relatively small—about two million (though some estimates are higher), or 0.5 percent of America's population—is increasing rapidly. Arab-Americans are concentrated in New York City, Detroit, and Los Angeles, and the largest group is of Lebanese descent. It is a heterogeneous group marked by cultural and religious diversity and does not yet enjoy the political influence that other national and ethnic groups such as Greek-Americans and Jewish-Americans have acquired. The two principal Arab advocacy groups are the American-Arab Anti-Discrimination Committee and the Arab American Institute, both of which defend the rights of Arab-Americans. An Arab American Political Action Committee was established in Michigan in 1998 to promote Arab-American political candidates and the community's political causes.

Overall, however, American foreign-policy involvement in the Arab world is relatively recent compared to European countries like Great Britain and France. Indeed, the contemporary Arab world had its origins in the demise and partition of the Ottoman Empire by the European victors in World War I. That empire, already known before the war as "the sick man of Europe," entered the conflict on the side of Germany and Austria-Hungary—the Triple Alliance. Arrayed against Germany, Austria-Hungary, and Ottoman Turkey were Britain, France, and Russia—the Triple Entente—and, after 1915, Italy.

THE ARABS: WORLD WAR I AND AFTER

Encouraged by the British and with the aid of T. E. Lawrence ("Lawrence of Arabia"), Hussein bin Ali, Sharif of Mecca and leader of the Hashemite clan that claimed descent from the Prophet Muhammad, together with his sons Feisal, Abdullah, and Zeid, triggered a revolt against the Ottomans by the Arabs of the Hejaz of western Arabia. The uprising was based on the understanding that under his leadership the Arabs would form a large homeland between Syria and Yemen, governed by Islamic law. By 1917 the revolt had driven the Turks from Arabia and Syria, as well as from Jerusalem.

On May 16, 1916, the world's two leading imperial powers, Britain and France, with Russian agreement signed a secret treaty negotiated by Sir Mark Sykes representing the British government and François Georges-Picot representing the French government. The Sykes-Picot Agreement, made public by the Bolsheviks after the Russian Revolution, allocated the Ottoman-ruled Arab Middle East to Britain and

Prince Feisal (center front) and T. E. Lawrence (second from right, center row) at Versailles

James A. Cannavino Library, Marist College

France. The agreement divided Syria, Iraq, Lebanon, and Palestine into French- and British-administered areas. Britain would administer southern Iraq, including Baghdad, Transjordan (the land east of the River Jordan in what is now the state of Jordan), and Palestine (the land west of the River Jordan, encompassing modern Israel, the Gaza Strip, and the West Bank). France acquired Lebanon, Syria, southeastern Turkey including Adana and Cilicia, and northern Iraq, while Russia would gain part of Armenia. A confederation of Arab states or a single independent Arab state divided into French and British spheres of influence would be established between the new British and French territories, with specific boundaries to be negotiated later. The negotiators intended to divide the region among the different religious and ethnic groups but failed because the straight lines that served as borders left communities such as Sunni and Shia Arabs and Christians in separate countries. In the initial agreement reached before the 1917 revolution, Tsarist Russia would receive the Armenian provinces of Erzurum, Trebizond, Van, and Bitlis.[5]

The secret Sykes-Picot Agreement conflicted with British promises given earlier to Hussein, as did the British government's commitment in 1917 to establishing a Jewish homeland in Palestine (the Balfour Declaration). When the Sykes-Picot Agreement became public it seemed a betrayal of the commitments made by Sir Henry McMahon, Britain's high commissioner in Egypt, in letters to Hussein. McMahon had declared that, while taking account of French interests, "Great Britain is prepared to recognize and support the independence of the Arabs in all the regions within the limits demanded by the Sharif of Mecca,"[6] and "We declare once more that His Majesty's Government would welcome the resumption of the Kalifate by an Arab of true race."[7] Lawrence sought to make London keep its word to its Arab allies, even refusing to accept the medals awarded him by Britain's King George V, and persuaded Prince Feisal to join him at the Versailles Conference in 1919 to plead the Arab cause in the name of President Wilson's principle of national self-determination. The victorious allies, however, were not prepared to overturn their secret wartime agreement.

In 1917 Hussein declared himself king of the Hejaz on behalf of the Hashemites but was deprived of the prize he had sought and was driven out by a rival Arab clan, the Saudis, led by Abd al-Aziz ibn Saud. The Saudis' campaign to unite Arabia under their control had begun in 1902. The Hejaz was conquered by ibn Saud in 1924–1925, and in 1932 it was united with the Nejd to form the kingdom of Saudi Arabia, which became an absolute monarchy based on the principles of Wahhabism, a puritanical and conservative branch of Sunni Islam established in the eighteenth century by Abdul Wahhab. Wahhabism would also become the form of Islam observed by many radical Muslims.

The Sykes-Picot Agreement was reaffirmed at the 1920 San Remo Conference attended by Britain, France, Italy, and Japan, with the United States as an observer, and was confirmed when in 1922 the League of Nations authorized the victorious allies to administer as League mandates former German and Ottoman territories, thereby providing a fig leaf for European imperialism. Class A mandates included the former Ottoman provinces of Iraq, Syria, Lebanon, and Palestine that were given provisional independence under British and French administrative control. Britain administered Mesopotamia (Iraq), Transjordan, and Palestine under a British high commissioner. Syria and Lebanon were made French mandates. Ottoman Turkey finally accepted these arrangements in the 1920 Treaty of Sèvres, which officially abolished the Ottoman Empire. Hostilities followed between a Turkish army commanded by the country's wartime hero Mustafa Kemal Atatürk, who opposed the treaty, and British, French, and Greek forces that occupied areas of Turkish Anatolia. The conflict ended with the 1923 Treaty of Lausanne that confirmed the independence and boundaries of the modern Republic of Turkey, with its capital moved from Istanbul to Ankara and with Mustafa Kemal as its first president.

MAP 3.2   1916 Sykes-Picot Middle East Partition

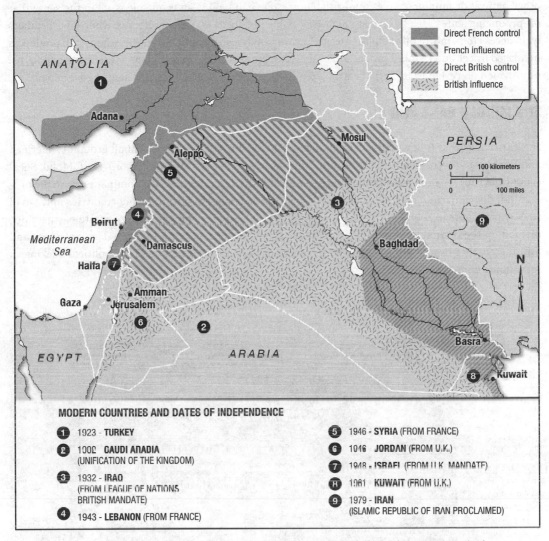

MODERN COUNTRIES AND DATES OF INDEPENDENCE

1 1923 - **TURKEY**

2 1902 - **SAUDI ARABIA**
(UNIFICATION OF THE KINGDOM)

3 1932 - **IRAQ**
(FROM LEAGUE OF NATIONS
BRITISH MANDATE)

4 1943 - **LEBANON** (FROM FRANCE)

5 1946 - **SYRIA** (FROM FRANCE)

6 1946 - **JORDAN** (FROM U.K.)

7 1948 - **ISRAEL** (FROM U.K. MANDATE)

8 1961 - **KUWAIT** (FROM U.K.)

9 1979 - **IRAN**
(ISLAMIC REPUBLIC OF IRAN PROCLAIMED)

Source: The Global Education Project, http://www.theglobaleducationproject.org/mideast/Info/maps/sykes-picot-map.html

"It was an era," writes David Fromkin, "in which Middle Eastern countries and frontiers were fabricated in Europe. Iraq and what we now call Jordan . . . were British inventions, lines drawn on an empty map by British politicians after the First World War; while the boundaries of Saudi Arabia, Kuwait, and Iraq were established by a British civil servant in 1922, and frontiers between Moslems and Christians were drawn by France in Syria–Lebanon and by Russia on the borders of Armenia and Soviet Azerbaijan."[8]

Perhaps the most crucial interest the United States and its European and Asian allies have perceived in the Arab Middle East is oil. The importance of oil made it the economic lifeblood of many of the region's countries, including Saudi Arabia, Iraq, Iran, Algeria, Libya, and Kuwait, many of which had few other natural or human sources of wealth. On the one hand, oil is an economic issue in the sense that oil-producing states seek to earn as much as possible as long as they have reserves, while oil consumers want access to plentiful oil at stable prices. However, oil is also a political issue, as when Arab producers increased prices and reduced production to show sympathy with the Palestinians in the 1960s and 1970s, or provided oil revenues to Egypt in 2013 after the overthrow of that country's Islamist government.

THE MIDDLE EAST AND OIL

In the decades that followed the development of the region's oil industry, a small group of American and European international oil companies, "the Seven Sisters"—Esso (later Exxon), Gulf, Mobil, Socal (later Chevron), Texaco, Royal Dutch Shell, and British Petroleum—played a dominant role in the production, distribution, and pricing of oil, and paid governments of oil-producing countries only small royalty payments in return for concessions to extract oil. Single companies or corporate partnerships divided up the region, thereby enhancing their bargaining leverage with individual governments and limiting competition with one another. In addition, the companies enjoyed the political backing of their home countries.

Royal Dutch Shell (shown here) is one of the Seven Sisters of international oil, along with Exxon, Gulf, Mobil, Chevron, Texaco, and British Petroleum.

Eduardo Luzzatti Buyé/iStock

Inflation during and after World War II reduced the value of the fixed royalties paid to governments, and in 1945 Venezuela forced the oil companies to pay it 50 percent of their profits. Some years later Saudi Arabia forced the American consortium Aramco (officially the Saudi Arabian Oil Company) to accept a 50–50 split of profits under threat of nationalization, and by the 1950s most oil-producing countries had reached similar agreements. When Iran's government demanded a similar arrangement British Petroleum refused, and in 1951 Iran set out to nationalize the British-owned Anglo–Iranian Oil Company. Fearful that other oil-producing countries would emulate Iran's nationalization, the West imposed a global boycott of Iranian oil and overthrew Iran's government.

The power of the major oil companies to set prices was further eroded by the entry of new oil companies—notably Amoco, Occidental, and Getty—as well as a Japanese consortium (the Arabian Oil Company). These companies cut prices and therefore the profits of the larger firms that had to compete. The latter in turn reduced posted prices (the price that they would accept for their oil), which reduced the taxes they paid to oil-producing countries. Lower prices globally also reduced the profits from domestic oil production in the United States, which in turn led to a decline in domestic production. Indeed, after 1948 the United States began to import more oil than it exported. In response to these developments, Washington mandated oil import quotas in 1959 to shelter domestic producers from inexpensive imported oil, an action that further diluted the power of the large international companies.

In order to prevent oil companies from further reducing prices and therefore their revenues, Iraq hosted a meeting of several oil-producing countries (Iran, Iraq, Kuwait, Saudi Arabia, and Venezuela) that established the Organization of the Petroleum Exporting Countries (OPEC) in September 1960, with headquarters initially in Geneva and then in Vienna, where members meet twice annually. Other oil-producing countries joined OPEC in the years that followed. During the 1960s OPEC was reasonably successful in stabilizing the price of oil, although increased production and inflation gradually decreased oil's "real price." ("Real prices" are prices adjusted for inflation, in contrast to "nominal prices," which are not adjusted for inflation.)

Following the 1967 Six-Day War, the Arab producers placed an embargo of oil exports to countries that had supported Israel. Although the embargo increased oil prices, the effort ultimately failed when the United States and non-Arab countries like Iran increased oil production, thereby depriving Arab countries of much of their oil revenue. Owing to the embargo's failure, OPEC's Arab members formed an Organization of Arab Petroleum Exporting Countries (OAPEC) within OPEC the following year to coordinate regional objectives. In addition, OPEC increased the posted price of members and set a minimum taxation rate of 55 percent on profits.

By the 1970s OPEC appeared able to prevent additional reductions in posted oil prices and enjoyed leverage over both industrialized and developing countries. Libya was the first oil-producing country to force companies to challenge existing arrangements, especially the equal division of profits. Col. Muammar Qaddafi, who had seized power in Libya from King Idris in late 1969, threatened in early 1970 to seize the assets of oil companies unless they raised the price of Libyan crude and reduced the amount being pumped. Their efforts to defy Qaddafi's demand collapsed when Occidental Petroleum, the largest oil company in the country, broke ranks after Qaddafi threatened to cut its permissible production from 800,000 to 500,000 barrels a day and Occidental was unable to obtain additional oil from major companies that it needed to meet contractual commitments. Libya's success led other oil-producing countries to demand similar increases and, trying to stabilize prices, the oil companies sought to engage the oil-producing governments in multilateral negotiations to set a common price. In 1971 Iran followed Libya's example and, because Iran's shah was a close ally of the United States, Washington was not prepared to do anything about it.

In the following years several factors conspired to produce an upward price spiral: global demand, devaluation of the U.S. dollar, the 1973 Yom Kippur War, and the second Arab oil embargo. In the absence of increasing supply and declining U.S. oil production, along with growing U.S. demand, prices moved higher. The U.S. dollar devaluations in 1971 and 1973, however, pushed real oil prices in the other direction and diluted profits because major industrialized countries paid for oil in dollars. Although OPEC members had more dollars, these were worth less, thereby leading them to demand higher nominal prices as they limited supply by assigning production quotas to members.

In the meantime, several Arab oil producers, including Algeria and Libya, nationalized oil production in 1971. The "North African nationalizations . . . demonstrated the extent of the changes in the structure of the system" that would make nationalization feasible, and "actions by the more militant producers also served to increase pressure on other regimes to respond in kind."[9] Thus, Iraq and Iran soon followed the Algerian–Libyan example, and in late 1972 Kuwait, Qatar, Saudi Arabia, and the United Arab Emirates reached an agreement to increase state control over the industry in ten years from 25 to 51 percent. Full or majority state control would be achieved by the mid-1970s, with the companies largely limited to managing operations.

Following the 1973 Yom Kippur War, the Arab states, having given ample warning of their intent before the war, sought to use the oil weapon to make industrialized countries change their policies and press Israel to make concessions. OPEC raised its posted oil price by more than $2 a barrel and OAPEC agreed to cut production by 5 percent each month to force Israel to withdraw from territories it had occupied in 1967. After the Nixon administration asked Congress for emergency military aid for Israel, Saudi Arabia reduced oil production significantly and placed an embargo on sales to the United States. Thereafter, a selective oil embargo was imposed on the United States, the Netherlands, and Portugal until March 1974. Although the transfer of oil among companies permitted non-Arab oil to flow to America, spot shortages and gas lines appeared in the United States despite rationing, lowering speed limits, abandoning oil import quotas, and other measures. From 1970 to 1974, the nominal price of oil jumped from $1.21 to $11.00,[10] and economic costs in the United States as reflected by unemployment and slow economic growth were high. Politics and economics had combined to boost the price of oil (the first "oil shock"), the profits of the oil-producing states, and the costs to oil consumers. "These price increases produced the largest 'peacetime' international transfer of wealth in history,"[11] triggering a global economic recession in 1974.

Nevertheless, divisions among Arab oil producers were becoming apparent. Iran sought to raise prices quickly to ensure political and social stability for its large population. By contrast, Saudi Arabia, with a smaller population and larger oil reserves, preferred smaller price increases. In addition, Iran's post-revolutionary regime viewed America as an enemy against which the oil weapon could be used and believed that this weapon would also help it Islamize other countries, like Iraq. By contrast, the conservative Saudi monarchy regarded Washington as a staunch ally in maintaining regional stability and resisting radical and aggressive leaders in Iran and Libya. Moreover, Iran had become the leader of Shia Islam, while Saudi Arabia was staunchly Sunni. The fissures in OPEC grew wider after Iraq and Iran went to war in 1980.

Between 1973 and 1980 supplies remained tight. OPEC discipline held, and prices continued to rise. In 1979–1980 oil prices again shot up (the second "oil shock"). Although OPEC had agreed in late 1978 to a program of price increases, it was quickly overtaken by events. The Iranian revolution of 1979 that reduced the flow of Iranian oil and the subsequent war between Iraq and Iran that heightened concerns about disruption in oil supplies triggered dramatic hikes in both the nominal and real price of oil.

Prices peaked in 1981 after the second "oil shock" and then began to fall because of economic recession, conservation efforts in consuming countries, the breakdown of discipline in the OPEC cartel, and resulting overproduction. Non-OPEC producers—Norway, Mexico, Britain, Russia, and Oman—also began to account for a larger share of oil production and export. By April 1994 real oil prices had dropped to about where they had been in 1973. Declining oil revenues and their political consequences played a role in events leading to Iraq's invasion of Kuwait in 1990. Kuwait sought to pressure Iraq to repay the huge debt of about $30 billion incurred during Iraq's war with Iran, a debt Saddam Hussein argued was the result of a war it had waged against an aggressive "Persian" Shia foe on behalf of the entire "Arab" world. In addition to Kuwait's "ingratitude," Iraq charged that Kuwait was profiting by exceeding its OPEC production quota and was pumping more than its share of oil from the disputed Rumaila oil field that straddled their common border. Control of Iraq and Kuwait gave Saddam control of 20 percent of the world's known oil reserves. From the perspective of Washington, what was worse was that it moved Iraq's army to the Saudi border, endangering an additional 25 percent. Although the invasion of Kuwait pushed prices up, the rise was temporary, especially after it became clear that Saddam's threat to Saudi Arabia had dissipated.

Other factors contributed to the erosion of OPEC's influence. Political conflicts among members were exacerbated by oversupply, which was partly the result of widespread cheating on production quotas by its members. Higher levels of production were a source of wealth as long as prices remained stable, but excessive supply reduced profits over time as prices declined. As the leading source of Middle East oil, Saudi Arabia played a crucial role in maintaining OPEC production levels. As prices fell in the 1980s and 1990s, the Saudis increased production to increase their market share, thereby keeping prices low until the Asian financial crisis of 1998. Thereafter, a combination of factors drove oil prices dramatically higher. These included OPEC production cuts and reduced cheating on national production quotas, cooperation between OPEC and non-OPEC producers, a general strike in Venezuela in 2002–2003 that closed down the country's state-owned oil and natural gas company, the 2003 U.S. intervention in Iraq, the 2006 conflict between Israel and Hezbollah, sanctions against Iran, and the 2011 civil war in Libya. However, the most important factor was the surging demand for energy from Asia, especially China and India. In March 2008 the nominal price of oil almost reached $104 a barrel, which, adjusted for inflation, exceeded the previous record set during the second "oil shock" in 1980. Thereafter, prices dropped as America's financial crisis became global and American oil production soared. Simultaneously, Saudi Arabia and OPEC more generally refused to cut oil production to retain market shares in the developed world. The result was a precipitous reduction in the price of oil, which slowed economic growth in countries like Russia, Iran, and Venezuela that relied heavily on oil exports to pay their bills.

China's average growth rate of 10 percent a year between 2000 and 2011 and its lower but still relatively high growth rate after 2011 were accompanied by a high demand for energy. By 2011 China imported about 5.5 million barrels of oil a day, or over half its daily consumption, and its domestic oil production had peaked. Its growing demand for oil accounted for more than half the increase in global demand that year and pushed prices higher. Despite the Great Recession the real price of oil remained high by historical standards. The demand for oil also increased the geopolitical importance of the Middle East for Beijing, especially since Saudi Arabia is its largest source of oil imports. And China's demand for energy is likely to continue to increase once it overcomes its 2016 economic slowdown. Per capita energy consumption of the country's 1.3 billion people remains far lower than that of Americans and will rise as the country develops economically. Global energy demand spurred mainly by China and India is predicted to increase by a third by 2035, and China for the first time surpassed the United States as the largest oil importer in 2015.

Another element in the politics of oil has been the increase in U.S. shale-oil and shale-gas production owing to the introduction of hydraulic fracturing, or "fracking"—creating fractures in rock formations by injecting fluid into cracks that allow oil and gas to flow to where it can be extracted. This process became commercially viable in areas like North Dakota's Bakken Shale and Texas's Eagle Ford because of oil's increased price. Between 2008 and 2011, America increased oil production by 14 percent and natural gas production by 10 percent, overtaking Russian energy production in 2013. America's declining reliance on oil imports, declared Henry Kissinger, is "of huge strategic consequence."[12]

The International Energy Agency predicted that America would pass Saudi Arabia as the world's largest oil producer by 2020 and could become energy independent and even a net oil exporter by 2030.[13] However, that agency also predicted that, by the mid-2020s, non-OPEC production would begin to decrease. Its director concluded, "We expect the Middle East will come back and be a very important producer and exporter of oil, just because there are huge resources of low-cost light oil."[14] Moreover, Saudi Arabia's Aramco has invested in the Motiva oil refinery, America's largest producer of petroleum products. "The Saudis are securing a home for their heavy crude," declared an analyst. "But there is no question that security is also part of the equation." Added another: "The Motiva relationship guarantees the Saudis an important but subtle footprint in the United States, and they want to have some negotiating strength when geopolitical issues in the Middle East and elsewhere arise."[15] Declining oil prices, however, combined with the end of OPEC quotas for individual members in 2012, have eroded the global influence of Saudi Arabia and OPEC.

Energy security had been a key issue during World War II and became even more so during the Cold War. "Oil provided the point at which foreign policy, international economic considerations, national security, and corporate interests would all converge."[16] The world had witnessed rapid expansion of global oil production, and oil as a crucial element of national power was viewed as a critical natural resource.

THE COLD WAR AND THE ARAB WORLD

During the Cold War, Washington's principal objectives in the Arab Middle East were access to the region's oil and preventing Soviet penetration of the area. Soviet involvement in the Middle East accompanied a growing U.S. presence there and was part of Moscow's global effort to maintain a balance of power with the United States. For a variety of reasons the Middle East became the site of intense Soviet–American competition during the Cold War.

As the influence of the European colonial powers, Britain and France, waned in the decade after World War II, the United States and the USSR competed to replace them and sought regional clients and friends. Moscow sought to aid communist movements and establish military facilities in the region, especially Egypt and Syria, that would balance American military assets in allied countries in the region's "Northern Tier"—Greece, Turkey, and Iran—while avoiding direct confrontation with America, which would risk escalation. At various times, Moscow enjoyed warm relations with Arab nationalist leaders in Egypt, Syria, Libya, and Iraq, exploiting their enmity toward Israel, providing economic and military assistance, and supporting their regional political aspirations. It also acquired naval access to the Arabian and Red Seas, with facilities at Aden and the Yemeni island of Socotra. "Khrushchev's strategy," according to John Campbell, "was primarily a manipulation of local forces to the detriment of Western positions rather than a campaign to intimidate local governments" and "exploited the new dynamic Arab nationalism and its distrust of the West."[17] "It was," he concludes, "a working relationship from which both sides profited, but neither had full faith and trust in the other."[18] Although communist ideology held little attraction for Arab nationalists, Soviet arms sales and political support intensified Arab ambitions to seek a military solution to their conflict with Israel.

At the outset of the Cold War, American support for Greece and Turkey aimed to prevent Moscow from expanding into the Middle East, and both countries were admitted to NATO in 1952. By the early 1950s, a period in which Soviet leader Josef Stalin largely ignored the developing world—including the Middle East—and Arab states were more concerned about Israel and British colonialism, Washington feared the prospect of Soviet influence in a region that President Dwight Eisenhower regarded as strategically vital to American interests. With U.S. encouragement, in 1955 Britain, Iraq, Turkey, Iran, and Pakistan established an alliance called the Baghdad Pact, aiming to strengthen the "Northern Tier" countries close to the Soviet Union and preventing the extension of Soviet influence in the Middle East. Although the United States was not a member of the organization, it concluded bilateral treaties with all of its members.

The catalyst for Soviet–American competition in the Arab world was Egyptian leader Gamal Abdel Nasser. Nasser had been a key figure in the overthrow of Egypt's King Farouk in 1952 by a group of military officers and had maneuvered to become the country's prime minister in 1954. He transformed Egypt into a one-party secular socialist republic and pursued expansionist pan-Arab nationalism that led to a temporary union of Egypt and Syria (the United Arab Republic) between 1961 and 1971. Nasser also became a leading opponent of European colonialism in the Middle East and North Africa, and a prominent figure in the nonaligned movement during the Cold War. He was also a persistent foe of conservative Arab governments in countries like Saudi Arabia, Jordan, and Iraq (until that country's monarchy was overthrown in 1958). Nasser was the target of an assassination attempt by members of the Muslim Brotherhood, and he vigorously repressed the group.

As a nationalist, Nasser sought to end British control of the Suez Canal, energize Egypt's economy by building a high dam at Aswan to irrigate the fertile Nile valley, and confront Israel militarily. Among Nasser's early achievements was a treaty with Britain in October 1954 under which British troops would leave Egypt by June 1956, and Egypt would respect free passage through the canal. The agreement also stipulated that British troops could return in the event that the canal was threatened by another country.

Nasser sought to play off Moscow against Washington. In an effort to obtain financial aid and arms from America, he arranged for a massive purchase of Soviet arms by Egypt in September 1955 from Czechoslovakia, then a Soviet satellite—a deal that China's foreign minister, Zhou Enlai, helped arrange. As an element in Moscow's effort to woo developing countries, this event brought the Cold War into the heart of the Arab world. Despite Secretary of State John Foster Dulles's dislike of Nasser, the Eisenhower administration responded in December 1955 to growing Soviet influence in Egypt with an offer of financial aid to build the Aswan Dam.

Nasser's continued dalliance with the Soviet Union, however, caused Washington to withdraw its offer in July 1956. "Eisenhower and Dulles had reached the limits of their patience with Nasser: he was undermining the Baghdad Pact, he had impeded an Arab–Israeli settlement, he had invited Soviet influence into the Middle East, and in May he had even recognized the People's Republic of China."[19] Moscow willingly stepped in to provide the needed funding for the dam, and Soviet leader Nikita Khrushchev would join Nasser in May 1964 to celebrate completion of the first stage of the dam's construction. In addition, Soviet naval vessels were given access to Egyptian ports in Alexandria and Port Said.

A week after Washington canceled the Aswan offer, Nasser nationalized the Suez Canal. "This in turn alarmed the British and French, who, without consulting Washington, hatched a plot with the Israelis to have them attack the canal, thereby giving London and Paris the right to 'protect' it—the real intention was to depose Nasser altogether."[20] The operation in October 1956 took place virtually at the same time as the unsuccessful Hungarian uprising against Soviet occupation and was a disaster that "almost broke up the NATO alliance."[21] Eisenhower, who was irate, viewed it as a revival of European colonialism and a threat to Western relations with the Arab world. Threatening economic sanctions, he demanded that Britain and France withdraw from the canal and Israel retire from the Sinai Peninsula, which it had occupied. Khrushchev threatened to "rain rockets" upon Paris and London. "The real winner, though, was Nasser, who kept the canal, humiliated the colonialists, and balanced Cold War superpowers against one another, while securing his position as undisputed leader of Arab nationalism."[22] Thereafter, U.S.–Soviet competition in the Middle East intensified as Moscow exploited Arab nationalism and the Arab conflict with Israel and used local proxies to undermine American influence. Soviet leaders gave their support to regimes that sought to alter the region's political complexion, especially in opposition to conservative, oil-rich monarchies allied with the West. Soviet influence spread beyond Egypt owing to instability in Syria in 1957 and the 1958 overthrow of the Iraqi monarchy.

Only months after Egypt purchased Soviet weapons, Syria did the same. Its government and ruling Syrian Ba'ath Party fully backed Egypt during the Suez crisis. Following Nasser's diplomatic triumph in the Suez affair, Syria began to be viewed in the West as in danger of becoming part of a pro-Soviet bloc in the Middle East. Syria's government, especially its Ba'ath Party, sought to copy Nasser's anticolonialism, pan-Arab nationalism, and socialist policies, as well as Egypt's adherence to nonalignment. Due to growing Soviet influence in Egypt and Syria after the Suez crisis, in January 1957 President Eisenhower announced the Eisenhower Doctrine. In the spirit of the earlier Truman Doctrine, it promised military and/or economic aid "to secure and protect the territorial integrity and political independence" of any Middle Eastern country needing help in resisting communist aggression.

In April 1957 a political crisis erupted in Jordan after the country's ruler, King Hussein, claimed to have discovered a plot by pro-Nasser politicians and army officers to overthrow him, and he declared martial law. Because of aid provided by Bedouins loyal to Hussein's Hashemite clan, the planned coup was averted, and Syrian troops that had begun to move toward the Jordanian border turned back. "Through private channels, Hussein made it clear to the Eisenhower administration that his regime would not accept Egyptian or Soviet dominance. American moral and financial support was . . . a crucial factor when the king moved to confront the radicalized elements in the Jordanian army and the Nabulsi government in April 1957."[23]

During the summer Syria's economic, political, and military cooperation with the Soviet Union intensified, alarming President Eisenhower and Secretary of State Dulles. A meeting in September, in which Nasser sought to persuade the U.S. ambassador in Cairo that neither Egypt nor Syria would become Soviet satellites, did little to calm Washington's fears, and Turkey—a NATO ally—began massing troops along its border with Syria despite Saudi efforts to mediate between Syria and Washington. The following month a small number of Egyptian troops arrived in Syria as a symbol of Egypt's—especially Nasser's—growing role in the Arab world. By that time, it had become clear that the United States would not intervene owing to the risks involved, including the military involvement of Turkey, Jordan, and Iraq, and the possibility of a U.S.–Soviet confrontation. "From this point onwards," concludes a British Middle East specialist, "it was apparent that Western policy in the Middle East based on the Eisenhower Doctrine had come to a dead end"[24] because pro-Western Arab regimes were confronting popular sentiment that favored Nasser's pan-Arab nationalism. Nevertheless, the threat of American military force was raised once more in September 1970 to deter Syrian forces that again threatened Jordan.

An additional challenge to the Eisenhower Doctrine came in 1958 in Lebanon, where the threat to the government was not armed aggression. The country's president, Camille Chamoun, asked for American aid to resist what appeared as an effort to overthrow the government by pro-Nasser elements, some of whom were believed to have communist leanings. Eisenhower responded to Chamoun's request by sending U.S. troops into Lebanon, where they remained for several months to maintain stability while the U.S. Sixth Fleet dominated the eastern Mediterranean. Although Washington never directly invoked the Eisenhower Doctrine, the U.S. action had the dual purpose of supporting Lebanese independence and indicating to Moscow America's resolve to act vigorously to protect its regional interests.

Washington's concern about the security of Western oil interests in the Persian Gulf intensified after the rapid British withdrawal from east of Suez between 1968 and 1972. Other factors added to this concern and led to an updating of U.S. policy toward the Arab world. Moscow was able to cultivate close relations with Iraq, Syria, and South Yemen. In Iraq, Soviet influence grew after its 1958 revolution overthrew its pro-Western monarchy, and in Libya Muammar Qaddafi's coup in 1969 triggered huge Soviet arms sales to that country that provided Moscow with much-needed hard currency.

In the early 1970s the Eisenhower Doctrine and its stress on direct American intervention was replaced by the Nixon Doctrine, which emphasized assisting local friends to help themselves. As originally applied under the label *Vietnamization* in the later stages of the Vietnam War, the administration sought to reduce America's military presence in that country and train and assist the South Vietnamese to defend themselves. In a speech in November 1969, President Richard Nixon explained his policy:

- First, the United States will keep all of its treaty commitments.

- Second, we shall provide a shield if a nuclear power threatens the freedom of a nation allied with us or of a nation whose survival we consider vital to our security.

- Third, in cases involving other types of aggression, we shall furnish military and economic assistance when requested in accordance with our treaty commitments. But we shall look to the nation directly threatened to assume the primary responsibility of providing the manpower for its defense.[25]

In the context of the Middle East and Persian Gulf, the Nixon Doctrine involved strengthening regional allies, especially Iran and Saudi Arabia, as a barrier to Soviet influence or aggression in the region and allowing those countries to acquire state-of-the-art American weapons. Although the Ford administration adhered to the Nixon Doctrine in its policy toward the Middle East, President Jimmy Carter was more concerned with brokering an Arab–Israeli settlement and involving the Soviet Union in this effort. Two events pushed the Carter administration in a different direction. The first was the Iranian revolution and the seizure of the American embassy in Tehran that began on November 4, 1979, events that preoccupied the administration for the remainder of its time in office. The second was the Soviet invasion of Afghanistan. Both had implications for U.S. interests in the oil-rich Persian Gulf. The first turned the administration's focus to the danger posed by Iran's shift from being a U.S. ally to becoming its leading adversary in the Persian Gulf, and the second brought a halt to U.S. cooperation with Moscow owing to the prospect of Soviet expansion toward the region. American concern about Soviet ambitions in the Persian Gulf would persist until the Cold War ended.

In his 1980 State of the Union address, Carter articulated his own doctrine for the region: "An attempt by any outside force to gain control of the Persian Gulf region will be regarded as an assault on the vital interests of the United States of America, and such an assault will be repelled by any means necessary, including military force."[26] The Reagan administration pursued a similar policy after 1981, emphasizing the Soviet danger and superpower rivalry and encouraging cooperation with and arms sales to Egypt, Saudi Arabia, and Pakistan until the reformist policies of Soviet leader Mikhail Gorbachev, which included Soviet withdrawal from Afghanistan, brought an end to the Cold War. In the following years, Moscow sought an equal role in the Israeli–Palestinian peace process and, after trying to persuade Saddam to withdraw from Iraq, joined the United States in condemning Iraq's 1990 invasion of Kuwait. Under Gorbachev, the USSR also reduced its ties to clients like Libya and Syria. Libyan–Russian relations were renewed in April 2008 with a visit by President Vladimir Putin, probably reflecting Russian desire for better economic ties after Libya's reconciliation with the West some years earlier.

The end of the Cold War reduced great power tension in the Middle East and North Africa. On the negative side, however, the constraints that the superpowers had placed on their respective clients vanished, freeing countries like Iraq to adopt dangerously aggressive policies. In the case of Egypt, Moscow staunchly supported Nasser until his death in September 1970, and in May the following year signed a fifteen-year treaty of friendship with Nasser's successor, President Anwar al-Sadat. The Soviet Union provided crucial political and military backing during Egypt's Yom Kippur War with Israel in 1973, saving Egypt's army from impending disaster. After that war, however, it became apparent to Sadat that Moscow's political, economic, and military largesse in the years before 1973 had been insufficient, as had been its commitment to Egyptian interests. He wrote in his autobiography, "the Soviet Union had planned to provide us with just enough [assistance] to meet our most immediate needs and at the same time maintain its role as our guardian and ensure its presence in the region—a more important goal from the Soviet point of view,"[27] a view reinforced by Moscow's refusal to reschedule Egypt's debt obligations in 1975. He also realized that only Washington could persuade Israel to surrender Egypt's Sinai Peninsula. Sadat's decision was a major blow to Soviet ambitions in the region. After Gorbachev assumed power in the mid-1980s, he sought to restore close relations with Cairo, especially in the realm of increasing aid and trade, but the effort was incomplete by the time the Soviet Union collapsed.

Sadat was also keenly aware of the relatively greater assistance that America had provided Israel, including timely intelligence information, and concluded that Washington could provide greater assistance in dealing with Israel than could Moscow. Thus, in 1976 Sadat canceled the 1971 Egyptian–Soviet treaty and began a process of improving relations with the United States and Israel that climaxed in his historic visit to Jerusalem, the 1978 Camp David agreements, and the Egyptian–Israeli peace treaty. Sadat also abandoned Nasser's pan-Arab and socialist policies and sought foreign investment. After Sadat's assassination on October 6, 1981, by Islamic extremists, Vice President Hosni Mubarak, whose foreign policy in the ensuing decades was "characterized by stability, moderation, and predictability,"[28] was elevated to the presidency. Mubarak could be trusted to maintain peace with Israel, oppose Syria and post-revolutionary Iran, and repress Islamism at home. For these reasons Washington strongly backed Mubarak and his authoritarian regime until they were swept from power during the first phase of the Arab Spring.

With the end of the Cold War, American preoccupation with Soviet penetration of the Arab Middle East gave way to preoccupation with the Iran–Iraq balance of power and the security of oil-rich friends like Saudi Arabia. The attraction of the sort of pan-Arab nationalism associated with Nasser was also ebbing in the Arab world. An alternative to pan-Arab nationalism was political Islam—that is, an ideology advocating that Muslim societies be governed in accordance with Islamic law and custom.

POLITICAL ISLAM

Political Islam refers to the views of those who are frequently described as "Muslim fundamentalists"— believers in the literal truth of their holy book, the Koran, and governance according to Islamic religious law, or Sharia.

The Aims of Political Islam

Islamic fundamentalists want Muslims everywhere to be governed according to the Koran and the writings and practices of the Prophet Muhammad in the seventh century CE and Muhammad's caliphs ("successors"), who combined secular and religious authority to rule an Islamic empire or caliphate that expanded to embrace the world's Islamic community. No distinction between the religious and the secular was imaginable in the Islamic community founded by the Prophet or in the caliphate that succeeded him between the seventh and thirteenth centuries, as well as in the later Ottoman Empire. Some seek to transform their own country into an Islamic state while others, including the violent terrorists in al-Qaeda and in the Islamic State in Iraq and Syria (ISIS), seek to restore a global version of the ancient caliphate.

Muslim rulers were expected to continue Muhammad's rule and govern subjects in accordance with his precepts and the laws revealed to him by Allah, "the one true God," which defined individual and collective virtue:

> From the very opening of the Quran [Koran] and the plea that the Lord of the universe show the faithful the straight path to the assurance that He has made of Muslims 'a balanced nation that [they] may be witnesses to people' and on the promise that He will bring victory to those who enter His religion, the close link between Islam and power is evident.[29]

Islamic law was to be explained and interpreted by Islamic jurists and theologians like the medieval Muslim philosopher al-Mawardi (972–1058 CE) and were to be applied to individual behavior as well as laws that would guide subjects to act rightly.

Such interpretations, however, may vary significantly, and that is why some Muslims become militants while others like the Muslim Brotherhood, who are our principal concern in this section, are more political and are prepared to work in nonviolent ways to transform their societies into Islamic polities. Such movements "seek the Islamic reform of society and state" with the goal of "a moral community governed by *Shari'a*, or Islamic law."[30] Indeed, some groups may not even seek political power but only wish to promote Islamic public morality.

Contemporary Western governments, including that of the United States, take issue with Islamic fundamentalists on a variety of issues such as gender equality, the separation of church and state, freedom of religion and speech, and the primacy of secular law. And some critics question the commitment of Islamic fundamentalists to democratic principles, expressing concern that if elected to office advocates of political Islam would raise the role of religious institutions and principles at the expense of democratic institutions and principles in political life and government. The source of this concern is the apparent tension between the supremacy of law based on religious revelation and the rights of citizens and their elected representatives to decide freely what laws and policies they wish.

Putting religion at the center of political life is hardly unique to Islam. No distinction was made between religious and secular obligations during Europe's Middle Ages, and the Church defined what permissible and proper behavior was for faithful Christians. Until the seventeenth century, much of Europe was governed by religious law and institutions, and secular princes struggled to become autonomous of those institutions and laws in their own realms. Most American colonies were also founded on the basis of and governed in accordance with religious scripture. Indeed, it was only in the eighteenth century, after the American and French Revolutions, that secular rule and individual rights became dominant in the West and took precedence over religiously based laws and principles. Even today, tension exists in the United States and Europe between those who oppose or believe in strict separation of church and state. Those who favor the infusion of religious principles for governing the ethical and moral life of individuals and communities remain influential and resist the belief that government should be secular and based on an obligation to protect the right of individuals to enjoy moral autonomy.

Let us examine some of the early influential advocates of political Islam and the evolution of the Muslim Brotherhood. That group would become an influential actor throughout the Arab world and a crucial participant in the Arab Spring.

Political Islam and the Muslim Brotherhood

Recent decades have witnessed a revival of political Islam in the Muslim world. This revival owes much to two individuals—Abul A'la Maududi and Hasan al-Banna. Although both were also sources of ideas for extremists like Osama bin Laden, we include them here because of their crucial role in formulating political Islam, a vision deeply enmeshed in the Arab Spring.

Maududi, who was born in British India, was a vigorous opponent of secular values and sought to restore the role Islam had played in India before Britain conquered India's Muslim Moghul Empire.

With the establishment of Muslim Pakistan after India's partition in 1947, Maududi and the political party he had founded in 1941, Jamaat-e-Islami, opposed declaring jihad against India because of its occupation of the disputed territory of Kashmir. In his view, jihad did not mean war but exertion of "one's utmost endeavor in promoting a cause"[31]—that is, establishing a world Islamic state. He also opposed the establishment of democratic institutions in Pakistan, arguing that a genuinely Islamic state had to be governed by Islamic law and custom, which he believed could be applied to all issues of daily life.

Some years later, Jamaat-e-Islami, with branches in India, Kashmir, Sri Lanka, as well as Pakistan, decided to seek power by participating in Pakistani elections but was prevented from doing so by the military coup of Gen. Ayub Khan. In the following years Khan sought to westernize his country, to the dismay of Maududi. In Maududi's view, Islamic culture was superior to other cultures, and Muslims should not be permitted to adopt non-Muslim customs. Maududi "produced an all-inclusive worldview, an internally consistent ideological perspective and a novel perspective of religious exegesis and political analysis" that "shaped the concept of the 'Islamic state.'"[32] But this aim, he argued, had to be achieved by evolution, not revolution.

A second important figure in the emergence of political Islam was Hasan al-Banna, a schoolteacher who founded the Muslim Brotherhood (or *Ikhwan*) in Ismailia, Egypt, in 1928 and who has been called the "founding father of modern Islamic fundamentalism."[33] At that time Egypt was governed as a British "protectorate"—that is, an autonomous territory that is protected by another state. Egypt's significance lay in Britain's dependence on the Suez Canal, its naval bases in the eastern Mediterranean, and its proximity to the oil-rich Arab areas around the Persian Gulf.

Al-Banna rebelled against British colonialism and Western cultural influence, which he viewed as responsible for the decline and corruption of Islamic civilization. He emphasized that Muslim countries should free themselves from the paternalistic West and its claim to cultural superiority. Al-Banna believed that secular mores had eroded the Islamic values of his coreligionists, and he was wary of secular trends in Turkey and Iran. He sought to transform Egypt into an Islamic state based on the Koran and the teachings of the Prophet. The Brotherhood's slogan became "Islam is the solution." The return to an earlier and purer form of Islam, in his view, would reverse the religion's decline. For al-Banna, Islam "was the final arbiter in politics as well as religion, in the things of the market place as well as in those of the state."[34]

Less philosophical than Maududi and less extreme than Sayyid Qutb, al-Banna was "more nearly a charismatic orator/preacher and a gifted organizer than a creative and consistent thinker."[35] And although the group retained its Egyptian core, it came to reflect al-Banna's beliefs that Islam and the Islamic community transcended national boundaries and should not be divided by nationalism. Instead, Muslims should seek to restore the ancient caliphate that had united that community. Al-Banna argued that achieving these objectives demanded patience and could only be attained gradually in a process that included propagating the Brotherhood's ideas to raise political consciousness, organizing the movement and training of activists, and, finally, imposing Islamic law. Unlike the contemporary jihadists we will examine in Part II, al-Banna, like Maududi, saw the process of Islamization as one of evolution.

As the Muslim Brotherhood spread across Egypt, al-Banna built a complex organization of provincial branches headed by an administrative board linked to the Brotherhood's center in Cairo. The group's

Cairo headquarters developed specialized departments dealing with matters such as propaganda, education, labor, social services, and relations with Muslims outside Egypt. At the top were three committees: a Founding Assembly to determine general policy, an Executive Office to execute policy, and a Membership Committee to select members of the Executive Office and supervise members of the Assembly.

In the 1930s the Brotherhood established branches across the Middle East and North Africa, and its membership in Egypt and elsewhere grew during World War II partly because of Britain's preoccupation with its conflict with Germany and Italy. The Brotherhood thus became the first and most successful Islamic mass movement to contest secular beliefs and demand a return to the puritanical version of its distant past in which Sharia law would govern society. In addition to its pan-Islamic ideological appeal, the Brotherhood's popularity was enhanced by its sponsorship of welfare and charitable work. Although al-Banna conceived the Brotherhood as "an all-embracing organization, transcending political parties, indeed making them unnecessary," he was also a pragmatist and skilled propagandist who "was not averse to playing by the prevailing political rules" when the group could "thereby gain in strength."[36]

During its early years, the Brotherhood abjured violence and emphasized propaganda. But although al-Banna generally considered violence counterproductive, his views on this idea were inconsistent. Resorting to violence, he believed, might be justified if government repression were severe or if the Brotherhood saw victory within its grasp; therefore, the group formed an armed militia, the Special Apparatus. A militant version of jihad might be acceptable if other means had failed, and al-Banna invoked that usage in 1945 when the British and Egyptian governments intensified their efforts to suppress the Brotherhood. The group, which had been involved in the 1936–1939 protests against Jewish immigration to Palestine, declared a violent jihad again in 1948 against the newly independent Jewish state of Israel.

Al-Banna remained the group's leader as it expanded in the 1930s and 1940s until he was assassinated in Cairo in February 1949, possibly by an agent of the Egyptian government, following the banning of the Brotherhood and subsequent assassination of Egypt's prime minister by a member of the group. The Brotherhood continued to extend its reach, establishing additional branches elsewhere in the region and beyond during the following decade.

Al-Banna was succeeded by Hasan al-Hudaybi, and the Brotherhood recognized that it should continue eschewing violence in favor of joining Egypt's political process if it were to survive government repression and remain faithful to al-Banna's philosophy. It therefore abandoned its pursuit of jihad against Egypt's government, which in turn became willing to reach a compromise with the group. Hudaybi was prepared to support the Egyptian military officers, including the future presidents of the country, Nasser and Sadat. Indeed, the members of the Brotherhood "were attracted by the soldiers' nationalist stance and Islamic rhetoric"[37] and were prepared to forgo pursuit of a global caliphate in favor of an Islamic democracy in Egypt. Thereafter, however, the group was alienated by the new government's failure to promulgate a constitution that enshrined both democracy and Islamic law. Thus, in early 1954 the Brotherhood helped organize demonstrations against Nasser, and in October of that year a member of the group's Special Apparatus tried unsuccessfully to assassinate him. Thereafter, "the greatest crackdown of the Brotherhood in Egypt began, with perhaps 20,000 detained in newly built concentration camps in the desert, and only 1,050 officially tried."[38]

In consequence, the Brotherhood turned its back on democracy and deemed existing political parties unable to unite Egypt or cope with its problems. In 2008 it boycotted local elections; in parliamentary elections in 2010 its participation was blunted by government harassment, and the pro-Mubarak National Democratic Party won 209 of 211 seats in the first round of voting. Thereafter, the Brotherhood boycotted the second round of voting and began to advocate "a non-partisan Islamic system."[39] Another consequence of Egypt's repression of the Brotherhood was to radicalize some of its members, notably Sayyid Qutb, who joined the Brotherhood in the 1950s and contributed to its reputation for being a violent or even terrorist group.

Qutb declared that officials in Egypt who repressed the Brotherhood were apostates and not true Muslims, and therefore should be the objects of violent jihad. Qutb's views, however, were repudiated by the Brotherhood, and Hudaybi declared that only God could declare a person's faith. "Within the Brotherhood, Hudaybi's tolerant view—in line with al-Banna's founding vision—prevailed, cementing the group's moderate vocation," while Qutb, "who breathed his last on Nasser's gallows in 1966 went on to become the prophet and martyr of jihad."[40] In the ensuing years the Brotherhood "followed the path of toleration and eventually came to find democracy compatible with its notion of slow Islamization," and "its road to power" was not revolutionary but depended "on winning hearts and minds through gradual and peaceful Islamization," even if that required allying with secular and liberal politicians. Furthermore, it had become "a collection of national groups," all of which rejected "global jihad while embracing elections and other features of democracy."[41] Those members who adhered to Qutb's views left the Brotherhood to join militant jihadist groups like Hamas and al-Qaeda, and by the 1980s the group sought to rejoin the country's political mainstream.

Prior to the Arab Spring, the Muslim Brotherhood sought to establish a genuine party base, first running "independent" candidates for parliament in 1984, though boycotting the 1990 elections owing to government limits on democratic participation. In addition to seeking to establish Islamic law as the basis for government, the Brotherhood in Egypt and its affiliates elsewhere focused on publicizing human-rights abuses, political corruption, and economic development.[42] During the Mubarak years, many student activists joined the Brotherhood. Although its members were sometimes arrested and harassed, the group was tolerated by the government, which nevertheless demonized it publicly in order to retain American political support. As the number of the Brotherhood's elected representatives in Egypt grew, it became the best-organized and most popular opponent of Mubarak, emerging as the largest opposition bloc in 2000 and winning eighty-eight seats as "independents" in the Egyptian parliament in 2005 despite being officially banned. It viewed "the election campaign as an ideal apparatus for promulgating the message of Islam as a solution."[43]

CONCLUSION: POLITICAL ISLAM AND DEMOCRACY

Nevertheless, when the Arab Spring spread to Egypt and elsewhere, there were observers who feared that Bernard Lewis was right when he wrote, "For Islamists, democracy, expressing the will of the people, is the road to power, but it is a one-way road, on which there is no return, no rejection of the sovereignty of God, as exercised through His chosen representatives. Their electoral policy has been classically summarized as 'One man (men only), one vote, once.'"[44] Lewis meant that Islamists like the Muslim Brotherhood were not genuinely committed to democracy but viewed it as a tactic to gain power, after which there would be no further elections. In contrast, as Middle East specialist Steven Cook suggests, although the members of the Brotherhood are Islamists, "the majority of them are first and foremost doctors, lawyers, pharmacists, and engineers" who "think of themselves as a vanguard that is uniquely qualified to rebuild Egypt and realize its seemingly endless quest for modernization."[45]

Those who fear that Islamists only advocate democracy as a temporary expedient cite how Iran has not held genuinely free elections since it became an Islamic republic in 1979 (forgetting that it had not been democratic under the shah). In Algeria, the Islamic Salvation Front, which like the Brotherhood sought to establish an Islamic state governed by Sharia law, triumphed in 1990 local elections and then won 188 of the 231 seats in the first round of voting for the country's National Assembly in December 1991. The Algerian army, fearful that the group would establish a dictatorship, canceled the election and arrested its leaders. The consequence was an insurgency led by the radical Armed Islamic Group, which lasted much of the decade, involved bloody atrocities on both sides, and cost some 200,000 lives before coming to an end.

By contrast, Turkey's Islamist Justice and Development Party (AKP) and its founder, President Recep Tayyip Erdoğan, have won democratic elections since 2002. Although it has Islamic roots, the AKP did not overturn the country's secular ideology established by the country's founder, Mustafa Kemal. That fact, along with its moderate Islamic policies, appeals to the emerging Muslim middle class in Turkey, as well as to its pious constituents in rural Anatolia. Thus, it escaped the fate of earlier Islamic parties that were outlawed or shut down by Turkey's secular authorities. Fortunately, unlike Algeria, Turkey's Islamic parties did not become clandestine or violent groups.[46] Indeed, Turkey, the United States, and other donors jointly established a fund in mid-2014 to reduce the appeal of violent jihadism in the Islamic world. Although Erdoğan has become increasingly authoritarian in recent years, the AKP's larger democratic legitimacy remained unquestioned, notwithstanding his ill-tempered arrogance.

The next chapter examines the outbreak and evolution of the Arab Spring beginning in 2011.

4

America and the Evolution of the Arab Spring

Chapter 4 begins by examining the background and onset of changes in the Arab world called the "Arab Spring." It continues by examining key countries affected by the Arab Spring and Washington's involvement in those events. The first case is Tunisia, in which the transition to democracy, though rocky, proved relatively successful in comparison to the second, the bloody events in Libya and that country's civil war and subsequent chaos. After describing the Libyan case and NATO intervention, the chapter turns to Egypt and the high tide of the Arab Spring, a revolution that overthrew President Hosni Mubarak, and the ensuing military counterrevolution that ousted the country's elected Islamic leaders. After examining Egypt and America's alienation of both Egyptian secularists and Islamists, the chapter turns to the bloodiest episode of the Arab Spring and its worst outcome, the long civil war in Syria, a war in which Washington sought to avoid becoming embroiled.

The shift in American foreign policy toward the Arab states and its 370 million people began several years earlier with an eagerly anticipated speech titled "A New Beginning" delivered by recently elected president Barack Obama at Al-Azhar University on June 4, 2009, in Cairo, a city regarded by many as the center of the Arab world. In an eloquent address the president sought to distance himself from his predecessor and alter anti-American views of the United States that were widely held in the Arab world owing to U.S. support of authoritarian Arab leaders, its pro-Israel stand in the Israeli–Palestine conflict, and its 2003 intervention in Iraq. The president praised Islam's historical contributions to culture, religion, and civilization and denounced political extremism and terrorism, describing the latter as a violation of the Koran. He also indicated a change in U.S. policy—from supporting dictatorial regimes in the Middle East toward supporting a transition to democracy.

It almost seemed Obama was inviting the events that would follow and constitute the Arab Spring.

THE ARRIVAL OF SPRING

On December 17, 2010, Mohamed Bouazizi, a Tunisian vegetable peddler with a university degree, set himself ablaze after a policewoman who slapped him seized his cart. "Events in Tunisia inspired protesters in Egypt and then in the rest of the Arab world. Tunisia shared many properties with its neighbors—high unemployment, a corrupt regime, a frustrated public, and more information about the regime from outside the country. WikiLeaks—the international organization founded by Julian Assange that

KEY DOCUMENT

President Barack Obama's Speech in Cairo[1]

We meet at a time of tension between the United States and Muslims around the world—tension rooted in historical forces that go beyond any current policy debate. . . . The attacks of September 11th, 2001 and the continued efforts of these extremists to engage in violence against civilians has led some in my country to view Islam as inevitably hostile not only to America and Western countries, but also to human rights. . . . I have come here to seek a new beginning between the United States and Muslims around the world; one based upon mutual interest and mutual respect; and one based upon the truth that America and Islam are not exclusive, and need not be in competition. . . . I do have an unyielding belief that all people yearn for certain things: the ability to speak your mind and have a say in how you are governed; confidence in the rule of law and the equal administration of justice; government that is transparent and doesn't steal from the people; the freedom to live as you choose. Those are not just American ideas, they are human rights, and that is why we will support them everywhere. . . . No matter where it takes hold, government of the people and by the people sets a single standard for all who hold power: you must maintain your power through consent, not coercion; you must respect the rights of minorities, and participate with a spirit of tolerance and compromise; you must place the interests of your people and the legitimate workings of the political process above your party. Without these ingredients, elections alone do not make true democracy.

publishes leaked news and classified information from anonymous sources on its website—turned out to be somewhat of a trigger, as Tunisians learned that their regime was considered to be more corrupt than they had expected."[2]

At the time most Arab states (plus Iran) were "authoritarian,"[3] but the death of Bouazizi triggered a revolutionary contagion of protests that swept across North Africa and the Middle East and toppled longtime dictatorships in Tunisia, Egypt, Libya, and Yemen. The contagion also threatened conservative regimes in the Persian Gulf, whose rulers hastened to grant political concessions and increase public spending in order to mollify their citizens. Throughout the Arab world, people—especially the young—gathered in massive demonstrations to spread their message that the "people demand the fall of the regime," seeking democracy, civil rights, social equality, and economic reform. It appeared that the Arab states would follow the path of the Soviet bloc in ridding itself of tyrants and achieving "people power."

The rapid spread of democratic aspirations from country to country was facilitated by modern information and communication technologies and social media like Facebook, combined with the growing skills of young people in using them effectively. Tunisia may have been "the first of this cascade because it had the highest internet access in North Africa, and, more importantly, this access made information about their success easier to get out to inspire protesters elsewhere."[4] Protesters "were middle-class, educated, and underemployed, relatively leaderless and technology-savvy youth," and "digital media appeared to have an important role in the ignition of social protest, the cascade of inspiring images and stories of success across the countries of the region, and the peculiar organizational form that Arab Spring uprisings had."[5]

Social media were less vulnerable to censorship by dictatorships than were other forms of communication. They provided "the entry points for young activists to explore democratic alternatives," "allowing for political discourse and even direct interventions with state policy, and coordinating mechanism that supports synchronized social movements through marches, protests, and other forms of collective action."[6] Google made adjustments to its speak2tweet technology to evade interference from the Egyptian and Syrian governments. Mobile phones played a key role in coordinating the activities of regime opponents and were "one of the key ingredients in parsimonious models for the conjoined combinations of causes behind regime fragility and social movement success."[7]

As the Arab Spring spread and took root, governments willingly or unwillingly rewrote constitutions to meet the aspirations of protesters demanding individual rights and democracy. "All the codes, however, had two major features in common. First, they generally detailed the aspirations of the state, for example, to be part of the Arab *Umma* [community] and uphold the principles of Islam. Such constitutions are in direct contrast to the U.S. one, which aims to limit the state. Second, like Western constitutions, Arab constitutions tended to be laden with strong guarantees for civil and political rights."[8] The combination of secular political rights for individuals and Islamic principles produced growing tensions within these societies between secularists and Islamists.

Between 2011 and 2012, although twelve regimes in the region remained authoritarian, significant changes had already taken place. Three countries (Libya, Egypt, and Morocco) had moved from the category of *authoritarian*, with Libya experiencing the most significant democratic gains among all the countries reviewed. Events in Libya and Egypt illustrated how "long-serving, geriatric leaders" may be overthrown by "young and restless populations."[9] Yet only months later counterrevolution engulfed Egypt, bloody civil war convulsed Syria, and democratic reforms virtually ceased elsewhere.

"All the people in those countries," declared a Lebanese journalist, "lived under similar suppression despite the differences in their regimes, so the uprisings were contagious," but "the new regional order is being drawn in blood."[10] What began as a springtime of hope, optimism, and peaceful change was transformed in only three years into instability and violence, highlighted by bloody revolution and civil war in Libya and Syria and the overthrow of a democratically elected government in Egypt by the country's army. Political Islam discovered that opposing authoritarian leaders was in many ways easier than governing countries. Eradicating earlier corruption did not prevent new leaders from being corrupt, and assuming power was not itself sufficient to solve their countries' complex and daunting economic, political, and social challenges. Thus, protests in Tunisia, Libya, and, most important, Egypt indicated growing disillusionment with political Islam in the Arab world.

The Arab Spring had bloomed in contexts not prepared for profound political changes that failed to improve their daily lives by providing jobs, health care, and greater opportunity. In the words of one analyst, "The Arab Spring is the canary in the mine shaft for a broader problem—fragmented countries, too much population growth, terrible education systems, too little water—these countries arc the losers."[11]

These tragic events threatened to revive the flagging fortunes of both authoritarian leaders and Islamic extremists throughout the region and reopened contested questions regarding the relationship between military and civilian rule and the role of religion in politics and society. Such issues fueled violent conflicts between Shia and Sunni Muslims and between adherents of secularism and those favoring Islamic rule. "This is political polarization on steroids." "You've got both sides trying to banish each other from politics."[12]

The story of the Arab Spring is not over, and the aspirations of those who thronged the centers of cities like Cairo, Tunis, and Tripoli only a few years ago may yet be realized. It is possible that those countries that witnessed revolutionary changes after 2010 may flourish in coming decades, and that those in turmoil will regain stability. This happened in Europe after the French Revolution and the dictatorship of Napoléon, the revolutions of 1848 and their repression by Russian and Prussian troops, and in the United States after the Civil War. In what follows we shall trace these momentous events in the countries in which they took place and explore America's reaction to them.

The regional transformation that began in Tunisia was most keenly felt in three countries—Libya, Egypt, and Syria. Violence engulfed all three, though for different reasons, and their future continues to preoccupy U.S. policy-makers. Libya experienced an insurrection that overthrew the authoritarian rule of Muammar Qaddafi; Egypt witnessed two dramatic changes in government; and Syria was the victim of a bloody civil war between the government of President Bashar al-Assad and his Sunni adversaries. Among the countries that have been affected by the Arab Spring, Tunisia, where it all began, weathered the political storm better than most of the Arab world, and we begin our examination of individual countries with what happened there after the suicide of Mohamed Bouazizi.

Tunisia: Cradle of the Arab Spring

After weeks of protests following Bouazizi's death, President Zine al-Abine Ben Ali, who had governed since 1987, resigned in January 2011 in Tunisia's "Jasmine Revolution." He was the first of the region's strongmen to fall victim to the Arab Spring. About 300 Tunisians were killed during protests against corruption, economic decline, and authoritarian rule, and in June 2012 Ben Ali was sentenced in absentia to life in prison for their deaths. Following Ben Ali's ouster Salafi Muslim leaders demanded that the country be subject to Islamic law. More moderate Islamic politicians, however, largely contained the extremists.

In October 20l1 multiparty democratic elections to a Constituent Assembly that would draft a new constitution were held. "Just as many Tunisian citizens protested peacefully in streets and squares to claim their rights," declared President Obama, "today they stood in lines and cast their votes to determine their own future."[13] The moderately Islamic Ennahda ("Renaissance") movement won a large plurality. The party, which had been inspired by Egypt's Muslim Brotherhood, had been banned by President Ben Ali in 1992 and was only legalized by the country's interim government in March 2011.

A coalition government led by Ennahda and including the runner-up Congress for the Republic (CPR), a secular party, was formed with Ennahda's deputy leader as prime minister. The daughter of Ennahda's leader and founder Rached al-Ghannouchi noted, "The inspiration for our values is Islam but we're concerned to address the modern daily concerns of Tunisians, within the context of modern culture."[14] In 2012 Ennahda declared it would not seek to make Islamic law the main source of legislation. Nevertheless, though the Ennahda movement remained a moderate party, claiming to emulate Turkey's ruling Islamist Justice and Development Party, its popularity raised the same suspicions in Tunisia regarding Islamism that appeared elsewhere in the Arab world.

Although Tunisia had become democratic, economic and social conditions improved little during the following years, and paradoxically, Tunisians' relative freedom and high education encouraged many of its young people to join the terrorist group Islamic State of Iraq and Syria (ISIS). In the year after Ben Ali's ouster, unemployment rose from 13 to 18 percent, including large numbers of college graduates, and the economy remained in a downward spiral. Unrest culminated in renewed protests in December 2012 led by the country's influential Tunisian General Labour Union (UGTT). Demonstrators were attacked by members of the Leagues for the Protection of the Revolution, militias whom critics claimed were associated with Ennahda—a claim the party denied. Militant Salafi Muslim groups also grew more influential, ransacking the U.S. embassy in Tunis and attacking a hotel for serving alcohol. Ennahda's leaders continued to profess moderation, and its leader insisted, "We don't believe the state has the right to impose its views on what people wear, eat or drink, what they should believe in."[15] Nevertheless, according to an analyst, after the Salafi attack on the embassy "people said, 'Enough with these bearded people.'"[16]

Matters further deteriorated when a leading secular politician, Chokri Belaid, who had accused Ennahda of refusing to stand up to hard-line Salafis, was assassinated in 2013. Belaid had claimed that Ennahda had given "an official green light" to political violence and accused "Ennahda mercenaries and Salafists"[17] of attacking a meeting of his supporters. Thereafter, street protests against Ennahda erupted around the country. Thousands attended Belaid's funeral, a general strike was declared, and the CPR announced it would leave the coalition. Arguing that "some rushed to accuse Ennahda Party and its leader Rached Ghannouchi without any evidence, driven by blind hatred and avoidance of revealing the real perpetrators,"[18] Ennahda turned down a proposal supported by Prime Minister Hamadi Jebali to form a national unity government of technocrats, and Jebali was forced to resign.

In May 2013 violence followed the government's ban of a meeting of the Salafi group Ansar al-Sharia (Tunisia), and an arrest warrant was issued for the group's leader. A Tunisian secular activist who had received death threats from jihadists contended, "Radical Islamists are flourishing in the new Tunisia."[19] Influenced by the ouster of Egypt's Islamist president in July 2013, secular groups in Tunisia began to organize opposition to the ruling Islamists in their country. Then a second opposition leader and head of the People's Movement Party, Mohamed Brahmi, was murdered in front of his family by an assassin using the same gun that had killed Belaid, an event that triggered the resignation of sixty opposition members in parliament and renewed calls for a nonparty government. Observed historian George Trumbull, "The danger of this is that it's an attack on democratic institutions" and "has a potential to divide Tunisia into purely secular and purely Islamist poles and to further alienate Islamist supporters committed, at the moment, to the democratic process."[20] Tunisian officials accused Salafi extremist and arms smuggler Boubaker Hakin, a member of a small jihadist cell linked to al-Qaeda in the Islamic Maghreb (AQIM), of both murders. A month later Prime Minister Ali Laarayedh accused Ansar al-Sharia (Tunisia) of involvement in the assassinations as well as well as a lethal ambush of an army patrol. "It is responsible," he charged, "for a weapons storage network, it is responsible for planning assassinations, and attacks against security and army posts."[21] In February 2014 the assassin of Belaid and Brahmi was killed in a police raid.

The country still confronts serious challenges. Security remains poor. Following the murder of two policemen by terrorists, protesting police drove President Moncef Marzouki and Prime Minister Ali Laarayedh from a memorial ceremony for the victims. A few days later militants in Ansar al-Sharia (Tunisia) died in a firefight with security forces. Economic reform has been slow. The country declared a state of emergency in July 2015 (a year after canceling it) following terrorist attacks aimed at foreign tourists outside the National Bardo Museum in Tunis and a beachfront hotel in Sousse. Nevertheless, in Tunisia an Islamist party had kept its commitment to democracy. "Although Tunisia benefits from some unique characteristics, other Arab countries should seek to emulate its homegrown national dialogue, its political coalition-building, and its bottom-up approach to reform," which allow "for broad reconciliation and a real evolution in Tunisian society."[22]

Thus, Tunisia's transition from authoritarian to democratic rule was difficult. Extremists with weapons from neighboring Libya, some of whom have pledged allegiance to the Islamic State (ISIS), still threaten the country's security. Fear of Islamism remains high, partly because Tunisia is the most secular society in the Arab world. However, the leaders of Ennahda have scrupulously adhered to their commitment to inclusive rule and a coalition government, and have negotiated in good faith with secular parties to overcome the division created by the two assassinations. In October 2013, after mediation by the UGTT between Ennahda and its political foes, Ennahda agreed to accept a nonparty caretaker government to prepare for parliamentary and presidential elections. The arrangement was also to allow for a "national dialogue," with the minister of industry serving as interim prime minister until elections in October 2014. In these, Ennahda trailed a secular party, Nidaa Tounes (Call for Tunisia), whose leader, Beji Caid Essebsi, won election as president in December.

Tunisia's new constitution declared Islam the country's religion, but in most respects it was a liberal contrast to what had existed before. It reflected a balance between religious and secular principles. Its preamble described Tunisia as "a free, independent and sovereign state. Islam is her religion, Arabic her language and republic her regime," but Tunisia is also "a state of civil character based on citizenship, the will of the people and primacy of law."[23]

If Tunisia's political evolution from authoritarian to democratic rule was difficult, what took place in neighboring Libya was more ominous. That country would descend into full-scale civil war.

Libya and Western Intervention

During most of Muammar Qaddafi's longtime dictatorship that began after the overthrow of King Idris in 1969, U.S.–Libyan relations were characterized by open hostility. Qaddafi's link to international terrorism during much of the 1970s led Washington to label Libya as a state sponsor of terrorism. Libya's connection to an attack on U.S. servicemen in a Berlin discotheque led to an American bombing attack on Tripoli in April 1986. Libyan meddling in several African states like Chad and Qaddafi's responsibility for the 1988 bombing of Pan Am Flight 103 over Lockerbie, Scotland, that killed 270 passengers as well the bombing of a French plane over Niger the following year made the Libyan dictator an international pariah. Libya's efforts to acquire nuclear weapons further estranged the country from the West. After Libya turned over two of its citizens to be tried for the Pan Am bombing in 1999, however, U.S. relations with Libya began to thaw. Thereafter, Qaddafi cut his ties to Palestinian terrorists, agreed to compensate the victims of the Pan Am bombing, and in late 2003 voluntarily renounced efforts to acquire weapons of mass destruction, inviting international inspectors to dismantle the country's chemical and nuclear weapons programs.

Although relations remained cool, the United States renewed diplomatic relations with Libya in 2004 and a year later ended sanctions against Tripoli. Thereafter, Libya's relations with the West were normalized, and the Qaddafi regime remained in power until the Arab Spring spread from Tunisia in early 2011, triggering violent demonstrations against corruption in the country's second-largest city, Benghazi, and elsewhere. Benghazi as well as other cities in eastern Libya was home to anti-Qaddafi tribal groups, and although the center of the country's oil-producing region, its residents were among the poorest in the country.

Demonstrations in Benghazi were met with government violence, and security forces were driven from the city as well as from Bayda, the country's fourth-largest city. Within days the country's third-largest city, Misrata, fell to the rebels, and from February until late May the city was the scene of bloody battles in what had become a civil war. Aerial attacks against demonstrators and use of deadly force by snipers and artillery had triggered a country-wide insurrection starting in eastern Libya and spreading westward to the capital, Tripoli. Qaddafi dismissed his opponents as "cockroaches" and "rats," declaring, "All my people love me. They would die to protect me," a remark that American UN delegate Susan Rice called "delusional."[24] Although the regime tried to shut down the Internet and cell-phone service, cell-phone videos still managed to be uploaded onto YouTube.

By the end of February a national council of Qaddafi's foes had been established in Benghazi by former justice minister Mustafa Mohamed Abdel Jalil. A spokesperson declared, "We will help liberate other Libyan cities, in particular Tripoli through our national army, our armed forces, of which part have announced their support for the people."[25] The council declared it would draft a democratic constitution, ensure political pluralism, guarantee human and civil rights, and prepare for free elections. The rebels ranged from middle-class professionals and troops and police who had deserted the government to Islamists, some with ties to al-Qaeda, including an individual who had been interned in America's internment camp in Guantánamo Bay, Cuba. As the heartland of the insurrection, Benghazi and Misrata became particular targets for Qaddafi's military forces.

At first the UN Security Council imposed economic sanctions on Qaddafi and his inner circle and an arms embargo against Libya, calling for an investigation into "widespread and systemic attacks" against Libyan citizens. According to Luis Moreno-Ocampo, prosecutor of the International Criminal Court (ICC), "War crimes are apparently committed as a matter of policy."[26] The ICC issued an arrest warrant for the Libyan leader in late June. After the government began to use indiscriminate force against civilians and sent armed columns toward Benghazi in March in what threatened to become a massacre and in response to rebel appeals, the Security Council unanimously authorized a no-fly zone and humanitarian intervention (Resolution 1973), including "all necessary measures" except the dispatch of ground troops to protect civilians. Although Russia and China voted in favor of the resolution, both emphasized their preference for a peaceful resolution of the conflict. The Security Council based its decision on the doctrine of "responsibility to protect" (R2P), under which states may intervene to prevent governments from committing atrocities against their citizens. It was the first time the Security Council had invoked the doctrine.

Proposals by the African Union for a cease-fire without requiring the removal of Qaddafi were rejected, and NATO responded to the UN resolution by authorizing air strikes against Qaddafi's military forces around Benghazi and enforcing a no-fly zone. Qaddafi's army drew heavily from members of his own Qadhadfa tribe as well as sub-Saharan migrants working in Libya. An immense refugee problem ensued, as thousands of foreign workers employed in Libya sought to flee to their own countries. After Qaddafi's death fighters from Mali who had fought for him returned home with their weapons and helped overthrow the government of that country in 2012. Economic conditions in Libya rapidly worsened as oil production virtually ceased. Tribal and regional hostilities intensified during the conflict as the Qadhadfa fought members of the Magariha and Warfalla tribes.

American and British cruise missile strikes began NATO's "Operation Odyssey Dawn" (Map 4.1). "I want the American people to know that the use of force is not our first choice and it's not a choice I make lightly," declared President Obama. "But we cannot stand idly by when a tyrant tells his people that there will be no mercy."[27] NATO attacks sought to degrade the offensive capabilities of Qaddafi's armed forces as well as their command and control capacity. Before NATO's air campaign ended seventeen countries were involved in aerial attacks on Qaddafi's forces, enforcing the no-fly zone and a maritime blockade, and/or providing logistical support.

By August 2011 the tide had begun to turn as rebel forces advanced westward toward Tripoli. Qaddafi fled Tripoli, and in September the United Nations recognized the rebel National Transitional Council as the legal successor to the Qaddafi regime. Qaddafi himself was caught and killed a month later after his home city of Sirte fell to the rebels. The civil war officially ended on October 23, with the council serving as a transitional legislature. President Obama called it a "momentous day" for Libya.

Elections to the General National Congress in July 2012 proved relatively successful, neither bringing Islamists to power nor triggering significant violence. The main Islamist party, Justice and Construction, with ties to Egypt's Muslim Brotherhood, gained 17 of the 80 seats in contrast to a coalition of liberals and moderate Islamists—the National Forces Alliance, headed by Mahmoud Jibril—that won 39 seats and became the largest bloc in the government formed in November. Of the other 120 seats reserved for individuals running as independents, about 60 joined the Justice and Construction caucus.

Establishing an effective government proved more difficult owing to regional rivalries and the virtual autonomy of some of Libya's cities, feeble government bureaucracies, the growing influence of Islamic extremists, the appearance elsewhere in North Africa—Algeria, Mali, Mauritania, Niger, and Libya itself—of arms including man-portable air-defense systems and SAM-7 missiles taken from stockpiles of the old regime, and the refusal of heavily armed militias established during the civil war to lay down their arms and demobilize. Some of the arms that disappeared fell into the hands of the terrorist group al-Qaeda in the Maghreb (AQIM). Some militant groups remained active in western areas of the country and others in eastern regions; some were Islamist and others were secular. Assassinations of military

MAP 4.1   Operation Odyssey Dawn

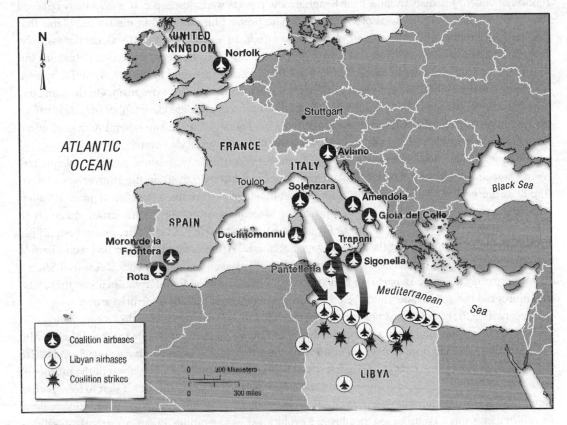

Source: Reuters.

and police officers, including the commander of the military police's investigative division, heightened Libya's insecurity.

Owing to the atmosphere of insecurity, foreign investors remained fearful of doing business in Libya. And in late 2013 the critical oil industry ground to a halt owing to protests and strikes. Oil terminals and ports were blockaded for six months, costing the country about $130 million a day and crippling its economy. Libya's prime minister warned tankers against buying from the country's militias and ordered the arrest of strike leaders, but the government lacked the resources to implement his orders. One militia began to ship oil on its own in March 2014. The government's failure to prevent the militia's tanker from sailing led to the ouster of Libya's prime minister, and the tanker was finally seized by a U.S. Navy SEAL team near Cyprus.

The dangers posed by Libyan jihadists were revealed in the murder of U.S. ambassador Christopher Stevens and three other Americans at what was thought to be a safe house near the U.S. consulate by assailants in Benghazi on September 11, 2012. Hillary Rodham Clinton described the event as her "biggest regret"[28] as secretary of state. Although there had been intelligence reports of violent jihadists training near Benghazi, the reports were unspecific. It was initially believed that local militias reflecting widespread Muslim anger over a film produced in the United States that insulted the Prophet Muhammad had planned the attack. In a speech to the UN General Assembly, President Obama described the film as "crude and disgusting" and "an insult not only to Muslims, but to America as well" but noted that the U.S. Constitution protected the right to free, even hateful, speech. And he pointed out that "Muslims have suffered the most at the hands of extremism. On the same day our civilians were killed in Benghazi, a Turkish police officer was murdered in Istanbul only days before his wedding; more than ten Yemenis were killed in a car bomb in Sana'a; and several Afghan children were mourned by their parents just days after they were killed by a suicide bomber in Kabul."[29]

When it became clear that the assault had been carried out by a well-armed group of Islamic terrorists associated with the al-Qaeda–linked group Ansar al-Sharia (Libya) on the anniversary of 9/11, Republican presidential candidate Mitt Romney and his supporters charged the Obama administration with trying to cover up the facts and with providing inadequate protection for American diplomats in Libya. A "prime suspect" in the murder of Ambassador Stevens was "an eccentric, malcontent militia leader, Ahmed Abu Khattala,"[30] the leader of Ansar al-Sharia. Witnesses declared they had seen Khattala lead the attack. Libyan officials were unwilling to arrest Khattala or other members of Ansar al-Sharia. In January 2013 the State Department offered a reward of $10 million for information about those who had murdered the ambassador, and a year later designated Ansar al-Sharia a terrorist group.

Responding to the continued presence of terrorists in Libya, Washington launched a commando raid on October 2013, spiriting away a senior member of al-Qaeda, Nazih Abdul-Hamed al-Ruqai (a.k.a. Abu Anas al-Libi), who had been indicted in 2000 in connection with the 1998 bombings of U.S. embassies in East Africa, but failing to capture Khattala or others believed to have been involved in the murder of Ambassador Stevens. Ruqai was interrogated aboard a U.S. naval vessel before being sent to New York to stand trial. A few days later Libyan prime minister Ali Zeidan was briefly kidnapped from a luxury hotel by militiamen from a group called the Libyan Revolutionaries Operations Room, apparently in retaliation for the capture of al-Ruqai, and a month later the country's deputy intelligence chief was also briefly kidnapped. Finally, in June 2014 Khattala was seized by U.S. commandos in Libya, taken to the United States, and indicted by a grand jury on eighteen counts, including murder.

Libya witnessed continued violence after the overthrow of Qaddafi. Extremist Salafi Muslims attacked the shrines and graves of Sufi Muslims whose perspective is mystic and pacific. Salafis in groups like Ansar al-Sharia regarded the worship of such shrines as idolatrous.

Tribal fighting also reflected the country's instability and insecurity. Such insecurity may have reflected the sympathies of members of the government as well as the inefficiency of and divisions within the Supreme Security Committee, a force of between 90,000 and 100,000 established by the transitional council, which attracted many militiamen who retained their local ties. In addition, militias that were raised in cities to fight Qaddafi and that were used by the government repeatedly and violently clashed with one another and engaged in gunrunning and drug trafficking. For its part, Washington was considering training Libyan personnel that would include militia veterans to create a security force.

In 2013 militias including Benghazi's powerful Libya Shield shut down the country's Ministries of Justice and Foreign Affairs to force passage of a law excluding former Qaddafi-era officials from holding office, and some months later the militias killed dozens of unarmed civilians in Tripoli who were protesting the fighting among the militias. "The strategy of trying to dismantle the regional militias while simultaneously making use of them as hired guns," wrote one observer, "might be sowing the seeds for the country's descent into warlordism," and "has also given local brigades and their political patrons leverage over the central government."[31] Local militias and tribal leaders retained authority at the expense of the central government, and most Libyans had little trust in political parties. In November 2013 militias from Misrata were forced out of Tripoli, and Ansar al-Sharia was driven out of Benghazi after an intense battle with a local military unit.

Libya remained unstable. In July 2013 over 1,000 prisoners escaped from a prison near Benghazi following violence that claimed the life of a prominent critic of the militias. "Libya's fragile transition is at stake, if political killings go unpunished,"[32] declared an official of Human Rights Watch. In October gunmen southeast of Tripoli killed fifteen soldiers, and continued violence led the country's prime minister, Ali Zeidan (November 2012–March 2014), and his successor, Abdullah al-Thinni (March–April 2014), to ask the West or the UN to lend assistance in bringing peace and ending the spread of arms from Libyan stockpiles seized by extremists. In sum, two years after NATO's intervention into Libya, the country was fast becoming a failed state. Libya's government unsuccessfully struggled to rebuild the country's economy and cities, while foreign donors, wary of growing terrorism, left

Prime Minister Zeidan had enjoyed the loyalty of the country's liberal and secular elements but not that of Islamists, who viewed him and his supporters as "remnants" of the Qaddafi regime, a perception reinforced when Zeidan had a friendly meeting with Egypt's general Abdel Fattah al-Sisi, who had overthrown Egypt's Islamist president. In February 2014 elections for a committee to draft a new constitution triggered violence by Islamic extremists, and some days later armed rioters stormed the Libyan parliament in Tripoli as frustration with the country's slow political transition boiled over. A militia called the Libyan National Army led by a participant in Libya's revolution, former general Khalifa Haftar, attacked the parliament again in May. Despite the government's opposition, Haftar was determined to defeat the Islamist militias and perhaps carry out a coup against the government, but his particular target was the Libyan branch of the Muslim Brotherhood. Violence raged in Benghazi between Haftar's forces and Islamists, and the former general attracted supporters from Libyan military units and anti-Islamist militias and politicians, including former prime minister Zeidan, who had been forced to resign in March.

Although an anti-Islamist majority was elected to parliament in June 2014, the danger of state collapse was reflected in an attack by Libyan militants on Egyptian soldiers near Egypt's border with Libya and violent clashes between Islamist and secular militias for control of Tripoli's airport. "What began . . . as localized clashes between rogue brigades for control of Tripoli International Airport" became "an all-out battle for control of the entire capital. Since then, the violence has rippled outward, setting the stage for a countrywide showdown between the anti-Islamist and Islamist blocs."[33] Two rival governments competed for control of the country, including its central banks, its funds, and its oil. One, the internationally recognized government, was in Bayda in eastern Libya, with some of the former members of parliament allied with Haftar and aided by Egypt and the United Arab Emirates. The other, the self-described National Salvation Government, was Islamist-led in Tripoli and supported by Turkey and Qatar. Amid the violence, U.S. diplomats, protected by military aircraft, were evacuated to Tunisia, and several Libyan extremist groups pledged allegiance to the Islamic State of Iraq and Syria and seized control of the city of Sirte.

Egypt: Revolution and Counterrevolution

Hosni Mubarak, Egypt's president after the assassination of Anwar Sadat in 1981, was a regional ally of the United States, reinforcing his status by stoking fears of Islamic extremism if he were replaced and abiding by Egypt's peace treaty with Israel. As described by Middle East analyst Marina Ottaway, Mubarak was "an ideal partner for the United States, as long as Washington focused on stability in the present without much thought about long-term implications."[34] Without American support Mubarak would not have remained in power for over forty years.

The contagion reached Egypt, the center of the Arab world, in January 2011, when demonstrators gathered in Cairo and elsewhere to protest unemployment, government corruption, and the Mubarak dictatorship. As in Tunisia, the trigger was a particular incident—the death of Khaled Said after a beating by police. Within days, Facebook, YouTube, Twitter, and cell phones spread the story across Egypt. Thereafter, the country experienced three revolutions: "Egypt's first revolution was to get rid of the dead hand, the second revolution was to get rid of the deadheads and the third revolution was to escape from the dead end."[35] The uprising took eighteen days to force Mubarak from office.

Revolution January 25 was described as a "day of rage" as thousands gathered in the center of Cairo—especially Tahrir Square, as well as in other cities—using social media like Twitter and Facebook to coordinate their activities. The government blamed the Muslim Brotherhood for the disturbances and sought to disrupt Internet and mobile phone services. Violence erupted in ensuing days across Egypt. President Obama phoned Mubarak, urging him to act quickly, and Mubarak interrupted the American president, responding, "You don't understand this part of the world. You're young."[36]

Says George Joffé, "At the beginning of 2011, the Obama administration faced two main problems in Egypt. Former president Hosni Mubarak had been a faithful U.S. ally, serving as a pillar of stability in the Middle East. But at the same time, once the Tahrir protests began in earnest, it was clear that history was passing the regime by. The foremost policy challenge in Washington was how to embrace change while maintaining order."[37]

Mubarak dismissed his cabinet and appointed the country's former intelligence chief, Omar Suleiman, as vice president while declaring he would meet the protesters' concerns, but refusing to resign. The government warned it would take "decisive measures" as protesters burned down the headquarters of the governing party. After phoning Mubarak, Obama declared, "I just spoke to him after his speech and told him he has a responsibility to give meaning to those words, to take concrete steps and actions that deliver on that promise. Violence will not address the grievances of the Egyptian people. Suppressing ideas never succeeds in making them go away. This moment of volatility has to be turned into a moment of promise."[38] It seemed as though Washington had decided to support reform and was considering abandoning Mubarak. Unrest across Egypt persisted during the following days until the numbers of protesters had reached about a quarter of a million.

As demands for Mubarak's resignation spread, Israeli officials showed concern that his ouster might endanger regional stability, notably Egypt's treaty with Israel. Mubarak did announce he would not run for reelection but would not step aside and would reform the country's 1971 constitution to foster competitive elections. President Obama commended "the Egyptian military for the professionalism and patriotism" it had shown thus far "in allowing peaceful protests while protecting the Egyptian people." But he made it clear that Washington was abandoning Mubarak, declaring "we have spoken out on behalf of the need for change" and, although "it is not the role of any other country to determine Egypt's leaders," it was his "belief that an orderly transition must be meaningful, it must be peaceful, and it must begin now."[39]

On the following day Internet services were restored, even as violence exploded in Tahrir Square between Mubarak supporters and protesters. The violence continued for several days, and Egypt's government sought to bank the fires of rebellion by raising salaries and pensions and announcing legislative reforms, but the protesters, with the addition of labor unions, remained unappeased. Washington's efforts to persuade Mubarak to step down continued. In Munich, Germany, Secretary of State Hillary Clinton declared, "The region is being battered by a perfect storm of powerful trends. This is what has driven demonstrators into the streets of Tunis, Cairo, and cities throughout the region. The status quo is simply not sustainable." President Obama pointedly urged Mubarak to "make the right decision."[40]

On February 10 Mubarak's announcement that he would remain in office until September further inflamed the demonstrators. Finally, on the following day Vice President Suleiman announced that Mubarak had resigned and the army would assume power with a cabinet led by a Mubarak-era air force general. Egypt's Supreme Council of the Armed Forces committed its members to changing the country's constitution, which they had suspended, and electing a new government within six months. The turmoil took an immediate toll on Egypt's economy, as the country's tourism industry collapsed, its currency's value plummeted, foreign currency reserves dropped, crime increased, and unemployment soared.

The Islamic Interregnum Parliamentary elections between November 2011 and February 2012 gave the Muslim Brotherhood's Freedom and Justice Party about 40 percent of the vote, with the ultra-orthodox Salafi Islamic bloc led by the al-Nour Party receiving almost 29 percent. This gave the Brotherhood about half the seats in the lower house and 90 percent of the seats in the upper house. Although demonstrations continued, Mubarak's ouster had made the country's military leaders popular among Egyptians. As the election of a new president approached in June, Egypt's military leaders consolidated their political power, shutting down the new parliament and claiming the right to issue laws even after a new president took office.

Promising "stability, security, justice and prosperity," U.S.-educated Mohamed Morsi of the Muslim Brotherhood was narrowly elected Egypt's fifth president in a runoff in June 2012, with 51.7 percent of the vote. Morsi was the first Islamist to be elected in any Arab country. "I grew up with the Muslim Brotherhood," he declared. "I learned my principles in the Muslim Brotherhood. I learned how to love my country with the Muslim Brotherhood. I was a leader of the Muslim Brotherhood."[41] Once elected, the Brotherhood was faced with the task of balancing the aspirations of its religiously conservative Islamic base, which wished to impose Islamic law and moral values, with the aspirations of the liberal and secular sectors that, while unhappy with corruption and economic malaise under Mubarak, remained wary of the Islamists.

Shortly after his election President Morsi set out to limit the influence of Egypt's military services. He fired the defense minister, Field Marshal Mohamed Tantawi, and other military leaders, apparently to gain support among a younger generation of officers, including the American-trained general Abdel

Fattah al-Sisi, who was named to replace Tantawi. Morsi then recalled the elected parliament that the generals had dissolved and nullified their claim to make laws, asserting his authority to govern to preserve unity and protect the revolution, and to assume control of drafting a new constitution.

Thereafter, Morsi extended his control over state institutions, especially the judicial system. He decreed an end to the power of judicial review, giving himself authority to issue laws that were "final and unchallengeable" until the new constitution took effect, and the "power to take all necessary measures and procedures"[42] against potential threats to the revolution. This act ignited a train of events that ultimately led to Morsi's downfall. Morsi also fired the country's prosecutor-general, whose successor reopened criminal investigations of Mubarak and his family and proclaimed that no court could dismiss the assembly that was writing the new constitution. Morsi's arbitrary actions brought tens of thousands of protesters back into the streets, declaring the slogan they had voiced with regard to Mubarak, "The people want the fall of the regime!"—this time in opposition to their new government. And in December Morsi's supporters physically prevented the country's Supreme Constitutional Court from ruling on the legitimacy of the Constituent Assembly that had written the new constitution. In June 2013, only days before his ouster, Morsi appointed seventeen provincial governors, including seven members of the Brotherhood and another, Adel al-Khayyat, who was associated with a militant group that had murdered fifty-eight tourists in 1997 near Luxor; at this time he also added loyalists to the state prosecutor's office. Collectively, these actions suggested that Morsi was seeking to monopolize power.

The government's heavy-handed stifling of dissent produced growing uneasiness among secularists about the new president's commitment to democracy, leading to their formation of the National Salvation Front in November 2012 to coordinate the efforts of opposition groups. It also prompted a leading Egyptian liberal, former head of the UN International Atomic Energy Agency and 2005 winner of the Nobel Peace Prize, Mohamed ElBaradei, who had originally supported Morsi, to tweet, "Morsi today usurped all state powers & appointed himself Egypt's new pharaoh. A major blow to the revolution that could have dire consequences."[43]

The draft of a new constitution was adopted by the Constituent Assembly over the objections of secular political parties and Egypt's Coptic Christian Church, and was approved by only a fifth of eligible voters in a referendum in December 2012 in which fewer than a third of eligible voters cast ballots. Although it included term limits for the president, strengthened parliament, and added guarantees of human rights, according to critics it did not end military trials of civilians or adequately protect freedom of expression and religion; nor did it meet secularist demands for separation of church and state.

The Brotherhood-inspired constitution, like the one it replaced, declared Islam to be the religion of the state, adding that the state should "ensure public morality." "The principles of Sharia include general evidence and foundations, rules and jurisprudence as well as sources accepted by doctrines of Sunni Islam and the majority of Muslim scholars."[44] It implicitly extended Islamic law by ambiguous commitments "to preserving the true nature of the Egyptian family" and protecting "ethics and morals and public order."[45] Although the Brotherhood's Supreme Guide, Mohammed Badie, argued that Sharia only "polishes morals, though persuasion and education, with no coercion whatsoever," and "totally rejects the concept of a theocracy,"[46] the constitution's language and the Brotherhood's growing concentration of power stoked fears of an emerging Islamic dictatorship. "The decision of constituent assembly leaders to move a flawed and contradictory draft to a vote is not the right way to guarantee fundamental rights or to promote respect for the rule of law," concluded the deputy Middle East and North Africa director at Human Rights Watch. "Rushing through a draft while serious concerns about key rights protections remain unaddressed will create huge problems down the road that won't be easy to fix."[47] The UN high commissioner for human rights argued that the new constitution, while guaranteeing equality, failed to prohibit discrimination.

The sequence of events that ended in the overthrow of President Morsi predated his election. When Mubarak was ousted in 2011 Egypt's military leaders "set a dangerous precedent. Claiming 'revolutionary legitimacy,' the army said that, until the new constitution was written, the rules of the game were whatever the army said they were—even if the army changed its mind. When Morsi was elected before the constitution was written, he claimed the same power. Then, when he shoved through his own constitutional declaration in November 2012 in order to rush the process ahead, he was only following in the generals' footsteps."[48]

Despite generous loans from Qatar, Saudi Arabia, Turkey, and Libya, the Egyptian economy remained in free fall. During his brief tenure, the new president and his government failed to cope with the country's growing economic and social problems and alienated Egypt's liberals and secularists. Fuel shortages that raised food prices and caused electricity blackouts plagued the country, and a shortage of hard currency needed to import wheat, plummeting foreign investment, a spiraling increase in crime, and declining tourism produced a crisis. Urging economic reforms, Secretary of State John Kerry declared, "It is paramount, essential, urgent that the Egyptian economy get stronger, that it gets back on its feet."[49]

Negotiations for a large IMF loan for debt relief were suspended after the new government failed to introduce significant reforms, notably reducing government subsidies on staples like food and oil and halting wage increases to government workers. (Subsidies for fuel were reduced in 2014 after General Sisi became president.) The country's population control program virtually ceased, and the government reversed IMF-supported tax increases shortly after having imposed them. Attacks on anti government demonstrators led a State Department spokesperson to denounce "cases of extreme police brutality."[50]

Even as Morsi sought to tighten his control over the Egyptian government by installing Brotherhood supporters in key bureaucratic and judicial positions, secret meetings were being held between the president's secular opponents and military personnel. The country's "deep state," as the professional bureaucrats and military, police, and intelligence apparatus was termed, was quietly resisting the new regime. "What you have," argues Nathan Brown, "is kind of underneath the surface of politics, this underlying set of structures that's running things."[51]

Counterrevolution A year after his election as Egypt's president Morsi was ousted in a military coup following massive street demonstrations organized by the Tamarod ("Rebellion"), a grassroots movement that claimed to have collected twenty-two million signatures demanding the president's resignation, revocation of Egypt's new constitution, and formation of an inclusive government of national unity.

In late November 2012 tens of thousands of demonstrators protested outside the presidential palace and in Tahrir Square against the president's growing power, and clashes between pro- and anti-government demonstrators erupted. Additional demonstrations took place in January–February 2013, especially in Port Said near the Suez Canal after the sentencing to death of soccer fans who had rioted at a match.

Many of the demonstrators were "male, urban, young, and unemployed."[52] "Since the start of the 2011 revolution in Tahrir Square, every time the Muslim Brotherhood faced a choice of whether to behave in an inclusive way or grab more power, true to its Bolshevik tendencies it grabbed more power and sacrificed inclusion. This was true whether it was about how quickly to hold elections (before the opposition could organize) or how quickly to draw up and vote on a new constitution (before opposition complaints could be addressed) or how broadly to include opposition figures in the government (as little as possible)."[53]

Morsi scheduled parliamentary elections for April 2013, and his opponents declared they would boycott them. "The National Salvation Front," declared an opposition spokesperson, "decided not to take part in the upcoming parliamentary elections because we were not consulted about the election law."[54] The elections were then postponed by the country's Administrative Court for review by the Supreme Constitutional Court of the constitutionality of the electoral law. At the end of June, growing tension in Egypt exploded when millions of Egyptians—more than had protested against Mubarak in 2011—loudly and in some cases violently demonstrated for the ouster of the president.

Demonstrators, many of whom were young and secular, opposed what they saw as Morsi's arbitrariness, his refusal to subject himself or his policies to judicial review, his unwillingness to embrace political pluralism, and his government's inept economic policies. "Morsi's miscalculation—which both he and the Brotherhood later compounded—was to think that everyone understood the results of the Egyptian elections the way the Brothers did"—that is, "that they gave him and his party a mandate to rule with little regard for those who might disagree."[55] "God's will and elections," Morsi declared, "made me the captain of this ship."[56]

Repeatedly, Washington counseled Morsi to be more inclusive, but America had little influence as it tried to avoid publicly criticizing the elected government and thereby destabilizing it. As Morsi's hold on power weakened, President Obama told the Egyptian leader, "The United States is committed to the democratic process in Egypt and does not support any single party or group."[57] Even as they became disillusioned with President Morsi, U.S. officials sought to find a silver lining in the Muslim Brotherhood's moderateness. "Indeed, the contemporary Muslim Brotherhood takes offense at the charge that it engages in violence and terrorism against the state and civilians" and "is proving to be a highly pragmatic organization that has rejected violence and calls for the expansion of democracy within a state ruled by Islamic legislation."[58] Consequently, according to a former assistant secretary of state for Near Eastern affairs, "The administration was slow to recognize that Morsi was not governing in a way that was creating conditions for a sustainable democracy."[59]

In December 2012, after Egypt's president refused to delay the referendum on Egypt's new constitution, the Egyptian army warned that it had a responsibility "to preserve the higher interests of the country" and would intervene to prevent Egypt from "sliding into a dark tunnel of conflict, internal fighting, civil war, sectarian discord and the collapse of state institutions."[60] Until then the Brotherhood and the country's military leaders had enjoyed a mutually beneficial relationship, with the government refusing to impose parliamentary oversight on the military budget and allowing the army to try civilians in military courts. Egypt's military leaders were nonideological, seeing themselves as the central institutional pillar of the state and prepared to work with civilian leaders who could ensure stability. Egypt's military officers form "a tightly knit group," noted Robert Springborg. "They tend to think alike and they are a force to be reckoned with because, besides the Brotherhood, they are really the only cohesive institution in the country."[61]

Morsi's foes declared that June 30 should be his final day in office, even as one pro-Brotherhood observer claimed, "Those who back the 30 June coup are traitors and puppets in the hands of the Americans. They are part of the American–Zionist project to wreak havoc across Egypt."[62] Massive demonstrations took place that day. Then, on July 1, 2013, Egypt's armed forces gave President Morsi an ultimatum, declaring that he had forty-eight hours to meet popular demands or they would intervene and "enact a roadmap for the future." Morsi bluntly refused to alter the course he had set, and Egypt's army carried out its threat two days later.

Morsi had failed to co-opt General Sisi, who declared, "All honorable Egyptians must take to the street to give me a mandate and command to end terrorism and violence."[63] In late July, the general publicly called upon Egyptians to "do me a favor" and take to the streets to show their support for the army. Claiming that the country was descending into anarchy, Sisi announced the suspension of Egypt's constitution and declared that the president of the Supreme Constitutional Court, Adly Mansour, would serve as interim president until new parliamentary and presidential elections could be held. Morsi, declared General Sisi, was "not a president for all Egyptians, but a president representing his followers and supporters."[64] No Islamists were appointed to the new cabinet.

A number of factors suggested that Egypt's "deep state" had indeed been involved in subverting the elected government. These included the rapid end of the fuel and consumer shortages and power cuts; the reappearance of police on the streets of Cairo after having previously failed to provide security at Brotherhood offices; the appointment of generals as governors of most of Egypt's provinces; and the affirmation in the new government's Constitutional Declaration of July 8, 2013, granting the country's armed forces independence from civilian oversight. The ouster of Morsi produced a wave of nationalist enthusiasm among his secular and liberal opponents across Egypt. ElBaradei, who became the country's acting vice president, declared, "We just lost two and a half years." "As Yogi Berra said, 'it's déjà vu all over again,' but hopefully this time we will get it right." President Morsi was placed under house arrest; the Brotherhood's Supreme Guide, Badie, and other Islamic leaders were arrested; and the Brotherhood's

Heng, International Herald Tribune

Counterrevolution
in Egypt

media outlets were shut down. In response, the Brotherhood declared it would "refuse to participate in any action with power usurpers" and called supporters to rise against those who "steal their revolt with tanks and massacres."[65]

In mid-August, after promising to disperse Brotherhood supporters in encampments in Cairo gradually and peacefully, the security services used armored vehicles, bulldozers, live ammunition, and snipers—killing over 500 Brotherhood supporters and injuring over 3,700—and restored the Mubarak-era state of emergency. Additional violence followed, with anti-Islamic civilians and police tracking down members of the Brotherhood in Cairo and other cities. "What is different," declared a researcher for Human Rights Watch, "is that the police feel for the first time in two and a half years, for the first time since January 2011, that they have the upper hand, and they do not need to fear public accountability or questioning."[66] Interim president Mansour defended the soldiers and police as "martyrs," saying, "They are the same men, army and police, who sacrifice their lives every day in Sinai and in all parts of Egypt to protect the security of the country and the dignity of its citizens, and to fight terrorism targeting the country's stability."[67]

The bloodshed triggered the resignation of interim vice president ElBaradei, who admitted, "We have reached a state of harder polarization and more dangerous division, with the social fabric in danger of tearing, because violence only begets violence. The beneficiaries of what happened today are the preachers of violence and terrorism, the most extremist groups, and you will remember what I am telling you."[68] President Obama warned Egypt's new leaders, "While we want to sustain our relationship with Egypt, our traditional cooperation cannot continue as usual when civilians are being killed and rights are being rolled back."[69]

Egypt's military leaders were portraying the Brotherhood as a terrorist group, preparing to crush it. In December 2013 the Egyptian government declared the Brotherhood a terrorist organization, and Saudi Arabia did the same some months later. In September 2013 the Brotherhood was dissolved and its assets confiscated by an Egyptian court, complicating the prospect of its participation in any new government. Historian Khaled Fahmy concluded that Morsi's overthrow was "an existential crisis, and it's much more serious than what they [the Brotherhood] were subjected to by Nasser or Mubarak."[70] Everybody abandoned us, without exception,"[71] admitted a Brotherhood leader.

Morsi's trial for incitement of murder began in November 2013. As it opened the former president proclaimed, "There is a military coup in the country," adding, "I am the president of the republic, according to the Constitution of the state, and I am forcibly detained!"[72] He accused General Sisi of "treason against God" and "treason against the whole nation by driving a wedge among the people of Egypt."[73] The military government seemed sufficiently unperturbed that in November it lifted the state of emergency that it had imposed in August 2013. Nevertheless, clashes on the third anniversary of the 2011 uprising against President Mubarak the following January led to large numbers of deaths. In September 2013 Morsi was also charged with conspiring with foreign groups, including Hamas and Hezbollah, to commit terrorism, and the next month was charged with a plot to free prisoners with the help of foreign groups. The latter charge resulted in a death sentence in May 2015. Egyptian courts also handed down mass death sentences to members of the Muslim Brotherhood in show trials in 2014, though the sentences were subsequently lightened for many of the accused.

Nevertheless, cracks began to appear within the ranks of the Brotherhood's opponents. After a law was passed regulating protest demonstrations and enabling authorities to ban them, attacks on security personnel increased and 150 police officers were killed between August and December 2013. Egypt's interim prime minister argued that, notwithstanding the right to protest, "practicing this right must be met with a sense of responsibility so it won't damage security or terrorize or assault establishments."[74]

In the end, Washington found itself a helpless bystander as Morsi and the Muslim Brotherhood were swept from power, and dissenters were arrested. According to General Sisi the U.S. ambassador had asked him to postpone for a day or two ousting President Morsi. The Obama administration, which had unsuccessfully advised Egypt's military leaders not to overthrow Morsi and negotiate an agreement between the army and president, refused to call the military coup a "coup" because by U.S. law that required an immediate cessation of America's annual military and economic assistance to Egypt. Egypt's ambassador to the United States argued it was not a coup but "a popular uprising. The military stepped in in order to avoid violence."[75] And Hillary Clinton's successor, Secretary of State Kerry, echoed the ambassador: "The military was asked to intervene by millions and millions of people" and had been "restoring democracy."[76]

"What was driving this decision," according to a senior administration official, "was what's in the best interest of the United States going forward and how can we have the most leverage to promote our interests in a very volatile situation."[77] Rep. Howard Berman (D-CA) got it right when he observed, "The law by its terms dictates one thing, and sensible policy dictates that we don't do that."[78] In response, an advisor to President Morsi accused the Obama administration of "verbal acrobatics," adding, "We're going to get into some really Orwellian stuff here."[79] The administration had chosen pragmatism over idealism, and as Elliott Abrams, a former deputy security advisor, commented, "If you said to people you can cast a secret ballot on whether to turn back the clock and have Morsi in power again, I don't think very many people in Washington would turn back that clock."[80]

Nevertheless, President Obama expressed "deep concern" at the actions of Egypt's military leaders, and the administration showed its disapproval by delaying the delivery of F-16 fighter jets to Egypt, reducing delivery of military hardware (though a partial reversal was announced in April 2014), and canceling biennial joint military exercises ("Bright Star 14") with the Egyptian army planned for September 2013. In addition, members of the U.S. Senate began to reconsider military aid to Egypt. "I'm not prepared to sign off on the delivery of additional aid for the Egyptian military," declared Sen. Patrick J. Leahy (D-VT). "I'm not prepared to do that until we see convincing evidence the government is committed to the rule of law."[81]

The regime's opponents concluded that the Obama administration was supporting the Islamists, while the Islamists concluded that the administration favored the military coup because nobody "who knows Egypt is going to believe a coup could go forward without a green light from the Americans."[82] Thus, President Obama admitted, "We've been blamed by supporters of Morsi. We've been blamed by the other side, as if we are supporters of Morsi."[83] Summarizing Washington's dilemma, a former State Department official concluded, "We've managed now to alienate both sides in Egypt."[84]

Although President Morsi's authoritarianism and the army's ouster of his government and its repression of the Muslim Brotherhood slowed the Arab Spring, its bloodiest casualty was Syria. There the government's violent response to protests triggered a full-scale civil war, pitting President Bashar al-Assad, who had assumed power in 2000 after three decades of rule by his father, Hafez, and his

Alawite (a branch of Shia Islam) supporters against a largely Sunni insurrection. The Syrian civil war generated considerable disagreement within the U.S. foreign-policy community about whether Washington should involve itself in the conflict and, if so, to what extent. This debate reflected President Obama's caution and indecision about the issue, especially in light of U.S. wars in Iraq and Afghanistan.

Syria: Civil War

The Arab Spring arrived in Syria early in 2011. The first major protests for democratic reform and release of prisoners took place in the city of Daraa in mid-March. Assad's supporters suppressed the protests, and the regime tried to conciliate opponents by releasing political prisoners and agreeing to initiate a "national dialogue." Additional dissent was met with mass arrests, violence, and brutal torture, and the government began to employ large-scale ground forces supported by tanks, aircraft, and helicopter gunships, as well as a paramilitary militia called the *shabiha* against opponents. Regime opponents, too, took up arms, provided initially by army deserters. "The first significant armed resistance of the current crisis was a local insurrection near the border with Turkey in June."[85] Thereafter, there began what would become a flood of refugees into neighboring Jordan, Lebanon, and Turkey. Many would later make their way to Europe via Turkey, creating a major crisis for the European Union. Turkish leaders who had formerly been on good terms with President Assad became outspoken foes and a source of arms to the rebels, and after Russia's intervention in Syria in 2015, Turkey triggered a crisis by shooting down a Russian warplane that Turkey claimed had violated its airspace. The event reflected the profound gap between Russian and Turkish policies toward Syria: the former support for the Assad regime, the latter opposition to it.

Syrian President
Bashar al-Assad

Louai Beshara/AFP/Getty

The Civil War Intensifies The United States and the European Union imposed sanctions on Syria in May as the Syrian army intensified its use of military force to crush the rebellion. In late July a number of former Syrian military officers established the Free Syrian Army (FSA), which included a variety of armed groups opposing the Assad regime. In August Syria's Sunni prime minister, Riad Hijab, defected. The government labeled its foes "terrorists" and "armed gangs."

At this point, U.S. officials and intelligence agencies believed that the Assad regime would not survive, and President Obama released a statement on August 18, 2011, declaring, "The future of Syria must be determined by its people, but President Bashar al-Assad is standing in their way. For the sake of the Syrian people, the time has come for President Assad to step aside."[86] In November the Arab League suspended Syrian membership and imposed sanctions after the regime turned down the League's proposed peace plan. At a 2013 summit, the Arab League declared the "right" to arm and aid anti-Assad rebels, including the FSA.

The issue of Syria's civil war became a central concern for the United Nations in 2012. Earlier, Russia and China had vetoed UN Security Council resolutions condemning the Assad regime, fearing that they might be used to bring about forcible regime change much as NATO had done to legitimize intervening in Libya. The Security Council did, however, approve a milder statement endorsing a nonbinding six-point peace plan drafted by former secretary-general Kofi Annan that called on the regime to "cease troop movements towards, and end the use of heavy weapons in, population centers"; "ensure timely provision of humanitarian assistance to all areas affected by the fighting"; and "intensify the pace and scale of release of arbitrarily detained persons."[87]

Annan's effort to bring about a cease-fire failed. Instead, Syrian forces stepped up the use of heavy weapons in urban areas, leading to Security Council condemnation in May 2012 and the expulsion of Syrian diplomats from several Western countries. Annan resigned, and Algerian diplomat Lakdar Brahimi replaced him as the UN and Arab League special envoy to seek an end to the violence in Syria. By then the bloodshed had engulfed the capital, Damascus, and much of Aleppo, Syria's largest city. The battle for Aleppo began in July 2012 and continued into 2016.

International Links

As the Syrian civil war intensified, members of the international community began to take sides. Iran and Russia provided funding and arms to the Assad regime, and Iranian proxy Hezbollah openly intervened to turn the tide in Assad's favor. Influenced by Iran, Iraq did little to prevent the flow of Iranian arms to Assad.

The rebels, however, were not receiving many heavy arms such as anti-tank mines, long-range rockets, or surface-to-air missiles capable of neutralizing the government's airpower. "Erratic flows of weapons, ammunition and money in turn," declared one report, "have given rise to a messy landscape of factions vying for resources, fighting over spoils and reshuffling their alliances. Newly-minted guerrilla fighters tend to flock to whatever group has more guns and bullets, irrespective of its ideological leaning; offers superior opportunities for personal enrichment; or, in contrast, enjoys the most impeccable reputation."[88]

Despite escalating violence in Syria, the Obama administration was reluctant to become deeply involved, owing partly to concern lest Washington find itself in the midst of a civil war and partly to doubts about the legality of such assistance. In one instance, a senior U.S. official who had told supporters of Syrian rebels in 2012 that "all options are on the table" recalled that "as I was mouthing the words,

I began to wonder if I was doing the right thing." He added, "It was always a struggle to keep up [rebel] morale without misleading anyone."[89] "Nobody could figure out what to do," admitted a Pentagon official. Washington preferred to plan policy for the post-Assad era. Thus, another observer noted, "It was clear to all participants that this was what the White House wanted, as opposed to really focusing on key questions of how do you get to the post-Assad period."[90]

In February 2013 the administration announced it would provide humanitarian assistance to rebels in areas under its control, leading an opponent of the Assad regime to comment acidly, "Nonlethal assistance—blankets and cellphones—do not topple a regime," adding, "Only Allah knows how Washington works."[91] Finally, in mid-2013 President Obama signed a secret order backing a CIA plan to provide small arms to Assad's foes, and in June 2014 he requested $500 million from Congress to "train and equip vetted elements of the Syrian opposition to help defend the Syrian people, stabilize areas under opposition control, facilitate the provision of essential services, counter terrorist threats and promote conditions for a negotiated settlement."[92] Responding to the threat of ISIS, in September 2014 Obama authorized additional U.S. aid and dispatched about 400 troops to train and arm 5,000 moderate Sunni rebels a year, even though an internal CIA study found that covert aid to insurgents usually failed without the presence of American advisors on the ground.[93]

Turkey's moderate Islamic government of Prime Minister (now President) Recep Tayyip Erdoğan opposed Assad's use of force against fellow Sunni Muslims from the onset of the conflict. Syrian–Turkish tensions were fueled by several incidents along their common border, including the downing of a Turkish F-4 Phantom jet in what Turkey charged was international airspace, leading Erdoğan to threaten to invoke NATO Article 5, which requires countries in the alliance to come to the aid of a member under attack. NATO did deploy six Patriot missile batteries in southern Turkey. Other incidents included the death of Turkish civilians owing to Syrian mortar fire in October 2012, interception of a Syrian plane that Turkey claimed was carrying arms from Russia, and the explosion of two car bombs in May 2013 in the border town of Reyhanli that killed over fifty Turks. Turkey indicted thirty-three suspects described as terrorists with ties to the Turkish People's Liberation Party, which had links with the Syrian army. In September 2013 a Syrian helicopter in Turkish airspace was shot down by Turkish warplanes. "I don't regard Bashar Assad as a politician anymore," fumed Erdoğan in October. "He's a terrorist carrying out state terrorism."[94] Erdoğan was also angered by Washington's failure to carry out its threat to use force against Syria after the regime used chemical weapons against civilians, and he sought to induce Washington to toughen its position toward Assad as a condition for acting against ISIS.

Turkey's effort to bring down Assad proved elusive, and some of the arms Turkey was sending to Syrian rebels found their way into the hands of radical jihadists. For Ankara, the prospect of Syria's civil war spilling into and destabilizing Turkey was worrisome. Thus, after Washington backed away from its threat to strike Syria in response to the use of chemical weapons, and the possibility of a thaw in U.S.–Iranian relations appeared in late 2013, Turkish leaders "felt they were hung out to dry."[95]

Despite President Obama's secret order to provide arms to anti-Assad forces, the arms shipments were delayed. By June 2013 the tide had begun to turn in favor of the Assad government as Syrian forces, aided by Hezbollah, brought about a collapse of rebel resistance in western Syria. The rebels' deteriorating situation led to a debate within the administration about whether to intervene actively in support of the anti-Assad forces, but no decision was reached.

American Intervention?

At a meeting in October 2012 Secretary of Defense Leon Panetta, Secretary Clinton, and CIA director David Petraeus had argued for arming Syrian rebels. Clinton recalled that "Petraeus and I argued that there was a big difference between Qatar and Saudi Arabia dumping weapons into the country and the United States responsibly training and equipping a nonextremist rebel force," but the "President's inclination was to stay the present course and not take the significant further course of arming rebels."[96]

Then in June 2013 Secretary Kerry informed President Obama that Assad's forces had used chemical weapons against civilians and that if Washington failed to "impose consequences" the Syrian regime would view it as a "green light for continued CW use."[97] This prediction was borne out when the Syrian government launched a massive sarin nerve gas attack against civilians on August 21, 2013—an event largely corroborated by a UN report—which violated the president's warning a year earlier at a press conference: "We have been very clear to the Assad regime, but also to other players on the ground, that a red line for us is we start seeing a whole bunch of chemical weapons moving around or being utilized. That would change my calculus. That would change my equation."[98] According to one U.S. official, "The idea was to put a chill into the Assad regime without actually trapping the president into any predetermined action," but according to another official, "what the president said in August was unscripted" and the "nuance got completely dropped."[99] In fact, chemical weapons had been used on several occasions before the August attack.

The president's threat may have confused the actors in the Syrian drama rather than clarify American policy:

> The rebels in Syria could be excused for wondering what U.S. policy toward them might be. At times, President Barack Obama has implied that the United States can't do much to help them because none of them has been gassed. By threatening "enormous consequences" should the Syrian regime use chemical weapons, he seemed to be saying that the first chemical attack would bring the Americans running in, guns blazing. Although understandable, that is likely to be a substantial misreading of the message coming out of Washington.[100]

Having made a commitment in 2012, the president's credibility was on the line. With support from U.S. allies Britain and France, he decided to launch a military strike against Syrian forces in retaliation, declaring on September 4, "First of all, I didn't set a red line; the world set a red line. The world set a red line when governments representing 98 percent of the world's population said the use of chemical weapons are [sic] abhorrent and passed a treaty forbidding their use even when countries are engaged in war."[101] However, after the British Parliament defeated a government motion to join Washington in attacking Syria, and Russia and China threatened to veto any Security Council resolution authorizing an attack, President Obama overruled his advisors and decided to seek congressional authorization to legitimize the proposed strike. It was a gamble the president was likely to lose, as those in Congress who favored an attack thought the proposed strike would be too weak to be effective, and opponents believed a strike would get America bogged down in another endless civil war while withdrawing troops from Afghanistan.

In the end, a Russian proposal—which required Syrian approval—for destroying Syria's chemical weapons, and a unanimous Security Council resolution requiring this, allowed Obama to escape the dilemma he confronted. The resolution "prohibited Syria from using, developing, producing, otherwise acquiring, stockpiling or retaining chemical weapons, or transferring them to other States or non-State actors."[102] At Russian insistence, however, the resolution did not endorse the automatic use of force in the event of noncompliance by the Assad regime, although it noted that coercive measures could be recommended under Chapter VII of the UN charter in another resolution.

Responsibility for the elimination of Syria's chemical weapons was turned over to the Organization for the Prohibition of Chemical Weapons (OPCW)—"the implementing body of the Chemical Weapons Convention (CWC), which entered into force in 1997"[103]—and required the destruction of such weapons. The OPCW was to complete its work by mid-2014, a tight schedule because the weapons were located in areas in which fighting was continuing. "We have urged all parties in Syria to be cooperative and to contribute positively to this mission," declared the OPCW's director-general. "Much depends on the situation on the ground," he said, and its achievement required "some cooperation by all parties."[104]

Although President Obama's defenders attributed the Russian proposal, Assad's willingness to cooperate, and an accompanying push to hold a proposed peace conference in Geneva, Switzerland, to the president's threat to use coercion, the episode reflected the administration's indecision. Presidential advisor Benjamin J. Rhodes described the problem that Syria presented: "We need to be realistic about our ability to dictate events in Syria. In the absence of any good options, people have lifted up military support for the opposition as a silver bullet, but it has to be seen as a tactic—not a strategy."[105] Less charitable was the comment of Syrian National Council leader George Sabra, who declared, "The international community has focused on the murder weapon, which is the chemical weapons, and left the murderer unpunished and forgotten the victims."[106]

A Divided Opposition   As the Syrian civil war ground on, rebel groups remained divided and proved unable to form a stable anti-Assad coalition. Divisions existed between opposition politicians residing outside Syria and militant groups fighting inside the country. A second schism separated moderate Sunni groups and growing numbers of radical jihadists fighting the regime, and a third divided those willing to negotiate with President Assad and those opposed to doing so.

In June 2011 a National Co-ordination Committee (NCC) for Democratic Change was formed. It consisted of several left-leaning and secular political groups and Kurdish political parties. Unlike other opposition factions, the NCC favored a cease-fire followed by negotiations with the regime, and was opposed to foreign intervention. The NCC also opposed the influence of the Muslim Brotherhood within other groups, including the Syrian National Council (SNC).

The SNC was established in October 2011 by a coalition of anti-government exiles and government opponents meeting in Istanbul, Turkey. It was a loose umbrella coalition of groups of many hues united only by a desire to overthrow Assad, and was backed by the Turkish government. The group promised to make Syria into a "democratic, pluralistic, and civil state; a parliamentary republic with sovereignty of the people based on the principles of equal citizenship with separation of powers, smooth transfer of power, the rule of law, and the protection and guarantee of the rights of minorities."[107] The SNC, however, proved ineffective and quarrelsome. It failed to attract support within Syria's Christian or Alawite minorities and was viewed with suspicion by those who were concerned about its Islamic links. In November 2012 Secretary Clinton declared that the SNC could "no longer be viewed as the visible leader of the opposition" and called for a new political group that could "speak to every segment and every geographic part of Syria."[108]

In September 2013, eleven of Syria's strongest rebel brigades, including militant and moderate Sunni fighters, announced their rejection of the SNC and its political leaders living outside of Syria, declaring, "All groups formed abroad without having returned to the country do not represent us."[109] The State Department reacted by expressing regret at the decision, emphasizing that Washington would continue to seek unity among anti-Assad groups. "At this stage," observed Middle East analyst Noah Bonsey, "the political opposition does not have the credibility with or the leverage over the armed groups on the ground to enforce an agreement that the armed groups object."[110]

Thereafter, several groups meeting in Doha, Qatar, established the National Coalition for Syrian Revolutionary and Opposition Forces. Headed by Ahmad Jarba, it included insurgents within and outside Syria who hoped that a moderate Islamist organization would attract international recognition, become the main conduit of aid to the insurgency, administer areas controlled by rebel forces, and plan for a democratic post-Assad regime. Although SNC leader George Sabra responded that his group would not be "subsumed under anybody," the National Coalition swiftly acquired support. The members of the Gulf Co-operation Council (GCC) (Saudi Arabia, Kuwait, the United Arab Emirates, Qatar, Bahrain, and Oman) recognized the National Coalition as "the legitimate representative" of the Syrian people, as did the United States, France, Britain, and the European Union. The new group, however, proved as fractious as its predecessor, and inadequate financial resources and the meddling of sponsoring countries like Qatar and Saudi Arabia sustained its divisions. Thus, it proved unable to exert authority over the armed rebels, especially jihadist groups.

At first, moderates including Syrian army defectors had led the insurrection in Syria. Islamist groups, however, increasingly challenged the Free Syrian Army. Within Syria, the Supreme Military Council of the Free Syrian Army headed by Gen. Salim Idris, a defector from the regime, remained titular leader of rebels in the country but in reality enjoyed little authority over the disparate rebel brigades under its command. Some of its units were relatively nonideological, like the Martyrs of Syria Brigades, while others were regional, like the Northern Storm Brigade, which operated near the Turkish border. The Military Council became increasingly dysfunctional owing to internal factionalism. "Syria's exiled opposition and the United States have invested heavily in propping up the FSA as a counterweight to radical groups that emerged as key players in areas liberated from Bashar al-Assad's rule. But that effort is now circling the drain."[111]

The Syrian Islamic Liberation Front was another coalition of diverse fighters that was active in Syrian cities like Aleppo and Damascus. In 2013 members of this group joined with the Islamic Front, an alliance of seven hard-line Islamic groups, including some of the most effective anti-Assad fighters. The Islamic Front, though declaring it sought to build an orthodox Islamic state, was *not* linked to ISIS or its "caliphate." With militias that collectively had between 40,000 and 50,000 fighters, the Islamic Front was among the largest coalitions of rebel fighters. In December 2013 the group seized the Supreme Military Council's headquarters and supply depots in Syria, and General

Idris fled first to Turkey and then to Qatar, triggering a temporary suspension of America's nonlethal aid to the rebels.

Using suicide tactics and operating throughout the country, militant Islamic groups were the most effective fighters in the insurgency. According to one jihadist, "Most groups are a reaction to the regime, whereas we are fighting for a vision."[112] The effectiveness of the militant Islamists "puts the administration into a situation of having to choose between supporting moderate groups or effective ones."[113] "For all practical purposes," concluded a former State Department official, "the moderate armed opposition that the administration really wanted to support—although in a hesitant and halfhearted way—is now on the sidelines."[114]

The fighting abilities of the jihadists was one reason why they, rather than the Supreme Military Council, were recipients of millions of dollars in contributions from individuals in the Arab world, many of whom were not themselves extremists. Fund-raisers using social media were especially effective in this regard. "Once upon a time we cooperated with the Americans in Iraq," said a Kuwaiti donor. "Now we want to get Bashar out of Syria, so why not cooperate with al-Qaeda?" The journalist Robert Worth recalled meeting a young woman at a Syrian club: "When I asked her about the opposition, she said: 'I am ashamed to say it, but the opposition has lost its meaning. Now it is only killing, nothing but killing. The jihadis are speaking of a caliphate, and the Christians are really frightened.' There was a pause, filled by the churn of Arab pop music. 'I waited all my life for this revolution,' she said. 'But now I think maybe it shouldn't have happened. At least not this way.'"[115] The militant jihadists in Syria fought not only the Assad regime, but also Sunni moderates and even other militants. In this complex setting, some Islamist groups sought to exclude extremists linked to al-Qaeda.

Thus, the cleavages among Assad's foes, as well as their inability to obtain sophisticated weapons, were crucial in keeping the president in power, and some observers, noting that ISIS spent most of its energy fighting other groups opposed to the regime, believed the group was cooperating with Assad. Thus, in mid-2015 it appeared that Assad was actually aiding ISIS's advance toward Aleppo, Syria's largest city, by attacking other insurgent groups.

Assad Hangs On Two years of indecision took their toll. Had Washington acted decisively to arm and support the anti-Assad insurrection in 2011 or 2012, it might have saved lives and led to the swift overthrow of the Syrian regime. Between November 2012 and April 2013, the insurgency steadily gained ground against government forces.

Beginning in the spring of 2013, however, government forces started to push insurgents from strategic positions they had occupied earlier, and the Assad government began to regain the upper hand. Hezbollah's intervention was decisive in the regime's victory in the struggle for the strategic town of Qusayr in June, which severed a rebel supply route and opened a corridor between Damascus and western and northern Syria. Furthermore, Hezbollah's March 2014 victory in Yabrud, near the Lebanese border, allowed government forces to increase pressure on rebel-held areas further north in Homs and Aleppo, as well as in the suburbs of Damascus. Fighting between moderate and extremist rebel factions further weakened the anti-Assad forces. By late 2013 the struggle for Aleppo had also begun to tilt in favor of the government, and the city was virtually besieged a year later. In April 2014 Assad declared he was winning his "war on terror" and would again run for president in elections in June, thereby ending the prospect for further negotiations by precluding discussion on how to form a transitional government. Nevertheless, the war continued with no end in sight, but with sophisticated American anti-tank missiles beginning to reach insurgents from the United States and Saudi Arabia. The regime's recovery dimmed hopes for an end to the violence and increased disillusionment among Assad's foes. Declared a former fighter: "The ones who fight now are from the side of the regime or the side of the thieves. I was stupid and naive. We were all stupid."[116]

A peace conference on Syria's civil war was held in Geneva in January 2014. The Syrian regime agreed to send a delegation while declaring, "Our people will not let anyone steal their exclusive right to decide their future and their leadership."[117] UN secretary-general Ban Ki-moon described the conference as "the vehicle for a peaceful transition that fulfils the legitimate aspirations of all the Syrian people for freedom and dignity, and which guarantees safety and protection to all communities in Syria."[118] Islamist rebels inside Syria were less enthused. The leader of Jaish al-Islam declared that if the National Coalition attended the conference, it would amount to "treason" and his group would regard it as an enemy "the same as Bashar Assad's regime."[119] The National Coalition did attend under U.S. and British pressure (and later received diplomatic status from Washington), though it continued to insist that Assad should have no role in Syria's future. Members of the Free Syrian Army later joined it.

The conference opened on January 22. Although the opposition coalition presented a twenty-four-point plan that omitted any demand for Assad's resignation, the talks made no progress except to arrange for the evacuation of civilians from a besieged area in Homs. The initial American position was that Assad should play no role in Syria's political transition. Moscow rejected this as an effort to predetermine the outcome of the talks. Ryan Crocker, former U.S. ambassador to Iraq, concluded that America's initial determination to oust Assad in advance of negotiations was surreal: "'Assad must go.' Well, Assad isn't going to go."[120] Although Washington reversed its demand that Assad leave office prior to talks, Crocker went further, arguing that "we really need to be making more of an effort to talk to regime people."[121] After a week of wrangling the conference adjourned, the only positive result being that the two sides were in the same room. A second round of talks proved equally fruitless. The Syrian government refused even to discuss its adversary's demands, notably the need for a political transition while calling for "terrorism" in Syria to cease. Each side blamed the other and its backers in Washington and Moscow for the stalemate.

On September 30, 2015, in response to a request by Assad, Russia intervened militarily in Syria, launching cruise missiles and air strikes against rebel groups threatening Syria's Alawite stronghold along the Mediterranean coast. Although claiming its attacks were directed against Islamic State terrorists, they were largely directed against other rebels groups, including those supported by the United States. Declared President Obama: "I think Mr. Putin understands that . . . with Afghanistan fresh in the memory, for him to simply get bogged down in an inconclusive and paralyzing civil conflict is not the outcome that he's looking for."[122] Notwithstanding American protests, Russian president Vladimir Putin seemed determined that Moscow would play a decisive role in supporting Assad and deciding the outcome of the Syrian civil war.

In late October, Assad made an unannounced visit to Moscow, his first journey outside Syria since 2011. During their meeting President Putin made clear he still supported Assad, declaring, "On the question of a settlement in Syria, our position is that positive results in military operations will lay the basis for then working out a long-term settlement, based on a political process that involves all political forces, ethnic and religious groups."[123] Although Washington still opposed Russia's military intervention in Syria, it insisted that Assad would have to step down. It agreed to Moscow's suggestion that the two countries coordinate air strikes to avoid accidents and that another peace conference be held that did not specify Assad's role in Syria's political transition. In addition, the United States agreed that Assad's ally, Iran, be permitted to attend the meeting. Although the participants pledged to seek an end to the Syrian conflict, expectations remained low as the conference opened in Vienna on November 14, 2015.

With arms and training from Iran, Hezbollah involved in the fighting and Russia's intervention, and the regime's enemies divided, the opportunity to overthrow Assad may have passed. Additionally, with the growing influence of radical Islamists like ISIS among Assad's foes, the situation had grown even more complex because Assad's critics in America and elsewhere had grown less certain that his overthrow would be desirable. Indeed, the growing influence of Islamic extremists in the rebellion seemed to support Assad's consistent theme that if he were overthrown, they would come to power. Declared a former U.S. official: "We spent so much damn time navel gazing, and that's the tragedy of it."[124] By 2015 Washington had begun to contemplate that Assad would remain. Although a resurgence of regime foes and the reduction in the numbers of Syrian soldiers owing to casualties and desertions had made the regime increasingly vulnerable and dependent on Hezbollah, Russia continued to supply military aid and advisors to the regime. U.S. officials accused Russia of escalating the conflict by increasing its military support for Assad. Then, in March 2016, Putin surprised observers by announcing an end to Russian military intervention.

CONCLUSION: THE MIDDLE EAST IN AN ERA OF DECLINING AMERICAN POWER

In an era of declining American military and economic power, events in the Arab world have become less amenable to Washington's preferences. As the Arab Spring spread in 2011 the director of studies at Israel's Institute of Policy and Strategy had presciently warned:

> The U.S. can only try to project that the abandoning of the regimes in Tunisia and Egypt is not a precedent that will be applied in the cases of other countries. It can also try to modify the impression that it is willing to accept the rise— albeit through quasi-democratic processes—of radical Islamist forces in lieu of the regimes that have already fallen. This should be done not only through declarations and public diplomacy but also by deeds, such as active support of real, secular, pro-democracy forces in these countries. Such a message may strengthen the liberal and democratic forces in those countries. An American policy of supporting the fall of despotic, secular, pro-Western regimes in favor of equally despotic Islamic regimes would be historical irony and run counter to America's real interests.[125]

5

American Options in a Changing Arab World

In the final chapter in Part I, we will consider the prospects for the tumultuous Middle East raised by the major events in the Arab Spring. We will also examine American policy options for some of the leading issues associated with the evolution of these events. There are two paramount policy issues confronting Washington that are related to the Arab Spring. They are linked by the question of how the United States can balance its values, notably support for democracy and human rights, with its interests in fostering regional stability and maintaining positive relations with crucial regional partners in the Arab world.

- Should Washington pressure Egypt's military government in the direction of democratization? Should it allow events in Egypt to run their own course, with minimal American involvement? Or should it engage Egypt's military leaders and encourage them to adopt liberal political and economic policies? Indeed, should Washington remain committed to the security of Egypt or the oil-rich but authoritarian Arab states although America is achieving energy independence, or should America reduce its longtime commitment to the security of these countries?

- Should the United States provide arms to the Syrian opposition while trying to negotiate an end to the country's civil war that would result in a government without President Assad? Should it negotiate an end to the civil war that leaves President Assad and supporters in power? Or should Washington use force to overthrow Assad, even though the regime has apparently carried out its agreement to rid itself of chemical weapons?

Only a few years before the Arab Spring erupted scholars sought to alert Americans about the consequences of supporting Arab dictators while failing to take account of public opinion in the Arab world:

> The only way you can control the tide of public opinion is by being more repressive, even if you have these electoral exercises that we've witnessed. . . . The first casualty will be any idea that democracy or a more participatory kind of political system will emerge as a consequence of this widening gap that can be addressed in the short term by insecure governments only through increased repression. . . . Second,

while it is true that we can actually pressure governments to accept positions that go against public opinion, the cost of doing business is much higher. It takes a lot more power to do that. . . . Third, where you have public opinion going very strongly against you, it is very hard for you to fight your enemies.[1]

Since Mohamed Bouazizi's suicide, every country in North Africa and the Middle East has been affected to a greater or lesser extent, and authoritarian governments in countries like China and Iran sought to conceal from their own publics the revolutionary upheavals in the Arab world lest the contagion infect their populations. New constitutions were enacted in Algeria, Egypt, Libya, Morocco, Sudan, Syria, and Tunisia. And in some countries, such as Tunisia and Morocco, where King Mohammed VI brought the moderate Islamist Justice and Development Party into government, political reforms have been relatively successful. Although Persian Gulf monarchies such as Saudi Arabia and Dubai have seen little movement toward democracy, even they have experienced evolution that has altered the relations between leaders and citizens. In some cases even authoritarian leaders have become willing to be judged on their performance in dealing with practical economic, political, and social problems, and not merely whether they are sufficiently anti-Israeli or anti-Iranian. Even ultra-conservative Kuwait and Oman witnessed large demonstrations for reform. Nevertheless, regional instability and Islamic–secularist tensions have led to a retreat from democracy.

Elections in Algeria and Jordan did little to make governments more accountable, and elsewhere governments brutally resisted reform and repressed or reversed efforts to democratize. Political violence and civil strife have afflicted Bahrain, Egypt, Iraq, Lebanon, Libya, Syria, Tunisia, and Yemen, and violence has spawned massive flows of refugees. Despite the spread of democratic aspirations, specific national circumstances produced quite disparate outcomes in different countries, and violence greatly exacerbated sectarian tensions across the Arab world.

Revolution in Egypt was the high point of the Arab Spring and saw the election of an Islamist government. Several of the political parties that won elections during the Arab Spring were Islamic, and they discovered that governing was a difficult business, harder than ousting their predecessors. Secular elites and government bureaucrats in Arab societies remained suspicious of moderate Islamic parties, as Egypt's Muslim Brotherhood discovered when opponents took to the streets and the army again assumed power. Not only were their efforts to Islamize their societies sources of suspicion, but their incompetence in coping effectively with their countries' daunting economic and social challenges, their efforts to monopolize political power, and their unwillingness to compromise or engage with political foes produced a political backlash at home and in other Arab countries, as well as in Israel.

Events in Egypt encouraged the growing resistance of conservative leaders to liberalizing trends in countries like Jordan and Saudi Arabia (as well as Israel). Then Saudi King Abdullah wrote General (later President) Abdel Fatah Sisi, figuratively "shaking the hand" that had saved Egypt "from a tunnel whose extent only God knows."[2] The Saudi foreign minister declared, "Concerning those who announced stopping their assistance to Egypt or threatening to stop them, the Arab and Islamic nation is rich with its people and capabilities and will lend a helping hand."[3] "The Saudis," observed a Saudi columnist, "feel they need to create a diplomatic and economic bloc to support Egypt, or it will collapse."[4] Egypt was only one illustration of how growing political instability became endemic throughout the Middle East after the Arab Spring. Full-scale civil war engulfed Libya and Syria. Libya, having rid itself of Col. Muammar Qaddafi's tyranny, remained divided among regional militias and between secularists and Islamists, and had become a virtual failed state with rival governments in Tripoli and Bayda—a situation further inflamed by Islamic terrorists.

Iraq remained in the grip of Shia–Sunni violence to an extent not seen since the withdrawal of American troops from that unhappy country, and had fallen victim to the predations of the terrorists in the Islamic State of Iraq and Syria (ISIS) and its self-declared "caliphate." Syria was the scene of a brutal conflict between the Alawite supporters of President Bashar al-Assad and his Sunni adversaries, while the insurgents themselves were divided between political moderates and extremists affiliated with al-Qaeda or ISIS. By 2016 the carnage in Syria had exceeded 250,000 dead, including 76,000 in 2014 alone, and the Assad regime was seeking to blockade and starve communities that supported the rebels and to impede efforts to get humanitarian aid to civilians in need. Both the regime and its adversaries have massacred civilians, leading the UN high commissioner for human rights to declare the need to investigate repeated incidents. "We should not," she cautioned, "reach the point in this conflict where people become numb to the atrocious killing of civilians."[5] In late 2013 the UN Human Rights Council overwhelmingly condemned the regime's human-rights violations and demanded that the government admit a UN Commission of Inquiry to monitor the violations. That Commission of Inquiry concluded that the Assad regime had conducted "a campaign of terror" through enforced disappearances "as part of a widespread and systematic attack against the civilian population" that constituted "a crime against humanity."[6] China and Russia, however, vetoed a UN Security Council resolution to allow the International Criminal Court to investigate war crimes in Syria.

Frustrated by the difficulty in getting the Assad regime to distribute humanitarian aid, Washington sought ways to bypass the Syrian government. This policy was supported by UN secretary-general Ban Ki-moon, who had tried with little success to press the Assad regime to allow humanitarian assistance into the cities and communities it had besieged. The delivery of aid to those in need became even more difficult after President Assad's reelection in June 2014. Referring to the effort to provide humanitarian aid, Secretary of State John Kerry declared, "It's not getting to people. It's going through one gate, one entryway, and it's going through Damascus and/or controlled by the Assad regime. That's unacceptable. We need to be able to get aid more directly, and we're going to work to do that."[7] After blocking a resolution in the UN Security Council to back the U.S. position on assistance, Russia's foreign minister argued that "terrorism" in the country was an equally serious problem. In late February 2014 the Security Council passed a binding resolution to make the Syrian regime and its foes allow the delivery of humanitarian aid, but little reached the nine million Syrians in need in the months that followed. Finally, in June 2014 the Security Council unanimously authorized emergency aid without prior approval by the regime, and this began a month later.

The UN estimated that by 2014 some 6,000 Syrians were fleeing the country *every day*. Of the more than 4 million registered Syrian refugees who had fled to Lebanon, Turkey, and Jordan by mid-2015,[8] almost 1.2 million had fled to Lebanon alone.[9] This is equal to almost a third of its population, which had the "highest per capita concentration of refugees worldwide"[10] according to the UN refugee agency. Lebanon sought to limit the flood of refugees by requiring that Syrians have a Lebanese sponsor or pay $200 for a six-month residency permit.[11] About 1.8 million had entered Turkey, including 180,000 from the Syrian Kurdish city of Kobani, which was besieged by ISIS;[12] 629,000 moved to Jordan; and almost

250,000 fled to Iraq.[13] "This is the biggest refugee population from a single conflict in a generation, according to the UN high commissioner for refugees."[14] Many Syrians also joined the flood of refugees moving through Turkey and elsewhere toward Europe, where Hungary and then additional countries began erecting barriers to their entry and movement. Over 12.2 million Syrians needed humanitarian assistance, of whom 6.9 million were internally displaced persons, and Washington had provided over $4 billion in humanitarian aid since March 2011.[15]

Syria had virtually fragmented into several small sectarian ghettoes—Alawite, Sunni, and Kurdish (and ISIS). Islamist rebel groups had coalesced into a loosely organized umbrella group called the Army of Conquest. Syria's Kurdish political party, the People's Democratic Union and its military wing, formed an interim administration in northeast Syria, and its leader declared, "We now control 70% of Syrian Kurdish territory [and] have prepared plans to take control over all of it."[16] Syria's Kurds were in turn trying to halt the expansion of ISIS into their area of the country. There was a hint of Syria's coming fragmentation in the prediction of President Barack Obama's press secretary, Jay Carney, in July 2013: "While there are shifts in momentum on the battlefield, Bashar al-Assad, in our view, will never *rule all of Syria again*."[17] Nevertheless, in February 2014 even America's director of national intelligence, James R. Clapper, confirmed that Assad had strengthened his hold on power. Even if Assad only retained control of part of the country, especially the Alawite regions, it would be a victory of sorts, and his reelection as president in June 2014 with 90 percent of the vote (in government-controlled areas) confirmed his hold on power. Assad had reasons to feel confident: polls showed that by mid-2014, though Syria's neighbors still wished Assad to give up power, majorities everywhere were fearful of a jihadist victory and opposed Western military aid to Assad's foes.[18]

As Syria became a battlefield in the violence between ISIS and other Sunni opponents of the Assad regime, a new flood of refugees was unleashed. American airpower began striking ISIS in Syria without the permission of the Syrian government but was not being used against the regime itself. Washington was walking a tightrope. It was trying not to get involved in Syria's civil war, yet opposing the Assad regime while simultaneously though tacitly on the same side as Assad and his allies Iran, Russia, and Hezbollah as foes of ISIS. Indeed, both Syrian and American air strikes were launched against the group in Syria, and many Syrians found it difficult to understand how Washington could fight ISIS while refusing to intervene against the Assad regime they regarded as a more deadly enemy.

With Hezbollah having intervened in support of the regime and reinforced Assad, the Syrian conflict threatened to spill over into Lebanon. For its part, Israel feared instability on its Syrian border and, while opposed to the Syrian–Iranian–Hezbollah connection, it was equally concerned about the possibility of al-Qaeda extremists in Syria coming to power and had made it clear it would aid Syria's Druse inhabitants (a small, cohesive, and eclectic religious sect) if needed. Israel was also determined to prevent the movement of sophisticated Syrian arms to Hezbollah's sanctuary in Lebanon. In addition, the governments of Saudi Arabia, Turkey, and Qatar had provided aid to Assad's foes, and these countries were concerned about American passivity in the face of continued challenges in Syria and elsewhere in the region. "There is a lot of confusion and lack of clarity amongst U.S. allies in the Middle East regarding Washington's true intentions and ultimate objectives," declared a former State Department official. "There is also widespread unease throughout the Middle East, shared by many U.S. allies that the United States' primary objectives when it comes to Iran, Egypt or Syria are to avoid serious confrontation."[19]

Syrian refugees

Bulent Kilic/AFP/Getty

Robert Ford, who resigned as U.S. ambassador to Syria in February 2014, was more acerbic, noting that he could "no longer defend the policy in public." "We've consistently been behind the curve," he continued. "We need—and we have long needed—to help moderates in the Syrian opposition with both weapons and other nonlethal assistance."[20]

Let us now examine policy options for the United States in the wake of the Arab Spring. We will start with the Egyptian case, then turn our attention to Syria.

EGYPT

Egypt has always been at the center of the Arab political world. Its 1979 treaty with Israel remains a rare success in the peace process, and its defection from the Soviet embrace during the Cold War was a dramatic turning point in U.S.–Soviet relations in the Middle East. Thus, it is not surprising that the revolution that overthrew Egypt's President Hosni Mubarak and brought to power President Mohamed Morsi and the Muslim Brotherhood was viewed as the high tide of the Arab Spring. Similarly, some observers concluded that the ouster of Morsi by the country's military leaders marked the nadir of the Arab Spring and possibly the beginning of a new Arab Winter. The post-Morsi government undertook to rewrite the country's constitution in a manner that would prevent a political party like the Brotherhood's Freedom and Justice Party from receiving a large majority in parliament while winning only a plurality or small majority of the popular vote. The post-Morsi constitution marked a return to Egypt's 1971 constitution, though it provided citizens with protection of additional rights, made freedom of belief "absolute" rather than merely "protected," and banned political parties based on religion. Nevertheless, as of 2016 street violence and terrorism intensified despite military rule.

In contrast to Tunisia's constitution, Egypt's constitution reflected the views of its military leaders and the defeat, at least for the time being, of the country's Islamists. Even as the country's military rulers crushed its opponents, 38 percent of Egypt's voters went to the polls and over 98 percent of them voted in favor of the military-backed constitution in what Secretary Kerry described as the country's "polarized political environment."[21] "This time," said the founder of the Egyptian Initiative for Personal Rights, the regime "has surpassed Mubarak at the height of his authoritarianism."[22] The new constitution obliged the government to fight terrorism, and the powers it grants the government to do so "invite limitless interpretations and ensure that arbitrary and exceptional security measures remain the norm in Egypt."[23]

As we have seen, Washington's attitude toward the tumultuous events in Egypt was persistently ambiguous, reflecting a simultaneous desire to foster democracy and remain "on the side of history," with a strong preference for political stability in that country and its relations with its neighbors—especially Israel. Nevertheless, uncertainty remained about whether the empowerment of political Islam in Egypt augured a democratic future or an intolerant Islamic regime. In fact, it is difficult to imagine democracy or even long-term stability in Egypt without some willing participation of the Brotherhood, although it is likely that the group will fragment between those resorting to violence and those wishing to reform it peacefully to attract a larger constituency. The absence of clarity in U.S. policy reduced American influence in Egypt, alienating both sides in that country's political conflicts.

Egypt's military rulers were less dependent on U.S. aid than in the past, owing to support from the oil-rich countries in the region. They were also being wooed by Russia. When General Sisi visited Russia in February 2014 to arrange for the purchase of arms, Russian president Vladimir Putin declared, "I know that you, Mr. Defense Minister, have decided to run for president of Egypt," and "I wish you luck both from myself personally and from the Russian people."[24] Thereafter, Sisi announced he would run for the presidency, an election he won easily in late May 2014 despite a low voter turnout. During the short campaign Sisi made clear he would be a strong president, perhaps as authoritarian as his predecessors, and after his victory declared his government would be "inclusive." Secretary Kerry then visited Cairo and announced the resumption of U.S. aid to Egypt. Whether Sisi will succeed depends on his ability to end government corruption, provide security, and improve his country's economy.

General Sisi may be the wrong horse for Americans or Russians to bet on. "Sisi has no economic policies or political programs to speak of. The military-backed government's base is narrow, and since it has no way to incorporate dissenters, it will generate more dissent and state-generated violence."[25] And a RAND Corporation analyst adds,

> To be sure, one should be careful about betting against a regime with an over-whelming advantage in both firepower and public support, but the current order does have two Achilles' heels. First, as the threat of the Muslim Brotherhood reclaiming power recedes, it will become difficult for the new authorities to hold together a coalition that is built solely on its members' shared antipathy for the Islamist group. Second, the new regime might overreach in its suppression of the opposition, inviting a backlash.[26]

Policy Options

The policy options available to Washington are fraught with uncertainty about key questions such as which course of action promises to minimize American unpopularity in Egypt and in the Arab world, and whether U.S. policy can actually affect what happens in that country and therefore whether Washington should try to play an active role or remain passive in the face of events beyond its control. According to a former National Security Council (NSC) official, "Anything they do that is dramatic puts the United States in the middle of a story that we really don't want to be in the middle of."[27]

a. *Focus on the democratization process and demand that Egypt's military leaders swiftly establish an inclusive democratic system, using U.S. leverage like cutting off military aid to Egypt to achieve this goal.* After the ouster of President Mubarak, Washington chose to engage the Islamists in the Muslim Brotherhood and would continue trying to do so. Concerns that an Islamist government would jeopardize regional stability by adopting anti-Israeli policies or encouraging Islamic extremism—intensified by anti-Semitic remarks that Morsi had made before becoming Egypt's president—proved exaggerated. Indeed, with American encouragement President Morsi also helped broker a cease-fire between Israel and Hamas in 2012, dealt vigorously with jihadi extremists in the Sinai (who became increasingly active after Morsi's ouster), and publicly condemned the "oppressive regime" of Syria's President Assad, cutting diplomatic relations with that country. He welcomed American investment in his country and used his legislative authority to outlaw pretrial detention of those accused of media-related crimes. All this led one U.S. official to declare of Morsi and the Brotherhood, "They sound like Republicans half the time."[28]

After Morsi's overthrow and the suspension of Egypt's 2012 constitution, Egypt's military rulers laid out what they termed a "roadmap" for moving the country toward national reconciliation. The "roadmap is defined and fixed," declared General Sisi, and "we are marching forward in confident steps in absolute transparency."[29] The map involved installing an interim government with the head of the Constitutional Court as acting president, elections in 2014, an amended constitution, and establishment of a reconciliation commission. The roadmap was tarnished, however, by a widespread crackdown on Morsi supporters, and in July 2013 Deputy Secretary of State William J. Burns scolded Egypt's military leaders: "If representatives of some of the largest parties in Egypt are detained or excluded, how are dialogue and participation possible?"[30] On a visit to Cairo in November 2013, Secretary of State Kerry encouraged the Egyptian leaders to adhere to their "roadmap." "The roadmap," declared Kerry, "is being carried out to the best of our perception," adding, "I think it's important for all of us, until proven otherwise, to accept that this is the track Egypt is on and to work to help it be able to achieve that."[31]

Initially, U.S. engagement was partly driven by recognition that opposing the Brotherhood would radicalize its followers. One problem, however, with pressuring the military successors to Morsi was that Morsi's ouster constituted more than a simple military coup. It also reflected genuine unhappiness on the part of a substantial segment—perhaps a majority—of Egyptian society with the incompetence, authoritarianism, and Islamic inclinations of those whom the military ousted. Polls reflected a dramatic increase in Egyptian optimism after the ouster of Mubarak and an equally rapid decline in the country's mood after President Morsi assumed office—to the point, in fact, where dissatisfaction was almost as high as it had been with Mubarak. Having charged Morsi and other Brotherhood leaders with inciting murder, Egypt's military rulers would find it difficult to work with the country's Islamists. According to one anti-Morsi demonstrator, "We had to show Morsi that we could get rid of him if we didn't like him just like we got rid of the one before him."[32]

Although the Muslim Brotherhood might in time have become pragmatic and capable and more open to collaborating with other political groups, it is unclear whether democracy would best be served by restoring an Islamist government. However, U.S. pressure on Egypt's post-Morsi government to pursue democratic reforms is also risky and would probably end Egypt's close military cooperation with the United States, including fly-over rights across Egypt for tasks like supplying NATO forces in Afghanistan or conducting counterterrorist strikes and fast-track transit for U.S. naval vessels through the Suez Canal. "We need them for the Suez Canal, we need them for the peace treaty with Israel, we need them for the overflights, and we need them for the continued fight against violent extremists who are as much of a threat to Egypt's transition to democracy as they are to American interests,"[33] argued the former head of the U.S. Central Command. Pressure on President Sisi would also strain relations with American allies like Saudi Arabia, the United Arab Emirates, Jordan, and Israel, all of which support the new regime. By contrast, other U.S. regional allies such as Qatar and Turkey had close ties to the Muslim Brotherhood.

Egypt's military leaders were offended by Washington's cool reception to their overthrow of President Morsi and their violent repression of his supporters. As an official in the U.S. Chamber of Commerce observed, "It's important for the U.S. to give Egypt a reason to look to the West, as well as the East."[34] And according to a senior Arab official, "If the aid gets cut, you can be sure that Putin will arrive in Cairo in two or three months. And he will give aid with no strings attached."[35]

TABLE 5.1 Egyptians' Changing Views, 2010–2013

	2010 (%)	2011 (%)	2012 (%)	2013 (%)
Way things are going in the country				
Satisfied	28	65	53	30
Dissatisfied	69	34	41	62
Don't know	3	2	6	7
National economic conditions are . . .				
Good	20	34	27	23
Bad	80	64	71	76
Don't know	0	2	2	1
In next 12 months, economy will . . .				
Improve	25	56	50	29
Remain the same	35	26	28	26
Worsen	38	17	20	42

	2010 (%)	2011 (%)	2012 (%)	2013 (%)
Now that Mubarak is not in power, Egypt is . . .				
Better off	—	—	44	39
Worse off	—	—	26	30
Both/neither	—	—	26	20
Don't know	—	—	3	4
Way democracy is working in our country				
Satisfied	—	—	—	43
Dissatisfied	—	—	—	56
Don't know	—	—	—	1

Source: "Egyptians Increasingly Glum," Pew Research Global Attitudes Project, May 16, 2013, http://www.pewglobal.org/2013/05/16/egyptians-increasingly-glum/

b. *Let events in Egypt take their course,* a policy endorsed by one scholar who writes: "There are no longer any compelling reasons for Washington to sustain especially close ties to Cairo. What was once a powerfully symbolic alliance with clear advantages for both sides has become a nakedly transactional relationship—and one that benefits the Egyptians more than the Americans."[36] This option has the advantage of avoiding blame for what might happen in the future, but it involves the possibility of letting matters grow progressively worse in a country that is critical to America's security interests. Civil war between Islamists and Egypt's military, similar to that which wracked Algeria in the early 1990s after that country's government canceled democratic elections, is one dire possibility, accompanied by the spread of jihadist terrorism by groups like Ansar Bayt al-Maqdis ("Partisans of Jerusalem") in Sinai that are linked to al-Qaeda or ISIS. Thus, after Morsi's ouster al-Qaeda leader Ayman al-Zawahiri, who had loathed the Brotherhood, urged Egypt's "soldiers of the Koran to wage the battle of the Koran."[37] The radicalization of many Egyptian Islamists has already taken place, and the prospect of a radical Islamic government, while improbable, is also the worst possible outcome for U.S. interests. What transpires in Egypt, writes Robert Malley, from "popular attitudes toward the U.S., to its domestic economy, to relations between the Muslim Brotherhood and the army, to relations between Cairo and Jerusalem, to the situation in Sinai, will profoundly affect the region, and so will profoundly affect America's posture in the region."[38]

c. *Launch an active policy of engaging Egypt's military leaders and the country's transitional government, encouraging them to pursue liberal political and economic policies.* Robert Springborg sees promise in such engagement. He contends that President Sisi resembles Egyptian president Gamal Nasser before Nasser alienated American leaders and turned to the Soviet Union for help. He writes:

> The U.S.–Egyptian relationship is now essentially back to where it was in 1954, with Washington supporting an emerging military strongman who needs to demonstrate his bona fides to his most important constituency, the military, first,

and to the country as a whole, second. The challenge for both the United States and Sisi will be to recalibrate their expectations of the relationship so that they focus narrowly on the enduring overlap in strategic interests. . . . The United States needs a strong Egypt upon which to anchor its drifting policy in the region, while Sisi needs arms and money to fend off domestic challengers.[39]

Sisi, however, mixes nationalism and Islam, and like Nasser may be willing to switch horses in midstream—a fact reflected in the visit to Cairo in late 2013 of a high-ranking Russian delegation eager to sell arms to Egypt and deepen Egyptian–Russian military relations. Egypt's military leaders clearly were seeking a possible alternative to their dependence on American arms assistance and political support.

Although Washington learned to coexist with the Morsi government, several events and trends caused concern among U.S. leaders. In September 2012 mobs attacked the U.S. embassy in Cairo in reaction to an American-made film that insulted the Prophet. The government's failure to protect the embassy or criticize those who had attacked it triggered an angry phone call from President Obama. "The president," declared an American official, "made his point that we've been committed to the process of change in Egypt. But he made it clear how important it is that the Egyptian government work with us to lower the tension both in terms of the practical cooperation they give us and the statements they make."[40] Morsi also improved Egyptian relations with Iran, inviting Iran's anti-American president Mahmoud Ahmadinejad to attend a conference of the Organization of Islamic Cooperation in Cairo in February 2013.

Engaging the Sisi government means that Washington would encourage a transparent process in reviving secularism and an inclusive government, and economic and financial reforms to reduce unemployment, promote economic development and growth, reduce corruption, and eliminate wasteful subsidies. Morsi's successors find themselves like those whom they overthrew with popular demands to maintain uneconomic food subsidies that maintain domestic political stability. Egyptian institutions also need to be strengthened if stability is to be restored. To encourage reform Washington could foster investment in and trade with Egypt, contribute expertise and economic aid, and fulfill its 2012 pledge to forgive much of Egypt's debt to the United States. The objective of such a course of action would not be democratization as an end it itself but political stability and economic recovery.

SYRIA

Syria is a "wicked problem," as Hillary Rodham Clinton suggests, and what makes such problems "wicked" "is that every option seems worse than the next."[41] Syria's civil war presents Washington with a quandary. Should the United States sit back and permit the bloodstained government of President Assad to retain power and allow Syria to remain a crucial regional ally of Iran and Hezbollah? Or should America actively support the Sunni insurgency, and if so, to what extent and how? And if Washington does support the insurgents, how can it ensure that moderates rather than Islamic extremists will come to power? As one Syria analyst noted, "You are not going to find this neat, clean, secular rebel group that respects human rights and that is waiting and ready because they don't exist."[42] In February 2013 two research scholars concluded, "if the rebels were going to achieve a decisive military victory, they would have done so by now."[43] Indeed, in early 2016 Russian military intervention in Syria in support of President Assad further reduced the prospects of Assad's foes and sharply diminished the possibility of a negotiated settlement.

"Syria today," wrote Gen. Martin Dempsey, chair of the Joint Chiefs of Staff, in a letter to Congress, "is not about choosing between two sides but rather about choosing one among many sides," and "the side we choose must be ready to promote their interests and ours when the balance shifts in their favor. Today they are not."[44] Policy options in Syria were narrowed by the growing strength of Islamic extremists like ISIS that worked to Assad's advantage by giving substance to the claim that his adversaries were "terrorists" and impeded the efforts of the United States and others to aid Assad's moderate adversaries. The State Department derided Assad's claim: "The Assad regime is a magnet for terrorists. The regime's brutality is the source of violent extremism in Syria today."[45] A former advisor to the State Department summarized Washington's dilemma: "Some of the more extremist opposition is very scary from an American perspective, and that presents us with all sorts of problems. We have no illusions about the prospect of engaging with the Assad regime—it must still go—but we are also very reticent to support the more hardline rebels."[46]

Policy Options

a. *Provide arms to the Syrian opposition while seeking to negotiate an end to Syria's civil war that would result in a government without President Assad or his Alawite loyalists.* This is the policy that the Obama administration adopted after hesitating for a lengthy period, though relatively few American arms have reached their destination. Before June 2013 Washington provided only nonlethal aid, but thereafter began to open the arms spigot. Russia has moved away from rigidly demanding that Assad retain power, but it would continue to support the regime as long as it seems likely to survive. With tension between Washington and Moscow over Ukraine, Russia became less likely to cooperate with Washington in ending the Syrian civil war. In addition, it is becoming increasingly difficult to ensure that arms will be given only to moderate factions opposed to Assad rather than to radical jihadists. For many of the regime's opponents, Assad must step down before negotiations can occur. Were the rebels able to defeat Hezbollah decisively (or were Israel to do so), or were Iran's new president willing to urge Hezbollah to end its support for the Syrian regime, it would add significant pressure on Assad to find a way to step aside without loss of face.

Whether another peace conference will succeed also depends on whether the Syrian rebels participate and whether moderate elements in the rebel movement can dominate the insurgency. As former British foreign secretary William Hague concluded, "The reason we have to make sure we are supporting and dealing with the moderate opposition committed to a democratic, pluralistic, nonsectarian future for Syria is precisely because if they don't have a role, then all the Syrian people got left is a choice between Assad and extremists."[47]

b. *Negotiate an end to the conflict that leaves President Assad or his Alawite loyalists in power.* If Washington concludes that the civil war is likely to end with Sunni jihadists in power or in control of large areas of the country, it might prefer to leave Assad in power. This policy would reduce tensions between America on the one hand and Russia and Iran on the other. It would, however, further antagonize allies like Saudi Arabia and Turkey that fear the Iranian–Syrian axis, as well as domestic human-rights groups and the members of Congress appalled by the atrocities committed by the Assad regime. As part of an effort to end the bloodshed, Washington and Moscow agreed to cosponsor a peace conference in Geneva ("Geneva II"), but it proved difficult to persuade most anti-Assad militants to negotiate with the present regime, especially if forced to do so from a position of weakness.

Negotiations were renewed in Vienna in late 2015, with the aim of achieving a cease-fire between Assad and his opponents excluding "terrorists." They were suspendend shortly thereafter and renewed in early 2016 in Geneva. Assad and Russia, however, have far broader definitions of which rebels are terrorists. The United States agreed to permit Iran's participation in the talks, a shift advocated by Russia. In addition, even though Washington seemed reluctantly prepared to allow Assad to participate in a political transition in the country, Moscow continued to refuse discussing his replacement and continued bombing rebel groups supported by the United States and other opponents of the Syrian regime until March 2016. Negotiations were also complicated by differences among other key participants in the talks. Turkey and Saudi Arabia remained vigorously opposed to Assad (and his Iranian ally), while Iran continued to provide the Assad regime with money, arms, and military advisors. "There cannot be long-term peace with Assad, but on the other hand there cannot be a peace process that stipulates that Assad must go," noted Jean-Marie Guehenno, president of the International Crisis Group. He added, "How you square that circle has been the issue from the beginning and still is."[48] Additionally, Russian–Turkish relations have been poisoned by Moscow's bombing of ethnic Bayirbucak Turkmen opponents of the Syrian regime and Turkey's downing of a Russian Su-24 bomber it accused of violating its airspace.

Finally, leaving Assad or his followers in power would be seen at home and abroad as reflecting American weakness and unwillingness to continue playing the role of global leader. As long as Assad believed he was winning the conflict, he had little incentive to negotiate seriously. Thus, in all likelihood, "absent the credible application of force against the Syrian regime, a negotiated transition leading to Mr. Assad's departure is not going to happen."[49]

c. *Use force, even though Syria carried out its agreement to rid itself of chemical weapons.* American allies like Saudi Arabia and Turkey were angered by the Obama administration's failure to carry out threatened strikes against the Assad regime after it employed chemical weapons against civilians. Turkish leaders had taken the lead in encouraging an American military strike and felt that Washington had betrayed them. Saudi leaders were already disturbed by America's failure to endorse the ouster of President Morsi by the Egyptian army and the apparent thaw in U.S.–Iranian relations. Viewing as insufficient Washington's decision not to carry out its threatened reprisal after the regime had used chemical weapons, they increased their delivery of weapons to rebels in southern Syria.

Although Syria carried out its part of the bargain regarding chemical weapons, it is difficult to be certain whether Assad has revealed all of Syria's chemical weapons and facilities. If the Syrian government did hide some of these weapons, it is unlikely to use them. If it did so, Washington would be

MAP 5.1   Areas Reportedly Affected by August 21, 2013, Syrian Chemical Attack

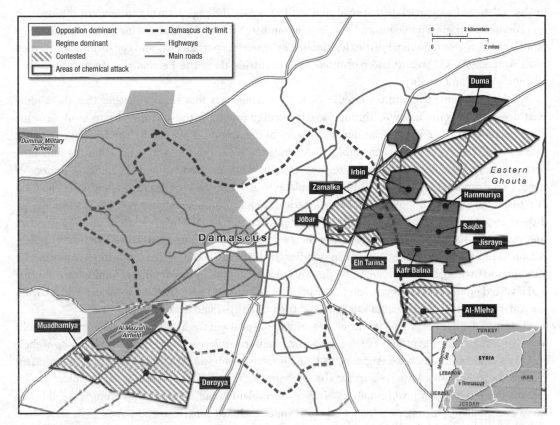

Source: The White House.

under considerable pressure at home and abroad to carry out reprisals. Congress might prove more willing to back the president if chemical weapons were used again, though that too is uncertain, and the basic argument remains that a limited strike on Syria's chemical weapons facilities would not be a game changer.

This course of action would entail a dramatic reversal in the caution shown by the Obama administration to date, and would threaten to trigger another "no-win" conflict without ensuring that the winning side would be those Syrians Washington prefers. Intervention would meet vigorous opposition domestically by public opinion and Congress, both of which are weary of major wars after those in Iraq and Afghanistan. It would also consume significant budgetary resources at a time of budget constraints and spread U.S. military power thinly, thereby reducing American ability to react to crises in East Asia or the Persian Gulf.

CONCLUSION: SPRING OR WINTER?

Much has happened in the tumultuous years since Mohamed Bouazizi set himself on fire in Tunisia, in December 2010—a spark that spread like wildfire across the region owing to modern information and communication technologies and online communities. Prior to the Arab Spring authoritarian ruling families or clan-based political parties legitimated by powerless parliaments and constitutions governed most Arab states. Oil wealth had permitted Arab countries along the Persian Gulf to purchase their citizens' loyalty and docility.

Washington cannot ignore the Middle East. "The problem is that history teaches that the Middle East doesn't like being ignored. Through soaring energy prices, or the scourge of terrorism, or some other calamity, it has a habit of insinuating itself onto the American agenda."[50] The few policy options available to Washington reflect the limits of American influence in the Arab world and the difficulty, perhaps the impossibility, of achieving regional stability while furthering the democratic aspirations of the region's rapidly growing and youthful populations. Even in the decades before and after the Cold War, as democratization took root in Latin America, Eastern Europe, and areas of sub-Saharan Africa, little changed in the Middle East and North Africa. "The demise of Middle Eastern authoritarianism may come eventually," says Seth Jones. "But there is little reason to think that day is near, and even less reason to think that the United States can significantly increase its chances of happening. Any effort by Washington to bring democracy to the region will fail if local social and economic conditions are not ripe and if vested interests in the countries oppose political reforms."[51] These are the lessons to be drawn from the American wars in Afghanistan and Iran, and from U.S. experience in Egypt and Syria.

A stable Egypt, for example, is crucial for maintaining peace in the Middle East and ensuring Israel's security. But a stable Egypt may require supporting military leaders who overturned the results of their country's democratic elections. And according to presidential advisor Benjamin Rhodes, "The president made a decision to side with democratic change," but "we made it clear that it is not our place to dictate the outcomes in any given country."[52] In Syria, President Assad's dictatorship brought stability but was a crucial link in the region's "Shia Crescent," which included American and Israeli adversaries Iran and Hezbollah. In sum, Washington had no clear geopolitical strategy for achieving both stability and democracy.

Has the Arab Spring ended? Sheri Berman summarized the situation well: "With Syria descending ever deeper into civil war, the Egyptian military stepping in to oust the country's increasingly authoritarian government, and little political progress elsewhere in the region, the heady early days of the Arab Spring are a distant and fading memory." Yet "the problems of the Middle East today" stem from "the inherent difficulty and complexity of building truly liberal democratic regimes. Getting rid of authoritarianism is a long and nasty process; in the Middle East, at least that process has finally begun."[53]

But the process of democratization remains contingent on national factors and will at best prove difficult. The Arab world can no longer rely on the sort of support for democratization that the Obama administration seemed to promise in 2011. As President Obama's national security advisor, Susan Rice, concluded, "We can't just be consumed 24/7 by one region, important as it is."[54] Democratization in Egypt and elsewhere in the region would have to take a backseat to overcoming the Israel–Palestinian dispute, ending the Syrian civil war, dealing with Iran's nuclear ambitions, engaging China, and curbing Russian ambitions in Central Europe and the Middle East.

In the end, it remains to be seen whether Walter Russell Mead's conclusion that the White House made "five big miscalculations" is correct: "It misread the political maturity and capability of the Islamist groups it supported; it misread the political situation in Egypt; it misread the impact of its strategy on relations with America's two most important regional allies (Israel and Saudi Arabia); it failed to grasp the new dynamics of terrorist movements in the region; and it underestimated the costs of inaction in Syria."[55] U.S.–Saudi relations soured owing to Washington's willingness to negotiate with Iran regarding that country's nuclear program, its failure to use military force against the Assad regime, and its willingness to accept the government of President Morsi and the Muslim Brotherhood in Egypt. As a result Saudi King Salman, who became the country's ruler in 2015, initiated policies without consulting Washington, including the possibility of a formal alliance of Sunni countries. Finally, with the failure of most moderate Islamists like the Muslim Brotherhood either to gain or retain influence in the region, Islamic extremists, who reject democratic norms, became more influential. The terrorist group and putative "caliphate" Islamic State of Iraq and Syria expressed the view of the extremists when it declared that Islamists must choose "the ammunition boxes over the ballot boxes."[56]

ISIS's emergence reflected how the Arab Spring produced chaos in much of the region and how nonstate groups—militias, religious sects, and terrorists—became growing competitors of states in the Arab world for individuals' identities and loyalties. Not only are many Arab states the artificial creations of European imperialists, but "the region's insecure, control-obsessed governments—sometimes dominated by minorities—have failed to integrate citizens within an inclusive sense of nationhood."[57] Several Arab states were engulfed by civil war—Syria, Iraq, Yemen, and Libya—while others remain plagued by sectarian and ethnic violence. Transnational nonstate identities and loyalties include Sunni, Shia, Christian, and Kurdish, and these in turn are divided into myriad subgroups reflecting regional and tribal affiliations, moderate or extremist belief systems, and Islamic or secular leanings. Thus, "small fractures between sects or tribes or ethnicities grew rapidly into wider cracks that are often exploited by external actors eager to exercise influence."[58]

The Arab Spring produced power vacuums in which, as we shall see, terrorist groups thrived. Former Jordanian foreign minister Marwan Muasher concluded, "No matter which political systems Arab countries adopt, the Arab world will miss a golden opportunity if it does not give diversity and pluralism the attention they deserve. This applies to civil and religious forces alike. A new culture needs to be nurtured. No individual or party can claim monopoly on the truth and still expect a prosperous society to emerge."[59] In sum, despite the Arab Spring, Arab societies remain economically and socially stagnant, caught between authoritarian and corrupt leaders and Islamic fanatics in failed or failing states.

II

Radical Islam

The death
of Osama bin Laden

The terrorist attacks of September 11, 2001, on New York's World Trade Center and the Pentagon in Washington, D.C., changed U.S. foreign policy with dramatic suddenness. America's foe challenged not only American security and its presence in the Middle East but also its basic values—democracy, secularism, capitalism, and modernity. The end of the Cold War had produced uncertainty about American objectives in what President George H. W. Bush termed "the new world order" characterized by superpower cooperation and the spread of liberal American values worldwide. Francis Fukuyama wrote of "the end of history," entailing "the ultimate triumph of Western liberal democracy," "an unabashed victory of economic and political liberalism," and the "triumph of the West, of the Western *idea*."[1]

For over four decades the USSR—the "Red Menace"—had provided a focus for U.S. foreign policy, and that focus had disappeared. Islamic extremism—the "Green Menace"—became a substitute after 9/11. The attacks set in motion a train of events in which Washington struggled to understand and react to the challenge posed by Islamic terrorism, a challenge that had emerged before the end of the Cold War. Osama bin Laden was the face of Islamic extremism that Americans associated with what came to be called the global War on Terror.

The 9/11 attacks had a profound impact on the United States. America seemed more vulnerable than at any time since the Cold War. September 11, 2001, and subsequent terrorist attacks in cities like London, Madrid, Mumbai, Denpasar, and Paris revealed that Islamic radicals had global reach and were prepared to use limitless violence to achieve their ends. These attacks forced Washington to rethink its national security strategy to include proactive and preemptive violence wherever terrorists might hide.

Timeline

620–2004

622 Muhammad declares the first jihad against foes

661–1258 The original Islamic caliphate

1885 Mahdists seize Khartoum, Anglo–Egyptian Sudan

September 1898 British defeat Mahdists in the Battle of Omdurman

1914 Ottoman Turkey proclaims jihad against Britain, France, and Russia

1966 Sayyid Qutb is executed

1978–1992 Islamic insurrection against Soviet forces and communist government in Afghanistan

1989 Establishment of al-Qaeda

1992 Al-Qaeda involved in deaths of nineteen U.S. soldiers in Somalia

1993 Bombing in basement of New York's World Trade Center

1996 Bombing of U.S. military facility in Saudi Arabia

1998 Bombing of U.S. embassies in Nairobi, Kenya, and Dar es Salaam, Tanzania

1998 Bin Laden calls on Muslims to kill Americans; Ayman al-Zawahari joins bin Laden

1998 U.S. cruise missile attacks against terrorist camps in Afghanistan and Sudan

2000 Al-Qaeda attacks the destroyer USS *Cole* off Aden, Yemen

September 11, 2001 Al-Qaeda airplane hijackers destroy the World Trade Center and damage the Pentagon; another plane crashes into a field in Shanksville, Pa.

2001–2017 U.S. war in Afghanistan

2002 Suicide bombings by Jemaah Islamiyah in Bali, Indonesia

2004 Attack on a Saudi Arabian oil company in Riyadh

9/11 also triggered America's military intervention in Afghanistan in 2001 in pursuit of bin Laden and his followers, leading to the overthrow of the Islamist government of that country, the Taliban. U.S. intervention became the longest war in American history, and terrorism was given as one reason for U.S. intervention in Iraq in 2003. Finally, fear of terrorism at home led to a reorganization of the U.S. government, including the establishment of the Department of Homeland Security and the Office of Intelligence Analysis, which centralized the U.S. intelligence community.

2004–2015

2004 CIA drone attacks against Islamic militants in Pakistan begin

2005 Bomb attacks on London's transport system

2008–2009 Numerous suicide attacks on U.S. soldiers in Iraq

2009 Nigerian citizen tries to destroy a U.S. flight by igniting explosives in his underwear

2009 Al-Qaeda in the Arabian Peninsula formed in Yemen and Saudi Arabia

2010 Car bomb discovered in New York's Times Square

2011 Death of Osama bin Laden

2012 Somalia's al-Shabab joins al-Qaeda

2012 Jihadists seize power in northern Mali; French intervene in early 2013

2013 Bombings at the Boston Marathon by two Chechen brothers

August 2013 Closure of U.S. embassies in Middle East and North Africa and global travel alert owing to a "significant" terrorist threat

September 2013 Al-Shabab attacks Westgate Mall in Nairobi, Kenya

2013–2014 Islamic State of Iraq and Syria (ISIS) declares a caliphate

August–September 2014 U.S.-led coalition initiates air strikes against ISIS in Iraq and Syria

September 2015 Russia begins bombing anti-Assad groups in Syria

October–November 2015 ISIS launches attacks in Beirut, Lebanon, and Paris, France; an ISIS bomb downs a Russian airliner in Egypt; AQIP attacks hotel in Bamako, Mali

November 2015 United States deploys additional Special Operations forces in Syria

6

Radical Islam

ORIGINS AND EVOLUTION

Our initial chapter in Part II deals with the origins and evolution of radical Islam. It begins by examining sources of American policy toward radical Islam followed by a brief survey of early Islam including the caliphate, the medieval Islamic empire that marked the acme of Islamic civilization. It then examines the sources and meaning of contemporary Islamic extremism and violent jihadism. Thereafter, it turns to the establishment of al-Qaeda ("the Base") and traces its activities before and after the group's flight to Afghanistan in 1996. The chapter concludes with a brief discussion of the hunt for Osama bin Laden and bin Laden's death a decade after 9/11.

SOURCES OF AMERICAN POLICY TOWARD RADICAL ISLAM

American policies toward Islamic terrorism have consistently been shaped by external factors, especially the attacks by al-Qaeda on Americans and American interests before and after 9/11. No American president could have refused to respond to those attacks, although whether it was wise to declare a "war" on terrorism rather than regard terrorist acts as a criminal problem requiring police action remains debatable. In addition, American interests in the security of friendly countries, particularly in the Middle East, South Asia, and Africa, were important considerations in Washington's robust response to terrorism.

Government factors, notably bureaucratic disagreement, repeatedly entered decisions dealing with the War on Terror. The Obama administration was divided over whether to leave Iraq in 2011. It was also divided over a "surge" in U.S. troop strength in Afghanistan requested by then head of Central Command, Gen. David Petraeus, and Gen. Stanley A. McChrystal, commander of U.S. forces in Afghanistan. According to Secretary of State Hillary Rodham Clinton, "The president welcomed a full range of opinions and invited contrary points of view. And I thought it was a very healthy experience because people took him up on it. And one thing we didn't want—to have a decision made and then have somebody say, 'Oh, by the way.' No, come forward now or forever hold your peace."[2] Siding with Petraeus and McChrystal were Clinton, Secretary of Defense Robert M. Gates, and Gen. Michael Mullen, chair of the Joint Chiefs of Staff. Opposed or doubtful about the proposed surge were Vice President Joe Biden, Special Representative to Afghanistan Richard C. Holbrooke, and Ambassador to Afghanistan Karl Eikenberry. Holbrooke, in particular, argued for negotiations with the Taliban and believed the administration was too preoccupied with domestic politics to design a clear strategy.

After three months of debate, President Barack Obama decided to send 21,000 additional troops and then begin their withdrawal a year later. As one critic put it, the result was neither a "fully resourced counterinsurgency approach" nor "a more limited counterterrorism strategy." Instead, it was a compromise driven by domestic forces. The "policy that emerged from the reassessment of strategy in 2009—increasing troop levels through the summer of 2011 and withdrawing at the end of 2014—was worse than either of the proposed options," allowing NATO forces "to fight the insurgency" but placing time limits that "kept the fighting from producing enduring political results." As a result, "only in southern Afghanistan and northwest Pakistan are there adherents to al-Qaeda's radical ideology less than a day's drive from the world's least secure [Pakistan's] nuclear arsenal."[3]

In a different context, Secretary Clinton recalled how she and Leon Panetta, then CIA director, collaborated in designing a four-part counterterrorism strategy for President Obama: "Some of the White House national security staff supported our plan but others were concerned. They wanted to be sure State wasn't trying to usurp the White House's role as the primary coordinator of activity across the various agencies" in combatting "extremist propaganda."[4] This incident reflected Secretary Gates's criticism of the overcentralization of decision-making in the Obama administration: "The controlling nature of the Obama White House and the NSS [National Security Council] staff took micromanagement and operational meddling to a new level."[5]

The impact of role variables upon U.S. officials was evident when Panetta defended his agency against charges of "poor tradecraft" after several agents had been killed by a suicide bomber in Afghanistan. "That's like saying," wrote Panetta, "Marines who die in a firefight brought it upon themselves because they have poor war-fighting skills," and he added, "The CIA cannot speak publicly about its major victories—the plots foiled, the terrorists neutralized. In the past year, we have done exceptionally heavy damage to al-Qaeda and its associates."[6] John Brennan in his role as CIA director warned the Obama administration that extremists in Syria's civil war could pose a threat to America: "We are concerned about the use of Syrian territory by the Al Qaeda organization to recruit individuals and develop the capability to be able not just to carry out attacks inside of Syria, but also to use Syria as a launching pad."[7] Director of National Intelligence James Clapper supported Brennan, stressing that some of the groups in Syria sought to attack America's homeland. Brennan also defended his agency against the 2014 Senate report regarding the CIA's use of torture of terrorist suspects.

Societal factors had a major impact on the War on Terror. Thus, the American public initially supported U.S. involvement in Iraq in 2003 but had turned against the war by 2009. Similarly, there initially was overwhelming public support for America's entry into Afghanistan in pursuit of Osama bin Laden in 2001, but support declined as the war dragged on. America's return to Iraq after the murder of two U.S. citizens in 2014 was strongly supported.

In addition, corporate interests sought to profit from the War on Terror. Responding to congressional debate about how failing to control the Mexican border and illegal migration threatened America's homeland security, major U.S. defense corporations competed in offering expensive "solutions." Seeing an opportunity to profit from the fight against terrorism in an era of declining defense budgets, military contractors such as Raytheon, Lockheed Martin, and General Dynamics vigorously competed to secure a Homeland Security Department contract for radar and long-range camera systems to strengthen border security. Meanwhile, Northrop Grumman offered an automatic tracking device mounted on aerial drones, and General Atomics, a manufacturer of drones, sought to double the number available for border surveillance. In the words of an academic economist, "There are only so many missile systems and Apache attack helicopters you can sell. This push toward border security fits very well with the need to create an ongoing stream of revenue."[8]

Individual factors were apparent in disagreements among high officials about the review of decisions to use drone strikes against individuals suspected of terrorism. Hillary Clinton recalled that sometimes she supported particular strikes and other times she objected, and that "my good friend Leon Panetta, the Director of the Central Intelligence Agency, and I had a shouting match over one proposed strike."[9] And Panetta criticized President Obama for vacillation and lacking "fire": "Too often, in my view, the president relies on the logic of a law professor rather than the passion of a leader."[10]

Let us now turn to early Islam and the seeds of jihadism.

EARLY ISLAM

The caliphate—the Islamic empire after the Prophet Muhammad's death—expanded dramatically during the centuries after Islam's emergence, conquering the Middle East, North Africa, Persia, Armenia, and

MAP 6.1   The Umayyad Caliphate

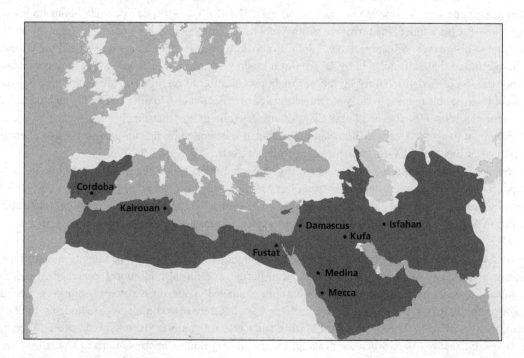

Spain in Europe for Islam. Many Muslims regard the rule of the Prophet and the first four caliphs ("successors") who followed him as a "golden age of pure Islam." The caliphate saw its greatest political, military, and cultural achievements during the rule of two dynasties—the Umayyads (661–750 CE) in Damascus and the Abbasids (750–1258 CE) in Baghdad. In 1258, however, the Mongols sacked Baghdad, and thereafter the caliphate was divided into rival Muslim communities. The Ottoman Empire's last sultan, Mehmed VI, was also Islam's last caliph. In 1924, after Turkey became a republic under Kemal Atatürk, the caliphate was abolished. In reality, however, "the caliphate is a political or religious idea whose relevance has waxed and waned according to circumstance," and "by conflating the nineteenth-century Ottoman royal family with these caliphs from a millennium ago or more, Western pundits and nostalgic Muslim thinkers alike have built up a narrative of the caliphate as an enduring institution, central to Islam and Islamic thought between the seventh and twentieth centuries."[11]

As of 2013 there were some 1.6 billion Muslims worldwide, a figure expected to grow to 2.2 billion by 2030—that is, from about 23 percent to over 26 percent of the world's population, a growth rate roughly twice that of non-Muslims.[12] As recently as 1990, Muslims constituted less than 20 percent of the world's population. As Table 6.1 and Map 6.2 illustrate, many of the world's Muslims live in a band of states in the southern hemisphere stretching across Africa and the Middle East to South Asia. Indonesia is the world's largest single Muslim country, and 93 percent of the inhabitants of the Middle East and North Africa are Muslim. The number of Muslim residents in Europe, North America, and sub-Saharan Africa is also growing rapidly. However, the world Islamic community is not united. In addition to divisions among political moderates and extremists and Islamists and secularists, it consists of a number of sects that frequently engage in sectarian violence, the most important of which are Shia (10–13%) and Sunni (87–90%).

TABLE 6.1   World Muslim Population by Region

	Estimated 2010 Muslim Population	Estimated 2010 Total Population	Population That Is Muslim (%)
Asia-Pacific	985,530,000	4,054,990,000	24.3
Middle East–North Africa	317,070,000	341,020,000	93.0
Sub-Saharan Africa	248,110,000	822,720,000	30.2
Europe	43,490,000	742,550,000	5.9
North America	3,480,000	344,530,000	1.0
Latin America–Caribbean	840,000	590,080,000	0.1
World Total	**1,598,510,000**	**6,895,890,000**	**23.2**

Population estimates are rounded to the ten thousands. Percentages are calculated from unrounded numbers. Figures may not add exactly due to rounding.

Source: Pew Research Center's Forum on Religion & Public Life, "The Global Religious Landscape," December 2012.

MAP 6.2 Major Muslim Communities

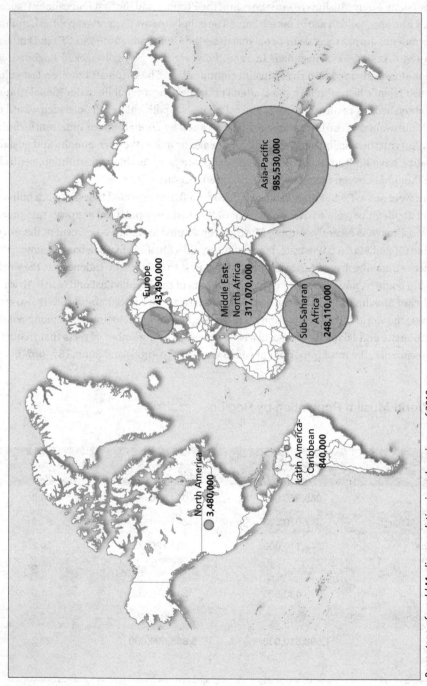

Asia-Pacific
985,530,000

Europe
43,490,000

Middle East-
North Africa
317,070,000

Sub-Saharan
Africa
248,110,000

North America
3,480,000

Latin America-
Caribbean
840,000

Percentage of world Muslim population in each region as of 2010

2.7 Europe   Sub-Saharan Africa   15.5

0.2 North America

0.1 Latin America-Caribbean

19.8   Middle East-North Africa

61.7   Asia-Pacific

Source: Pew Research Center's Forum on Religion & Public Life, "The Global Religious Landscape," December 2012.

Population by region as of 2010. Population estimates are rounded to the ten thousands. Percentages are calculated from unrounded numbers. Percentages may not add to 100 due to rounding.

As in other religions, many Muslims believe they should be governed in accordance with the dictates of their religion, but few are extremists or terrorists. We must keep in mind the difference between "political Islam" (described in chapter 3), which refers to Muslim groups that are prepared to work peacefully within existing political systems to bring about a transition to governments that rely on Islamic or Sharia law, and extremist Islam, which refers to groups whose objectives are to transform the interstate system into a vast Islamic empire or caliphate and are willing to use violence to achieve this end.

Islamic extremism, like religious extremism more generally, has appeared periodically over the centuries. For example, Muḥammad Aḥmad ibn al-Sayyid 'Abd Allā was declared the "Mahdi" ("Right-Guided One") in the Sudan in the late nineteenth century and succeeded in establishing an Islamic empire that stretched from central Africa to the Red Sea. In 1885, after defeating several Egyptian armies, the Mahdi besieged and captured the Sudanese capital, Khartoum, resulting in the death of British general Charles "China" Gordon when a British relief force failed to arrive on time. Thirteen years later, a British army under Sir Herbert Kitchener defeated the army of Abdullah al-Taashi, the successor to the Mahdi, in the Battle of Omdurman, a conflict at which young Winston Churchill was present and that showed the power of modern arms such as machine guns, rifles, and artillery against a foe lacking such weapons.

SOURCES AND MEANING OF RADICAL ISLAM

Radical, extremist, or *jihadist,* as we use these terms in this chapter, refer to a commitment to spread by force a fundamentalist version of Islam that will govern according to "pure" or strict religious doctrine that its adherents believe existed when the religion was originally established.

Islamic militants, including Osama bin Laden and his followers, are largely adherents of Salafi Islam (a relatively recent offshoot of Wahhabism, which has dominated Saudi Arabia for two centuries) who have become politicized throughout the Middle East and North Africa. Salafism is an ultraconservative version of Islamic fundamentalism, embracing those who seek to identify and follow the practices and beliefs of Islam as it was when founded by Muhammad (*salaf* means "predecessor"). Salafis believe that the Islamic community has declined since the collapse of the original seventh-century caliphate. In their view, most Islamic countries are not governed according to rigorous Islamic practices and law (Sharia) and have fallen under the influence of the secular West. Most Salafis are not violence prone, and some Salafi groups have competed in elections in countries like Tunisia and Egypt in recent years.[13]

Salafi jihadists, who constitute about 1 percent of the world's Muslims, perceive the world as divided between Islam (*dar al-Islam*) and the land of conflict or war (*dar al-harb*).[14] Many see themselves as involved in a violent struggle with moderate Islamic governments and with Muslims who support political and religious toleration. They seek the violent overthrow of these "apostate" governments (the "near enemy") and wish to unite Muslims in a restored caliphate in which Muslims will be governed according to strict Islamic law. Some Salafis are also prepared to use violence, including suicide bombings against the West (the "far enemy"), especially Israel and the United States (the "Zionist–Crusader alliance"), which they regard as obstacles to Islamic unity. Unlike other Muslims, they regard killing civilians, including fellow Muslims, as permissible. Salafis are

KEY DOCUMENT

**Osama bin Laden,
"Declaration of Jihad" (August 23, 1996)[15]**

It is no secret to you, my brothers, that the people of Islam have been afflicted with oppression, hostility, and injustice by the Judeo–Christian alliance and its supporters. This shows our enemies' belief that Muslims' blood is the cheapest and that their property and wealth is merely loot. Your blood has been spilt in Palestine and Iraq. . . . The massacres that have taken place in Tajikistan, Burma, Kashmir, Assam, the Philippines, Fatani, Ogaden, Somalia, Eritrea, Chechnya, and Bosnia-Herzegovina send shivers down our spines and stir up our passions.

All this has happened before the eyes and ears of the world, but the blatant imperial arrogance of America, under the cover of the immoral United Nations, has prevented the dispossessed from arming themselves. . . . Men of the radiant future of our *umma* of Muhammad, raise the banner of *jihad* up high against the Judeo–American alliance that has occupied the holy places of Islam. . . . And the *al-Jami al-Sahih* notes that the Prophet said: "The best martyrs are those who stay in the battle line and do not turn their faces away until they are killed."

Sunni Muslims, and they regard the Shia minority as infidels and nonbelievers against whom the use of violence is permissible.

There are several distinct meanings to the Arabic term *jihad* ("struggling or striving"), which is regarded as an obligation of all Muslims. According to the Muslim holy book, the Koran, and the sayings of the Prophet and his followers, jihad may be carried in any of four ways—by the heart, the tongue, the hand, or the sword. The first involves a personal struggle against evil desires. The second and third consist of doing what is right. It is the fourth meaning, the jihad of the sword—waging holy war against "infidels" or unbelievers and against Islam's enemies—that is the creed of Muslim extremists. Those who emphasize this meaning of jihad (*mujahideen*) believe that Islamic "warriors" are martyred and will go to Paradise in the afterlife.

Jihads have been periodically declared against the enemies of Islam for centuries. Muhammad declared the first jihad against his Arab foes in Mecca in 622 CE, and it has been associated thereafter with efforts to spread Islam by force and subdue its enemies. Thus, at Germany's urging, its ally Ottoman Turkey proclaimed jihad against Great Britain, France, and Russia on November 12, 1914, shortly after the beginning of World War I, and appealed to non-Ottoman Muslims in their foes' empires to rise up against their European masters. Osama bin Laden declared "holy war" or jihad in *fatwas* (Islamic religious decrees) against America in August 1996 and against "Jews and Crusaders" in February 1998.

Among those who promulgated the idea of jihad as holy war and inspired jihadists like bin Laden was an Egyptian scholar named Sayyid Qutb. Qutb, who studied in America in the late 1940s, intensely disliked American customs, especially the independence of women. On returning to Egypt he joined the Muslim Brotherhood and was imprisoned for a decade. After members of the Muslim Brotherhood tried to assassinate Egyptian leader Gamal Abdel Nasser, Qutb was arrested once more and was tried and executed in 1966.

Qutb was a prolific writer whose targets were other Muslims like President Nasser and the Jordanian and Saudi monarchs he believed did not follow genuine Islamic law and were dictators who had been infected by Western beliefs and practices that harmed their subjects. Such Muslims, he argued, were like pre-Islamic Arabs, who were ignorant pagans and against whom jihad could and should be waged. Indeed, Qutb concluded that such Muslims were apostates—traitors to Islam—and invoking *takfir* (apostates subject to death). True Muslims, he argued, should work toward a revolution within the Islamic community, or *umma,* using violence when necessary to impose the religion's original values on those who had become "infidels." It was this view of jihad that motivated Islamic extremists to assassinate Egypt's president Anwar Sadat in 1980 and inspired later terrorists like bin Laden and his successor Ayman al-Zawahiri.

Those who followed Qutb's beliefs argued that any "government not ruling solely by Sharia is apostate; democracy is not just a mistaken tactic but also an unforgivable sin, because it gives humans sovereignty over Allah."[16] The revolution that Qutb had sought was launched first in Egypt in the 1940s, was brutally suppressed, and then rekindled in the mountains of Afghanistan after that country was invaded by the Soviet Union in December 1979.

THE ORIGINS AND EARLY EVOLUTION OF AL-QAEDA ("THE BASE")

Osama bin Laden, the Egyptian extremist Ayman al-Zawahiri, and the Palestinian scholar and cleric Abdullah Yusuf Azzam organized al-Qaeda in the early summer of 1989 among Muslim veterans from around the world who had participated in the resistance against Soviet occupation of Afghanistan and who had taken an oath of loyalty to bin Laden. Many of these so-called "Arab Afghans" or foreign jihadists had received financial aid and arms from Saudi Arabia and America's CIA to wage war against the Soviet occupiers. Al-Qaeda's leader, bin Laden, who had provided financial backing to the Afghan resistance, was the son of a wealthy Saudi builder and had been profoundly influenced by Azzam. Azzam, who argued that Muslims were obliged to wage jihad to liberate Muslim lands from foreign occupation, was assassinated in Peshawar, Pakistan, in 1989. Azzam believed that Muslims should not kill one another and advocated focusing al-Qaeda's efforts on liberating Palestine, but al-Zawahiri sought the overthrow of Arab governments like those of Egypt and Saudi Arabia, which he contended had betrayed Islam. In this disagreement, bin Laden followed al-Zawahiri rather than Azzam.

According to a Jordanian journalist with links to al-Qaeda, the group had a seven-stage strategy. The first, of which 9/11 was a key element, was to "awaken" Muslims. The second was to transform al-Qaeda into a larger Islamic movement. The third and fourth stages involved attacks on Israel and organizing local and regional jihadist groups to gain power in Arabic countries. During the fifth and six phases,

Osama bin Laden and Ayman al-Zawahiri

Ausaf/epa/Corbis

al-Qaeda would declare a universal caliphate or Islamic state that would declare war on nonbelievers. With the United States overextended globally, the final stage—forecast for the year 2020—would be "definitive victory."[17]

Even before September 11, 2001, al-Qaeda had begun to undertake terrorist operations. With financial aid from wealthy Saudis and other Arabs and a "Bureau of Services" that recruited followers, the group operated from Sudan between 1989 and 1996. Bin Laden issued a fatwa decrying U.S. involvement in Somalia, and al-Qaeda was probably involved in the downing of two American helicopters in that country's capital, Mogadishu, in 1993 in a battle between U.S. rangers and a Somali militia.

Al-Qaeda apparently also had links with Ramzi Ahmed Yousef, who planted a bomb that exploded in the parking garage of the World Trade Center in New York City on February 26, 1993, injuring over 1,000 people and forcing the evacuation of some 50,000 others. Two years later the group claimed responsibility for a car bomb outside a U.S. training facility in Riyadh, Saudi Arabia, that killed five Americans, and the following year either al-Qaeda or the Shia group Hezbollah in the Hejaz bombed the U.S. Air Force's Khobar Towers barracks in Saudi Arabia, killing 19 American soldiers and injuring over 500 others.[18] Such incidents produced mounting international pressure on Sudan, which forced bin Laden and his followers to return to Afghanistan, where the Taliban could protect him and from where in 1998 he and al-Zawahiri issued a fatwa announcing jihad against America and Israel. The fatwa declared that the "crimes and sins committed by the Americans are a clear declaration of war on God, his messenger, and Muslims," and that the "ruling to kill the Americans and their allies—civilians and military—is an individual duty for every Muslim who can do it in any country in which it is possible to do it."[19] The fatwa also served to announce that al-Qaeda was the central actor in global terrorism. In 1999 Washington imposed financial sanctions on Afghanistan for refusing to extradite bin Laden to America.

Those who, like bin Laden and al-Zawahiri, waged jihad were known as *mujahideen,* a term associated with the Muslim guerrillas in Afghanistan who had resisted the Soviet invasion of that country. Moscow's invasion marked the beginning of CIA assistance to the anticommunist Islamic resistance movement in Afghanistan. American arms included shoulder-fired antiaircraft missiles, many of which have never been recovered. In an interview, President Jimmy Carter's national security advisor, Zbigniew Brzezinski, confirmed a claim that covert CIA aid to the mujahideen had begun before Moscow's invasion:

> According to the official version of history, CIA aid to the Mujahadeen began during 1980, that is to say, after the Soviet army invaded Afghanistan, 24 December 1979. But the reality, secretly guarded until now, is completely otherwise. Indeed, it was July 3, 1979 that President Carter signed the first directive for secret aid to the opponents of the pro-Soviet regime in Kabul. And that very day, I wrote a note to the president in which I explained to him that in my opinion this aid was going to induce a Soviet military intervention.

Brzezinski had no regrets:

> That secret operation was an excellent idea. It had the effect of drawing the Russians into the Afghan trap and you want me to regret it? The day that the Soviets officially crossed the border, I wrote to President Carter, "We now have the opportunity of giving to the USSR its Vietnam War". Indeed, for almost 10 years, Moscow had to carry on a war unsupportable by the government, a conflict that brought about the demoralization and finally the breakup of the Soviet empire.[20]

The Taliban ("Students of Islamic Knowledge Movement"), which remains America's militant foe, was established in Afghanistan during the resistance to the Soviet occupation by groups of mujahideen and devout Muslim religious students, many of whom had been educated in refugee camps in Pakistan by poorly educated *mullahs* (Islamic clergy) in the region's strict version of Islam, similar to Saudi Wahhabism. These groups of loosely organized religious students sought to end the civil strife among competing warlords that followed the withdrawal of Soviet forces and impose Islamic law throughout the country. They coalesced into a movement led by Mullah Mohammed Omar, which seized the city of Kandahar in 1994. The Taliban "were a *pathogenic* force whose view of the world conspicuously omitted the pragmatic moderation of tribal and religious codes in Afghan society."[21] The ability of the Taliban under Omar (who was reported to have died of natural causes in Pakistan in 2013) to restore security and order to the country made it widely popular, and it occupied Kabul and established a fundamentalist Islamic emirate in September 1996, the same year that Osama bin Laden returned to Afghanistan.

Other al-Qaeda terrorist acts planned in Afghanistan followed. Among these were an attack on the U.S. embassies in Nairobi, Kenya, and Dar es Salaam, Tanzania, in August 1998 that killed over 200 people and injured more than 5,000. In retaliation, President Bill Clinton authorized cruise missile strikes from American ships against an al-Qaeda training site in Afghanistan and the Al Shifa pharmaceutical plant in Khartoum, Sudan, which was believed to be producing nerve gas. "Countries that persistently host terrorists," declared the president, "have no right to be safe havens."[22]

Then, on October 12, 2000, a small boat carrying explosives rammed the destroyer USS *Cole* while at anchor in the Yemeni port of Aden, ripping open its hull and killing seventeen American sailors. During this period al-Qaeda operatives were also involved in numerous other plots directed against American interests, including Ramzi Yousef's 1995 abortive plan to place time bombs on U.S. aircraft flying across the Pacific and a plot in 2000 to bomb the Ramada Hotel in Amman, Jordan, where many Americans stayed. Then, in 2001, al-Qaeda terrorists hijacked three airliners and, as the world watched, undertook the infamous attacks on September 11 in New York and Washington.

CONCLUSION: AMERICAN FOREIGN POLICY AND THE "GREEN MENACE"

In 1986 the CIA had already established a Counterterrorist Center and ten years later created a unit that included FBI agents to learn more about bin Laden and capture or kill him. The "Bin Laden Issue Station," as it was called, headed by CIA analyst Michael Scheuer, "was the first to target an individual rather than a country."[23] Aided by an al-Qaeda defector and remote-controlled reconnaissance drones, the station had learned much about bin Laden and his activities before 9/11. The Clinton administration was aware that al-Qaeda was targeting the United States and intensively searched for its leader. "There was never a terrorist group," related Scheuer in 2005, "which we knew more about in terms of goals, organization, method of operation, personnel than Al Qaeda. And that was not only true in 2001, but by the summer of 1998, we had accumulated an extraordinary array of information about this group and about its intentions."[24] The hunt for bin Laden did not end until 2011.

In the dead of night on May 2, 2011, almost a decade after the terrorist attacks on the World Trade Center in New York and the Pentagon in Washington, D.C., a team of U.S. Navy SEALs avenged 9/11. Flying 120 miles from Afghanistan in two stealth helicopters, Team 6, as it was known, raided a compound in Abbottabad, Pakistan ("Operation Neptune Spear"); broke through several walls to gain entry; and shot dead Osama bin Laden, the founder and leader of al-Qaeda, along with four other inhabitants in the house, including one of bin Laden's sons. Bin Laden, who for years had been sought in the mountains of Afghanistan and the isolated frontier region of Pakistan, had been living in the Abbottabad compound, located near a Pakistani military base, for five years. After American intelligence intercepted a phone call to Abu Ahmed al Kuwaiti, an al-Qaeda courier, in Pakistan in 2010 and placed the compound under surveillance from satellites, a stealth drone, and a CIA safe house, bin Laden was finally located. Less than an hour after the raid had begun and after destroying one of the helicopters that had been damaged when landing in the compound, the U.S. team left with bin Laden's body, as well as documents, computer hard drives, and memory sticks, and returned to the American base in Bagram, Afghanistan. Afterward, bin Laden was buried at sea from a U.S. aircraft carrier.

Pakistan's government had not been informed of the planned raid. When asked why, President Obama answered, "I didn't tell most people here in the White House. I didn't tell my own family. It was that important for us to maintain operational security. If I'm not revealing to some of my closest aides what we're doing, then I sure as heck am not going to be revealing it to folks who I don't know."[25] Indeed, there was widespread suspicion that Pakistan's Inter-Services Intelligence (ISI) agency knew where bin Laden was living and had not shared this information with U.S. officials. The Pakistani air force scrambled several jet fighters on learning that its airspace had been violated, and they only turned back after American officials informed the Pakistanis that an operation was underway against "a high-value target." The U.S. operation had been meticulously planned, but President Obama approved the operation believing that "this was still a 55/45 situation." The president is reported to have called waiting for the outcome of the raid the longest forty minutes of his life, and he declared "we got him" on learning that it had been successful.[26] U.S. relations with Pakistan, however, were seriously damaged by what Pakistani military and civilian leaders regarded as a flagrant violation of their country's sovereignty. Pakistan's parliament and its prime minister after June 2013, Nawaz Sharif, publicly demanded an end to U.S. drone strikes on its territory (unless directed at Pakistan's own foes in the Afghan Taliban) to appease domestic anger, claiming they constituted an infringement of Pakistani sovereignty.

In the next chapter, we examine the War on Terror and its consequences, and look at several of the major Islamic terrorist groups that threaten Americans and American interests.

7

America and the War on Terror

Chapter 7 opens with a discussion of America's War on Terror and the changing nature of the terrorist threat. It describes the erosion of al-Qaeda's capabilities and the emergence of regionally based al-Qaeda affiliates around the world. Among the most dangerous are al-Qaeda in the Arabian Peninsula, a group centered in Yemen that seeks to strike the American homeland; al-Shabab in Somalia; al-Qaeda in the Land of the Islamic Maghreb in North Africa; and Boko Haram in Nigeria. The chapter then examines how al-Qaeda in Iraq was transformed into the Islamic State in Iraq and Syria (called ISIS, as well as ISIL and Daesh). Taking advantage of civil strife in Iraq and Syria, ISIS declared itself a caliphate and dropped "Iraq and Syria" from its name to indicate it had no geographic limits. Its murderous actions provoked Washington to initiate military operations against the group in both countries. The growing threat of ISIS also increased the threat of individual terrorists—"lone wolves"—who are influenced by jihadist propaganda. Thereafter, the chapter turns to domestic consequences of the War on Terror, including the establishment of the Department of Homeland Security and the Directorate of National Intelligence, as well as issues of human rights and surveillance raised by American efforts to combat terrorism.

THE WAR ON TERROR BEGINS

The 9/11 attacks triggered the beginning of the War on Terror. In retrospect, it may seem odd that a superpower decided to wage global war against a small group of Islamic fanatics. And since 9/11 America has been free from major terrorist attacks, though it has been the target of increasing numbers of violent acts by sympathizers of extremist groups like ISIS. However, 9/11 was a shock to Americans and augured a violent future punctuated by similar incidents at home and abroad that required the mobilization of U.S. capabilities. Although the War on Terror was never officially declared, a joint resolution of Congress, "Authorization for the Use of Military Force," was passed on September 18, 2001:

> The President is authorized to use all necessary and appropriate force against those nations, organizations, or persons he determines planned, authorized, committed or aided the terrorist attacks that occurred on September 11, 2001, or harbored such organizations or persons, in order to prevent any future acts of international terrorism against the United States.[1]

President George W. Bush described America's response on June 1, 2002, at the United States Military Academy at West Point: "America was attacked by a ruthless and resourceful enemy. You graduate from this academy in a time of war, taking your place in an American military that is powerful and is honorable. . . . Our war on terror is only begun. . . . We must take the battle to the enemy, disrupt his plans and confront the worst threats before they emerge."[2] The War on Terror would remain U.S. policy for twelve years until President Barack Obama declared it had ended. Nevertheless, though al-Qaeda had been weakened, it had survived, terrorist incidents continued, and America maintained its vigilance.

The 9/11 attacks were quickly traced to al-Qaeda and its leader, Osama bin Laden. Americans demanded that the Taliban, an Islamic group controlling Afghanistan, hand over bin Laden and other al-Qaeda leaders. Although the Taliban suggested that bin Laden leave, it refused to make him do so, and Washington invaded the country. Efforts to capture bin Laden and other al-Qaeda leaders who had fled Kabul proved frustrating. Afghan and American forces tracked the fugitives to Tora Bora, a series of mountain caves near the Pakistani border, destroying al-Qaeda's network of training camps and bombing the caves but always remaining a step behind the terrorists until the trail grew cold. "He's either dug in some tunnel, or he's alive," declared then secretary of defense Donald Rumsfeld of bin Laden. "And if he's alive, he's either in Afghanistan or he isn't. And it does not matter; we'll find him one day."[3]

In 2004 the Bush administration began employing CIA-controlled unmanned aerial vehicles (drones) to attack al-Qaeda safe havens in the border areas in northwest Pakistan that were beyond the control of the Pakistani government. Owing to civilian casualties and their violation of Pakistani sovereignty, Pakistani public opinion opposed drone strikes. And while quietly allowing the CIA to launch strikes from bases in Pakistan, its government loudly protested them.

After coming to office, the Obama administration intensified the strikes, viewing them as a way to reduce U.S. casualties and attack terrorist sanctuaries while limiting America's military "footprint." Between 2004 and 2013, when President Obama announced the drone campaign in the region would be reduced as America prepared to leave Afghanistan, the United States launched some 360 strikes against insurgents in Pakistan, killing senior al-Qaeda figures and other jihadists.

AL-QAEDA AND ISLAMIC EXTREMISM AFTER 9/11

The global response to 9/11 and America's War on Terror over time sharply eroded the capability of al-Qaeda as a centralized and hierarchical group financing, arming, and training local cells to launch complex terrorist attacks like 9/11. The war in Afghanistan and U.S. drone attacks and special operations there and in Pakistan eliminated many of al-Qaeda's leaders and foot soldiers, culminating in the death of bin Laden and isolating the remaining jihadists in remote areas of Pakistan. The last successful operation in which bin Laden was involved is believed to have been the bombings of London's transit system in July 2007 that resulted in the deaths of fifty-two civilians and four suicide bombers and many more injuries. Evidence found in bin Laden's compound in Abbottabad, Pakistan, suggests he was "immersed in operational details," and the London plot was "the last successful operation Osama bin Laden oversaw."[4] However, as one terrorist analyst observed, al-Qaeda "was never a mass movement; it was always meant to be a vanguard. So even with the first generation of leaders largely gone, it's very difficult to declare the movement dead."[5]

Increasingly, local jihadist groups or "franchises" that identified with and/or were inspired by al-Qaeda carried out terrorism. Such groups tended to have local objectives like seizing power in their own countries or regions rather than striking America, "the far enemy," or establishing a global Islamic caliphate. "Lone wolves" also carried out terrorist acts, many living in non-Islamic countries, inspired by jihadist propaganda or angered by what they saw as persecution of Muslims in their countries or in conflicts such as the Afghan and Iraq wars. "Al Qaeda is kind of a ready-made kit now," declared William McCants. "It is a portable ideology that is entirely fleshed out, with its own symbols and ways of mobilizing people and money to the cause. In many ways, you don't have to join the actual organization anymore to get those benefits." "There is really not one Al Qaeda anymore," declared another analyst. "It has taken on the local flavor of wherever it is, although none of the groups have really disavowed transnational jihad."[6]

Thus, jihadist violence became increasingly decentralized, and the Internet and social media became potent tools for communicating among terrorists, spreading jihadist ideas and propaganda in videos and publications to radicalize and recruit individuals, and sending practical information about how to make bombs or identify targets to attack. Both bin Laden and Zawahiri repeatedly used the Internet to broadcast videos. ISIS was especially effective in using communication technologies, prompting the UN human-rights commissioner to say, "The way it has spread its tentacles into other countries, employing social media and the Internet to brainwash and recruit from across the globe, reveals it to be the product of a perverse and lethal marriage of a new form of nihilism with the digital age."[7] ISIS video productions are, according to two media experts, "a generation ahead" of other groups.[8] Violence in Iraq and Syria attracted some 22,000 foreign fighters from around the world.[9] These included Chechens whom Russia may have permitted to go to the Middle East and leave the Caucasus despite Moscow's support for Syrian president Bashar al-Assad.[10]

The appearance of local groups associated with al-Qaeda also reflected declining coherence among jihadists after the death of bin Laden. "Like any sprawling organization," writes McCants, "al-Qaeda has seen its fair share of bureaucratic infighting. But the squabbling has reached fever pitch since Ayman al-Zawahiri began his tenure as head of the organization."[11] Al-Qaeda's problem was described as an "organizational challenge in precisely calibrating violence" that "stems from the fact that political and ideological leaders, or the principals, must delegate certain duties—such as planning attacks, soliciting funds, and recruiting—to middle-men or low-level operatives, their agents. Such delegation is problematic as agents in terrorist organizations often see the world differently than their leaders and tend to disagree with them on both how best to serve the cause and how to carry out specific missions."[12]

Local jihadist groups became more dangerous, especially in failed or failing states where central authority was weak such as Somalia, Yemen, and Mali, or where governments were incompetent and corrupt such as Nigeria, Iraq, and Syria. And "lone wolves" have appeared in many countries, including America and France. Jihadist groups emerged in Asia, the Arabian Peninsula, the Maghreb, and the Middle East, especially after the Arab Spring undermined longtime dictators in countries like Libya and Egypt. Thus, following the overthrow of Egypt's elected president, jihadist terrorism resumed in that country, especially in the Sinai Peninsula, where a terrorist group pledged loyalty to ISIS and declared itself the Islamic State's "Sinai Province." "The problem we face today," declared Bruce Riedel, "is there are probably more al-Qaeda cells than there have ever been before because of the chaos that's followed the Arab Spring."[13]

REGIONAL TERRORIST GROUPS

Al-Qaeda and other groups have been involved in numerous terrorist plots since 9/11. Among the best known were an unsuccessful effort to shoot down an Israeli jetliner with shoulder-fired missiles in Mombasa, Kenya (2002); car bomb attacks on residential compounds in Saudi Arabia (2003); bomb attacks on commuter trains in Madrid, Spain, that killed almost 200 and injured 1,800 others (2004); the bombing of three trains on the London Underground and a bus that killed 52 and injured over 700 (2005); the assassination of former Pakistani prime minister Benazir Bhutto (2007); and the attempted bombing of a Detroit-bound flight (2009). Increasingly, plots were hatched of jihadist groups not under al-Qaeda's control. According to a State Department report, "2013 saw the rise of increasingly aggressive and autonomous AQ affiliates and like-minded groups in the Middle East who took advantage of the weak governance and instability in the region to broaden and deepen their operations."[14]

Localization of terrorist groups caused Washington to alter its counterterrorism strategy. Although still concerned about terrorist attacks on America's homeland, there was growing concern about attacks on Western targets overseas and efforts to destabilize local governments in Mali, Algeria, Nigeria, and Somalia. Although American commandos continued to carry out raids, Washington increasingly relies on indigenous proxies in Africa and the Middle East, providing them with training, intelligence, reconnaissance, and logistics. In 2014 President Obama asked Congress for $5 billion to fund a Counterterrorism Partnership Fund as part of a strategy "that matches this diffuse threat; one that expands our reach without sending forces that stretch our military too thin, or stir up local resentments."[15]

Al-Qaeda in the Arabian Peninsula

Al-Qaeda in the Arabian Peninsula (AQAP)—established in Saudi Arabia in 2003 by a former aide to bin Laden, Nasser al-Wuhayshi—merged in 2009 with Yemeni jihadists. The group participated in an insurrection in southern Yemen with a local offshoot, Ansar al-Sharia ("Supporters of Islamic Law"), which emerged amid Yemen's political instability in 2011. AQAP also developed links with al-Shabab, a militant jihadist group operating in Somalia across the Gulf of Aden from Yemen.

Although most AQAP operations were directed against Yemeni government officials and installations, individual foreigners, and Yemeni Shiites, it also tried to attack American targets and bomb U.S. aircraft. With bomb maker Ibrahim Hassan Asiri, "AQAP has the technical capacity to build bombs that made it past airport security."[16] AQAP was responsible for a 2009 effort to blow up a Detroit-bound Northwest jetliner by the "underwear bomber," Umar Farouk Abdulmutallab; a 2010 plot involving bombs hidden in Hewlett-Packard desktop printer cartridges that were addressed to synagogues in Chicago but were discovered during stopovers in London and Dubai; and another underwear bomb plot in 2012. Those responsible for killing twelve people in Paris in 2015 had been trained and/or influenced by AQAP.

The closing of U.S. embassies and consulates in August 2013 and an accompanying global travel alert were triggered by an intelligence intercept concerning an AQAP plot linked to the group's bomb-making skill. Communications intercepted between Zawahiri and Wuhayshi (killed in a U.S. military strike in 2015) revealed what U.S. intelligence officials described as one of the most serious plots against American interests since 9/11. The revelation of the intelligence coup forced al-Qaeda to develop new ways to encrypt online and telephone messaging. Another alert involving an AQAP plot with other foreign extremists in 2014 led Attorney General Eric Holder to declare, "That's a deadly combination, where you have people who have the technical know-how along with the people who have this kind of fervor to give their lives in support of a cause that is directed at the United States and directed at its allies."[17]

Washington assumed an active role in helping Yemen cope with AQAP, seeking to eliminate its leaders and strengthening Yemen's counterterrorism capability. America launched drone strikes from a base in Saudi Arabia against AQAP militants, including the first outside Afghanistan in November 2002, which killed al-Qaeda's top operative in Yemen, Qaed Salim Sinan al-Harethi, a suspect in the 2000 bombing of the USS *Cole*, and Kamal Derwish, the first reported American death to result from the drone campaign. Aircraft strikes and Special Operations teams to train Yemeni security personnel augmented drone strikes, but these left amid growing civil war in 2015. AQAP took advantage of the violence to occupy large areas in southern Yemen and seize an oil terminal and large stores of arms.

In Yemen, jihadists employed video propaganda to paint U.S. drone strikes as a threat to innocent civilians. Gregory Johnson, a Yemen expert, noted that militant jihadists "believe that the side that kills the most Yemeni civilians loses. So they are trying to show that, 'Look, in this war we are more careful about Yemeni civilian lives than the United States is. That is what we have been telling you all along, and this is why you should join our side.'"[18]

Drones

Dave Granlund

Africa, too, is home to jihadists. Sudan is a haven for extremists, and Tanzania is a transit for European terrorists. U.S. drone strikes from Djibouti, where America's Combined Joint Task Force–Horn of Africa is located, have killed militants in Somalia as well as Yemen. Jihadist terrorism has also infected a number of sub-Saharan countries including Cameroon, the Central African Republic, Chad, Eritrea, Ethiopia, Kenya, Mali, Mauretania, Niger, Nigeria, Somalia, Sudan, Tanzania, Uganda, and several countries in West Africa.[19] Thus, the joint task force also trains military units from Ethiopia, Djibouti, Kenya and other African countries in counterterrorism, and American commandos have conducted antiterrorist raids in Somalia and Libya and have helped Uganda and Nigeria fight terrorism.

Al-Shabab

Somalia became a failed state in the 1990s. America's intervention (1992–1994) failed to end the violent chaos that had torn the country apart after the Cold War. Somalia proved fertile soil for Islamic jihadists, many of whom had previously fought in Afghanistan. Al-Shabab ("The Youth"), originally the militant wing of the Somali Council of Islamic Courts, gained control of southern Somalia in late 2006 and sought to create an Islamic emirate in East Africa. The group imposed harsh Islamic punishments in areas it governed, stoning to death women accused of adultery and cutting off the hands of thieves. It was financed by extortion, ivory and charcoal smuggling (from acacia wood for shisha pipes), kidnappings, and even piracy. "They calculate your income, they do the math," said a former Somali official. "And then you have to obey. Otherwise, they kill you."[20]

With the aid of Ethiopian forces, Shabab was defeated in a brief war that ended in 2007. Ethiopian intervention attracted additional recruits to Shabab, which continued to wage guerrilla war and terrorism in much of Somalia. By 2009 its 5,000 fighters controlled half the country and "was the only self-proclaimed Al-Qaeda ally controlling large territories."[21] The group created havoc elsewhere in Somalia and governed the country's capital, Mogadishu, until driven out by Somalia's Transitional Federal Government (TFG) in 2011, aided by the 22,000-member African Union Mission in Somalia (AMISCOM). The following year Shabab's leader, Ahmed Abdi Godane, formally pledged loyalty to Zawahiri, bin Laden's successor as leader of al Qaeda. In 2015, Shabab shifted its allegiance to ISIS.

U.S. officials feared Somalia could become a sanctuary for terrorist groups seeking to attack American interests or destabilize countries like Ethiopia and Kenya, and its retreat reignited conflict among Somali warlords and warring clans. The group successfully recruited over forty Somali-Americans, many from Minneapolis, after 2007, and there was concern some might return to carry out attacks in America as Australian-Somalis unsuccessfully tried to do in Australia after returning home.

AMISCOM was authorized by the UN Security Council in 2007 and funded by the European Union (EU). It consisted mainly of troops from Uganda, Burundi, and Kenya. (Outside of Somalia, Kenya sent more fighters than any other country to fight for al-Shabab and has experienced domestic Muslim unrest as a consequence of involvement in Somalia.) After 2011, pressured by AMISCOM, al-Shabab retreated from most Somali towns and cities. American drones, air strikes, and Special Operations teams aided AMISCOM. After meeting with Somalia's president in January 2013, Secretary of State Hillary Rodham Clinton applauded what she called "the extraordinary partnership between the leaders and people of

Somalia, with international supporters" that had driven al-Shabab "from Mogadishu and every other major city in Somalia."[22] In 2014 AMISCOM drove Shabab from the southern port of Barawe, and a U.S. air strike killed Godane, an event described by a Pentagon official as "a major symbolic and operational loss."[23]

Although weakened, the group coordinated suicide bombings in Uganda's capital, Kampala, in 2010, killing 74 people. It continued to launch deadly attacks in Mogadishu, including one on the UN compound in January 2013 and another at a popular restaurant some months later. Kenya was the victim of Shabab attacks on the upscale Westgate mall in Nairobi in September 2013, killing 68, including the nephew of Kenya's president. The group used Twitter to claim responsibility for its brutal act. A U.S. analyst interpreted the attack, however, as "the latest sign of the group's weakness. It was a desperate, high-risk gamble by Shabab to reverse its prospects."[24] Shabab attacked Kenya's Garissa University in April 2015, resulting in 147 deaths. A UN official observed, "This is Shabab still trying to carry out a Somali agenda, attacking countries that are contributing to the Somalia mission."[25] Thus, "with continuing losses on the battlefield, a new AMISON [sic] offensive, shrinking finances, and now the death of their charismatic leader,"[26] Shabab's influence had eroded. There remains concern that Shabab may collaborate with other jihadist groups, including AQAP, North Africa's al-Qaeda in the Land of the Islamic Maghreb, and Nigeria's Boko Haram, to which we now turn.

Al-Qaeda in the Land of the Islamic Maghreb (AQIM)

AQIM has roots in Algeria's Armed Islamic Group, which led an insurgency against that country's military leadership after it canceled a second round of parliamentary elections in 1992 that threatened to bring Islamists to power. There followed a bloody civil war in which 200,000 died. In 1998 a faction of the Armed Islamic Group broke away to form the Salafist Group for Call and Combat. By September 2006 that group was in disarray, owing to the government's combination of repression and amnesty, and it declared its union with al-Qaeda. Some months later it renamed itself al-Qaeda in the Islamic Maghreb. After 2006 AQIM broadened its objectives to include attacking Western interests and establishing Islamic governments across the region in Algeria, Tunisia, Libya, Mali, Mauritania, Morocco, Senegal, and Niger. It identified as "far enemies" Spain and France, calling for Islam's reconquest of the former and declaring war on the latter.

AQIM, many of whose leaders had participated in the anti-Soviet resistance in Afghanistan, moved south into the Sahel region of North Africa, where it used improvised explosive devices to attack convoys of oil workers and diplomats. It launched attacks on UN offices in Algiers (2007) and the Israeli embassy in Mauritania (2008), and increasingly used suicide bombings. With 600 to 800 militants in Europe and Algeria, it forged links with suspected terrorists in Europe. Some of its members became involved in the Iraq war after 2003. For funding, the group relied on drug smuggling and ransom payments by European governments to free citizens who had been kidnapped, and two French hostages died during an unsuccessful 2011 rescue operation.

Political instability in Mali offered AQIM opportunities. In 2012 military officers unhappy with President Amadou Toumani Touré's failure to quell a rebellion by nomadic Tuaregs seized power. Many of the Tuaregs had returned home after the overthrow of Libya's Muammar Qaddafi, for whom they had fought. In the ensuing chaos AQIM, in collaboration with Ansar al-Din ("Movement of Defenders of the Faith") and with arms looted from Libya, seized control of northern Mali, including cities such as Timbuktou, Gao, and Kidal, and imposed a harsh version of Islamic law that alienated many Malians, including the Tuaregs. The jihadists then moved south toward the capital city of Bamako. Mali's former colonial ruler, France, intervened in January 2013 with UN approval, forcing AQIM to flee into the mountains along the Algerian border and neighboring Niger, where French forces continued to chase them. Thereafter, remaining French soldiers were integrated into a UN-approved peacekeeping force consisting of African troops sent by the Economic Community of West African States. Franco–American cooperation on terrorism in North Africa was close. Although Washington did not directly participate in the Mali conflict, it aided France by providing giant C-17 transport planes to airlift French troops and supplies and aerial intelligence gathered by surveillance drones. Washington also dispatched a small team of soldiers to train African countries that sent troops to Mali, and with France has sought to engage Algeria more fully in the fight against AQIM. Washington was less concerned that AQIM posed an immediate threat to homeland security than its potential for providing a sanctuary for other terrorists in North Africa.

In retaliation for Algeria's willingness to allow France to use its airspace, a group called al-Mulathameen ("Masked Men Brigade") led by "one-eyed" Mokhtar Belmokhtar (who had left AQIM), aided by Libya's Ansar al-Shariah, and armed with looted Libyan weapons, attacked an energy production facility in southern Algeria. The facility was operated by Britain's BP, Norway's Statoil, and Algeria's state oil and gas company Sonatrach. The terrorists took foreign employees as hostages, and when Algerian troops regained control of the facility, thirty-eight hostages including three Americans were killed. Belmokhtar is also believed to have been responsible for two suicide attacks—one against a military base and the other against a French-run uranium mine in Niger, which had granted Washington use of its territory to launch drone missions. He also planned the attack on the Radisson Blu hotel in Bamako, Mali, in late 2015, which some observers believe was intended to show that al-Qaeda, which he supports, remains a major factor in global terrorism despite the growing threat of its competitor, the Islamic State.[27] Referring to Belmokhtar's breakaway from AQIM, Bruce Hoffman noted, "Splinters can become even more consequential than their parent organization."[28]

An FBI official described Belmokhtar as a "fanatical jihadist leading an extremist vanguard of an extremist ideology,"[29] and the State Department offered a reward of $5 million for information leading to his location. In August 2013 the "Masked Men Brigade" and the Mali-based "Movement for Oneness and Jihad in West Africa" formed a new group called al-Murabitun ("Movement for Unity and Jihad in West Africa"), described by the State Department as "the greatest near-term threat to U.S. and Western interests"[30] in North Africa. Belmokhtar financed operations by kidnapping and by smuggling arms, drugs, and cigarettes.

AQIM may also have been involved in the September 2012 attack on the U.S. consulate in Benghazi, Libya. Referring to AQIM, Secretary Clinton declared, "With a larger safe haven and increased freedom to maneuver, terrorists are seeking to extend their reach and their networks in multiple directions. And they are working with other violent extremists to undermine the democratic transitions under way in North Africa, as we tragically saw in Benghazi."[31] In congressional hearings shortly after the French intervention in Mali, Clinton warned that anarchy in Libya after Qaddafi's death had opened a "Pandora's box of weapons." "There's no doubt that the Algerian terrorists had weapons from Libya. There's no doubt that the Malian remnants of al-Qaida in the Islamic Maghreb has weapons from Libya," and she forecast that North Africa would pose problems as had Afghanistan: "This is going to be a very serious ongoing threat because if you look at the size of northern Mali, if you look at the topography, it's not only desert, it's caves—[it] sounds reminiscent. We are in for a struggle. But it is a necessary struggle. We cannot permit northern Mali to become a safe haven."[32] Nevertheless, with inept leaders, Mali remained unstable. With few military assets in this vast region, Washington, according to a former CIA analyst, "is facing a security environment in Africa that is increasingly more complex and therefore more dangerous."[33]

Boko Haram

Among the terrorist groups to which AQIM has provided funding and training is Boko Haram ("Western Education Is Sacrilegious"), which seeks to transform Nigeria into an Islamic state, attacks Christian churches, and opposes Western practices including voting and secular education. The group was founded by a Muslim cleric, Mohammed Yusuf, in the northeastern Nigerian city of Maiduguri, capital of Borno state, in 2002 using an Islamic school to recruit adherents mainly from ethnic Kanuri fishermen from near Lake Chad. In 2009 it attacked police stations and government buildings in Maiduguri, spreading violence in the city's streets in which hundreds of its supporters died.

Although Yusuf was later killed and Nigeria's government claimed the group had been defeated, Boko Haram reappeared in 2010 under a new leader, Abubakar Shekau, who claimed he communicated with God and was described as being "unhinged."[34] The group's followers began to shoot and bomb government officials and schools and kidnap children in cities and towns across the impoverished region, heightening tensions between Nigeria's Christians and Muslims. The group, numbering 5,000 to 10,000 fighters, also attacked UN offices in Abuja, Nigeria's capital, and looted heavy weapons from army garrisons. Between 2009 and 2015 the group massacred thousands of Nigerians, including 185 in Kano, northern Nigeria's largest Muslim-majority city, in one day in 2012, and 2,000 in the town of Baga in 2015, when it also systematically razed towns along the shore of Lake Chad. Referring to Baga, Shekau declared, "This is just the beginning of the killings. What you've just witnessed is a tip of the iceberg. More deaths are coming."[35]

In 2013 Boko Haram terrorists murdered 50 college students in their sleep, and the following year killed 50 children at a soccer match and 75 people in a bombing in Abuja, stepping up assaults on towns throughout the region. The group murdered hundreds of civilians in Gamboru Ngala in 2014 and took women and children hostage for whom it demanded ransom. It abducted 200 girls from a boarding school in Chibok May 2014, an action that even other jihadists criticized, triggering a massive but unsuccessful search involving U.S. reconnaissance assistance.

Boko Haram also extended its operations beyond Nigeria into Cameroon, where it kidnapped a French priest on the same day that the State Department declared the group a foreign terrorist organization. Some months later the group began occupying major towns and, aping ISIS, declared areas in Borno state as a "Muslim territory" or caliphate and the Islamic State's "West Africa Province," triggering a flight of refugees to Cameroon and Niger and later attacking Chad, where its suicide bombers killed large numbers of Nigerians who had fled for safety. Shekau declared that Allah "commands us to rule the rest of the world, not only Nigeria, and now we have started."[36] As a result, five West African countries—Nigeria,

Benin, Cameroon, Chad, and Niger—agreed to share intelligence and cooperate in fighting Boko Haram; the African Union authorized a regional force of 7,500; and Nigeria hired South African mercenaries to fight the group. To aid the African Union, Obama sent 300 U.S. soldiers to Cameroon in October 2015 to provide what the president called "intelligence, surveillance and reconnaissance."[37] And shortly thereafter Cameroon's army killed over 100 terrorists and freed hostages being held by Boko Haram. Two years earlier the American undersecretary of defense for intelligence had described the group as looking like ISIS: "How fast their trajectory can go up is something we're paying a lot of attention to. But certainly in their area, they're wreaking a lot of destruction."[38] Thus, in 2014 Boko Haram was responsible for 6,664 deaths, more than any other terrorist group including the more widely publicized Islamic State.[39]

Indiscriminate reprisals by Nigerian security forces and poverty were sources of recruitment for the group among Nigerian Muslims, prompting a U.S. analyst to conclude, "Military and police heavy-handedness in the north is core to the story of Boko Haram's emergence. You can't discount the effects of the state's brutality in the north."[40] An army counterattack led to 500 deaths after a mass jailbreak. After President Goodluck Jonathan declared a state of emergency in northeast Nigeria in May 2013, Secretary of State John Kerry observed that Washington was "deeply concerned about the fighting" there, adding that "we are also deeply concerned by credible allegations that Nigerian security forces are committing gross human rights violations, which, in turn, only escalate the violence and fuel extremism."[41]

Although Washington regards Nigeria as a regional power and trading partner and a bulwark against Islamic extremism, there has been a lack of trust between the two governments. U.S. officials were reluctant to share intelligence with Nigerian officials because of the penetration of Nigerian security agencies by Boko Haram informants. To date Boko Haram has largely targeted Nigerian officials, but a congressional report declared that its links with other terrorist groups "combined with the increased sophistication of attacks . . . have led to concerns from the U.S. intelligence community over the sect's intent and capability to strike Western targets in Nigeria, throughout Africa, and, most importantly, the U.S. homeland."[42] President Jonathan's elected successor, Muhammadu Buhari, however, criticized the U.S. refusal to sell Nigeria arms because of its army's violation of human rights, arguing that the policy aided Boko Haram. Under President Buhari, who fired Nigeria's military chiefs and sought to root out corruption in Nigeria's army, U.S.–Nigerian cooperation against Boko Haram improved significantly, and the group began to lose ground.

Asian Terrorist Groups

Jihadists have also made inroads in Asia. Al-Qaeda is suspected of contacts in Afghanistan with leaders of Jemaah Islamiyah, a terrorist group first discovered in Singapore in 2001 that seeks to establish an Islamic state throughout Southeast Asia, and more recently ISIS has managed to infiltrate the Afghan Taliban. Jemaah Islamiyah was responsible for violence in the Philippines and Indonesia, notably the bombing of two Bali nightclubs in October 2002 that took 202 lives, including many Australians and Britons, and suicide bombings in Indonesia's capital, Jakarta, at the JW Marriott and Ritz-Carlton hotels (2003) and outside the Australian embassy (2004). Since then governments in the region have arrested many of the group's leaders and members, and an elite U.S.–Australian-trained counterterrorist squad called Detachment 88 has aided Indonesia. Nevertheless, Jemaah

Islamiyah remained a threat with links to the Sunni Movement Indonesian Society, or HASMI, that planned to bomb the American and Australian embassies in Jakarta until the plot was discovered in 2012. Other violent Southeast Asian groups include the Abu Sayyaf Group, which seeks an independent Islamic state in the Philippines consisting of western Mindanao and the Sulu Archipelago, and Jemmah Anshorut Tauhid, a splinter of Jemaah Islamiyah that seeks an Islamic caliphate in Indonesia and has urged attacking Americans.

In South Asia, Pakistan's Jaish-e-Mohammed ("The Army of Muhammad") has carried out terrorist attacks in Indian-occupied Kashmir as well as a 2009 attack on a bus carrying a Sri Lankan cricket team and declared war on America. Another Pakistani group, Laskar-e-Taiba ("Army of the Righteous"), also seeks to unite Kashmir with Pakistan and carried out widely publicized terrorist acts including an attack on India's parliament in New Delhi in 2001, an attack on commuter trains in Mumbai in 2006 that killed over 180, and attacks in Mumbai in 2008 that killed over 160 and threatened to trigger a war between India and Pakistan. An American, David Headley, was convicted and sentenced to thirty-five years in prison for scouting targets in Mumbai for Laskar-e-Taiba before its 2008 attacks. In 2014 al-Qaeda leader Zawahiri announced the establishment of al-Qaeda in the Indian Subcontinent, where ISIS was already recruiting militants, as al-Qaeda's fifth branch, others being North Africa, East Africa, Yemen, and Syria.

"Lone Wolves"

Al-Qaeda and regional terrorists have also encouraged individuals to carry out solo attacks against the United States and its friends. Al-Qaeda, observed a former CIA psychiatrist, has "made a particular effort to recruit lonely people who are looking for a cause."[43] Jihadist sites online and publications like *Inspire*, an English-language magazine published by American Samir Khan for AQAP, spread anti-U.S. propaganda and provided information about how to make bombs and where to launch attacks.

The bombs set off during the 2013 Boston Marathon by two Chechen brothers, Tamerlan and Dzhokhar Tsarnaev, killed 3 and injured over 200 others. The bombs were made from readily available items like pressure cookers, nails, and gunpowder from fireworks, and were probably based on information in a jihadist Internet manual called the "Lone Mujahid Pocketbook." As President Obama declared, "One of the dangers that we now face are self-radicalized individuals who are already here in the United States," and their attacks "are in some ways more difficult to prevent."[44] Examples include Nidal Hasan, a U.S. Muslim of Palestinian descent who murdered thirteen soldiers and wounded almost three dozen others at Fort Hood in Texas in November 2009; Faisal Shahzad, a naturalized U.S. citizen who unsuccessfully tried to set off a car bomb in New York's Times Square in 2010; and Ahmed Abassi, a Tunisian accused in 2013 of plotting to establish a terrorist cell to poison a water system.

Particularly brutal were the murders of a British soldier in 2013 on a London street by two "lone wolves" who were British citizens of Nigerian origin, two Canadian soldiers in 2014 by converts to Islam, two Australians by an Iranian immigrant in 2014, and fourteen Americans by a married couple in San Bernardino, California, in late 2015. It the latter case, the woman, Tashfeen Malik, had apparently pledged allegiance to ISIS in a Facebook posting, and ISIS described the couple as "soldiers of the caliphate." Nevertheless, it is thought that while influenced by the terrorist group, they were not directly associated with it. Coming early in America's presidential campaign, the incident drew different responses from candidates, with Democrats ascribing the attacks to the availability of guns in the United States and Republicans pointing to the need for improving mental health facilities.

Some young Muslims living in non-Muslim societies, especially second-generation immigrants, lack a sense of self-identity, feeling neither at home in their parents' adopted countries nor members of the societies from which their families emigrated. Such "lone wolves," according to a former U.S. counterterrorism official, are "angry kids with a veneer of ideology that's about skin-deep," and are frequently social failures who "sometimes latch onto a cause that makes their anger legitimate."[45] Their anger is focused on Muslim grievances elsewhere in the world such as the wars in Afghanistan and Iraq, America's use of drones against Muslim militants, Washington's support for Israel, or the repression of Chechen Muslim separatists in Russia. Most are single males, and many are unemployed and living alone. Some have histories of mental illness.

Civil strife in Iraq and Syria has provided training for some of these individuals. A threat is posed by the "backflow" of the 3,000 jihadists from America and Europe who went to Syria, which is easy to enter via Turkey, and who received training before joining the uprising against the regime. "Syria," according to the director of America's National Counterterrorist Center, "has become really the predominant jihadist battlefield in the world," and there is concern about individuals who have Western passports "returning as part of really a global jihadist movement to Western Europe and, potentially, to the United States."[46] "It's possible," observed Paul Cruickshank, "that new recruits could get training like what we saw al Qaeda in Pakistan giving—showing people how to make high-explosive bombs made of chemicals bought at beauty or home good stores and detonate them. All they would need to do is return to Europe, buy what they need and carry out an attack."[47] The British security minister noted his agency monitored "very closely people seeking to travel [to Syria]—and also people traveling back," and the Dutch national coordinator for security and counterterrorism declared the jihadists were a threat "because they can and will return battle hardened, further radicalized, traumatized."[48] European concerns regarding the problem were dramatically heightened by a massacre in Paris in November 2015 by a terrorist team associated with ISIS that included several individuals who had travelled back and forth between Syria and Europe in the massive upsurge of refugees from Syria in 2014-2015. Among its results were growing calls in Europe for additional border controls, greater cooperation with Turkey to halt the migration of Syrians to Europe, and greater surveillance and intelligence cooperation.

The toxic combination of jihadists and a civil war awash with arms from external sources makes Syria a major threat to U.S. national security. Dozens of Americans have tried to join the Syrian jihadists, and an American intelligence official noted, "It's a very steady increase, and I expect that to continue as long as the fighting there continues."[49] Added a counterterrorism official, "We know Al Qaeda is using Syria to identify individuals they can recruit, provide them additional indoctrination so they're further radicalized, and leverage them into future soldiers, possibly in the U.S."[50] Thus, America's FBI director considered tracking Americans returning from Syria a high priority, and America's attorney general urged Europeans to adopt laws like America's that prevent individuals from traveling to Syria before they leave. The agency has begun apprehending suspects in the United States as quickly as possible to prevent attacks.[51]

IRAQ AND SYRIA

Al-Qaeda in Iraq

Abu Musab al-Zarqawi established al-Qaeda in Iraq with Pakistani and Afghan fighters and later with Iraqis. He sought to establish a transnational Islamic state based on Islamic law. Although Zarqawi declared allegiance to al-Qaeda in 2004, al-Qaeda had not been involved with Zarqawi. The dissolution of Iraq's army and the ban on members of Saddam's political supporters from government by the transitional authority established in Iraq by Washington contributed to the pool of potential followers of al-Qaeda in Iraq. Funded by contributions from sympathizers in Saudi Arabia, Syria, Jordan, and Iran, and by smuggling and extortion, Zarqawi developed "a four-pronged strategy to defeat the American-led coalition"—isolate America's forces by attacking its coalition partners, attack Iraqi security forces and politicians, attack aid workers and civilian contractors, and ignite a Shia–Sunni civil war.[52] In 2005 bin Laden questioned the wisdom of Zarqawi's strategy of attacking Shiite holy sites. Zarqawi was killed in 2006 by a U.S. air strike, and Iraqi security forces killed his successor in 2010.

Despite severe losses during the war, al-Qaeda in Iraq was responsible for an upsurge in anti-Shia terrorism in Iraq aimed at reigniting Shia–Sunni conflict in that country, assisted by Sunni reaction to the authoritarianism of Iraq's Shia-dominated government. After leaving office Secretary Leon Panetta wrote, "It was clear to me—and many others—that withdrawing all our forces would endanger the fragile stability then barely holding Iraq together."[53] A dramatic surge in terrorist attacks in Iraq followed America's withdrawal, and sectarian violence in 2013 reached levels not seen for five years, with over 7,000 civilian deaths.

Al-Qaeda in Iraq aided by foreign jihadists from 74 countries including Pakistan, Egypt, Saudi Arabia, Indonesia, and Russia sent volunteers to help jihadists in Syria and Iraq, and Washington sponsored a UN resolution requiring countries to take action to prevent citizens from joining terrorist groups. Thousands of foreign fighters including 150 Americans and many more French, British, Belgian, and Swedish Muslims have traveled to the region since 2011, and about 1,000 additional recruits continue to enter Syria and Iraq each month, many of whom may return home.[54]

Al-Qaeda in Iraq's successor, al-Qaeda in Iraq and Syria (ISIS)—later the Islamic State—became the world's most violent and disruptive terrorist group, attracting thousands of recruits from around the world including America by occupying large swaths of territory in Syria and Iraq and imposing early Islamic customs. (We will continue to use "ISIS" to refer to the group.) Washington offered a reward of $10 million for information about its leader, Abu Bakr al-Baghdadi, who according to a Pentagon official "was a street thug when we picked him up in 2004." It was hard to imagine he would "become head of ISIS."[55] Until reentering Iraq, al-Baghdadi remained in Syria, where in addition to fighting the regime, ISIS fought both moderate and extremist foes of Assad. In Syria, al-Qaeda in Iraq also established the Jabhat al-Nusra, another Sunni jihadist group with Muhammad al-Jolani as leader. Declared a masked al-Nusra fighter, "We are Syrian mujahideen, back from various jihad fronts to restore God's rule on the Earth and avenge the Syrians' violated honor and spilled blood."[56]

"Syria," argues Cruickshank, "is now the fuel for the jihadist movement and some of the most experienced operatives from Pakistan and Iraq have relocated there."[57] Referring to Syrian jihadists, a U.S.

official declared, "We encourage all responsible actors to speak out against and distance themselves from extremists seeking to hijack the Syrian struggle for their own ends."[58]

The Islamic State

In April 2013 Baghdadi announced a merger of al-Qaeda in Iraq and Jabhat al-Nusra into a single group, al-Qaeda in Iraq and Syria, thereafter called the Islamic State. Proclaimed Baghdadi, "The time has come for us to announce to the people of the Levant and to the whole world that al-Nusra Front is merely an extension of the Islamic State of Iraq and a part of it."[59] However, Jolani and Zawahiri denied that a merger had occurred, and Zawahiri "sent a private message ruling that both men had erred: Baghdadi by not consulting Jawlani [Jolani], and Jawlani by refusing to join ISIS and giving his direct allegiance to Zawahiri without permission from al Qaeda central."[60] In early 2014 al-Qaeda denied it had links to ISIS and condemned the group for killing fellow jihadists and disobeying Zawahiri by operating in Syria. Baghdadi responded: "I have chosen the command of my Lord over the command in the message that contradicts it."[61] Some months later Zawahiri also criticized ISIS for beheading hostages and posting videos of the executions because it created public revulsion.

The Assad regime seemed to welcome ISIS because it bore out its narrative of events in Syria as a war against "terrorism." "The presence of Islamists in the country," argued a Syrian Christian activist, "benefits the regime because it confirms the theory it was promoting from the first minute."[62] Thus, Russia's military intervention in Syria in 2015, though mainly aimed at aiding Assad, also reflected concern about the number of Chechen extremists in the Russian Caucasus, and was justified by Russian president Vladimir Putin as attacking "terrorists." Hence, a former U.S. ambassador concluded, "We need to start talking to the Assad regime again" about counterterrorism because "bad as Assad is, he is not as bad as the jihadis who would take over in his absence."[63]

The ISIS–Nusra dispute was over strategy. Unlike Jabhat al-Nusra, which cultivated popular support in Syria, ISIS attacked other Syrian rebels and "implemented draconian Islamic law in the towns that it has captured, both of which have alienated Syrians."[64] "Nusra," wrote an analyst, "is really embedding itself in the Islamic landscape, working with other groups and trying to compromise, while ISIS has been doing the opposite, which is why they have no more friends."[65] "For al-Qaeda," argued an observer, "violence is a means to an end; for ISIS, it is an end in itself."[66] Another concluded, "It is clear that the first and second generation that started Al Qaeda, most of them are supporting Zawahiri, but the new generation is more radical and closer to ISIS."[67]

The dispute "is not just about bureaucratic power; it is also about strategy and the future of al Qaeda's global jihad."[68] Unlike ISIS, which sought global jihad, Jabhat al-Nusra had the limited goal of creating an Islamic state in Syria, and al-Nusra has attacked small, moderate, American-trained rebel groups in Syria, undermining the U.S. efforts to create a viable anti-extremist group in that country. Both groups recruited foreign jihadists to Syria, making that country a haven for terrorists—including thousands from the West, of whom some were American. In addition, America was reluctant to aid powerful anti-ISIS groups in Syria like Ahrar al-Sham ("Free Men of Syria") that declared a willingness to work with the West because of its suspected ties to al-Qaeda. "They are in a gray zone," noted Robert Ford, a former

U.S. ambassador to Syria, "but in a civil war if you are not willing to talk to factions in the gray zone, you'll have precious few people to talk to."[69]

Other insurgents initially avoided confronting ISIS in order to maintain unity against Assad, but ISIS made this impossible. "They want to carve out a jihadi state," concluded terrorist analyst Bruce Hoffman, "and obviously anything above that is gravy, like overthrowing the Assad regime."[70] ISIS sought to transform Syria along with Iraq and Lebanon into a caliphate of the Levant and then establish a global caliphate, threatening to attack America afterward.

After seizing Syrian territory around Raqqa near Iraq's border, occupying Syria's oilfields, and selling fuel on the Turkish and Syrian black markets, ISIS expanded operations back into Iraq. There, terrorist violence spiked as Iraqi parliamentary elections approached in April 2014 and continued after Nuri al-Maliki's Shia bloc won a plurality but not a majority of parliamentary seats. Maliki's "self-defeating strategy in the Sunni-majority areas during his second term in office [had] squandered the security gains enabled by the United States' military surge between 2007 and 2009,"[71] alienating Iraqi Sunnis. By 2013 American intelligence had come to recognize the threat ISIS posed in Syria, "but," noted an intelligence official, "the White House just didn't pay attention to it. They were preoccupied by other crises." Added a former State Department official, "I'm not suggesting anyone was asleep at the switch necessarily," but ISIS "definitely achieved strategic surprise when it rolled into Iraq."[72]

ISIS had "spent two years" in Iraq "breaking senior leaders out of prison and re-establishing a professional command and control structure; expanding operational reach, including into Syria, and exploiting rising Sunni discontent with the Shiite-led government of Iraqi Prime Minister Nuri al-Maliki, thereby encouraging sectarianism."[73] It had developed a sophisticated administrative structure and harnessed technology, using social media like Twitter, WordPress, and YouTube. By early 2014 ISIS militants, aided by former Sunni followers of Saddam Hussein, had returned to Iraq and seized control of Falluja and sometime later Ramadi, the capital of Anbar Province. In June ISIS drove the Iraqi army from Mosul, the country's second largest city; continued to Tikrit, where it murdered numerous Shia prisoners, and Tal Afar, the country's second largest city; and temporarily seized Iraq's largest oil refinery, in Baiji. ISIS also looted some $400 million in currency from Mosul's central bank and robbed banks elsewhere as it advanced. At the same time, it began providing services in the cities and towns in Syria like Raqqa, its de facto capital, and Deir al-Zour and Palmyra, which it occupied. Hundreds of thousands of Iraqis were displaced in Anbar alone, and about 500,000 fled Mosul. As ISIS moved deeper into Iraq, Secretary Clinton recalled, "I never thought it was just a Syrian problem. I thought it was a regional problem. I could not have predicted, however, the extent to which ISIS could be effective in seizing cities in Iraq and trying to erase boundaries to create an Islamic state."[74] In both countries a power vacuum allowed ISIS to flourish.

Like the Americans some years before, the Iraqi army sought to mobilize the tribes under the name of the Sunni Awakening that had rejected jihadi extremism but that Iraq's Shia leaders then ignored. Maliki's repression of Sunni unrest reversed the security gains of America's 2007–2009 "surge." Sunni soldiers in the Iraqi army deserted in large numbers, with four divisions fleeing in disorder. Inasmuch as Washington had spent $25 billion to train and equip the Iraqi army, its swift collapse—a "psychological collapse," declared U.S. officials—came as a surprise. Its training and preparedness had declined after America's withdrawal from Iraq, and it had been infiltrated by Sunni extremists. According to retired general James Dubik, who had trained Iraqi forces, "There are pockets of proficiency, but in general, they have been made fragile over the past three to four years, mostly because of the government of Iraq's policies."[75] Thus, an army of 200,000 soldiers, with an additional 500,000 paramilitary personnel, fled from ISIS.

After consolidating control of Iraq's "Sunni Triangle," ISIS advanced toward Baghdad, seized Iraq's border crossings with Syria and Jordan, occupied Kurdish towns in northern Iraq, fought Lebanese troops, and temporarily captured Iraq's largest dam. As ISIS advanced, its fighters massacred Shia soldiers, videotaping its atrocities. "Our Islamic State forces are still fighting in all directions," ISIS declared, "and we will not step down until the project of the caliphate is established, with the will of God."[76] Responding to the invasion, Iraq's leading Shia cleric, Grand Ayatollah Ali Sistani, called followers to defend their country and its religious sites. Thousands of Shias, many in Iranian-supported anti-American militias, heeded his call to take up arms, some returning from Syria, where they had fought to defend Assad. Ayatollah Sistani declared he was trying to defend all Iraqi communities from ISIS, not just his Shia followers. His effort threatened to split the Shia community after Moktada al-Sadr, a Shia cleric who between 2006 and 2008 induced his powerful militia, the "Mahdi Army," to fight U.S. troops in Iraq, called his followers to join the fight against ISIS.

After symbolically leveling a berm along the Syrian–Iraqi border, ISIS declared itself "the State of the Islamic Caliphate"—with Baghdadi as "Caliph Ibrahim"—consisting of the areas in both countries under its control. In taking this step, ISIS claimed to be righting historical wrongs committed by the West in dividing the Middle East into states after World War I. "Now that there is an actual caliphate with a caliph," noted a Brookings Institution analyst, "a lot of Muslims are going to have to talk about what that means, and there is going to be some sympathy."[77] Thus, in addition to its presence in Syria and Iraq, the Islamic State acquired additional adherents in Afghanistan, Algeria, Egypt, and Libya (all of which it declared to be provinces of the Islamic State), as well as individuals in Europe, Kosovo, Chechnya, and elsewhere. In Libya, ISIS's presence was estimated at 2,000 fighters. All this led the director of America's Defense Intelligence Agency to conclude that the group was "beginning to assemble a growing international footprint."[78] Many of the leaders of the Afghan ISIS group, which had split from the Taliban, were killed in a U.S. drone strike in July 2015, and U.S. air strikes against ISIS in Libya were launched in 2016.

In declaring a territorial caliphate, ISIS achieved what al-Qaeda had not. Observers objected to ISIS's new name. "This is a terrorist group and not a state," declared French foreign minister Laurent Fabius. "I do not recommend using the term Islamic State because it blurs the lines between Islam, Muslims, and Islamists." A French Muslim demonstrator was blunter: "I call them terrorists because that's what they are. One has to call a dog a dog. One can't play with words."[79] Nevertheless, ISIS began to assume the trappings of a territorial state, including ministries and bureaucrats who maintained day-to-day services for those in the cities and towns it had conquered. In addition, al-Baghdadi allowed his close associates significant authority in order to ensure that even if he were killed the Islamic State would continue to function.

Thus, U.S. counterterrorist specialists began to debate whether al-Qaeda or ISIS was a greater threat to America. While conceding that ISIS constituted a constant danger to America's homeland by encouraging individuals to commit violent acts, those preoccupied by al-Qaeda emphasized the group's ability to plan "mass-casualty" attacks, especially aided by affiliates like AQAP. America's director of the

National Counterterrorism Center noted, "There's a greater likelihood of ISIL being linked to attacks in the homeland right now. That said, we still look at AQAP as more capable of carrying out larger-scale attacks against the homeland, including against aircraft coming here."[80]

The Maliki government requested U.S. aid as the threat grew, but President Obama resisted providing help until Prime Minister Maliki made his government inclusive. Obama held out the possibility that U.S. airpower might be used if Iraq's leaders empowered Sunnis and Kurds.

The president acknowledged that "the American people and the American taxpayers made huge investments and sacrifices in order to give the Iraqis the opportunity to chart a better course, a better destiny."[81] He then dispatched 300 military advisors to provide intelligence for potential American air strikes while simultaneously U.S. and Saudi diplomats sought a replacement for Maliki. Maliki finally acceded, and in August 2014 Haider al-Abadi replaced him as prime minister, a step endorsed by America, Iran, and Saudi Arabia. The Saudis, who had opposed Washington's 2003 intervention in Iraq, its support of Egypt's Islamists, and its negotiations with Iran, were pleased by Washington's pressure on Iraq to enhance the status of the country's Sunnis and its willingness to aid moderate Sunni opponents of ISIS. The dispatch of even the few advisors aroused unease among Americans, and a poll revealed that only a small majority of Americans approved of sending those troops, while over half disapproved of how the president was dealing with violence in Iraq.[82] In addition, Abadi had little success in creating an effective Iraqi government and became increasing dependent on Iranian support.[83]

After ISIS routed Kurdish fighters in August 2014, threatening a massacre of Yazidi refugees and the safety of U.S. diplomats in Erbil, the Kurdish capital, Obama authorized limited air strikes. "I know that many of you are rightly concerned about any American action in Iraq, even limited strikes like these," the president declared, promising, "As commander in chief, I will not allow the United States to be dragged into fighting another war in Iraq."[84] Recognizing that ISIS could not be defeated except by extending U.S. attacks into Syria, President Obama authorized aerial surveillance of Syria, and ISIS responded by publicly beheading two Americans, producing a dramatic rise in public and congressional support for U.S. intervention. With bipartisan congressional approval, Washington extended its bombing campaign against ISIS to Syria, began aiding moderate Syrian insurgents, and assembled an anti-ISIS coalition of Western allies and Arab states. "The strength of this coalition," declared the president, "makes clear to the world that this is not just America's fight alone."[85]

Describing ISIS as a "cancer," the president said the coalition would "take the fight" to terrorists "who are unique in their brutality" and "degrade and ultimately destroy"[86] ISIS. Initial attacks included carrier- and land-based aircraft and cruise missiles. These were followed by attacks on Syrian oil refineries, a key source of ISIS funding according to the Treasury Department's counterterrorism office. Simultaneously, U.S. air strikes targeted another shadowy group, the "Khorasan Group," whose leader, a Kuwaiti, had been sent by Zawahiri from Pakistan to Syria to plan terrorist attacks against America. Of that group James Clapper, director of national intelligence, warned, "In terms of threat to the homeland, Khorasan may pose as much of a danger as the Islamic State."[87] In Turkey, America's secret Military Operations Command began to aid moderate Sunni foes of ISIS.

Having asked that the 2001 "Authorization for the Use of Military Force" be rescinded, Obama used it as authorization to extend America's fight against ISIS to Syria, a claim vigorously contested by some in

Congress like Sens. Tim Kaine (D-VA) and Chris Murphy (D-CT), who demanded explicit congressional approval for the action. In November 2014 the president agreed to seek congressional authorization for America's campaign against ISIS. In the absence of either a UN Security Council resolution or a request from Syria's government, Secretary Kerry invoked the right of "hot pursuit" for strikes in Syria to avoid charges of violating Syrian sovereignty. This was not sufficient to persuade America's European allies to go beyond aiding Iraq, which unlike Syria had requested foreign assistance. Syria offered to help fight ISIS while condemning American "aggression." For Washington, the dilemma was how to fight ISIS without aiding Assad.

ISIS's foes found it difficult to cooperate against what Secretary Kerry described as "an ambitious, avowed, genocidal, territorial-grabbing, caliphate-desiring, quasi state with an irregular army."[88] America and Iran were at odds over Syria; Iran, Qatar, and Saudi Arabia were engaged in a proxy war in Syria; and the Kurds sought autonomy. Turkey, though initially paying lip-service to fighting ISIS and a NATO ally, seemed more interested in limiting Kurdish autonomy and bringing down Syria's Assad regime, and stood by as Syrian Kurds were massacred by ISIS in Kobani just across its border from where 100,000 Syrians sought refuge. Iraq, its political and military institutions in ruins, was poised on the verge of full-scale sectarian war that could spread and become region-wide. However, ISIS attacks on Turkish soldiers persuaded Ankara to retaliate in July 2015 and to allow American aircraft to use Turkish air bases to strike the Islamic State, something it had previously refused to do. In addition, Turkey and the United States agreed to work with moderate Syrian insurgents to establish a "safe zone" for refugees in Syria beyond the Turkish border, although it remained unclear whether the Turks were more concerned about the Islamic State or Kurdish groups seeking to establish a Kurdish state.[89]

Owing to coalition air strikes and aid to allies like Iraq's Kurds in Iraq and Syria, ISIS began to shift its focus in 2015 to a greater emphasis on overseas "external" targets.[90] These included the bombing of a Russian airliner over the Sinai desert in late October by ISIS's Egyptian affiliate that killed all 224 people on board; mid-November suicide bombings in Beirut, Lebanon, that took 43 lives; and a series of coordinated attacks in Paris, also in November, that took 130 lives and injured 300 others. Other attacks in Yemen, Saudi Arabia, and Tunisia were also claimed by ISIS. "They [ISIS] have crossed some kind of Rubicon," declared McCants. "They have definitely shifted in their thinking about targeting their enemies."[91]

France was traumatized by the massacre in Paris, and President François Hollande told his citizens, "It is an act of war that was committed by a terrorist army, a jihadist army, Daesh, against France."[92] Hollande then invoked European Union article 42.7, a clause never before used that obliged other EU states to aid France, and visited Washington and Moscow in an effort to intensify and coordinate the campaign against ISIS. Thereafter, the French and British Parliaments approved extending air strikes to Syria, and Germany agreed to send a naval vessel and provide reconnaissance and mid-air fueling capacity (though no combatants) in the fight against ISIS.

Iran had a great interest in the fate of Iraq and its Shia majority. Tehran began two daily flights of military equipment to Baghdad and delivered several attack aircraft and surveillance drones to provide intelligence. Iranian president Hassan Rouhani promised to protect Shia sacred sites in Iraq, and Gen. Qassim Suleimani, commander of Iran's elite Quds Force of the Revolutionary Guards, met with Iraqi leaders to advise them, much has he had done in Syria to aid the Assad regime. His visit signaled growing Iranian involvement in Iraq. Americans tacitly coordinated air strikes with Iran, which conducted air strikes in a buffer zone it established in Iraq, and President Obama wrote a secret letter to Iran's supreme leader offering conditions for cooperation against ISIS. "Iran," suggested terrorism expert Charles Lister, "is likely to be playing somewhat of an overarching command role within the central Iraqi military apparatus, with an emphasis on maintaining cohesiveness in Baghdad and the Shia south and managing the reconstitution of Shia militias,"[93] known as the Hashid al-Shabi or "popular mobilization units,"[94] many controlled by Iran.

Critics of America's policy, including Hillary Clinton, faulted U.S. indecision and passivity as partly to blame for the growing influence of ISIS in Syria. "The failure to help build up a credible fighting force of the people who were the originators of the protests against Assad—there were Islamists, there were secularists, there was everything in the middle—the failure to do that left a big vacuum, which the jihadists have now filled."[95] "In cases like this," Anthony Cordesman concluded, "we have to choose between the least bad options. The whole idea that we have some magic wand hasn't worked out that well."[96]

In addition to the global consequences of America's War on Terror, the conflict had profound domestic consequences.

THE "WAR ON TERROR"

Unlike previous wars, in which enemy combatants were fighting America in the name of another government, the War on Terror was characterized by a different kind of adversary. Traditional military strategies and conventional military operations were unsuited for dealing with terrorist groups. The conduct of the War on Terror required new strategies: a massive reorganization of the country's civilian security and intelligence agencies; the creation of new security legislation; the implementation of new rules for identifying, detaining, and interrogating enemy combatants who were not fighting on behalf of another sovereign government; and the use of "targeted" and "extrajudicial" killings of terrorism suspects, often by unmanned drones. These efforts, designed to increase homeland security and prevent attacks against U.S. interests abroad, were controversial, especially to critics who believed they entailed invasions of individual privacy and violations of individual rights.

The Department of Homeland Security and the Director of National Intelligence

Congress established the Department of Homeland Security, headed by a cabinet-level secretary, in 2002. It was the most extensive reorganization of the government's executive branch since consolidation of the military services into a single Defense Department and the various intelligence agencies into a single Central Intelligence Agency in the 1940s in response to the onset of the Cold War. The idea was to unify nonmilitary agencies involved in protecting U.S. security to avoid the intelligence gaps that prevented U.S. officials from anticipating and thwarting the 9/11 attacks and improve America's ability to respond to and recover from human-made and natural disasters.

Among the twenty-two agencies placed in the new department were the Secret Service, the Coast Guard, Customs and Border Protection, Immigration and Customs Enforcement, the Federal Emergency Management Agency (FEMA), and the Transportation Security Agency, which is familiar to Americans who have been screened at U.S. airports. The new department brought together agencies that had previously been in other executive departments such as Agriculture, Commerce, Justice, Health and Human Services, Treasury, Energy, Transportation, and Defense.

FIGURE **7.1** Organization of the Department of Homeland Security

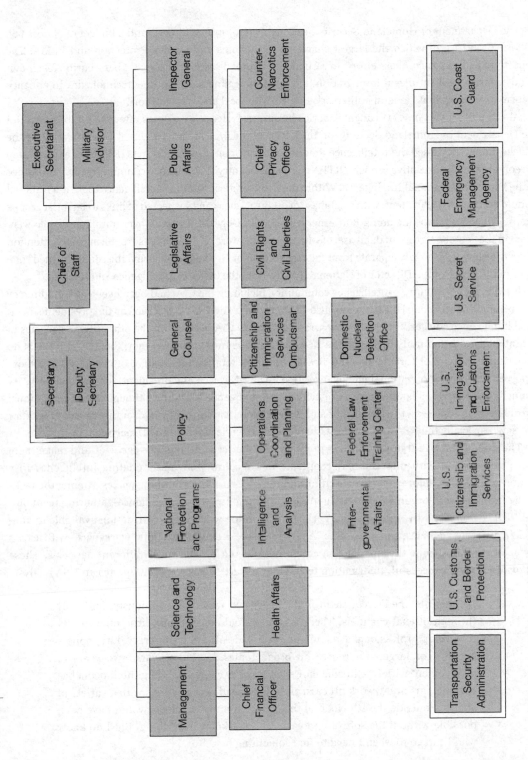

Source: U.S. Department of Homeland Security, 2015.

The Department of Homeland Security has roughly 240,000 employees and a budget of almost $65 billion (FY 2016), of which the largest shares go to Customs and Border Protection and FEMA. The department's tasks encompass efforts to respond to natural disasters, improve cybersecurity, foster aviation security, prevent illegal immigration and drug smuggling, develop new technologies to enhance security, and coordinate federal antiterrorist efforts with local and state authorities.

Al-Qaeda's attacks on 9/11 caught America by surprise. Hence, two years after the establishment of the Department of Homeland Security, on the advice of the 9/11 Commission that was investigating the attacks, Congress passed the Intelligence Reform and Terrorism Prevention Act (IRTPA) as another step in reorganizing the executive branch. IRTPA placed the country's intelligence community under an Office of the Director of National Intelligence. Within the Directorate of National Intelligence there is a National Counterterrorism department, with a database of 20,800 Americans suspected of links to terrorist groups like AQAP and 47,000 (including 800 Americans) on a no-fly list. In total, over a million people were listed in the center's terrorism database, of whom 680,000 were on "watch lists" requiring extra attention when traveling.[97] Although separate from the Department of Homeland Security, the center "owned" one piece of the Office of the Director of National Intelligence—the Office of Intelligence and Analysis.

Previously, the country's intelligence community, including the CIA, had been overseen by a director of central intelligence, or DCI (who was also CIA director). The DCI also served as the president's principal intelligence advisor. Under the new arrangement, the CIA, along with the other fifteen agencies in the intelligence community including the NSA, the Defense Intelligence Agency, the FBI, and the State Department Bureau of Intelligence and Research, with a total annual budget of close to $50 billion, report to the director of national intelligence (DNI). The DNI briefs the president, the National Security Council, and the Homeland Security Council on all intelligence matters. Although the organizational reform had some success, the DNI lacked authority to exercise strong control over the agencies the office oversaw, especially the NSA and the military intelligence services within the Department of Defense.

The intent of the reorganization was to integrate America's intelligence agencies and make them share information with one another, cooperate in collecting and disseminating intelligence to a greater extent than before, and reduce cultural differences in the different agencies. Among the tasks of the intelligence reorganization was funding and developing new intelligence-gathering technologies. This led in 2005 to "Intellipedia," consisting of online wikis with information available to analysts in different agencies, and in 2008 to "Analytic Space," a common online "workspace" with access for analysts throughout the intelligence community to the databases of different agencies. These innovations were successful. Information technology expert Andrew McAfee quotes an NSA analyst:

> Before Intellipedia, contacting other agencies was done cautiously, and only through official channels. There was no casual contact, and little opportunity to develop professional acquaintances—outside of rare [temporary duty] opportunities, or large conferences on broad topics. . . . After nearly two years of involvement with Intellipedia, however, this has changed. Using Intellipedia has become part of my work process, and I have made connections with a variety of analysts outside the IC. None of the changes in my practices would have been possible without the software tools. . . . I don't know everything. But I do know who I can go to when I need to find something out.[98]

FIGURE 7.2   Organization of the Office of the Director of National Intelligence

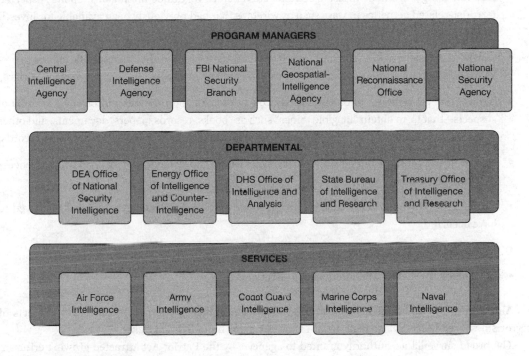

Source: Office of the Director of National Intelligence, 2015.

Although the post-9/11 reorganization increased the efficiency of U.S. counterterrorism, the War on Terror involved several questionable practices involving alleged human-rights violations. The USA Patriot Act signed by President Bush on October 26, 2001, remained a particular subject of controversy.

The Patriot Act and Growing Surveillance

The USA Patriot Act was passed just six weeks after 9/11. Fourteen of the law's seventeen provisions were permanently renewed after lengthy delay in 2006, and the remaining three were renewed by Congress for an additional four years in 2011, hours before they were to expire. The act reduced restrictions on intelligence gathering by government agencies in the United States, enabled the government to detain and deport terrorism suspects more easily, and expanded Washington's authority to regulate financial transactions. The American public was deeply divided over the 2011 renewal, with 42 percent regarding it as a necessary tool to help the government find terrorists and 34 percent describing it as going too far and posing a threat to civil liberties.[99]

Specific provisions of the Patriot Act included the following:

- Allowed the government to use electronic surveillance to gather intelligence about suspected terrorist-related activities in ways such as wiretaps that had previously been available for investigating other criminal activities;

- Legalized the use of "roving wiretaps" linked to individual suspects rather than specific phones to prevent suspects from evading surveillance by changing cell phones and/or moving from place to place;

- Allowed the government to obtain a secret court order for the personal and business records of suspects—that is, to obtain "tangible things" such as "books, records, papers, documents, and other items" ranging from purchases in stores or online, to hotel records, to credit card and library records;

- Removed barriers preventing different agencies—law enforcement, defense, and intelligence—from sharing information;

- Enabled officials to obtain a search warrant wherever terrorism-related activity was believed to have occurred;

- Prohibited harboring terrorists; and

- Eliminated the statute of limitations for terrorism crimes.

Although these provisions enhanced the government's ability to prevent or react swiftly to acts of terrorism, some observers also regarded them as infringing on individual rights.

The broad surveillance authority granted to agencies by the Patriot Act attracted growing criticism at home and abroad after Edward Snowden revealed to a British newspaper, *The Guardian,* the existence of a highly classified program by which America's National Security Administration (NSA) was carrying out a vast covert electronic surveillance program within the United States. Snowden claimed that his position as "infrastructure analyst" for the government contractor Booz Allen Hamilton granted him "access to lists of machines all over the world the NSA hacked."[100] The program existed by virtue of the 1978 Foreign Intelligence Surveillance Act (FISA), which allowed eavesdropping on foreigners as well as Americans thought to be "agents of foreign powers" (suspected terrorists), as amended by section 215 of the Patriot Act (its "business records" provision) and the 2008 FISA Amendments Act. Meant to apply to those suspected of terrorist-related activities, the surveillance program had become increasingly sophisticated after 2005. It had also been expanded by a ruling of the secret, eleven-member Foreign Intelligence Surveillance Court (FISC) that "relevant" material could encompass entire databases of records on millions of persons. In a series of cases, the FISC expanded the "special needs" doctrine allowing an exception to the Fourth Amendment's requirement of a warrant for searches and seizures in the event of imminent danger to the public. Initially applied only to drug testing of railway workers, it was expanded to include terrorism suspects. "It seems like a legal stretch," declared a national security law expert. "It's another way of tilting the scales toward the government in its access to all this data."[101] Thus, only 12 of 34,000 surveillance requests made to the secret court were refused.[102]

The Obama administration defended the program it had inherited from the Bush administration as vital to prevent terrorism, declaring that Congress was aware of it and insisting that the NSA was exercising care in using information it gathered, while admitting that the agency was collecting from companies like Verizon millions of Americans' telephone records, including telephone and calling card numbers, serial numbers of phones, and duration of calls but not content.[103] (The NSA claimed it asked for *detailed* information on only 300 phone numbers among the millions of records surveyed in 2012.) The government was also using an Internet monitoring program called Prism to tap into the servers of nine Internet companies—Microsoft, Yahoo, Google, Facebook, PalTalk, AOL, Skype, YouTube, and Apple[104]—to oversee foreigners' e-mail and online postings. By law these companies could not reveal how many data requests from law enforcement authorities were related to national security.

Leading members of both parties in Congress joined President Obama in defending the NSA and condemning Snowden, and the NSA claimed its surveillance program helped prevent "dozens of potential terrorist plots here in the homeland and in more than 20 countries around the world."[105] The president declared that, unlike his predecessor, his concern had "always been not that we shouldn't do intelligence gathering to prevent terrorism, but rather are we setting up a system of checks and balances?" People should understand that these programs "have disrupted plots, not just here in the United States but overseas as well," thereby "increasing our chances of preventing a catastrophe."[106] NSA director Keith Alexander claimed the surveillance program had prevented "potential terrorist events over 50 times since 9/11," including at least ten "homeland-based threats."[107]

DNI James Clapper argued that "unauthorized disclosure" of the surveillance program "threatens potentially long-lasting and irreversible harm to our ability to identify and respond to the many threats facing our nation," and the program was "designed to facilitate the acquisition of foreign intelligence information concerning non-U.S. persons located outside the United States" and "cannot be used to intentionally target any U.S. citizen, any other U.S. person, or anyone located within the United States."[108] In March 2013, however, in response to Sen. Ron Wyden's (D-OR) question about whether the NSA collected "any type of data on millions or hundreds of millions of Americans?" Clapper responded disingenuously, "No sir. Not wittingly."[109] He later explained that he was constrained about revealing classified information in public.

The revelation triggered a firestorm of criticism by others across the political spectrum. Former vice president Al Gore tweeted, "Is it just me, or is secret blanket surveillance obscenely outrageous?" while Republican senator Rand Paul (R-KY) denounced the surveillance as "an astounding assault on the Constitution"[110] and Vermont's Independent senator, Bernie Sanders, declared, "To simply say in a blanket way that millions and millions of Americans are going to have their phone records checked by the U.S. government is to my mind indefensible and unacceptable."[111] Senators Wyden and Mark Udall (D-CO) proposed legislation requiring that data collection be preceded by a "demonstrated link to terrorism or espionage."[112] Thereafter, the EU demanded assurances that Europeans were not being targeted by the surveillance program. A Gallup Poll indicated that a majority of Americans (53 percent)—especially Republicans (63 percent) and Independents (56 percent)—disapproved of NSA surveillance, while only 37 percent of those questioned approved of it.[113] Other polls indicated that despite their concerns about privacy, Americans viewed the government's data collection effort as necessary to fight terrorism.[114]

The revelations about surveillance should not have been surprising. A 2006 story in *USA Today* had revealed, "The National Security Agency has been secretly collecting the phone call records of tens of millions of Americans, using data provided by AT&T, Verizon and BellSouth,"[115] and journalist Bob Woodward asserted in 2010 that the NSA had developed a "breakthrough eavesdropping capability."[116] Two years later an article in *Wired* described an NSA installation called the Utah Data Center, a "project of immense secrecy," in which the agency could decipher coded information from databases consisting of "all forms of communication, including the complete contents of private emails, cell phone calls, and Google searches, as well as all sorts of personal data trails—parking receipts, travel itineraries, bookstore purchases, and other digital 'pocket litter.'" It also reported that the NSA had "established listening posts throughout the nation to collect and sift through billions of email messages and phone calls, whether they originate within the country or overseas."[117]

After the House of Representatives narrowly voted (217–205) in July 2013 to retain the NSA's domestic phone surveillance program, the Obama administration released previously classified briefing papers to Congress from 2009 and 2011 that described the NSA's collection of "metadata" of domestic phone calls and e-mails of Americans as an "early warning system." "Both of these programs operate on a very large scale," declared one briefing paper, but "only a tiny fraction of such records are ever viewed by NSA intelligence analysts."[118]

Notwithstanding Washington's assertion that the NSA took care to follow the rules for surveillance, John Bates, then chief judge of the FISC, revealed in 2011 that the court was "troubled that the government's revelations regarding NSA's acquisition of Internet transactions mark the third instance in less than three years in which the government has disclosed a substantial misrepresentation regarding the scope of a major collection program."[119] Reacting to Judge Bates's opinion, an NSA critic suggested it "illustrates that the way the court is structured now it cannot serve as an effective check on the NSA because it's wholly dependent on the representations that the NSA makes to it" and "has no ability to investigate."[120]

The Guardian also revealed additional information that Snowden provided about another NSA program called XKeyscore, which "allows analysts to search with no prior authorization through vast databases containing emails, online chats and the browsing histories of millions of individuals," including those of Americans, and that it explained Snowden's claim that sitting at his desk, he could "wiretap anyone, from you or your accountant, to a federal judge or even the president, if I had a personal email."[121] Although the NSA claimed that by 2008 XKeyscore had provided intelligence leading to the capture of 300 terrorists, *The Guardian* declared that "training materials for XKeyscore detail how analysts can use it and other systems to mine enormous agency databases by filling in a simple on-screen form giving only a broad justification for the search. The request is not reviewed by a court or any NSA personnel before it is processed." Thus, "XKeyscore, the documents boast, is the NSA's 'widest reaching' system developing intelligence from computer networks," and "One presentation claims the program covers 'nearly everything a typical user does on the internet', including the content of emails, websites visited and searches, as well as their metadata."[122]

It was also revealed that the NSA had over 61,000 hacking operations worldwide. It had spied on European Union offices and computer networks in America and Europe, including those of the EU's permanent UN mission in New York, and had monitored the phones of thirty-eight embassies and missions, including those of friendly countries like France, Italy, Greece, Japan, South Korea, and India, and thirty-five world leaders, including those of German chancellor Angela Merkel and Brazilian president Dilma Rousseff.[123] Foreign officials and publics were outraged. President Rousseff abruptly canceled her scheduled visit to Washington and argued before the UN General Assembly that "[t]ampering in such a manner in the lives and affairs of other countries is a breach of international law and, as such, it is an affront to the principles that should otherwise govern relations among countries, especially among friendly nations."[124]

Many Americans were also appalled by the extent of NSA surveillance and began to advocate greater privacy protection. Thus, as sections 215, 206, and 6001 were about to expire in 2015, a federal appeals court ruled that the Patriot Act did not allow the collection of bulk telephone metadata (records of length, time, and frequency of calls and who calls whom). Then, over the opposition of Senate hard-liners, Congress passed the USA Freedom Act, ending the NSA's bulk phone data collection. While retaining much of the existing system, including roving wiretaps, it created a less intrusive system that leaves metadata in the hands of phone companies like Verizon and AT&T and requires the government to ask a special court for permission to obtain those data. In addition, the formerly secret Foreign Intelligence Surveillance Court must declassify earlier decisions. President Obama welcomed and signed the new law, chastising those in Congress who had delayed its passage for several days, and claiming that "enactment of this legislation will strengthen civil liberty safeguards and provide greater public confidence in these programs."[125] Nevertheless, Sen. Rand Paul, then a candidate for Republican presidential nomination, denounced the president for continuing "to conduct an illegal program," referring to the decision of the federal appeals court that the original data collection program in the Patriot Act had been legally collected. And shortly later it was revealed that with the president's approval, the NSA had secretly expanded its warrantless surveillance of Americans' international e-mails to hunt for computer hackers—that is, criminals but not suspected terrorists.

HUMAN RIGHTS AND THE WAR ON TERROR

Other consequences of Washington's reaction to 9/11 included a significant rise in anti-Americanism, especially in the Muslim world but also in countries that were U.S. friends and allies. There also was a belief that Washington was acting as a unilateral bully, flouting U.S. and international law by denying "unlawful combatants" the rights of prisoners of war. These included detaining prisoners at Guantánamo Bay, Cuba, for lengthy periods with no trial or constitutional rights, and using torture in interrogations and "extraordinary rendition"—that is, apprehending and transferring suspected terrorists to other countries where they could be imprisoned without trial, interrogated about terrorist plans, and sometimes tortured.

Illegal Combatants

Identification and treatment of combatants posed significant challenges in the effort to balance the need to protect U.S. security and act with regard to human rights. Soldiers fighting for another country's army are considered lawful combatants under international law and are protected by the Geneva Conventions if taken prisoner. Terrorists, according to U.S. officials, who wear no uniform, fight for no recognized authority, and ignore the laws of war are illegal combatants and lack the protection of the Geneva Conventions.

As part of the War on Terror, President Bush signed a presidential finding giving the CIA discretion to detain or kill terrorists wherever they were found, thereby avoiding trying terrorist suspects captured in Afghanistan or elsewhere. Moreover, the White House legal counsel sought a legal framework under which, without prior approval of the president or the Departments of Justice or State, suspects could be held indefinitely without trial in secret locations as "illegal combatants." In 2006 Congress passed the Military Commissions Act giving the president authority to identify "unlawful enemy combatants" who could be tried by military commissions and would not be entitled to prisoner-of-war status and the protection of the Geneva Conventions.[126] "To qualify for protection, a person must wear a uniform, or at least a distinctive sign recognizable at a distance, wear arms openly, be under a proper command, and abide by the rules of the law of war," but "a suspected terrorist, if a civilian of whatever nationality, who does not fulfill the requirements of being a privileged combatant falls altogether *outside the protection of the Geneva Conventions*."[127]

The Supreme Court, however, ruled in 2004 and 2010, respectively, that as U.S. citizens, Yaser Hamdi and José Padilla could not be denied such constitutional rights as seeing an attorney and a prompt and fair trial in a U.S. court. Although the Court upheld a president's right to detain citizens as enemy combatants during a military conflict, such prisoners could challenge the merits of their imprisonment before a neutral fact-finder. The majority opinion also declared that war was not "a blank check" for the government, and "an unchecked system of detention carries the potential to become a means for oppression and abuse of others who do not present that sort of threat."[128] Thereafter, Combatant Status Review Tribunals were established to decide whether individual prisoners were enemy combatants, and an Administrative Review Board was established to recommend whether individual prisoners should be detained, released, or returned to their own countries.

In *Hamdan v. Rumsfeld* (2006), the Supreme Court ruled that military commissions were not "competent tribunals" to try "enemy combatants" and their use violated the prisoner's rights under the Third Geneva Convention, which prohibited "the passing of sentences and the carrying out of executions without previous judgment pronounced by a regularly constituted court affording all the judicial guarantees which are recognized as indispensable by civilized peoples."[129] The Court declared that it made no difference that al-Qaeda—to which Salim Ahmed Hamdan, a Yemeni citizen and former chauffeur of bin Laden, belonged—had not signed the convention, because it applied to individuals in "international conflicts" within states (e.g., Afghanistan) that were signatories. Thus, even those detained as illegal combatants, many of whom were imprisoned without trial in secret CIA prisons, enjoyed protection under the Geneva Conventions.

Extraordinary Rendition and "Black Sites"

Following 9/11 some fifty-four countries participated in the CIA's secret detention and extraordinary rendition programs, allowing the agency to run interrogation prisons in their territory and/or use their airports for refueling while transporting captives.[130] Although "there is a conceptual distinction between secret detention and extraordinary rendition operations, there is little practical difference: both entailed the abduction and disappearance of detainees, their extra-legal transfer on secret flights to undisclosed locations around the world, followed by their incommunicado detention, interrogation, torture, and abuse."[131]

Overseas, CIA prisons or "black sites" circumvented U.S. laws that prohibited holding prisoners in secret in an extrajudicial manner in America. One U.S. official declared: "We don't kick the [expletive] out of them. We send them to other countries so they can kick the [expletive] out of them."[132] Some suspects were initially detained by U.S. agencies, but many were seized by local security personnel at the behest of the CIA or FBI. Although some were held in local prisons, others were detained in covert "black sites" in Afghanistan, Lithuania, Poland, Morocco, Romania, Thailand, and Guantánamo Bay,

Cuba. Among the many countries cooperating with America's extraordinary renditions were Canada, Britain, Italy, and Germany. In 2003 CIA agents abducted a radical Muslim cleric in Milan, Italy, and transferred him to Egypt. In this instance, the CIA agents responsible were tried and convicted in absentia of kidnapping in Italy, and Robert Lady, CIA station chief at the time, was arrested in Panama in 2013 on an international warrant issued by Italy but released shortly afterward and returned to the United States.

Among those seized and held in this manner was Khalid Shaikh Muhammad, described as "the principal architect of the 9/11 attacks" by the 9/11 Commission Report, who was captured in Pakistan in 2003 and interned in Guantánamo Bay. Several captives, however, including Khaled al Masri, who was seized by local authorities in Skopje, Macedonia, were cases of mistaken identity or "erroneous renditions." Masri, a German citizen of Arab descent, was flown to a CIA prison in Afghanistan where he claimed an interrogator told him: "You are here in a country where no one knows about you, in a country where there is no law. If you die, we will bury you, and no one will know."[133] According to a U.S. intelligence officer, the prison system was never part of "a grand strategy" but was instead "very reactive." "That's how you get into a situation where you pick people up, send them into a netherworld and don't say, 'What are we going to do with them afterwards?'"[134]

After President Bush publicly acknowledged America's secret prisons in 2006, pressure grew at home and in Europe to curb their abuses. Congressional hearings were held in April 2007, and in July Sen. Joe Biden (D-DE) introduced legislation to "prohibit extraterritorial detention and rendition," but the bill was not adopted. That same year, Sen. Barack Obama (D-IL), in an article in *Foreign Affairs*, wrote: "To build a better, freer world, we must first behave in ways that reflect the decency and aspirations of the American people. This means ending the practices of shipping away prisoners in the dead of night to be tortured in far-off countries, of detaining thousands without charge or trial, of maintaining a network of secret prisons to jail people beyond the reach of the law."[135] Efforts by victims of extraordinary rendition to have U.S. courts hear their cases failed because presidents invoked the "state secrets privilege" to stop lawsuits.[136]

Although President Obama ordered the closure of CIA "black sites" in 2009, the administration did not end the practice of rendition of suspects to other countries provided they were treated humanely. Two Somalis who were Swedish citizens and a Somali resident of Britain with suspected ties to al-Shabab were arrested in Djibouti in August 2012, questioned by U.S. agents, and transferred to America to stand trial. Nor did the president prevent the CIA from detaining individuals for short periods before they could be transferred elsewhere. However, the issue of detention became less contentious when the administration intensified the campaign of using aerial drones to kill terrorists overseas.

Targeted Killings

Drones can be either "personality" strikes, that is, targeted killings aimed at particular individuals, or "signature" strikes, aimed at suspected terrorists who may not be identified but who "bear the characteristics of al-Qaeda or Taliban leaders on the run."[137] Aided by John Brennan, his counterterrorism advisor who later became CIA director, Obama took personal charge of authorizing the targeted killing of individual terrorists in Pakistan, Somalia, and Yemen. According to President Obama's former chief of staff, William

Daley, the president called his decision to have Anwar al-Awlaki killed by drones based in Saudi Arabia in September 2011 "an easy one."[138] Awlaki, an American citizen in Yemen, was described by Obama as having taken "the lead role in planning and directing the efforts to murder innocent Americans" and "the leader of external operations for al-Qaeda in the Arabian Peninsula,"[139] whose "citizenship should no more serve as a shield than a sniper shooting down on an innocent crowd should be protected from a swat team."[140]

Awlaki had publicly called for attacks against America, and several of the 9/11 hijackers had attended his sermons in the United States. He had also "operationally" aided terrorists like the "underwear bomber," Umar Farouk Abdulmutallab, and the Kouachi brothers responsible for the 2015 massacre at the newspaper *Charlie Hebdo* in Paris; and he had supported a plot to send hidden PETN (pentaeryth-ritol tetranitrate) bombs from Yemen to Chicago in 2010.[141] Awlaki had also been in contact with others, including Nidal Hasan, about whom Awlaki wrote on his Web site, "Fighting against the US army is an Islamic duty today," and the "only way a Muslim could Islamically justify serving as a soldier in the U.S. army is if his intention is to follow the footsteps of men like Nidal."[142]

The president realized that most of these decisions were more difficult to make, leading Daley to con-clude, "He realizes this isn't science. This is judgments made off of, most of the time, human intelligence. The president accepts as a fact that a certain amount of screw-ups are going to happen, and to him, that calls for a more judicious process."[143] As Brennan noted, "The purpose of these actions is to mitigate threats to U.S. persons' lives. It is the option of last recourse. So the president, and I think all of us here, don't like the fact that people have to die. And so he wants to make sure that we go through a rigorous checklist: The infeasibility of capture, the certainty of the intelligence base, the imminence of the threat, all of these things."[144]

Although the drone strikes decimated al-Qaeda's leadership and required a small military presence, they produced a popular backlash in countries that were targeted and among Muslims elsewhere owing to "collateral damage" in which innocent bystanders were sometimes victims. Thus, the Times Square bomber, Faisal Shahzad, told a judge, "When the drones hit, they don't see children."[145] Whether right or wrong, President Obama's resort to drone strikes was a way to reduce the incidence of torture in "black sites" that he had closed.

Torture

The issue of torture became a focus of U.S. concern after photographs taken by soldiers in 2003 show-ing the abuse of prisoners in Iraq's Abu Ghraib prison became public. As a result of the outcry, the Justice Department decided to review how torture was defined in a forty-six-page "Torture Memo" written in 2002 by Assistant Attorney General Jay Bybee to Presidential Counsel Alberto Gonzales to prohibit physical abuse during interrogations. The memo was a response to a CIA request to use "more aggressive" interrogation techniques of terrorist suspects outside America. The memo gave the agency what it sought, declaring that to constitute torture, "Physical pain must be equivalent in intensity to the pain accompanying serious physical injury, such as organ failure, impairment of bodily function, or even death." According to Bybee, even if the president authorized interrogation that could be defined as torture, "in the circumstances of the current war against al-Qaeda and its allies," criminal prose-cution under America's antitorture statute would represent "an unconstitutional infringement of the

President's authority to conduct war."[146] A second memo in December 2004 disavowed torture but in a footnote reiterated the conclusions reached in 2002. Even though coercive interrogation techniques were of dubious value in eliciting useful information, two additional memos in May 2005 reaffirmed the interrogation methods previously authorized, and a third indicated that interrogation methods that had been authorized earlier did not violate the UN Convention against Torture.

According to investigative journalist Seymour Hersh, the torture problem stemmed from a decision by Rumsfeld:

> The roots of the Abu Ghraib prison scandal lie not in the criminal inclinations of a few Army reservists but in a decision, approved last year by Secretary of Defense Donald Rumsfeld, to expand a highly secret operation, which had been focused on the hunt for Al Qaeda, to the interrogation of prisoners in Iraq. Rumsfeld's decision embittered the American intelligence community, damaged the effectiveness of élite combat units, and hurt America's prospects in the war on terror.[147]

A 2008 report by the Senate Armed Services Committee confirmed Secretary Rumsfeld's role in approving "enhanced interrogation techniques." Although the Justice Department declared torture "abhorrent," Gonzales, Vice President Dick Cheney, and Attorney General Michael Mukasey defended the practice of "waterboarding"—a procedure in which water is forced into a captive's mouth and nose to induce the sensation of drowning—as an acceptable "enhanced interrogation technique." President Bush admitted authorizing waterboarding three high-level terrorists.[148] Nevertheless, an internal review ordered by director Leon Panetta in 2009 concluded that the CIA had exaggerated the value of intelligence gained from enhanced interrogation.

Under public pressure Congress passed the Detainee Treatment Act in late 2005 to follow the interrogation standards set in the Army Field Manual, which President Bush threatened to veto because it contained an amendment offered by Sen. John McCain (R-AZ) outlawing "cruel, inhuman and degrading treatment" of suspected terrorists. McCain, who had been tortured while a prisoner of war in North Vietnam, declared: "The image of the United States was very badly harmed by the pictures of prisoner abuse. We have to send a message to the world that we will not ever allow such kind of treatment to be repeated."[149] The president finally signed the bill but issued a "signing statement," declaring he would interpret its language in the context of his constitutional powers as commander in chief. In July 2007 the White House agreed to let the CIA resume several of the interrogation methods used in its secret prisons, asserting these were lawful both under the Third Geneva Convention, which the Supreme Court had ruled was applicable to the War on Terror, and under the Detainee Treatment Act, which barred "cruel, inhuman and degrading treatment" of anyone in American custody, whether within or outside America. In May 2006 President Bush announced that fourteen of the detainees held in "black sites" had been sent to Guantánamo Bay, where representatives of the International Committee of the Red Cross (ICRC) could visit them and, if accused of a crime, would have access to defense lawyers. In subsequent interviews with the ICRC, the detainees claimed they had indeed been tortured while in CIA prisons.

Distancing himself from the policies of the Bush administration, President Obama in January 2009 issued an executive order intended to "improve the effectiveness of human intelligence gathering, to promote the safe, lawful, and humane treatment of individuals in United States custody and of United States personnel who are detained in armed conflicts, to ensure compliance with the treaty obligations of the United States, including the Geneva Conventions."[150] The executive order required that individuals "shall in all circumstances be treated humanely and shall not be subjected to violence to life and person (including murder of all kinds, mutilation, cruel treatment, and torture), nor to outrages upon personal dignity (including humiliating and degrading treatment), whenever such individuals are in the custody or under the effective control of an officer, employee, or other agent of the United States Government or detained within a facility owned, operated, or controlled by a department or agency of the United States."[151] It also required U.S. officials to ensure that individuals transferred to other countries be treated humanely.

In late 2014, after five years of investigation, the Senate Select Committee on Intelligence released the executive summary of a blistering 600-page report. It concluded that the CIA had not properly overseen what its interrogators were doing, had not revealed how brutal its interrogations were, had underreported the number of suspects it tortured, had misled both Congress and the White House about interrogation techniques, had wrongfully detained suspects, and had overstated the information gained by "enhanced interrogation." Moreover, CIA personnel who objected to the use of torture were routinely overruled.[152] The committee chair, Sen. Dianne Feinstein (D-CA), declared that although the CIA was under pressure to prevent another terrorist attack, "such pressure, fear and expectation of other terrorist plots do not justify, temper or excuse improper actions taken by individuals or organizations in the name of national security" and "the intelligence community's actions must always reflect who we are as a nation, and adhere to our laws and standards."[153] Although George W. Bush and Dick Cheney denounced the report and several conservative Republicans objected to revealing details that might incite violence against Americans, President Obama supported its release. Moscow and Beijing used the occasion to suggest that the report revealed Washington's hypocrisy regarding human rights.

During the following year, it was revealed that a number of psychologists in the American Psychological Association, including its ethics director, had refused to condemn CIA interrogation techniques as torture. A report written by a team at the request of the psychological association concluded that the association's ethics office had "prioritized the protection of psychologists—even those who might have behaved in unethical behavior—above the protection of the public,"[154] and the team's authors had sought to ingratiate themselves with CIA and Pentagon officials by doing so.

Guantánamo Bay: "Un-American by Any Name"

In January 2002 the Bush administration established a camp consisting of three facilities (one later closed) at Guantánamo Bay to hold enemy combatants captured in Afghanistan and elsewhere at a site outside the United States and therefore not in U.S. legal jurisdiction. The facility at Guantánamo Bay, leased in perpetuity to Washington by Cuba in 1903 and reaffirmed in a 1934 treaty, has long been a focus for criticism of U.S. policies.[155] Based on the Military Commissions Act, a federal appeals court ruled against lawsuits filed on behalf of Guantánamo detainees who were demanding hearings in an American court, where they would enjoy U.S. constitutional guarantees. However, in a 5–4 decision, the Supreme Court ruled in *Boumediene v. Bush* (2008) that Guantánamo detainees were protected by the

Constitution and had the right to appeal to U.S. civilian courts to challenge their detention. Based on this decision, several prisoners successfully sought their release.

Whether to keep the Guantánamo Bay detention camp open remained controversial. Human-rights groups like Amnesty International and Human Rights Watch; organizations like the UN, the EU, and the Organization of American States; and leaders of America's European allies have criticized the Guantánamo internments. In 2004 the ICRC confirmed the use of torture at Guantánamo, a charge denied by the Defense Department. But, according to former president Jimmy Carter, "American authorities have revealed that, in order to obtain confessions, some of the few being tried (only in military courts) have been tortured by waterboarding more than 100 times or intimidated with semiautomatic weapons, power drills or threats to sexually assault their mothers."[156] Of the most important prisoners, three had been convicted by a military court, and eight had been charged under the Military Commissions Act that was declared unconstitutional in 2008. Of the roughly 800 detainees in Guantánamo, most had been released or sent to other countries by spring 2011, and 6 had committed suicide. One problem was that some 20 countries that were asked to give detainees asylum refused to do so, leaving detainees with nowhere to be released. "We are aggressively reaching out to a wide variety of countries," said a State Department spokesperson. "The support of our friends and allies is critical to achieving our goal of reducing the detainee population and ultimately closing the detention facility."[157]

Over the years, the status of Guantánamo became increasingly controversial as demands grew that the camp be closed and its prisoners either freed or tried in U.S. courts. In January 2009 President Obama suspended the proceedings of the Guantánamo military commission for 120 days, but the order was reversed by a military judge. Obama also ordered that the facility be closed within the year, and in his 2009 Cairo speech, he declared that "Just as America can never tolerate violence by extremists, we must never alter our principles. 9/11 was an enormous trauma to our country. The fear and anger that it provoked was understandable, but in some cases, it led us to act contrary to our ideals. We are taking concrete actions to change course. I have unequivocally prohibited the use of torture by the United States, and I have ordered the prison at Guantánamo Bay closed by early next year."[158]

Nevertheless, Guantánamo remained open. Indeed, the Obama administration sought to limit lawyers' access to detainees but was rebuffed in a 2012 judicial decision because such limits would impede detainees' access to the courts. Declared Judge Royce Lambeth: "The government wants to place itself as the sole arbiter of when a habeas petitioner is 'seeking' to challenge their own detention and when a habeas case is 'impending,' and thus when they can have access to counsel. But access to the Court means nothing without access to counsel." "Had, for example, the Obama administration closed the Guantánamo Bay detention facility as it promised," added the judge, "the court's protective order would no longer have any effect."[159] As of late 2015 the Obama administration had not shut down the facility, and his secretaries of defense, Chuck Hagel and Ashton B. Carter, had made few decisions to transfer individual detainees to other countries.[160]

Few detainees have been tried, and some for whom there were no plans to charge or who were to be released remained in detention because the administration contended it did not know what to do with detainees for whom there was insufficient evidence to use in a civilian or military court, or to whom other countries would not grant asylum. Moreover, there was strong domestic opposition to moving detainees to maximum-security U.S. prisons or try them in U.S. courts because, as former FBI director

Robert Mueller told Congress, "concerns we have about individuals who may support terrorism being in the United States run from concerns about providing financing, radicalizing others," and "the potential for individuals undertaking attacks in the United States."[161] "The American people don't want these men walking the streets of America's neighborhoods," declared Sen. John Thune (R-SD) and "don't want these detainees held at a military base or federal prison in their backyard, either."[162] Congress refused to fund closing Guantánamo in the absence of an acceptable plan to release or transfer detainees.

An effort by the administration to move Guantánamo detainees to a prison in Illinois failed in the face of congressional objections, and in 2011 Congress again voted not to permit moving detainees to the United States and prevent their transfer to countries "unless specified conditions are met" that, according to President Obama, "would hinder the conduct of delicate negotiations with foreign countries and therefore the effort to conclude detainee transfers in accord with our national security."[163] Thereafter, the president authorized a resumption of military trials that comply with the Geneva Conventions, and, on signing the National Defense Authorization Act for Fiscal Year 2012, he reiterated his objections to congressional renewal of "the bar against using appropriated funds for fiscal year 2012 to transfer Guantánamo detainees into the United States for any purpose. I continue to oppose this provision, which intrudes upon critical executive branch authority to determine when and where to prosecute Guantánamo detainees, based on the facts and the circumstances of each case and our national security interests."[164] In November 2012 Congress again voted against transferring prisoners to U.S. facilities.

Guantánamo's closure had not begun when most detainees embarked on a hunger strike in February 2013 to protest their indefinite detention. The strike continued for months as authorities force-fed some through a greased nasal tube, a procedure the president of the American Medical Association argues violates the "core ethical values of the medical profession."[165] In May 2013 the administration created a new Pentagon position to facilitate the transfer of detainees for whom transfer had been approved if they posed no further danger, and named an attorney as the State Department's special envoy to close the camp. By 2016, after several prisoners were sent to Slovakia, Georgia, Uruguay, Kazakhstan, Oman, the United Arab Emirates, and Afghanistan, only 93 detainees remained in Guantánamo, 34 of whom were cleared for release if other countries accept them.[166]

CONCLUSION: AN EVOLVING THREAT

After coming to office, President Obama ended American intervention in Iraq and began the process of removing U.S. forces from Afghanistan (though deciding in October 2015 to keep 5,500 U.S. troops there until the end of his term). He also led an intensive campaign against al-Qaeda, killing Osama bin Laden and containing regional terrorist groups. In addition, the president repeatedly sought authorization to close the Guantánamo detainment camp and committed himself publicly to ending controversial anti-terrorist policies of the Bush administration. The jihadist threat to America and American interests has not ended. Indeed, in some respects the threat has grown again with the spread of ISIS in Iraq, Syria, and elsewhere, and its growing overseas terrorist activities. In the following chapter we examine outstanding issues and policy alternatives available to Washington.

8

An End to the War on Terror?

Chapter 8 examines alternative policies for Washington in approaching issues involved in the War on Terror. Although President Barack Obama declared the conflict at an end in May 2013, in some respects it has intensified, especially with the establishment of a caliphate by the Islamic State. Is the War on Terror over? To what extent do militant jihadist groups still pose a threat to the United States? Will American intervention in Iraq and Syria reduce the threat of terrorism, or will problems in those countries continue to fester and pose new threats to American interests? What are America's future policy options in the struggle against Islamic radicalism, and what are their relative costs and benefits? This chapter examines policy options for the following issues:

- How to deal with al-Qaeda and its regional affiliates in the Middle East, Africa, and Asia such as al-Qaeda in the Arabian Peninsula, al-Shabab, al-Qaeda in the Land of the Islamic Maghreb, and Boko Haram.

- How to cope with the threat posed by the Islamic State (ISIS).

- How to manage the terrorist threat posed by "lone wolves."

- Whether to provide Americans with greater privacy from government surveillance resulting from the War on Terror.

- How to deal with human-rights concerns raised by the War on Terror, ranging from targeted drone strikes to the use of torture.

- Whether to transform the War on Terror into an issue of law enforcement.

In May 2013 President Obama in a speech at the National Defense University in Washington, D.C., recalled, "With the collapse of the Berlin Wall, a new dawn of democracy took hold abroad, and a decade of peace and prosperity arrived at home. For a moment, it seemed the 21st century would be a tranquil time. Then, on September 11th 2001, we were shaken out of complacency. . . . And so our nation went to war." He then added, "We have now been at war for well over a decade," and concluded that "our systematic effort to dismantle terrorist organizations must continue. But this war, like all wars, must end. That's what history advises. That's what our democracy demands."[1]

To this end the president asked Congress to repeal the "Authorization to Use Military Force" that it passed after 9/11 to provide a legal basis for the War on Terror. He also justified his use of drones (though only against those shown to pose a threat to Americans), again called on Congress to close down the Guantánamo detainment camp, and again rejected the use of torture in interrogating terrorist suspects. In fact, the president's use of drones and his failure to close down Guantánamo continued to enjoy public support in America.[2] What really mattered was that the president was declaring an end to the War on Terror, and in doing so hoped to raise the country's moral stature in the eyes of foreign observers.

Although generally well received, Obama's speech was criticized on the one hand by civil libertarians who thought the president did not sufficiently restrict the use of drones, and on the other by congressional Republicans who saw no reason to alter the way drones were used, believed the Guantánamo facility should remain open, and thought declaring an end to the War on Terror was premature. One conservative Republican senator declared, "This is the most tone-deaf president I ever could imagine, making such a speech at a time when our homeland is trying to be attacked [sic] literally every day."[3] To preclude charges of being weak toward terrorists, the president responded, "Ask Osama bin Laden and the 22 out of 30 Al Qaeda leaders who've been taken off the field whether I engage in appeasement."[4] In reality, as one observer argued, the president's speech portended "few concrete changes," and its "main aims were to conserve the arc of the secret war that Obama has presided over and to help deflect responsibility for the inherited problems that he has been unable to fix."[5] What is clear is that America's struggle against terrorism is far from over, and President Obama's commitment of American airpower in Iraq and Syria in 2014 reflects this fact.

AL-QAEDA AND ITS REGIONAL AFFILIATES

The death of Osama bin Laden was a major factor in the erosion of al-Qaeda's capabilities that began after 9/11. Its current leaders may inspire and even advise others, but al-Qaeda no longer has the capabilities it had in 2001. The ending of America's wars in Afghanistan (in 2017) and Iraq eliminated key sources for rallying al-Qaeda followers with the shared narrative that Washington is at war with Islam, although both Iraq and Afghanistan run the risk of becoming terrorist sanctuaries again. Brokering a peace between Israel and the Palestinians would also reduce the attraction of militant jihadism.

Increasingly, the terrorist danger became decentralized and the challenges became more localized and diffuse. Most groups pursued local objectives, but as we have seen, several posed a danger to American interests. Overall, U.S. counterterrorist operations and drone strikes were directed principally at jihadists in Somalia, Yemen, and North Africa, and away from Afghanistan and Pakistan as the U.S.–NATO presence in Afghanistan wound down. Nevertheless, al-Qaeda remained dangerous, a fact brought home by a wave of prison breaks in Iraq, Pakistan, and Libya in July 2013 that the group may have coordinated to free its operatives; the closure of U.S. diplomatic posts across the Middle East and North Africa in August 2013; and the issuing of a worldwide travel alert for Americans owing to "credible threats" that we noted earlier.

U.S. surveillance drones operated from Niger in North Africa and Djibouti in East Africa, aiding weak governments in Mali, Somalia, Libya, Niger, Mauritania, and elsewhere to resist jihadist violence, and American Special Operations troops were training counterterrorism forces in Libya, Niger, Mauretania, and Mali. Oil-rich Nigeria is beset by Boko Haram, and Islamic extremists have appeared along Africa's east coast in Kenya, Tanzania, and Mozambique. In addition to older militant groups like Hezbollah, Hamas, Islamic Jihad, the Abu Nidal Organization, the Popular Front for the Liberation of Palestine, the Popular Front for the Liberation of Palestine–General Command, and al-Qaeda in Iraq, the Middle East witnessed a proliferation of individual jihadists and jihadi groups spawned by the Arab Spring in Syria, Libya, Egypt, and elsewhere. In Asia, in the Philippines, Pakistan, Indonesia, and Malaysia, militant Islamic groups remain dangerous. Finally, in Europe, North America, Russia, and even China, angry individuals or small groups seduced by online propaganda or extremist clerics have gone overseas for terrorist training, have joined groups like al-Shabab in Somalia or ISIS in Syria and Iraq, or have plotted violence at home.

Policy Options

Policy options for the United States in dealing with the remnants of al-Qaeda and its regional and local sympathizers are not clearly etched because of local differences in these groups and because the threats they pose to Americans and American interests vary.

a. *Respond to al-Qaeda affiliates vigorously by stationing units of U.S. Special Forces and drone bases overseas, where they can respond to terrorist threats and actions, aiding and training local security personnel, and sanctioning countries that facilitate al-Qaeda or its affiliates.* This robust policy would reduce the global terrorist threat and strengthen links with friendly governments. It would, however, entail a significant commitment of American resources during a time of declining budgets and war weariness at home, spread American forces thinly, and continue the War on Terror. It might also place Washington in the position of helping dictators in countries like Uzbekistan that are faced by jihadist threats.

b. *Tailor U.S. involvement to fit the level of importance of different threats.* Americans are probably at greatest risk from disaffected Muslims at home, especially those influenced by the Islamic State. Indeed, that is a principal reason for the proliferation of surveillance in homeland security. Thus, al-Qaeda in the Arabian Peninsula (AQAP) poses a threat to the American homeland, while the presence of ISIS in Syria and Iraq generated support for Syrian president Bashar al-Assad and led to the establishment of a transnational and extremist regional Sunni "caliphate." ISIS and groups like al-Shabab and Boko Haram may pose future threats to America's homeland, while AQAP is already trying to attack America directly. However, today's most important threats may not be tomorrow's. A strategy that focuses on "less important" threats may fail to anticipate emerging dangers, especially those posed by new nonstate actors.

c. *Rely to a greater extent on American allies and regional friends.* This is an option that can be combined with either of the first two alternatives. NATO's role in Afghanistan lent legitimacy to that conflict that was missing in America's intervention in Iraq, and NATO's involvement in the 2011 Libyan civil war allowed Washington to limit its role to imposing diplomatic and economic sanctions, logistical assistance, enforcement of a no-fly zone, and bombing missions to protect anti-Qaddafi insurgents and civilians. A light American military "footprint" in support of French intervention in Mali in 2013 also proved politically popular at home and abroad. The United States could continue providing arms and training local security forces in counterterrorism in the Middle East, East and Southeast Asia, and the Horn of Africa and North Africa.

ISIS terrorists
in Iraq

Reuters/Diaa Al-Din

ISLAMIC STATE

Although the war in Iraq ended, that country failed to achieve political stability after America's with-drawal. Sectarian strife persisted even as President Nuri al-Maliki became increasingly authoritarian and excluded Sunnis from positions of authority. ISIS had already seized large areas in Syria from rival jihad-ists and moderate foes of the Assad government when it returned to Iraq. As ISIS advanced deeper into Iraq's "Sunni Triangle," Kurdish forces took advantage of the invasion to seize control of the disputed oil-rich city of Kirkuk, thereby emphasizing their region's autonomy, and reasserted the right to sell oil in their region without the agreement of Iraq's central government until a compromise was reached in late 2014. Despite Secretary John Kerry's appeal that they help unite the country, the Kurds and their president, Masoud Barzani, also assumed the trappings of statehood in Erbil, their capital city. Maliki's Shia-dominated government also moved closer to Shia Iran and claimed it was unable to stop Iranian arms shipments to the Assad government in Syria or prevent Shia Iraqis from going to Syria to aid Assad.

Policy Options

a. *Avoid involvement in Iraq and Syria.* President Obama successfully extricated American forces from Iraq and refused to use force in Syria even after the Assad regime used poison gas against its citi-zens. Following the ISIS offensive in Iraq that resulted in its capture of Mosul and other cities, and the threat it posed to Iraq's Kurds, the Obama administration made it clear that additional American support depended on Iraq's Shia-dominated government taking steps to empower Sunni and Kurdish politicians and giving their communities equal responsibility for the country's future. Thus, Washington was involved in bringing about Maliki's replacement. "There is no military solution that will solve Iraq's problems," declared the White House press secretary, "which is why we've been urgently pressing Iraq's leaders across the political spectrum to govern in a nonsectarian manner, to promote stability and unity among Iraq's diverse populations, to address the legitimate grievances of Iraq's Sunni, Kurd and Shia communities, and build and invest in the capacity of Iraq's security forces."[6]

Although willing to let the president authorize air strikes against ISIS after Maliki's removal, Congress and the American public would probably resist committing significant ground forces in those countries even in the face of the challenge posed by ISIS. Thus, it may be tempting for Washington to limit U.S. involvement in Iraq and Syria and allow violence there to continue. The violence in these countries, however, threatens to spill over into neighboring Lebanon, Jordan, and Turkey, and trigger sectarian Sunni–Shia violence across the region. A "hands-off" policy would probably exacerbate political instability throughout the Middle East, and ISIS could become a direct threat to American interests in the region and beyond in the coming years.

b. *Intervene unconditionally against ISIS.* Although terrorist attacks in Paris and California moved some Americans to change their minds, public opinion and Congress, as we noted, would oppose large-scale U.S. intervention in Iraq or Syria. President Obama tacitly recognized his error in describing ISIS as a "jayvee" team (in terms of terrorism) in an interview published in January 2014, when he agreed to U.S. air strikes against ISIS in Iraq and Syria later that year. Committing large ground forces, however, would be a political minefield for the president, who declared, "We're not going to allow ourselves to be dragged back into a situation in which, while we're there, we're keeping a lid on things."[8] However, air strikes without Iraqi and Syrian ground forces will not defeat ISIS, although they may impede its advance. Therefore, defending his policies, President Obama seemed to up the ante in December 2014 when he declared, "Our coalition isn't just going to degrade this barbarous terrorist organization, we're going to destroy it."[9] Although American leaders made it clear they regarded the prospect of either a victory by radical Sunni insurgents associated with ISIS or continued civil war in Iraq and Syria as inimical to U.S. interests, they recognized that Iraq's Shia-dominated government would find it difficult to keep the country united or defeat ISIS, and that Washington alone could not bring peace to Syria.

Large-scale intervention would necessarily lead to another asymmetric conflict in which Americans may be fighting an elusive enemy that uses terrorism and guerrilla tactics, replicating U.S. experiences in the Vietnam War, in Afghanistan after 2001, and in Iraq after 2003—conflicts in which brute conventional force failed. Even worse, it would mean intervening in civil wars in failed states. Military historian Andrew J. Bacevich is probably correct in concluding that "the lessons of these failures" tend to be forgotten because Americans cling "to the illusion that because we have a splendid military, putting it to work will make things come out all right in the end." Bacevich also argues that even if ISIS were destroyed, "a similar organization will likely arise in its place, much as ISIS emerged to take the place of Al Qaeda in Iraq."[10] Bacevich's view is similar to President Obama's.

In addition, unconditional intervention by the United States in Iraq and Syria would seem to fulfill Islamic prophecies cited by ISIS of an apocalyptic battle in Dabiq and al-Amaq in northern Syria against Western invaders before Islam's final triumph. Declared a French academic specialist on the Middle East, Jean-Pierre Filiu, "I have said it repeatedly: Because of these prophecies, going in on the ground would be the worst trap to fall into. They [ISIS] want troops on the ground." He added, "It's a very powerful and emotional narrative. It gives the potential recruit and the actual fighters the feeling that not only are they part of the elite, they are also part of the final battle."[11]

c. *Limit intervention in Iraq and Syria.* American air strikes, combined with Special Operations to provide intelligence and advisors to begin rebuilding Iraq's army and train moderate Syrian insurgents in Saudi Arabia, may repel ISIS's advance. Some of the small force of Special Operations troops are now permitted to conduct raids, free hostages, and eliminate or capture ISIS leaders. U.S. intervention, however, had to avoid appearing anti-Sunni, and without Sunni allies on the ground it would not defeat ISIS. Antiwar Democrats in Congress were wary of military involvement, while Republicans like Sen. John McCain and House Speaker John Boehner criticized American air strikes as insufficient to meet the ISIS threat. Boehner commented, "Like many Americans, I am dismayed by the ongoing absence of a strategy for countering the grave threat ISIS poses to the region."[12]

d. *Cooperate with Russia in fighting ISIS.* Russia, as noted in an earlier chapter, intervened in Syria militarily in late September 2015 and justified its air strikes as directed against terrorists. In fact, its major objective was to prop up the Syrian government of Bashar al-Assad, as well as possibly reduce friction with the West over Ukraine.[13] Initially, most of its attacks were directed at Sunni groups supported by the United States, and the gap between Western and Russian perceptions of Assad seemed insurmountable. Despite an agreement to share information that would reduce the likelihood of accidents involving U.S. and Russian manned aircraft and drones over Syria, there was little mutual trust between Washington and Moscow regarding Syria. Two atrocities involving ISIS, however, altered Western and Russian views to some extent about possible cooperation: the bombing of a Russian passenger plane in Egypt and the massacre in Paris, both in late 2015. After the latter, French president François Hollande journeyed to Washington and Moscow in an effort to promote a coalition against the Islamic State. Nevertheless, the prospects for genuine cooperation remain unclear. As former deputy secretary of state Strobe Talbott said, "Maybe it's getting through to them. They keep talking about being part of a solution. But they talk the talk of being part of the solution and they walk the walk of being part of the problem."[14]

Following coalition air strikes in late 2014, Kurds, Shia militias, and some Sunni tribes joined the fight against ISIS, which could no longer concentrate or move fighters in large groups. "The airstrikes have been very helpful, and now the ISIS fighters are confused and don't know where to go,"[15] declared an Iraqi police chief. In November, President Obama authorized the dispatch of 1,500 additional troops to Iraq, doubling the American presence, and said he would ask Congress for $5 billion for military operations against ISIS, including $1.6 billion to train and equip Iraq's army. Iraqi officials publicly welcomed U.S. security cooperation and assistance to deal with the country's continued violence, and Iraq sought U.S. personnel to help train Iraqi security forces to cope with terrorism and limit the spillover of additional violence to and from neighboring Syria.

"LONE WOLVES"

"Lone wolves" pose a particularly difficult terrorist challenge. Surveillance at home and abroad has provided valuable intelligence, but the challenge will grow as Western jihadists return from Iraq and Syria.

"ISIS' stunning battlefield victories lent the organization credibility and enhanced its allure for the small but important Western community of young radicals it seeks to court."[16] Some observers believe we "can expect that Westerners currently in Iraq and Syria will continue to commit atrocities abroad and will come home and attempt some kind of terrorist plot."[17] Not all agree. According to two analysts, "the vast majority of Western Muslims who set out to fight in the Middle East today will not come back as terrorists. Many of them will never go home at all, instead dying in combat or joining in new military campaigns elsewhere, or they will return disillusioned and not interested in bringing the violence with them."[18] Nevertheless, the murder of fourteen Americans in San Bernardino, California, by two radicalized Muslims in December 2015 led Jeh Johnson, the U.S. secretary of homeland security, to declare, "We have moved to an entirely new phase in the global terrorist threat and in our homeland security efforts." Alluding to ISIS, he added that terrorists have "in effect outsourced attempts to attack our homeland. We've seen this not just here but in other places. This requires a whole new approach, in my view."[19]

Policy Options

Americans enjoy freedom to travel around the world except where such travel is expressly prohibited. The State Department advised Americans not to travel to Iraq except when it was "essential" and noted that "travel within Iraq remains dangerous given the security situation."[20] The State Department also advised Americans to leave Syria as soon as possible and reminded "U.S. citizens that the security situation remains volatile and unpredictable as a civil war between government and armed anti-government groups continues throughout the country, along with an increased risk of kidnappings, bombings, murder, and terrorism."[21] Nevertheless, over 100 Americans have gone or tried to go to Syria since its civil war began in 2011.

It is not illegal for Americans to travel to these countries; nor is it illegal for them to fight in another country's army unless they are fighting against America, which would be treason. It is, however, illegal for Americans to fight for a "foreign terrorist organization." Americans who do so may also be prosecuted for "providing material support to terrorists," "providing material support or resources to designated terrorist organizations," "conspiracies to engage in violence against people or property overseas," "terrorist attacks against United States nationals," or "receiving military-type training from a foreign terrorist organization."[22]

a. *Prevent American citizens from travelling to Iraq or Syria.* American jihadist sympathizers become more dangerous if persuaded by radical clerics or jihadist propaganda to travel overseas to join violent extremists. Merely criminalizing travel to Iraq, Syria, or other terrorist sites, however, is likely to have little impact. Travel to Cuba was illegal for decades, but the law has been easily evaded by first traveling to third countries. Individuals wanting to travel to Iraq or Syria have done the same, in particular via Turkey. Sharing data with Turkey about potential American jihadists would be valuable. Even more effective would be an effort to mobilize clerics and parents in Muslim communities to dissuade potential jihadists from joining extremist groups. Thus, the parents of an American who knew their son had travelled to Syria, where he died as a suicide bomber, failed to notify U.S. authorities of his journey: "They didn't notify law enforcement and now their son is dead," said a U.S. official. "You have to get involved early—the results may not be pleasant, but it's better than having a dead son."[23]

A more robust approach was the effort to use surveillance and informants to identify individuals who are in contact with foreign terrorists and expressed a desire to join or aid terrorist groups. The FBI arrested a young man in Chicago who told an undercover agent he intended to join the Nusra Front, and he was charged with "attempting to provide material support to a foreign terrorist organization."[24] To arrest such individuals the government must show they intend to help a terrorist group.

b. *Seek to capture or kill Americans fighting for a foreign terrorist organization.* If Americans who have joined terrorist groups fail to return home, it would be possible in some cases to locate and capture them, or even kill them. Anwar al-Awlaki, an American citizen and a senior operative in AQAP, was the victim of a targeted U.S. drone strike in Yemen in September 2011. Awlaki had been in contact with the Fort Hood gunman, Nidal Hassan; had helped prepare Umar Farouk Abdulmutallab for his effort to blow up a Detroit-bound airliner; and had met with Chérif and Said Kouachi, who later killed twelve people in Paris. Although Awlaki had not been tried in a court of law, the Obama administration justified his death because he was fighting for al-Qaeda and was an "imminent threat" to U.S. security.

The justification was, however, vigorously criticized by civil rights advocates and was the subject of a thirteen-hour filibuster in the Senate by Rand Paul against the Obama administration's nomination of John Brennan as CIA director. An alternative to "bringing the most hardened Western foreign fighters to justice would require their capture and rendition on a large scale,"[25] a practice that was criticized as a human-rights abuse. In addition, Pakistan's arrest of a suspected terrorist and U.S. citizen, Mohanad Al Farekh, and his extradition to the United States to stand trial in April 2015—only months after Washington contemplated a drone strike to kill him—revived the issue of whether it was necessary to resort to targeted killings of U.S. citizens overseas.

c. *Counter jihadist propaganda and prevent individuals from trying to attack American interests.* "The Internet," writes journalist Peter Bergen, "has had as great an impact on Holy War, Inc. as it has on many other concerns."[26] Thus, the online Global Islamic Media Front advised viewers to attack Spain just months before the 2004 bombings in Madrid, and *Inspire* provided a hit list of anti-Muslim Westerners before the murderous 2015 attack on the Paris office of the satirical newspaper *Charlie Hebdo*. And on the anniversary of the 9/11 attacks in 2013, Zawahiri, bin Laden's successor as leader of al-Qaeda, released an audio speech on the Internet calling on Muslims to launch "a few disparate attacks" on American territory by "lone wolves" like the Boston Marathon bombers, and to "bleed America economically" by provoking the United States "to continue in its massive expenditure on its security."[27]

d. *Disrupt the use by terrorists of social media to seduce Americans and others in the West to commit acts of violence at home or aid groups like the Islamic State.* ISIS, writes Jared Cohen, is the first terrorist group "to hold both physical and digital territory" and "dominates pockets of the Internet with relative impunity." To combat this reality, he recommends "digital counterinsurgency" "to marginalize the Islamic State online."[28] Although ISIS ridicules such efforts,[29] Cohen provides a complex strategy that would require cooperation among governments, tech companies, and international organizations. He describes how such cooperation would need to "separate the human-run accounts on social networks from the automated ones"; "zero in on the Islamic State's digital central command, identifying and suspending the specific accounts responsible for setting strategy, and giving orders to the rest of its online army"; and, finally, "push the remaining rank and file into the digital equivalent of a remote cave."[30]

In an effort to counter jihadi media directed at recruiting Americans, the State Department's Center for Strategic Counterterrorism Communications began a program in December 2013 aimed at discouraging potential young, English-speaking jihadists on English-language Web sites and social media like Facebook, YouTube, and Twitter. Social media are used by ISIS to make susceptible young Americans feel like they are part of a community. Ali Amin, a teenager in Virginia, noted, "For the first time, I felt I was not only being taken seriously about very important and weighty topics, but was actually being asked for guidance."[31] Referring to jihadist sites, Alberto Fernandez, the center's coordinator, declared, "They were setting the narrative and had a free shot at the audience for radicalizing people," and "Nobody was calling them" on it.[32] Richard Stengl, a former *Time* editor who became undersecretary of state for public diplomacy, described meeting Arab officials to establish "a communicational coalition, a messaging coalition, to complement what's going on the ground."[33]

e. *Investigate and maintain surveillance on citizens returning from Iraq or Syria.* Surveillance of social media like Facebook and Twitter can identify at least some of those who have returned from war zones as well as provide information about friends and sympathizers. It may also help facilitate counseling for returnees to prevent their carrying out terrorist acts at home and reintegrating them into society. The necessary surveillance, however, raises the controversial issue of government invasion of individual privacy.

SURVEILLANCE

The surveillance of telephone calls, e-mails, and Internet activity of Americans and non-Americans by the NSA as disclosed by Edward Snowden poses additional dilemmas for Washington. Several options exist, but none is entirely satisfactory.

Policy Options

a. *Continue operating the same way as before Snowden's revelations.* Domestic surveillance is controversial but to some extent necessary for homeland security. American officials need to identify and monitor returning jihadists as well as individuals with the potential to become "lone wolves." However, this risks alienating growing numbers of Americans and American legislators who are uneasy about a program that violates their privacy and may violate the Constitution's Fourth Amendment protection against unreasonable search and seizure by their government. It also would anger many citizens in friendly countries in Europe who deeply value their privacy (even though their governments have benefited from intelligence collected by the NSA and by their own intelligence agencies). Following the massacres in Paris and San Bernardino, politicians in Europe and the United States began to reverse themselves and demand intensified intelligence surveillance of potential terrorists. Republican presidential candidates Marco Rubio, Jeb Bush, Chris Christie, and Lindsey

Graham spoke of eliminating restrictions placed on the NSA by the 2015 USA Freedom Act, which limited its collection of phone data.

b. *Maintain NSA surveillance programs but make their procedures more transparent and subject to greater scrutiny by courts and officials accountable to the public to safeguard individual privacy.* The present system is highly classified, and it is unclear how the secret FISA Court operates and what the criteria are for demanding that companies like Verizon turn over records, or for identifying specific groups and individuals for surveillance of the content of their communications. President Obama alluded to these concerns when he referred to the "instinctive bias of the intelligence community to keep everything very close," and declared, "Let's just put the whole elephant out there, and examine what's working."[34] Thus, it has been suggested that the appointment of judges to the FISA Court, currently made by the chief justice of the Supreme Court, should be made by the president in a transparent way, and that the procedure the FISA Court uses to authorize surveillance should be clarified.

If limitations are too strict, however, crucial information may be unavailable—an argument Senate Republicans used in November 2014 to defeat a bill that would have limited NSA collection of telephone metadata from U.S. phone companies. The importance of information collected by the NSA was shown by the intercept of messages between al-Qaeda and AQAP in August 2013 that led to the widespread closure of U.S. diplomatic posts around the world. It is unclear how much information can be made public without endangering security against terrorism like the 9/11 attacks, the murder of the U.S. ambassador to Libya in Benghazi in 2012, or the al-Qaeda plot to bomb the New York City subway—the world's largest public transportation system—just before the eighth anniversary of 9/11. Thus, the president was vigorously criticized for the lack of forewarning of the events in Benghazi, and the political backlash against the U.S. government would be enormous if a plot such as that against the New York subway succeeded and was attributed to inadequate intelligence.

c. *Close down the NSA programs and require law enforcement officials to follow the same procedures and rules they had in the past for acquiring warrants to listen in on specific individuals.* This shift would reduce public concerns about privacy, and suspects would be granted additional rights under U.S. law, the Constitution, or the Geneva Conventions. It might complicate the government's ability to obtain accurate and timely intelligence about some terrorist planning. However, it would enhance America's "soft power" ("the ability to get what you want through attraction rather than through coercion or payments"[35]), which was reduced by America's 2003 intervention in Iraq, and its propensity to act unilaterally in the War on Terror. While desirable from the perspective of protecting the civil rights of individuals and ensuring the privacy of most Americans and non-Americans, this option is probably inadequate for protecting the public here and abroad from technologically resourceful and dedicated terrorist groups.

HUMAN RIGHTS: DRONE STRIKES

For the most part, Washington has forsworn activities like torture and extraordinary rendition that most offend human-rights activists. Targeted drone strikes, however, continue, and they remain controversial. They are a form of assassination, and they are alleged to result in the deaths of innocent victims that produce negative reactions in countries like Yemen, Somalia, and Pakistan—claims that are both hotly contested.[36]

Policy Options

a. *End such strikes.* Doing so, however, would eliminate a crucial military asset in regions where there is a diminishing or nonexistent U.S. military presence. Such strikes reduce the likelihood that terrorist groups will take control of large areas and operate openly in countries that are failed or failing states.

b. *Turn over the drone program to local governments*, using U.S. drones only for surveillance and providing the information they afford to help local military forces act against terrorists or to give the targeted country a final say about whether to strike particular targets. The difficulties with giving other countries direct control over the drones include revealing their technology. There is also the assumption that targeted countries see the terrorist threat as does Washington, and that they view their interests as does the United States. In the case of Pakistan, neither is the case.

c. *Ignore local objections.* Although the governments of countries such as Pakistan and Yemen tacitly accept Washington's use of drones, ignoring local perceptions runs the risk of alienating populations on which governments rely for information about terrorists and whose support on the ground is crucial in conflicts with jihadist groups. In the words of a White House official, "We've got this technology, and we're not going to be the only ones who use it," and thus, "We have to set standards so it doesn't get abused in the future."[37]

Nevertheless, President Obama seemed willing to limit such strikes when he declared in his speech of May 23, 2013, that they would be used only "against terrorists who pose a continuing and imminent threat to the American people, and when there are no other governments capable of effectively addressing the threat. And before any strike is taken, there must be near certainty that no civilians will be killed or injured—the highest standard we can set."[38] In what may have reflected an interagency dispute between the State Department and the CIA, shortly after Secretary Kerry declared that he hoped drone strikes in Pakistan would end soon, a State Department spokeswoman emphatically stated, "In no way would we ever deprive ourselves of a tool to fight a threat if it arises."[39] As one observer put it, "There's nothing that indicates this administration is going to unilaterally end drone strikes in Pakistan, or Yemen for that matter."[40] And in late 2013 the Pakistani government revised significantly downward the number of civilian casualties allegedly caused by U.S. drone strikes in that country since 2008, declaring that of the 2,227 killed in such strikes only 67 were civilians rather than militants (past estimates claimed as many as 300 civilian deaths).[41]

THE WAR ON TERROR

Although U.S. tactics have changed—notably reliance on Special Forces, selective air strikes, and drones rather than large-scale military intervention—and America's focus is moving away from Afghanistan and Pakistan and toward Iraq, Syria, Yemen, Somalia, and North Africa, the global conflict with Islamic extremists continues, and in the foreseeable future may encompass other unstable countries. In the case of many (though not all) al-Qaeda affiliates, it is local governments that are threatened by jihadists rather than the U.S. homeland, though some groups like al-Qaeda in the Arabian Peninsula continue to seek ways to attack America directly. In addition, the threat of "lone wolves" in the United States persists, especially in view of the sophisticated online propaganda of the Islamic State.

Homeland security thus remains of great concern. Although the Obama administration has dealt with some of the concerns regarding violations of human rights associated with the War on Terror, it continues to rely on counterterrorist agencies and policies put in place by the Bush administration. The Department of Homeland Security will remain; efforts to enhance airport and port security continue; international and domestic surveillance and intelligence, though controversial, persist; and commando operations and drone strikes, though modified to reduce CIA involvement, remain in use despite the claim that such strikes intensify anti-American sentiment in the countries where they take place.

Policy Options

a. *Transform the "war" on terror into a "police action" against international criminals.* Such a change in language may imply little in terms of actual behavior but would encourage a more multilateral approach toward the problem and assuage concerns among America's overseas friends and allies about U.S. unilateralism. It would also appear less hostile to Islam in general and would attract greater support from Muslims at home and abroad. In addition, adopting this option would have legal implications, for example, related to the rights of terrorist suspects and perhaps to drone strikes as well. These would meet with approval from civil-rights advocates at home and abroad but would invite criticism by hard-liners for being "weak" on terrorism. For such reasons, the option would prove divisive domestically. It might also be regarded by jihadi extremists as an invitation to step up efforts against other governments because their actions would not violate U.S. law.

b. *Continue acting as though it were a "war"*—that is, responding robustly to threats overseas *and* at home, much as in recent years. With the end of large-scale involvement in Iraq and Afghanistan, the new status quo is less expensive and intrusive than policies followed after 9/11 and enjoys more support from a war-weary public than would major military operations. It would not, however, solve domestic controversy over homeland security.

CONCLUSION: TERRORISM PERSISTS

The focus of U.S. foreign policy shifted dramatically after the attacks of 9/11. Islamic radicalism, a threat that had received little attention previously, was suddenly elevated to the top of Washington's foreign-policy agenda. As we have seen, American leaders employed military force in Iraq, Afghanistan, Pakistan (in the latter by means of unmanned drones), and elsewhere, trying to reduce or eliminate Islamic terrorism in the Middle East, Africa, and Central Asia. U.S. policies also involved fostering bureaucratic and legal reforms at home to reveal potential terrorists and foil their plans before they could be implemented. American policies came at enormous financial and human cost, and we are still evaluating their benefits: Have these measures reduced the threat of Islamic terrorism? Or have they fueled radicalism, producing new jihadists who may be more determined than ever to attack the United States?

Although Osama bin Laden is dead and al-Qaeda significantly weakened, regional jihadist groups remain dangerous, and failed and/or failing states like Syria remain potential sanctuaries for terrorist groups even as they are eliminated elsewhere. The souring of the Arab Spring brought new recruits to violent jihadist groups. According to the State Department, in 2014 there were about 13,500 terrorist incidents (up from 10,000 in 2013) involving 33,000 deaths (up from 18,000 in 2013).[42] Over 60 percent of these incidents and most of these deaths occurred in five countries—Iraq, Afghanistan, Pakistan, Nigeria, and India[43]—all sites of active jihadist groups. Following the massacres in Paris and San Bernardino in 2015, some European and American politicians demanded greater examination and even exclusion of refugees from the Middle East, especially Syria. Some sought greater surveillance of Muslim citizens, and one Republican presidential candidate even demanded that Muslims be refused entry into the United States. Such suggestions will likely radicalize additional Muslims and recruit additional volunteers to terrorist groups like ISIS because they seem to bear out the narrative of a Western war against Islam as a religion, while also violating America's Constitution.

Although President Obama declared an end of the War on Terror in 2013, has the conflict against jihadi terrorism ceased? The answer, of course, is no, and the president seemed to reverse course when in May 2014 he declared, "For the foreseeable future, the most direct threat to America at home and abroad remains terrorism."[44] In September he admitted, "We can't erase every trace of evil from the world and small groups of killers have the capacity to do great harm. That was the case before 9/11, and that remains true today. And that's why we must remain vigilant as threats emerge."[45] In November 2014 alone jihadists killed 5,000 people in 664 attacks in fourteen countries around the world.[46] Ultimately, the threat of terrorism, whether religious or secular in nature, is impossible to eliminate completely, and that threat will remain high on America's foreign-policy agenda in one form or another in the coming years.

III

Israel and Palestine

U.S. president Barack Obama and Israeli prime minister Benjamin Netanyahu

Mark Wilson/Getty

The conflict between Israel and the Arab Palestinians is among the most durable of Washington's preoccupations with the Middle East. America has been a staunch friend of Israel since its birth in 1948. Americans view Israel as a rare Middle Eastern democracy and an outpost of U.S. values. Both are economically developed and democratic countries with dense economic and social ties. They support human rights (though Israel has violated Palestinian rights) and stress individualism and free-market capitalism. Although sentiment and shared values explain much of the relationship, Israel is also a stable, powerful, and valuable geopolitical ally in an unstable and violent region, where it fosters American interests. Israel has been and remains a close U.S. ally and has many friends in the United States who have simultaneously sought to reassure and enhance Israel's security while brokering a resolution to the Israeli–Palestinian conflict.

The U.S.–Israeli relationship is complex. During the 2012 U.S. presidential campaign, Israel's hard-line prime minister, Benjamin Netanyahu, made little secret of his preference for Republican candidate Mitt Romney, and Israel's oldest newspaper, *Haaretz,* accused Netanyahu of "interfering grossly, vulgarly and unreservedly in the campaign."[1] Netanyahu and Romney were close friends who had worked together in 1976 as advisors to the Boston Consulting Group and had maintained close ties afterward. By contrast, Netanyahu and Barack Obama differed significantly on several vital issues, including how to respond to Iran's effort to acquire nuclear weapons, Netanyahu's unwillingness to compromise with the Palestinians, and the expansion of Israeli settlements on the West Bank and East Jerusalem on land occupied by Israel after the 1967 Six-Day War and financed by the Israeli government and Zionist organizations.

Timeline

Before 1950

1000–587 BCE The Kingdom of Israel

6–135 CE The Roman province of Judea

70 Roman destruction of the Temple in Jerusalem

1893 Nathan Birnbaum coins the term *Zionism*

1897 The First Zionist Congress is held in Basel, Switzerland

1917 Balfour Declaration

1933–1945 The Holocaust

1947 Partition of Palestine

1948 Founding of Israel

1950–1990

1956 Suez War

1964 Formation of the PLO

1967 Six-Day War

1973 Yom Kippur War

1977 Right-wing government in Israel; President Anwar Sadat visits Israel

1979 Israeli–Egyptian Peace Treaty

1982 Israeli invasion of Lebanon

1987 First intifada

1988 PLO accepts "two-state" solution

The two leaders seemed to dislike each other personally. Speaking of Obama, one observer concluded, "My sense is that he both dislikes and distrusts Israeli Prime Minister Netanyahu, and that he is more likely to use his new momentum to settling scores than to settling issues."[2] And after Obama's electoral triumph an Israeli political strategist argued, "Netanyahu backed the wrong horse. Whoever is elected prime minister is going to have to handle the U.S.–Israel relationship, and we all know Netanyahu is not the right guy."[3] Shortly before the 2013 Israeli election, which returned Netanyahu as prime minister for a third time, Obama was quoted as declaring privately, with Netanyahu in mind, "Israel doesn't know what its own best interests are." Netanyahu responded, "I think everyone understands that only Israeli citizens will be the ones who determine who faithfully represents the vital interests of Israel."[4] Relations worsened after Netanyahu denounced U.S.–Iranian negotiations in March 2015 during Israel's election campaign and, after returning home, declared he would oppose a two-state solution as long as he was prime minister. After his reelection he suggested he was misunderstood. The president, nevertheless, phoned Netanyahu. "I indicated to him that given his statements prior to the election, it is going to be hard to find a path where people are seriously believing negotiations are possible,"[5] he said. And in March 2016 Netanyahu effectively refused Obama's invitation to meet him in Washington.

1990–2009

1993 Oslo Accords

1995 Assassination of Yitzhak Rabin

2000 Second intifada

2002 West Bank reoccupied by Israel

2003 United States sponsors "roadmap" to peace

2005 Israel leaves Gaza

2006 Hamas wins election in Gaza; Israel–Hezbollah war

2007 Hamas coup in Gaza

2008–2009 Israel–Hamas war

2010–2015

2010 Israelis attack Gaza relief flotilla

2012 Israel–Hamas war

March 2013 Obama visits Israel

2013 Israeli–Palestinian talks resume

2014 Israeli–Palestinian talks collapse; third Gaza war

2015 Outbreak of Palestinian–Israeli killings

9

America and the Evolution of the Israeli–Palestinian Conundrum, 1948–1967

Our first chapter in Part III deals with the evolution of U.S.–Israeli relations and events in the region from the birth of the Jewish state in 1948 until its triumph in the 1967 Six-Day War. It opens with Israel's establishment and then examines the sources of U.S. policy toward Israel. The conflict was originally an "Arab–Israeli" issue and, as we shall see, following the partition of the region called Palestine, Israel and its Arab neighbors engaged in a series of conflicts culminating in the Six-Day War. We explore the immense consequences of the Six-Day War, including the disagreement over the meaning of Security Council Resolution 242 and the Palestine Liberation Organization's effort to promote a Palestinian state from territories occupied by Israel in return for peace. The Palestinian question reflects durable nationalist, cultural, and religious passions. Its conflicts are rooted in history—ancient and modern.

THE BIRTH OF ISRAEL

U.S.–Israeli relations have been close since Israel was established. Israel's founding grew out of a belief in Zionism, a national movement for the return of the Jewish people to their homeland and the resumption of Jewish sovereignty in the biblical Land of Israel that was a reaction to the nineteenth-century spread of anti-Semitism in Europe. Israeli claims to Palestine were rooted in biblical rule until the Roman conquest in the first century BCE. Among the leading figures in the early Zionist movement were Theodor Hertzl and Chaim Weizmann. The British government was especially indebted to Weizmann, who was a chemist, because he provided Great Britain with a process to extract acetone, a key ingredient of cordite (which replaced gunpowder) from grain. During World War I a letter written by British foreign secretary Arthur Balfour to Lord Rothschild, to be transmitted to the British Zionist Federation, declared,

> His Majesty's government view with favour the establishment in Palestine of a national home for the Jewish people, and will use their best endeavours to facilitate the achievement of this object, it being clearly understood that nothing shall be done which may prejudice the civil and religious rights of existing non-Jewish communities in Palestine, or the rights and political status enjoyed by Jews in any other country.[6]

This letter, the Balfour Declaration, which gave incompatible assurances to both sides, became the basis for a Jewish homeland in Palestine that Britain administered as a League of Nations mandate.

Growing Jewish settlements in Palestine in the 1930s produced conflict with Palestinian Arabs. Britain had limited Jewish immigration to placate the Arabs who had aided their defeat of the Ottoman Turks in World War I who had governed the region. World War II was looming, and the oil-rich region was geopolitically crucial, linking British India and the Mediterranean Sea. The wartime Holocaust produced global sympathy for Jewish survivors who emigrated to Palestine, but that influx triggered additional violence, as Palestinians did not wish to surrender land to compensate for crimes committed in Europe.

Britain's efforts to maintain order in Palestine produced additional violence by Jewish militias against the British, who decided to surrender the mandate and turn the issue over to the United Nations. On November 29, 1947, the General Assembly voted to partition Palestine into two states, one Jewish and the other Arab, each with a majority of its own population. The Jewish leadership accepted the plan, but the Arabs rejected it. As the British withdrew from Palestine, the Jewish State of Israel declared its independence on May 14, 1948, and five Arab armies invaded Israel.

There followed Israel's triumphal war of independence against the five Arab armies that sought to crush the new Jewish state, which occupied almost three-quarters of what had been the British Mandate under the League of Nations. Jordan controlled East Jerusalem and the West Bank of the River Jordan, and Egypt occupied the Gaza Strip on the Mediterranean coast, bordering Israel. The war also produced hundreds of thousands of Arab Palestinian refugees, many settling in camps in Jordan, Syria, Lebanon, and Gaza, where they became wards of the United Nations Relief and Works Agency. Some had fled voluntarily, while others were driven out by Israeli forces. The establishment of Israel and the flight of Arab Palestinians became collectively known to Arabs as *al-Nakba* ("the catastrophe"). Israel's Arab neighbors refused to recognize the new Jewish state. This was the first of many wars that Israel and the Arabs would fight during ensuing decades.

America has been deeply involved in relations between Israelis and Arabs since the United Nations (UN) recommended the partition of Palestine. Washington recognized Israel's independence eleven minutes after it had been declared. Since then U.S. leaders have tried to balance their support for Israel's security and independence without alienating American friends in the Arab world, and have used their influence to reconcile Israeli and Palestinian interests to bring about a resolution of the issues that divide them. The territory over which the two sides quarrel is, however, small, and a solution that satisfies both sides, ensuring their mutual security and overcoming their grievances, remains elusive.

SOURCES OF U.S. POLICY TOWARD ISRAEL AND THE PALESTINIANS

External factors were less central to American policy toward Israel and its neighbors in the 1940s and 1950s than in other issues. The failure of the Roosevelt administration to assist European Jews before World War II and the wartime Holocaust produced guilt and sympathy in the United States for the plight of those who had survived and for Israel as a small democratic country surrounded by much larger Arab enemies.

Individuals were significant in mobilizing support for Israel in the 1940s, ranging from President Harry Truman to Supreme Court justices Louis Brandeis and Felix Frankfurter, among others. "A sentimental attachment to the ancient Hebrews infused the religious upbringing of Harry Truman and Lyndon Johnson, the two presidents who did most to cement American ties with Israel."[7] More recently, some Israeli leaders with close links to America have been popular in the United States. An example was Israeli prime minister Golda Meir (1969–1974), who was raised and educated in Milwaukee, Wisconsin, and later taught high school in that city. By contrast, key government agencies, including the Departments of State and Defense, argued that recognizing Israeli independence would harm relations with the Arab states that controlled much of the world's oil.

Sensitive to societal factors like the voting strength of ethnic minorities in key constituencies, Congress supported a pro-Israeli policy. The Israel lobby is a source of controversy. Although there are numerous lobbying groups that seek close U.S.–Israeli ties, they are divided over how to achieve this goal. Some would like Washington to back all Israeli policies, however hard-line—for example, Christians United for Israel. Others, such as J Street, Americans for Peace Now, the Israel Policy Forum, and the Tikkun Community, while pro-Israeli, argue that Israel should do more to accommodate Palestinian interests. Such groups provide campaign contributions to U.S. politicians, both Democratic and Republican, who support Israel. In recent years contributions from pro-Israeli groups have been directed increasingly to conservative congressional Republicans, unlike in earlier decades, when liberal congressional Democrats were the major recipients. This change is owed in part to perceived criticisms of Israeli policies by the Obama administration.

The best-known pro-Israeli group is the American Israel Public Affairs Committee (AIPAC), with over 100,000 members in all fifty states. The group describes its mission as strengthening "the ties between the United States and its ally Israel."[8] It "empowers pro-Israel activists across all ages, religions and races to be politically engaged and build relationships with members of Congress from both sides of the aisle to promote the U.S.–Israel relationship."[9] American politicians routinely consult with or attend meetings of AIPAC, as did Vice President Joe Biden in March 2013. Biden reassured his audience of U.S. willingness to use force against Iran if that country acquired nuclear weapons.

AIPAC is usually careful not to be seen as promoting policies that are unpopular in the United States. At the height of the debate in America in 2013 over whether to attack Syria in response to its use of chemical weapons, AIPAC cautiously lobbied Congress to support President Obama but did not want the Israeli government to be perceived as taking sides in America's domestic debate. A senior Israeli official observed, "It is a major dilemma. We don't want to be identified with pressing for a strike. This is not for us—we don't want anybody to think this is for us. But if the president asks us for assistance, who are we to refuse?"[10] Nor does the group always get what it seeks. Its effort to get Congress to pass legislation for additional sanctions against Iran—opposed by the president in the midst of negotiating with Iran— narrowly fell short of mobilizing sufficient votes in the Senate to override a presidential veto or to sustain a filibuster. Its virulent and well-financed effort to mobilize congressional opposition to the Iranian deal led President Obama to denounce "lobbyists"—a reference to the group—and reflected growing hostility between AIPAC and the administration. As a former Middle East advisor to the Obama administration observed, "There's almost a bunker mentality on both sides."[11]

Despite the Israel lobby, American policy toward Israel has repeatedly shifted. Thus, President Bill Clinton pressed "Israel to make far-reaching concessions on the West Bank," while the Bush administration altered the policy, standing "by Israeli Prime Minister Ariel Sharon as he rejects all talk of territorial concessions."[12] Pro-Israeli groups routinely urge Washington to provide Israel with economic and military assistance, but such aid would probably be forthcoming anyway owing to a convergence in U.S.–Israeli strategic interests, including opposition to Islamic terrorists and regional instability.

Following Israeli independence, pro-Israeli sentiment in the United States was centered among liberals in the Democratic Party and labor unions, which admired Israeli democracy and the socialist leanings of Israel's leftist political parties and leaders like David Ben-Gurion, Golda Meir, and Yitzhak Rabin. The societal sources of U.S. support for Israel shifted after Israel's Labor Party ceded political dominance in 1977 to hard-liners associated with the right-wing Likud Party such as Menachem Begin, Yitzhak Shamir, Ariel Sharon, and Benjamin Netanyahu.

Increasingly, Israel's American advocates were conservatives associated with evangelical Christianity and the Republican Party. Known as "Christian Zionists" and organized in groups like Christians United for Israel, they believed that the return of the Jewish people to Palestine was God's will and a precondition for the second coming of Christ as foretold by the Hebrew prophet Ezekiel. They also believed that God would judge them according to their treatment of the Jewish people. American Protestants were among the first Zionists to settle in Palestine, and evangelical leaders like Pat Robertson, Jerry Falwell, and Dr. James Dobson were vocally pro-Israeli. At a meeting of evangelicals in July 2006 attended by Republican politicians, the Rev. John Hagee called support for Israel "God's foreign policy."[13] In a 2011 poll, nearly two-thirds of America's evangelical Protestants and conservative Republicans thought that protecting Israel was an important foreign-policy goal, in contrast to roughly a third of mainline Protestants and Catholics.[14]

Some domestic groups, however, oppose Israel's continued occupation of the West Bank and East Jerusalem, and its construction of settlements in those areas. The movement "Boycott, Divestment, and Sanctions" (BDS) emerged to pressure Israel to cease settlement construction and leave the occupied territories. In 2014 the Presbyterian Church (U.S.A.) at its general convention narrowly voted to divest three American companies—Caterpillar, Hewlett-Packard, and Motorola Solutions—that sold Israel equipment used for settlement expansion, while reaffirming Israel's right to exist and denying it was part of the BDS movement. The action divided America's Jewish community, with 1,700 rabbis declaring in an open letter that it placed "all the blame on one party, when both bear responsibility," and increased "conflict and division instead of promoting peace."[15] Following the 2014 Hamas–Israeli war, the boycott movement gained steam among Europeans, leading an Israeli analyst to comment that "after the casualties and the destruction," the conflict "could make it very easy for the BDS campaign to isolate Israel and call for more boycotts."[16] In 2014 Sweden became the first European state to recognize a Palestinian state, despite Israeli protests, and the British, Irish, Spanish, French, and European Union parliaments followed with nonbinding votes recognizing an independent Palestine.

During the 1950s Israel's leading foes were neighboring Arab states like Egypt and Syria, and the United States and Israel sought to limit Soviet influence in the Middle East. In general, however, both superpowers restrained their regional clients during the Cold War. Washington and Moscow joined briefly to bring an end to the Anglo–French invasion of the Suez Canal and Israel's occupation of the Sinai Peninsula in 1956. The superpowers also cooperated in helping end the Six-Day War, and in preventing the Yom Kippur War from triggering a superpower conflict.

THE YOM KIPPUR OR OCTOBER WAR

Regarding Egypt and Syria as Soviet pawns, the Nixon administration provided Israel with significant military equipment in the early 1970s. Although Egyptian president Anwar Sadat sought closer relations with the United States and expelled Soviet advisors from his country in 1972—a year after signing a friendship treaty with Moscow—Washington, then preoccupied by the Vietnam War, failed to respond. Thus, Egypt and Syria remained dependent on the USSR for arms. Sadat came to believe that military action was necessary to acquire additional political leverage to force Israel from territory occupied in 1967. On October 6, 1973—Yom Kippur, the holiest day in the Jewish calendar—Egypt and Syria launched a surprise though poorly coordinated attack against Israel. Egyptian troops initially swept across the Sinai Peninsula and Syrian forces briefly recovered the Golan Heights until Israel counterattacked and seemed ready to move toward Damascus, Syria's capital. The war ended with a cease-fire on October 26 after Israel had driven back Egyptian forces, crossed the Suez Canal, and threatened the annihilation of Egypt's Third Army.

The war produced an American–Soviet confrontation. Washington viewed the conflict through the prism of U.S. need for Middle East oil and, more generally, the credibility of U.S. support for its allies. Both Washington and Moscow resupplied their respective allies with massive amounts of military equipment during the war, and America provided Israel with invaluable intelligence information. U.S. aid to Israel produced an effort by OAPEC (the Arab members of the Organization of Petroleum Exporting Countries) to embargo oil exports to America and its allies, thereby causing a spike in oil prices worldwide. Israel's advances into Egypt heightened tension between the superpowers, leading Washington to raise the level of its nuclear alert. It also induced Secretary of State Henry Kissinger to persuade Israel to permit the resupply of Egyptian forces, thereby confirming Sadat's belief in the political benefit of what had become a lost war. The war raised Arab morale and revealed that Israel had become increasingly dependent on American political, military, and economic support.

Kissinger helped Egypt and Israel reach a cease-fire, and then a partial Israeli withdrawal from the Sinai in January 1974. This paved the way for Sadat's dramatic visit to Jerusalem and Egypt's peaceful reacquisition of the entire Sinai. Kissinger's role in the settlement made clear that Washington would remain a key player in subsequent events. "Sometime in the mid-1970s the term *peace process* began to be widely used to describe the American-led efforts to bring about a negotiated peace between Israel and its Arab neighbors. The phrase stuck, and ever since it has been synonymous with the gradual step-by-step approach to resolving one of the world's most difficult conflicts."[17]

During most of the Cold War, the Palestinians enjoyed little autonomous influence, and were manipulated by their Arab sponsors for their own ends. In 1964 Egypt and the Arab League—an international organization of Arab states (including Palestine) founded in 1945—established the Palestinian Liberation Organization (PLO) as an umbrella group to coordinate the activities of Palestinian guerrilla and political organizations. After the 1967 Six-Day War, the PLO became increasingly independent of its Arab state sponsors and came to be widely viewed as the representative of the Palestinians.

THE SIX-DAY WAR AND ITS CONSEQUENCES

Israel's victory during the 1967 Six-Day War against Egypt, Syria, and Jordan transformed the Middle East. Israel's occupation of the Sinai Peninsula, the Gaza Strip, the West Bank, the Golan Heights, and the city of Jerusalem doubled its territory, and it became the region's military superpower. Thereafter, while remaining Israel's closest ally, Washington sought to broker a regional settlement that, while recognizing Israel's legitimate security concerns, would lead to the resolution of the territorial disputes caused by Israel's 1967 triumph.

Since 2001 Washington has supported establishing an independent Palestinian state. For American leaders, these objectives proved difficult and posed a dilemma: How could Washington maintain its support for Israel while simultaneously earning the trust of Israel's Arab neighbors and bringing about a "two-state" solution (Israel and Palestine) in the region? At some moments peace has seemed tantalizingly close, only to prove illusory.

From November 7 to November 26, 1967, the UN Security Council sought to draft a resolution to deal with the consequences of the Six-Day War. Alternative versions were proposed by the United States, India, the USSR, and Britain. In the end, the British resolution was unanimously adopted. This was Resolution 242, and it would shape almost all subsequent debate and negotiation concerning the issue. Resolution 242 was adopted under Chapter VI of the UN Charter, "Pacific Resolution of Disputes"—thus labeling neither Israel nor its Arab neighbors as aggressors. In consequence, the resolution required the adversaries to negotiate both the resolution's meaning and implementation. Negotiation was necessary to establish "a just and lasting peace in the Middle East" that would be based on "withdrawal of Israeli armed forces from territories occupied" during the war and "respect for and acknowledgment of the sovereignty, territorial integrity and political independence of every State in the area and their right to live in peace within secure and recognized boundaries free from threats or acts of force." Thus, Israel was expected to leave those territories it had conquered in June in exchange for peace. In return, Israel's sovereignty and the security of its boundaries would be recognized by its Arab neighbors. For its part, Israel declared that a united Jerusalem—including East Jerusalem, with its Palestinian population—was Israel's capital. In 1980 it passed a law to this effect, even though the Palestinians also claimed East Jerusalem as their capital.

Resolution 242 remained a topic of fierce debate owing to the adversaries' different interpretations. What constituted "secure and recognized boundaries"? First, inasmuch as the Arabs had rejected the original UN partition plan, and Israel's initial boundaries in 1949 were the outcome of war and cease-fires rather than a treaty, those boundaries could be considered temporary. Second, Israel argued that for its boundaries to be "secure" it had to retain some of the territory occupied in 1967—for instance, the Golan Heights that dominate the Syrian border, or West Bank areas near Jerusalem. Third, in declaring the "inadmissibility of the acquisition of territory by war," but not requiring Israel to leave "*all* occupied territories," did Resolution 242 imply that Israel could remain in some of those territories it deemed necessary for its security? Finally, "Palestinians" were not mentioned in the resolution except in its allusion to "a just settlement of the refugee problem." What settlement would be "just"? Did this phrase grant the right of return to Israel to all Palestinian refugees, or only to some, and did a "just" settlement mean integrating Palestinians into the Arab societies to which they had fled? Did a "just" settlement require the establishment of a sovereign Palestinian state in the region? Such contested issues continued to bedevil Israeli–Palestinian relations. But the ambiguity of the resolution at the time suited President Lyndon Johnson, who wished to allow Israel to retain its conquests until its Arab neighbors were prepared to agree to peace with the Jewish state.

MAP 9.1 Occupied Territories, Israeli Settlements, and Palestinian Refugee Camps

Source: Adapted from http://www.theglobaleducationproject.org/mideast/info/maps/israel-and-occupied-territories-map.html

KEY DOCUMENT

UN Resolution 242,[18] November 22, 1967

The Security Council, Expressing its continuing concern with the grave situation in the Middle East, *Emphasizing* the inadmissibility of the acquisition of territory by war and the need to work for a just and lasting peace in which every State in the area can live in security, *Emphasizing further* that all Member States in their acceptance of the Charter of the United Nations have undertaken a commitment to act in accordance with Article 2 of the Charter,

1. *Affirms* that the fulfillment of Charter principles requires the establishment of a just and lasting peace in the Middle East which should include the application of both the following principles:

   (i) Withdrawal of Israel armed forces from territories occupied in the recent conflict;

   (ii) Termination of all claims or states of belligerency and respect for and acknowledgment of the sovereignty, territorial integrity and political independence of every State in the area and their right to live in peace within secure and recognized boundaries free from threats or acts of force;

2. *Affirms further* the necessity

   (a) For guaranteeing freedom of navigation through international waterways in the area;

   (b) For achieving a just settlement of the refugee problem;

   (c) For guaranteeing the territorial inviolability and political independence of every State in the area, through measures including the establishment of demilitarized zones;

3. *Requests* the Secretary-General to designate a Special Representative to proceed to the Middle East to establish and maintain contacts with the States concerned in order to promote agreement and assist efforts to achieve a peaceful and accepted settlement in accordance with the provisions and principles in this resolution,

4. *Requests* the Secretary-General to report to the Security Council on the progress of the efforts of the Special Representative as soon as possible.

CONCLUSION: CONSEQUENCES OF THE SIX-DAY WAR

The Six-Day War did not only alter the Middle East. It also traumatized the Palestinians, who recognized that their Arab sponsors were pursuing their own interests. Some years before, al-Fatah (the Movement for the National Liberation of Palestine) was secretly established with the avowed aims of destroying Israel and establishing a Palestinian state. Fatah, aided by Syria, began launching terrorist attacks against Israel from Gaza, Lebanon, and Jordan in 1965. Led by Yasser Arafat, Fatah became the most powerful group in the PLO, and in 1969 Arafat became PLO chair. In the ensuing years, Palestinian groups intensified attacks against Israelis, including the murder of Israeli athletes by the terrorist group Black September at the 1972 Munich Olympics. Other PLO groups such as the Marxist-oriented Popular Front for the Liberation of Palestine (PFLP) and the Democratic Front for the Liberation of Palestine (DFLP), a militant faction of Fatah, also carried on an armed struggle against Israel. In 1974 the UN General Assembly granted the PLO "observer entity" status, recognizing it as the "representative of the Palestinian people"; thereafter, the PLO took tentative steps toward negotiating a diplomatic solution with Israel while still calling for that country's destruction. Thus, the PLO was and remains viewed as a future government for a Palestinian state. It has a legislature, the Palestinian National Council, whose Executive Committee was headed by Arafat until his death in 2004, when he was succeeded by Mahmoud Abbas.

Our next chapter examines the evolution of Palestinian–Israel relations and the peace process from 1967 to the present. It charts the ups and downs of that process and the role of the United States in seeking peace in the Middle East.

10

America, Israel, and Palestine

THE ELUSIVE ROAD TO PEACE

Chapter 10 examines the Israeli–Palestinian issue following the Six-Day War, focusing on the "peace process"—notably, American efforts to mediate a resolution of the differences between the adversaries. It begins with the 1973 Yom Kippur War launched by Egypt's president Anwar Sadat and describes how Sadat decided to make a historic journey to Jerusalem that set the stage for the Camp David Accords and a peace treaty between Israel and Egypt, which though an initial step toward peace, had little impact on Israeli–Palestinian relations. It then describes how Washington sought to end the Israeli–Palestinian logjam with the Oslo Accords and the ensuing Camp David summits hosted by President Bill Clinton that led to increased Palestinian autonomy on the West Bank and brought the adversaries closer to a final deal than ever before or since. After negotiations again failed, Israeli–Palestinian relations quickly soured and deteriorated into the violence of the second intifada, or uprising. Another American initiative, the "roadmap" to peace, also ended in failure, and Prime Minister Ariel Sharon unilaterally withdrew Israeli forces and settlers from the Gaza Strip.

The chapter then describes how Gaza, which along with the West Bank constituted the Palestinian territories, fell under the control of the militant Islamic group Hamas, leading to three wars between Hamas and Israel in less than a decade. With Hamas in Gaza and the Shia militant group Hezbollah controlling southern Lebanon, the prospect for peace became increasingly remote. Nevertheless, in 2013 Secretary of State John Kerry cajoled Israeli prime minister Benjamin Netanyahu and Palestinian president Mahmoud Abbas to open negotiations that again ended in rancor in April 2014, sorely straining U.S.–Israeli relations.

AMERICAN POLICY AND THE ISRAELI–PALESTINIAN PEACE PROCESS

Violence would continue to define Israel's relations with its neighbors, and Washington would play a major role in aiding Israel and thereafter in seeking to promote a peace settlement. The Six-Day War made Israelis overconfident about their military supremacy while intensifying Egyptian and Syrian desire to recover their lost territories. Egypt's president Anwar Sadat concluded that military action was necessary to recover territory lost to Israel in 1967. In time, events transformed the central issue in the Middle East from territorial disputes between Israel and its Arab neighbors into an effort by Palestinians to end Israel's occupation of the West Bank, Jerusalem, and Gaza, and create their own sovereign state.

The Peace Process Begins

The prospect of Egyptian–Israeli peace persuaded President Jimmy Carter to go beyond Secretary of State Henry Kissinger's shuttle diplomacy during and after the Yom Kippur War and seek a more comprehensive settlement, and the president visited Israel, Egypt, and Jordan during his first year in office. He then convened a multinational meeting in Geneva to negotiate Israel's withdrawal from the occupied territories, Arab recognition of Israel and its need for security, and the reunification of Jerusalem. However, on November 20, 1977, Sadat altered the politics of the Middle East by paying an official three-day visit to Israel, where he was met by Israeli prime minister Menachem Begin and spoke before the Knesset (Israel's parliament). "We really and truly welcome you," declared Sadat, "to live among us in peace and security."[1] Sadat's visit entailed a tacit recognition of the State of Israel, the first by an Arab neighbor.

Sadat made it clear that he was less interested in the multilateral Geneva talks than in a bilateral agreement with Israel that would sidestep the Palestinian issue. President Carter, who had no advance knowledge of Sadat's visit to Israel, then organized a meeting between Sadat and Begin at the presidential retreat at Camp David in Maryland. For Begin, a bilateral meeting was also preferable because he would not have to address Israel's continued occupation of the West Bank. For Sadat, it offered the prospect of economic aid from the West, friendship with the United States instead of the USSR, the return of the Sinai Peninsula to Egypt, and the possibility that other Arab states would follow Egypt's example. The Camp David meeting, which lasted thirteen days, climaxed with a three-part agreement entitled the Framework for Peace in the Middle East (the "Camp David Accords") that was signed on September 17, 1978. Carter had worked hard to make the talks succeed, and the accords became possible when Begin agreed to allow Israel's parliament to decide the fate of Israeli settlements in the Sinai and Carter ceased trying to resolve the status of the West Bank.

The Camp David Accords consisted of two bilateral agreements. The first committed participants to negotiate about providing "full autonomy" and "a "self-governing authority" for Palestinians in Gaza and the West Bank, which would lead to a withdrawal of Israeli troops. The second sketched out the terms for a 1979 Egyptian–Israeli peace treaty. Under the treaty Egypt formally recognized Israel, limited its military presence in the Sinai, and gave Israel access to the Suez Canal and Red Sea via the Straits of Tiran in return for Israeli withdrawal of its armed forces and civilian settlers from the Sinai. A third accord proffered a similar peace process between Israel and other Arab neighbors, but was rejected by the Arab states and the Palestinian Liberation Organization (PLO) on the grounds that they were not involved in the process and it did not meet all their demands. For its part, Washington agreed to provide economic and military aid to both Egypt and Israel. Both Begin and Sadat were awarded the Nobel Peace Prize, and the treaty has remained in effect since. The two countries exchanged ambassadors in February 1980. Egypt also began to sell oil to Israel, and Israel began a staged evacuation of the Sinai that was completed in 1982. The treaty was unpopular in much of the Arab world, and Egypt was expelled from the Arab League in 1979 and not readmitted for a decade.

Although the American-mediated Camp David Accords were a step toward regional peace, it was a narrow agreement between two states that had little impact on the relationship between Israel and the Palestinians. In 1988 Jordan surrendered its authority over the West Bank and East Jerusalem, leaving the Palestinians to negotiate directly with Israel. Following the defeat of Iraq in the Persian Gulf War and the liberation of Kuwait in 1991, U.S. influence seemed unchallenged in the Middle East.

From Madrid to Oslo

The PLO was isolated, having supported Iraq during the Persian Gulf War. Washington had persuaded Israel to restrain itself from involvement in that war, and the Soviet Union, though cooperative politically, had not been a member of the coalition that had fought Iraq. Under the circumstances, the administration concluded it could resolve the Israel–Palestinian issue. The Cold War had ended and the USSR would shortly disintegrate, but Washington and Moscow cooperated to sponsor multilateral negotiations between Israel and the Palestinians, Jordan, Lebanon, and Syria in Madrid, Spain, in 1991 and in Washington in 1992.

President George H. W. Bush and Secretary of State James Baker, having decided to increase pressure on Israel to resolve the Palestinian issue, were largely responsible for organizing the multilateral conference in Madrid. Although the Reagan administration had held talks with the PLO, Bush and Baker were determined to press Israel to surrender land and give up settlements in the occupied territories in exchange for peace. Initially, the Israelis—led by Prime Minister Yitzhak Shamir, the Likud hard-liner who had succeeded Begin as prime minister—angrily resisted until Baker threatened to withhold $10 billion in U.S. loan guarantees for resettling Russian Jewish immigrants in Israel. The threat mobilized pro-Israeli domestic groups and aroused fierce domestic debate in America. The issue remained a sore point in U.S.–Israeli relations, as the Bush administration linked the loan request to Israeli willingness to cease settlement expansion in the West Bank and Gaza, and Congress refused to overrule the president. The loan dispute also played a role in the 1992 electoral victory of Yitzhak Rabin, who was committed to ending settlement expansion. Congress agreed to the loan guarantees in October 1992.

The Madrid conference was the first direct negotiation between Israel and its adversaries except Egypt. "To much pomp and publicity, the peace conference opened on October 30, 1991 in the Spanish capital. Millions around the world delighted to the sight of Israeli and Arab leaders gathered in the rococo Royal Palace (from which a portrait of Charles V massacring Moors had been hastily removed) and seated around the same ornate table."[2] The Palestinians were linked to the Jordanian delegation in order to evade Israel's objections to a separate Palestinian presence. Despite the animosity of the participants, the U.S. representatives managed to get agreement on a two-tier framework of bilateral and multilateral negotiations over a wide range of issues. Bilateral talks between Israelis and Palestinians were based on a proposed two-step process—interim Palestinian self-government followed by permanent status talks.

The Israelis, however, refused to budge regarding occupied territory in Gaza and the West Bank, while the Palestinians continued to demand the establishment of a Palestinian state in those two areas. Nor could Syria and Israel bridge their disagreement over Israeli occupation of the Golan Heights. In the face of these differences the ambitious multilateral negotiations concerning contentious issues including refugees, economic development, and resources were unsuccessful. By 1994 it was clear the talks had failed. Baker later described the conference as "a rich tale of determination, false starts, personal and political courage, blind alleys, perseverance, misjudgments, lost tempers, endless negotiations, scores of creative compromises, and both good faith and bad."[3] Even as the Madrid negotiations continued fitfully in public, secret back-channel meetings between Palestinians and Israelis were occurring in Oslo, Norway, sponsored by the Norwegian government.

The Oslo Accords and Camp David Summits

On September 13, 1993, Israeli prime minister Rabin and PLO chair Yasser Arafat signed the Declaration of Principles on Interim Self-Government Arrangements at the White House. As a result, along with Israeli foreign minister Shimon Peres, they would receive the 1994 Nobel Peace Prize. Standing next to President Bill Clinton, Arafat declared: "We must realize the prophecy of Isaiah, that the cry of violence shall no more be heard in your land, nor wrack nor ruin within your borders." Rabin responded: "Let me say to you, the Palestinians, we are destined to live together on the same soil in the same land," and "we say to you today, in a loud and clear voice: enough of blood and tears. Enough!"[4]

The Declaration of Principles was followed in 1994 by an Israeli–Jordanian peace treaty that President Clinton mediated, and the two countries normalized their relations and commenced trading with each other. Thereafter, an Interim Agreement concerning steps to carry out the Oslo Accords[5] was signed by Rabin and Arafat in September 1995. It recognized the PLO as the legitimate representative of the Palestinians; established a self-governing Palestinian Authority (PA) in the West Bank; and reaffirmed a "mutual commitment to act, in accordance with this Agreement, immediately, efficiently and effectively against acts or threats of terrorism, violence or incitement, whether committed by Palestinians or Israelis."[6] Administratively, the West Bank was divided into three areas: Area A, where the PA enjoyed full civil and security control; Area B, under Palestinian civil control and joint Palestinian–Israeli security control; and Area C, encompassing strategically sensitive locations that remained under Israeli control. Article 31 declared, "Neither side shall initiate or take any step that will change the status of the West Bank and the Gaza Strip pending the outcome of the permanent status negotiations."[7] The Palestinians interpreted Article 31 as requiring the cessation of Israeli settlement construction in Gaza, Jerusalem, and the West Bank. In October 1998 the two parties signed the Wye River Memorandum (negotiated in Wye, Maryland) in the company of President Clinton, by which they agreed to take additional steps toward carrying out the 1995 Interim Agreement.

The Oslo Accords and the Interim Agreement marked a high point in the peace process. In ensuing years, the Palestinian Authority (PA) formally recognized Israel, and took control of local government and internal security in Gaza and in major cities like Jericho in the West Bank. Ramallah served as the PA's de facto administrative capital. Self-government was supposed to last five years, after which a permanent agreement would take effect.

Although the accords focused on security issues, overshadowing economic concerns that had been raised earlier in the talks, Israel recognized that economic cooperation and development were important if the Palestinians were to embrace a peaceful settlement. Thus, the Oslo Accords called for such cooperation and economic development for the entire region as well as multilateral economic assistance for the Palestinians involving the United States, the European Union (EU), and other donors like Saudi Arabia and Japan. By 1997 foreign aid accounted for 15 percent of the Palestinian gross national product, and the Clinton administration expected dramatic regional economic improvement and an inflow of private investment once a final status agreement was reached.

The Oslo Accords also triggered the assassination of Israeli prime minister Rabin in November 1995 and eroded Palestinian support for Arafat. Thereafter, the peace process ground to a halt, and planning for additional regional economic development ended after Israeli elections the following May brought to power a hard-line coalition led by the Likud Party with Netanyahu as prime minister. Terrorism had not ceased in Gaza or the West Bank, and a wave of suicide attacks by Palestinian groups took place before Israel's election. Netanyahu accused the PLO of inciting the violence in violation of the Interim Agreement and threatened to end the peace process if it continued.

Although Rabin and his immediate successors, Shimon Peres and Netanyahu, had slowed construction of Israeli settlements in the occupied territories at the request of Secretary of State Madeleine Albright, their expansion continued—at least in existing settlements. Elections in 1999 saw the victory of a moderate Labor Party led by Ehud Barak, who continued expanding existing settlements to the dismay of Arafat, who regarded this as contrary to the spirit of Article 31 of the Oslo Accords and the Interim Agreement, and prejudicial to a final territorial settlement.[8]

The closest that Israelis and Palestinians came to a final agreement owed much to President Clinton's efforts at summit conferences with Barak and Arafat at Camp David in 2000. Under terms proposed by Clinton and accepted by Israel, the Palestinians would receive all of Gaza and most of the West Bank except for a small area that was the site of heavily populated Jewish settlement blocs, in exchange for which an equivalent area in Israel would be added to Gaza. Arab neighborhoods in Jerusalem would be turned over to the Palestinians, and both sides would declare the city their capital. Reparations would be paid to Palestinian refugees, and desalination facilities to provide fresh water would be provided for the Palestinians.

Talks between Barak and Arafat at Taba in the Sinai Peninsula in early 2001 were a last effort to reach agreement. Israel demanded sovereignty over settlement blocs containing 80 percent of Jewish residents in the West Bank and Gaza, which comprised about 6 percent of these territories, in return for territorial compensation elsewhere. At a White House meeting in December 2000, President Clinton proposed the parameters for a territorial swap in which between 94 and 96 percent of the West Bank territory should constitute a Palestinian state. "The land annexed by Israel should be compensated by a land swap of 1–3 percent"[9] that would minimize annexed areas and the number of Palestinians affected.

Disagreement persisted, however, over the extent of Israel's "security" settlements, and the talks ended owing to an imminent election in Israel that brought to power a hard-line coalition led by Prime Minister Ariel Sharon in February. In the end, for reasons that remain obscure, Arafat—whom Clinton blamed for the failed outcome—balked, sacrificing what were the most generous terms for a settlement offered until that time by an Israeli leader. Under pressure from Clinton, whose presidential term was ending, Arafat and Barak came painfully close to what would have been a final status agreement. The failure of negotiations also ended progress in Israeli–Palestinian economic cooperation.

The Second Intifada

Complicating Israeli–Palestinian negotiations was the onset of a second Palestinian intifada in September 2000, during which some 3,000 Palestinians and 1,000 Israelis died. Arafat may have planned the uprising after realizing his demands would not be met at Camp David. The failure of the Camp David negotiations and continued expansion of Israeli settlements in the West Bank heightened tensions between Israel and the Palestinians, and increased the Palestinians' desire for their own state, but the trigger for violence was pulled on September 28 when Sharon, then a candidate for Israeli prime minister, escorted by 1,000 police officers, provocatively visited Jerusalem's Temple Mount, site of the Dome of the Rock and the al-Aqsa Mosque (Islam's third-holiest site). Both sites were holy to Jews and Muslims. Sharon declared the area would remain under Israel's control and that he only wished to pray at the Temple Mount: "It's my absolute right to be there. I'm not hurting anyone and I had no intention of visiting the mosques."[10]

Sharon was a controversial figure, and whatever his purpose, the event incited Palestinians to violence. There followed car bombs, riots, kidnappings, guerrilla attacks, rocket attacks from Gaza, and suicide attacks in Israeli cities by Hamas and Islamic Jihad that Israelis regarded as Palestinian terrorism and Palestinians saw as justifiable national resistance to an illegal occupation. In response, Israeli forces demolished the homes of the families of suicide bombers, reoccupied West Bank towns, used air strikes, and resorted to mass arrests and targeted killings of foes like Hamas leader Sheikh Ahmed Yassin and his successor, Abdel Aziz al-Rantissi. Matters worsened after the failure of the Taba meeting. Fierce fighting took place in West Bank cities like Jenin and Bethlehem. The violence continued until 2005, dooming any prospect for a peace settlement during that time.

The second intifada and the many suicide bombings within Israel triggered Israel's decision to build a security barrier, or wall, that would run over 400 miles along the West Bank. In some places it enclosed and therefore annexed Palestinian lands within it. For this reason the wall was deemed illegal in an advisory opinion of the International Court of Justice in 2004. The ICJ concluded, "Israel must respect the right of the Palestinian people to self-determination and its obligations under humanitarian law and human rights law. Israel must also put an end to the violation of its international obligations flowing from the construction of the wall in the Occupied Palestinian Territory and must accordingly cease forthwith the works of construction of the wall, dismantle forthwith those parts of that structure situated within the Occupied Palestinian Territory."[11]

The Failed "Roadmap" to Peace

Under these conditions, the peace process virtually ground to a halt. Israel turned down negotiations proposed by Arab leaders in Beirut in 2002. A "roadmap" for peace that would lead to a Palestinian state was proposed by the United States along with Russia, the EU, and the UN in July 2002, following the appointment of Mahmoud Abbas as the first prime minister of the Palestinian Authority and after the United States and Israel refused to deal with Arafat any longer owing to his association with violent elements in the PLO. Arafat was besieged in Ramallah for several weeks by Israeli forces in 2002 and remained largely isolated until his death in 2004.

The roadmap involved a series of reciprocal steps by each side—the first an end to Palestinian violence, followed by a cessation of Israeli settlement construction—and, if all went well, culminating in establishment of a democratic Palestinian state, which President George H. W. Bush hoped could be achieved by 2005. Bush, Sharon, and Abbas met in Aqaba, Jordan, in June 2003, but the cease-fire they declared proved transitory. At a summit at Sharm el-Sheikh, Egypt, in February 2005, attended by Jordan's king Abdullah and Egypt's president Hosni Mubarak, Sharon publicly committed his country to the establishment of a Palestinian state, and Abbas called for an end to the intifada. Owing to a resumption of Palestinian violence and Israeli retaliation after a period of calm, however, the parties were unable to continue the peace process, and Israel unilaterally continued constructing its barrier on the West Bank to protect it from Palestinian attacks. In another unilateral decision, Sharon announced in early 2004 that Israeli settlements in Gaza would be dismantled followed by a withdrawal of Israeli troops.[12] Despite settler protests, the unilateral Israeli disengagement took place in August 2005, creating a vacuum Hamas would later fill. Thereafter, a peace conference in November 2007 organized by President George W. Bush in Annapolis, Maryland, failed like so many prior efforts to bridge Israeli–Palestinian differences.

Among the efforts to achieve a peaceful settlement during these years was an unofficial conference that brought prominent Israeli and Palestinian politicians together in Geneva in 2003. Building on the Camp David and Taba talks, the negotiators went beyond the incremental roadmap and sought a comprehensive "final status" agreement that would confront issues such as the status of Jerusalem, Israeli settlements in the occupied territories, and the "right of return" of Palestinian refugees. The negotiations produced a nonbinding Draft Permanent Status Agreement, also known as the Geneva Accord, which called for a two-state solution in which each side recognized the legitimacy of the other's right to exist, territorial boundaries that would give Palestinians much of the Gaza Strip and the West Bank, and the principle that both "shall have their mutually recognized capitals in the areas of Jerusalem under their respective sovereignty." In addition, "The state of Israel shall be responsible for resettling the Israelis residing in Palestinian sovereign territory outside this territory" and the two sides "recognize that, in the context of two independent states, Palestine and Israel, living side by side in peace, an agreed resolution of the refugee problem is necessary for achieving a just, comprehensive and lasting peace between them."[13]

Additional efforts to revive the peace process were complicated by the emergence of two extremist groups—Hamas, an offshoot of Egypt's Muslim Brotherhood, and Hezbollah, a Shia Islamic group backed by Iran and Syria. Neither group recognized Israel's right to exist. Both threatened Israeli security and were designated terrorist groups by America and the EU (until the EU's General Court removed this designation of Hamas in late 2014). Following his election, President Obama sent former senator George Mitchell on a fact-finding visit to the Middle East, where he conferred with Israeli and PA leaders. Since Washington refused to negotiate with Hamas, however, that organization dismissed the Mitchell mission, which in the end had few tangible results.

Hamas ("Islamic Resistance Movement")

Hamas was founded in December 1987 by Sheikh Ahmed Yassin during the first intifada and drew support from Palestinians who regarded Arafat and the PLO as increasingly authoritarian, corrupt, and ineffective. Hamas abandoned the Muslim Brotherhood's policy of nonviolence while retaining the goal of establishing an *Islamic* Palestinian state. Its 1988 covenant committed the group to "raise the banner of Allah over every inch of Palestine" (Article 6) and declared, "so-called peaceful solutions and international conferences, are in contradiction to the principles of the Islamic Resistance Movement" (Article 13).[14]

Hamas's military wing—the Izz ad-Din al-Qassam Brigades, established in 1991—was responsible for guerrilla attacks against Israel and a high proportion of suicide bombings in Israel after 1993, especially during the second intifada. Ahmed Jabari commanded the Qassam Brigades until he died in an Israeli air strike in late 2012. Hamas opposed the Oslo Accords and repeatedly sought to undermine the peace process between Israel and the PLO.

In 2006 Hamas won an electoral majority in the Palestinian parliament and then, after a series of violent clashes with supporters of Fatah, a more moderate secular group, it carried out a coup and seized power in Gaza in June 2007, leaving Fatah to administer Palestinian communities in the West Bank. This led to the division of Palestinian territory and continuing tension between Hamas and Fatah. Subsequent Arab-sponsored efforts to get Hamas and Fatah to form a united government failed. Meanwhile, Hamas's efforts to provide social welfare, charity, and health care to the Palestinians in Gaza have increased its popularity. After taking control of Gaza, Hamas also introduced new textbooks into Gaza's schools to replace the PLO's curriculum and to intensify hatred of Israel among young Palestinians.

With Hamas in power, Israel and Egypt isolated Gaza economically, and Washington cut off financial assistance to Palestinians in Gaza. Since Hamas took control of Gaza, its relations with Israel have seesawed between spasms of violence and uneasy cease-fires. Periodic efforts by outsiders like Egypt to overcome the rift between Fatah and Hamas have failed to reunite the two factions. Violence in Gaza (as well as rockets fired into Israel by Palestinian militants located in Gaza) led Israel to blockade the territory and try to destroy the myriad tunnels built to smuggle weapons into the area. That blockade, according to the UN, produced an economic and humanitarian crisis in Gaza, and in May 2010 triggered a crisis with Turkey after nine Turks who were trying to break the blockade died in a skirmish with Israeli soldiers who boarded their vessel.

After the coup in Gaza, prospects for a peaceful settlement grew increasingly remote because of the deep division among the Palestinians. That division complicated negotiations for establishing a single coherent Palestinian state. Neither the United States nor Israel was prepared to negotiate with a group they considered to be terrorists, though Hamas's leaders, Khaled Meshal and Ismail Haniyeh, have implied on occasion that the group might consider a two-state solution based on Israel's pre–June 1967 borders. Whether Meshal and Haniyeh meant they would accept a permanent solution or merely a lengthy cease-fire was unclear.

Intermittent rocket fire from Gaza followed by Israeli retaliation continued between 2005 and 2008, when Egypt mediated a cease-fire. Israel continued to hold Hamas responsible for the actions of all Palestinians in Gaza and demanded the release of an Israeli soldier kidnapped by Hamas in 2006. (The soldier, Gilad Shalit, remained a hostage from 2006 until 2011, when he was exchanged for over 1,000 Palestinians imprisoned by Israel.) In December 2008, in an effort to suppress rocket fire into Israel, destroy Hamas's stockpiles of weapons, and end weapons smuggling into Gaza, the Israel Defense Forces invaded Gaza and launched air strikes against Hamas ("Operation Cast Lead") in an effort to degrade Hamas's capabilities and deter additional attacks from Gaza.

Three weeks after its incursion, Israel withdrew from Gaza, leaving Hamas in power and more popular among Palestinians than before. Owing to the high number of Palestinian civilian casualties (1,300–1,400 deaths), the question of whether Israeli forces had committed war crimes during the conflict became a topic of heated debate. Thereafter, episodic violence continued. And after a number of Egyptian soldiers were killed near the Gaza border in August 2012, Egyptian security forces clamped down on the movement of goods through tunnels linking Gaza to Egypt, thereby squeezing the already weak economy of the Palestinians in Gaza.

Another effort in May 2011 to bridge the Palestinian schism led Hamas to agree that its resistance would be peaceful, but the group was unwilling or unable to suppress militants in other Palestinian factions from using violence. After the firing of Iranian-supplied Fajr-3 and Fajr-5 missiles from Gaza with the range to reach Tel Aviv and Jerusalem, Israel initiated a brief but intensive bombing campaign against Hamas's installations in November 2012; employed with considerable success its U.S.-financed mobile Iron Dome anti-missile system; and seemed on the verge of invading Gaza again until Secretary of State Hillary Rodham Clinton rushed to the region from Southeast Asia, where she had been accompanying President Obama, and—aided by Egypt's president, Mohamed Morsi—persuaded the Netanyahu government to desist.

The revolution in Egypt that brought Morsi and the Muslim Brotherhood to power in 2012 strengthened Hamas because the new government was more sympathetic to the group and its aims than President Mubarak. However, the overthrow of Morsi a year later again isolated Hamas and eroded its influence within the Palestinian movement as Egypt's new military rulers shut down its smuggling tunnels into Gaza, cutting off the source of much of Hamas's funds and slowing the movement of people to and from Gaza. Hamas had already severed relations with the Syrian government, from which it had received money and weapons owing to its support of the anti-Assad insurgency. Syria's patron, Iran, also cut off funding to Hamas and began to channel funds to the extremist group Islamic Jihad. By late 2013 Hamas was virtually bankrupt. Nevertheless, a senior Hamas official declared, "Unlike the Muslim Brotherhood, we will not be good victims."[15]

The third and bloodiest Israeli–Hamas war erupted in 2014. Three Israeli teenagers were kidnapped and murdered on the West Bank by members of Hamas, and a Palestinian teenager was killed in retaliation. Israel jailed Hamas supporters in the West Bank, and Netanyahu declared the events showed that Israel would have to maintain a long-term presence there. Hamas resumed missile attacks into Israel, including its major cities (temporarily closing Tel Aviv's airport), and Israel retaliated with air strikes and sent its soldiers once more into Gaza in "Operation Protective Edge," seeking to end the missile attacks and close down tunnels through which Hamas was infiltrating militants into Israel. In a violent repeat of earlier wars with Hamas, there were numerous Palestinian civilian casualties, though Hamas inflicted considerably greater losses on Israel than in previous conflicts. A UN human-rights official suggested that both sides might have committed war crimes by indiscriminate attacks on civilians.

It was a difficult moment for Hamas, which had renewed hostilities because of its political isolation, financial woes, and inability to achieve its objectives. "All these achievements of Hamas, if they strike a deal without achieving something for the people of Gaza, they will lose everything and will bury themselves,"[16] declared a Palestinian political scientist. Netanyahu had responded under domestic political pressure, notably, "a growing segment of the Israeli public" that "is susceptible to fits of religious ultranationalism."[17]

With hostile regimes in Egypt and Syria, Hamas remained isolated. "The Arab states' loathing and fear of political Islam is so strong," concluded one analyst, "that it outweighs their allergy to Benjamin Netanyahu."[18] "In all the other invasions and assaults on Gaza," added another, "there was at least some government that would come out and talk about how what Israel was doing was illegal and show some support. This time around, there's been nothing."[19] Protests in sympathy with Gaza's residents took place in several countries, as well as eruptions of ugly anti-Semitic incidents in Europe. Israel's sense of insecurity had deepened, domestic fissures had reopened, and Netanyahu had lost his reputation for keeping Israel secure.

After fifty days and several abortive cease-fires, an open-ended and vaguely worded truce was reached. Neither side had achieved its objectives: Israel had sought to disarm Hamas, destroying its arsenal of rockets and the tunnels it had built into Israel, and Hamas had hoped to end Israel's blockade of Gaza. Hamas declared victory, and an Israeli minister described the cease-fire as "a reasonable arrangement."[20] The conflict, the longest and bloodiest of those between Israel and Hamas, further strained U.S.–Israeli relations as American leaders vigorously criticized the deaths of civilians in Gaza. "This is the most sustained period of antagonism in the relationship," declared a former U.S. ambassador to Israel. "I don't know how the relationship recovers as long as you have this president and this prime minister."[21] With public opinion and Congress supporting Israel's military operation and Arab governments remaining silent, the Obama administration had little influence over Israel.

If Hamas was a security threat on Israel's southern border, the paramilitary group Hezbollah, located in southern Lebanon on Israel's northern border, posed as great a threat owing to its links with Shia Iran and its global reach—a reach reflected by the group's terrorist bombing of a Jewish synagogue in Argentina in 1994.

Hezbollah ("Party of God")

Lebanon's population is a religious and ethnic mosaic. Its Muslim majority is divided into Sunni, Shia, and Druze communities. Lebanon's Christians include Maronites, Greek Orthodox, and Greek Catholics. There is also a large Palestinian and Syrian refugee population in the country. Lebanon's constitution reserves parliamentary seats for different sects. The country's president must be a Maronite Christian, its prime minister a Sunni Muslim, and the Speaker of parliament a Shia Muslim.

Lebanon's communities view one another with suspicion and have their own political parties, territorial strongholds, and paramilitary militias. Between 1975 and 1990 the country descended into a bloody and confused civil war that pitted these groups against one another. Syria intervened in 1976 in northern Lebanon and dominated Lebanese politics until 2005, when it was accused of a series of assassinations including that of former Lebanese prime minister Rafik Hariri, which triggered massive anti-Syrian demonstrations. Israel invaded the country in 1978 and again in 1982 in efforts to set up a security zone in south Lebanon. The 1982 intervention, "Operation Peace for Galilee," led by then Israeli defense minister Ariel Sharon, climaxed with Israel's siege of Lebanon's capital, Beirut; the massacre of Palestinians in the Sabra and Shatila refugee camps by Israeli-supported Christian forces; and the expulsion of the PLO from Lebanon. Although a cease-fire was reached, it soon collapsed, throwing the country into chaos once again. Israeli forces withdrew from much of Lebanon in 1985, retaining only a buffer zone in the south. These events were the background for Hezbollah's emergence.

Hezbollah attracted the support of Lebanon's Shia population, the poorest and fastest growing of the communities. Most Lebanese Shiites were located in southern Lebanon, Baalbek in the eastern Beqaa Valley, and the southern suburbs of Beirut. An estimated 300,000 Palestinian refugees resided in Lebanon, and Hezbollah, though not a Palestinian organization, championed the Palestinian cause. The group became a significant actor after Iran's 1979 Shia Islamic revolution that overthrew that country's shah and Israel's 1982 invasion of Lebanon. Following Israel's invasion, some 800 American Marines entered Lebanon as part of a multinational force sent to oversee the PLO withdrawal. In April, Hezbollah car-bombed the U.S. embassy in Beirut, and in October it launched devastating suicide attacks against American and French troops in the city. Hezbollah's suicide bombing of the Marine barracks resulted in the largest one-day loss of Marine lives since the World War II battle of Iwo Jima. President Ronald Reagan withdrew the remaining Marines in February 1983.

Hezbollah, which remained closely aligned with the Assad regime in Syria and with Iran, sought to drive Israel out of Lebanon, erode Israel's political and military power, and aid the Palestinian cause. During Lebanon's civil war, Hezbollah sought to consolidate its political power among Lebanese Shiites by eliminating rival Shia political groups. While gaining favor in the Shia community by providing social services, Hezbollah kidnapped Westerners and increasingly became an Iranian pawn. Following the end of Lebanon's civil war, Syrian forces in the country allowed Hezbollah to retain its arms, and the group continued attacks against Israeli soldiers until all Israeli forces were withdrawn from Lebanon in 2000. Claiming responsibility for ending Israel's presence in the country, the group and its leader, Hassan Nasrallah, acquired unrivaled popularity within Lebanon's Shia community. Thereafter, Hezbollah's dependence on arms and funding from Iran and Syria grew as it harassed Israeli forces in cross-border raids. Hezbollah also funded itself from the South American cocaine trade and drug smuggling in West Africa, laundering funds using two Lebanese money exchange houses to move tens of millions of dollars in drug profits through American banks on behalf of the group. "Hezbollah is operating like a major drug cartel,"[22] declared an agent for the U.S. Drug Enforcement Agency. Comparing the group to the Mafia, another law-enforcement officer noted, "They operate like the Gambinos [a New York City crime family] on steroids."[23]

Following Hezbollah's abduction of two Israeli soldiers in July 2006 to barter for the release of Lebanese imprisoned by Israel, Israel mounted large-scale attacks against Hezbollah that lasted over a month, resulting in over 1,000 Lebanese deaths and destruction of large areas of Beirut. In retaliation, Hezbollah fired Iranian rockets at Israeli cities, including Tiberias and Haifa, resulting in 55 Israeli deaths.[24] A UN-brokered truce went into effect in August, and Security Council Resolution 1701 provided for additional UN peacekeepers in southern Lebanon and demanded that Hezbollah disarm. Hezbollah refused to lay down its arms and, owing to its successful resistance against Israel's incursion, was acclaimed in much of the Arab world. The group was rearmed by Iran, acquiring sophisticated Iranian missiles that threatened Israeli cities.

Israeli military leaders believe another war with Hezbollah is only a matter of time. Alluding to the threat to Israel on the Lebanese border, Israeli general Herzl Halevi observed, "I don't think there is the war or the operation that will solve the problem. . . . The interesting issue is how you create a longer gap between the wars." Halevi concluded that the next war would not "be a simple one," but "We are ready to pay this price to make a very decisive and strong war to make the gap as long as possible."[25] Hezbollah continued to act as Iran's surrogate, a role reflected in terrorist attacks against Israeli citizens in India, Thailand, and elsewhere in retaliation for Israeli-sponsored assassinations of Iranian nuclear scientists and cyberattacks against Iranian nuclear facilities.

In recent years, Hezbollah used its popularity to increase its political power in Lebanon and was responsible for assassinating several high-ranking Lebanese political opponents. After several violent clashes with Lebanon's armed forces and continuing political opposition to the Lebanese government, the group emerged in 2008 as the country's power broker—a state within the state—with a capacity to veto government policies. And in November 2009 Hezbollah entered Lebanon's government. With the onset of the Syrian civil war in 2011, however, Hezbollah found itself facing the prospect that its principal supporter along with Iran, the Syrian regime of Bashar al-Assad, might be overthrown. Hezbollah, therefore, intervened in Syria to assist the Assad regime, alienating Sunnis in both Syria and Lebanon and muddying its reputation as a stalwart foe of Israel, but gaining fighting skills that could be used against Israel.

Israel avoided involvement in Syria's civil war, but its leaders were dismayed by U.S. reluctance to respond militarily to Syria's use of chemical weapons, believing that Iran would conclude that American threats to prevent its acquiring nuclear weapons were not credible. A former Israeli UN ambassador concluded that U.S. indecision regarding Syria made it appear that "America's allies cannot rely on it that its enemies can do what they want and nothing will happen to them."[26]

Israel also made it clear it would not permit the transfer of sophisticated weapons from Syria to Hezbollah and attacked Syrian convoys and storage facilities to prevent Hezbollah from acquiring "game-changing" weapons such as surface-to-sea missiles, surface-to-air missiles, and Iranian mobile surface-to-surface missiles. These attacks were part of Israel's continuing conflict with Iran and Hezbollah rather than efforts to alter the outcome of Syria's civil war.

The Kerry Round of Negotiations

Frustrated in efforts to achieve Palestinian statehood through negotiation, in 2011 the PLO, which had nonstate observer status in the UN since 1974, sought to be recognized as a sovereign state. The Obama administration opposed the PLO's effort, and its bid failed when the Security Council was unable to assemble the minimum of nine of the fifteen votes necessary to pass a resolution. Even had it done so, Washington would have used its veto as a permanent council member to prevent the resolution's passage. In late November 2012, however, a majority in the General Assembly agreed to admit the PLO as a nonmember observer state, a status also enjoyed by the Vatican. As such, the PLO could participate in assembly debates and would find it easier to enter other UN agencies like the International Criminal Court (ICC). Although pleased with a symbolic victory that showed that most countries supported Palestinian statehood, the PLO insisted it would continue seeking UN recognition as a sovereign country.

In Israel's January 2013 elections, Netanyahu's electoral bloc, though remaining the largest in Israel's parliament, fared worse than predicted. The prime minister's coalition excluded the country's ultra-Orthodox parties while including his Likud Party as well as the right-wing and nationalist Jewish Home Party led by Naftali Bennett and the secular and centrist Yesh Atid Party headed by Yair Lapid. As Moshe Arens, a former Israeli minister of foreign affairs, once observed: "U.S.–Israeli relations are close to the heart of the Israeli electorate. If one party is perceived to be the source of friction in that relationship, then it may pay a price at the ballot box."[27]

Although Israelis and Palestinians disagreed on many issues, including how they viewed Washington, many on both sides wanted President Obama "to play a larger role in resolving the Israeli–Palestinian stalemate."[28] Thus, in February 2013 Israel grudgingly succumbed to pressure from Secretary Kerry to reopen negotiations with the Palestinians, for which Bennett criticized Netanyahu so vociferously that the prime minister demanded an apology. According to an Israeli analyst, "The more serious these negotiations get, the more fragile this coalition is."[29] Kerry had "gotten them into the pool," noted a Middle East expert. "Right now they're in the very shallow end, and they're going to have to swim in deeper waters—and they can be treacherous. It's still an achievement that he's gotten them into the pool."[30] Kerry followed up with several trips to the region, engaging in shuttle diplomacy between Palestinian and Israeli leaders. He had previously also proposed a plan to encourage private investment in the West Bank to reduce Palestinian unemployment and increase the West Bank's gross domestic product by 50 percent within three years. For its part the PLO, on the verge of bankruptcy, was pressed by the Americans and the Arab League to reopen talks with Israel. Referring to Abbas and Netanyahu, Kerry commented, "Both leaders have demonstrated a willingness to make difficult decisions that have been instrumental in getting to this point."[31]

The resumption of Israeli–Palestinian peace talks in August 2013 began on several sour notes. One condition set by the PLO for a resumption of talks was the release of imprisoned Palestinians. Israel met the condition, but only minimally, by initially releasing twenty-six Palestinian prisoners. In addition, Israel announced shortly before the talks began that it was building an additional 1,000 housing units in East Jerusalem and was adding the number of settlements in the West Bank eligible for government subsidies. Moreover, settlement construction announced earlier, if carried out, would effectively sever East Jerusalem from the West Bank. "The Israeli government," declared Hanan Ashrawi, a member of the PLO executive committee, "has approved a confidence-destruction measure."[32] A Palestinian expert in national security added: "Jerusalem has to be negotiated. Israel is determining the outcome of the negotiation before it has started."[33] And a British-Israeli historian noted sarcastically that Netanyahu "is like a man who, while negotiating the division of a pizza, continues to eat it."[34] By contrast, the Israeli director of an organization dedicated to increasing the Jewish population in Jerusalem declared, "What has happened since 1967 in the Old City [East Jerusalem] and around the Old City has made any discussion of dividing Jerusalem the way the Arabs see it irrelevant, because on the ground it ain't going to happen."[35]

As with previous efforts, even agreement over principles proved elusive, and as the round of negotiations approached its end in April 2014, the effort was near collapse. Although Abbas conceded that Israeli soldiers could remain in the West Bank for as long as five years and a U.S.-led NATO force could remain in a Palestinian state indefinitely, Kerry no longer referred to achieving a comprehensive settlement but limited his objective to a vague "framework agreement" of principles that Israel's defense minister harshly criticized. A State Department official responded, "The remarks of the defense minister, if accurate, are offensive and inappropriate, especially given all that the United States is doing to support Israel's security needs."[36]

Other events contributing to a deteriorating atmosphere included Israel's failure to release a fourth group of Palestinian prisoners until Abbas agreed to extend negotiations beyond the deadline. The PLO denied that extending negotiations was linked to prisoner release and submitted applications to join several international organizations as steps toward acquiring sovereign recognition. These applications were in violation of an earlier agreement not to take such actions as long as negotiations continued. Israel responded by halting the transfer of taxes it collected for the Palestinian Authority to pay its debts for Israeli utilities, bringing the PA to the brink of bankruptcy.

The next step in this increasingly hostile tit-for-tat interaction was a threat by President Abbas to disband the PA and give Israel full responsibility for maintaining security on the West Bank. Simultaneously, the PLO and Hamas renewed negotiations for unifying the Palestinian movement, and Netanyahu responded by suspending peace talks, declaring that Abbas could "have peace with Israel or a pact with Hamas—he can't have both."[37] Abbas wished to reinvigorate the Palestinian movement and regain control of Gaza, while Hamas sought to avoid bankruptcy and end its isolation in Gaza. Abbas "did a huge favor to Bibi [Netanyahu]," declared a former Israeli national security advisor. "Since we are in this blame game now, it is easier for him to say, 'This is not our fault, look at our potential partner.'"[38]

Abbas "had shut down," declared an American official. "His experience in the last nine months, of settlements gone wild has just, I think, convinced him that he doesn't have a partner."[39] A further meeting between Abbas and Israeli justice minister Tzipi Livni in London in May 2014 failed to overcome the breech caused by the PLO–Hamas negotiations, and Abbas formed a new government that included four ministers from Gaza. Even Pope Francis sought to overcome the rift by sponsoring a ceremony of "peace prayers" for Israeli and Palestinian leaders at the Vatican.

Secretary Kerry argued that both sides shared the blame for the end of talks, but that Israel's announcement of additional apartment construction in Gilo, East Jerusalem—a decision that deeply divided Israeli politicians—was the final straw. "Poof," he said, "that was sort of the moment,"[40] a remark that drew an angry response from Israeli officials. Kerry further angered Israel when he compared it to pre-1993 South Africa, declaring that the country risked becoming an "apartheid state."[41] Kerry, responded an Israeli official, "knows that it was the Palestinians who said 'no' to continued direct talks with Israel in November; who said 'no' to his proposed framework for final status talks; who said 'no' to even discussing recognition of Israel as the nation-state of the Jewish people; who said 'no' to a meeting with Kerry himself; and who said 'no' to an extension of the talks."[42] Washington declared a "pause" in its efforts to reconcile the adversaries, and Shlomo Avineri, formerly director general of Israel's foreign ministry, captured the essence of the problem: "The gap between the most moderate position in Israel and the most moderate position in the Palestinian leadership is too far right now."[43] "We worked very hard," said President Obama. "But, frankly, the politics inside of Israel and the politics among the Palestinians as well made it very difficult."[44]

With the breakdown of negotiations and the effort by Abbas to reunite the Palestinian movement, it appeared little would happen soon. After the formation of a new Palestinian cabinet consisting of non-political experts and Abbas's promise that it would adhere to his policy of nonviolence and follow earlier Israeli–Palestinian agreements, however, Israel's leaders were in for a shock. Instead of refusing to have anything to do with a Palestinian government that enjoyed the support of Hamas, the Obama administration said it was ready to deal with that government. Washington was prepared for new Palestinian elections and emphasized that no Hamas members were in the new Palestinian cabinet. "With what we know now," declared a State Department spokesperson, "we will work with this government."[45] A senior U.S. official proclaimed, "We're not naïve. We understand that this could be Hamas's nose under the tent, that it could lead Hamas to get a foothold in the West Bank, that terrorist cells could spring up in the West Bank again under a looser regime. So we're watching all of that very carefully to ensure that it doesn't happen."[46]

Israel's ambassador in Washington angrily responded, "With suits in the front office and terrorists in the back office, it should not be business as usual," while Israel's previous ambassador contended, "It delivers a blow to American credibility, and American credibility is cardinal here. Because at the end of the day, if Israel is going to make concessions for peace, is going to take risks for peace, we have to rely on our alliance with the United States. There has to be deep trust."⁴⁷ Pro-Israeli American members of Congress were outraged by the decision of the Obama administration, and the Israeli government swiftly approved additional settlement construction in the West Bank and East Jerusalem.

Following the collapse of the Kerry initiative, however, the new Palestinian government failed to wrest control in Gaza from Hamas, and with the third Hamas–Israeli war the cycle of violence had resumed. Palestinian frustration over the lack of progress in reaching a "two-state solution" with Israel and tension over Jerusalem's Temple Mount boiled over. Beginning in late 2015, individual Palestinians began to attack individual Israelis, frequently with knives. In response, Israeli security forces acted with growing lethality. This led some observers to fear a third intifada, or "stabbing intifada," was imminent.⁴⁸ As he stepped down as America's mediator between Israel and the Palestinians, Martin Indyk sadly noted, "It's the distrust between the leaders and between the people that holds us up and makes it difficult" after "20 years of distrust."⁴⁹

CONCLUSION: WHAT NEXT?

The Middle East status quo has evolved in recent years, though the basic clash among religions and nationalities persisted. The future became even cloudier owing to the angry breakdown in negotiations between Israel and the Palestinians in 2014. Speaking to the UN in September 2014 Palestinian president Abbas declared it was impossible "to return to the cycle of negotiations that failed to deal with the substance of the matter and the fundamental question."⁵⁰ An effort by the PLO to get a binding Security Council resolution demanding an Israeli withdrawal from the occupied territories was blocked. "There is aggression practiced against our land and our country," declared Abbas, "and the Security Council has let us down—where shall we go?"⁵¹ Thereafter, the PLO applied for admission to the ICC. Washington then threatened to cut off financial assistance to the Palestinians, and Israel withheld tax revenues it collects for the PA that are vital for it to provide public services. The PLO became an ICC member in April 2015.

The two-state solution, which Prime Minister Netanyahu reluctantly accepted, enjoyed little support in the prime minister's cabinet, although it was supported by a majority of Israelis. Netanyahu could probably cobble together a parliamentary majority that would include the Labor Party as well as a number of smaller groups in favor of two states, but only if he abandoned the Likud Party as Ariel Sharon did when he left Likud in November 2005 to found a new and more flexible centrist party, Kadima. Netanyahu, however, was unwilling to follow Sharon's example. Instead, he fired moderate members in his cabinet, called a new election for March 2015, accelerated settlement expansion, and demanded military control of the Jordan Valley in the West Bank. His demand that Palestinian leaders acknowledge Israel as a "Jewish state" implied Palestinian refugees would have to surrender the "right of return" prior to a comprehensive settlement. With a coalition that had only a single-vote majority, Israel's prime minister's government would likely fall if he made concessions to the Palestinians, notably taking steps toward establishing an independent Palestinian state. Netanyahu's position created a dilemma for Abbas, who could make additional concessions only at the risk of being ousted by his own hard-liners.

Israelis crave security in an insecure and changing region. Among Israeli concerns, the most important were the growing role of Islamic extremists, American indecisiveness toward Syria and

Iran, and—most significant—Iran's progress toward acquiring nuclear weapons (chapter 13). The latter was regarded by Israelis as an impermissible existential threat. "Israel does not oppose Iran having a peaceful nuclear energy program," declared Israel's security cabinet in a statement. "But as has been demonstrated in many countries, from Canada to Indonesia, peaceful programs do not require uranium enrichment or plutonium production. Iran's nuclear program does."[52]

Although Israel remained a Middle East superpower, its position was complicated by events in Egypt and Syria. In some ways it was in a stronger position as a result, at least in the short term. Among these changes was the emergence of new governments in Egypt, where President Hosni Mubarak had been briefly replaced by a government dominated by the Muslim Brotherhood, which was in turn overthrown by the army. Although the Brotherhood had honored the Egyptian–Israeli peace treaty, it did not provide Israel the security it had enjoyed under Mubarak, who loathed Islamists and refused to aid Hamas. Israel was pleased by the army coup, sensing it would be more secure with Egypt's anti-Islamist military leaders who viewed Hamas as a militant arm of the Brotherhood. And divisions between Fatah and Hamas, the former controlling the West Bank and the latter controlling Gaza, had set back the Palestinian cause.

In addition, neighboring Syria was riven by civil war. The Assad regime, though Israel's avowed enemy, had avoided direct confrontation over the Golan Heights and maintained stability along its border with Israel. If it collapsed, there was a risk of Islamic extremists creating havoc along that border. Syria's chaotic condition created the additional prospect of that country's stockpile of advanced weapons falling into the hands of extremists or Israel's nemesis, Hezbollah. In addition, the Palestinian cause remained weakened by internal divisions. Instability in Syria and Egypt had reduced the prospect of a conventional interstate war but increased the threat to Israel posed by nonstate groups such as Hamas, Hezbollah, and Egyptian jihadists, encouraging the Israel Defense Forces (IDF) to restructure itself. "The IDF," declared a Likud politician, "relies on cheap manual labor instead of specialization and technology and this harms the country's defenses."[53] The plan would transform it from a conscript army toward becoming a professional army of volunteers and from relying on manpower-intensive armored forces and investing in its air force, intelligence collection, and cyberwarfare.

President Obama sought to make progress in resolving the Israeli–Palestinian stalemate during his first term, thereby reducing Muslim animosity toward America. In Cairo in 2009, the president had said:

> Too many tears have flowed. Too much blood has been shed. All of us have a responsibility to work for the day when the mothers of Israelis and Palestinians can see their children grow up without fear; when the Holy Land of three great faiths is the place of peace that God intended it to be; when Jerusalem is a secure and lasting home for Jews and Christians and Muslims, and a place for all of the children of Abraham to mingle peacefully together as in the story of Isra, when Moses, Jesus, and Mohammed (peace be upon them) joined in prayer.[54]

And in Israel in 2014, Obama warned that if "Palestinians come to believe that the possibility of a contiguous, sovereign Palestinian state is no longer within reach, then our ability to manage the international fallout is going to be limited."[55]

Washington failed to make headway in resolving the Israeli–Palestinian deadlock. Obama did not visit Israel until his second term, and the president found himself dealing with an Israeli leader who, having agreed to a two-state solution in 2009, had done little to accomplish this goal and who reversed his position during Israel's 2015 electoral campaign. In 2010 Obama set September 2011 as his deadline for achieving a two-state solution. In addition, Obama and Netanyahu, noted Martin Indyk, "have a fraught relationship and it's fuelled by a belief on the part of both of them that the other is trying to screw them, trip them up, thwart their policies, corner them, ambush them."[56] Their dislike of each other was clear during the debate over whether to conclude a deal with Iran over that country's nuclear program. Once the deal had been completed, Netanyahu and Obama tried to patch up their relations in a meeting in Washington in November 2015, but in fact they would never fully overcome their differences.

Indeed, by the time of his reelection Obama was widely disliked by Israelis and was no longer trusted by Palestinians, for whom little had changed during the president's first term. The president had no desire to get bogged down in a Middle East quagmire but could not ignore the region.

11

Is Israeli–Palestinian Peace Possible?

Chapter 11 outlines the issues that divide Israel and the Palestinians and examines alternative policies available to America in dealing with them. The peace process has become even cloudier owing to the breakdown in negotiations between Israel and the Palestinians in April 2014. Key issues we will examine separating Israel and Palestine include:

- Whether Israelis and Palestinians should live in two states or one.

- How to overcome the problem posed by Israeli settlements in the West Bank and Jerusalem.

- How to respond to Palestinian demands for the return of refugees displaced in wars with Israel.

- How to deal with Hamas, Gaza, and a divided Palestinian movement.

- How to find a solution for Palestinian–Israeli differences over disputed resources like water and underwater natural gas deposits.

There are a variety of alternative policies available to Washington in dealing with Israel and the Palestinians and the issues that divide them. "There is no such thing as benign neglect when it comes to the Middle East,"[1] as one Middle East specialist declared. Thus, Washington is pursuing a dual policy of seeking to ensure Israel's security, in President Barack Obama's words, while not turning "our backs on the legitimate Palestinian aspiration for dignity, opportunity, and a state of their own."[2]

The possibility of a settlement remains hostage to Israeli and Palestinian hard-liners. In Israel, conservative intelligence and military officials enjoy an influential role in policy-making, and settlers in the occupied territories oppose efforts to make them withdraw or cease expanding. In 1994 an Israeli hard-liner, American-born Baruch Goldstein, undermined the peace process when he murdered twenty-nine Muslim worshippers in a mosque at the Cave of the Patriarchs in the West Bank city of Hebron. "I am shamed," declared Prime Minister Yitzhak Rabin, "over the disgrace imposed upon us by a degenerate murderer."[3]

Rabin himself was assassinated in 1995 by a hard-line right-wing student, Yigal Amir, who argued the Israeli prime minister was responsible for the Oslo Accords and was prepared to surrender some of the territory that Israel had occupied in 1967. And Egypt's president, Anwar Sadat, was assassinated in 1981 by members of an extremist Islamic group led by a radical Egyptian military officer who was incensed by Sadat's visit to Jerusalem and subsequent peace treaty with Israel. Sadat's assassination took place on the anniversary of Egypt's crossing of the Suez Canal during the 1973 Yom Kippur War. Hamas and Hezbollah, as we have seen, are both extreme anti-Israeli groups and have repeatedly undermined efforts at reaching a settlement. Extremism begets extremism in the Israeli–Palestinian relationship.

Israel wants its foes to recognize the country's sovereign legitimacy as a Jewish state, with secure borders and Jerusalem as its capital. Although some Palestinians refuse to recognize Israel's right to exist, most seek an independent state consisting of Gaza and the West Bank with Jerusalem as its capital, but without the Israeli settlements established after 1967. They also seek the right of return for Palestinian refugees and their descendants. Each side demands control of their religion's holy sites in Jerusalem—for Jews the Wailing Wall (or Western Wall), which formed part of the enclosure of Herod's temple near the most sacred area of the ancient First and Second Temples of Jerusalem and at which Jews traditionally gather for prayer, and for Muslims the al-Aqsa Mosque ("the Noble Sanctuary"), the destination of the Prophet Muhammad's night journey from Mecca on a spirit horse. In recent years, in violation of a tacit arrangement under which Jews remained below at the Wailing Wall, small Jewish groups ascended the Temple Mount, the thirty-seven-acre site of both al-Aqsa and the ancient Jewish temple, and Palestinian leaders called on Muslims to prevent such "incursions." In 2014 Israel's closure of al-Aqsa for several days triggered violent Palestinian demonstrations. Persistent differences over management of the Temple Mount triggered additional violence in 2015. What Muslims regard as provocative, Jews see as the right to pray at their holiest site.

TWO STATES OR ONE?

The first and most crucial issue in Israeli–Palestinian relations is whether the two sides are prepared to accept two sovereign states living side by side and what the boundaries of those states should be. This solution was initially advanced in the original UN partition plan and was central to a plan put forward by the Arab League at a 2002 summit that was based on "the land-for-peace principle, and Israel's acceptance of an independent Palestinian state with East Jerusalem as its capital, in return for the establishment of normal relations in the context of a comprehensive peace with Israel."[4] In 2013 the Arab League softened the terms of the original plan by suggesting that Israel and the Palestinians could trade land ("land swaps") rather than reinstate the precise pre–1967 war boundaries.

Israel lives in a dangerous neighborhood:

> The PowerPoint maps that Israeli military briefers use for Sinai, Gaza, Lebanon and Syria today consist of multicolored circles, and inside each are clusters of different armed groups . . . with nonstate actors, armed with rockets, dressed as civilians and nested among civilians on four out of its five borders. . . . But the status quo is not neutral. Israel needs to do all it can to avoid turning itself into a kind of forced binational state—with a hostile minority in its belly—by permanently holding onto the West Bank and its 2.5 million Palestinians. That's exactly the kind of states blowing up in the world of disorder.[5]

The Palestinians have been divided on the two-state question, the PLO having agreed to two states and Hamas remaining ambiguous. Israeli prime minister Benjamin Netanyahu declared that any Palestinian state must be "demilitarized" and any peace agreement subject to an Israeli referendum. Palestinian Authority (PA) chair Mahmoud Abbas responded that Israeli soldiers could remain in the West Bank for a period of time and a U.S.-led NATO force could remain "wherever they want, not only on the eastern borders, but also on the western borders, everywhere." He also agreed that a Palestinian state would not have an army. "We will be demilitarized. Do you think we have any illusion that we can have any security if the Israelis do not feel they have any security?"[6]

Hamas's 1988 charter called for eliminating Israel and establishing a single Islamic state. In March 2006, however, the group suggested that the Palestinian people could vote to decide the question of recognizing Israel. That year, Ismail Haniyeh, Hamas's prime minister in Gaza, also began to speak publicly about the possibility of a long-term truce with Israel, perhaps for as long as twenty years, and a "temporary two-state solution" if Israel left the occupied territories, but added, "We will never recognize the usurper Zionist government and will continue our jihad-like movement until the liberation of Jerusalem."[7] Two years later Khaled Meshal, chair of the Hamas Political Bureau, told Jimmy Carter that the group could accept a two-state solution based on Israel's boundaries before June 1967 if approved by Palestinians in a referendum but "without recognizing Israel." Meshal also added the condition that Israel permit the return of all Palestinian refugees.

Most Israelis favor a two-state solution, but not within the country's pre-1967 borders. The fate of Jerusalem poses a particularly knotty territorial issue. Israeli prime ministers including Ariel Sharon and Ehud Olmert recognized that Israel might become a segregated or apartheid state if it failed to surrender the occupied territories. The Palestinians refused to accept Prime Minister Netanyahu's demand that they recognize Israel as a *Jewish* state because it undermined their "right of return." Netanyahu had grudgingly endorsed a two-state solution in 2009 at Bar-Ilan, which he repeated in 2014 when noting that he remained committed to "a vision of peace of two states."[8] But he denied that Israeli security should rely on a third party like NATO, declaring, "I think the Israeli people understand now what I always say: that there cannot be a situation, under any agreement, in which we relinquish security control of the territory west of the River Jordan."[9]

During Israel's 2015 election campaign, Netanyahu reversed himself, abruptly declaring he would not agree to a two-state solution while prime minister. Then after his reelection he again changed course: "I never retracted my speech in Bar-Ilan University six years ago calling for a demilitarized state that recognizes the Jewish state. What has changed is the reality."[10] An angry President Obama, nevertheless, suggested that Washington might have to rethink its policy toward Israel: "We take him at his word that it wouldn't happen during his prime ministership, and so that's why we've got to evaluate what other options are available to make sure we don't see a chaotic situation in the region."[11]

Although Netanyahu described his demand that the Palestinians recognize Israel as a *Jewish* state as the real key to peace, Palestinian leaders refused to concede this point because it undermined their "right of return." Palestinian negotiator Saeb Erekat argued, "I've never heard in the history of mankind that others must participate in defining the nature of others. It's really ridiculous."[12] Thus, according to a former senior Israeli intelligence officer, "There's an antagonistic convergence between Bibi [Netanyahu] and Hamas. He says he's against a bi-national single state, but is not ready to pay the price for two."[13]

Israeli politicians remained divided. Israeli diplomat Dore Gold concluded, "There's the idea of a two-state solution and there's converting it into a map. Israelis want negotiations, they want to see a settlement that addresses the issue, but they also have certain red lines that they don't want any arrangements to cross."[14] By contrast, Danny Danon, a member of the Likud Party, insisted that a majority of Israelis had "given up the idea of land for peace" and that "the fate of Palestinian settlement 'blocks' should be determined in an agreement with Jordan."[15] Several Palestinians retorted that Danon was voicing Netanyahu's view and was intentionally undermining Israeli–Palestinian negotiations, a claim reinforced by Netanyahu's tortured comments on a two-state solution during and after Israel's 2015 election campaign.

Policy Options

a. *Back Israeli hard-liners who prefer a one-state solution.* Although many Israeli hard-liners oppose an independent Palestinian state and are members of a "Greater Israel Caucus" that regards the West Bank as forever part of Israel, few American politicians could support this option because it would mark a dramatic reversal of U.S. policy. Nevertheless, there are variations of this argument. For some, a one-state solution implies that Palestinians in the West Bank should either move across the River Jordan to the East Bank (Jordan) or that Palestinian areas on the West Bank should be placed under Jordanian sovereignty, as all of the West Bank had been between 1949 and the Six-Day War. The position might also imply returning Gaza to Egypt, which oversaw it before 1967.

In July 1988, however, Jordan's King Hussein formally surrendered his country's legal claim to the West Bank and East Jerusalem and ceded its sovereignty to the PLO. Indigenous Arab Bedouins constitute the major political element upon which the country's rulers rely. By contrast, for decades Jordan's rulers have suspected the loyalty of Palestinian refugees, who account for almost a third of Jordan's population, and they had no interest in increasing the number of Palestinians in their country. As for Gaza, Egypt occupied the area between 1948 and 1967, but in signing the 1978 Camp David Accords indicated that it had no wish to control Gaza again. A more benign one-state vision was provided by Israeli writer Daniel Gavron, who argued, "Israeli and the Palestinian territories can be merged into a dynamic, multi-ethnic, culturally rich nation with new forms of co-existence between its different constituents."[16] Even some Palestinians, including the son of President Abbas, have contemplated a one-state solution in which Jews and Palestinians would be citizens with the same rights. If Israel were to annex the West Bank, however, or even if Palestinians and Israelis agreed to form a single democratic state, it would erode the Jewish identity of the country in which, in time, Palestinians would outnumber Israelis. Thus, in late 2015 Secretary of State John Kerry remarked, "The one-state solution is no solution at all for a secure, Jewish, democratic Israel living in peace. It is simply not a viable option."[17] His comment triggered an angry response from hard-line Israeli politicians.

b. *Press Israel to accept a two-state solution,* an option that enjoys considerable official American support. "Negotiations will be necessary," declared President Obama, "but there is little secret about where they must lead—two states for two peoples."[18] Even some hard-line Israelis like former Likud minister Dan Meridor recognized this imperative: "It is a sword of Damocles hanging over our heads. We are living on illusions. We must do everything we can on the ground to increase the separation between us and the Palestinians so that the idea of one state will go away. But we are doing nothing."[19] Some, however, like Israeli commentator Yoaz Hendel, would have Israel *unilaterally* decide what the boundaries of the two states should be: "Sometimes the stronger actor should decide for the other because the other cannot decide for itself. If we decide for ourselves, if we put the vision, the world will accept it."[20]

As we have seen, on several occasions Palestinians and Israelis came close to achieving this outcome, but differences regarding settlements, boundaries, and the status of Jerusalem have stymied a final agreement, especially because of the hard-liners in the Israeli government and Netanyahu's dependence on them to maintain a parliamentary majority. Land swaps might overcome part of the problem, and expanding Jerusalem's boundaries to accommodate a Palestinian capital, combined with internationalizing the city's holy sites, could move the two sides closer to an agreement. It would, however, be necessary to negotiate with a united Palestinian movement and require a plan to end Gaza's isolation and improve the economic well-being of its inhabitants.

c. *Support the status quo, in which Israel continues to share borders with autonomous but nonsovereign Palestinian communities in Gaza and Areas A and B of the West Bank.* Although this situation has existed for many years, Palestinians assumed it was an interim condition on the road to an independent state. If that prospect disappeared, it would likely lead to renewed violence between the two sides. Extremist Palestinian groups might again resort to violent protests and terrorism, and Israel would become increasingly besieged and isolated.

ISRAELI SETTLEMENTS

Israeli settlements in the occupied territories and the "right of return" for Palestinian refugees are emotional and explosive issues for both, and violence frequently occurs between Israeli settlers and

Israel's Ma'ale Adumim settlement near Jerusalem

Reuters/Ammar Awad

Palestinians. Israel's settlers and those who support them claim they seek to fulfill the promise of Zionism throughout biblical Israel, including ancient Judea and Samaria (the West Bank). Arab Palestinians contend that every settlement encroaches on their land and is part of an illegal Israeli effort to create "facts on the ground" like settler colonies and Jewish-only roads to strengthen Israel's hand in preparation for a final negotiation of territorial differences. Thus, even as Israeli–Palestinian talks resumed in 2013, the Israeli government first announced a plan to add 1,500 apartments to a settlement in East Jerusalem and later another plan to construct 20,000 new apartments in West Bank settlements. "This is not going to be tolerated," declared Saeb Erekat. "Either they revoke this order or they will be held responsible for the end of the peace process."[21] Secretary of State John Kerry also criticized the Israeli announcement, asking, "If you say you're working for peace and a Palestine that is a whole Palestine that belongs to the people who live there, how can you say, 'We're planning to build in the place that will eventually be Palestine'? It sends a message that somehow, perhaps, you're not really serious. If you announce planning, I believe it is disruptive to the process."[22]

By 2013 in the region of the West Bank designated Area C, where Israel retained full military and political control, there were over 300,000 Jewish settlers in more than 100 settlements (some of which had existed before the establishment of the State of Israel) and about 200,000 more in settlements annexed by Israel in East Jerusalem. And Naftali Bennett, the leader of the hard-line Jewish Home Party, publicly suggested that Israel annex all of Area C. The United States has several alternative, though complementary, policy options regarding the settlements.

Policy Options

a. *Intensify U.S. pressure on Israel to cease expansion of existing settlements or establishment of new ones,* which are regarded as illegal by most countries as well as the United Nations and the International Court of Justice. Previous U.S. presidents including Jimmy Carter and Ronald Reagan expressed concern about settlement expansion. And in his 2009 speech in Cairo, President Obama unequivocally stated, "Israelis must acknowledge that just as Israel's right to exist cannot be denied, neither can Palestine's. The United States does not accept the legitimacy of continued Israeli settlements. This construction violates previous agreements and undermines efforts to achieve peace. It is time for these settlements to stop. Israel must also live up to its obligations to ensure that Palestinians can live, and work, and develop their society. And just as it devastates Palestinian families, the continuing humanitarian crisis in Gaza does not serve Israel's security; neither does the continuing lack of opportunity in the West Bank. Progress in the daily lives of the Palestinian people must be part of a road to peace, and Israel must take concrete steps to enable such progress."[20] Four years later he argued, "Israelis must recognize that continued settlement activity is counterproductive to the cause of peace, and that an independent Palestine must be viable—that real borders will have to be drawn."[24]

The European Union has tried to pressure Israel by refusing to give the same preferential status to imports from the occupied territories that it does to goods produced within Israel. In 2014 Sweden became the first European state to recognize a Palestinian state, despite Israeli protests, and the Vatican announced in May 2015 that it would do so as well. In addition, the British, Irish, Spanish, French, and EU parliaments followed with nonbinding votes recognizing an independent Palestine.

Although Washington has leverage with its ally Israel, the degree of pressure needed to force Israel to cease expansion of settlements or, even more, to force Israel to withdraw from some settlements as a confidence measure would doubtlessly produce intense domestic opposition among Israel's supporters in America, including Congress. Moreover, if Israel did not give way and Washington failed to impose sanctions, it would be widely perceived as reducing U.S. credibility and declining influence in the Middle East.

b. *Encourage and help finance intensive Jewish settlement in Israel's Negev Desert*, which some have suggested be given to the Palestinians in return for West Bank settlements. Although this might be a bargaining chip, it probably would not resolve the problem because it would not satisfy the aspirations of Israel's religious nationalists. Even if it slowed the expansion of settlements in the West Bank, it would not persuade existing settlers to surrender their homes. It would also produce additional friction between Israelis and the roughly 200,000 Bedouin Arabs who live in the Negev.

c. *Persuade Israel to abandon most of the West Bank settlements while permitting it to retain those it regards as vital to the country's security*, especially the larger settlements in which 60 percent of Israeli settlers in the West Bank live (Ma'ale Adumim, Modiin Ilit, Ariel, Gush Etzion, and Givat Ze'ev). These are located close to the 1967 border (the "Green Line"), and recent settlement construction has been limited mainly to those areas. The settlement blocs involve about 2 percent of the territory of the West Bank, and Israel could compensate the Palestinians by swapping land elsewhere in Israel in exchange for retaining these settlements. President Bill Clinton put forward this idea in December 2000, and the Arab League adopted it later. Even Israeli foreign minister Avigdor Lieberman, a hard-liner, proposed that settlement blocs be annexed by Israel in exchange for Arab-populated areas inside Israel, an idea that some Israeli moderates and Israeli Arabs found attractive. Washington could encourage such an exchange by providing financial aid to cover the costs involved and helping provide funds to those Palestinians displaced by the settlements.

d. *Endorse Israel's retention of settlements in the occupied territories.* In a letter to Israeli prime minister Sharon in 2004, President George W. Bush, after endorsing his "vision of two states living side by side in peace and security as the key to peace," seemed prepared to let Israel unilaterally annex major settlement blocs. Bush declared, "As part of a final peace settlement, Israel must have secure and recognized borders, which should emerge from negotiations between the parties in accordance with UNSC Resolutions 242 and 338. In light of new realities on the ground, including already existing major Israeli population centers, it is unrealistic to expect that the outcome of final status negotiations will be a full and complete return to the armistice lines of 1949, and all previous efforts to negotiate a two-state solution have reached the same conclusion."[25] This position, however, did not sit well with Palestinians, who regarded Bush as too pro-Israeli.

REFUGEES

Another impediment to resolving Palestinian–Israeli differences is the status of the millions of Palestinian refugees displaced in the course of the wars since 1948. The Palestinian demand for the "right of return" was related to a belief that Israel was not prepared to accept a two-state solution and that Palestinians would have no option but to resettle within a single state—Israel. Given their number—almost 5 million including descendants of those who originally left Israel—Palestinians along with the 670,000 Arabs already living in Israel would swamp the country's 6 million Jewish citizens. Currently, about one-third of registered Palestinian refugees—more than 1.4 million people—live in fifty-eight refugee camps in Jordan, Lebanon, Syria, the Gaza Strip, and the West Bank.

Policy Options

a. *Press Israel to grant all Palestinian refugees the right of return.* Some Palestinians continue to demand the right of all Palestinians to return to Israel. As we have seen, however, most Israelis and their American supporters would regard this alternative as unacceptable because Israel would no longer be a Jewish state. Thus, Israeli novelist Amos Oz declared, "The right of return is a euphemism for the liquidation of Israel. Even for a dove like myself this is out of the question." And the imprisoned Palestinian leader Omar Barghouti seemed to agree: "If the refugees were to return, you would not have a two-state solution, you'd have a Palestine next to a Palestine."[26]

b. *Support Israel's sovereign right to refuse any right of return.* Although most Palestinians recognize that Israel would almost certainly refuse to grant *all* Palestinian refugees a right of return and that Washington would not force Israel to do so, it would be difficult to get Palestinians to surrender the *principle* of returning to their former homes. To do so would divide the Palestinian movement even more than at present, rendering any settlement impossible.

c. *Seek a compromise by which Palestinians would enjoy a "symbolic" right of return.* This option has been widely discussed among American, Israeli, and Palestinian negotiators. It would entail the return of a relatively small number of Palestinians, thereby abiding by the *principle* while not endangering the status of Israel as a Jewish state. In 2008 PA chair Mahmoud Abbas was reported to have been ready to agree with then Israeli prime minister Ehud Olmert to accept the return of between 40,000 and 60,000 over a period of years. According to Olmert, Abbas declared, "I can tell you one thing. We are not aspiring to change the nature of your country," and Stephen Hadley, President George W. Bush's national security advisor, recalled, "Our reading was that there was a deal to be done on [the refugee issue]."[27] In January 2010 Saeb Erekat is said to have privately told a State Department official that the Palestinians would accept a "symbolic number" of refugees returning to Israel.

Chairman Abbas later declared he had personally given up his right of return, an admission that was widely criticized by fellow Palestinians. But he expressed clearly what he wanted in return for that concession: "Palestine now for me is '67 borders, with East Jerusalem as its capital. This is now and forever," and "I am a refugee, but I am living in Ramallah. I believe that the West Bank and Gaza is Palestine and the other parts are Israel."[28] In other words, a compromise on the right of return was inseparable from a larger compromise on other issues including a two-state solution and removal of most Israeli settlements. In this, Abbas's views reflect what were the views of American leaders and many moderate Israelis.

HAMAS AND GAZA

When Israeli prime minister Sharon announced in December 2003 that his country would unilaterally withdraw from Gaza, he expected that the Palestinian Authority under Abbas would administer the area while Israel continued to control its borders, coastline, and airspace. The decision would also, he believed, show that Israel was committed to a peaceful settlement of its conflict with the Palestinians. The takeover of Gaza in 2007 by Hamas, which was dedicated to the destruction of Israel, undermined Sharon's vision and led to a deep split between Hamas and the Fatah-dominated PA, rocket attacks from Gaza into Israel, an Israeli blockade, and the Gaza war of 2008 that was followed by two later conflicts. Although the Israeli–Gaza border grew quieter after the 2014 Israeli–Hamas war and the 2013 overthrow of Egypt's elected Islamic government again isolated Hamas, the group retained significant influence among Palestinians. Despite the formation of a unity government by Fatah and Hamas in 2014, it was doubtful their schism was bridged. The absence of a single entity representing all Palestinians significantly complicates the peace process. What policy should Washington adopt toward Hamas?

Policy Options

a. *Do not recognize Hamas.* Although Hamas is one of the two principal Palestinian political groups, Washington declared it a foreign terrorist organization in October 1997. Hamas continued to advocate violence against Israel and refused to recognize Israel's right to exist. Washington's nonrecognition of Hamas is popular among Israelis and domestically in America, but it virtually precludes negotiation with a single Palestinian entity that could assume power in a Palestinian state. Possibly an agreement could be reached with the PA in the West Bank to establish a "rump" state that would legally encompass Gaza but from which Gaza would remain independent until Hamas were ousted or persuaded to cooperate with the Fatah-dominated PA.

b. *Seek to reconcile Hamas and Fatah.* Despite signing an agreement to reconcile in 2011, the two groups remained divided, with Hamas initially opposing Abbas's efforts to gain UN recognition for a Palestinian state. Forming a single legitimate Palestinian entity would advance the peace process because Israel would have only one group with which to negotiate, and successful negotiations could produce a united Palestinian state (e.g., a two-state solution). Hamas, however, was loathed by Israel, and the PLO's resumption of unity talks with Hamas in 2014 was the excuse Netanyahu used to end negotiations with the Palestinians. Abbas's efforts to form a coalition government with Hamas prompted an Israeli official to observe that if this took place, the PLO and Abbas would be held responsible for any violence by Hamas. Following the kidnapping and murder of three Israeli boys on the West Bank in June 2014, war again erupted between Israel and Hamas. Moreover, Washington is not trusted by Hamas, and efforts by Arab countries friendly to America such as Egypt and Saudi Arabia failed to persuade Hamas to moderate its policies or bridge the differences between the two Palestinian groups.

c. *Negotiate with Hamas.* This option might lead to an easing of hostility between Washington and Hamas, but only if Hamas were prepared to forgo violence and recognize Israel's right to exist. Moreover, such negotiations, unless entirely secret, would be vigorously opposed by Israel, domestic lobbying groups like the American Israel Public Affairs Committee (AIPAC) and others committed to Israel's security, and leading members of both political parties. It would also make American leaders vulnerable to accusations of pandering to "terrorists."

ECONOMIC AND RESOURCE ISSUES

A final set of issues involves regional economic development and the distribution of natural resources between Israel and the Palestinians. Israel is a developed state economically and technologically, and the United States and Israel enjoy a high level of economic and technological interdependence. Israel ranks high on global measures of economic competitiveness and ability to exploit opportunities offered by information and communications technologies. Its citizens have a per capita gross domestic product (GDP) of over $32,000. America and Israel have had a free-trade agreement since 1985, spurring trade and investment between the two. Thus, the United States is Israel's largest single trading partner, and each has large direct investments in the other, especially in high-tech manufacturing. Many American and Israeli firms have collaborated in commercial and military research and development, and Washington provides Israel over $3 billion in military assistance each year.

By contrast, per capita Palestinian GDP in 2012 was less than $1,700. The unemployment rate in Gaza in 2013 was almost 28 percent, and in the West Bank almost 17 percent. U.S.–Palestinian trade is negligible. The PA depended heavily on foreign assistance to pay its bills, and Palestinians were among the world's largest per capita recipients of foreign aid. According to one U.S. analysis, "From FY2008 to the present, annual regular-year U.S. bilateral assistance to the West Bank and Gaza Strip has averaged around $500 million, including annual averages of approximately $200 million in direct budgetary assistance and $100 million in non-lethal security assistance for the PA in the West Bank. Additionally, the United States is the largest single-state donor to the U.N. Relief and Works Agency for Palestine Refugees in the Near East (UNRWA)."[29] Were there a regional peace settlement, both Israelis and Palestinians would greatly benefit economically. Indeed, it is ironic that Israeli settlers in the West Bank employ about 20,000 Palestinians to help build their settlements and that, at least before the second intifada, many Palestinians were employed as agricultural workers in Israel. Currently, almost 100,000 Palestinians are employed in Israel and the occupied territories.

Israel and the Palestinian Authority also have conflicts over natural resources. One involves deposits of natural gas that were discovered in the eastern Mediterranean off Israel and Gaza. To date, Israel has relied on gas imports from Egypt, but in recent years these were repeatedly sabotaged. Offshore gas in its Tamar and Leviathan gas fields promise to make Israel energy independent, and a partnership between the American company Noble Energy and two Israeli firms to exploit the two major gas fields off Israel's coast led Israel to agree in October 2014 to export gas to Jordan and the PA, which may improve Israeli–Palestinian relations. Both the Palestinians and Lebanese contended, however, that some of these reserves were located in their economic zones.

In 1994, however, the PA was ceded a twenty-mile maritime zone off Gaza's coast, but five years later Britain's BG Group gained the rights to develop Gaza's offshore gas reserves that would be provided to the Palestinians only if they gave Israel "full security control" of the sea off Gaza. According to one source, the United States and Britain, "who are the major players in this deal, see it as a possible tool to improve relations between the PA and Israel. It is part of the bargaining baggage."[30]

A second resource issue involves the distribution of scarce water resources. Israel retains control of the Jordan River basin and almost nine-tenths of the West Bank's underground aquifers. According to a Palestinian human-rights group, the 500,000 Israeli settlers in the West Bank and East Jerusalem used six times the amount of water used by the area's 2.6 million Palestinians, and had prevented Palestinian development of additional water resources.[31] In late 2013, however, a modest agreement was reached between Israel, Jordan, and the PLO to enable construction of a desalination plant using hydroelectric power in Aqaba, Jordan, for 200 million cubic meters of water that would be pumped from the Red Sea to the Dead Sea, which has been drying up. Israel also agreed to supply additional water to the West Bank and to Jordan.

Policy Options

a. *Support the status quo.* One option is for Washington to continue funneling aid to the PA to help it survive and maintain security in the West Bank, while backing Israel's control of energy and water resources in the region as part of continued support for Israel as an ally. This cautious policy, however, while promising stability in the short run would not advance the peace process significantly and would do little to prod Israel to negotiate seriously with the Palestinians on economic and resource issues.

b. *Provide development assistance to the Palestinians.* The Obama administration, as we noted earlier, has advocated a plan to encourage investment in the West Bank. U.S. investment and aid afford Washington with additional political leverage with the PA and will help to persuade it to continue negotiating with Israel. However, it is at best a means to maintain the peace process on life support and does nothing to resolve resource disputes unless it includes investment aimed at helping the Palestinians to develop their existing water and energy resources.

c. *Encourage Israeli–Palestinian economic cooperation and resource redistribution, along with U.S. investment in and aid to the region.* This option is the most ambitious of the alternatives and could be an incentive toward a final settlement of the Israeli–Palestinian conflict. It should be offered only in conjunction with a resolution of other outstanding issues such as territorial boundaries of Israel and establishing a Palestinian state, Israeli settlements, and refugees. The investment and aid would be directed toward enlarging the overall economic "pie" and expanding regional water and energy resources to facilitate a redistribution of benefit to Palestinians while minimizing what Israel would have to surrender. Thus, U.S. investment in advanced desalination facilities such as those that use a reverse osmosis process and in exploitation of deep-sea oil and gas resources in the eastern Mediterranean would increase total resources. Such investment would make it easier to expand Israeli–Palestinian cooperation regarding resource issues and create conditions in which both sides could benefit economically. And if a final resolution to the conflict emerges, it should prove possible to negotiate trade and labor agreements that could also benefit both parties.

CONCLUSION: WILL IT EVER END?

Above all, Israelis crave security in an insecure and rapidly changing neighborhood. A radically different Arab world is emerging. "What we have to understand," declared Israel's former national security advisor, "is going to be changed—to what, I don't know," but the collapse of the idea of the national Arab state "means that we will be encircled by an area which will be no man's land at the end of the day." This required a strategy of "wait and keep the castle."[32] Such Israeli "strategic conservatism," according to Middle East analyst Natan Sachs, stems from "a belief that there are currently no solutions to the challenges the country faces and that seeking quick fixes to intractable problems is dangerously naïve. Kicking problems down the road until some indefinite future point at which they can be tackled more successfully therefore does not reflect a lack of Israeli strategy; rather, it defines Israeli strategy."[33]

According to the director of Washington's Israel Institute, Israel's concern about U.S. foreign policy stemmed from three developments: "First, the Arab Spring has revealed popular tendencies toward Islamist politics in the region, which give Arab politicians who attempt to ride popular will [*sic*] significantly less inclination to accommodate Israel than the autocrats who preceded them. . . . Second, Israel's ability to deter aggression is eroding. . . . Third, the lack of U.S. resolve on Syria and Iran leaves the impression that the United States is seeking to disentangle from the Middle East as its gaze turns elsewhere."[34]

U.S. diplomat Dennis Ross sadly concluded, "Most Israelis and Palestinians today simply don't believe that peace is possible." On the one hand, "Israelis feel that their withdrawal from territory (like southern Lebanon and the Gaza Strip) has not brought peace and security; instead it has produced only violence." On the other hand, "Palestinians discount what Israelis say about two states and believe instead that the Israelis will never accept Palestinian independence,"[35] a belief fostered by expansion of Israeli settlements in the West Bank.

Partly to overcome the pessimism of those like Ross, President Obama visited Israel and the West Bank in March 2013. During his visit, the president spoke eloquently to a group of young Israelis on the virtues of peace with the Palestinians: "I believe that Israel is rooted not just in history and tradition, but also in a simple and profound idea: the idea that people deserve to be free in a land of their own." He reiterated America's commitment to the security of Israel. Peace, he declared, was crucial for Israel's security: "the only path to true security." "And given the march of technology, the only way to truly protect the Israeli people is through the absence of war—because no wall is high enough, and no Iron Dome is strong enough, to stop every enemy from inflicting harm." Then he added, "But the Palestinian people's right to self-determination and justice must also be recognized. Put yourself in their shoes—look at the world through their eyes. It is not fair that a Palestinian child cannot grow up in a state of her own, and lives with the presence of a foreign army that controls the movements of her parents every single day. It is not just when settler violence against Palestinians goes unpunished. It is not right to prevent Palestinians from farming their lands; to restrict a student's ability to move around the West Bank; or to displace Palestinian families from their home. Neither occupation nor expulsion is the answer. Just as Israelis built a state in their homeland, Palestinians have a right to be a free people in their own land."[36] Perhaps John Kerry will prove right in the end. Alluding to the example of Nelson Mandela, who brought peace to South Africa, he noted, "The naysayers are wrong to call peace in this region an impossible goal," adding, "It always seems impossible until it is done."[37]

The Shia Crescent

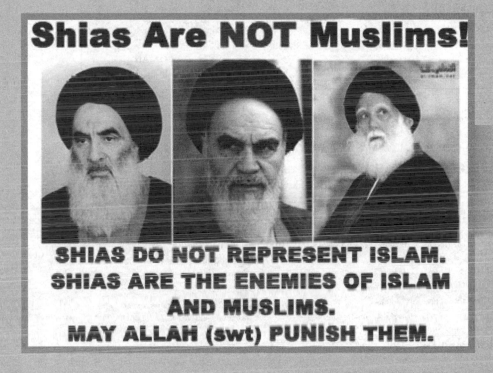

Shias Are NOT Muslims!

SHIAS DO NOT REPRESENT ISLAM.
SHIAS ARE THE ENEMIES OF ISLAM
AND MUSLIMS.
MAY ALLAH (swt) PUNISH THEM.

The Sunni–Shia divide: Sunni Islamic extremists believe that followers of Shia Islam are not "true" Muslims and regard them as apostates.

Part IV of the book focuses on American relations with the Shia Islamic states—Iran and Iraq. It examines the thorny U.S.–Iranian relationship, the links of both America and Iran to Iraq and other Shia Muslims in the Middle East, and the hostility between Sunni and Shia Muslims. Unlike most of the Arab world, which is Sunni Muslim, non-Arab Iran is largely Shia, as is Arab Iraq, with about 60 to 65 percent Shia and 32 to 37 percent Sunni Muslims. Around 15 to 20 percent of Iraqis are ethnic Kurds who are predominantly Sunni and who share a common language and history. Many Iraqis also have close tribal links.

MAP IV.1   The Shia Crescent

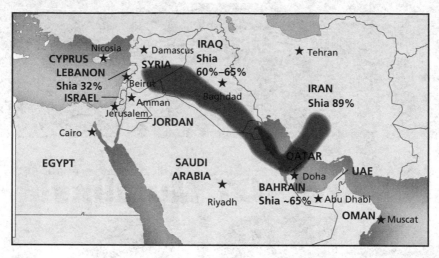

Source: "Shia Crescent," Cambridge Forecast Group Blog, December 10, 2007, https://cambridgeforecast.wordpress.com/2007/12/10/shia-crescent/

Timeline

1900–1950

1907 Iran divided into Russian–British zones of influence

1908–1909 Oil discovered in Iran and the Anglo–Persian Oil Company is established

1917 British occupation of Iraq

1919 Britain and Iran sign the Anglo–Persian Agreement

1920 Britain establishes the State of Iraq; Iraqis rebel against British occupation

1927 Oil discovered around Mosul, Iraq

1932 Iraq becomes an independent state

1939–1945 British reoccupation of Iraq

1941 U.S.–Soviet occupation of Iran

1946 Cold War crisis over Soviet presence in northern Iran

1951–1988

1951 Iran nationalizes its oil industry

1953 United States and Britain carry out a coup overthrowing Iranian prime minister Mossadeq

1955 Baghdad Pact signed

July 1958 Revolution brings an end to Iraq's monarchy, introducing a republic under military rule

1972 Iraq nationalizes the Iraq Petroleum Company

1974–1978 Shah Mohammad Reza Pahlavi, with U.S. aid, initiates an Iranian nuclear program for peaceful purposes

1975 Construction of Bushehr Nuclear Power Plant begun in Iraq; construction ceases in 1979

1978 Iranian revolution overthrows the shah and Ayatollah Khomeini assumes power

1979–1980 Iranian hostage crisis; Saddam Hussein becomes president of Iraq

1980–1988 Iran–Iraq War

1981 Israel destroys Iraqi nuclear facility

The schism between Sunni and Shia Muslims emerged after the Prophet's death in 632 CE. Those who believed Muhammad's son-in-law Ali was his legitimate successor and that caliphs should only be direct descendants of Ali and Fatima (Muhammad's daughter) took the name Shiat Ali ("partisans of Ali"). Sunni Muslims do not insist that caliphs be descended from Muhammad, and they follow the Prophet's customs (*sunna*) and Islamic law as established by those customs and by the Koran. During the rule of the initial successors or "caliphs" after Muhammad's death, Ali was critical of what he believed were non-Islamic customs in the caliphate. He finally became caliph in 656 but was assassinated five years later. The "partisans of Ali" believe he was followed by twelve legitimate successors, the last of whom—the Twelfth or Hidden Imam—will someday reappear. Ali's son, Hussein, was killed in a revolt in 680. Shia Muslims still venerate Ali and Hussein, but Sunnis regard them as heretics who worship idols and who should be exterminated.

Unlike most of the Arab states in the Middle East, modern Iran was not an artificial creation of the West. It is the heir to the ancient civilization and empire of Persia (which also included Mesopotamia—that is, Iraq, Kuwait, and part of Syria), ruled by the Persian kings Darius and Xerxes, rulers of the Achaemenid Empire. It fought to conquer classical Greece, and was itself conquered by Alexander the Great in the fourth century BCE and by nomadic Muslim Arabs in the seventh century CE. Modern Iranians are not ethnic Arabs but ethnic Persians, and many have contempt for Arab culture. As the early caliphate grew weaker and Arabic power ebbed, Shiism became deeply rooted in Iran, becoming the state religion early in the sixteenth century. "Iranians were already bound together by a shifting geography, a

1988–2000

March 1988 Saddam uses poison gas against Iraqi Kurds

1990–1991 Iraq invades Kuwait and is driven out by a U.S.-led coalition

1991 Iraq becomes subject to weapons inspection program

April 1991 UN-approved safe haven established for Iraqi Kurds

August 1992 A no-fly zone is established in southern Iraq to protect Shia Iraqis

June 1993 U.S. cruise missile attack against Baghdad in retaliation for attempted assassination of former president George H. W. Bush

1994 Iran and Russia agree to construct Iran's first commercial nuclear power plant at Bushehr

December 1998 Anglo–American bombing campaign to destroy Iraqi WMD programs

2001–2015

2002 President Bush labels Iran, Iraq, and North Korea an "axis of evil"

2003 Construction of Iran's first nuclear reactor begins

2003 Anglo–American invasion of Iraq

2003–2011 Iraq war and sectarian violence in Iraq

2009 Iran admits building a uranium enrichment facility, rejecting an offer for enriching its uranium abroad

2011 Iran's Bushehr Nuclear Power Plant opens

2013 Iran signs a Joint Plan of Action to negotiate a comprehensive nuclear agreement

2014 ISIS invades Iraq; United States and allies begin bombing ISIS in Iraq and Syria

2015 P5+1 and Iran announce agreement on a comprehensive nuclear deal

language, and a collective memory of ancient glory, but none of these ties evoked anything close to the unifying fervor of Shiism. By embracing this faith, Iranians accepted Islam but not in the way their Sunni Arab conquerors had wished."[1]

Iraq's fate has always been linked to that of Iran, its large neighbor. Iraq, unlike Iran, was an artificial creation carved out of three Ottoman provinces that sought to knit Shia and Sunni Muslims and non-Arabic ethnic Kurds in a single state, despite the provision for an independent Kurdistan in the 1920 Sèvres Treaty with Ottoman Turkey that Kurdish leaders rejected because it failed to include the Van region in eastern Turkey. After World War I "there was no Iraqi people; history, religion, geography pulled the people apart, not together. Basra looked south, toward India and the Gulf; Baghdad had strong links with Persia; and Mosul had closer ties with Turkey and Syria. Putting together the three Ottoman provinces and expecting to create a nation was, in European terms, liking hoping to have Bosnian Muslims, Croats, and Serbia make one country. . . . There was no Iraqi nationalism, only Arab."[2] Like Iran, Iraq is largely Shia, but until Saddam Hussein was overthrown during America's 2003 war with Iraq, Iraq was governed by a Sunni Muslim minority that repressed the Shia majority. Since then Iran has become increasingly influential in Iraq.

12

Early American Relations
with Iran and Iraq

This first chapter in Part IV focuses on the evolution of Iran and Iraq, the major Shia states in the Middle East. It examines Iran's tumultuous relations with the United States and its allies from the discovery of oil in Iran and describes Anglo–American efforts to overthrow Prime Minister Mohammad Mossadeq, and U.S. support for Iran's shah until the 1979 Iranian revolution and subsequent hostage crisis. It also describes the founding of Iraq after World War I and American relations with that country before and after the revolution that ended the monarchy, the rise of Saddam Hussein, and Saddam's disastrous war with Iran during the 1980s.

American policies toward Iran and Iraq have reflected a mix of interests and values. In both cases access to oil has played a role, as both countries are major oil producers and are strategically located in the Middle East on the Persian Gulf. Both played a significant role in the Cold War and as adversaries of America's ally, Israel. Washington also sought to export its values to both countries—by opposing German expansion in World War II and countering British imperialism and Soviet communism after the war, and most recently by actively seeking to export democratic values to both countries.

SOURCES OF AMERICAN POLICY TOWARD IRAN AND IRAQ

External factors have always been present in shaping U.S. policy toward Iran and Iraq, especially after the world navies shifted from coal- to oil-powered vessels. In both cases the United States has long sought access to oil and its free flow through the Persian Gulf. During the Cold War, Washington also sought to contain the threat of growing Soviet influence in these countries. More recently, the foreign policies of both Iran and Iraq have been key external factors influencing U.S. foreign policy in the Middle East. Iran's transformation from a secular monarchy allied to America to a revolutionary theocracy opposed to U.S. allies like Saudi Arabia and Israel and U.S. policies and interests throughout the Middle East, as well as its ambition to a acquire nuclear weapons, have been crucial in U.S.–Iranian relations. Iraqi efforts to balance Iranian power and the aggressive ambitions of its dictator, Saddam Hussein, including his occupation of oil-rich Kuwait in 1990, have been important determinants of U.S. policy.

Government factors range from strong congressional and Defense Department opposition to Iran's acquisition of nuclear weapons and support for Israel, to Homeland Security's concern about American jihadists returning to the United States after undergoing terrorist training in Iraq. The U.S. military and intelligence services depended on Iran and Iraq as reliable barriers to Soviet expansion until revolutions in both countries severed Cold War links. President Barack Obama in his role as commander in chief ordered American aircraft to bomb jihadists in Iraq (and Syria) in 2014. Furthermore, in July 2015 John Kerry in his role as secretary of state went before the Senate Foreign Relations Committee to explain and defend the controversial nuclear arms control deal the administration had negotiated with Iran.

Societal factors also affect American policy toward Iraq and Iran. When the United States withdrew from Iraq in 2011, 75 percent of Americans polled approved, including 96 percent of Democrats.[3] However, some believe this decision produced a power vacuum that allowed al-Qaeda in Iraq and Syria (ISIS, which later split from al-Qaeda) to seize large areas of Iraq in 2014. Therefore, after ISIS decapitated two American journalists in 2014, a large majority of Americans regarded the group as a serious threat to U.S. interests and supported air strikes in Iraq and Syria.[4]

Other societal involvement includes the pro-Israel lobby in America, which is forcefully anti-Iranian. American conservatives—politicians and citizens—continued to support sanctions and even military action against Iran after negotiations to limit Iran's nuclear program had begun between Washington and Tehran following the election of President Hassan Rouhani in 2013. These groups also supported President George W. Bush's decision to invade Iraq in 2003 and overthrow the government of Saddam Hussein.

Individual predilections have consistently been important in relations with both countries. President Harry Truman and Secretary of State Dean Acheson both disliked British imperialism and opposed British plans to overthrow the Iranian government in the early 1950s. By contrast, their successors in the Eisenhower administration, notably Secretary of State John Foster Dulles, were more concerned about the spread of communism, which they felt was a real risk in Iran. More recently, neoconservatives in the George W. Bush administration like Secretary of Defense Donald Rumsfeld and Vice President Dick Cheney personally felt strongly about strengthening presidential prerogatives and spreading democracy, and thus supported the 2003 U.S. war in Iraq that undermined that country's regime. President George W. Bush's father, President George H. W. Bush, later concluded that Rumsfeld and Cheney were too hawkish and bore much of the responsibility for America's 2003 intervention. Of Cheney, the elder Bush declared, "The reaction [to 9/11], what to do about the Middle East. Just iron-ass. His seeming knuckling under to the real hard-charging guys who want to fight about everything, use force to get our way in the Middle East."[5]

IRAN, AMERICA, AND BRITAIN UNTIL THE IRANIAN REVOLUTION

Persian culture reached its peak in the sixteenth century with construction of its capital city, Isfahan, which housed the shah's Peacock Throne. The country's decline followed under the Turkmen Qajar dynasty, which ruled from 1779 to 1925 with its capital in Tehran.

Iran before the Shah's Overthrow

Iran increasingly became entangled in the imperial rivalry of Great Britain and Russia during the nineteenth century. As part of an agreement to settle imperial quarrels, Britain and Russia agreed in 1907 to divide Iran into spheres of influence, with Russia controlling the north and Britain the south and a neutral zone in the middle. With the collapse of the Russian and Ottoman Empires in World War I, Britain emerged as the dominant imperial power in Iran. In 1919 Britain and Iran signed the Anglo–Persian Agreement, under which Iran was made a virtual British protectorate, with key institutions including its army and treasury under British supervision. The failure of Iran's parliament to approve the agreement and the revelation that leading Iranian politicians had accepted bribes from London, however, led Iran to abrogate the agreement in 1921.

With an eye to the security of India, Britain obtained economic concessions in the country that incensed Iranian nationalists. The discovery of oil in Iran in 1908 by William Knox D'Arcy, who had obtained "a special and exclusive privilege to search for and obtain, exploit, develop, render suitable for trade, carry away and sell natural gas, petroleum, asphalt and ozokerite"[6] throughout the country for sixty years, dramatically increased Iran's geopolitical value. Interest in oil was sparked by the shift from coal-fired to oil-driven naval vessels. The U.S. experience in the Spanish–American War when four ships were absent for recoaling when the Spanish fleet successfully ran the American blockade of Santiago, Cuba, provided impetus to shift to oil, which produced more energy per pound than coal and therefore required less refueling.

Oil was plentiful and accessible in America. By contrast, the British navy depended on foreign sources of oil, especially as World War I approached. "To commit the Navy irrevocably to oil," declared Winston Churchill, then First Lord of the Admiralty, "was indeed to take 'arms against a sea of troubles.'"[7] D'Arcy sold his concession to the Burmah Oil Company in 1904, and it became the Anglo–Persian Oil Company in 1909 (renamed the Anglo–Iranian Oil Company in 1935 and the British Petroleum Company in 1954), which under the Anglo–Persian Agreement was given exclusive drilling rights and access to Iran's oil fields. That agreement undermined Iranian sovereignty, involved exploiting its resources, and fueled Iranian nationalism. In 1914 the British government became the company's majority stockholder, as well as the principal target of Iranian nationalism. The company piped crude oil to Abadan, a facility it built on an island near the Persian Gulf and Iran's border with Iraq. By 1938 it had become the world's largest refinery, with tens of thousands of workers from Iran, surrounding countries, and elsewhere. Living and working conditions in Abadan were dreadful. Iranian nationalists came to view Britain as the enemy and demanded Iran take back control of its oil. In response, Reza Khan, an Iranian officer of the Persian Cossack Brigade, launched a coup in 1921, seizing power, ousting the last Qajar ruler, and becoming Reza Shah Pahlavi in 1926—a position he would occupy until World War II.

Reza Shah sought to modernize his country and demanded that it be known as Iran rather than Persia. An authoritarian leader, he was attracted by fascism, and notwithstanding Iran's neutrality in World War II appeared to favor Adolf Hitler's Germany. Thus, the Soviet Union and Britain again occupied northern and southern Iran respectively in 1941, shortly after Hitler invaded the USSR, and Reza Shah abdicated in favor of his son Mohammad Reza Shah Pahlavi. In 1942 Iran, the USSR, and Britain signed a treaty guaranteeing Iranian sovereignty and agreeing that Soviet and British troops would depart within six months after the war's end. Nevertheless, following Germany's surrender, Soviet troops remained in the Iranian province of Azerbaijan and encouraged pro-communist and Kurdish separatists. Only under intense American diplomatic pressure did Moscow withdraw its troops in 1946 in what was one of the earliest crises of the Cold War.

Six years later Iran's parliament decreed an end to concessions to foreign companies and demanded a renegotiation of arrangements with Anglo–Iranian. The charismatic politician and nationalist most responsible for this initiative was Mohammad Mossadeq. Led by Mossadeq, Iranian nationalists then formed a popular electoral alliance called the National Front, and Mossadeq was named chair of the parliamentary oil committee to conduct negotiations with the Anglo–Iranian Oil Company. Negotiations, however, proved fruitless, as neither the company nor the British government was prepared to compromise about sharing profits with Iran or improving workers' conditions. The stalemate triggered growing sentiment in Iran for nationalizing the company, and in March 1951 parliament (the Majlis) voted to nationalize Anglo–Iranian. Britain reacted by sending naval vessels to the Persian Gulf. On May 1 the shah signed into law the revocation of the company's concession and established the National Iranian Oil Company in its place. A few days later Mossadeq was named Iran's prime minister.

The British government was incensed by Iran's action and sought to persuade the United States to join it in pressuring Iran to rescind nationalization of Anglo–Iranian. Washington's initial reactions reflected the skepticism of President Truman and Secretary of State Acheson regarding European colonialism in the developing world. They sought to persuade the British government and the Anglo–Iranian Company to make concessions to Tehran that would facilitate a compromise. Like Truman, Acheson, and their special envoy to Iran Averell Harriman in 1951, American ambassador Henry Grady believed "the United States has tragically failed to insist that the British adopt what must clearly be the only policy that would keep this vital country on the side of the West," and "we went along with the British and supported them in their efforts to bring Iran to Britain's terms by pressures that are steadily weakening the economy of the country." Grady concluded that "Mossadeq grew in power as the oil dispute continued because of British intransigence."[8] The Truman administration vigorously opposed British plans to use the threat of force to undo Iran's nationalization of the company, urging a 50–50 split of profits with Iran, and America's National Security Council warned that the conflict and the possible British resort to force threatened to divide the West and increase Soviet influence in Iran. Truman regarded these issues as far more central than controlling Iranian oil and suggested U.S. mediation by a team led by Harriman. Britain, however, imposed an embargo on Iranian oil, and Iranians began to view Washington in the same light as London.

The Iranian Coup

In May 1951 the British government began to consider military intervention, and might have done so if Washington were not opposed. However, British leaders, including Foreign Minister Herbert Morrison and Britain's ambassador to Iran, began to contemplate overthrowing Mossadeq. In August Britain placed additional economic sanctions on Iran, including withdrawal of British technicians from Abadan and cutting off Tehran's access to hard currency and British exports. The failure of Harriman's mediation and the increasing belligerence of Britain angered Acheson and Truman and prompted a warning to Washington from Britain's ambassador in the United States. This led the British to consider once again the possibility of covert actions including sabotage of Iranian oil production. The British also decided to bring the issue of Iranian nationalization to the United Nations, and Mossadeq decided to participate in the debate personally.

Thereafter, political changes in London and Washington altered the situation significantly. In Britain, general elections in October 1951 ousted Labour prime minister Clement Attlee. Conservative prime minister Winston Churchill, who regarded Mossadeq as "an elderly lunatic bent on wrecking his country and handing it over to the Communists,"[9] and Foreign Secretary Anthony Eden were determined to act decisively, and the new government tightened the oil embargo, intercepting tankers carrying Iranian oil. In July 1952, owing to friction with the shah, Mossadeq resigned as prime minister and was replaced by Ahmad Qavam. Qavam sought to negotiate with the British, triggering violent demonstrations that persuaded the shah to reappoint Mossadeq, who was more popular than ever and who in October severed diplomatic relations with London.

In November 1952 Republican Dwight Eisenhower was elected U.S. president and appointed two ardent anticommunists to his Cabinet: Secretary of State John Foster Dulles and his brother, CIA director Allen Dulles. The British almost immediately sought to sell their version of events in Iran as part of a communist conspiracy to the new and more receptive U.S. administration, sending the chief of their Iran intelligence station to consult with CIA leaders in Washington. The result was an agreement to plan a covert operation ("Operation Ajax") to overthrow Mossadeq. Shortly after Eisenhower took office in January 1953, American diplomats in Tehran began seeking Iranians opposed to Mossadeq. Although Eisenhower initially sought to compromise with Mossadeq, the Iranian leader remained unwilling to do so, and the CIA assumed leadership of Ajax from Britain's MI6 and began recruiting Iranian allies. In July 1953 Churchill and Eisenhower approved plans to oust Mossadeq.

Kermit Roosevelt, grandson of President Theodore Roosevelt and chief of the CIA's Near East and Africa Division, was the architect of the coup. After persuading the shah to sign decrees ousting Mossadeq, Roosevelt organized massive street demonstrations against the prime minister to be followed by a military takeover, but the plot launched August 15, 1953, initially failed. Mossadeq's putative successor, Gen. Fazlollah Zahedi, went into hiding, and the shah fled to Baghdad. Roosevelt, however, launched a second effort, which succeeded two days later. Thereafter, the shah returned, and Mossadeq, convicted of treason, remained under house arrest until his death in 1967. Despite its effort to restore its former dominance, the Anglo–Iranian Oil Company (now British Petroleum), with 40 percent ownership, became part of an international consortium that included five U.S. oil companies (Gulf, Exxon, Chevron, Mobil, and Texaco, with 8 percent each), Royal Dutch/Shell (14 percent), and Compagnie Française de Petroles (6 percent). It retained the name National Iranian Oil Company and agreed to split profits equally with Iran.

Iran to the Revolution

The Iranian coup guaranteed over two decades of stability in Iran as a loyal ally of the United States, but its ultimate consequences were less benign. Writes Mark Gasiorowski:

> In retrospect, the United States–sponsored *coup d'état* in Iran of August 19, 1953, has emerged as a critical event in postwar world history. The government of Prime Minister Mohammad Mossadeq that was ousted in the coup was the last popular, democratically oriented government to hold office in Iran. The regime replacing it

was a dictatorship that repressed all forms of popular political activity, producing tensions that contributed greatly to the 1978–1979 Iranian revolution. If Mossadeq had not been overthrown, the revolution might not have occurred. . . . [T]he U.S. role in the coup and the subsequent consolidation of the shah's dictatorship were decisive for the future of U.S. relations with Iran. . . . As the dire consequences of the revolution for U.S. interests continue to unfold, one can only wonder whether this has been worth the long-term cost.[10]

Indeed, American leaders have come to recognize these consequences, and both Presidents Bill Clinton and Barack Obama admitted their country's involvement in the 1953 coup. For its part, the CIA released a classified document declaring, "The military coup that overthrew Mossadeq and his National Front cabinet was carried out under CIA direction as an act of U.S. foreign policy, conceived and approved at the highest levels of government."[11] In March 2000 Secretary of State Madeleine Albright virtually apologized for the government's past role:

In 1953 the United States played a significant role in orchestrating the over-throw of Iran's popular Prime Minister, Mohammed Mossadeq. The Eisenhower Administration believed its actions were justified for strategic reasons; but the coup was clearly a setback for Iran's political development. And it is easy to see now why many Iranians continue to resent this intervention by America in their internal affairs.[12]

Following the coup, Shah Mohammad Reza Pahlavi became increasingly authoritarian, strengthened Iran's military forces, and sought to modernize and westernize his country as rapidly as possible. Dissent was crushed by the secret police, the Savak, and the shah's foes were imprisoned or exiled, as was Ayatollah Ruhollah Khomeini in 1964. Under the shah, Iran became a bastion of anticommunism as a member of the U.S.-supported Baghdad Pact (later the Central Treaty Organization, or CENTO) and a base for U.S. intelligence and reconnaissance facilities. CENTO was dissolved after the 1979 Iranian revolution.

In the 1960s and 1970s President Richard Nixon and Secretary of State Henry Kissinger viewed Iran rather than Saudi Arabia as America's proxy in the Middle East. Iran "was transformed from a client to a partner of the United States in the global struggle to contain the Soviet Union"[13] following Britain's retreat as an imperial power in the Persian Gulf. "Kissinger's staff saw Iranian primacy in the Persian Gulf as a sound choice, given that Iran was 'the most powerful and stable state in the area.'"[14] Meanwhile, the shah used the CIA to provide covert aid for a Kurdish revolt in northern Iraq and, as we shall see, persuaded Washington to help begin Iran's nuclear program.

Iran's 1979 Islamic revolution was triggered by Ayatollah Khomeini, "a charismatic cleric distin-guished as much by his mystical cast of mind as by his ferocious opposition to the shah."[15] Iran, enriched by high oil prices in the 1970s that created immense disparities in wealth—and challenges from social and economic turmoil resulting from rapid population growth, urbanization, and the imposition of Western values and mores—was buffeted by unrest when a recession began in 1975. Tension increased after rumors spread that the government was responsible for the sudden death of Ayatollah Khomeini's son in 1977. Demonstrations in January 1978 led by theology students in the holy city of Qom were violently suppressed, and protests spread across the country. Khomeini, who was still in exile, began to call for the shah's overthrow. Despite the imposition of martial law, Tehran was the scene of additional violent protests in September that were suppressed brutally by Iran's army. In the following months, strikes paralyzed the country, climaxing in a general strike on November 6. The shah sought to placate his foes by naming moderate prime ministers, freeing political prisoners, and arresting the former chief of the Savak, but on December 11 over a million protesters demonstrated in Tehran. By then Washington had begun to have doubts about the shah's political survival. President Jimmy Carter's national security advisor warned Carter that anarchy was engulfing Iran "with the result that our position in the [Persian] Gulf would be undermined."[16]

On January 16, 1979, the shah and his wife left the country for a "vacation," and his opponents took to the streets to demand he step down. "The Shah had constructed the state machine around his person. Once the Shah had lost the will to fight, the state crumbled from within and out of its own lack of momentum."[17] Prime Minister Shapour Baktiar sought to quell the protesters by abolishing the secret police, ordering the army to avoid using force, freeing additional political prisoners, and allowing Ayatollah Khomeini to return to Iran. Khomeini, whose speeches had been spread by smuggled tapes, arrived on February 1, calling for the government's overthrow and naming Mehdi Bazargan prime minister of an Islamic government. Thereafter, fighting erupted between pro-Khomeini and pro-shah elements in the armed forces, and the shah's government resigned on February 11.

On October 21, 1979, President Carter agreed to allow the shah, who was suffering from cancer, to enter the United States. U.S. diplomats in Tehran strongly opposed the decision. Before seeking asylum in America, the shah had unwisely spent time in Egypt and Morocco, leading Zbigniew Brzezinski to comment that this "pause" in his journey "proved to be disastrous" and "generated an issue where none should have existed."[18] What had changed was a brief seizure of America's embassy in Tehran on February 14, 1979, an action that greatly complicated U.S. policy toward Iran and its former shah. As a result, Washington and its diplomats in Tehran believed that the shah's entry into the United States would endanger American interests and personnel in Iran. Thus, the shah journeyed to the Bahamas in March and then to Mexico in June. Brzezinski, Kissinger, and others pressed Carter to admit him as a matter of principle even though the president, Secretary of State Cyrus Vance, and Deputy Secretary of State Warren Christopher were trying to normalize relations with the new Iranian government. By October, however, the shah's health had deteriorated, which persuaded the president to go ahead and allow the shah to fly to New York to receive medical care. The shah left the United States in December 1979 and died in Egypt in July 1980.

On November 4 radical Iranian students demanding that the shah be extradited seized the U.S. embassy in Tehran, taking dozens of Americans hostage of whom fifty-two were held for 444 days. In the ensuing days Iran abrogated its military agreement with Washington and the Iranian government resigned, ceding authority to Ayatollah Khomeini and his Revolutionary Council. President Carter then imposed economic sanctions on Iran, the UN Security Council demanded the hostages' release, and on April 7, 1980, Washington severed diplomatic ties with Tehran. An effort to rescue the hostages in a raid on April 24 proved a fiasco after eight U.S. servicemen were killed in the collision of a helicopter and a transport plane. Finally, after Ronald Reagan had defeated President Carter in the November presidential election, an agreement was reached on January 19, 1981, to free the hostages in return for turning over Iranian assets frozen by Washington. According to Bruce Laingen, then embassy chargé d'affaires, "There were uproarious cheers as we cleared the runway, more when champagne was broken

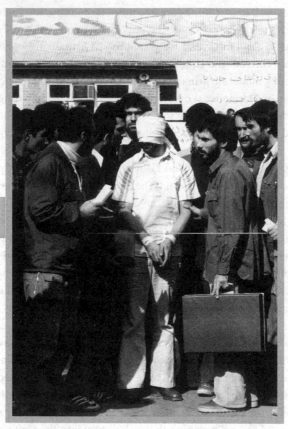

American hostages
in Tehran

Kaveh Kazemi/Getty

out when we crossed the Turkish border, and then the beginning of a flight to freedom we can never forget, nor can we forget the constant hospitality of that Algerian aircraft's crew."[19]

The Iranian hostage crisis was the end of a chain of events that had begun in the early 1950s and that transformed U.S.–Iranian relations from one of allies to that of enemies. "The hostage episode," writes Stephen Kinzer, "changed the course of American political history and poisoned relations between Iran and the United States."[20] Iran's revolutionary regime began to arm and finance Hamas and Hezbollah, and was possibly involved in the 1983 bombings that killed over 200 marines in Beirut, Lebanon, and the 1994 bombing of a Jewish center in Argentina. As we shall see, events in Iran also affected U.S. relations with Iraq.

THE BIRTH AND EVOLUTION OF IRAQ

Iraq became Islamic owing to its conquest by Arabic Muslims in the seventh century CE. It was the site of the death of Muhammad's grandson, Hussein, a key event in the development of Shia Islam, and Baghdad became the brilliant capital of the Abbasid caliphate. Following a war between Persia and the Ottoman Turks in the sixteenth century, Iraq was absorbed by the Sunni Ottoman Empire that ruled the region until the end of World War I. Nevertheless, Persian (Iranian) influence persisted in Iraq owing partly to their link as Shia-majority societies and Iran's location, which abuts southern Iraq—site of many of the country's Shiites. During World War I Britain occupied Iraq to protect it from Ottoman Turkey, and following the war, Iraq became a British League of Nations colonial "mandate" under which Britain was supposed to prepare Iraq for self-government.

Iraq's Political Evolution from a Monarchy to Saddam Hussein

In 1920 the British selected Feisal, son of Hussein bin Ali, sharif of Mecca, as king of Greater Syria, but he went into exile after France occupied that country. The following year Britain chose Feisal to be king of the new country of Iraq, in which Sunni Muslims dominated the government. It included the northern region around Mosul, where oil was discovered in 1927, and London obtained an oil concession under which the Iraq Petroleum Company was established. Anti-British resentment in Iraq sparked an insurrection in that country in 1920 that lasted four years. With the aid of aircraft, the insurgency was brutally suppressed, and Iraq was granted formal independence in 1930 in the Anglo–Iraqi Treaty that became operative upon Iraq's entry to the League of Nations in 1932. Feisal reigned until his death in 1933 and was succeeded by his son Ghazi, who reigned until he died in 1939. Ghazi's son, Feisal II, succeeded him until he was killed in 1958 by Iraqi officers who established the Republic of Iraq. Although a majority of Iraqis were Shiites, Iraq's governing elite remained largely Arab Sunni.

Between 1920 and 1958 Iraqi politics was dominated by a king, the British who provided him support, and Arab Sunni politicians, many of whom were nationalists who constituted the country's major political opposition. Although the mandate ended after the 1930 treaty under which Iraq became a member of the League of Nations, Britain continued to exercise paramount influence in that country through pro-British politicians—notably Nuri al-Said, who was prime minister during much of the period. Britain's continued influence and its reoccupation of Iraq in World War II fueled Iraqi nationalism in subsequent decades, especially among young officers in the country's army, which became a key political player after a 1936 coup. Iraqi nationalism intensified with the emergence of conflict in British-administered Palestine. Following Iraq's return to civilian rule, another military coup in 1941 brought pro-German military officers to power, triggering British occupation of the country after a brief conflict. Prime Minister Rashid Ali was then replaced by pro-British Nuri al-Said, who served as prime minister until 1944 and again from 1946–1947, 1949, 1950–1952, 1954–1957, and 1958, becoming increasingly authoritarian as he aged.

Following World War II, pan-Arabism and nationalism were fostered by a revolution in Egypt in 1952 that ultimately bought Abdel Gamal Nasser to power, the rise and subsequent overthrow of Mossadeq in Iran, and the partition of Palestine. In addition, communists became increasingly influential, and the Cold War began to have an impact on the country. Thus, in 1955 at the urging of Secretary Dulles, Iraq, Iran, Turkey, Pakistan, and Britain formed an alliance—the Baghdad Treaty organization—as part of Washington's policy of containing the USSR. This action alienated Nasser, who opposed the Western presence in the region, and split the Arab world between pro- and anti-Western states, a split further exacerbated by the Anglo–French invasion of Egypt during the 1956 Suez War.

By the mid-1950s Iraq's nationalist officers were increasingly opposed to the regime. Following civil strife in Lebanon in May 1958 involving pro-Nasser elements, the government dispatched troops to neighboring Jordan to protect that country from a similar fate. Instead, in what came to be called the

July Revolution, the military seized power in Baghdad, and the king, his family, and Prime Minister al-Said were killed. Gen. Abd al-Karim Qasim and Col. Abdul Salam Arif imposed a military dictatorship, although they later became political rivals. The ensuing decade was characterized by persistent political instability and sectarian and tribal divisions in Iraq, and by a nationalist and increasingly pro-Soviet and anti-American tilt in foreign policy. During this time the Arab Socialist Ba'ath Party that had originated in Syria became a significant factor in Iraqi politics by advocating popular nationalist policies. Saddam Hussein was among the Ba'athists who unsuccessfully plotted against the Qasim regime in 1959. In 1963 the Ba'athists finally overthrew Qasim. Ba'athist rule lasted only a year until it lost power to Iraq's military leaders, but with the aid of army officers led by Gen. Ahmed Hassan al-Bakr, the party regained power in a successful coup in 1968. Saddam Hussein and others from Saddam's home city of Tikrit assumed control of the country's security forces. Between 1968 and 1979, when he became Iraq's president, Saddam remained in al-Bakr's shadow while gathering the reins of power in his own hands and giving the Ba'ath Party a monopoly of authority.

Iraq's Shifting Foreign Policy

In 1959 Iraq's military regime withdrew from the Baghdad Pact, which was then renamed the Central Treaty Organization (CENTO). Iraq's regime further isolated itself in 1961 by claiming ownership of the former British protectorate of Kuwait. This action triggered a return of British troops to Kuwait and produced hostility toward Iraq in much of the Arab world. Thereafter, the Soviet–Iraqi relationship warmed significantly, and Moscow opposed efforts by Iraq's Communist Party to seize power. Iraq's pro-Soviet shift produced tensions with neighboring Turkey and Iran. Iraq's hostility toward the West intensified after the Arab defeat in the 1967 Six-Day War, while Soviet–Iraqi relations were strengthened between 1972 and 1975 owing to the growing military power of neighboring Iran, Soviet aid in developing Iraq's oil industry, and the 1973 Yom Kippur War. In April 1972 the two countries signed a Treaty of Friendship and Cooperation, and Iraq increased its purchase of arms from the USSR.

The regime nationalized the Iraq Petroleum Company in 1973, and higher oil prices and a lowering of tension with Iran in the 1970s reduced Iraq's dependence on Moscow. Nevertheless, after 1968 the Ba'ath-dominated government was loudly anti-American because of Washington's ties to Israel and Iran. Relations with Iran further deteriorated after Washington stepped up military aid to Tehran as part of the "Nixon Doctrine" to use regional proxies when possible. Iran's own defense spending soared, and America's military presence in the Persian Gulf increased. Both Iran and Iraq began to aid Kurdish separatists in the other country. Iran provided Iraq's militant Kurdish separatists with heavy weapons in the mid-1970s and even sent troops into northern Iraq, while the Nixon administration provided Iraqi Kurdish groups with clandestine financial support.

Thereafter, Saddam Hussein became a fixture in the "rejectionist front" of those who wanted no compromise with Israel and sought to undermine Iran's Shia regime, a policy that led ultimately to a disastrous war with that country in 1980. In addition, Iraq's competition with Syria (which became a Soviet client after 1966) for leadership of the Arab world, as well as Baghdad's rapprochement with Sadat's Egypt and disputes with Moscow about oil prices and Moscow's support of Iraq's Kurds, eroded Soviet influence in Iraq after 1975. This did not, however, prevent a massive Soviet arms deal with Iraq the following year. However, relations with Moscow deteriorated significantly after the Soviet invasion of Afghanistan in December 1979.

Iran–Iraq War

Iraq's relations with Iran were complicated by the Iranian revolution, that country's subsequent unwillingness to prevent Kurds from crossing into Iraq, and Ayatollah Khomeini's effort to export his revolution to Iraq and foster Shia Iraqi discontent. Iraq's Shiites were inspired by the cleric Muhammad Baqir al-Sadr, who was executed in 1980.

Saddam Hussein regarded Ayatollah Khomeini as a threat to his authority. The ensuing Iran–Iraq War was partly the consequence of a lengthy dispute over the narrow Shatt al-Arab that divides southern Iraq and Iran and affords Iraq with its only access to the Persian Gulf, through which much of its oil as well as Iran's is exported. Iran came to view the 1937 treaty that had surrendered to Iraq control of the ship channel as unfair. In 1969 it repudiated the agreement, claiming that the boundary ran in the middle of the entire length of the channel. Iran's claim was recognized in a 1975 agreement between the two countries, the Algiers Accords. Growing Iranian–Iraqi hostility was followed by Iraqi demands for

MAP 12.1   Iran, Iraq, and Kuwait

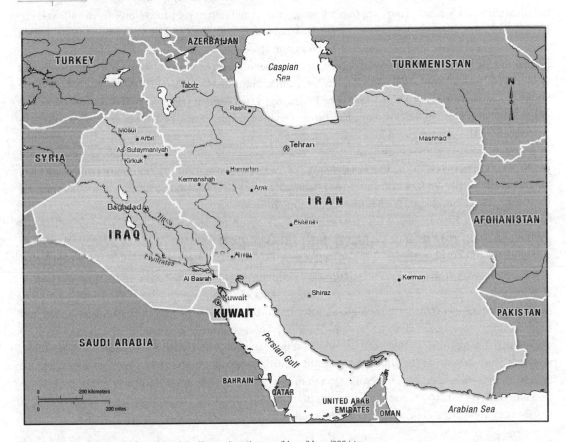

Source: Adapted from World Sites Atlas: http://www.sitesatlas.com/Maps/Maps/606.htm

two strategic Kuwaiti islands in the Persian Gulf, resorting to force in 1973 and ceasing only after Saudi Arabia intervened to assist neighboring Kuwait.

Following Iranian bombardment of Iraqi border areas in September 1980, Saddam abrogated the 1975 agreement, bombed Iranian bases, and invaded Iran. What followed was an eight-year war of attrition that bled both countries and ended in a stalemate. It was a brutal war in which Iraq used missiles against Iranian cities and poison gas against Iranian troops and its country's Kurds (notably against the city of Halajba in 1988), while Iran launched human-wave attacks against Iraq's defenses. Iraq's ports were destroyed and its oil pipeline to Syria was blocked, forcing Bagdad to appeal to other Arab states for financial support against their common Persian foe. Iran also began organizing Shia Iraqis in exile into a Supreme Council for the Islamic Revolution in Iraq in order to establish an Islamic regime in Baghdad. Concern about Iranian and Iraqi ambitions and a desire to strengthen relations with Washington led Gulf countries (Saudi Arabia, Kuwait, the United Arab Emirates, Bahrain, Qatar, and Oman) to establish the Gulf Cooperation Council in 1981.

Beginning in 1983 Washington began to "tilt" toward Iraq and sought to cut the flow of foreign arms to Iran's revolutionary regime while permitting arms exports to Iraq and providing Baghdad with intelligence information. After Iraq began bombing Iranian oil tankers, Iran attacked tankers heading toward Saudi Arabia and Kuwait—Iraq's supporters—triggering American naval protection for Kuwaiti vessels. In May 1987 the U.S. frigate *Stark* was struck by Iraqi missiles, and in October an Iranian missile struck a Kuwaiti tanker flying the American flag. Washington struck several Iranian facilities in retaliation. The following year U.S.–Iranian relations deteriorated further after an Iranian mine struck a U.S. vessel, and Washington struck Iranian offshore oil facilities. Iranian ships then attacked offshore oil platforms of the United Aram Emirates, and U.S. naval vessels destroyed two Iranian frigates. This tit-for-tat sequence climaxed in July 1988 in the downing of an Iranian civilian airliner by the USS *Vincennes,* which mistakenly assumed the plane was a military aircraft.

Although the Security Council called for a cease-fire in July 1987, the war continued for another year. Saddam Hussein's desire to take advantage of Iran's post-revolutionary instability to dominate the Persian Gulf had turned to ashes, and in the aftermath of the war Iraq sought to strengthen relations with Washington and its regional friends like Jordan and Turkey.

CONCLUSION: CHANGING ERAS OF FRIENDSHIP AND HOSTILITY

U.S. relations with Iran and Iraq and relations between the latter have reflected complex domestic events in all three countries and have witnessed changing eras of friendship and hostility. Iranian hostility toward America has roots in Washington's role in overthrowing Iran's government in the 1950s and in its Islamic revolution, whose leaders saw the United States as the "Great Satan." Relations with Iraq were warm during the Cold War until Baghdad left the Baghdad Pact and turned to Moscow. Thereafter, relations warmed during the Iran–Iraq War but chilled as the nature of Saddam Hussein's regime and Saddam's ambitions became clearer. For much of the period following the Iranian revolution until the Persian Gulf War in 1990, containment—or, more accurately, "dual containment"—was employed to isolate Iraq and Iran and prevent either from dominating the Middle East.

13

America and the Shia Crescent

IRAQ AND IRAN

President George
W. Bush announces
start of U.S.-led
invasion of Iraq in
2003

Official White House Photo by Paul Morse

Chapter 13 begins by describing U.S.–Iraqi relations from the Cold War including Washington's response to Iraq's 1990 invasion of Kuwait and the 1990–1991 Persian Gulf War, the U.S. invasion of Iraq in 2003, and its subsequent partial return to Iraq in 2013. It then examines the claim of the George W. Bush administration that Saddam Hussein had links to al-Qaeda, a claim given as one justification for Washington's overthrow of Saddam. The chapter then turns to U.S.–Iranian relations after Iran's Islamic revolution. It looks at the spread of Iranian influence in the Middle East, including Iran's links with the Syrian regime of Bashar al-Assad, which Washington opposed, and its Shia allies in Yemen and Bahrain. It then describes anti-Iranian attitudes of Sunni states, especially Saudi Arabia and the conservative Sunni monarchies along the Persian Gulf, and examines the evolution of U.S. relations with these states owing to the changing politics of oil. The chapter concludes with a description of American efforts to prevent Tehran from developing nuclear weapons as well as Israeli opposition to a U.S.–Iranian deal limiting Iran's ability to develop nuclear weapons.

IRAQ

American relations with Iraq began to worsen after that country left the Bagdad Pact and improved relations with Moscow. Although Washington "tilted" toward Iraq in its war with Iran, relations deteriorated rapidly after Iraq invaded Kuwait. Shortly before the invasion, U.S. ambassador April Glaspie met with Saddam. Some believe he intentionally deceived her, promising to settle the dispute with Kuwait peacefully, and others contend Glaspie led Saddam to believe Washington would not become involved, tacitly offering U.S. approval for Iraq's invasion of Kuwait. The reasons for Iraq's invasion included persistent border disputes with Iraq that involved Kuwaiti islands, which could impede Iraqi access to the Persian Gulf; Iraq's mountainous debt to Kuwait (and other Sunni states) owing to the war with Iran, for which Kuwait demanded repayment; and a dispute over Iraq's giant Rumaila oil field near Kuwait's border, from which Baghdad charged Kuwait was pumping oil by slant-drilling.

The Persian Gulf War

The first challenge to the post–Cold War world order was Saddam Hussein's invasion of Kuwait in 1990. The international community swiftly condemned Iraq's action. Washington also responded quickly, though some dissented from the decision to employ U.S. military power to compel Iraq to retreat from Kuwait. In what became known as the Powell Doctrine, Gen. Colin Powell, chair of the Joint Chiefs of Staff, argued that America should only commit forces to battle when a clear vital interest was threatened, other means of protecting that interest had been exhausted, there was a clear exit strategy, and the use of force enjoyed broad domestic and international support. Powell did not view Kuwait as a vital interest and believed other strategies, including containing Iraq, would serve U.S. interests better. His view did not prevail, and President George H. W. Bush began building a multilateral coalition, eventually comprising thirty states, to drive Iraq out of Kuwait should it not withdraw by the Security Council's deadline. While diplomatic efforts were under way, Bush began increasing U.S. troop levels in the Persian Gulf and diverting resources to the region while lobbying in the Security Council for economic and military sanctions against Iraq.

Despite pressure from Washington, the United Nations (UN), and others, and faced with declining oil prices, Saddam Hussein refused to comply with successive Security Council resolutions. In November 1990 the council authorized member states to "use all necessary means" to implement previous resolutions and restore international peace and security[1] should Iraq not withdraw from Kuwait by January 15, 1991. As the deadline approached, Congress authorized the use of American troops to force Iraq from Kuwait. On January 17 hostilities commenced with a massive bombing campaign over six weeks that targeted Iraq's war-related infrastructure—communication facilities, utilities, and military bases. On February 24 U.S. Marines invaded Iraq and Kuwait, beginning a ground offensive ("Operation Desert Storm"). Iraqi forces were outmatched, and coalition forces swiftly liberated Kuwait. Iraqi missile attacks against Israel, which many feared contained toxic gas, were intended to force Israel to retaliate, thereby rallying Arab states to Iraq's side. However, the Israelis refused to be drawn into the conflict, and the allied coalition remained united. Saddam also sought to use "ecoterrorism," setting fire to Kuwaiti oil fields.

The outcome of the Persian Gulf War affected U.S. military strategy for decades, partly because it left Saddam Hussein in power. The coalition achieved its aim of driving Iraq from Kuwait, and U.S. officials chose not to overthrow Saddam, whose ouster would likely produce a power vacuum in the region that would embolden revolutionary Iran. Saddam viewed, and celebrated, his survival as a victory, but U.S. officials hoped that his opposition would regard his loss as an opportunity to overthrow the regime. "Obviously," Bush reflected, "when the troops straggle home with no armor, beaten up, 50,000 . . . and maybe more dead, the people of Iraq will know."[2] Uprisings occurred in the Kurdish north and the Shia south of Iraq, but the regime responded with such brutality that the allied coalition established no-fly zones over those regions. U.S. failure to intervene more robustly in the south despite requests from Iraqi Shiites, however, left a residue of anger toward Washington among Shiites that became evident after 2003. Kurdish–American relations were warmer, and U.S. humanitarian relief and enforcement of a no-fly zone in northern Iraq fostered the relative autonomy of Iraq's Kurdish region. Saddam Hussein remained in power for more than another decade, but neither Iraqi Shiites nor Kurds were pacified.

The war was notable as an exercise in post–Cold War cooperation—only the second instance of collective security since the founding of the UN in 1945. It also demonstrated U.S. military superiority. America introduced F-117 stealth bombers, precision-guided munitions ("smart" bombs), infrared targeting, and global positioning system technology that made it possible to win the war quickly and with few U.S. casualties. (The Defense Department reported that 148 U.S. troops were killed in action or died of wounds.[3] Iraqi combat and civilian deaths were much greater.)

From the end of the Persian Gulf War until Washington's 2003 intervention in Iraq, Saddam's regime was largely unsuccessful as it sought to undo the no-fly zones, the economic sanctions, and the international weapons inspections imposed by the 1991 cease-fire and UN Security Council Resolution 687. In addition, Iraqi opponents of Saddam led by Ahmed Chalabi and Ayad Allawi were organized overseas, ready to return to Baghdad if the regime collapsed. These groups were funded in part by the CIA, which also sought unsuccessfully to organize a coup against Saddam.[4] After George W. Bush became president, Washington increased its funding to support Iraqi groups opposed to the regime.

The 2003–2011 Iraq War and Thereafter

When Iraq invaded Kuwait in 1990, U.S. leaders were already concerned about Iraq's effort to acquire weapons of mass destruction (WMD). Iraq had established a secret program for acquiring WMD in 1974 under Saddam Hussein, and in the same year purchased a nuclear reactor from France. Israeli agents destroyed nuclear reactor cores on their way to Iraq from France, and in 1981 Israel bombed and destroyed Iraq's French-built Osirak reactor. After Iraq started an enrichment facility in February 1990, Saddam feared another Israeli attack and claimed to have acquired chemical weapons to retaliate if Israel did so.

After the Persian Gulf War, a UN Special Commission (UNSCOM) was established to enforce Security Council Resolution 687 (1991), requiring Iraq to "unconditionally accept, under international supervision, the destruction, removal or rendering harmless of its weapons of mass destruction, ballistic missiles with a range over 150 kilometers, and related production facilities and equipment."[5] It also established a system to monitor Iraq's compliance with the ban on these weapons.

Between 1992 and 2003 there was continual friction between Iraq and UNSCOM regarding access to Iraqi military facilities and production sites. Security Council Resolution 1051 (1996) set up a system to monitor Iraq's exports and imports related to WMD, and Resolution 1284 (1999) established a new agency—the UN Monitoring, Verification and Inspection Commission (UNMOVIC)—to verify Baghdad's compliance with its obligation to eliminate chemical and biological weapons and illegal missiles, while the International Atomic Energy Agency (IAEA) did the same regarding nuclear weapons. Several uranium-enrichment sites were uncovered and destroyed, as were a number of stockpiles of chemical weapons. In the face of Iraqi obstruction, America and Britain launched three days of air and cruise-missile strikes ("Operation Desert Fox") in 1998 against Iraqi targets believed to contribute to Iraq's ability to produce, store, and deliver WMD. Thereafter, Iraqi officials ceased cooperating with UN inspectors, who were withdrawn until Iraq allowed them to return in 2002. In the meantime, economic sanctions remained in place because UNSCOM could not confirm that all banned weapons had been destroyed, although the agency believed that most of Iraq's WMD had been found. Owing to worsening conditions in Iraq, the sanctions regime was altered in 1996 to allow Baghdad to export some oil in return for imports of food.

Washington's concern that Baghdad was hiding WMD or the means to produce them served as the principal justification for the Anglo–American invasion of Iraq in 2003. At American insistence, the Security Council unanimously adopted Resolution 1441 in November 2002, declaring that Iraq "has been and remains in material breach" of its previous commitments and was being given "a final opportunity to comply with its disarmament obligations" and set up "an enhanced inspection regime." The Security Council also demanded that Baghdad provide "a currently accurate, full, and complete declaration of all aspects of its programs to develop chemical, biological, and nuclear weapons, ballistic missiles, and other delivery systems" and provide "immediate, unimpeded, unconditional, and unrestricted access to any and all, including underground, areas, facilities, buildings, equipment, records, and means of transport which they wish to inspect, as well as immediate, unimpeded, unrestricted, and private access to all officials and other persons whom UNMOVIC or the IAEA wish to interview." The resolution warned Iraq that, in the event of noncompliance, it would "face serious consequences as a result of its continued violations of its obligations."[6] The following year America, Britain, and Spain proposed an additional resolution, explicitly endorsing the use of force against Iraq, but it was withdrawn after it became clear that it did not have majority support and would be vetoed by Russia, China, and/or France.

Washington claimed that Resolution 1441, with its threat of "serious consequences," was sufficient to authorize the invasion—a claim that even some of America's closest allies rejected. In 2003 Washington launched "Operation Iraqi Freedom" to force Iraq to abide by a decade of Security Council resolutions, calling on it to reveal all weapons of mass destruction activities and verifiably dismantle its WMD programs, with an emphasis on nuclear disarmament. When U.S. troops failed to locate these weapons, their principal goal became "regime change"—overthrowing Saddam Hussein, who the Bush administration also claimed was linked to al-Qaeda. The initial military campaign that began March 19 ended with Iraq's defeat by May. In September 2004 UN secretary-general Kofi Annan declared the invasion "was not in conformity with the UN charter from our point of view, from the charter point of view, it was illegal."[7]

America's invasion of Iraq ("Operation Iraqi Freedom") commenced on March 19, 2003. U.S. and British troops swiftly overcame Iraqi resistance, and on May 1 President Bush declared "mission accomplished" from aboard the carrier USS *Abraham Lincoln*. Saddam Hussein's two sons were killed in July, and Saddam was captured in December. The real war, however, was just beginning. A violent insurgency erupted in the power vacuum left by the dismantling of Iraq's army and governing institutions. America's short-lived Office of Reconstruction and Humanitarian Assistance under Jay Garner accomplished little, and its successor, the Coalition Provisional Authority under Ambassador L. Paul Bremer, had little choice but to impose direct rule. U.S. nation-building efforts proved unsuccessful. "That effort—ideologically driven, ill-considered, and woefully understaffed—destroyed more than it built. It dismantled the entire institutional structure of the old regime but had too few resources, staff, or time—and too little understanding of the country—to construct the building blocks of the new Iraq it wished to create."[8]

In 2004 and 2005 violence across Iraq escalated and took on a sectarian character as Sunni insurgents, including former Iraqi military personnel, al-Qaeda-affiliated terrorists, and Shia militias, fought for control of towns and neighborhoods and attacked coalition forces. Shia militias aided by Iran—especially the Mahdi Army of Muqtadā al-Ṣadr, son of Grand Ayatollah Mohammad Mohammad Sadeq al-Sadr, who had been murdered by the regime in 1999—as well as Sunni militants including al-Qaeda in Iraq, also attacked U.S. troops. As a consequence, opposition to the war intensified in the United States. An interim Iraqi government was appointed in June 2004, but Iraqi elections in 2005 did little to reduce sectarian squabbling and, though hailed in Washington, contributed little to promoting the prerequisites of genuine democracy—tolerance of diverse views, willingness to accept election results, and readiness to compromise. Gradually, Iraq's government came to be dominated by Shia politicians, notably Prime Minister Nuri al-Maliki, who excluded Sunnis as much as possible and opposed autonomy for Sunni or Kurdish regions. Thus, in a letter to President Barack Obama shortly before Maliki visited America in late 2013 to request additional U.S. weapons, a bipartisan group of senators declared that a "failure of governance is driving many Sunni Iraqis into the arms of al-Qaeda in Iraq and fueling the rise of violence."[9] After meeting Maliki, one senator declared, "I did not feel like he seemed to internalize at all the concerns that we had, and was somewhat dismissive," and a colleague added, "I got the sense there was no acknowledgement of any of the challenges facing Iraqi society today."[10]

American forces, though sufficient to defeat Saddam's army, were insufficient to deal with the ensuing Shia and Sunni insurgencies, as some high-ranking U.S. officers had predicted. In November 2005 U.S. officials announced a new counterinsurgency strategy that emphasized reconstructing local institutions. Violence intensified until 2007, when a "surge" strategy promoted by Gen. David Petraeus, commander of the Multi-National Force in Iraq, added 30,000 troops. In addition, the "Sunni Awakening" that involved persuading Sunni tribes to fight insurgents helped reduce violence and enhance stability. America's "surge" occurred with a shift in strategy known as "clear, hold, build" introduced by Petraeus that emphasized reconstructing infrastructure, reducing sectarian violence, protecting local populations, and encouraging reconciliation among Sunnis, Shias, and Kurds. Violence was reduced and the country was sufficiently stable to allow parliamentary elections in 2010. However, following the withdrawal of U.S. forces from Iraq in 2011, sectarian violence reignited and Iraq's weak and corrupt political institutions were ill-equipped to cope with renewed terrorism started in 2014 by the Islamic State of Iraq and Syria (ISIS).

When he was elected president in 2008, Barack Obama inherited the wars in Iraq and Afghanistan, and U.S. military strategy, especially during Obama's first term in office, focused on conducting and winding down those wars. Obama came to office emphasizing multilateral and internationalist policies to advance U.S. interests. In practice, his military strategy was *less* multilateral and internationalist than his supporters hoped and *more* multilateral and internationalist than his critics wished. Nevertheless, after Obama became president, all U.S. troops left Iraq and were scheduled to leave Afghanistan. Both countries remained violent and unstable, but confronted by war fatigue, budget constraints, and other foreign-policy challenges, America remained unlikely to resume major military operations in those countries. Washington responded to Islamic terrorism not with boots on the ground, but with air and drone strikes, the latter a technology that allows America to target suspected terrorists without risk to U.S. soldiers. Thus, only a few years after U.S. troops left Iraq, terrorists were again operating there.

Nuri al-Maliki, who initially was highly regarded by officials in Washington for his promises to unify rival factions, pursue economic development, and partner with the United States in its 2007 surge, began losing favor by 2010. Unable to form a unity government, Maliki gradually became more authoritarian, taking control of key political institutions and using his new powers to punish critics and fuel sectarianism—and eventually a rebellion in Anbar and northwestern Iraq that left a foothold for ISIS forces. In its foreign policy, Maliki's Shia-dominated government moved closer to Shia Iran and claimed it was unable to stop Iranian arms shipments to the Assad government in Syria or prevent Shia Iraqis from going to Syria to aid Assad.

Washington urged Iraq's government to become inclusive and settle its disputes with the Kurds and those Sunnis who were prepared to work with it. American influence in Iraq, however, had waned after the U.S. withdrawal in December 2011, and thus U.S. options were limited. Equally important, ISIS's invasion again threatened to partition the country into predominantly Shia, Sunni, and Kurdish regions, an idea promoted in 2006 by then senator Joe Biden. "At least a third of the country is beyond Baghdad's control, not counting Kurdistan," declared one analyst. "But any effort to make that official would likely lead to an even greater disaster—not least because of the many mixed areas of the country, including Baghdad, where blood baths would surely ensue as different groups tried to establish facts on the ground."[11]

Maliki's successor, Haider al-Abadi, showed greater sensitivity to the interests of Iraq's Sunnis and Kurds, perhaps recognizing that if the government were willing to fight a full-scale sectarian war, it would have to allow greater autonomy to its three communities and persuade Sunnis in particular to help defend the country against ISIS. Former ambassador to Iraq Ryan Crocker had observed, "Either we intervene at the White House and the secretary of state level or this is going to devolve into a bloody stalemate, a line of demarcation between north and south, to be determined, but probably just north of Baghdad and the establishment of a de facto Al Qaeda state, and that's completely terrifying."[12] After ISIS declared a caliphate in June 2014—the Islamic State—and beheaded two American journalists, President Obama finally ordered air strikes against ISIS in Iraq and extended them to Syria when it became clear that the group had to be confronted in both countries.

Iraq and al-Qaeda: Any Connection?

Although over a decade has passed since America's invasion of Iraq, the country remains a virtual failed state, ranking twelfth among 178 states on *Foreign Policy*'s 2015 Fragile States Index.[13] Violent sectarian divisions undermined the fragile stability in Iraq following the U.S. withdrawal. "Sunni Arab Muslims, who resent Shiite political domination and perceived discrimination," were "escalating their political opposition to the government of Prime Minister Nuri al-Maliki through demonstrations as well as violence."[14] Without U.S. troops, sectarian violence had resumed, with almost 9,000 deaths in 2013, and Iraq's Shia-dominated government had come under the influence of neighboring Shia Iran. The uneasy combination of Shias, Sunnis, and Kurds that endangered the country's unity during the Iraq war again threatened to rip it apart.

One justification for America's 2003 invasion of Iraq was the belief that Saddam Hussein was linked to al-Qaeda. In a 2009 television interview, President George W. Bush declared: "Well, first of all, I do think Iraq is a central front in the war on terror and so does Osama bin Laden."[15] To what extent was this correct? And how did the Iraq war affect global terrorism?

Although President Bush and his advisors framed U.S. intervention in Iraq as part of the War on Terror, there was little evidence that Saddam Hussein had cooperated with al-Qaeda or jihadists. Although adopting Islamic rhetoric after the 1990–1991 war, Saddam governed largely as a secular ruler. His Ba'ath Party, far from seeking an Islamic theocracy, pursued secular, socialist, and pan-Arab goals. Nevertheless, in an interview, Vice President Dick Cheney insisted that "there is a pattern of relationships going back many years. And in terms of exchanges and in terms of people, we've had recently since the operations in Afghanistan—we've seen al-Qaeda members operating physically in Iraq and off the territory of Iraq. We know that Saddam Hussein has, over the years, been one of the top state sponsors of terrorism for nearly 20 years."[16] President Bush, Secretary of Defense Donald Rumsfeld, National Security Advisor Condoleezza Rice, and Secretary of State Colin Powell made similar allegations (though Powell retracted his in 2005). The president also sought to tie the alleged Saddam–bin Laden link to a claim that Iraq was developing nuclear weapons, arguing, "The danger is, is that al-Qaeda becomes an extension of Saddam's madness and his hatred, and his capacity to extend weapons of mass destruction around the world. Both of them need to be dealt with. The war on terror, you can't distinguish between al-Qaeda and Saddam when you talk about the war on terror."[17]

The president had described Saddam's Iraq as part of the "axis of evil," a term he also applied to Iran and North Korea, referring to their illicit efforts to acquire nuclear weapons. The administration cited alleged cooperation between al-Qaeda and Iraq in the years before 9/11, but there was no evidence of this. Instead, Saddam and bin Laden mistrusted each other, and al-Qaeda fostered opposition to Saddam among Iraqi Kurds. An alleged meeting between 9/11 hijacker Mohamed Atta and an Iraqi diplomat in Prague in 2001 probably never took place. And though there was a meeting between bin Laden and an Iraqi intelligence officer in Sudan in 1994 or 1995, its purpose was to end al-Qaeda's aid to anti-Saddam Kurds and inquire about possible al-Qaeda training camps in Kurdish Iraq.

One official report concluded that "a review of the White House's statements and interviews with current and former intelligence officials indicate[s] that the assertion was extrapolated from nuggets of intelligence, some tantalizing but unproven, some subsequently disproved, and some considered suspect even at the time the administration was making its case for war."[18] A Pentagon report concerning captured Iraqi documents and interrogation of Saddam Hussein "all confirmed" that the alleged link between al-Qaeda and Iraq did not exist. In 2002 the CIA determined, "Overall, the reporting provides no conclusive signs of cooperation on specific terrorist operations,"[19] an assessment reaffirmed in 2008 by the Senate Select Committee on Intelligence. According to the 9/11 Commission Report of 2004:

President Bush had wondered immediately after the attack whether Saddam Hussein's regime might have had a hand in it. Iraq had been an enemy of the United States for 11 years, and was the only place in the world where the United States was engaged in ongoing combat operations. . . [Anti-terrorism advisor Richard] Clarke has written that on the evening of September 12, President Bush told him and some of his staff to explore possible Iraqi links to 9/11. "See if Saddam did this," Clarke recalls the President telling them. "See if he's linked in any way.". . . Responding to a presidential tasking, Clarke's office sent a memo to Rice on September 18, titled "Survey of Intelligence Information on Any Iraq Involvement in the September 11 Attacks.". . . The memo found no "compelling case" that Iraq had either planned or perpetrated the attacks. . . Finally, the memo said, there was no confirmed reporting on Saddam cooperating with Bin Laden on unconventional weapons.[20]

It appears that the allegations regarding a bin Laden–Saddam Hussein link were spread by a report, later discredited, that Rumsfeld had Undersecretary of Defense Douglas Feith write and deliver to CIA director George Tenet in 2002. Feith apparently pulled together bits of raw intelligence to make the case he was to make. Thus, bureaucratic politics involving intelligence played a key role in justifying the Iraq war, and former CIA analyst Paul Pillar contended that the "administration used intelligence not to inform decision-making, but to justify a decision already made."[21]

Instead of curbing global terrorism, the Iraq war encouraged adherents to al-Qaeda and similar groups, as reflected in the emergence of al-Qaeda in Iraq. London's International Institute of Strategic Studies concluded that the occupation of Iraq became "a potent global recruitment pretext" for al-Qaeda,[22] and America's national intelligence officer for transnational threats described U.S.-occupied Iraq as "a training ground, a recruitment ground, the opportunity for enhancing technical skills," and as creating "the likelihood that some of the jihadists who are not killed there will, in a sense, go home, wherever home is, and will therefore disperse to various other countries."[23] The war radicalized many Muslims, some of whom joined the insurrection in Iraq. With the flight of bin Laden and Ayman al-Zawahiri from Afghanistan to Pakistan, al-Qaeda's role in global terrorism began to change. Shortly after bin Laden's death, Secretary of Defense Leon Panetta declared confidently that the United States was "within reach of strategically defeating" al-Qaeda, and that by eliminating the surviving leaders of the group in Pakistan, Somalia, and Yemen, "We can really cripple al-Qaeda as a threat to this country."[24] Panetta was overly optimistic.

Iran, to which we turn next, also had a great interest in the fate of Iraq and its Shia majority. In 2014 Tehran began shipping military equipment to Iraq. Its new president Hassan Rouhani guaranteed the security of Shia religious sites in Iraq, and key Iranian military personnel were sent to Iraq to advise the government and the Shia militias. Iran also conducted air strikes against ISIS forces near the Iranian frontier. All of this indicated growing Iranian concern about events in Iraq and a willingness to cooperate, at least tacitly, with Americans involved in the air strikes against the

Islamic State. Iran was clearly assuming a more direct role in Iraqi military operations, especially those of the Shia militias.[25]

IRAN

Iranian influence in the Middle East benefitted from America's wars in Iraq and Afghanistan, which had overthrown regimes hostile to Tehran. By mid-2015 Iranian influence in the region encompassed Shia allies in Syria, Iraq, Yemen, and Lebanon, where Hezbollah had become a major Iranian proxy and asset. Iran also had Shia allies in Bahrain and even Saudi Arabia. In Syria, Iran and Hezbollah propped up the Assad regime; and in Iraq, Iranian soldiers advised by the leader of Iran's Quds Force, Qassem Suleimani, complemented American airpower in the struggle against ISIS.

Iran and Syria

Iran and Russia were stalwart supporters of and sources of arms for the Assad regime, and the militant Shia group Hezbollah, an Iranian proxy based in Lebanon, intervened to assist Assad's military forces. Hezbollah's intervention was intended to prevent a changing balance of power against Shia Iran. Declared Secretary John Kerry, "Believe me, the bad actors, regrettably, have no shortage of their ability to get arms—from Iran, Hezbollah, from Russia, unfortunately."[26] By late 2013 Iran was believed to have provided $13 billion in financial aid to the Assad regime as well as members of the Quds Force, an elite arm of its Revolutionary Guard Corps. A commander in the corps admitted, "we are involved in fighting every aspect of a war, a military one in Syria and a cultural one as well."[27]

Despite American efforts to get Iraq to inspect flights from Iran to Syria, Iraq's Shia government, though not openly taking sides, remained a transit point for arms shipments to Syria. According to a U.S. official, "We urge Iraq to be diligent and consistent in fulfilling its international obligations and commitments, either by continuing to require flights over Iraqi territory en route to Syria from Iran to land for inspection or by denying overflight requests for Iranian aircraft going to Syria."[28] U.S. senators visiting Baghdad in September 2012 warned Iraqi leaders that allowing Iranian arms to fly weapons to Syria across their territory would harm relations with Washington. For his part, Prime Minister Nuri al-Maliki was concerned about the prospect of Sunni extremists coming to power in Syria: "Terrorists came back to Iraq when the conflict started in Syria."[29]

Shia versus Sunni: Yemen

Yemen, the poorest country in the Middle East, is strategically located at the southern tip of the Arabian Peninsula. Over half its population is Sunni Muslim, but a large minority is Shia, adherents of a branch called Zaydism that had ruled North Yemen for a millennium until 1962, when civil war erupted and the army ousted the country's ruling imam.

In early 2011 protests erupted against the country's autocratic president, Ali Abdullah Saleh, accompanied by a power struggle between governing factions. Saleh had enjoyed American support owing to his willingness to fight al-Qaeda-linked terrorists in his country. In June the president was badly wounded, and Vice President Abed Rabbo Mansour Hadi became acting president after Saleh left for Saudi Arabia for medical treatment. Following the formal transfer of power from President Saleh to Hadi in November 2011 in a deal brokered by the Gulf Cooperation Council, Hadi was himself elected president with no opposition.

After Hadi's election complex tribal and regional animosities—a rebellion by Shia Houthi rebels in the north seeking greater autonomy, a secessionist movement led by the Southern Movement (al-Hirak), and terrorists in al-Qaeda in the Arabian Peninsula (AQAP) in south Yemen—made the country increasingly ungovernable and a growing target of U.S. drone strikes. In early 2013 a ship stopped off Yemen's coast was found to be loaded with Iranian weapons that were of Chinese origin. The country's economy ground to a virtual halt, and in the words of a Yemeni political analyst, "at the helm, we have a leader who behaves like Saleh but doesn't even have his political skills."[30] Nevertheless, by the spring of 2013 Yemen seemed on a path toward a representative political system, owing to a lengthy process called the National Dialogue Conference. "We have not gotten to the solution," declared a Yemeni political analyst, but the conference "changed the political dynamic and the balance of power in the country."[31]

In August 2014 the Houthis, with Iranian backing and links with former president Saleh, again rose up in protest against the removal of subsidies that had aided Yemen's poor, and in September they seized control of Sanaa, Yemen's capital city, causing the country's prime minister to resign and triggering violence with tribal foes in the city. Additional violence in Sanaa in January 2015 led to the Houthi occupation of the presidential palace and the resignation of President Hadi and Prime Minister Khaled Baha. Hadi had been an American ally who, like his predecessor, had permitted U.S. drone strikes against AQAP. Washington feared that Hadi's ouster would impede U.S. counterterrorist actions in Yemen. Despite the Houthis' slogans that included "Death to America, death to Israel, damnation to the Jews,"[32] however, they were also enemies of the Sunni jihadists in AQAP, a position they shared with Washington. American diplomats, nevertheless, left Yemen to protest the government's overthrow.

Iran's regional foe, Sunni Saudi Arabia, had been funding Yemen but was unwilling to aid an ally of Iran and began to launch air strikes against Houthi forces advancing southward toward Aden in March 2015. The Saudis were joined by other Sunni states including Egypt. Washington provided logistical and intelligence support for the Saudis and their allies, and the presence of a U.S. aircraft group in the Arabian Sea apparently led Iran to turn around a convoy headed to Yemen to resupply the Houthi forces.

Shia versus Sunni: Bahrain

In February 2011 Shia–Sunni sectarian violence also engulfed Bahrain, a close U.S. military partner and home port of the U.S. Fifth Fleet, with responsibility for the security of the Persian Gulf. Bahrain and the other conservative monarchies in the region, including Qatar (another U.S. partner and host to a highly classified U.S. military facility called the Combined Air and Space Operations Center, which can track all aircraft over the region, including Syria, Afghanistan, and the Persian Gulf), sought to isolate themselves from the contagion of the "Arab Spring." As the Arab Spring spread, these governments increased repression of domestic dissidents.

Bahrain's ruling Sunni family declared martial law and called in aid from Saudi Arabia to crush Shia demonstrators who sought reforms establishing a constitutional monarchy. Although King Hamad bin Isa bin Salman al-Khalifa authorized a commission of inquiry that condemned the government's use of force, little was done to carry out its recommendations. Large protests again erupted in March and April 2013 in an effort to prevent the Formula 1 Grand Prix from taking place in Bahrain. In September 2013 some fifty Shia Muslims belonging to a group called the "14 February Coalition" were sentenced to long terms in prison for establishing a clandestine movement as the government sought to depict pro-democracy demonstrators as sectarian terrorists. With a marginalized and impoverished Shia majority, Bahrain's leaders risked causing the sectarian animosities they claimed to fear.

Elsewhere in the Persian Gulf, the United Arab Emirates (UAE), which bans political parties, arrested several Egyptians in 2013 and charged them with trying to form a Muslim Brotherhood cell and conspiring with Egypt's Brotherhood. In Saudi Arabia, King Abdullah bin Abdulaziz al Saud invested heavily, to the tune of $130 billion, to provide housing, education, unemployment benefits, and other welfare schemes to improve social welfare and thereby avoid domestic unrest.

MAP 13.1   Iran, Bahrain, and the Persian Gulf

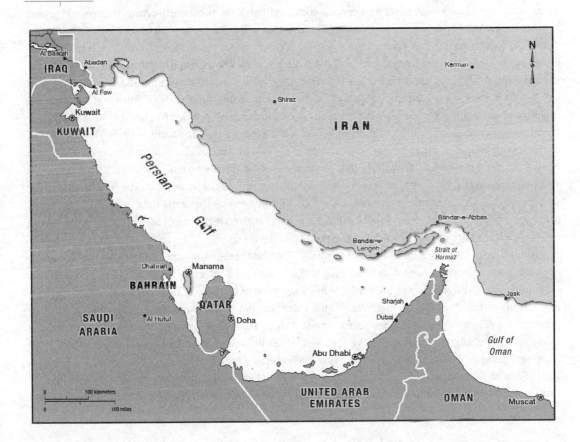

Iran's Sunni Foes

An anti-Iranian Sunni axis exists. It revolves around Saudi Arabia, long an American ally and a leading source of oil, and includes other oil-producing states in the Persian Gulf like Kuwait and the United Arab Emirates, countries ruled by conservative monarchs and fearful of the spread of political instability and Shia and Iranian influence in the region. Opposed to the Assad regime in Syria, they have sought to balance the influence of Iran and its proxy, Hezbollah, and were angered by America's unwillingness to use force against Assad after his use of chemical weapons against civilians and by Washington's willingness to negotiate with Iran regarding Tehran's nuclear aspirations.

Foes of the Assad regime included Jordan (where Washington secretly sent a small contingent of military specialists as well as a detachment of F-16 aircraft and Patriot antiaircraft missiles), Saudi Arabia, Bahrain, Kuwait, the United Arab Emirates, and Turkey. These governments viewed Syria as a battlefield for their conflict with Iran. "Saudi Arabia," observed a Saudi sociologist, "cannot afford to be encircled by Iran, from Iraq and Syria."[33] Iranian leaders, too, perceived the Syrian civil war as part of a larger regional conflict. "What is happening in Syria is not an internal Syrian issue," claimed the secretary of Iran's Supreme National Security Council, "but a conflict between the axis of resistance and its enemies in the region and the world."[34]

In August 2011 the conservative Arab monarchies recalled their ambassadors from Syria and demanded an end to the use of military force against civilians. Notwithstanding American warnings that arms could end up in the hands of extremists, Saudi Arabia and Qatar along with other Persian Gulf states shipped arms, including anti-tank missiles, to Syrian rebels as part of an effort to weaken Iranian influence and the links between Iran and Syria. Qatar, which successfully resisted instituting political reforms at home, began shipping arms via Turkey in early 2012, and some of these were made available to Sunni extremists battling Assad. Saudi Arabia was said to have paid for "thousands of rifles and hundreds of machine guns"[35] and other weapons for rebels from a Croatian source, aided by the CIA, which had been coordinating arms shipments from allies to Syrian rebels since 2012. The Saudis may also have supplied Syrian insurgents with more advanced weapons, as well as provided Lebanon with funding to acquire arms that could be used against Hezbollah—both signs of Saudi frustration with American restraint in equipping the insurgents with sufficient arms. In arming anti-Assad insurgents, the Saudis risked the possibility that weapons might fall into the hands of militant jihadi groups they opposed. Additional arms for rebel forces came from Libyan stockpiles left after the overthrow of Muammar Qaddafi, some paid for by Sunni opponents of Assad in Lebanon and elsewhere.

By early 2013 Assad's Sunni foes—aided by the CIA—had stepped up arms shipments via Turkey to opposition forces in Syria. According to an analyst of the Stockholm International Peace Research Institute, "The intensity and frequency of these flights are suggestive of a well-planned and coordinated military logistics operation."[36] And following Washington's decision not to use force against Assad after Russia's proposal for ridding Syria of its chemical weapons, Prince Turki al-Faisal, the brother of Saudi Arabia's foreign minister, angrily declared, "We've seen several red lines put forward by the president, which went along and became pinkish as time grew, and eventually ended up completely white." He added, "When that kind of assurance comes from a leader of a country like the United States, we expect him to stand by it."[37] And the Saudi ambassador to the United States commented, "The current charade of international control over Bashar's chemical arsenal would be funny if it were not so blatantly perfidious, and designed not only to give Mr. Obama an opportunity to back down but also to help Assad to butcher his people."[38]

The Saudis and other members of the Gulf Cooperation Council (GCC) that regarded the spread of democratic aspirations and Islamist values as potentially subversive were also angered by Washington's initial support of Egypt's Islamist government. The monarchies in the GCC concluded they were "only as strong as the weakest link in their chain," and if one of them succumbed to instability it could undo "the illusion of invincibility that the Gulf monarchies have so painstakingly built to distinguish themselves from the floundering Arab republics next door."[39]

After the overthrow of Egypt's Islamist government by the army in 2013, the members of the GCC were quick to provide its new military leaders with financial assistance. Saudi Arabia, Kuwait, and the United Arab Emirates pledged $12 billion to Egypt's military government in July and added additional assistance thereafter, partly reflecting their competition with Qatar, which along with Turkey had supported the Muslim Brotherhood. And several Arab states, including Egypt, Bahrain, the United Arab Emirates, and—most important—Saudi Arabia, recalled their ambassadors from Qatar in March 2014 owing to that country's support for the Muslim Brotherhood and other moderate Islamists.

As the 1990–1991 war against Iraq had shown, oil as well as geostrategic location made the Saudis crucial to America's Middle East calculations. U.S. relations in the Arab world were also complicated by the changing economics and politics of oil. Shifts in global demand for energy accompanied by a substantial increase in U.S. oil and gas production will affect American relations with the Persian Gulf states in expected and unexpected ways.

The politics of oil began to change and thus the relative influence of the Gulf States, including Saudi Arabia. In 2012 the real price of oil remained high, and the U.S. and Saudi Arabia were the global leaders in oil production, and the former was the leading global consumer of oil. Notwithstanding the economic crisis that began in 2007-2008, growing Chinese oil consumption remained high, and the region for China had assumed ever greater importance as the leading source of Chinese oil imports. Indeed, as indicated in Figure 13.1, it was anticipated that Chinese oil consumption would continue to rise and that China would soon pass America as the world's leading consumer of oil.

However, few observers recognized the importance of rapidly increasing shale oil and gas production in the United States and how in time this would push prices down globally. "Fracking," in North Dakota, Texas, and elsewhere had already increased U.S. oil and gas production by 14 and 10 percent respectively by 2011, and the U.S. was overtaking Russian oil and gas production.[40] Henry Kissinger among others recognized that growing American energy independence was of immense geopolitical importance.[41] Despite declining oil production owing to conflicts in other oil-producing countries like Libya, Iraq, and Syria and sanctions on Iran, economic problems in China and elsewhere, increasing U.S. energy production, and other factors like energy conservation and alternative energy sources like hydroelectric and solar power would cause a dramatic decline in energy prices in 2014 and thereafter. Among its consequences were a significant erosion of the economies of American foes including Russia and Venezuela as well as an economic bonanza for energy importers including China, India, and much of Europe.

FIGURE 13.1   China's Oil Production and Consumption, 1993–2016

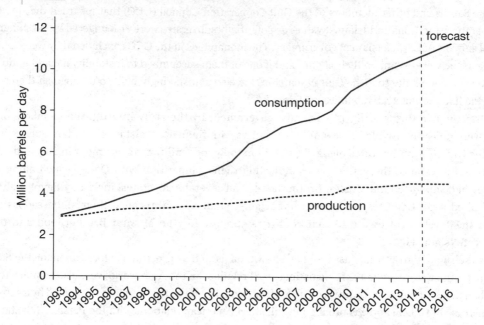

Source: U.S. Energy Information Administration, *International Energy Statistics and Short-Term Energy Outlook* (May 2015).

As recently as 2012, the International Energy Agency predicted that America would exceed Saudi Arabia as the world's largest oil producer by 2020 and could be energy independent or even a net oil exporter by 2030.[42] In fact, in 2014 the United States surpassed Saudi Arabia for the first time (see Table 13.1), but how long America will outproduce Saudi Arabia is uncertain. In its annual World Energy Outlook that agency also predicted that, although shale oil is having a significant impact on global energy supplies, "by the mid-2020s, non-OPEC production starts to fall back and countries from the Middle East provide most of the increase in global supply." The agency's director concluded, "We expect the Middle East will come back and be a very important producer and exporter of oil, just because there are huge resources of low-cost light oil."[43] Saudi Arabia's Aramco has invested heavily in the Motiva oil refinery in Port Arthur, Texas, the largest American producer of petroleum products. "The Saudis are securing a home for their heavy crude," declared an oil analyst. "But there is no question that security is also part of the equation. In Saudi Arabia, oil and politics always mix." Added another observer: "The Motiva relationship guarantees the Saudis an important but subtle footprint in the United States, and they want to have some negotiating strength when geopolitical issues in the Middle East and elsewhere arise."[44]

TABLE 13.1   Leading Oil Producers and Consumers, 2014

Producers (2014)

Country	Thousand barrels per day
United States	13,973
Saudi Arabia	11,624
Russia	10,853
China	4,572
Canada	4,383
United Arab Emirates	3,471
Iran	3,375
Iraq	3,271
Brazil	2,950
Mexico	2,812

Consumers (2013)

Country	Thousand barrels per day
United States	18,961
China	10,480
Japan	4,531
India	3,660
Russia	3,493
Brazil	3,003
Saudi Arabia	2,961
Canada	2,431
Germany	2,403
South Korea	2,324

Source: Data from the U.S. Energy Information Administration, "Total Petroleum and Other Liquids Production—2014," http://www.eia. gov/beta/international (accessed September 8, 2015).

The United States and Iranian Nuclear Aspirations

Iran also poses a serious proliferation challenge. Mohammad Reza Shah Pahlavi launched Iran's nuclear program in the 1950s. After Iran signed the Nonproliferation Treaty (NPT), it became a full participant in the nuclear nonproliferation regime. By the mid-1970s, however, the issue of control over uranium reprocessing had become a source of contention in U.S.–Iranian relations. The shah sought to turn Iran into a powerful, modern state and pursued an ambitious nuclear policy to enable the country to produce electrical power from nuclear power stations. While the shah insisted he did not seek nuclear weapons, he also asserted Iran's right to enrich its own nuclear fuel, a claim that contemporary Iranian leaders continue to make. U.S. officials viewed Tehran's intentions with skepticism, especially since no one in Tehran had "satisfactorily explained" how Iran expected "to absorb 23,000 megawatts-electric of additional power within the next 20 years."[45] Although Washington supported Iran's efforts to develop nuclear energy, it also tried to prevent Iran from pursuing fuel-cycle research that would give it its own plutonium reprocessing capability.[46]

After the shah's overthrow, the Islamic regime began to resurrect the nuclear program. In 1984 the Isfahan Nuclear Research Center opened with China's assistance and with aid from North Korea and from Pakistani nuclear scientist Abdul Qadeer Khan's nuclear black market network. Iran's nuclear program accelerated when Iran and Russia signed an agreement in 1994 to provide Iran with two 950-megawatt light-water reactors at Bushehr and the fuel to run them. In a separate, secret agreement, Russia offered Iran a large research reactor, a fuel fabrication plant, and a gas centrifuge facility to be used for peaceful, commercial purposes. After many delays, the Bushehr plant was opened in 2011.

Iranian officials insisted that nuclear power was needed to meet growing domestic demand for energy paid for with hard currency earned from oil and gas exports. They had long insisted that Iran was in compliance with the NPT, having declared all of its nuclear material and allowed inspectors to monitor its nuclear facilities, but the IAEA remained "unable to confirm that *all* nuclear material is in peaceful activities."[47] Was Iran seeking to develop nuclear weapons, as U.S. officials believed, or was it trying to develop commercial nuclear energy, as Iranian officials claimed? Resolving such questions was complicated by the mistrust between the two governments that had not had diplomatic relations since Iran's 1979 Islamic revolution.

Concern over Iran's nuclear ambitions began in 2002, when it was revealed that Iran was pursuing a clandestine nuclear program involving several undeclared nuclear facilities, including a uranium-enrichment facility and research lab under construction at Natanz, and a heavy-water reactor at Arak. The safeguards agreements negotiated with the IAEA in 1974 had only authorized its inspectors to monitor *declared* nuclear facilities. Moreover, countries were not required to report facilities until six months before nuclear material was introduced—at the time of the revelation there was no nuclear material at Natanz. Iran's efforts to conceal these facilities seemed to confirm U.S. suspicions that Iran was interested in building nuclear weapons. The IAEA began an investigation of Iran's nuclear program and called for a suspension of its uranium-enrichment activities while the investigation was under way.

For a time, it appeared that Iran might be willing to prove its peaceful intentions by entering into a voluntary agreement to halt its enrichment activities and signing an Additional Protocol with the IAEA granting the agency authority to inspect a wider range of undeclared nuclear-related facilities. It is difficult to say whether Iran's cooperation at that time reflected the policies of reformist president

MAP 13.2   Iranian Nuclear Facilities

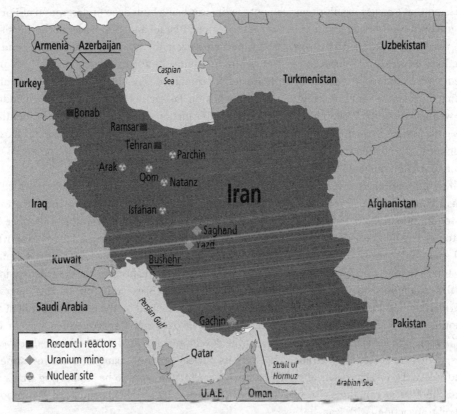

Source: Modified from CQ *Global Researcher*, "Rising Tension in Iran," February 7, 2012. Original map by Lewis Agrell.

Mohammad Khatami or was a reaction to America's 2003 invasion of Iraq. But Iran's accommodating stance only lasted until 2005, when the George W. Bush administration pressed Iran to abandon all enrichment activities, and Khatami was succeeded by Mahmoud Ahmadinejad, a hard-line conservative under whom enrichment activity was resumed. In the face of Iran's noncompliance, the IAEA referred the matter to the Security Council in 2006, after which Iran refused to implement the Additional Protocol. Later that year, China, France, Germany, Russia, Britain, and America—the P5+1, referring to the five permanent members of the Security Council plus Germany—offered incentives to Tehran to address the IAEA's concerns.

President Bush tried to halt Iran's progress toward a nuclear weapons capability by combining sanctions and international diplomacy—refusing face-to-face talks with Iranian officials unless Iran suspended uranium enrichment. As this proved unsuccessful, in July 2008 Washington decided to alter its policy and signaled that it was committed to a diplomatic path. From Iran's perspective, it was too little too late.

Although Barack Obama had run for office promising unconditional dialogue with Iran, events in 2009 made face-to-face talks politically impossible during his first administration. These included the regime's manipulation of Iran's 2009 presidential election and its harsh repression of ensuing protests, its admission that a covert uranium-enrichment facility was being built deep underground at Fordo, and tests of medium- and longer-range missiles that threatened Israel and U.S. bases in the Persian Gulf. Instead, Washington pursued a two-track policy, participating in the P5+1 multilateral effort and imposing sanctions to pressure Tehran to cease enriching uranium. In 2010 America and the UN imposed unprecedented sanctions. A year later, an IAEA report contained "credible evidence" that Tehran was conducting nuclear weapons research, including work on fast-acting detonators and an indigenous nuclear weapon design.[48] Washington again ramped up sanctions and, as the 2012 presidential campaign began, pressure to consider a military response mounted from both congressional hard-liners and Israeli leaders. Obama insisted "diplomacy backed by pressure" would work, but potential military action remained "on the table."

Washington combined several instruments to cripple Iran's nuclear program. It imposed robust sanctions to punish those who assisted Iran's development of WMD, advanced conventional weapons, or invested in industries with dual-use applications—including Iran's energy sector—to induce Iranian leaders to participate in multilateral talks. Multilateral pressure steadily increased after 2006 when the first UN sanctions were imposed. By 2013 there had been six Security Council resolutions demanding Iran to stop enriching uranium, open its facilities to international inspectors, and participate in multilateral talks to demonstrate its commitment to the NPT. Several U.S. executive orders and congressional acts provided the legal authority for sanctions that were implemented by the State Department's Office of Economic Sanctions Policy and Implementation and the Treasury Department's Office of Foreign Assets Control. U.S. legislation aimed to prevent the development of WMD and advanced conventional weapons, deny Iran access to materials to advance its nuclear program, ban trade and investment with Iran, and freeze the foreign assets of public and private actors believed to be supporting Iran's nuclear activities. Since 2010 sanctions also targeted Iran's oil sector by penalizing financial institutions that conduct oil transactions with Iran.

The EU imposed a similar list of sanctions. In July 2012 it embargoed Iranian oil and prohibited European companies from insuring Iranian oil shipments, most of which they had previously insured. By mid-2013 the EU embargo had pushed that country's oil exports to their lowest level in decades. Washington has credited the sanctions regime—which has cost Iran billions in oil revenue and investment in its oil sector and caused soaring inflation, unemployment, public debt, and a steep decline in the value of its currency—with bringing Iran to the negotiating table.

Along with sanctions, America's CIA tried unsuccessfully to sabotage Iran's nuclear program by feeding faulty parts into its supply chain. In 2006 a program named "Olympic Games" pursued a new strategy. In cooperation with a secret Israeli military unit known as "8200," NSA cyberexperts designed a sophisticated computer worm that instructed infected computers to accelerate abruptly or slow down, thereby making the highly sensitive centrifuges used to enrich uranium in Iran's Natanz facility spin out of control while its control room suggested that everything was normal. In mid-2010 an error in the computer code allowed the worm to spread beyond Iran. Computer security experts identified the worm as a cyberweapon called "Stuxnet." Stuxnet was originally believed to have destroyed a fifth of Iran's nuclear centrifuges and delayed its progress toward building nuclear weapons by several years, but some analysts believe its results were relatively limited. Iran, for its part, also developed sophisticated cyber-weapons that are more usable and deniable than WMD.

The surprising election of moderate cleric Hassan Rouhani as Iran's president in June 2013 raised hopes, however, that Iran might become more conciliatory. In a UN speech, Rouhani, though condemning America's "warmongering pressure groups," insisted that Iran would never seek nuclear weapons and expressed hope that "we can arrive at a framework to manage our differences."[49] As Rouhani prepared to leave New York he declared a desire to speak with President Obama. Obama phoned Rouhani, and their brief conversation led to an agreement to direct their governments to negotiate a deal over Iran's uranium-enrichment program. Obama later observed, "The very fact that this was the first communication between an American and Iranian president since 1979 underscores the deep mistrust between our countries . . . But it also indicates the prospect of moving beyond that difficult history."[50]

Following the historic phone call, Iran resumed negotiations with the IAEA and the P5+1. Initial talks achieved an agreement called the Joint Plan of Action, containing an interim agreement to curtail Iran's nuclear activities in return for $7 billion in sanctions relief and a framework for pursuing a permanent, comprehensive agreement by July 20, 2014. Iran agreed to eliminate its stockpile of 20 percent enriched uranium and take measures to ensure that its existing equipment would not be used to enrich more uranium at that level, and IAEA inspectors were authorized to visit enrichment facilities in Natanz and Fordo daily and observe centrifuge-production facilities. As the arrangement went into effect in January 2014, the IAEA's deputy director general indicated that Iran was cooperating and that "we have a very robust system in place with Iran"[51] to ensure its compliance.

The Joint Plan of Action had critics. Some observers believed Iran was already close to achieving a "critical capability," the point at which it could produce enough weapons-grade uranium from its stock of low-enriched uranium for one or more bombs without being detected. Congressional critics objected that the agreement allowed Iran to continue to enrich uranium to 5 percent to produce fuel for civilian reactors. Fuel enriched to this level is not weapons grade but can be enriched to 20 percent, which can quickly be enriched to the 90 percent purity needed for an atom bomb. Republicans also charged the president with trying to divert attention from the problems associated with implementing the Affordable Care Act. Congressional hard-liners believed Iran could not be trusted and had a record of deception. Others expressed concern that the deal benefitted Iran disproportionately by easing sanctions without requiring a comprehensive agreement to end uranium enrichment and undercut America's position in future negotiations. Critics were also concerned that sanctions relief would be difficult to undo if a comprehensive agreement were not reached by the end of the interim period. Administration officials insisted that sanctions would continue to put pressure on Iran, with Secretary of State Kerry contending that the sanctions relief was "just a drop in the bucket compared to the roughly $100 billion in foreign exchange holdings that are inaccessible to Iran."[52] Democrats, for the most part, applauded the agreement as a pragmatic step in the right direction, and President Obama declared, "For the first time in nearly a decade, we have halted the progress of the Iranian nuclear program, and key parts of the program will be rolled back."[53]

Iran's opaque decision-making process complicated efforts to understand that country's policies. The president is Iran's highest elected office but is constitutionally subordinate to Iran's supreme leader, Ayatollah Ali Khamenei. Any decision about Iran's nuclear program, however, needed the approval of Ayatollah Khamenei, who "suspects that even if all of Iran's nuclear facilities were closed down, or opened up to inspections and monitoring," its foes would not give up their efforts to overthrow Iran's Islamic regime and that it would suffer the same fate as Qaddafi in Libya and Saddam Hussein in Iraq, who "ended up having no nuclear weapons, and were eventually attacked, deposed, and killed."[54] Shifts in nuclear policy over the years have been attributed to the supreme leader, who insisted Iran had no interest in acquiring nuclear weapons, which he described as a crime against humanity. In the days leading up to the January 2014 negotiations over implementation, Ayatollah Khamenei, who had generally approved of the talks, broadcast a list of grievances against America and denied that sanctions had made Iran negotiate. President Rouhani also sent mixed signals, promising at the 2014 World Economic Forum that Iran had no desire to acquire a nuclear bomb and would pursue "constructive engagement" as long as world leaders respected Iran, while insisting that nuclear enrichment for commercial energy was Iran's sovereign right.

By the July 2014 deadline progress had been made, including stronger IAEA oversight and inspections, modifications to Iran's Arak heavy-water reactor to reduce its plutonium production, and a clearer explanation of sanctions relief. Major issues, however, remained unresolved, and the talks were extended for another four months so that negotiators could work out details about how much existing uranium-enrichment infrastructure Iran would have to destroy and for how long, and what kinds of research its scientists could legitimately pursue. While negotiations continued, America agreed to give Iran access to $2.8 billion in frozen assets and Tehran agreed to dilute more of its uranium or turn it into reactor fuel.

Then in April 2015 the talks produced unexpectedly detailed "Parameters for a Joint Comprehensive Plan of Action" of a final possible agreement to be completed by June 30, 2015, to remain in force between ten and fifteen years. Negotiators admitted that details had to be worked out and that differences remained. Both sides recognized they would have to sell the deal to domestic hard-liners. Among the parameters, Iran agreed to retain some 5,060 less-advanced centrifuges (far more than Washington had sought) of the 19,500 it had installed, with all of its centrifuges open to IAEA inspectors. Tehran also agreed to reduce its stockpile of low-enriched uranium from 8 tons to 600 pounds and, while retaining centrifuges at its underground Fordo site, these would not be used for uranium enrichment for fifteen years. IAEA inspectors would have access to Iran's major nuclear facilities as well as its uranium mines, and enjoy the right to investigate suspicious sites throughout Iran. Iran's unfinished Arak nuclear facility would be redesigned to prevent production of plutonium that could be used in nuclear weapons. In return, the P5+1 negotiators agreed to suspend the sanctions imposed on Iran in stages, and that Iran would retain all of its nuclear facilities and thus maintain the right to develop peaceful nuclear energy.

Secretary Kerry and Energy Secretary Ernest J. Moniz, a nuclear physicist, aided by a crash program at America's nuclear laboratories to estimate how rapidly Iran's nuclear centrifuges could enrich uranium,[55] contended that any clandestine cheating by Iran would be detected and that the agreement would prevent a "breakout" time of less than a year for Iran to acquire enriched uranium for a nuclear weapon. President Obama described it as "a historic understanding with Iran" that "cuts off every pathway" for Iran to develop nuclear weapons, while the former chief inspector of the IAEA declared, "It appears to be a fairly comprehensive deal with most important parameters" but that "Iran maintains enrichment capacity which will be beyond its near-term needs."[56]

For President Obama the deal was a triumph. "Right now, he has no foreign policy legacy," declared Cliff Kupchan, an Iran analyst. "He's got a list of foreign policy failures. A deal with Iran and the ensuing transformation of politics in the Middle East would provide one of the more robust foreign policy legacies of any recent presidencies." For Obama, "it's all or nothing."[57] Rhetorically, the president asked, "Do you really think that this verifiable deal, if fully implemented, backed by the world's major powers, is a worse option than the risk of another war in the Middle East?" He added that if Congress blocked the deal "then it's the United States that will be blamed for the failure of diplomacy."[58] Nevertheless, achieving a final agreement proved difficult, especially after Iran's supreme leader, Ayatollah Ali Khamenei, publicly declared he would not permit inspections of the country's military bases or interview Iranian nuclear scientists to find out how far the country's nuclear program had advanced,[59] and he demanded that Western sanctions be ended before Iran dismantles part of its nuclear infrastructure and before international inspectors verify that Tehran is meeting its commitments. He also declared himself unwilling to freeze on Iran's nuclear enrichment for as long as a decade.[60]

Finally, after two years of negotiations, including a last-minute push over eighteen days, U.S. and Iranian officials announced in July 2015 that they had reached a deal. The Joint Comprehensive Plan of Action (JCPOA) did not stray far from the agreement of the previous April. It reduced Iran's capability to produce weapons-grade uranium and plutonium, and put in place enhanced monitoring and verification mechanisms. Figure 13.2 identifies the key restrictions placed on Iran's nuclear program and offers a comparison of how long each is to be implemented. Specifically, the deal limited Iran to 5,060 "IR-1" (Iran's first-generation) centrifuges for a period of ten years and curbed research and development on more advanced centrifuges, which would allow for higher levels of enrichment, for thirteen years. Still more restrictions were to be implemented over fifteen years: Iran agreed to cut its stockpile of low-enriched uranium by 97 percent to 300 kilograms and to convert its Fordo enrichment facility to a medical research laboratory, to redesign its heavy-water reactor at Arak, and to refrain from building new heavy-water reactors, all to eliminate its ability to produce weapons-grade uranium and plutonium. Moreover, Iran committed to surveillance of its centrifuge production facilities and uranium mines and mills for twenty and twenty-five years, respectively, and to continued implementation of its NPT obligations, including its Additional Protocol.

In announcing the JCPOA to the American public, President Obama declared it would "cut off every pathway" for Iran to develop a nuclear weapon and, anticipating those who would claim he was too soft on Iran, "You don't make deals like this with your friends."[61] Indeed, the agreement incorporated an intrusive monitoring and verification system to "detect and deter Iranian noncompliance"[62] and "snap back" provisions to renew sanctions automatically in the event that Iran violated the agreement. For its part, Iran reluctantly accepted extensive monitoring provisions, including implementation of its Additional Protocol with the IAEA that allowed its inspectors to visit any suspicious sites, including military sites. One point on which the United States gave ground was "immediate access." Instead, the agreement gave Iran twenty-four days to comply with any IAEA inspections requests. A joint commission of representatives from Iran, P5+1, and the EU was also established to grant mandatory access to suspicious sites by a vote of 5–3, preventing Iran from denying access to any facility that a majority of partner states viewed as suspicious. This joint commission was also empowered to investigate any other allegations that Iran was cheating on the agreement and refer concerns to the UN Security Council.

FIGURE 13.2 Key Restrictions Will Last Well Over a Decade

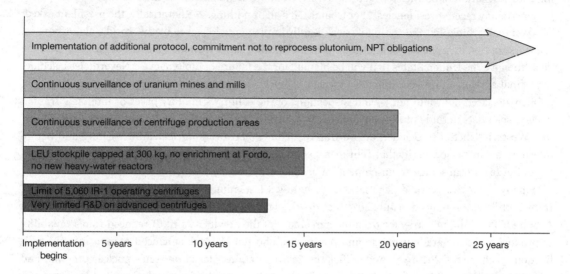

Source: Arms Control Association, http://www.armscontrol.org/files/ACA_Iran_Deal_fnl4_Updated_July_2015.pdf

Monitoring was to be ongoing, as described above, and wider inspections (consistent with Iran's NPT obligations) were made permanent. In return for Iran's concessions, the United States agreed to implement sanctions relief once Iran took verifiable steps to meet its obligations. Within days, the Security Council passed Resolution 2231, endorsing the nuclear deal and arranging to lift UN sanctions once the deal was implemented.

In the end, the agreement reflected a series of compromises. Sanctions were to be lifted sequentially—although some of the most important sanctions would also be some of the first to be rescinded—and could "snap back" if Iran failed to comply. Iran agreed to allow inspections of military facilities, but was given twenty-four days to comply with any such request. Iran was prohibited from developing advanced centrifuges (a U.S. demand), but only for ten years.

Supporters viewed the deal as a "net plus for nonproliferation," arguing that no better deal was to be found and that if both sides did comply it would "reduce the risk of a destabilizing nuclear competition in a troubled region and head off a potentially catastrophic military conflict over Iran's nuclear program."[63] According to one analyst, what mattered most in the deal is that "at a crucial moment and without a shot being fired, the United States and Iran have come to a turning point away from an era of outright hostility. The nuclear accord binds the two nations to years of engagement and leaves the door open to a fuller relationship."[64] For supporters, sustained cooperation over ten to fifteen years could yield long-term stability by ending Iran's isolation and welcoming it back into the community of nations. Opponents accused Obama of retreating from his goal of completely dismantling Iran's nuclear infrastructure, and in doing so giving "away the store."[65] They attacked the deal as too generous, fearing it would undermine proliferation, spark a nuclear arms race, and by the easing of sanctions enable Iran to ramp up support for regional actors like Hezbollah and Syria. Nonetheless, by early September the president had amassed enough support in the Senate to ensure Congress would not block the deal.

Israel and Iran's "Existential Threat"

Israel was intensely concerned that Iranian nuclear weapons would pose an existential threat to the Jewish state. Israel sought to blunt Iran's nuclear ambitions by assassinating prominent Iranian scientists involved in Iran's nuclear program and, with U.S. cooperation, launching a cyberattack in 2010 to infiltrate the computer system at Iran's Natanz nuclear facility. Iran's election of President Hassan Rouhani in 2013 to succeed the hard-line Holocaust-denier Mahmoud Ahmadinejad, together with Rouhani's overtures to the West (including greetings for the Jewish New Year sent on Twitter), raised hopes in Washington that progress might be made in negotiations with Iran on the nuclear issue that would avoid a military confrontation. Israeli leaders, however, remained profoundly suspicious that such "moderation" merely masked Iran's efforts to delay matters while progressing toward acquiring nuclear weapons.

A U.S. -Iranian deal was condemned by Israel and Saudi Arabia, both U.S. allies. Israeli prime minister Benjamin Netanyahu insisted the deal was "a historic mistake." "For the first time," he said, "the leading nations in the world agreed to the enrichment of uranium in Iran by ignoring the decisions of the (U.N.) Security Council that they themselves led."[66] The Saudis, Sunni foes of Shia Iran, feared the deal would bolster Iran's status in the region. Indeed, the April 2015 deal so angered the Saudis that King Salman along with several other Arab leaders refused to attend a meeting at Camp David in May 2015 to smooth over differences with President Obama over policies toward Iran, instead sending lesser officials. At that meeting the Saudis and several of their smaller Arab allies declared that if Iran were allowed to continue enriching uranium, they would also develop a similar capability. "We can't sit back and be nowhere as Iran is allowed to retain much of its capability and amass its research,"[67] declared one of the Arab leaders.

Although Washington and Israel agreed that Iran should not be permitted to acquire nuclear weapons, they differed over when military action would be necessary. Michael Oren, formerly Israeli ambassador to Washington, explained: "America's clock is large and slow, and our clock is small and fast. And what we have is this dialogue between clocks."[68] Whereas Prime Minister Netanyahu predicted that Iran would have overcome most impediments to build a nuclear weapon by the spring or summer of 2013, President Obama declared in March 2013 that it would take Iran a year or two to reach that objective. Shortly afterward Netanyahu argued that Rouhani's "only purpose" was "to distract attention from the fact" that Iran "continues to enrich uranium and build a plutonium reactor for the purpose of developing nuclear weapons that will threaten the state of Israel and the entire world."[69] Netanyahu argued that Rouhani was engaged in "media spin in order to keep the centrifuges spinning" and called Iran's new president a "wolf in sheep's clothing."[70] "We will not be fooled by half-measures that merely provide a smoke screen for Iran's continual pursuit of nuclear weapons," he said.[71]

Israeli anxiety led its leaders to denounce the six-month interim agreement reached at Geneva with Iran in late 2013 as a "historic mistake" and "a surrender," and Israel's moderate minister of justice, Tzipi Livni, observed, "We have six months to prevent a permanent agreement with Iran that will make it nuclear, and six months to reach a permanent agreement with the Palestinians which will secure a safe, Jewish and democratic Israel."[72] Israel's hard-line economy minister, Naftali Bennett, pointed even more directly at the ticking clock, arguing, "The focus has to be on what happens at the end of those six months. A, define what our objective is, and B, define now, in advance, as soon as possible, what happens if we don't meet those objectives. If it's just some open-ended vague negotiations, it's pretty clear that Iran will retain its nuclear program and revive its economy—the worst-case scenario." Finance Minister Yair Lapid expressed similar anxiety: "We've lost the world's ear . . . We have six months, at the end of which we need to be in a situation in which the Americans listen to us the way they used to listen to us in the past."[73]

Although both the United States and Israel repeatedly threatened to use military force to prevent Iran from acquiring weapons of mass destruction, given their divergent clocks, there were significant differences between the two governments about *when* a preventive attack should be launched, with Israel seeking to attack before Iran's nuclear program proceeded much further and the Obama administration prepared to wait to see if sanctions and diplomacy caused Iran to give way, using force only when Iran was on the verge of acquiring nuclear weapons. Netanyahu laid out Israel's perspective when he declared, "I think it's important to note that we (Israel) can't allow it to happen. Our clocks are ticking at a different pace. We're closer than the United States, we're more vulnerable, and therefore we'll have to address this question of whether to stop Iran before the United States does." He added, "There are many important issues that we have to deal with and I have a sense that there is no sense of urgency on Iran and yet Iran is the most important and the most urgent matter of all."[74]

Netanyahu demanded that Iran meet four conditions: (1) cease enriching uranium; (2) remove enriched uranium from the country; (3) close its nuclear fuel processing plant at Fordo, near Qum; and (4) renounce plutonium reprocessing. The interim agreement with Iran violated Israel's key requirement—the dismantling of Iran's nuclear program. One U.S. official pointed out that Netanyahu "will be satisfied with nothing less than the dismantlement of every scrap of the Iranian nuclear infrastructure," and "We'd love that too—but there's no way that's going to happen at this point in the negotiation. And for us, the goal is to make sure that we are putting limits and constraints on the program, and ensuring that if the Iranians decided to race for a bomb, we would know in time to react."[75]

During his visit to Israel in March 2013, President Obama encouraged Israelis to be patient and let sanctions do their work. "The Iranian government," he argued, "is now under more pressure than ever before, and that pressure is increasing. It is isolated. Its economy is in a dire condition. Its leadership is divided." He then voiced his belief that "peace is far more preferable to war, and the inevitable costs—and unintended consequences—that would come with it." If, however, Iran persisted in developing nuclear weapons despite all diplomatic efforts, Washington retained the option of using force. "Iran must know this time is not unlimited. And I have made the position of the United States of America clear: Iran must not get a nuclear weapon. This is not a danger that can be contained. As President, I have said to the world that all options are on the table for achieving our objectives. America will do what we must to prevent a nuclear-armed Iran."[76]

A month later, Secretary of Defense Chuck Hagel emphasized Israel's right to defend itself "in a very dangerous, combustible region of the world," but cautioned Israel to allow time for sanctions against Iran to bite and avoid attacking prematurely. U.S. leaders stressed that an Israeli strike by itself would at best probably delay Iran's acquisition of nuclear weapons. Hagel sought to minimize the gap in

U.S.–Israeli perceptions of the problem, declaring that "there is no daylight there at all—that Iran is prevented from acquiring that nuclear capacity." While offering to sell Israel additional advanced weapons that would help that country if it did attack Iran, Hagel added that military options, "most of us feel, ought to be the last option."[77]

Such comments seemed to placate Netanyahu during his visit to Washington in September 2013, but an American expert on Iran observed, "At this point, it's easy for them to agree. Should the Iranians offer something that the West finds attractive, and that the Israelis have problems with, then the rubber meets the road."[78] Some Israeli observers agreed with Obama's logic. One security analyst viewed his government's concern with the interim agreement as exaggerated: "They call it the deal, the deal, the deal—they should call it the initial deal that leads either to an acceptable deal or to the failure of the deal."[79] Another argued, "It seems like he [Netanyahu] thinks that this is the final agreement—it is not. The real judgment of whether it's a bad deal or an acceptable deal will be at the end of the negotiating period."[80]

Washington's agreement to cancel a military response to the Syrian government's use of toxic gas against its citizens in September 2013 was seen by some Israelis as reducing the credibility of America's commitment to use force against Iran if that country acquired nuclear weapons. "The determination the international community shows regarding Syria," declared Netanyahu, "will have a direct impact on the Syrian regime's patron, Iran."[81] To reassure Israel, President Obama declared that Iran's nuclear program was a "far larger issue" for Washington than Syria's use of chemical weapons. What Iran should recognize from the Syrian case is that "a credible threat of force, combined with a rigorous diplomatic effort"[82] would make a deal possible. Israeli leaders seemed prepared to accept the president's assurance. American diplomat and Middle East specialist Dennis Ross explained the relationship between American policy toward Syria and Iran pithily: "These two situations are deeply intertwined. If the Syrians are forced to give up their weapons, it will make a difference to the Iranian calculation," enhancing the prospects for a peaceful outcome to the Iranian issues. "If the Syrians can drag this out and give up just a little," he added, "that will send a very different message to the supreme leader [Ayatollah Khamenei]."[83]

On hearing of the P5+1 framework deal of March 2015 from President Obama, Netanyahu declared, "A deal based on this framework would threaten the survival of Israel."[84] Netanyahu called the final deal in July a "bad mistake of historical proportions,"[85] and the Israeli cabinet immediately expressed its disapproval by voting to reject it. As U.S. and Iranian negotiations were concluding, U.S. officials offered new military and diplomatic support packages to appease Israel's fears for its security, but Netanyahu rejected these offers, indicating in private that "he has no intention of taking a payoff in return for this agreement, and that there's no compensation—in money or kind—that can make up for turning Iran into a nuclear threshold state."[86] Some Israeli military and intelligence officials, however, privately conceded the deal was "not terrible" in that it would prevent Iran from proliferating for at least another ten years and supported accepting U.S. aid to begin preparing for "the day after."[87]

CONCLUSION: NAVIGATING THE SHIA–SUNNI DIVIDE

Shia–Sunni relations constitute a crucial divide in the Middle East. Washington has friends and foes on both sides of the divide and has sought to craft policies that will not foster sectarian hatred and violence. The Shia world is led by Iran, a country that since its Islamic revolution has regarded the United States as its enemy and that has enjoyed warm ties with Iraq's Shia majority. America, which had favored Iraq in its 1980–1988 war with Iran, turned against Iraq after Saddam Hussein invaded Kuwait in 1990; then, after another decade of U.S.–Iraqi hostility, it invaded that country in 2003, ostensibly as part of America's War on Terror.

Washington and Tehran disagree on major issues, notably the future of Syria and Iran's nuclear ambitions, and American efforts to curb those ambitions by negotiating with Tehran fostered serious tensions with America's allies (and Iran's enemies), Saudi Arabia and Israel. On at least one issue, however, U.S., Iranian, Saudi, and Israeli interests overlap: the fight against the Sunni terrorists in the Islamic State of Iraq and Syria.

14

American Options in Iran and Iraq

American, European,
Russian, and Iranian
negotiators

Fabrice Coffrini/AFP/Getty

Chapter 14 looks at several major issues in U.S. relations with Iraq and Iran.

- How can Washington shape counterinsurgency and counterterrorist strategies to cope with threats like those posed in Iraq and Syria by ISIS?

- What policy options are available to America for dealing with growing Iranian influence in Syria, Iraq, and elsewhere in the Middle East?

- How should Washington deal with major friends in the region like Saudi Arabia?

- How should the United States react to the rapidly changing issue of oil?

- What alternatives exist for Washington in responding to Iranian nuclear ambitions?

- How can Washington ease Israeli fears that Iranian nuclear ambitions pose a threat to Israel's survival?

COMBATING INSURGENCY IN IRAQ

As sectarian violence again spread across Iraq after America's troop withdrawal in 2011, the problem of dealing with the insurgency reappeared. Growing violence and terrorism climaxed in the invasion of Iraq from Syria by the Islamic State (ISIS). That invasion was followed by a U.S. bombing campaign against ISIS in both Iraq and Syria.

With the U.S. public weary of long, costly wars in remote Afghanistan and Iraq, it looked like large-scale ground wars were obsolete. As for regime change, "We went down that road in Iraq," President Barack Obama argued. "Regime change there took eight years, thousands of American and Iraqi lives, and nearly a trillion dollars."[1] Americans were averse to intervention in Syria in 2012—despite growing evidence that the Assad regime was using chemical weapons against civilians—and they continued to oppose military intervention even as ISIS, aided by thousands of foreign extremists, brutally took control of large swaths of Iraq and Syria. Public opinion only shifted after the release of video footage of the savage murders in 2014 of American journalists James Foley and Steven Sotloff. By February 2015 some 65 percent of Americans viewed ISIS as a major threat and 57 percent favored sending U.S. troops into Iraq and Syria to combat it.[2] Although ISIS was better organized than other insurgent groups in Iraq and Afghanistan, any larger conflict would be asymmetrical. Should the United States conduct future asymmetrical warfare in the future, and if so, how?

Policy Options

a. *Improve counterinsurgency (COIN) warfare.* Some analysts argue that COIN was successful in Iraq and Afghanistan to the extent it was actually employed. COIN cannot be effective, they insist, if strategy is limited by political constraints. Political leaders must be willing to commit enough troops to get the job done. In Iraq, at the height of the "surge" fewer than 170,000 troops were stationed in that country, whereas some observers argue that around 400,000 were needed to accomplish U.S. goals. In Afghanistan, troop levels never exceeded 100,000, and U.S. troop rotations that brought troops home after about a year further undermined COIN by removing experienced soldiers from conflict zones. It is also necessary, these analysts insist, to persuade local leaders to support U.S. COIN efforts. In Iraq, for example, removal of all employees of the former regime and dismantling the Iraqi army left political and military institutions without competent officials. Finally, COIN warfare requires more than military force to clear and hold territory. It also involves winning over the local population and rebuilding political and economic institutions. Military forces, used to achieve these goals in Iraq and Afghanistan, were not well suited to those tasks. Nonetheless, Washington was reluctant to commit civilian resources or integrate them with military efforts to accomplish successful nation-building.

b. *Reduce reliance on counterinsurgency.* Not everyone agrees that COIN could have been done better in Iraq and Afghanistan. Counterinsurgency warfare is costly, hard to control, and slow to produce results. Moreover, victory is always elusive; it is never decisive until functioning and legitimate political and economic institutions are established. Nation-building involves more than restoring political and economic institutions that enable the state to fulfill basic functions like providing security, enforcing the rule of law, and collecting taxes. As one analyst contends, "Political engineering by outsiders seldom succeeds in radically altering the underlying conditions responsible for the state's ineffectiveness."[3] Militarily, such warfare is also difficult to conduct. Strategy and tactics must constantly evolve to counter innovations employed by the adversary and win over local populations. Armies are often fighting the last war and rarely demonstrate the flexibility to respond deftly to new methods of warfare. Done poorly, counterterrorist and counterinsurgent strategies perpetuate power vacuums that fuel sectarianism and extremism. Given the high costs over the time required to achieve success, it is difficult to sustain domestic political support for such conflicts.

c. *Focus counterterrorist strategies on efforts to protect Americans and U.S. interests at home and abroad.* A third policy that is compatible with the other two options would be to focus on enhancing counterterrorism to protect Americans at home and abroad by working to address the underlying conditions that give rise to extremism and terrorism—poverty, economic inequality, and repressive government. To a large extent, this requires nonmilitary tools and soft power. It can also involve military force, however, to identify and target known and potential terrorists. Like the previous option, this strategy requires a substantial commitment of time and resources to achieve success.

GROWING IRANIAN INFLUENCE IN SYRIA, IRAQ, AND ELSEWHERE IN THE MIDDLE EAST

In addition to the challenges posed by Iran's nuclear ambitions, that country leads an informal Shia coalition that is seen as threatening America's Sunni friends, and runs counter to U.S. policy toward Syria. Iran enjoys major influence in Syria and Lebanon directly owing to the funds and arms it sends, and indirectly through its proxy, Hezbollah. It is deeply involved in aiding Iraq's Shia-dominated government against ISIS and supports Shia partisans in Iraq, Lebanon, Bahrain, and Yemen.

The only issue on which Tehran and Washington have a common interest is in combating ISIS in Iraq and Syria. Washington is, however, wary about growing Iranian influence in Iraq, and leading Sunni states in the region are concerned that the military campaign against ISIS is strengthening the position of Syrian president Bashar al-Assad, whom they loathe.

Policy Options

a. *Cooperate with Iran against ISIS.* Iran has much to lose if the Shia-dominated government in Iraq is overthrown or if ISIS dominates Syria. After American troops withdrew from Iraq, its government served as a conduit of arms to Iran's ally, Syrian president Assad, and it had moved closer to becoming part of an Iranian-led Shia coalition in the Middle East. Iran was also well positioned to provide assistance on the ground to Iraq, and Iranian military leaders conferred with Iraqi leaders. Hundreds of "volunteers" from Iran's elite Revolutionary Guard Corps appeared in Iraq, aiding Shia militias including those involved in the assault against ISIS forces in Tikrit in 2015. As an ally of Iraq's Shia leaders, Iran began flying military equipment to Baghdad. Iran's president promised to protect Shia sacred sites, and the commander of Iran's elite Quds Force of the Revolutionary Guards advised Iraqi leaders and mobilized Shia militias fighting ISIS on the ground. For a time, Washington refused to provide airpower for the assault on Tikrit owing to the involvement of Iran and the fear that Shia militias would alienate the Sunni residents of the region. It finally did so, and though neither Washington nor Tehran admitted it, Iranian ground forces and American airpower tacitly supported each other to drive ISIS from Tikrit.

Iran had a dilemma in deciding how extensively it should become involved in Iraq. As one Iranian analyst observed, "Numerous sites could potentially be destroyed or taken hostage by Sunni extremists. They are traps for us, as for any incident there the Shiite world will be looking to us for action." And he added, "We are a Shiite country, but trying to be the leaders of the entire Muslim world. As a result we can't even act in our own backyard."[4] Moreover, American public opinion and congressional leaders, especially those with strong ties to Israel, would loudly resist cooperating with a country that is Israel's enemy and that had retained its potential to acquire nuclear weapons. It would be politically toxic if observers saw U.S.–Iranian cooperation as weakening American resolve on the nuclear issue.

b. *Foster a nonsectarian government in Iraq and seek to erode Iranian influence in that country.* Washington has sought to persuade Iraq's leaders of the need to be more inclusive, and its pressure helped force Nuri al-Maliki from power. His successor as prime minister, Haider al-Abadi, has made an effort to overcome friction among Iraq's major groups and has also tried to maintain close links with both Iran and the United States. He is unlikely to sever ties to Iran, which would alienate the Shia politicians on whom he relies and eliminate an important source of foreign economic, political, and military support to Iraq's Shia-dominated government. Although coalition air strikes and Shia militias have stopped ISIS's expansion in Iraq, that group is not likely to be defeated without the support of Iraqi and Syrian Sunni and Kurdish forces on the ground. Therefore, eroding Iranian influence may be counterproductive as long as ISIS poses a threat in the region.

Washington's flirtation with Iran, however, has eroded its longtime close relationship with Saudi Arabia and other Sunni states in the Middle East. The Saudis may soon begin developing nuclear weapons, aided by Sunni Pakistan, to balance Iranian efforts to acquire WMD. A U.S.–Iranian nuclear deal "will open up the Saudi appetite and the Turkish appetite for more nuclear programs," declared a Saudi journalist. "But for the time being Saudi Arabia is moving ahead with its operations to pull the carpet out from under the Iranians in our region."[5]

AMERICA AND ITS SUNNI FRIENDS

America's Sunni friends in the Middle East, notably Saudi Arabia, Egypt, Kuwait, and other Persian Gulf states, were adamantly opposed to growing Iranian influence in the region, and Tehran's nuclear potential. Notwithstanding the impressive increase in domestic U.S. oil and gas production, the Persian Gulf remains a major source of energy for America and even more so for U.S. allies in Europe and Asia.

Most of these conservative Sunni governments were disturbed by America's initial embrace of the Arab Spring and its willingness to desert Egyptian president Hosni Mubarak. The Obama administration further angered them, especially Saudi Arabia, by not immediately supporting the post-Brotherhood military regime in Egypt and failing to take stronger steps against Iran for seeking to acquire nuclear weapons, or against the Assad regime in Syria. The Saudis showed their displeasure in late 2013 by turning down their country's election as a temporary member of the UN Security Council, a status they had long sought with American help. To reassure the Saudis, Secretary John Kerry visited the country the following month, playing down their differences by declaring, "There are some countries in the region that wanted the United States to do one thing with respect to Syria, and we have done something else. Those differences on an individual tactic on a policy do not create a difference on the fundamental goal of the policy. We all share the same goal that we have discussed; that is, the salvation of the state of Syria."[6]

Sunni Arab states agreed to form a military force as protection against Iran and ISIS. In 2015, without consulting Washington, Saudi Arabia initiated air strikes in Yemen against Houthi (Shia) rebels advancing southward toward Aden, whom they charged were aided by Iran. In 2011 the Saudis had aided Bahrain's Sunni government to put an end to Shia demonstrations, and in 2014 Egypt's military regime, which received significant funding from the Saudis and other Persian Gulf states, allowed the United Arab Emirates to launch air strikes against Islamists in Libya without warning Washington. The Saudis, along with Turkey, also aided Sunni insurgents opposed to Syria's president Assad, which along with Hezbollah in Lebanon were funded and armed by Iran. All the while, Washington was reluctant to get involved in the Syrian imbroglio except to act against the Sunni extremists in ISIS.

Policy Options

a. *Aid the Sunni insurrection against Assad and his ally, Hezbollah.* After the onset of the Syrian civil war in 2011, America's Sunni friends, including Saudi Arabia and Turkey, sought to persuade Washington to provide greater assistance to the Syrian insurgency. Although Washington has supplied some aid to Sunni "moderates," it feared that arms would fall into the hands of Sunni extremists—and, indeed, the extremists have gained ascendancy in the insurrection. Additional U.S. aid would likely be insufficient to save moderate groups and might also fall into the hands of extremists, and those like ISIS would be the principal beneficiaries if the Assad regime were overthrown. This option became even less likely by late 2015 following ISIS-sponsored or inspired attacks in Paris and San Bernardino, California. The focus of U.S. policy in the region shifted toward combatting ISIS, rather than Assad, and to building a Syrian Arab coalition of ground forces and actively pursuing peace talks to end Syria's civil war.

b. *Intervene in Yemen.* A sectarian civil war has engulfed Yemen, which is strategically located south of Saudi Arabia where the Red Sea meets the Gulf of Aden, which empties into the Arabian Sea. Saudi air strikes against Houthi rebels supported by Iran, and who had taken control of much of the country, were a prelude to possible ground forces from Sunni states. Washington has an additional concern about events in Yemen, namely, that the collapse of the Yemeni state will give the terrorists in al-Qaeda in the Arabian Peninsula (AQAP) greater freedom of action, especially after the small contingent of U.S. Special Forces in that country was forced to leave. Washington has provided intelligence and logistical aid to the Saudis, and a larger military footprint would improve relations with the Sunni world and restore America's ability to fight AQAP. Sending troops would, however, further stretch American forces at a time when they are involved in striking ISIS, are not yet out of Afghanistan, and must meet additional challenges in Europe and East Asia.

c. *Increase pressure to reduce Iran's influence.* We noted above the delicate situation in which Iraq's Shia-dominated government finds itself. Vigorous efforts to force that government to act against Iran, while pleasing America's Sunni friends, would likely exacerbate violence between Iraq's Shia and Sunni communities, while reducing the pressure on ISIS.

U.S. SECURITY COMMITMENTS TO OIL-RICH SUNNI FRIENDS

Pleasing Sunni governments in the Persian Gulf region has long supported American interests, which also involve oil. We have discussed the crucial role that access to Middle Eastern oil has played in American foreign policy and how regional crises and conflicts have affected the price and availability of oil imported by America. As recently as 1991 the United States went to war to liberate Kuwait from Iraqi occupation and protect Saudi Arabia and its oil reserves from Saddam Hussein. And notwithstanding the rapidly expanding domestic production of oil in America in recent years, which reduced U.S. imports from an average of about 400,000 barrels a month between 2004 and 2008, the United States still imported over 300,000 barrels a month in much of 2013, compared to between 170,000 and 190,000 barrels a month in 1981.[7]

The impact of growing U.S. energy production as well as greater energy efficiency and introduction of additional sources of renewable energy will continue to be felt globally, and nowhere more so than in the Arab world, at least for another decade. For one thing, the Arab oil weapon will no longer be available until non-OPEC oil production falls, and in the interim OPEC is likely to enjoy significantly less global influence. The Saudis are also coming to recognize the significance of rising U.S. shale-oil production.[8] A related consequence will be greater American ability to stabilize energy prices during crises in the Middle East and elsewhere like Iran, and low oil prices harm Iran, the Saudis' archenemy. In the near future Washington will enjoy greater flexibility in designing policies toward the region, and it may choose to pay less attention to the Middle East, especially as it "pivots" to Asia. Minimally, Washington will have the luxury of adopting policies toward the Arab states, with less concern about the region's oil.

Whether growing oil production in the United States and elsewhere, combined with energy conservation and renewable energy sources, will stay abreast of global oil consumption in the developing world remains unclear. Not surprisingly, much depends on China and India. According to energy analyst Chris Nelder:

Right now, all of the new oil consumption in the world is coming from out-side . . . the developed world. It's largely coming from . . . China and India. And that new oil demand is now being met, almost exactly, by declining demand in North American [*sic*] and Europe. . . . The growing economies of Asia get so much more marginal economic utility out of a gallon of fuel than we do. In a poorer coun-try, you might have a couple guys on a moped, burning one gallon of fuel to get to the market and back. They get so much more economic value out of doing that than a construction worker in the U.S. gets in his pickup truck burning 5 gallons per day.[9]

Thus, the oil-rich Arab Middle East will remain an important and contested geopolitical region and may become more so in coming decades. America retains a significant stake in the stability of the Persian Gulf region. Nevertheless, declining oil prices and growing energy production in America give Washington greater flexibility toward the oil-rich monarchies of the region than at any time in recent decades.

Policy Options

a. *Remain committed to the security of the oil-rich Arab states and reassure them that America will protect them from Iran.* For decades Washington has provided security for the conservative, oil-rich states of the Middle East such as Saudi Arabia, Kuwait, Qatar, the United Arab Emirates, and Bahrain against potential threats including Iran. Energy as well as military bases in Bahrain, Qatar, Kuwait, Oman, Saudi Arabia, and the United Arab Emirates can defend U.S. interests against regional threats like Iran or ISIS.

America's growing gas and oil production at home reduces but does not eliminate U.S. dependence on Middle East oil. Although Canada (3.39 million barrels per day), Mexico (0.84 million bpd), and Venezuela (0.79 million bpd) contributed significantly to U.S. oil imports in 2014, the Persian Gulf countries also remained a crucial source. Countries in that region still accounted for much of America's imported oil in 2014, with Saudi Arabia alone providing 1.17 million barrels per day.[10]

b. *Reduce American commitment to the security of the oil-rich Arab states.* Even if America's need for Middle East oil continues to drop, threats to the security of major oil producers like Saudi Arabia can have dramatic consequences on energy prices, especially for U.S. allies in Europe and Asia like Japan that rely heavily on oil imports and would find it difficult to fill the resulting security vacuum. Another dangerous possibility is that in the absence of a U.S. security umbrella, Saudi Arabia might feel compelled to acquire its own weapons of mass destruction owing to the threat posed by the prospect of a nuclear-armed Iran. Egypt or Turkey might be tempted to do the same to balance Iran, thereby creating enormous instability throughout the Middle East.

In 2015 China became the world's leading oil importer, slightly edging out the United States. If America reduces or severs its commitment to the security of the oil-producing Persian Gulf states, China will be tempted to fill the security vacuum to protect its access to the energy that its growing economy

MAP 14.1   U.S. Military Facilities in the Persian Gulf

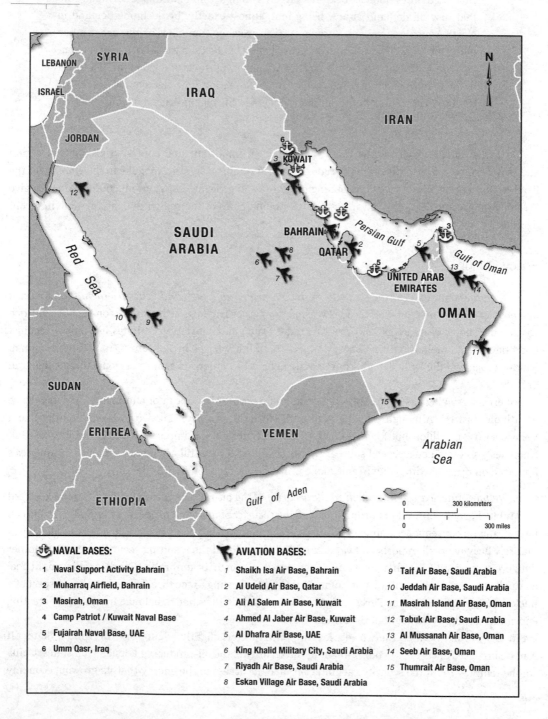

NAVAL BASES:

1. Naval Support Activity Bahrain
2. Muharraq Airfield, Bahrain
3. Masirah, Oman
4. Camp Patriot / Kuwait Naval Base
5. Fujairah Naval Base, UAE
6. Umm Qasr, Iraq

AVIATION BASES:

1. Shaikh Isa Air Base, Bahrain
2. Al Udeid Air Base, Qatar
3. Ali Al Salem Air Base, Kuwait
4. Ahmed Al Jaber Air Base, Kuwait
5. Al Dhafra Air Base, UAE
6. King Khalid Military City, Saudi Arabia
7. Riyadh Air Base, Saudi Arabia
8. Eskan Village Air Base, Saudi Arabia

9. Taif Air Base, Saudi Arabia
10. Jeddah Air Base, Saudi Arabia
11. Masirah Island Air Base, Oman
12. Tabuk Air Base, Saudi Arabia
13. Al Mussanah Air Base, Oman
14. Seeb Air Base, Oman
15. Thumrait Air Base, Oman

TABLE 14.1   Oil Imports to America

Country	Imports	% of Total in 2013	% of Change since 2003
Canada	2.57	33.3	65.8
Saudi Arabia	1.33	17.2	−23.2
Mexico	0.85	11.0	−45.8
Venezuela	0.76	9.8	−36.2
Colombia	0.37	4.8	121.1
Iraq	0.34	4.4	−29.1
Kuwait	0.33	4.2	56.7
Nigeria	0.24	3.1	−71.3
Ecuador	0.23	3.0	64.0
Angola	0.20	2.6	−44.4

Source: Data from Energy Information Administration.

requires. In fact, Beijing is already building links to Central Asia to give it access to sources of oil imports that do not require American naval protection.

IRAN'S NUCLEAR AMBITIONS

Iran poses another challenge for U.S. policy in the Middle East. As it has not declared a nuclear capability, it remains possible for proliferation to be prevented, but the obstacles are great. Iran's domestic politics are complicated and opaque, and even as Iran negotiated with the P5+1 it was unknown how committed the regime was to a nuclear deal. Both Ayatollah Khamenei and President Rouhani sent mixed signals, but in July 2015 the P5+1 negotiators and Iran announced a final and detailed agreement. By September, there was enough support for the deal in the Senate to ensure Congress could not prevent it from being implemented, even as significant opposition remained in both houses. In Iran, however, there was a backlash against the deal as hard-liners who viewed the agreement as "a submission to foreign powers" and feared that it "is a precursor to a breakdown in the old revolutionary leadership" not only criticized President Rouhani, his aides, and even some leading conservatives who were not entirely hostile to the deal,[11] but also arrested journalists, activists, and business people who supported the deal or who had ties to the United States. Iran also escalated computer espionage directed against targets in the Obama administration in a series of attacks that were, according to a State Department official, "very carefully designed and showed the degree to which they understood which of our staff was working on Iran issues now that the nuclear deal is done."[12] U.S. options to manage Iran's nuclear ambitions include allowing Iran to pursue nuclear weapons and preventing Iran from acquiring nuclear weapons, either by threat of force or enhanced sanctions.

Policy Options

a. *Let Iran acquire nuclear weapons.* The nuclear deal negotiated in July 2015 does not permanently close the door on Iran's nuclear ambitions, as critics of the agreement were quick to point out. Proliferation is the option least favored by U.S. officials, but it does have academic proponents. Political scientist Kenneth Waltz argued that those who are afraid of a nuclear Iran have misread the history of the nuclear era and misunderstand Iran's leaders, who are neither irrational nor wish to pursue policies that undermine their regime's security. A nuclear and therefore secure Iran, in Waltz's view, would moderate its belligerence. Iran's entry into the nuclear club need not start a nuclear arms race. "Should Iran become the second Middle Eastern nuclear power since 1945," claimed Waltz, "it would hardly signal the start of a landslide. When Israel acquired the bomb in the 1960s, it was at war with many of its neighbors. Its nuclear arms were a much bigger threat to the Arab world than Iran's program is today. If an atomic Israel did not trigger an arms race then, there is no reason a nuclear Iran should now."[13]

It would, however, be difficult to persuade Israel or domestic critics in Congress to agree to this outcome, and it would trigger a domestic firestorm on the part of those who would see it as abandoning Israel, a longtime ally in the region. It would also reduce the credibility of American commitments in the Middle East and Asia, where a belief would take root that Washington could not be trusted to ensure security.

b. *Threaten force to prevent Iran from acquiring nuclear weapons.* The threat of force to deter Iran from acquiring nuclear weapons continues to have proponents, even as U.S. officials proceed with the Joint Comprehensive Plan of Action (JCPOA). American foreign policy expert Michael Mandelbaum argues that a traditional deterrence policy is "justified, feasible, and indeed crucial to protect vital U.S. interests," and "the U.S. military has or can develop the tactics and munitions necessary to cause enough damage to lengthen the time Iran would need to build a bomb by years, even without the use of any ground troops."[14] The greatest obstacle to successful deterrence, he contends, is demonstrating credibility when successive U.S. administrations have "tolerated" Iran's slow but continuing progress toward a nuclear weapon.

Washington, however, has concluded that an attack would only delay Iran's acquisition of nuclear weapons. American leaders have been in no hurry to attack Iran, especially once Iran's newly elected president Rouhani initiated what appeared to be serious negotiations with Washington. In July 2015 those negotiations culminated in a comprehensive agreement to limit Iran's enrichment activities and prevent it from achieving a breakout capability for at least another ten years. By September 2015 President Obama had secured the votes of enough Senate Democrats to ensure Congress could not block the agreement. Much rides on whether Israel can be persuaded to accept that final agreement and whether Iran is willing to abide by all of its terms. If Tehran does not meet its obligations, Washington would be left with only two options: increasing economic sanctions, and if these fail to bring Iran to its knees, going to war—a course of action officials believe is likely to reinforce Iran's determination and only temporarily delay its ability to acquire nuclear weapons.

c. *Ratchet up sanctions to prevent Iran from acquiring nuclear weapons.* In the 1990s Washington began applying pressure through expanded sanctions to get Tehran to curb its nuclear activities. During the Bush and Obama administrations sanctions weakened Iran's economy, including its oil sector and its financial institutions, but sanctions appear to work best when coupled with a diplomatic process that clearly defines what behavior by the targeted state will end them. A balance of "sticks" and "carrots" like those in the 2015 agreement are more likely than coercion alone to produce change.

Nonetheless, opponents of the 2015 agreement argue that it was sanctions that brought Iran to the negotiation table, and sustained—and possibly even stronger—sanctions are necessary to compel Iran to abandon its nuclear ambitions completely. They faulted the agreement for relieving sanctions while Iran retained a capacity to enrich uranium, even at low levels. Others see problems with enhanced sanctions. First, they argue, there is no clear evidence that sanctions alone were responsible for Iran's new interest in diplomacy. Iran's policy reversal, they say, was a result of sanctions *and* a domestic political climate in which economic pain was intensified by frustration with the effects of economic and political mismanagement. (Indeed, some even contend that the sanctions relief promised in the deal will accomplish fewer benefits than expected unless the regime backs legal and regulatory reforms to attract foreign investment.[15]) Second, successful sanctions require widespread participation. By the time the 2015 nuclear deal was announced, many of America's diplomatic partners were skeptical of the value of maintaining—let alone increasing—sanctions against Iran while it was engaged in multilateral diplomacy. New or sustained sanctions would revitalize U.S. relations with Israel and the Sunni oil states, but they would be unlikely to force the Iranian leaders to capitulate on an issue central to them. And unless Iran were to reject entirely or violate the terms of the 2015 agreement, they would make the United States, not Iran, look recalcitrant.

ISRAEL AND IRAN'S "EXISTENTIAL THREAT"

The United States and Israel remained far apart on how to deal with Iran. Israel demanded that Iran renounce *any capability* to make a weapon. The Obama administration sought to prevent Tehran from *obtaining* a nuclear weapon, while allowing Tehran to retain capabilities that could allow it to construct such a weapon later. Negotiations with Iran on the nuclear issue were perceived by some Israelis as raising questions about the reliability of Washington's commitment to Israel's security, while Washington regarded Israel's position as unattainable short of a war. "It's a distinction with a huge difference," declared a former State Department official. "It defines two different approaches to dealing with Iran that today may be fundamentally irreconcilable."[16]

Israelis remained suspicious of Rouhani's sincerity, dismissed by Netanyahu as "the face of the sweet-talk and the onslaught of smiles." And Israeli academic Uzi Rabi declared, "Part of the [Iran's] plan is to drive a wedge between Americans and Europeans and Israel."[17] Although a senior U.S. official argued that U.S.–Israeli differences over Iran merely involved "a tactical disagreement" that could be managed, Middle East analyst Aaron David Miller concluded, "When the U.S. and Israel are at fundamental odds, it weakens U.S. power in the region and sends very bad signals to America's other allies." The problem was made worse because some of America's Arab allies were as concerned as Israel about Iran's nuclear ambitions, leading Miller to observe, "Israel has more in common now with Saudi Arabia. It exacerbates an already fractious region."[18] It may be that the United States and Israel simply have diverging interests regarding Iran and therefore cannot agree on a single course of action. Thomas Friedman posed this possibility bluntly:

> But there is something else that goes without saying, but still needs to be said loudly: We, America, are not just hired lawyers negotiating a deal for Israel and the Sunni Gulf Arabs, which they alone get the final say on. We, America, have our own interests in not only seeing Iran's nuclear weapons capability curtailed, but in ending the 34-year-old Iran–U.S. cold war, which has harmed our interests and those of our Israeli and Arab friends.[19]

Negotiations with Iran had to deal with a variety of issues, including Iran's willingness to give inspectors access to its nuclear installation, Tehran's right to have peaceful nuclear energy, and the ending of diplomatic and economic sanctions against Iran. Such negotiations were time consuming, and hard-liners in Israel and America viewed them as a "delaying tactic" by Iran to give it time to "go nuclear." Israeli anxiety will increase over time, and American hard-liners and domestic supporters of Israel will likely intensify pressure on Washington to act before it becomes too late. "As a result of the sanctions," wrote an Iranian-Israeli analyst, "the regime in Iran is under real pressure, and Rouhani comes to save the regime, and I think there is a chance. If Rouhani does the work, this is good for Israel. If the Iranians do the job, our pilots and soldiers don't have to."[20] President Obama described the July 2015 framework agreement as "an historic opportunity" and "the best, most effective, most rigorous mechanism whereby it is very, very, very difficult for Iran to cheat," and the "definitive path by which Iran will not get a nuclear weapon,"[21] but many in Israel were not convinced.

Policy Options

a. *Offer additional strategic support to reassure Israel in a changing strategic environment.* This policy is consistent with U.S. policy in the region and was the policy Obama adopted as the United States and Iran were approaching a deal. In fact, Obama attempted to reassure skeptical Israelis by promising "to go further than any other administration's gone before in terms of providing [Israel] additional security assurances from the United States."[22]

b. *Let Israel go it alone to attack Iran once it has crossed Israel's "red line."* The United States might tacitly let Israel unilaterally try to eliminate the Iranian nuclear program. President Obama recognized this possibility when he declared, "We all prefer to resolve this issue diplomatically. Having said that,

Iran's leaders should have no doubt about the resolve of the United States, just as they should not doubt Israel's sovereign right to make its own decisions about what is required to meet its security needs."[23] Washington could facilitate Israel's success by providing stealth aircraft, air refueling tankers, and advanced "bunker buster" bombs—30,000-pound "Massive Ordnance Penetrators" that would be able to penetrate Iran's Fordo nuclear enrichment complex, which is buried under a mountain. "Hopefully we never have to use it," declared a senior U.S. official. "But if we had to, it would work."[24] Even with these weapons, Israel might not have the capability to do the job by itself, and the result would be disastrous—a regional war with Iran developing nuclear weapons as quickly as possible and with pro-Israeli groups accusing Washington of having betrayed a close ally. In the end, Washington might have no choice but to join the conflict to ensure the security of Israel and America's Arab friends in the Persian Gulf. Indeed, Israel and the Gulf States may discover they have common security interests in the threats posed by Iran and militant jihadists in Syria and Iraq.

Netanyahu's demand that Iran be forbidden any enrichment of nuclear fuel, plus his insistence that Tehran recognize Israel's right to exist as part of a final agreement concerning Iran's nuclear ambitions, was likely "aimed to ensure that no deal is struck at all" because "Netanyahu and much of Israel's security establishment view the status quo—ever-increasing sanctions that cripple Iran's economy, combined with the ever-present threat of war—as preferable to any realistic diplomatic deal." However, "Improved U.S.–Iranian relations, with tangible steps to end Iran's isolation on the condition that it shifts its behavior, could divorce Iran's ideological and strategic impulses. If that happens, Iran would have compelling incentives to disentangle itself from anti-Israeli hostilities."[25]

　　c.　*Coordinate a joint attack with Israel* that would probably include providing Israel with additional weaponry and enhance the prospect for achieving its military objective. This option has been removed from the table unless Iran were to renege on the 2015 agreement. By the time this option would be implemented, Iran would be closer to acquiring nuclear weapons, but economic sanctions and diplomatic negotiations would have been permitted to run their course. However, a joint attack would nonetheless trigger fierce debate between American "hawks" and "doves," and an attack would set off a destabilizing regional conflict in the Persian Gulf and elsewhere in the Middle East.

CONCLUSION: POLICY DILEMMAS

The Sunni–Shia divide in the Middle East confronts the United States with a number of dilemmas. Washington seeks to prevent the spread of sectarian violence that will destabilize a region of geostrategic importance and a leading global source of oil. Several countries are already suffering sectarian tensions or even conflicts—Syria, Iraq, Lebanon, Yemen, and Bahrain. If Washington takes sides in these conflicts, it risks alienating either Sunni or Shia communities or their key external supporters, Iran or Saudi Arabia and Turkey. The alternative, however, is for America to remain on the sidelines, conceding its leadership and reducing the credibility of its commitments to regional friends.

Reaching an acceptable final agreement to limit Iran's effort to acquire nuclear weapons was Washington's most important goal. The alternative is likely to be a regional war and a regional nuclear arms race. Such an agreement might also persuade Iran to restrain its efforts to meddle in Syria, Iraq,

Yemen, and Lebanon, and begin a process of reconciliation between Tehran and Washington. By contrast, the agreement raised further suspicions of Sunni governments like Saudi Arabia, and might persuade them to act unilaterally rather than in concert with Washington, and accelerate their own efforts to acquire nuclear weapons. Individual regional contests also offer unpalatable choices for the United States. For example, how can America confront ISIS without giving comfort to Syria's president Assad as well as Iran, Hezbollah, and anti-American Shia militias in Iraq, while further alienating Assad's Sunni foes?

Although America's new domestic energy sources leave it less dependent on the Arab Middle East, it does not obviate the need for Washington to make choices. Regional instability and failed states are invitations to Islamic terrorists, and may in the future produce greater interventions by potential American rivals like China and Russia that also have interests in the region. In sum, the Middle East continues to pose challenges that have no easy solution and for which no grand strategy seems applicable—challenges that are not likely to vanish in the near future.

15

Conclusion

AMERICA AND THE COMPLEX MIDDLE EAST

President Obama at West Point commencement, May 2014, emphasizing the crucial role of America's global leadership

Official White House Photo by Peter Souza

This text has described the trends characterizing American foreign policy in the Middle East in the past and present, as well as future alternatives. Perhaps the most outstanding features of the country's foreign policy visible in the Middle East during President Barack Obama's two terms in office have been:

1. A greater concern for "realist" power and security, though mixed with a desire to spread "liberal" values.

2. A shift from the unilateralism of the George W. Bush years to greater multilateralism in dealing with Syria and Iran.

3. Greater caution in use of force in light of public weariness with long wars in Afghanistan and Iraq, and political pressures at home to reduce the budget deficit and husband available resources.

4. Corresponding pressures to use new military technologies and strategies such as drones, cyberwarfare, and Special Forces to manage complex threats cost-effectively without placing large numbers of troops in harm's way.

5. The withdrawal of America's troop presence in Iraq (2011), a drawdown in Afghanistan, and continuing efforts to provide military support to those governments without putting boots on the ground.

6. A greater willingness to negotiate with regional rivals like Iran while containing Iran's regional ambitions in cooperation with the Sunni states of the Persian Gulf.[1]

7. Failure to mediate a settlement in the Israeli–Palestinian dispute and willingness to deal with a PLO–Hamas coalition government under certain conditions, and growing frustration with Israel's hard-line policies.

8. Continuation of the global fight against terrorism and the proliferation of dangerous regional groups, especially the Islamic State (ISIS), despite the president's declaration of an end to the "War on Terror."

9. An effort to reduce U.S. policies adopted during the War on Terror that were viewed as violations of human rights.

10. A declining focus on democratization and human rights in the Middle East following the chaos and sectarian violence between Shia and Sunni Muslims and Iranian- and Saudi-led blocs produced by the Arab Spring.[2]

THE EVOLUTION OF AMERICAN FOREIGN POLICY BEFORE THE COLD WAR

American foreign policy underwent a dramatic shift in the twentieth century after the country had already become an economic superpower. Presidents like Theodore Roosevelt and Woodrow Wilson declared their desire that America participate to a greater extent throughout the world. World War I precipitated an expansion of American interests owing to U.S. sympathy for the cause of democracy and the European balance of power. America had already become democracy's arsenal when German submarines and inept diplomacy brought the United States into the war in 1917. Following the war, Americans rejected the Versailles Treaty and the League of Nations and sought, as in earlier centuries, to avoid military entanglements in Europe or Asia, though not in the Western Hemisphere.

... and the Wolf chewed up the children and spit out their bones ...
But those were Foreign Children and it really didn't matter."

Isolationism

American public opinion accepted what Wilson's successor, Warren Harding, advocated in Boston in May 1920: "America's present need is not heroics, but healing; not nostrums, but normalcy; not revolution, but restoration; not agitation, but adjustment; not surgery, but serenity, not the dramatic, but the dispassionate; not experiment, but equipoise; not submergence in Internationality, but sustainment in triumphant nationality."[3] Americans sought to avoid involvement overseas—a desire heightened by the Great Depression—because they believed those conflicts did not affect their core interests. Instead, others were urged to emulate America's example. Although President Franklin Roosevelt had tried to persuade Americans that their fates were linked to those in Europe who were fighting Nazi tyranny, isolationism only ended after Japan bombed Pearl Harbor on December 7, 1941, bringing America into World War II.

The world changed in myriad ways after the emergence of America as a superpower in World War II. The war persuaded Americans and their leaders that they had global responsibilities and that without their active participation in world affairs, democracy and global order could not be secured. Hence, America joined the United Nations, sought to restore the devastated economies of Europe and Asia, and as the Cold War with the USSR and its allies deepened, became increasingly committed to the security of those believed to be endangered by Moscow and infected by its ideology. America's grand strategy, as articulated by diplomat George Kennan, "must be that of a long-term, patient but firm and vigilant containment of Russian expansive tendencies" in the form of "the adroit and vigilant application of counter-force at a series of constantly shifting geographical and political points, corresponding to the shifts and maneuvers of Soviet policy" that will, in the end, "promote tendencies which must eventually find their outlet in either the breakup or the gradual mellowing of Soviet power."[4]

American leaders militarized Kennan's version of containment, and military commitments to a host of allies around the world played a role in their strategy. America remained protected by two great oceans, and its remoteness from Europe and Asia reassured those who sought American protection that the United States would remain a "benign" hegemon rather than an acquisitive imperialist power. "This new American grand strategy for the postwar world," concludes political scientist Robert Kagan, "could not have been a more radical departure from 'normalcy'" because it involved "the promotion of a liberal world order that would defend not only America's interests but those of many other nations as well."[5] In the end, Kennan proved correct, and the American-led "free world" won the Cold War, and the Soviet Union finally collapsed.

AFTER THE COLD WAR

With the end of the Cold War, the United States appeared to stand alone as the unchallenged hegemon in a global system in which globalization had made people interdependent economically, politically, and culturally. The proliferation of nongovernmental groups advocating solutions to collective problems like global warming has fostered global civil society and promised global governance of a variety of issue areas. Under American hegemony, an open global economy flourished as barriers to trade and investment were reduced, corporations became increasingly transnational, and international economic organizations such as the World Bank, the World Trade Organization, and the International Monetary Fund were established to maintain economic order. American leadership produced the United Nations and other international agencies to maintain peace and cope with challenges to human security and well-being.

After the Cold War, with American encouragement, democracy spread to the developing world and the countries of the former Soviet bloc. Concern for human rights deepened, and even authoritarian regimes felt it necessary to pay lip service to this concern. All this led optimists like G. John Ikenberry to conclude that "the liberal principles that Washington has pushed enjoy near-universal appeal, because they have tended to be a good fit with the modernizing forces of economic growth and social advancement," while Washington's chief foes such as Islamic extremists "aren't just up against the United States; they would also have to contend with the most globally organized and deeply entrenched order the world has ever seen, one that is dominated by states that are liberal, capitalist, and democratic."[6]

There is, however, a darker side to world affairs that is reflected in the views of Kagan, who argues that the liberal order was created by and continues to depend on the power and determination of America.[7] Although he believes that the United States is not in decline, other observers are persuaded that America is growing ever less dominant relative to countries like China and Russia, and is less able to maintain order and control outcomes in the Middle East and elsewhere. Nevertheless, public fear of American decline, combined with the multiple foreign-policy crises of the Obama years, ensured that foreign policy would be a central concern during the nominating process and subsequent 2016 presidential election.

However, with the passage of time since the Cold War, the erosion of American hegemony, and the emergence of an increasingly multipolar world, America has retreated from its one-time role as the world's police officer. "America," argues political scientist William Martel, "does not have a coherent, functioning grand strategy" as it did during the Cold War, when "containment" guided America's foreign policy:

> Without one, the nation, its leaders, and people will experience a sense of drift and confusion. How do we know what is important, what threatens our interests, when we should act, and what instruments of power should we use? According to Ralph Waldo Emerson, "A foolish consistency is the hobgoblin of little minds, adored by little statesmen and philosophers and divines," but, a coherent grand strategy provides the United States with an overarching sense of purpose in its international affairs. It helps to build domestic support and provide international clarity for its foreign policies.[8]

What is happening, according to political scientist Randall Schweller, is a transition from "an age of order to an age of entropy"[9]—that is, disorder.

Can a global leader exercise hegemony "from behind"? Kagan thinks not: "The United States, in short, was the 'indispensable nation,' as Bill Clinton would proclaim—indispensable, that is, to the liberal world order,"[10] and it is hard to imagine that the "indispensable nation" can lead "from behind." Power—both "hard" and "soft"—is crucial to leadership, yet in recent years American power has declined in a relative sense economically and (to a lesser extent) militarily, and U.S. strategy has relied more heavily on local proxies trained and armed by America. Although this approach reflects American public opinion, it has not always achieved what Washington sought, whether in replacing Bashar al-Assad as Syria's president or in the rapid collapse of Iraq's army in 2014. Kagan criticizes the Obama foreign-policy establishment and the generation it represents when he writes of a "sense of futility" that followed the country's financial crisis and reflects what one scholar calls the "Iraq syndrome,"[11] the fear that America could be dragged into another Middle East civil war. "Senior White House officials," writes Kagan, "especially the younger ones, look at problems like the struggle in Syria and believe that there is little if anything the United States can do. This is the lesson of their generation, the lesson of Iraq and Afghanistan: that America has neither the power nor the understanding nor the skill to fix problems in the world." And he adds that this "is also escapism"[12] because such officials, including the president, may not appreciate what is at stake and how quickly the liberal global order could disappear. Responding to such criticism, Obama's final National Security Strategy included ninety-four references to American leadership.

CONTEMPORARY MIDDLE EAST CHALLENGES

The complexity of political life in the Middle East is daunting and makes it almost impossible for Washington to formulate a coherent strategy. Regional analysts Steven Simon and Jonathan Stevenson contend, "Political and economic developments in the Middle East have reduced the opportunities for effective American intervention to a vanishing point, and policymakers in Washington have been recognizing that and acting accordingly."[13] They conclude that the intractability of regional issues justifies a "moderate U.S. pullback, at least in the absence of a serious threat to core U.S. interests."[14] In addition, lack of economic development, overpopulation, and poor governance limit the attraction of American investment in the Arab world while fostering Islamic extremism.

In the absence of a clear ends-and-means strategy, however, allies in the Middle East became concerned about America's commitment to their security and the credibility of its deterrence of Iran. Thus, political scientist Michael Mandelbaum reached the pessimistic conclusion, "To keep nuclear weapons out of Tehran's hands will require . . . a credible commitment by the United States to respond to significant cheating by using force to destroy Iran's nuclear infrastructure."[15] The administration of George W. Bush had been widely regarded by allies as well as domestic foes as overly eager to use military force in fighting the War on Terror after 9/11 and in the effort to spread democracy and foster regime change in Afghanistan and the Middle East. However, it is frequently forgotten that prior to 9/11 President Bush had tried to limit America's overseas commitments, including humanitarian interventions in which the Clinton administration had become involved. America, declared diplomat Richard Haass, would become a "reluctant sheriff,"[16] involving itself only when local powers could not maintain peace. But neither the War on Terror nor the invasions of Afghanistan and Iraq constituted a coherent global strategy, nor did America's allies see them as such. Instead, as Kagan suggests, "the rest of the world saw the United States not as a global leader seeking the global good but as an angry Leviathan narrowly focused on destroying those who had attacked it," and "the only thing worse than a self-absorbed hegemon is an incompetent self-absorbed hegemon."[17]

President Obama assumed office committed to ending the "bad" war in Iraq and pacifying and reforming Afghanistan in a "good" war. In neither case did Washington realize its objectives. Iraq is in the midst of a sectarian war between Shia and Sunni Muslims, with little to show after a decade of U.S. intervention. As one observer concludes, perhaps "Washington should accept the fractious reality on the ground, abandon its fixation with artificial borders, and start allowing the various parts of Iraq and Syria [e.g., Shia, Sunni, Kurdish, Arab, Persian, Alawite, and so forth] to embark on the journey to self-determination."[18] "This would mean," he continues, "openly encouraging confederal decentralization across Iraq and Syria,"[19] rather than trying to prop up their central governments. Afghanistan is still threatened by the Taliban-led insurrection against a government installed by America and may descend into civil war among ethnic groups and warlords after all American troops leave in 2017, and that might allow al-Qaeda militants to return to their Afghan sanctuaries. The president reluctantly contributed airpower to assist America's European allies in protecting Libyans from Muammar al-Qaddafi. Qaddafi was overthrown, but America's ambassador was murdered in the violent chaos that followed and has made Libya a failed state.

Unlike President George W. Bush, President Obama became convinced that the United States should resort to military force sparingly and only when vital interests were at stake. In a 2009 speech at West Point he announced plans to beef up American forces in Afghanistan, while in a later speech there in 2014 he declared, "You are the first class to graduate since 9/11 who may not be sent into combat in Iraq or Afghanistan."[20] He observed, "Since world war two, some of our most costly mistakes came not from our restraint, but from our willingness to rush into military adventures without thinking through the consequences,"[21] contending that unless critical interests are at stake, "the threshold for military action must be higher."²² Obama's position reflected American public opinion, at least unless events somewhere posed such a threat. "I would betray my duty to you, and to the country we love," the president continued, "if I sent you into harm's way simply because I saw a problem somewhere in the world that needed to be fixed or because I was worried about critics who think military intervention is the only way for America to avoid looking weak."²³

Thus, the president declared an end to the War on Terror while continuing to use drones and Special Forces against terrorists in Pakistan, Yemen, Somalia, Libya, Iraq, and Syria, and putting forward a plan to fund counterterrorist partnerships with countries under threat from terrorist groups. Nevertheless, ISIS seized large areas in Syria and Iraq over which their governments had lost control. Daniel Byman, an analyst on jihadi terrorism, criticizes the American counterterrorist efforts. He observes that, although Americans are reluctant to see their country intervene in the Middle East, they make an exception for terrorism. However, he notes that "the long-term security capacity of states in the Middle East will be vital to preventing terrorism,"²⁴ but requires state-building, which American officials are generally unprepared to undertake.

The president also sought to end human-rights abuses associated with the War on Terror by closing the internment camp at Guantánamo Bay (which remained open owing to congressional opposition to housing prisoners in America) and ending policies like "extraordinary rendition" of suspected terrorists, but American efforts to end massive human-rights violations in Syria, Egypt, and South Sudan have been minimal.

It was President Obama's misfortune that he was simultaneously confronted with challenges in Ukraine, Iraq, Syria, Israel, and elsewhere that made a coherent strategy virtually impossible to design and drove his domestic foreign-policy rating to new lows. While differing with Shia Iran over the future of Syria and negotiating an agreement to curb Iran's nuclear ambitions, he was finding common ground

Obama's Mideast strategy

with Tehran over ISIS even as he sought a coalition against ISIS consisting of Sunni states and opponents of Syria's president, Bashar al-Assad.

All the while Russia provided Assad's regime with military support, including surface-to-air missiles, combat aircraft, and military advisors, that compelled Washington to ask if Russia really intended to support Assad's fight against extremists or instead sought to help Assad defend his regime from eventual external intervention. In September 2015 U.S. and Russian defense officials met to make sure American and Russian forces would not accidently come into conflict and to start a broader diplomatic process "to define some of the different options that are available" in Syria.[25] Simultaneously the president sought to reassure Israel while condemning its war in Gaza, and seeking a two-state solution and an end to settlement expansion. A former Obama advisor admitted, "You name it, the world is aflame. Foreign policy is always complicated. We always have a mix of complicated interests. That's not unusual. What's unusual is there's this outbreak of violence and instability everywhere."[26] Let us briefly examine some of Obama's policies in a disorderly world.

The death of Osama bin Laden during a raid by U.S. Navy SEALs was probably President Obama's most memorable foreign-policy triumph until the July 2015 comprehensive agreement with Iran. Nevertheless, in the Middle East, recent American policy has seemed irresolute, a vivid contrast to the militancy of the Bush administration and its "neoconservatives." Having threatened to use force against Syrian president Assad if he employed chemical weapons, the Obama administration backed off in return for a deal with Assad brokered by Russia for destroying Syria's remaining chemical weapons. At the same time, Washington, while initially refusing to aid Assad's foes, ultimately began to contribute nonlethal aid and weapons covertly to Syria's Sunni opposition, but only after Assad was in the driver's seat again, aided by Russia, Iran, and Hezbollah, with the opposition involved in its own civil war and without fear of overt American intervention. Indeed, U.S. intervention to overthrow Assad would have sabotaged Washington's efforts to reduce friction with Iran and might have triggered a regional Shia–Sunni conflict.

Only after ISIS made the region tremble did Washington agree to help train "moderate" Sunni rebels. President Obama had previously dismissed the claim that aid to "what was essentially an opposition made up of former doctors, farmers, pharmacists and so forth" would have made a difference in Syria as "a fantasy."[27] "The concern," declared former Obama defense secretary Leon Panetta, "is the president's defining what America's role in the world is in the 21st century hasn't happened."[28] The result, Obama's critics believe, "has been a policy designed to answer the political exigency to act with minimal action."[29]

Elsewhere, having supported the overthrow of a military regime in Egypt by the Muslim Brotherhood in the name of democracy, Washington said little about the new government's antidemocratic policies and even less after that government was ousted in a military coup. There were claims that America had supported the coup against Egypt's Islamist government as well as claims that Washington had tried to prevent it. In either case, President Abdel Fatah al-Sisi's military government of Egypt paid little attention to U.S. advice.

In failing to carry out its threat against Assad, supporting an Islamic government in Egypt, and negotiating with Iran over that country's nuclear program, Washington incensed its long-term ally, Saudi Arabia, and intensified Israeli suspicion of American motives. Relations between Israel and the United

States had been close during Bush's presidency, but they began to sour after President Obama took office and unsuccessfully urged Israel to stop building settlements in the occupied territories and show flexibility in negotiating with the Palestinians. A new round of peace negotiations prompted by Secretary of State John Kerry yielded little and collapsed in mutual recriminations exacerbated by Washington's willingness to consider dealing with a Palestinian government after Hamas and the PLO undertook efforts to unify their movement. Shortly thereafter a third Israel–Hamas war erupted. However, after the agreement with Iran to curb that country's nuclear program had been reached, the United States and Israel began efforts to reduce the friction between them.

America's passivity during Syria's civil war and Egypt's turmoil also enhanced Islamic extremists in the Middle East and North Africa, and the region has become the "chief cauldron of contemporary disorder."[30] Islamic radicalism has fostered the spread of a pan-Islamic Sunni identity. If America's 2003 intervention in Iraq had radicalized Muslims, Washington's indecisiveness mobilized al-Qaeda affiliates around the world. In the meantime, Iraq had descended into renewed sectarian violence, with a Shia government that had grown more dependent on Iran as it grew less dependent on America, which had installed it in the first place.

Washington also entered into negotiations and completed a final agreement with Iran in July 2015 to curb that country's nuclear ambitions—an outcome that raised profound concern in Israel and in America's conservative Sunni allies including Saudi Arabia, Jordan, Egypt, and the United Arab Emirates—even while Iran continued to provide arms, fighters, and funding to Syria's president Assad and supported the Shia Houthis in Yemen. In the months that followed, the United States set about offering military and economic assistance to allies in the region to reassure them of Washington's commitment to their regimes and to stability in the Middle East. Simon and Stevenson suggest that the improvement of U.S.–Iranian relations might "reinvigorate multinational talks on Syria's transition" that would foster "a power-sharing body with executive authority that could marginalize ISIS and Jabhat al-Nusra."[31]

WHAT NEXT?

When President Obama accepted the Nobel Peace Prize early in his first term, he admitted, "We must begin by acknowledging the hard truth: We will not eradicate violent conflict in our lifetimes. There will be times when nations acting individually or in concert—will find the use of force not only necessary but morally justified." And he touched upon the dilemma he would face in the following years: "So part of our challenge is reconciling these two seemingly irreconcilable truths—that war is sometimes necessary, and war at some level is an expression of human folly."[32] It was a dilemma that became manifest in the Middle East, where countries questioned American commitments and in so doing posed threats to the post–Cold War international order. The president's caution was apparent when he defended his foreign-policy legacy by asking, "Why is it that everybody is so eager to use military force after we've just gone through a decade of war at enormous cost to our troops and to our budget? And what is it exactly that these critics think would have been accomplished?" Furthermore, he expressed what may someday be called the Obama Doctrine with a baseball analogy: "You hit singles, you hit doubles; every once in a while we may be able to hit a home run. But we steadily advance the interests of the American people and our partnership with folks around the world."[33] Obama's policy of restraint was reasoned and thoughtful but led a former national security official in his administration to conclude rather tersely and pointedly, "We're seeing the 'light footprint' run out of gas."[34]

In the *Aeneid* (6.851 ff), written after Augustus became emperor of Rome, the poet Virgil challenges his countrymen: "Roman, be this thy care—these thine arts—to bear dominion over the nations and to impose the law of peace, to spare the humbled and to war down the proud!" Kagan would have Americans follow the arduous task Virgil set for Romans. What he fears is that, in the face of economic crisis, renewed assertiveness by foes, and setbacks overseas, American foreign policy reveals that "Americans would like a world order that was essentially self-regulating and self-sustaining" because it "is the answer to the conundrum of power and interest that so bedevils them—how to create a world conducive to American ideals and interests without requiring the costly and morally complex exercise of American power."[35]

President Obama's answer to Kagan could well have been his comment, "Apparently people have forgotten that America, as the most powerful country on earth, still does not control everything around the world."[36] "Indeed," argues Richard Haass, "with U.S. hegemony waning but no successor waiting to pick up the baton, the likeliest future is one in which the current international system gives way to a disorderly one with a larger number of power centers acting with increasing autonomy, paying less heed to U.S. interests and preferences. This will cause new problems even as it makes existing ones more difficult to solve. In short, the post–Cold War order is unraveling, and while not perfect, it will be missed."[37]

Notes

CHAPTER 1

1. Hillary Rodham Clinton, "Leading through Civilian Power: Redefining American Diplomacy and Development," *Foreign Affairs* 89:6 (November/December 2010), 15.

2. This typology is derived from James N. Rosenau, "Pre-Theories and Theories of Foreign Policy," in R. Barry Farrell, ed., *Approaches to Comparative and International Politics* (Evanston, IL: Northwestern University Press, 1966), 27–92.

3. Gideon Rachman, "American Decline: This Time It's Real," *Foreign Policy* 184 (January/February 2011), 63, 60.

4. Joseph S. Nye Jr., "The Future of American Power: Dominance and Decline in Perspective," *Foreign Affairs* 89:6 (November/December 2010), 3, 12.

5. Office of the Press Secretary (May 8, 2009), "Briefing by White House Press Secretary Robert Gibbs," www.whitehouse.gov/the_press_office/Briefing-by-White-House-Press-Secretary-Robert-Gibbs-5-8-09

6. Kimi Lynn King and James Meernik, "The Supreme Court and the Powers of the Executive: The Adjudication of Foreign Policy," *Political Research Quarterly* 52:4 (December 1999), 818.

7. Roger Hilsman, *To Move a Nation* (Garden City, NY: Doubleday, 1967), 5.

8. Graham Allison and Philip Zelikow, *Essence of Decision*, 2nd ed. (New York: Longman, 1999), 143.

9. Cited in Peter Baker, "How Obama Came to Plan for 'Surge' in Afghanistan," *New York Times*, December 5, 2009, http://www.nytimes.com/2009/12/06/world/asia/06reconstruct.html?pagewanted=all

10. Cited in Richard E. Neustadt, *Presidential Power and the Modern Presidents* (New York: Free Press, 1990), 10. Emphasis in original.

11. Warner R. Schilling, "The Politics of National Defense: Fiscal 1950," in Schilling, Paul Hammond, and Glenn Snyder, eds., *Strategy, Politics, and Defense Budgets* (New York: Columbia University Press, 1962), 230.

12. Cited in Dina Badie, "Groupthink, Iraq, and the War on Terror: Explaining U.S. Policy Shift toward Iraq," *Foreign Policy Analysis* 6:4 (October 2010), 279.

13. Ibid., 283.

14. Alexis de Tocqueville, *Democracy in America*, ed. J. P. Mayer, trans. George Lawrence (New York: Anchor Books, 1969), 228–229.

15. Alexander Hamilton, "Speech on the Constitutional Convention on a Plan of Government," in Morton J. Frisch, ed., *Selected Writings and Speeches of Alexander Hamilton* (Washington, DC: American Enterprise Institute, 1985), 108.

16. Walter Lippmann, *The Public Philosophy* (New York: Mentor Books, 1955), 29.

17. Gabriel Almond, *The American People and Foreign Policy* (New York: Praeger, 1960), 53.

18. George F. Kennan, *American Diplomacy: Expanded Edition* (Chicago, IL: University of Chicago Press, 1984), 66.

19. "A World of Troubles," *The Economist*, October 6, 2012, 15; "Arms and the Men," *The Economist*, October 6, 2012, 18.

20. Chris Cillizza, "Winners and Losers from Election 2012," *Washington Post*, November 7, 2012, http://www.washingtonpost.com/blogs/the-fix/wp/2012/11/07/winners-and-losers-from-election-2012/

21. Niccolò Machiavelli, *The Prince*, trans. Luigi Ricci (New York: Mentor Books, 1952), 93.

22. William R. Caspary, "The 'Mood Theory': A Study of Public Opinion and Foreign Policy," *American Political Science Review* 64:2 (June 1970), 546. Emphasis in original.

23. Almond, *The American People and Foreign Policy*, 5.

24. George F. Kennan, *Memoirs 1925–1950* (Boston: Little Brown, 1967), 53.

25. Robert D. Putnam, "Diplomacy and Domestic Politics: The Logic of Two-Level Games," *International Organization* 42:3 (Summer 1988), 434.

26. Jane Mayer, "Covert Operations," *The New Yorker*, August 30, 2010, http://www.newyorker.com/magazine/2010/08/30/covert-operations?currentPage=all

27. Library of Congress, Bill Text, 112th Congress (2011–2012), S.RES.399. IS, http://thomas.loc.gov/cgi-bin/query/z?c112:S.RES.399:

28. Robert J. Art, *The TFX Decision, McNamara, and the Military* (Boston: Little Brown, 1968), 166.

29. George W. Bush, "Graduation Speech at West Point," June 1, 2002, *Voices of Democracy,* http://vod.academicwebpages.com/bush-graduation-speech-speech-text/

30. Steve Smith, "Policy Preferences and Bureaucratic Position: The Case of the American Hostage Rescue Mission," *International Affairs* 61:1 (Winter 1984), 24.

31. Thomas Carlyle, Lecture I, The Hero as Divinity (May 5, 1840), "On Heroes, Hero-Worship, and the Heroic in History," *The Project Gutenberg EBook*, July 26, 2008, http://www.gutenberg.org/files/1091/1091-h/1091-h.htm

32. Harold D. Lasswell, *Psychopathology and Politics* (Chicago, IL: University of Chicago Press, 1930), 75.

33. Harold D. Lasswell, *Power and Personality* (New York: W. W. Norton, 1948), 120.

34. Garry Wills, *Nixon Agonistes: The Crisis of the Self-Made Man* (New York: Houghton Mifflin, 2002), 412.

35. Alexander L. George and Juliette L. George, *Woodrow Wilson and Colonel House: A Personality Study* (New York: Dover Publications, 1964), 11. Emphasis in original.

36. John G. Stoessinger, *Crusaders and Pragmatists* (New York: W. W. Norton, 1985), 27, 289, 290.

37. Cited in Ron Suskind, "Faith, Certainty and the Presidency of George W. Bush," *New York Times Magazine,* October 17, 2004, http://www.nytimes.com/2004/10/17/magazine/17BUSH.html

38. Ole R. Holsti, "The 'Operational Code' Approach to the Study of Political Leaders: John Foster Dulles' Philosophical and Instrumental Beliefs," *Canadian Journal of Political Science* 3:1 (March 1970), 130.

39. David Rothkopf, "National Insecurity," *Foreign Policy* 204 (September/October 2014), 49.

40. Cited in Michael D. Shear, "With Foreign Leaders, Obama Keeps It Mostly Business," *New York Times*, March 10, 2015, http://www.nytimes.com/2015/03/11/us/politics/with-foreign-leaders-obama-keeps-it-mostly-business.html

41. Cited in Peter Baker, "In Book, Panetta Recounts Frustration with Obama," *New York Times,* October 6, 2014, http://www.nytimes.com/2014/10/07/world/middleeast/ex-defense-secretary-panetta-tells-of-frustrations-with-obama.html

42. Arthur M. Schlesinger Jr., *The Coming of the New Deal* (New York: Houghton Mifflin, 1958), 502, 527–528.

43. Cited in Scott Shane, "Petraeus's Quieter Style at C.I.A. Leaves Void on Libya Furor," *New York Times,* November 2, 2012, http://www.nytimes.com/2012/11/03/world/africa/petraeuss-lower-profile-at-cia-leaves-void-in-benghazi-furor.html

44. Arnold Rogow, *James Forrestal: A Study of Personality, Politics, and Policy* (New York: Macmillan, 1963), 351.

CHAPTER 2

1. Barack H. Obama, "Nobel Lecture: A Just and Lasting Peace," December 10, 2009, http://www.nobelprize.org/nobel_prizes/peace/laureates/2009/obama-lecture_en.html

2. Chris Good, "Obama Stresses Multilateralism in Announcing Libya Strikes," *The Atlantic,* March 19, 2011, http://www.theatlantic.com/politics/archive/2011/03/obama-stresses-multilateralism-in-announcing-libya-strikes/72738/

3. B. Liddell Hart, *Strategy* (New York: Praeger, 1967), 333–372.

4. Paul Kennedy, "Grand Strategies in War and Peace: Towards a Broader Definition," in *Grand Strategies in War and Peace*, ed. Paul Kennedy (New Haven: Yale University Press, 1992), 5.

5. Hal Brands, "The Promise and Pitfalls of Grand Strategy," Strategic Studies Institute External Research Associates Program Monograph, August 2012, 4, http://www.strategicstudiesinstitute.army.mil/pubs/display.cfm?pubid=1121

6. William C. Martel, "America's Dangerous Drift," *The Diplomat*, February 25, 2013, http://thediplomat.com/2013/02/25/americas-dangerous-drift/

7. Manfred Jonas, "Isolationism," in Alexander DeConde, ed., *Encyclopedia of American Foreign Policy* (New York: Charles Scribner's Sons, 1978), 496.

8. Robert J. Art, *A Grand Strategy for America* (Ithaca, NY: Cornell University Press, 2003), 173.

9. Andrew Johnstone, "Isolationism and Internationalism in American Foreign Relations," *Journal of Transatlantic Studies* 9:1 (2011), 11.

10. George C. Herring, *From Colony to Superpower: U.S. Foreign Relations since 1776*, vol. 12 (New York: Oxford University Press, 2008), 1.

11. John Lewis Gaddis, *Surprise, Security, and the American Experience* (Cambridge, MA: Harvard University Press, 2004), 24.

12. Jonas, "Isolationism," 498.

13. Johnstone, "Isolationism and Internationalism in American Foreign Relations," 13.

14. Glenn Hastedt, *Encyclopedia of American Foreign Policy* (New York: Facts on File, 2004), 325–326.

15. David C. Hendrickson, *Union, Nation, or Empire: The American Debate over International Relations, 1789–1941* (Lawrence, KS: University Press of Kansas, 2009), 6.

16. J. Simon Rofe and John Thompson, "'Internationalists in Isolationist Times'—Theodore and Franklin Roosevelt and a Rooseveltian Maxim," *Journal of Transatlantic Studies* 9:1 (2011), 47.

17. David M. Malone and Yuen Foong Khong, "Unilateralism and U.S. Foreign Policy," in Malone and Khong, eds., *U.S. Foreign Policy: International Perspectives* (Boulder, CO: Lynne Rienner, 2003), 3.

18. Robert O. Keohane, "Multilateralism: An Agenda for Research," *International Journal* 45:4 (Autumn 1990), 731.

19. John Ruggie, "Multilateralism: The Anatomy of an Institution," *International Organization* 46:3 (Summer 1992), 571, 572.

20. Malone and Khong, "Unilateralism and US Foreign Policy," 3.

21. Doris A. Graber, "Intervention and Nonintervention," in DeConde, ed., *Encyclopedia of American Foreign Policy*, 482.

22. Ibid., 483.

23. Ronald E. Powaski, *Toward an Entangling Alliance: American Isolationism, Internationalism, and Europe, 1901–1950* (New York: Greenwood Press, 1991), xi.

24. Michael B. Oren, *Power, Faith, and Fantasy: America in the Middle East, 1776 to the Present* (New York: W. W. Norton & Company, 2011), 78.

25. "Washington's Farewell Address 1796," The Avalon Project, Yale Law School, http://avalon.law.yale.edu/18th_century/washing.asp

26. A. Kalaitzidis and G. W. Streich, *U.S. Foreign Policy: A Documentary Resource Guide* (Santa Barbara, CA: Greenwood, 2011), xix.

27. "Monroe Doctrine; December 2, 1823," The Avalon Project, http://avalon.law.yale.edu/19th_century/monroe.asp

28. Walter A. McDougall, *Promised Land, Crusader State: The American Encounter with the World since 1776* (New York: Houghton Mifflin, 1997), 57.

29. Cited in Harold Temperley, *The Foreign Policy of Canning 1822–1827,* 2nd ed. (Abingdon, Oxford, UK: Frank Cass, 1966), 381.

30. See Hendrickson, *Union, Nation, or Empire,* 278.

31. Herring, *From Colony to Superpower*, 180.

32. Dwight Marsh, cited in Oren, *Power, Faith, and Fantasy,* 130.

33. Ibid., 130–131.

34. Jerald A. Combs, *The History of American Foreign Policy,* 3rd ed. (Armonk, NY: M. E. Sharpe, 2008), 57–8.

35. Ibid., 182.

36. Cited in ibid., 207.

37. Rofe and Thompson, "'Internationalists in Isolationist Times,'" 48.

38. Transcript of Theodore Roosevelt's Corollary to the Monroe Doctrine, http://www.ourdocuments.gov/doc.php?doc=56&page=transcript

39. Cited in Carlos F. Diaz-Alejandro, "Direct Investment in Latin America," in Charles P. Kindleberger, ed., *The International Corporation* (Cambridge, MA: MIT Press, 1970), 320.

40. Rofe and Thompson, "'Internationalists in Isolationist Times,'" 48.

41. Herring, *From Colony to Superpower*, 406.

42. Justus D. Doenecke, "American Internationalism, 1939–1941," *The Journal of Libertarian Studies,* 1:3–4 (Summer/Fall 1982), 201, http://mises.org/journals/jls/6_3/6_3_1.pdf

43. "Franklin D. Roosevelt: Proposal for Lend-Lease," http://www.britannica.com/presidents/article-9116959

44. Henry R. Luce, "The American Century," *Life Magazine,* February 1941, http://www.informationclearinghouse.info/article6139.htm

45. James M. Lindsay, "George W. Bush, Barack Obama, and the Future of US Global Leadership," *International Affairs* 87:4 (2011).

46. Cited in John Dumbrell, "Unilateralism and 'America First'? President George W. Bush's Foreign Policy," *Political Quarterly* 73:3 (July 2002), 284.

47. Michael Hirsh, "Bush and the World," *Foreign Affairs* 81:5 (September/October 2002), http://www.foreignaffairs.com/articles/58244/michael-hirsh/bush-and-the-world

48. George H. W. Bush, Address to the Nation on the Invasion of Iraq, January 16, 1991, http://millercenter.org/scripps/archive/speeches/detail/3428

49. *National Security Strategy of the United States, 1994–1995: Engagement and Enlargement* (Washington, DC: Potomac Books, 1994), 5.

50. Michael T. Klare, "The Clinton Doctrine," *The Nation,* April 1, 1999, http://www.thenation.com/article/clinton-doctrine#

51. Francine Kiefer, "Clinton 'Doctrine:' Is It Substance or Spin?" *Christian Science Monitor,* June 28, 1999, http://www.csmonitor.com/1999/0628/p2s1.html

52. "To Paris, U.S. Looks Like a 'Hyperpower,'" *New York Times*, February 5, 1999, http://www.nytimes.com/1999/02/05/news/05iht-france.t_0.html

53. Mott Spetalnick, "Obama Rules Out U.S. Troops on Ground to Fight Islamic State," Reuters, November 16, 2015, http://www.reuters.com/article/2015/11/16/us-g20-turkey-obama-strategy-idUSKCN0T51QS20151116

54. Lindsay, "George W. Bush, Barack Obama, and the Future of US Global Leadership," 769.

55. Cited in ibid.

56. Inaugural Address by George W. Bush, published January 20, 2005, *New York Times,* http://www.nytimes.com/2005/01/20/politics/20BUSH-TEXT.html

57. Melvyn P. Leffler, "Bush's Foreign Policy," *Foreign Policy* 144 (September/October 2004), 22.

58. James M. Lindsay, "Rally Round the Flag," Brookings Daily War Report, March 25, 2003, http://www.brookings.edu/research/opinions/2003/03/25iraq-lindsay

59. James Kitfield, "Can Mitt Romney Recover the Soul of Republican Foreign Policy?" *The Atlantic*, August 27, 2012, http://www.theatlantic.com/international/archive/2012/08/can-mitt-romney-recover-the-soul-of-republican-foreign-policy/261602/

60. Barack Obama, "Renewing American Leadership," *Foreign Affairs* 86:4 (July/August 2007), 2, 2–4.

61. Lindsay, "George W. Bush, Barack Obama, and the Future of U.S. Global Leadership," 773.

62. Ryan Lizza, "The Consequentialist: How the Arab Spring Remade Obama's Foreign Policy," *The New Yorker*, May 2, 2011, http://www.newyorker.com/reporting/2011/05/02/110502fa_fact_lizza

63. "The Nobel Peace Prize 2009—Press Release," Nobelprize.org (October 9, 2009), http://www.nobelprize.org/nobel_prizes/peace/laureates/2009/press.html

64. Cited in Guy Chazan and Alistair MacDonald, "Nobel Committee's Decision Courts Controversy," *Washington Post*, October 11, 2009, http://online.wsj.com/article/SB125509603349176083.html

65. Cited in Scott Wilson, "President Obama Wins Nobel Peace Prize," *Washington Post,* October 10, 2009, http://www.washingtonpost.com/wp-dyn/content/article/2009/10/09/AR2009100900914.html

66. Martin S. Indyk, Kenneth G. Lieberthal, and Michael E. O'Hanlon, "Scoring Obama's Foreign Policy," *Foreign Affairs* 91:3 (May/June 2012), 30.

67. "Obama's Speech to the United Nations General Assembly," *New York Times,* September 23, 2009, http://www.nytimes.com/2009/09/24/us/politics/24prexy.text.html

68. "Obama's Second Inaugural Speech," *New York Times,* January 21, 2013, http://www.nytimes.com/2013/01/21/us/politics/obamas-second-inaugural-speech.html

69. Daniel W. Drezner, "Does Obama Have a Grand Strategy?" *Foreign Affairs* 90:4 (July/August 2011), http://www.foreignaffairs.com/articles/67919/daniel-w-drezner/does-obama-have-a-grand-strategy

70. Cited in John Mueller, "The Iraq Syndrome Revisited," *Foreign Affairs,* March 28, 2011, http://www.foreignaffairs.com/articles/67681/john-mueller/the-iraq-syndrome-revisited

71. "The Price of Detachment," *The Economist,* March 23, 2013, http://www.economist.com/news/united-states/21573970-shunning-foreign-entanglements-does-barack-obama-risk-losing-his-global-bully

72. Jeffrey M. Jones and Nathan Wendt, "Americans Say UN Is Needed, but Doubt Its Effectiveness," *Gallup Politics,* March 28, 2013, http://www.gallup.com/poll/161549/americans-say-needed-doubt-effectiveness.aspx

73. Gordon N. Bardos, "The High Cost of U.S. Foreign Policy," *The National Interest,* July 9, 2013, http://nationalinterest.org/commentary/the-high-cost-us-foreign-policy-8704

74. Stephen G. Brooks, G. John Ikenberry, and William C. Wohlforth, "Lean Forward," *Foreign Affairs* 92:1 (January/February 2013), http://www.foreignaffairs.com/articles/138468/stephen-g-brooks-g-john-ikenberry-and-william-c-wohlforth/lean-forward

75. On shapers and restrainers/retrenchers, see James M. Parent and Paul K. MacDonald, "The Wisdom of Retrenchment," *Foreign Affairs* 90:6 (November/December 2011), 32–4, and Charles Kupchan, "Grand Strategy: The Four Pillars of the Future," *Democracy Journal* 27 (Winter 2012), 9–18.

76. Barry Posen, "Pull Back," *Foreign Affairs* 92:1 (January/February 2013), http://www.foreignaffairs.com/articles/138466/barry-r-posen/pull-back

77. Peter J. Spiro, "The New Sovereigntists: American Exceptionalism and Its False Prophets," *Foreign Affairs* 79:6 (November/December 2000), http://www.foreignaffairs.com/articles/56621/peter-j-spiro/the-new-sovereigntists-american-exceptionalism-and-its-false-pro

78. Barry Posen, "Pull Back," *Foreign Affairs* 92:1 (January/February 2013), http://www.foreignaffairs.com/articles/138466/barry-r-posen/pull-back

CHAPTER 3

1. Edward D. Mansfield and Jack Snyder, "Democratization and the Arab Spring," *International Interactions* 38:5 (2012), 723.

2. Cited in "Syria Conflict: Top U.S. General Outlines Military Options," BBC News, July 23, 2013, http://www.bbc.co.uk/news/world-middle-east-23414906

3. Cited in Ryan Lizza, "The Consequentialist," *The New Yorker,* May 2, 2011, http://www.newyorker.com/reporting/2011/05/02/110502fa_fact_lizza?printable=true&currentPage=all

4. Ibid.

5. Recent scholarship suggests Russia was more influential in negotiating the agreement than most historians have recognized. See Sean McMeekin, *The Ottoman Endgame: War, Revolution, and the Making of the Modern Middle East, 1908–1923* (New York: Penguin Press, 2015), 280.

6. "Modern History Sourcebook: Sir Henry McMahon: Letter to Ali ibn Husain, 1915," http://www.fordham.edu/halsall/mod/1915mcmahon.html

7. Cited in Isaiah Friedman, *British Pan-Arab Policy, 1915–1922* (New Brunswick, NJ: Transaction Books, 2010), 23.

8. David Fromkin, *A Peace to End All Peace: The Fall of the Ottoman Empire and the Creation of the Modern Middle East* (New York: Henry Holt, 1989), 9.

9. Stephen J. Kobrin, "Diffusion as an Explanation of Oil Nationalization: Or the Domino Effect Rides Again," *Journal of Conflict Resolution* 29:1 (March 1985), 26.

10. Statista, "Average Prices for OPEC Crude Oil from 1960 to 2013," http://www.statista.com/statistics/262858/change-in-opec-crude-oil-prices-since-1960/

11. Robert S. Walters and David H. Blake, *The Politics of Global Economic Relations* (Englewood Cliffs, NJ: Prentice-Hall, 1987), 184.

12. Cited in "Analysis: Awash in Oil, U.S. Reshapes Mideast Role 40 Years after OPEC Embargo," Reuters, October 17, 2013, http://www.reuters.com/article/2013/10/17/us-usa-energy-geopolitics-analysis-idU.S.BRE99G14P20131017

13. Mark Thompson, "U.S. to Become Biggest Oil Producer—IEA," CNNMoney, November 12, 2012, http://money.cnn.com/2012/11/12/news/economy/us-oil-production-energy/index.html

14. Cited in Matthew L. Wald, "Shale's Effect on Oil Supply Is Not Expected to Last," New York Times, November 12, 2013, http://www.nytimes.com/2013/11/13/business/energy-environment/shales-effect-on-oil-supply-is-not-expected-to-last.htm

15. Cited in Clifford Krauss, "Texas Refinery Is Saudi Foothold in U.S. Market," New York Times, April 4, 2013, http://www.nytimes.com/2013/04/05/business/texas-refinery-is-saudi-foothold-in-us-market.html

16. Daniel Yergin, The Prize: The Epic Quest for Oil, Money, and Power (New York: Free Press, 2008), 392.

17. John C. Campbell, "The Soviet Union and the United States in the Middle East," Annals of the American Academy of Political and Social Science 401 (May 1972), 127.

18. Ibid., 133.

19. John Lewis Gaddis, We Now Know: Rethinking Cold War History (Oxford, UK: Oxford University Press, 1997), 171.

20. John Lewis Gaddis, The Cold War: A New History (New York: Penguin Press, 2005), 127.

21. Ibid.

22. Ibid., 128.

23. Stephen Blackwell, British Military Intervention and the Struggle for Jordan: King Hussein, Nasser, and the Middle East Crisis, 1955–1958 (New York: Routledge, 2009), 51.

24. Philip Anderson, "'Summer Madness': The Crisis in Syria, August–October 1957," British Journal of Middle East Studies 22:1/2 (1995), 34.

25. Richard Nixon, "Address to the Nation on the War in Vietnam," November 3, 1969, http://www.nixonlibrary.gov/forkids/speechesforkids/silentmajority/silentmajority_transcript.pdf

26. Jimmy Carter, "State of the Union Address Delivered before a Joint Session of the Congress," January 23, 1980, The American Presidency Project, http://www.presidency.ucsb.edu/ws/?pid=33079

27. Anwar al-Sadat, In Search of Identity (New York: Harper & Row, 1978), 187, cited in NSA, "Moscow's Realignment with Cairo: A Look at Gorbachev's New Political Thinking," Cryptologic Quarterly, n.d., unclassified, 3, http://www.nsa.gov/public_info/_files/cryptologic_quarterly/Moscows_Realignment_with_Cairo.pdf

28. Ali E. Hillal Dessouki, "Regional Leadership: Balancing off Costs and Dividends in the Foreign Policy of Egypt," in Bahgat Korany and Ali E. Hillal Desouki, eds., The Foreign Policies of Arab States: The Challenge of Globalization (Cairo, Egypt: The American University of Cairo Press, 2008), 169.

29. Charles E. Butterworth, "Political Islam: The Origins," Annals of the American Academy of Political and Social Science 524 (November 1992), 29.

30. Carrie Rosefsky Wickham, "The Path to Moderation: Strategy and Learning in the Formation of Egypt's Wasat Party," Comparative Politics 36:2 (January 2004), 205.

31. Abul A'la Maududi, Jihad in Islam (Beirut, Lebanon: The Holy Koran Publishing House, n.d.), 5, ww.muhammadanism.org/Terrorism/jihah_in_islam/jihad_in_islam.pdf

32. Seyyed Vali Reza Nasr, Mawdudi and the Making of Islamic Revivalism (Oxford, UK: Oxford University Press, 1996), 68.

33. Beverley Milton-Edwards, Islamic Fundamentalism since 1945 (New York: Routledge, 2005), 27.

34. Rupe Simms, "'Islam Is Our Politics': A Gramscian Analysis of the Muslim Brotherhood (1928–1953)," Social Compass 49:4 (December 2002), 573.

35. Leon Carl Brown, Religion and State: The Muslim Approach to Politics (New York: Columbia University Press, 2000), 146.

36. Ibid.

37. Robert S. Leiken and Steven Brooke, "The Moderate Muslim Brotherhood," Foreign Affairs 82:2 (March/April 2007), 109.

38. Hazem Kandil, *Soldiers, Spies, and Statesmen: Egypt's Road to Revolt* (London, UK: Verso, 2012), 40.

39. Simms, "'Islam Is Our Politics,'" 574.

40. Leiken and Brooke, "The Moderate Muslim Brotherhood," 110.

41. Ibid., 110, 111, 108.

42. Its Syrian branch, however, rose up in 1982 in the city Hama against the regime of Hafez al-Assad, which crushed it at the cost of about 25,000 lives.

43. Sana Abed-Kotob, "The Accommodationists Speak: The Goals and Strategies of the Muslim Brotherhood of Egypt," *International Journal of Middle East Studies* 27:3 (August 1995), 331.

44. Bernard Lewis, *The Crisis of Islam: Holy War and Unholy Terror* (New York: Random House, 2003), 111–112.

45. Steven A. Cook, "Morsi's Mistake," *Foreign Affairs,* December 2, 2012, http://www.foreignaffairs.com/articles/138472/steven-a-cook/morsis-mistake

46. The earlier Welfare Party, which won the largest bloc in parliament in 1994 and was forced from power by the army in 1997, had links with Egypt's Muslim Brotherhood.

CHAPTER 4

1. Excerpted from "Text: Obama's Speech in Cairo," *New York Times,* June 4, 2009, http://www.nytimes.com/2009/06/04/us/politics/04obama.text.html

2. Stephen M. Saideman, "When Conflict Spreads: Arab Spring and the Limits of Diffusion: Empirical and Theoretical Research in International Relations," *International Interactions* 38:5 (2012), 717.

3. Economist Intelligence Unit, "Democracy Index 2010: Democracy in Retreat," Table 3, p. 5, http://www.eiu.com/Handlers/WhitepaperHandler.ashx?fi=Democracy_Index_2010_Web.pdf&mode=wp&campaignid=demo2010. Three Arab states were ranked as "hybrid regimes," a category just above "authoritarian" but below "flawed democracies."

4. Saideman, "When Conflict Spreads," 717.

5. Muzammil M. Hussain and Philip Howard, "What Best Explains Successful Protest Cascades? ICTs and the Fuzzy Causes of the Arab Spring," *International Studies Review*, 15 (March 2013), 49.

6. Ibid., 51.

7. Ibid., 64.

8. Anthony Billingsley, "Writing Constitutions in the Wake of the Arab Spring," *Foreign Affairs,* November 30, 2011, http://www.foreignaffairs.com/articles/136699/anthony-billingsley/writing-constitutions-in-the-wake-of-the-arab-spring

9. Cited in Kavitha A. Davidson, "Democracy Index 2013: Global Democracy at a Standstill, the Economist Intelligence Unit's Annual Report Shows," *Huffington Post*, March 21, 2013, http://www.huffingtonpost.com/2013/03/21/democracy-index-2013-economist-intelligence-unit_n_2909619.html

10. Cited in Ben Hubbard and Rick Gladstone, "Arab Spring Countries Find Peace Is Harder Than Revolution," *New York Times,* August 14, 2013, http://www.nytimes.com/2013/08/15/world/middleeast/egypt-bloodshed-may-be-ill-omen-for-broader-region.html?pagewanted=all

11. Ibid.

12. Ibid.

13. Cited in "Tunisia Counts Votes in Historic Free Election," BBC News, October 24, 2011, http://www.bbc.co.uk/news/world-africa-15425407

14. Cited in Allan Little, "Renaissance Party Offers Clean Break to Tunisian Voters," BBC News, October 25, 2011, http://www.bbc.co.uk/news/world-africa-15453466

15. Cited in Lyse Doucet, "Tunisians' Frustrations, Two Years On," BBC News, December 10, 2012, http://www.bbc.co.uk/news/world-20663981

16. Cited in "It's Hard Being in Charge," *The Economist*, March 9, 2013, 41.

17. Cited in Monica Marks and Kareem Fahim, "Tunisia Move to Contain Fallout after Opposition Figure Is Assassinated," *New York Times,* February 6, 2013, http://www.nytimes.com/2013/02/07/world/africa/chokri-belaid-tunisian-opposition-figure-is-killed.html

18. Cited in Lyce Doucet, "Clouds Gather over Bellwether Tunisia," BBC News, February 10, 2013, http://www.bbc.co.uk/news/world-africa-21402778

19. Cited in Ahmed Maher, "Tunisia's Radical Divide over Salafi Agenda," BBC News, June 6, 2013, http://www.bbc.co.uk/news/world-africa-22771536

20. Cited in Carlotta Gall, "Second Opposition Leader Assassinated in Tunisia," New York Times, July 25, 2013, http://www.nytimes.com/2013/07/26/world/middleeast/second-opposition-leader-killed-in-tunisia.html

21. Cited in "Tunisia Declares Ansar al-Sharia a Terrorist Group," BBC News, August 27, 2013, http://www.bbc.co.uk/news/world-africa-23853241

22. Ibrahim Sharqieh, "Tunisia's Lessons for the Middle East," Foreign Affairs, September 17, 2013, http://www.foreignaffairs.com/articles/139938/ibrahim-sharqieh/tunisias-lessons-for-the-middle-east#

23. Cited in David D. Kirkpatrick and Carlotta Gall, "Arab Neighbors Take Split Paths in Constitutions," New York Times, January 14, 2014, http://www.nytimes.com/2014/01/15/world/middleeast/arab-neighbors-take-split-paths-in-constitutions.html

24. Cited in Maria Golovnina, "World Raises Pressure on Libya, Battles for Key Towns," Reuters, February 28, 2011, http://www.reuters.com/article/2011/02/28/us-libya-protests-idUSTRE71G0A620110228

25. Cited in "Libyan Opposition Launches Council," Aljazeera, February 27, 2011, http://www.aljazeera.com/news/africa/2011/02/2011227175955221853.html#

26. Cited in Marlise Simons and Neil MacFarquhar, "Hague Court Seeks Warrants for Libyan Officials," New York Times, May 4, 2011, http://www.nytimes.com/2011/05/05/world/africa/05nations.html

27. Cited in Devin Dwyer and Luis Martinez, "U.S. Tomahawk Cruise Missiles Hit Targets in Libya," ABC News, March 19, 2011, http://abcnews.go.com/International/libya-international-military-coalition-launch-assault-gadhafi-forces/story?id=13174246#.T35yGdI0SZR

28. Cited in Amy Chozick, "Clinton Calls Benghazi Her 'Biggest Regret' as Secretary," New York Times, January 27, 2014, http://www.nytimes.com/2014/01/28/us/politics/clinton-calls-benghazi-attack-her-biggest-regret-as-secretary.html

29. "Obama's Speech to the United Nations General Assembly—Text," New York Times, September 25, 2013, http://www.nytimes.com/2012/09/26/world/obamas-speech-to-the-united-nations-general-assembly-text.html

30. David D. Kirkpatrick, "A Deadly Mix in Benghazi," New York Times, December 28, 2013, http://www.nytimes.com/projects/2013/benghazi/#/?chapt=0

31. Frederic Wehrey, "Libya's Militia Menace," Foreign Affairs, July 12, 2012, http://www.foreignaffairs.com/articles/137776/frederic-wehrey/libyas-militia-menace

32. Cited in Suliman Ali Zway, "Amid Protests, Inmates Escape from Libyan Prison," New York Times, July 27, 2013, http://www.nytimes.com/2013/07/28/world/africa/libyans-turn-on-islamists-and-liberals-after-killings.html

33. Jason Pack, "Libya on the Brink," Foreign Affairs, July 28, 2014, http://www.foreignaffairs.com/articles/141666/jason-pack/libya-on-the-brink

34. Cited in Yolande Knell, "The Complicated Legacy of Egypt's Hosni Mubarak," BBC News, January 25, 2013, http://www.bbc.co.uk/news/world-middle-east-21201364

35. Thomas L. Friedman, "Egypt's Three Revolutions," New York Times, July 23, 2013, http://www.nytimes.com/2013/07/24/opinion/friedman-egypts-three-revolutions.html

36. Cited in Helene Cooper and Robert F. Worth, "In Arab Spring, Obama Finds a Sharp Test," New York Times, September 24, 2012, http://www.nytimes.com/2012/09/25/us/politics/arab-spring-proves-a-harsh-test-for-obamas-diplomatic-skill.html

37. George Joffé, "Navigating the Nile," Foreign Affairs, September 21, 2012, http://www.foreignaffairs.com/articles/138128/george-joffe/navigating-the-nile

38. Cited in "Obama: I Told Mubarak He Must Deliver on His Promises," CNN World, January 28, 2011, http://www.cnn.com/2011/WORLD/africa/01/28/egypt.protests.u.s.response/index.html

39. "Remarks by the President on the Situation in Egypt," The White House, February 1, 2011, http://www.whitehouse.gov/the-press-office/2011/02/01/remarks-president-situation-egypt

40. Cited in Andrew Quinn, "Clinton Warns of 'Perfect Storm' in Middle East," The Independent, February 5, 2011, http://www.independent.co.uk/news/world/politics/clinton-warns-of-quotperfect-stormquot-in-middle-east-2205407.html

41. Cited in David D. Kirkpatrick and Steven Erlanger, "Egypt's New Leader Spells Out Terms for U.S.–Arab Ties," New York Times, September 22, 2012, http://www.nytimes.com/2012/09/23/world/middleeast/egyptian-leader-mohamed-morsi-spells-out-terms-for-us-arab-ties.html?pagewanted=all

42. Cited in "Egypt: Who Holds the Power?" BBC News, July 3, 2013, http://www.bbc.co.uk/news/world-middle-east-18779934

43. Cited in Hamza Hendawi, "Morsi's Constitutional Declarations Grant Egypt's President Far-Reaching Powers," Huffington Post, November 22, 2012, http://www.huffingtonpost.com/2012/11/22/morsi-constitutional-declaration_n_2175651.html

44. Cited in "Comparison of Egypt's Suspended and Draft Constitutions," BBC News, November 30, 2012, http://www.bbc.co.uk/news/world-middle-east-20555478

45. Cited in Human Rights Watch, "Egypt: New Constitution Mixed on Support of Rights," November 30, 2012, http://www.hrw.org/news/2012/11/29/egypt-new-constitution-mixed-support-rights

46. Cited in David D. Kirkpatrick, "A Vague Role for Religion in Egyptian Draft Constitution," New York Times, November 9, 2012, http://www.nytimes.com/2012/11/10/world/middleeast/draft-egyptian-constitution-adopts-a-role-for-religion.html

47. Cited in Human Rights Watch, "Egypt: New Constitution Mixed on Support of Rights."

48. Nathan J. Brown, "Redoing the Egyptian Revolution," Foreign Affairs, July 3, 2013, http://www.foreignaffairs.com/articles/139555/nathan-j-brown/redoing-the-egyptian-revolution

49. Cited in Michael R. Gordon and David D. Kirkpatrick, "Kerry Is Hoping to Nudge Egypt toward Reforms," New York Times, March 2, 2013, http://www.nytimes.com/2013/03/03/world/middleeast/kerry-hoping-to-nudge-egypt-toward-reforms.html

50. Cited in Kareem Fahim, "Diplomatic Incident Arises over Egyptian Comedian," New York Times, April 2, 2013, http://www.nytimes.com/2013/04/03/world/middleeast/diplomatic-incident-arises-over-egyptian-comedian.html

51. Cited in "Egypt in Crisis," Frontline, http://www.pbs.org/wgbh/pages/frontline/foreign-affairs-defense/egypt-in-crisis/the-deep-state-how-egypts-shadow-state-won-out/

52. Elijah Zarwan, "Back Street's Back," Foreign Affairs, February 4, 2013, http://www.foreignaffairs.com/features/letters-from/back-streets-back

53. Thomas L. Friedman, "The Belly Dancing Barometer," New York Times, February 19, 2013, http://www.nytimes.com/2013/02/20/opinion/friedman-the-belly-dancing-barometer.html

54. Cited in David D. Kirkpatrick, "Opposition Will Boycott Egypt's Vote for Assembly," New York Times, February 26, 2013, http://www.nytimes.com/2013/02/27/world/middleeast/opposition-in-egypt-will-boycott-elections.html

55. Steven A. Cook, "Morsi's Mistake," Foreign Affairs, December 2, 2012, http://www.foreignaffairs.com/articles/139472/steven-a-cook/morsis-mistake

56. Cited in Kareem Fahim and David D. Kirkpatrick, "Clashes Break Out after Morsi Seizes New Power in Egypt," New York Times, November 23, 2013, http://www.nytimes.com/2012/11/24/world/middleeast/amid-protest-egypts-leader-defends-his-new-powers.html

57. Cited in Mark Landler, "Political Turmoil in Egypt Is Replay for White House," New York Times, July 2, 2013, http://www.nytimes.com/2013/07/03/world/middleeast/political-turmoil-in-egypt-is-replay-for-white-house.html

58. Sana Abed-Kotob, "The Accommodationists Speak," *International Journal of Middle East Studies* 27:3 (August 1995), 322, 332, 337.

59. Cited in Adam Entous, Jay Solomon, and Peter Nicholas, "U.S.'s Stance Was Product of Yearlong Shift," *Wall Street Journal,* July 4, 2013, http://online.wsj.com/article/SB10001424127887324260204578585910863051042.html

60. Cited in Jeff Martini, "The Egyptian Military's Playbook," *Foreign Affairs,* July 2, 2013, http://www.foreignaffairs.com/articles/139547/jeff-martini/the-egyptian-militarys-playbook

61. Cited in Ben Hubbard, "Military Reasserts Its Allegiance to Its Privileges," *New York Times,* July 3, 2013, http://www.nytimes.com/2013/07/04/world/middleeast/Egyptian-military-reasserts-its-allegiance-to-its-privileges.html

62. Cited in "Egypt Deeply Polarised as Morsi Marks First Year," BBC News, June 27, 2013, http://www.bbc.co.uk/news/world-middle-east-23077898

63. Cited in Patrick Martin, "Why Political Islamic Movements Are under Fire," *The Globe and Mail*, August 6, 2013, http://www.theglobeandmail.com/news/world/why-political-islamic-movements-are-under-fire/article13605860/?page=all

64. Cited in ibid.

65. Cited in Zachary Laub, "Egypt's Muslim Brotherhood," Council on Foreign Relations, updated August 28, 2013, http://www.cfr.org/egypt/egypts-muslim-brotherhood/p23991?cid=nlc-dailybrief-daily_news_brief-link7-20111122

66. Cited in David D. Kirkpatrick, "Egypt Widens Crackdown and Meaning of 'Islamist,'" *New York Times*, August 24, 2013, http://www.nytimes.com/2013/08/25/world/middleeast/egypt-widens-crackdown-and-meaning-of-islamist.html?pagewanted=all

67. Cited in David D. Kirkpatrick, "Egypt to Vote Next Month on New Constitution," *New York Times*, December 14, 2013, http://www.nytimes.com/2013/12/15/world/middleeast/egypt-to-vote-next-month-on-new-constitution.html?_r=0

68. Cited in David D. Kirkpatrick, "Hundreds Die as Egyptian Forces Attack Islamist Protesters," *New York Times,* August 14, 2013, http://www.nytimes.com/2013/08/15/world/middleeast/egypt.html?pagewanted=all

69. Cited in Mark Landler and Peter Baker, "His Options Few, Obama Rebukes Egypt's Leaders," *New York Times,* August 15, 2013, http://www.nytimes.com/2013/08/16/world/middleeast/obama-statement-on-egypt.html

70. Cited in David D. Kirkpatrick and Kareen Fahim, "Depth of Discontent Threatens Muslim Brotherhood and Its Leader," *New York Times,* July 2, 2013, http://www.nytimes.com/2013/07/03/world/middleeast/depth-of-discontent-threatens-muslim-brotherhood-and-its-leader.html

71. Cited in ibid.

72. Cited in David D. Kirkpatrick and Mayy El Sheikh, "Egypt's Ex-President Is Defiant at Murder Trial," *New York Times,* November 4, 2013, http://www.nytimes.com/2013/11/05/world/middleeast/egypt.html

73. Cited in "Morsi Warns of Egypt Instability without Reinstatement," BBC News, November 13, 2013, http://www.bbc.co.uk/news/world-middle-east-24927100

74. Cited in David D. Kirkpatrick, "New Egypt Law Effectively Bans Street Protests," *New York Times,* November 25, 2013, http://www.nytimes.com/2013/11/26/world/middleeast/egypt-law-street-protests.html

75. Cited in Peter Baker, "A Coup? Or Something Else? $1.5 Billion in U.S. Aid Is on the Line," *New York Times,* July 4, 2013, http://www.nytimes.com/2013/07/05/world/middleeast/egypts-arrests-of-islamists-pose-test-to-us-over-military-aid.html

76. Cited in Michael R. Gordon and Kareem Fahim, "Kerry Says Egypt's Military Was 'Restoring Democracy' in Ousting Morsi," *New York Times,* August 1, 2013, http://www.nytimes.com/2013/08/02/world/middleeast/egypt-warns-morsi-supporters-to-end-protests.html

77. Cited in Adam Entous, "White House's Egypt Debate Heralds Shift," *Wall Street Journal,* July 30, 2013, A6.

78. Cited in Baker, "A Coup? Or Something Else?"

79. Ibid.

80. Cited in Peter Baker, "Egypt Crisis Finds Washington Largely Ambivalent and Aloof," *New York Times,* July 5, 2013, http://www.nytimes.com/2013/07/06/world/middleeast/egypt-crisis-finds-washington-ambivalent-and-aloof.html

81. Cited in Jonathan Weisman, "Military Aid to Egyptians Loses Support in the Senate," *New York Times,* April 29, 2014, http://www.nytimes.com/2014/04/30/us/politics/egypt.html

82. Cited in David D. Kirkpatrick and Mayy El Sheikh, "Morsi Spurned Deals, Seeing Military as Tamed," *New York Times,* July 6, 2013, http://www.nytimes.com/2013/07/07/world/middleeast/morsi-spurned-deals-to-the-end-seeing-the-military-as-tamed.html?pagewanted=all

83. Cited in Kim Ghattas, "U.S. Credibility 'in Tatters' over Egypt Crisis," BBC News, August 16, 2013, http://www.bbc.co.uk/news/world-middle-east-23721918

84. Cited in Entous, Solomon, and Nicholas, "U.S.'s Stance Was Product of Yearlong Shift."

85. Joseph Holliday, "The Struggle for Syria in 2011," *Middle East Security Report 2,* 7, December 2011, http://www.understandingwar.org/sites/default/files/Struggle_For_Syria.pdf

86. Cited in Scott Wilson and Joby Warrick, "Syria's Assad Must Go, Obama Says," *Washington Post,* August 18, 2011, http://articles.washingtonpost.com/2011-08-18/politics/35271355_1_syrian-government-assets-syrian-president-bashar-al-assad-syrian-people

87. Kofi Annan, "Annan's Peace Plan for Syria," Council on Foreign Relations, March 2012, http://www.cfr.org/syria/annans-peace-plan-syria/p28380

88. Cited in "Saudis Struggling to Supply Syrian Rebels; 'We Are Not in the Arms Dealing Business,'" WorldTribune.com, October 13, 2013, http://www.worldtribune.com/2013/10/13/saudis-struggling-to-supply-syrian-rebels-we-are-not-the-the-arms-dealing-business/

89. Cited in Adam Entous, "Inside Obama's Syria Debate," *Wall Street Journal,* March 30–31, 2013, A10.

90. Cited in ibid.

91. Cited in Ibid.

92. Cited in Helene Cooper, "Obama Seeks Money to Train 'Appropriately Vetted' Syrian Rebels," *New York Times,* June 26, 2014, http://www.nytimes.com/2014/06/27/world/middleeast/obama-seeks-500-million-to-train-and-equip-syrian-opposition.html?_r=0

93. Mark Mazzetti, "C.I.A. Study of Covert Aid Fueled Skepticism about Helping Syrian Rebels," *New York Times,* October 14, 2014, http://www.nytimes.com/2014/10/15/us/politics/cia-study-says-arming-rebels-seldom-works.html

94. Cited in Lazar Berman, "Erdogan Calls Assad a 'Terrorist,' Blasts Kerry," *The Times of Israel,* October 7, 2013, http://www.timesofisrael.com/erdogan-calls-assad-a-terrorist-blasts-kerry/

95. Cited in Tim Arango, "Erdogan, Syrian Rebels' Leading Ally, Hesitates," *New York Times,* October 17, 2013, http://www.nytimes.com/2013/10/18/world/middleeast/erdogan-syria-rebels-leading-ally-hesitates-31-months-in.html

96. Hillary Rodham Clinton, *Hard Choices* (New York: Simon & Schuster, 2014), 463, 464.

97. Cited in Mark Mazzetti, Robert F. Worth, and Michael R. Gordon, "Obama's Uncertain Path amid Syria Bloodshed," *New York Times,* October 22, 2013, http://www.nytimes.com/2013/10/23/world/middleeast/obamas-uncertain-path-amid-syria-bloodshed.html?hp

98. Cited in Glenn Kessler, "President Obama and the 'Red Line' on Syria's Chemical Weapons," *Washington Post,* September 6, 2013, http://www.washingtonpost.com/blogs/fact-checker/wp/2013/09/06/president-obama-and-the-red-line-on-syrias-chemical-weapons/

99. Cited in Peter Baker, Mark Landler, David E. Sanger, and Anne Barnard, "Off-the-Cuff Obama Line Put U.S. in Bind on Syria," *New York Times,* May 4, 2013, http://www.nytimes.com/2013/05/05/world/middleeast/obamas-vow-on-chemical-weapons-puts-him-in-tough-spot.html

100. John Mueller, "Erase the Red Line," *Foreign Affairs,* April 30, 2013, http://www.foreignaffairs.com/articles/139351/john-mueller/erase-the-red-line

101. Cited in Susan Jones, "Obama: 'I Didn't Set a Red Line' on Syria," *The Telegraph,* October 23, 2013;

Cnsmnew.com, September 4, 2013, http://www
.cnsnews.com/news/article/susan-jones/obama-i-
didnt-set-red-line-syria

102. United Nations, "Security Council Requires
Scheduled Destruction of Syria's Chemical
Weapons, Unanimously Adopting Resolution
2118 (2013)," September 27, 2013, http://www
.un.org/press/en/2013/sc11135.doc.htm

103. "About the OPCW," Organisation for the
Prohibition of Chemical Weapons, http://www.
opcw.org/about-opcw/

104. Cited in "Chemical Weapons Watchdog Urges
Cooperation in Syria to Carry Out UN-Joint
Mission," UN News Centre, October 9, 2013,
http://www.un.org/apps/news/story
.asp?NewsID=46229#.Uo0AHuKwVgE

105. Cited in Mazzetti, Worth, and Gordon, "Obama's
Uncertain Path amid Syria Bloodshed."

106. "Syrian National Council Rejects Geneva Peace
Talks," BBC News, October 13, 2013, http://www
.bbc.co.uk/news/world-middle-east-24513538

107. Cited in "Syria Crisis: Guide to Armed and
Political Opposition," BBC News, October 17,
2013, http://www.bbc.co.uk/news/world-middle-
east-15798218

108. Cited in ibid.

109. Cited in "Islamist Rebels in Syria Reject National
Coalition," BBC News, September 25, 2013,
http://www.bbc.co.uk/news/world-middle-
east-24239779

110. Cited in Ben Hubbard and Michael R. Gordon,
"Key Syrian Rebel Groups Abandon Exile
Leaders," New York Times, September 25, 2013,
http://www.nytimes.com/2013/09/26/world/
middleeast/syria-crisis.html

111. Cited in Hassan Hassan, "The Army of Islam
Is Winning in Syria," Foreign Policy, October
1, 2013, http://www.foreignpolicy.com/
articles/2013/10/01/the_army_of_islam_is_
winning_in_syria?page=0,0

112. Cited in "The Hard Men on Both Sides Prevail,"
The Economist, May 18, 2013, 53.

113. Cited in "Syria Crisis: Guide to Armed and
Political Opposition," BBC News, October 17,
2013, http://www.bbc.co.uk/news/world-middle-
east-24403003

114. Cited in Michael R. Gordon, Mark Landler, and
Anne Barnard, "U.S. Suspends Nonlethal Aid to
Syria Rebels," New York Times, December 11,
2013, http://www.nytimes.com/2013/12/12/world/
middleeast/us-suspends-nonlethal-aid-to-syrian-
rebels-in-north.html

115. Robert F. Worth, "The Price of Loyalty in Syria,"
New York Times, June 19, 2013, http://www.
nytimes.com/2013/06/23/magazine/the-price-of-
loyalty-in-syria.html?pagewanted=all&_r=0

116. Cited in Anne Barnard, Mohammad Ghannam,
and Hwaida Saad, "Disillusionment Grows among
Syrian Opposition as Fighting Drags On," New
York Times, November 28, 2013, http://www
.nytimes.com/2013/11/29/world/middleeast/
syria-war.html

117. Cited in Ben Hubbard, "Syria Will Attend Geneva
Peace Talks," New York Times, November 27,
2013, http://www.nytimes.com/2013/11/28/world/
middleeast/syria.html

118. Cited in "Q&A: Geneva II Peace Conference," BBC
News, November 25, 2013, http://www.bbc.co.uk/
news/world-middle-east-24628442

119. Cited in "Still No Hint of Compromise," The
Economist, November 9, 2013, 51.

120. Cited in Anne Barnard, "Syrians on Both Sides
of the War Increasingly See Assad as Likely to
Stay," New York Times, November 8, 2013, http://
www.nytimes.com/2013/11/09/world/middleeast/
syrians-and-observers-increasingly-see-assad-as-
likely-to-stay.html

121. Cited in ibid.

122. Cited in Kevin Liptak, "Obama Warns Putin on
Intervening in Syria's Civil War," CNN Politics,
December 1, 2015, http://www.cnn.com/2015/12/01/
politics/obama-paris- press-conference/

123. Cited in Neil MacFarquhar, "Assad Makes
Unannounced Trip to Moscow to Discuss Syria
with Putin," New York Times, October 21, 2015,
http://www.nytimes.com/2015/10/22/world/
middleeast/assad-putin-syria-russia.html?_r=0

124. Cited in Mazzetti, Worth, and Gordon, "Obama's
Uncertain Path amid Syria Bloodshed."

125. Shmuel Bar, "America's Fading Middle East
Influence," Policy Review 166 (Hoover Institution),
http://www.hoover.org/publications/policy-review/
article/73161

CHAPTER 5

1. Shibley Telhami, Brian Katulis, Jon B. Alterman, and Milton Viorst, "Middle Eastern Views of the United States: What Do the Trends Indicate? *Middle East Policy* 13:3 (2006), 2.

2. Cited in Ellen Knickmeyer, "Saudis Gain amid Islamist Setbacks," *Wall Street Journal,* July 8, 2013, A11.

3. Cited in Rod Nordland, "Saudi Arabia Promises to Aid Egypt's Regime," *New York Times,* August 19, 2013, http://www.nytimes.com/2013/08/20/world/middleeast/saudi-arabia-vows-to-back-egypts-rulers.html

4. Cited in ibid.

5. Cited in Nick Cumming-Bruce, "U.N. Rights Chief Urges Faster Action to End Fighting in Syria," *New York Times,* May 10, 2013, http://www.nytimes.com/2013/05/11/world/middleeast/syria-human-rights.html

6. Cited in Nick Cumming-Bruce, "U.N. Panel Cites 'Terror' Campaign against Syrian Civilians," *New York Times,* December 19, 2013, http://www.nytimes.com/2013/12/20/world/middleeast/syria.html

7. Cited in Michael R. Gordon, "U.S. Seeks to Bypass Assad So More Aid Can Reach Syrian Civilians," *New York Times*, May 15, 2014, http://www.nytimes.com/2014/05/16/world/middleeast/us-seeks-ways-to-make-aid-reach-syrian-civilians.html

8. Nick Cumming-Bruce, "Number of Syrian Refugees Climbs to More Than 4 Million," *New York Times*, July 9, 2015, http://www.nytimes.com/2015/07/09/world/middleeast/number-of-syrian-refugee-climbs-to-more-than-4-million.html?_r=0; United Nations High Commissioner for Refugees, "Syria Regional Refugee Response," July 9, 2015, http://data.unhcr.org/syrianrefugees/regional.php

9. United Nations High Commissioner for Refugees, "Syria Regional Refugee Response," November 26, 2014, http://data.unhcr.org/syrianrefugees/country.php?id=122

10. Cited in "Million Syria Refugees Registered in Lebanon–UN," BBC News, April 3, 2014, http://www.bbc.com/news/world-middle-east-26864485

11. "Outstaying Their Welcome," *The Economist,* May 23, 2015, 39.

12. "More Funds Needed for Million Syrian Refugees in Turkey: UNHCR," Reuters, October 9, 2014, http://www.reuters.com/article/2014/10/09/us-foundation-syria-turkey-refugees-idUSKCN0HX1YC20141009

13. Cumming-Bruce, "Number of Syrian Refugees Climbs to More Than 4 Million."

14. Cited in ibid.

15. USAID, "Syria," June 25, 2015, http://www.usaid.gov/crisis/syria

16. Cited in Joe Parkinson and Ayla Albayrak, "Syria Kurds Move toward Autonomy," *Wall Street Journal*, November 16–17, 2013, A10.

17. Cited in Mark Landler and Thom Shanker, "Pentagon Lays Out Options for U.S. Military Effort in Syria," *New York Times,* July 22, 2013, http://www.nytimes.com/2013/07/23/world/middleeast/pentagon-outlining-options-to-congress-suggests-syria-campaign-would-be-costly.html. Emphasis added.

18. "Syria's Neighbors Want Assad to Step Down, but No Appetite for Aid to Rebels," Pew Global Attitudes Project, June 10, 2014, http://www.pewglobal.org/2014/06/10/syrias-neighbors-want-assad-to-step-down-but-no-appetite-for-aid-to-rebels/

19. Cited in Michael R. Gordon, "'Criticism of United States' Mideast Policy Increasingly Comes from Allies," *New York Times*, October 23, 2013, http://www.nytimes.com/2013/10/24/world/middleeast/kerry-reassures-israel-on-iran-but-divisions-remain.html

20. Cited in Anne Barnard, "Victory in Syrian Election Is Show of Assad's Control," *New York Times,* June 4, 2014, http://www.nytimes.com/2014/06/05/world/middleeast/former-syria-ambassaor-ford-criticizes-us.html

21. Cited in David D. Kirkpatrick, "Overwhelming Vote for Egypt's Constitution Raises Concern," *New York Times,* January 18, 2014, http://www.nytimes.com/2014/01/19/world/middleeast/vote-validates-egypts-constitution-and-military-takeover.html

22. Cited in David D. Kirkpatrick and Carlotta Gall, "Arab Neighbors Take Split Paths in Constitutions,"

New York Times, January 14, 2014, http://www.
nytimes.com/2014/01/15/world/middleeast/arab-
neighbors-take-split-paths-in-constitutions.html

23. Mara Revkin, "Worse Than Mubarak," *Foreign Affairs*, February 11, 2014, http://www
.foreignaffairs.com/articles/140729/mara-revkin/
worse-than-mubarak

24. Cited in David D. Kirkpatrick, "Putin Encourages Egyptian's Presidential Ambitions," *New York Times,* February 13, 2014, http://www.nytimes.
com/2014/02/14/world/middleeast/putin-
encourages-presidential-ambitions-of-egypts-ruler.
htm

25. Joshua Stacher, "Can a Myth Rule a Nation?" *Foreign Affairs*, January 31, 2014, http://www
.foreignaffairs.com/articles/140706/joshua-stacher/
can-a-myth-rule-a-nation

26. Jeff Martini, "The Egyptian Regime's Achilles' Heel," *Foreign Affairs,* February 11, 2014, http://www
.foreignaffairs.com/articles/140730/jeff-martini/the-
egyptian-regimes-achilles-heel

27. Cited in Mark Landler and Peter Baker, "His Options Few, Obama Rebukes Egypt's Leaders," *New York Times,* August 15, 2013, http://www
.nytimes.com/2013/08/16/world/middleeast/
obama-statement-on-egypt
.html?ref=middleeast

28. Cited in Steven Lee Myers, "To Back Democracy, U.S. Prepares to Cut $1 Billion from Egypt's Debt," *New York Times,* September 3, 2012, http://www
.nytimes.com/2012/09/04/world/middleeast/us-
prepares-economic-aid-to-bolster-democracy-in-
egypt.html?pagewanted=all

29. Cited in David D. Kirkpatrick and Rick Gladstone, "Egypt's Leaders Select Premier and Plan for Quick Elections," *New York Times,* July 9, 2013, http://
dir.groups.yahoo.com/neo/groups/OurWorldView/
conversations/topics/13488

30. Cited in David D. Kirkpatrick and Kareem Fahim, "U.S. Warns Egypt's Generals against Jeopardizing 'Second Chance' at Democracy," *New York Times,* July 15, 2013, http://www.nytimes.com/2013/07/16/
world/middleeast/us-steps-up-public-diplomacy-in-
egypt-crisis.html

31. Cited in Michael R. Gordon, "Egyptians Following Right Path, Kerry Says," *New York Times,*

November 3, 2013, http://www.nytimes
.com/2013/11/04/world/middleeast/kerry-egypt-
visit.html

32. Cited in Ben Hubbard, "Hardening Split in Egypt as Islamists Stage Huge Demonstrations," *New York Times,* July 12, 2013, http://www.nytimes
.com/2013/07/13/world/middleeast/egypt-morsi
.html

33. Cited in Thom Shanker and Eric Schmitt, "Ties with Egypt Army Constrain Washington," *New York Times,* August 16, 2013, http://www.nytimes
.com/2013/08/17/world/middleeast/us-officials-
fear-losing-an-eager-ally-in-the-egyptian-military
.html

34. Cited in Myers, "To Back Democracy, U.S. Prepares to Cut $1 Billion from Egypt's Debt."

35. Cited in Landler and Baker, "His Options Few, Obama Rebukes Egypt's Leaders."

36. Michael Wahid Hanna, "Getting over Egypt," *Foreign Affairs* 94:6 (November/December 2016), 67.

37. Cited in "The Unquenchable Fire," *The Economist,* September 28, 2013, 22.

38. Cited in Helene Cooper and Mark Landler, "Egypt May Be Bigger Concern Than Libya for White House," *New York Times,* September 13, 2012, http://www.nytimes.com/2012/09/14/world/
middleeast/egypt-not-libya-may-be-bigger-
challenge-for-white-house.html?pagewanted=all

39. Robert Springborg, "The Nasser Playbook," *Foreign Affairs,* November 5, 2013, http://www
.foreignaffairs.com/articles/140242/robert-
springborg/the-nasser-playbook

40. Cited in David D. Kirkpatrick, Helene Cooper, and Mark Landler, "Egypt, Hearing from Obama, Moves to Heal Rift from Protests," *New York Times,* September 13, 2012, http://www.nytimes
.com/2012/09/14/world/middleeast/egypt-hearing-
from-obama-moves-to-heal-rift-from-protests.
html?pagewanted=all

41. Hillary Rodham Clinton, *Hard Choices* (New York: Simon & Schuster, 2014), 461.

42. Cited in Ben Hubbard, Eric Schmitt, and Mark Mazzetti, "U.S. Pins Hope on Syrian Rebels with Loyalties All Over the Map," *New York Times,*

September 11, 2014, http://www.nytimes
.com/2014/09/12/world/middleeast/us-pins-hope-
on-syrian-rebels-with-loyalties-all-over-the-map.
html

43. J. Michael Quinn and Madhav Joshi, "Settling
Syria," *Foreign Affairs,* February 6, 2013, http://
www.foreignaffairs.com/articles/138833/j-michael-
quinn-and-madhav-joshi/settling-syria

44. Cited in Thom Shanker, "General Says Syrian
Rebels Aren't Ready to Take Power," *New York
Times,* August 21, 2013, http://www.nytimes
.com/2013/08/22/world/middleeast/general-says-
syrian-rebels-arent-ready-to-take-power.html

45. Cited in Anne Barnard and Nick Cumming-Bruce,
"Syrian Talks Disrupted by Congress's Approval
of Aid to Rebels," *New York Times,* January 28,
2014, http://www.nytimes.com/2014/01/29/world/
middleeast/syria.html

46. Cited in Ben Hubbard, "Islamist Rebels Create
Dilemma on Syria Policy," *New York Times,* April 27,
2013, http://www.nytimes.com/2013/04/28/world/
middleeast/islamist-rebels-gains-in-syria-create-
dilemma-for-us.html

47. Cited in Michael R. Gordon and Alan Cowell,
"Syrian Opposition Undecided on Talks, John
Kerry Says," *Boston Globe,* October 23,
2013, http://www.bostonglobe.com/news/
world/2013/10/22/kerry-says-syrian-opposition-
still-undecided-peace-conference-next-month/
U2wL0mYR10i6UW8sg0oSIK/story.html

48. Cited in Somini Sengupta, "World Powers Try Anew
for Syria Cease-Fire, but Path Is Tortuous," *New
York Times,* November 19, 2015, http://www
.nytimes.com/2015/11/20/world/middleeast/world-
powers-try-anew-for-syria-cease-fire-but-path-is-
tortuous.html

49. Michael Ignatieff, "With Syria, Diplomacy Needs
Force," *New York Times,* February 25, 2014, http://
www.nytimes.com/2014/02/26/opinion/with-syria-
diplomacy-needs-force.html

50. Gerald F. Seib, "Few Good Choices for U.S. in
Mideast," *Wall Street Journal,* July 30, 2013, A4.

51. Seth Jones, "The Mirage of the Arab Spring," *Foreign
Affairs* 92:1 (January/February 2013), 56.

52. Cited in David D. Kirkpatrick, "Benghazi and Arab
Spring Rear Up in U.S. Campaign," *New York

Times,* October 21, 2012, http://www.nytimes
.com/2012/10/22/us/politics/benghazi-and-arab-
spring-rear-up-in-us-campaign.html

53. Sheri Berman, "The Continuing Promise of the Arab
Spring," *Foreign Affairs,* July 17, 2013, http://www
.foreignaffairs.com/articles/139586/sheri-berman/
the-continuing-promise-of-the-arab-spring

54. Cited in Mark Landler, "Rice Offers a More Modest
Strategy for Mideast," *New York Times*, October 26,
2013, http://www.nytimes.com/2013/10/27/world/
middleeast/rice-offers-a-more-modest-strategy-for-
mideast.html

55. Walter Russell Mead, "Our Failed Grand Strategy,"
Wall Street Journal, August 24–25, 2013, C1.

56. Cited in David D. Kirkpatrick, "As Moderate
Islamists Retreat, Extremists Surge Unchecked,"
New York Times, June 18, 2014, http://www
.nytimes.com/2014/06/19/world/middleeast/
as-moderate-islamists-retreat-extremists-surge-
unchecked.html

57. "The Rule of the Gunmen," *The Economist*, October
11, 2014, 57.

58. Ibid.

59. Marwan Muasher, *The Second Arab Awakening and
the Battle for Pluralism* (New Haven: Yale University
Press, 2014), 27.

CHAPTER 6

1. Francis Fukuyama, "The End of History," *The
National Interest* 16 (Summer 1989), 3. Emphasis in
original.

2. Cited in Peter Baker, "How Obama Came to Plan for
'Surge' in Afghanistan," *New York Times,* December
5, 2009, http://www.nytimes.com/2009/12/06/
world/asia/06reconstruct.html?pagewanted=all

3. Paul L. Yingling, "An Absence of Strategic
Thinking," *Foreign Affairs,* December 16, 2011,
http://www.foreignaffairs.com/articles/134033/paul-
l-yingling/an-absence-of-strategic-thinking

4. Hillary Rodham Clinton, *Hard Choices* (New York:
Simon & Schuster, 2014), 190.

5. Robert M. Gates, *Duty: Memoirs of a Secretary at
War* (New York: Knopf, 2014), 587.

6. Leon Panetta, "The CIA Is Proud to Be on the Frontlines against al-Qaeda," *Washington Post*, January 10, 2010, http://www.washingtonpost.com/wp-dyn/content/article/2010/01/08/AR2010010803588.html

7. Cited in Clinton, *Hard Choices*, 469.

8. Cited in Eric Lipton, "As Wars End, a Rush to Grab Dollars Spent on the Border," *New York Times*, June 6, 2013, http://www.nytimes.com/2013/06/07/us/us-military-firms-eye-border-security-contracts.html?pagewanted=all

9. Clinton, *Hard Choices*, 184.

10. Cited in Peter Baker, "In Book, Panetta Recounts Frustration with Obama," *New York Times*, October 6, 2014, http://www.nytimes.com/2014/10/07/world/middleeast/ex-defense-secretary-panetta-tells-of-frustrations-with-obama.html

11. Nick Danforth, "The Myth of the Caliphate," *Foreign Affairs*, November 19, 2014, http://www.foreignaffairs.com/articles/142379/nick-danforth/the-myth-of-the-caliphate

12. "Muslims," Pew Research Religion & Public Life, December 18, 2012, http://www.pewforum.org/2012/12/18/global-religious-landscape-muslim/

13. "Politics and the Puritanical," *The Economist*, June 27, 2015, 38–39.

14. Bruce Livesey, "The Salafist Movement," *Frontline*, n.d., http://www.pbs.org/wgbh/pages/frontline/shows/front/special/sala.html

15. Osama bin Laden, "Declaration of *Jihad*," in Bruce Lawrence, ed., *Messages to the World: The Statements of Osama bin Laden* (New York: Verso, 2005), 25, 29.

16. Robert S. Leiken and Steven Brooke, "The Moderate Muslim Brotherhood," *Foreign Affairs* 82:2 (March/April 2007), 110–111.

17. See Bill Roggio, "The Seven Phases of the Base," *The Long War Journal*, August 15, 2005, http://www.longwarjournal.org/archives/2005/08/the_seven_phase.php

18. See "Al Qaeda Is Now Suspected in 1996 Bombing of Barracks," *New York Times*, May 14, 2003, http://www.nytimes.com/2003/05/14/world/al-qaeda-is-now-suspected-in-1996-bombing-of-barracks.html

19. "Al Qaeda's Second Fatwa," *PBS NewsHour*, February 23, 1998, http://www.pbs.org/newshour/updates/military/jan-june98/fatwa_1998.html

20. "The CIA's Intervention in Afghanistan: Interview with Zbigniew Brzezinski," *Le Nouvel Observateur*, Paris, January 15–21, 1998, http://www.globalresearch.ca/articles/BRZ110A.html

21. William Malley, *The Afghanistan Wars*, 2nd ed. (New York: Palgrave Macmillan, 2002), 223. Emphasis in original.

22. Cited in Philip Shenon, "U.S. Fury on 2 Continents; Clinton's Words: 'There Will Be No Sanctuary for Terrorists'," *New York Times*, August 21, 1998, http://www.nytimes.com/1998/08/21/world/us-fury-2-continents-clinton-s-words-there-will-be-no-sanctuary-for-terrorists.html?n=Top%2fReference%2fTimes%20Topics%2fPeople%2fC%2fClinton%2c%20Bill

23. Ned Zeman, David Wise, David Rose, and Bryan Burrough, "The Path to 9/11: Lost Warnings and Fatal Errors," *Vanity Fair*, November 2004, http://www.vanityfair.com/politics/features/2004/11/path-to-9-11-200411

24. "Interview Michael Scheuer," *Frontline*, July 21, 2005, http://www.pbs.org/wgbh/pages/frontline/torture/interviews/scheuer.html

25. Cited in "Bin Laden Raid: Barack Obama Describes 'Huge Risks,'" BBC News, May 9, 2011, http://www.bbc.co.uk/news/world-us-canada-13331762

26. Cited in Adrian Brown, "Osama Bin Laden's Death: How It Happened," BBC News, September 10, 2012, http://www.bbc.co.uk/news/world-south-asia-13257330

CHAPTER 7

1. "S.J.Res. 23—107th Congress: Authorization for Use of Military Force," September 14, 2001, http://www.govtrack.us/congress/bills/107/sjres23

2. "Text of Bush's Speech at West Point," *New York Times*, June 1, 2012, http://www.nytimes.com/2002/06/01/international/02PTEX-WEB.html

3. Cited in Michael R. Gordon and Eric Schmitt, "A Nation Challenged: The Hunt; Marines and Army May Scour Caves, U.S. General Says," *New York Times*, December 20, 2001, http://www.nytimes

.com/2001/12/20/world/a-nation-challenged-the-hunt-marines-and-army-may-scour-caves-us-general-says.html. For a detailed description of the hunt for bin Laden in Tora Bora, see Peter Bergen, "The Battle for Tora Bora," *New Republic,* December 22, 2009, http://www.newrepublic.com/article/the-battle-tora-bora#

4. Cited in "7/7 London Bombings 'Were Osama bin Laden's Last Successful Operation,'" *The Guardian,* July 13, 2011, http://www.guardian.co.uk/uk/2011/jul/13/7-july-bin-laden-last-operation

5. Cited in Robert F. Worth, "Al Qaeda–Inspired Groups, Minus Goal of Striking U.S.," *New York Times,* October 27, 2012, http://www.nytimes.com/2012/10/28/world/middleeast/al-qaeda-inspired-groups-minus-goal-of-striking-us.html?pagewanted=all&_r=0

6. Cited in Ben Hubbard, "The Franchising of Al Qaeda," *New York Times,* January 25, 2014, http://www.nytimes.com/2014/01/26/sunday-review/the-franchising-of-al-qaeda.html

7. Cited in "Islamic State 'Being Driven Out of Syria's Kobane,'" BBC News, October 16, 2014, http://www.bbc.com/news/world-middle-east-29647314

8. Cited in "The Propaganda War," *The Economist,* August 15, 2015, 41.

9. "UN Says '25,000 Foreign Fighters' Joined Islamic Militants," BBC News, April 2, 2015, http://www.bbc.com/news/world-middle-east-32156541

10. "Caucasian Jihad," *The Economist,* July 4, 2015.

11. William McCants, "How Zawahiri Lost al Qaeda," *Foreign Affairs,* November 19, 2013, http://www.foreignaffairs.com/articles/140273/william-mccants/how-zawahiri-lost-al-qaeda

12. Jacob N. Shapiro, *The Terrorist's Dilemma: Managing Violent Covert Organizations* (Princeton, NJ: Princeton University Press, 2013), 4.

13. Cited in Adam Entous, "Regrouped Al Qaeda Poses Global Threat," *Wall Street Journal*, August 5, 2013, A8.

14. Cited in Eric Schmitt, "Qaeda Affiliates Gain Regional Influence as Central Leadership Fades," *New York Times*, April 30, 2014, http://www.nytimes.com/2014/05/01/world/middleeast/qaeda-affiliates-gain-regional-influence-as-central-leadership-fades.html

15. Cited in Mark Landler, "Obama Warns U.S. Faces Diffuse Terrorism Threats," *New York Times,* May 28, 2014, http://www.nytimes.com/2014/05/29/us/politics/obama-foreign-policy-west-point-speech.html

16. Cited in Ken Dilanian, "Al Qaeda in the Arabian Peninsula at Center of U.S. Cross Hairs," *Los Angeles Times,* August 7, 2013, http://www.latimes.com/news/nationworld/world/middleeast/la-fg-yemen-terror-20130808,0,3137705.story

17. Cited in Brian Knowlton, "Holder Voices 'Extreme Concern' about Terrorist Bomb Makers," *New York Times,* July 13, 2014, http://www.nytimes.com/2014/07/14/world/middleeast/holder-expresses-concern-about-terrorist-bomb-makers.html

18. Cited in Saeed Al Batati and David D. Kirkpatrick, "Qaeda Affiliate Steps Up Video Propaganda Push," *New York Times,* May 12, 2014, http://www.nytimes.com/2014/05/13/world/middleeast/qaeda-affiliate-steps-up-video-propaganda-push-in-yemen.html

19. "Jihafrica," *The Economist*, July 18, 2015, 38.

20. Cited in Jeffrey Gettleman and Nicholas Kulish, "Somali Militants Mixing Business and Terror," *New York Times,* September 30, 2013, http://www.nytimes.com/2013/10/01/world/africa/officials-struggle-with-tangled-web-of-financing-for-somali-militants.html?pagewanted=all

21. Stig Jarle Hansen, *Al-Shabaab in Somalia: The History and Ideology of a Militant Islamic Group, 2005-2012* (New York: Columbia University Press, 2013), 72.

22. Cited in Jay Solomon and Julian E. Barnes, "Terror Threat Prompts U.S. Rethink on Africa," *Wall Street Journal,* January 19–20, 2013, http://online.wsj.com/article/SB10001424127887324468104578250211314357762.html

23. Cited in Helene Cooper, Eric Schmitt, and Jeffrey Gettleman, "Strikes Killed Militant Chief in Somalia, U.S. Reports," *New York Times,* September 5, 2014, http://www.nytimes.com/2014/09/06/world/africa/somalia-shabab.html

24. Cited in Adam Nossiter, "Increase in Jihadi Attacks in Africa May Reflect Movement's

Weakness," *New York Times,* September 24, 2013, http://www.nytimes.com/2013/09/25/world/africa/increase-in-jihadi-attacks-in-africa-may-reflect-movements-weakness.html

25. Cited in Nicholas Kulish, Mark Mazzetti, and Eric Schmitt, "Kenya Mall Carnage Shows Shabab Resilience," *New York Times,* September 22, 2013, http://www.nytimes.com/2013/09/23/world/africa/kenya-mall-carnage-shows-shabab-resilience.html?pagewanted=all

26. Paul Hidalgo, "Al Shabab's Last Stand?" *Foreign Affairs,* September 11, 2014, http://www.foreignaffairs.com/articles/141975/paul-hidalgo/al-shababs-last-stand

27. Anne Barnard and Neil MacFarquhar, "Paris and Mali Attacks Expose Lethal Qaeda–ISIS Rivalry," *New York Times,* November 20, 2015, http://www.nytimes.com/2015/11/21/world/middleeast/paris-and-mali-attacks-expose-a-lethal-al-qaeda-isis-rivalry.html

28. Cited in Michael R. Gordon, "State Dept. Warns of New Terrorist Group Posing Threat to U.S. Interests in Africa," *New York Times,* December 18, 2013, http://www.nytimes.com/2013/12/19/world/africa/state-dept-warns-of-new-terrorist-group-posing-threat-to-us-interests-in-africa.html

29. Cited in Benjamin Weiser, "U.S. Charges Algerian in Deadly Gas Plant Attack," *New York Times,* July 19, 2013, http://www.nytimes.com/2013/07/20/nyregion/us-charges-algerian-in-deadly-gas-plant-attack.html

30. Cited in ibid.

31. Cited in Steven Lee Myers, "Clinton Suggests Link to Qaeda Offshoot in Deadly Libya Attack," *New York Times,* September 26, 2012, http://www.nytimes.com/2012/09/27/world/africa/clinton-cites-clear-link-between-al-qaeda-and-attack-in-libya.html?pagewanted=all

32. Cited in Chris McGreal, "Clinton Demands U.S. Takes Lead to Combat 'Jihadist Threat' in North Africa," *The Guardian,* January 23, 2013, http://www.guardian.co.uk/world/2013/jan/23/hillary-clinton-north-africa-jihadist-threat

33. Cited in Eric Schmitt, "Drones in Niger Reflect New U.S. Tack on Terrorism," *New York Times,* July 10, 2013, http://www.nytimes.com/2013/07/11/world/africa/drones-in-niger-reflect-new-us-approach-in-terror-fight.html?pagewanted=all

34. Cited in Adam Nossiter and David D. Kirkpatrick, "Abduction of Girls an Act Not Even Al Qaeda Can Condone," *New York Times,* May 7, 2014, http://www.nytimes.com/2014/05/08/world/africa/abduction-of-girls-an-act-not-even-al-qaeda-can-condone.html

35. Cited in "Boko Haram Leader Claims Massacre in Baga, Threatens More," *New York Times* January 21, 2015, http://www.nytimes.com/aponline/2015/01/21/world/africa/ap-af-nigeria-violence.html

36. Cited in "Nigeria: Militants Claim to Rule City 'by Islamic Law,'" *New York Times,* August 25, 2014, http://www.nytimes.com/2014/08/26/world/africa/nigeria-militants-claim-to-rule-city-by-islamic-law.html

37. Cited in Helene Cooper, "To Aid Boko Haram Fight, Obama Orders 300 Troops to Cameroon," *New York Times,* October 14, 2015, http://www.nytimes.com/2015/10/15/world/africa/obama-orders-300-troops-to-cameroon-to-support-fight-against-boko-haram.html

38. Cited in Helene Cooper, "Rifts between U.S. and Nigeria Impeding Fight against Boko Haram," *New York Times,* January 24, 2015, http://www.nytimes.com/2015/01/25/world/rifts-between-us-and-nigeria-impeding-fight-against-boko-haram.html

39. Dionne Searcey and Marc Santora, "Boko Haram Ranked Ahead of ISIS for Deadliest Terror Group," *New York Times,* November 18, 2015, http://www.nytimes.com/2015/11/19/world/africa/boko-haram-ranked-ahead-of-isis-for-deadliest-terror-group.html

40. Cited in Drew Hinshaw and Adam Entous, "On Terror's New Front Line, Mistrust Blunts U.S. Strategy," *Wall Street Journal,* February 27, 2013, A10.

41. Cited in Adam Nossiter, "In Nigeria, More Attacks on Militants," *New York Times,* May 17, 2013, http://www.nytimes.com/2013/05/18/world/africa/nigeria-steps-up-assaults-on-militants-in-northeast.html

42. U.S. House of Representatives Committee on Homeland Security Subcommittee on

Counterterrorism and Intelligence, "Boko Haram Emerging Threat to the U.S. Homeland," November 30, 2011, 2, http://homeland.house .gov/sites/homeland.house.gov/files/Boko%20 Haram-%20Emerging%20Threat%20to%20 the%20US%20Homeland.pdf

43. Cited in Scott Shane, "A Homemade Style of Terror: Jihadists Push New Tactics," *New York Times,* May 5, 2013, http://www.nytimes .com/2013/05/06/us/terrorists-find-online-education-for-attacks.html

44. Cited in ibid.

45. Ibid.

46. Cited in Eric Schmitt, "Worries Mount as Syria Lures West's Muslims," *New York Times,* July 27, 2013, http://www.nytimes.com/2013/07/28/world/ middleeast/worries-mount-as-syria-lures-wests-muslims.html?pagewanted=all

47. Cited in Ashley Fantz, "Still Out There and Growing—al Qaeda on the Rebound, Experts Say," CNN, December 28, 2013, http://www .cnn.com/2013/12/28/world/meast/al-qaeda-growing

48. Cited in Siobhan Gorman, Cassell Bryan-Low, and Maria Abi-Habib, "Return of Jihadists Threatens Europe," *Wall Street Journal,* December 5, 2013, A10.

49. Cited in Eric Schmitt, "U.S. Says Dozens of Americans Have Sought to Join Rebels in Syria," *New York Times,* November 20, 2013, http://www.nytimes.com/2013/11/21/world/ middleeast/us-says-dozens-of-americans-have-sought-to-join-rebels-in-syria.html

50. Cited in Michael S. Schmidt and Eric Schmitt, "Syria Militants Said to Recruit Visiting Americans to Attack U.S.," *New York Times,* January 9, 2014, http://www.nytimes.com/2014/01/10/ world/middleeast/syrian-groups-try-to-recruit-us-travelers.html

51. Matt Apuzzo and Michael S. Schmidt, "F.B.I Emphasizes Speed as ISIS Exhorts Individuals to Attack," *New York Times,* July 27, 2015, http:// www.nytimes.com/2015/07/28/us/fbi-emphasizes-speed-as-isis-exhorts-individuals-to-attack.html

52. M. J. Kirdar, "Al-Qaeda in Iraq," Center for Strategic and International Studies, June 2011,

http://csis.org/files/publication/110614_Kirdar_ AlQaedaIraq_Web.pdf, p. 4.

53. Leon Panetta, "How the White House Misplayed Iraqi Troop Talks," *Time,* October 1, 2014, http:// time.com/3453840/leon-panetta-iraqi-troop/

54. Eric Schmitt and Michael S. Schmidt, "West Struggles to Halt Flow of Citizens to War Zones," *New York Times,* January 13, 2015, https:// www.google.com/webhp?sourceid=chrome-instant&ion=1&espv=2&ie=UTF-8#q=Eric+Schm itt+and+Michael+S.+Schmidt%2C+%E2%80% 9CWest+Struggles+to+Halt+Flow+of+Citizens+ to+War+Zones%2C%E2%80%9D

55. Cited in Tim Arango and Eric Schmitt, "U.S. Actions in Iraq Fueled Rise of a Rebel," *New York Times,* August 10, 2014, http://www .nytimes.com/2014/08/11/world/middleeast/us-actions-in-iraq-fueled-rise-of-a-rebel.html

56. Cited in "Syria: Islamist Nusra Front gives BBC Exclusive Interview," BBC News, January 17, 2013, http://www.bbc.co.uk/news/world-middle-east-21061018

57. Cited in Fantz, "Still Out There and Growing."

58. Cited in Jay Solomon and Nour Malas, "U.S. Tries to Isolate Syria's Militant Islamists," *Wall Street Journal,* December 6, 2012, A12.

59. Cited in Hania Mourtada and Rick Gladstone, "Iraq's Branch of Al Qaeda Merges with Syria Jihadists," *New York Times,* http://www .nytimes.com/2013/04/10/world/middleeast/Iraq-and-Syria-jihadists-combine.html

60. McCants, "How Zawahiri Lost al Qaeda."

61. Cited in William McCants, "State of Confusion," *Foreign Affairs,* September 11, 2014, http://www. foreignaffairs.com/articles/141976/william-mccants/ state-of-confusion

62. Cited in Sam Dagher, "Islamist Rebels Take Fight to Suburbs of Syrian Capital," *Wall Street Journal,* November 1, 2013, A10.

63. Cited in Robert F. Worth and Eric Schmitt, "Jihadist Groups Gain in Turmoil across Middle East," *New York Times,* December 3, 2013, http:// www.nytimes.com/2013/12/04/world/middleeast/ jihadist-groups-gain-in-turmoil-across-middle-east.html

64. McCants, "How Zawahiri Lost al Qaeda."

65. Cited in Ben Hubbard, "Syrian Rebels Deal Qaeda-Linked Group a Reversal," *New York Times,* January 8, 2014, http://www.nytimes.com/2014/01/09/world/middleeast/syrian-rebels-said-to-oust-qaeda-linked-group-from-its-aleppo-headquarters.html

66. Cited in David D. Kirkpatrick, "ISIS' Harsh Brand of Islam Is Rooted in Austere Saudi Creed," *New York Times* September 24, 2014, http://www.nytimes.com/2014/09/25/world/middleeast/isis-abu-bakr-baghdadi-caliph-wahhabi.html

67. Cited in Ben Hubbard, "ISIS Threatens Al Qaeda as Flagship Movement of Extremists," *New York Times,* June 30, 2014, http://www.nytimes.com/2014/07/01/world/middleeast/isis-threatens-al-qaeda-as-flagship-movement-of-extremists.html. See also Joseph Krauss, "A Look at the Rivalry between Al-Qaida and IS," Associated Press, November 21, 2015, http://bigstory.ap.org/article/464b2e414b294278ab5fbb0f9dbfd59c/look-rivalry-between-al-qaida-and

68. McCants, "How Zawahiri Lost al Qaeda."

69. Cited in Ben Hubbard, "In Syria, Potential Ally's Islamist Ties Challenge U.S.," *New York Times,* August 25, 2015, http://www.nytimes.com/2015/08/26/world/middleeast/ahrar-al-sham-rebel-force-in-syrias-gray-zone-poses-challenge-to-us.html?_r=0

70. Cited in Ben Hubbard, "Qaeda Branch in Syria Pursues Its Own Agenda," *New York Times,* October 1, 2013, http://www.nytimes.com/2013/10/02/world/middleeast/in-pushing-its-own-agenda-for-syria-a-qaeda-franchise-turns-rebels-into-enemies.html

71. Omar Al-Nidawi, "How Maliki Lost Iraq," *Foreign Affairs,* June 18, 2014, http://www.foreignaffairs.com/articles/141579/omar-al-nidawi/how-maliki-lost-iraq

72. Cited in Peter Baker and Eric Schmitt, "Many Missteps in Assessment of ISIS Threat," *New York Times,* September 29, 2014, http://www.nytimes.com/2014/09/30/world/middleeast/obama-fault-is-shared-in-misjudging-of-isis-threat.html

73. Charles Lister, "ISIS a Fanatical Force—with a Weakness," CNN, June 17, 2014, http://www.cnn.com/2014/06/16/opinion/lister-isis-iraq

74. Cited in Tim Arango, Kareem Fahim, and Ben Hubbard, "Rebels' Fast Strike in Iraq Was Years in the Making," *New York Times,* June 14, 2014, http://www.nytimes.com/2014/06/15/world/middleeast/rebels-fast-strike-in-iraq-was-years-in-the-making.html

75. Cited in Eric Schmitt and Michael R. Gordon, "The Iraqi Army Was Crumbling Long before Its Collapse, U.S. Officials Say," *New York Times,* June 12, 2014, http://www.nytimes.com/2014/06/13/world/middleeast/american-intelligence-officials-said-iraqi-military-had-been-in-decline.html

76. Cited in Alissa J. Rubin and Tim Arango, "ISIS Forces Appear to Capture Iraq's Largest Dam," *New York Times,* August 7, 2014, http://www.nytimes.com/2014/08/08/world/middleeast/isis-forces-in-iraq.html

77. Cited in Hubbard, "ISIS Threatens Al Qaeda as Flagship Movement of Extremists."

78. Cited in Eric Schmitt and David D. Kirkpatrick, "Islamic State Sprouting Limbs beyond Its Base," *New York Times,* February 14, 2015, http://www.nytimes.com/2015/02/15/world/middleeast/islamic-state-sprouting-limbs-beyond-mideast.html

79. Cited in Dan Bilefsky, "In New Front against Islamic State, Dictionary Becomes a Weapon," *New York Times,* October 2, 2014, http://www.nytimes.com/2014/10/03/world/europe/islamic-state-isis-muslims-term.html

80. Cited in Eric Schmitt, "ISIS or Al Qaeda? American Officials Split over Top Terror Threat," *New York Times,* August 4, 2015, http://www.nytimes.com/2015/08/05/world/middleeast/isis-or-al-qaeda-american-officials-split-over-biggest-threat.html

81. Cited in Peter Baker, "Obama Finds He Can't Put Iraq War behind Him," *New York Times,* June 13, 2014, http://www.nytimes.com/2014/06/14/world/middleeast/obama-finds-he-cant-put-iraq-behind-him.html

82. Michael D. Shear and Dalia Sussman, "Poll Finds Dissatisfaction over Iraq," *New York Times,* June 23, 2014, http://www.nytimes.com/2014/06/24/world/middleeast/sharp-rise-in-disapproval-of-obamas-handling-of-foreign-policy-poll-finds.html

83. "Uneasy Lies the Head," *The Economist*, October 31, 2015, 47.

84. Cited in Peter Baker, "Obama, with Reluctance, Returns to Action in Iraq," *New York Times*, August 7, 2014, http://www.nytimes.com/2014/08/08/world/middleeast/a-return-to-action.html

85. Cited in Mark Landler, Ben Hubbard, and Helene Cooper, "U.S. Will 'Do What Is Necessary' against ISIS, Obama Says," *Boston Globe*, September 23, 2014, http://www.bostonglobe.com/news/world/2014/09/23/obama-scores-coalition-victory-with-arab-strikes/gV456QnSeLoybn1dLPlygK/story.html

86. "Transcript of Obama's Remarks on the Fight against ISIS," *New York Times*, September 10, 2014, http://www.nytimes.com/2014/09/11/world/middleeast/obamas-remarks-on-the-fight-against-isis.html

87. Cited in Mark Mazzetti, Michael S. Schmidt, and Ben Hubbard, "U.S. Suspects More Direct Threats beyond ISIS," *New York Times*, September 20, 2014, http://www.nytimes.com/2014/09/21/world/middleeast/us-sees-other-more-direct-threats-beyond-isis-.html

88. Cited in Helene Cooper, "U.S. and Allies Form Coalition with Intent to Destroy ISIS," *New York Times*, September 5, 2014, http://www.newsdiffs.org/diff/668927/668939/www.nytimes.com/2014/09/06/world/europe/nato-summit.html

89. Anne Barnard, Michael R. Gordon, and Eric Schmitt, "Turkey and U.S. Plan to Create Syria 'Safe Zone' Free of ISIS," *New York Times*, July 27, 2015, http://www.nytimes.com/2015/07/28/world/middleeast/turkey-and-us-agree-on-plan-to-clear-isis-from-strip-of-northern-syria.html

90. Eric Schmitt, "Paris Attacks and Other Assaults Seen as Evidence of a Shift by ISIS," *New York Times*, November 22, 2015, http://www.nytimes.com/2015/11/23/world/europe/paris-attacks-isis-threatens-west.html

91. Cited in Eric Schmitt and David D. Kirkpatrick, "Strategy Shift for ISIS: Inflicting Terror in Distant Lands," *New York Times*, November 14, 2015, http://www.nytimes.com/2015/11/15/world/europe/strategy-shift-for-isis-inflicting-terror-in-distant-lands.html

92. Cited in Adam Nossiter, Aurelien Breeden, and Katrin Bennhold, "Three Teams of Coordinated Attackers Carried Out Assault on Paris, Officials Say; Hollande Blames ISIS," *New York Times*, November 14, 2015, http://www.nytimes.com/2015/11/15/world/europe/paris-terrorist-attacks.html

93. Cited in Michael R. Gordon and Eric Schmitt, "Iran Secretly Sending Drones and Supplies into Iraq, U.S. Officials Say," *New York Times*, June 25, 2014, http://www.nytimes.com/2014/06/26/world/middleeast/iran-iraq.html

94. "The Caliphate Strikes Back," *The Economist*, May 23, 2015, 37.

95. Cited in Jeffrey Goldberg, "Hillary Clinton: 'Failure' to Help Syrian Rebels Led to the Rise of ISIS," *The Atlantic*, August 10, 2014, http://www.theatlantic.com/international/archive/2014/08/hillary-clinton-failure-to-help-syrian-rebels-led-to-the-rise-of-isis/375832

96. Cited in Peter Baker, "Grim Sequel to Iraq's War," *New York Times*, January 8, 2014, http://www.nytimes.com/2014/01/09/world/middleeast/grim-sequel-to-iraqs-war.html

97. Charlie Savage, "Secret Papers Describe Size of Terror Lists Kept by U.S.," *New York Times*, August 5, 2014, http://www.nytimes.com/2014/08/06/us/secret-papers-describe-size-of-terror-lists-kept-by-us.html

98. Cited in Andrew McAfee, "Enterprise 2.0 Is a Crock: Discuss," *Andrew McAfee's Blog*, September 2, 2009, http://andrewmcafee.org/2009/09/e20-is-a-crock-discuss

99. "Public Remains Divided over the Patriot Act," Pew Research Center, February 15, 2011, http://www.pewresearch.org/2011/02/15/public-remains-divided-over-the-patriot-act

100. Cited in Scott Shane and David E. Sanger, "Job Title Key to Inner Access Held by Snowden," *New York Times*, June 30, 2013, http://www.nytimes.com/2013/07/01/us/job-title-key-to-inner-access-held-by-snowden.html?pagewanted=all

101. Cited in Eric Lichtblau, "In Secret, Court Vastly Broadens Powers of N.S.A.," *New York Times*, July 6, 2013, http://www.nytimes.com/2013/07/07/us/in-secret-court-vastly-broadens-powers-of-nsa.html?pagewanted=all

102. "Reviewing the Surveillance State," *The Economist,* May 23, 2015, 22.

103. See "U.S. Confirms Verizon Phone Records Collection," BBC News, June 6, 2013, http://www.bbc.co.uk/news/world-us-canada-22793851

104. James Risen and Nick Wingfield, "Web's Reach Binds N.S.A. and Silicon Valley Leaders," *New York Times,* June 19, 2013, http://www.nytimes.com/2013/06/20/technology/silicon-valley-and-spy-agency-bound-by-strengthening-web.html?pagewanted=all

105. Cited in "U.S. NSA 'Probed Fewer Than 300 Phone Calls'," BBC News, June 16, 2013, http://www.bbc.com/news/world-us-canada-22925892

106. Cited in Peter Baker, "Obama Defends Authorization of Surveillance Programs," *New York Times,* January 17, 2013, http://www.nytimes.com/2013/06/18/us/politics/obama-defends-authorization-of-surveillance-programs.html

107. Cited in Charlie Savage, "N.S.A. Chief Says Surveillance Has Stopped Dozens of Plots," *New York Times,* June 18, 2013, http://www.nytimes.com/2013/06/19/us/politics/nsa-chief-says-surveillance-has-stopped-dozens-of-plots.html?hp

108. Cited in "U.S. Spy Chief Clapper Defends Prism and Phone Surveillance," BBC News, June 7, 2013, http://www.bbc.co.uk/news/world-us-canada-22809541

109. Cited in Scott Shane and Jonathan Weisman, "Earlier Denials Put Intelligence Chief in Awkward Position," *New York Times,* June 11, 2013, http://www.nytimes.com/2013/06/12/us/nsa-disclosures-put-awkward-light-on-official-statements.html?pagewanted=all

110. Cited in Peter Baker, "Even as Wars Fade, Obama Maintains Bush's Data Mining," *New York Times,* June 6, 2013, http://www.nytimes.com/2013/06/07/us/obamas-strong-embrace-of-divisive-security-tools.html

111. Cited in "U.S. Confirms Verizon Phone Records Collection."

112. Cited in Sabrina Siddiqui, "Mark Udall, Ron Wyden Introduce Bill Limiting Federal Government's Authority to Collect Data," *Huffington Post*, June 14, 2013, http://www.huffingtonpost.com/2013/06/14/mark-udall-ron-wyden-nsa_n_3442054.html

113. Frank Newport, "Americans Disapprove of Government Surveillance Programs," *Gallup Politics,* June 12, 2013, http://www.gallup.com/poll/163043/americans-disapprove-government-surveillance-programs.aspx

114. Jonathan Weisman, "House Defeats Effort to Rein in N.S.A. Data Gathering," *New York Times*, July 24, 2013, http://www.nytimes.com/2013/07/25/us/politics/house-defeats-effort-to-rein-in-nsa-data-gathering.html

115. Leslie Cauley, "NSA Has Massive Database of Americans' Phone Calls," *USA Today,* May 11, 2006, http://yahoo.usatoday.com/news/washington/2006-05-10-nsa_x.htm

116. Bob Woodward, *Obama's Wars* (New York: Simon & Schuster, 2010), 7.

117. James Bamford, "The NSA Is Building the World's Biggest Spy Center (Watch What You Say)," *Wired*, March 15, 2012, http://www.wired.com/threatlevel/2012/03/ff_nsadatacenter/all

118. Cited in Charlie Savage, "U.S. Outlines N.S.A.'s Culling of Data for All Domestic Calls," *New York Times,* July 31, 2013, http://www.nytimes.com/2013/08/01/us/nsa-surveillance.html?pagewanted=all

119. Cited in Charlie Savage and Scott Shane, "Secret Court Rebuked N.S.A. on Surveillance," *New York Times*, August 21, 2013, http://www.nytimes.com/2013/08/22/us/2011-ruling-found-an-nsa-program-unconstitutional.html

120. Cited in ibid.

121. Glenn Greenwald, "XKeyscore: NSA Tool Collects 'Nearly Everything a User Does on the Internet,'" *The Guardian,* July 31, 2013, http://www.theguardian.com/world/2013/jul/31/nsa-top-secret-program-online-data

122. Ibid.

123. "Edward Snowden: Leaks That Exposed U.S. Spy Program," BBC News, January 17, 2014, http://www.bbc.com/news/world-us-canada-23123964

124. "Statement by H. E. Dilma Rousseff, President of the Federative Republic of Brazil, at the Opening of the General Debate of the 68th Session of the

United Nations General Assembly," New York, September 24, 2013, http://gadebate.un.org/sites/default/files/gastatements/68/BR_en.pdf

125. Cited in Michael D. Shear, "In Pushing for Revised Surveillance Program, Obama Strikes His Own Balance," *New York Times,* June 3, 2015, http://www.nytimes.com/2015/06/04/us/winning-surveillance-limits-obama-makes-program-own.html

126. International Committee of the Red Cross (ICRC), "Geneva Conventions," http://www.icrc.org/eng/war-and-law/treaties-customary-law/geneva-conventions/index.jsp

127. Ingrid Detter, "The Law of War and Illegal Combatants," *The George Washington Law Review* 75:5/6 (August 2007), 1058, 1059–1060. Emphasis in original. For an opposing argument, see René Värk, "The Status and Protection of Unlawful Combatants," *Juridica International* XII (2005), 191–198, http://www.juridicainternational.eu/public/pdf/ji_2005_1_191.pdf

128. Cited in "Hamdi Voices Innocence, Joy about Reunion," CNN.com, October 14, 2004, http://www.cnn.com/2004/WORLD/meast/10/14/hamdi

129. Syllabus, *Hamdan v. Rumsfeld*, http://www.supremecourt.gov/opinions/05pdf/05-184.pdf, 5.

130. Scott Shane, "Report Says 54 Countries Helped C.I.A. after 9/11," *New York Times*, February 4, 2013, http://www.nytimes.com/2013/02/05/us/politics/report-says-54-countries-helped-cia-with-interrogations-after-9 11.html

131. Open Society Justice Initiative, *Globalizing Torture: CIA Secret Detention and Extraordinary Rendition* (New York: Open Society Foundation, 2013), 16.

132. Cited in Dana Priest and Barton Gellman "U.S. Decries Abuse but Defends Interrogations " *Washington Post*, December 26, 2002, http://www.washingtonpost.com/wp-dyn/content/article/2006/06/09/AR2006060901356.html

133. Cited in Dana Priest, "Wrongful Imprisonment: Anatomy of a CIA Mistake," *Washington Post*, December 4, 2005, http://www.washingtonpost.com/wp-dyn/content/article/2005/12/03/AR2005120301476.html

134. Cited in Dana Priest, "CIA Holds Terror Suspects in Secret Prisons," *Washington Post*, November 2, 2005, http://www.washingtonpost.com/wp-dyn/content/article/2005/11/01/AR2005110101644_2.html

135. Barack Obama, "Renewing American Leadership," *Foreign Affairs* 86:4 (July/August 2007), 14.

136. Paul Elias, "Court Sides with CIA on 'Extraordinary Rendition,' Grants President Broad 'State Secrets' Privilege," *Huffington Post*, September 9, 2010, http://www.huffingtonpost.com/2010/09/08/extraordinary-rendition-court-sides-with-cia_n_709911.html

137. Micah Zenko, cited in John Kaag and Sarah Kreps, *Drone Warfare* (New York: Wiley, 2014), 32.

138. Cited in Jo Becker and Scott Shane, "Secret 'Kill List' Proves a Test of Obama's Principles and Will," *New York Times*, May 29, 2012, http://www.nytimes.com/2012/05/29/world/obamas-leadership-in-war-on-al-qaeda.html?pagewanted=all

139. Cited in Mark Mazzetti, Eric Schmitt, and Robert F. Worth, "Two-Year Manhunt Led to Killing of Awlaki in Yemen," *New York Times*, September 30, 2011, http://www.nytimes.com/2011/10/01/world/middleeast/anwar-al-awlaki-is-killed-in-yemen.html?pagewanted=all

140. "Remarks of President Barack Obama," The White House, May 23, 2013, http://www.whitehouse.gov/the-press-office/2013/05/23/remarks-president-barack-obama

141. "Shoe Bomber" Richard Reid tried unsuccessfully to ignite PETN hidden in the hollowed-out bottoms of his shoes to destroy an American Airlines flight from Paris to Miami in 2001.

142. Cited in Sudarsan Raghavan, "Cleric Says He Was Confidant to Hasan," *Washington Post*, November 16, 2009, http://www.washingtonpost.com/wp-dyn/content/article/2009/11/15/AR2009111503160.html

143. Cited in Becker and Shane, "Secret 'Kill List' Proves a Test of Obama's Principles and Will."

144. Cited in Ibid.

145. Cited in Dilanian, "Al Qaeda in the Arabian Peninsula at Center of U.S. Cross Hairs."

146. "Memorandum for Alberto R. Gonzales Counsel to the President," August 1, 2002, http://www.justice.gov/sites/default/files/olc/legacy/2010/08/05/memo-gonzales-aug2002.pdf

147. Seymour M. Hersh, "The Gray Zone," *The New Yorker*, May 24, 2004, http://www.newyorker.com/archive/2004/05/24/040524fa_fact

148. George W. Bush, *Decision Points* (New York: Crown Publishers, 2010), 169–171.

149. Cited in "Senate Ignores Veto Threat in Limiting Detainee Treatment," CNN.com, October 6, 2005, http://www.cnn.com/2005/POLITICS/10/06/senate.detainees/

150. White House, "Executive Order 13491—Ensuring Lawful Interrogations," January 22, 2009, http://www.whitehouse.gov/the_press_office/EnsuringLawfulInterrogations

151. Ibid.

152. Jeremy Ashkenas, Hannah Fairfield, Josh Keller, and Paul Volpe, "7 Key Points from the C.I.A. Torture Report," *New York Times,* December 9, 2014, http://www.nytimes.com/interactive/2014/12/09/world/cia-torture-report-key-points.html

153. Cited in Carl Hulse, "For Dianne Feinstein, Torture Report's Release Is a Signal Moment," *New York Times*, December 9, 2014, http://www.nytimes.com/2014/12/10/us/politics/for-dianne-feinstein-cia-torture-reports-release-is-a-signal-moment.html

154. Cited in James Risen, "Outside Psychologists Shielded U.S. Torture Program, Report Finds," *New York Times,* July 10, 2015, http://www.nytimes.com/2015/07/11/us/psychologists-shielded-us-torture-program-report-finds.html

155. "Un-American by Any Name," *New York Times*, June 5, 2005, http://www.nytimes.com/2005/06/05/opinion/05sun1.html

156. Jimmy Carter, "A Cruel and Unusual Record," *New York Times*, June 24, 2012, http://www.nytimes.com/2012/06/25/opinion/americas-shameful-human-rights-record.html

157. Cited in Helene Cooper, "Obama Nears Goal for Guantánamo with Faster Pace of Releases," *New York Times,* January 5, 2015, http://www.nytimes.com/2015/01/06/us/obama-nears-goal-for-guantanamo-with-faster-pace-of-releases.html

158. "Text: Obama's Speech in Cairo," *New York Times*, June 4, 2009, http://www.nytimes.com/2009/06/04/us/politics/04obama.text.html?pagewanted=all

159. Cited in Warren Richey, "Guantánamo: Judge Rejects U.S. Bid to Limit Lawyers' Access to Detainees," *Christian Science Monitor*, September 6, 2012, http://www.csmonitor.com/USA/Justice/2012/0906/Guantanamo-Judge-rejects-US-bid-to-limit-lawyers-access-to-detainees

160. Charlie Savage, "Obama's Plan for Guantánamo Is Seen Faltering," *New York Times,* July 21, 2015, http://www.nytimes.com/2015/07/22/us/politics/obamas-plan-for-guantanamo-is-seen-faltering.html

161. Cited in Andrew Taylor, "Senate Votes to Block Funds for Guantánamo Closure," *The Guardian*, May 20, 2009, http://www.guardian.co.uk/world/feedarticle/8517772

162. Cited in ibid.

163. Barack Obama, "Statement on Signing the Ike Skelton National Defense Authorization Act for Fiscal Year 2011," January 7, 2011. Available online by Gerhard Peters and John T. Woolley, *The American Presidency Project*, http://www.presidency.ucsb.edu/ws/?pid=88886

164. Barack Obama, "Statement on Signing the National Defense Authorization Act for Fiscal Year 2012," December 31, 2011. Available online by Gerhard Peters and John T. Woolley, *The American Presidency Project*, http://www.presidency.ucsb.edu/ws/?pid=98513

165. Cited in "Enough to Make You Gag," *The Economist*, May 4, 2013, 12.

166. Camila Domonske, "With Latest Transfers, Guantanamo Now Holds Fewer Than 100 Detainees," NPR, January 14, 2016, http://www.npr.org/sections/thetwo-way/2016/01/14/463031323/with-latest-transfers-guantanamo-now-holds-fewer-than-100-detainees

CHAPTER 8

1. "Remarks of President Barack Obama," The White House, May 23, 2013, https://www .whitehouse.gov/the-press-office/2013/05/23/ remarks-president-barack-obama

2. Scott Wilson and Jon Cohen, "Poll Finds Broad Support for Obama's Counterterrorism Policies," *Washington Post,* February 8, 2012, http:// articles.washingtonpost.com/2012-02-08/ politics/35445649_1_drone-program-support-for-drone-strikes-drone-policy

3. Cited in Peter Baker, "In Terror Shift, Obama Took a Long Path," *New York Times,* May 27, 2013, http:// www.nytimes.com/2013/05/28/us/politics/in-terror-shift-obama-took-a-long-path.html?pagewanted=all

4. Cited in Ibid.

5. Jack Goldsmith, "Obama Passes the Buck," *Foreign Affairs,* May 23, 2013, http://www .foreignaffairs.com/articles/139403/jack-goldsmith/ obama-passes-the-buck

6. Cited in David S. Joachim, "Obama to Meet Congressional Leaders over Iraq," *New York Times,* June 18, 2014, http://www.nytimes .com/2014/06/19/world/middleeast/obama-Iraq.html

7. David Remnick, "Going the Distance," *The New Yorker,* January 27, 2014, http://www .newyorker.com/magazine/2014/01/27/going-the-distance-david-remnick. For an analysis of why ISIS was underestimated, see Ian Fisher, "In Rise of ISIS, No Single Missed Key but Many Strands to Blame," *New York Times,* November 18, 2015, http://www .nytimes.com/2015/11/19/world/middleeast/in-rise-of-isis-no-single-missed-key-but-many-strands-of-blame.html

8. Cited in Peter Baker, "Obama Finds He Can't Put Iraq War Behind Him," *New York Times,* June 13, 2014, http://www.nytimes .com/2014/06/14/world/middleeast/obama-finds-he-cant-put-iraq-behind-him.html

9. Cited in Peter Baker, "Obama Defends Progress against Extremists," *New York Times,* December 16, 2014, http://www.nytimes.com/2014/12/16/us/ politics/obama-says-coalition-forces-have-halted-islamic-state-momentum.html

10. Cited in Anne Barnard, "Lessons of the Past Hint at Hurdles in Fight to Stop ISIS," *New York Times,* December 8, 2015, http://www.nytimes .com/2015/12/09/world/middleeast/lessons-of-the-past-hint-at-hurdles-in-fight-to-stop-isis.html

11. Cited in Rukmini Callimachi, "U.S. Strategy Seeks to Avoid Ground War Welcomed by Islamic State," *New York Times,* December 7, 2015, http://www .nytimes.com/2015/12/08/world/middleeast/us-strategy-seeks-to-avoid-isis-prophecy.html

12. Cited in Julie Hirschfeld Davis and Jonathan Weisman, "Bipartisan Support, with Caveats, for Obama on Iraq Airstrikes," *New York Times,* August 8, 2014, http://www.nytimes.com/2014/08/09/us/ politics/bipartisan-support-with-caveats-for-obama-on-iraq-airstrikes.html

13. See Jeffrey Mankoff, "A Syrian Sleight of Hand," *Foreign Affairs,* October 13, 2015, https://www. foreignaffairs.com/articles/syria/2015-10-13/syrian-sleight-hand

14. Cited in Steven Erlanger and Peter Baker, "For France, an Alliance against ISIS May Be Easier Said Than Done," *New York Times,* November 18, 2015, http://www.nytimes.com/2015/11/10/world/europe/ for-france-an-alliance-against-isis-may-be-easier-said-than-done.html

15. Cited in Ben Hubbard, "ISIS Wave of Might Is Turning into Ripple," *New York Times,* November 5, 2014, http://www.nytimes.com/2014/11/06/world/ middleeast/isis-wave-of-might-is-turning-into-ripple.html

16. Daniel Byman and Jeremy Shapiro, "Homeward Bound?" *Foreign Affairs,* September 30, 2014, http://www.foreignaffairs.com/articles/142025/ daniel-byman-and-jeremy-shapiro/homeward-bound

17. Jytte Klausen, "They're Coming," *Foreign Affairs,* October 1, 2014, http://www .foreignaffairs.com/articles/142129/jytte-klausen/ theyre-coming

18. Byman and Shapiro, "Homeward Bound?"

19. Cited in Peter Baker and Eric Schmitt, "California Attack Has U.S. Rethinking Strategy on Homegrown Terror," *New York Times,* December 5, 2015, http://www.nytimes.com/2015/12/06/us/

politics/california-attack-has-us-rethinking-strategy-on-homegrown-terror.html

20. U.S. Department of State, "Iraq Travel Warning," August 10, 2014, http://travel.state.gov/content/passports/english/alertswarnings/iraq-travel-warning.html

21. U.S. Department of State, "Syria Travel Warning," May 5, 2014, http://travel.state.gov/content/passports/english/alertswarnings/syria-travel-warning.html

22. Cited in Gregory S. McNeal, "Americans Fighting for ISIS Could Face Array of Criminal Charges," *Forbes*, June 13, 2014, http://www.forbes.com/sites/gregorymcneal/2014/06/13/americans-fighting-for-isis-could-face-array-of-criminal-charges

23. Cited in Eric Schmitt and Michael S. Schmidt, "West Struggles to Halt Flow of Citizens to War Zones," *New York Times*, January 13, 2015, http://www.nytimes.com/2015/01/13/world/west-struggles-against-flow-to-war-zones.html

24. Marya Hannun, "How Countries Are Keeping Their Citizens from Fighting in Syria," *Foreign Policy*, April 24, 2013, http://blog.foreignpolicy.com/posts/2013/04/24/how_countries_are_keeping_their_citizens_from_fighting_in_syria

25. Klausen, "They're Coming."

26. Peter Bergen, *Holy War, Inc.: Inside the Secret World of Osama bin Laden* (London, UK: Phoenix, 2002), 38.

27. Cited in Alan Cowell, "Qaeda Leader Urges Muslims to Boycott and Attack U.S.," *New York Times*, September 13, 2013, http://www.nytimes.com/2013/09/14/world/al-qaeda-leader-ayman-al-zawahiri-urges-muslims-to-attack-america.html

28. Jared Cohen, "Digital Counterinsurgency," *Foreign Affairs* 94:6 (November/December 2015), 52, 55.

29. Nicole Perlroth and Mike Isaac, "Terrorists Mock Bids to End Use of Social Media," *New York Times*, December 7, 2015, http://www.nytimes.com/2015/12/08/technology/terrorists-mock-bids-to-end-use-of-social-media.html

30. Cohen, "Digital Counterinsurgency," 55.

31. Cited in Scott Shane, Matt Apuzzo, and Eric Schmitt, "Americans Attracted to ISIS Find an 'Echo Chamber' on Social Media," *New York Times*, December 8, 2015, http://www.nytimes.com/2015/12/09/us/americans-attracted-to-isis-find-an-echo-chamber-on-social-media.html?hp&action=click&pgtype=Homepage&clickSource=story-heading&module=first-column-region&region=top-news&WT.nav=top-news

32. Cited in Eric Schmitt, "A U.S. Reply, in English, to Terrorists' Online Lure," *New York Times*, December 4, 2013, http://www.nytimes.com/2013/12/05/world/middleeast/us-aims-to-blunt-terrorist-recruiting-of-english-speakers.html

33. Cited in Brian Knowlton, "Digital War Takes Shape on Websites over ISIS," *New York Times*, September 26, 2014, http://www.nytimes.com/2014/09/27/world/middleeast/us-vividly-rebuts-isis-propaganda-on-arab-social-media.html

34. Cited in Mark Mazzetti and Scott Shane, "Threats Test Obama's Balancing Act on Surveillance," *New York Times*, August 9, 2013, http://www.nytimes.com/2013/08/10/us/threats-test-obamas-balancing-act-on-surveillance.html?pagewanted=all

35. Joseph S. Nye Jr., *Soft Power: The Means to Success in World Politics* (New York: PublicAffairs, 2004), x.

36. For research that runs counter to this claim, at least in Yemen, see Christopher Swift, "The Drone Blowback Fallacy," *Foreign Affairs*, July 1, 2012, http://www.foreignaffairs.com/articles/137760/christopher-swift/the-drone-blowback-fallacy

37. Cited in Baker, "In Terror Shift, Obama Took a Long Path."

38. "Obama's Speech on Drone Policy," *New York Times*, May 23, 2013, http://www.nytimes.com/2013/05/24/us/politics/transcript-of-obamas-speech-on-drone-policy.html

39. Cited in Mark Mazzetti and Mark Landler, "Despite Administration Promises, Few Signs of Change in Drone Wars," *New York Times*, August 2, 2013, http://www.nytimes.com/2013/08/03/us/politics/drone-war-rages-on-even-as-administration-talks-about-ending-it.html?pagewanted=all

40. Cited in ibid.

41. "Pakistan Says Drone Strikes Killed 67 Civilians since 2008," *Al Jazeera America*, October 31, 2013,

http://america.aljazeera.com/articles/2013/10/31/pakistan-report-saysonly3percentofdronedeathiswerecivilians.html

42. "Global Terrorism Deaths Nearly Doubled in 2014—U.S. State Dept.," Reuters, June 19, 2015, https://www.rt.com/usa/268399-global-terrorism-attacks-deaths/

43. Institute for Economics and Peace, *Global Terrorism Index 2014*, http://www.visionofhumanity.org/sites/default/files/Global%20Terrorism%20Index%20Report%202014_0.pdf, 2.

44. Cited in Mark Landler, "Obama Warns U.S. Faces Diffuse Terrorism Threats," *New York Times*, May 28, 2014, http://www.nytimes.com/2014/05/29/us/politics/obama-foreign-policy-west-point-speech.html

45. "Transcript of Obama's Remarks on the Fight against ISIS," *New York Times*, September 10, 2014, http://www.nytimes.com/2014/09/11/world/middleeast/obamas-remarks-on-the-fight-against-isis.html

46. "Jihadism: Tracking a Month of Deadly Attacks," BBC News, December 10, 2014, http://www.bbc.com/news/world-30080914

CHAPTER 9

1. Cited in Sheera Frenkel, "Israel Worries about Netanyahu's Pro-Romney Stand Now That Obama's Won," *McClatchy DC*, November 7, 2012, http://www.mcclatchydc.com/2012/11/07/174023/israel-worries-about-netanyahus.html

2. Cited in Jodi Rudoren, "Netanyahu Rushes to Repair Damage with Obama," *New York Times*, November 7, 2012, http://www.nytimes.com/2012/11/08/world/middleeast/netanyahu-rushes-to-repair-damage-with-obama.html

3. Cited in ibid.

4. Cited in Isabel Kershner, "Netanyahu Issues Veiled Barb in Response to Reported Criticism from Obama," *New York Times*, January 16, 2013, http://www.nytimes.com/2013/01/17/world/middleeast/netanyahu-issues-veiled-response-to-criticism-from-obama.html

5. Cited in Julie Hirschfeld Davis, "Obama Says He Told Netanyahu That Talk Before Election Hurt

the Peace Process," *New York Times*, March 21, 2015, http://www.nytimes.com/2015/03/22/world/middleeast/obama-says-he-told-netanyahu-that-campaign-talk-hurt-the-peace-process.html

6. Modern History Sourcebook, "The Balfour Declaration," http://www.fordham.edu/halsall/mod/balfour.asp

7. Max Rodenbeck, "Midnight at the Oasis," *New York Times*, January 28, 2007, http://www.nytimes.com/2007/01/28/books/review/Rodenbeck.t.html

8. "Our Mission," AIPAC, http://www.aipac.org/about-aipac/our-mission

9. "How We Work," AIPAC, http://www.aipac.org/en/about-aipac/how-we-work

10. Cited in Jodi Rudoren and Isabel Kershner, "Lobbying Group for Israel to Press Congress on Syria," *New York Times*, September 9, 2013, http://www.nytimes.com/2013/09/10/world/middleeast/lobbying-group-for-israel-to-press-congress-on-syria.html

11. Cited in Julie Hirschfeld David, "Fears of Lasting Rift as Obama Battles Pro-Israel Group on Iran," *New York Times*, August 7, 2015, http://www.nytimes.com/2015/08/00/world/middleeast/fears-of-lasting-rift-as-obama-battles-pro-israel-group-on-iran.html

12. Walter Russell Mead, "Jerusalem Syndrome: Decoding the Israel Lobby," *Foreign Affairs* 86:6 (November/December 2007), 163.

13. Cited in David D. Kirkpatrick, "For Evangelicals, Supporting Israel Is 'God's Foreign Policy,'" *New York Times*, November 14, 2006, http://www.nytimes.com/2006/11/14/washington/14israel.html?pagewanted=all

14. Pew Research Center, "Evangelical Support for Israel," April 0, 2011, http://www.pewresearch.org/daily-number/evangelical-support-for-israel/

15. Cited in Laurie Goodstein, "Presbyterians Vote to Divest Holdings to Pressure Israel," *New York Times*, June 20, 2014, http://www.nytimes.com/2014/06/21/us/presbyterians-debating-israeli-occupation-vote-to-divest-holdings.html

16. Cited in Steven Erlanger, "With Gaza War, Movement to Boycott Israel Gains Momentum in Europe, *New York Times*, August 28, 2014, http://www.nytimes.com/2014/08/29/world/europe/with-gaza-war-

movement-to-boycott-israel-gains-momentum-in-europe.html

17. William B. Quandt, *Peace Process: American Diplomacy and the Arab–Israeli Conflict since 1967* (Washington, DC, and Berkeley, CA: The Brookings Institute and the University of California Press, 2005), 1. Emphasis in original.

18. United Nations Security Council, Resolution 242 (November 1967), http://unispal.un.org/unispal .nsf/0/7D35E1F729DF491C85256EE700686136

CHAPTER 10

1. Cited in "1977: Egyptian Leader's Israel Trip Makes History," BBC News, n.d., http://news.bbc. co.uk/onthisday/hi/dates/stories/november/19/ newsid_2520000/2520467.stm

2. Michael B. Oren, *Power, Faith, and Fantasy: America and the Middle East* (New York: Norton, 2008), 570.

3. Cited in ibid.

4. Cited in William Safire, *Lend Me Your Ears: Great Speeches in History* (New York: W. W. Norton, 2004), 171, 172.

5. See Jodi Rudoren, "What the Oslo Accords Accomplished," *New York Times,* September 30, 2015, http://www.nytimes.com/2015/10/01/world/ middleeast/palestinians-mahmoud-abbas-oslo-peace-accords.html

6. Israel Ministry of Foreign Affairs, "The Israel–Palestinian Interim Agreement," September 28, 2005, http://www.mfa.gov.il/MFA/Peace+Process/ Guide+to+the+Peace+Process/THE+ISRAELI-PALESTINIAN+INTERIM+AGREEMENT.htm

7. Ibid.

8. Baylis Thomas, *The Dark Side of Zionism: Israel's Quest for Security through Dominance* (Lanham, MD: Lexington Books, 2011), 137.

9. The Jewish Peace Lobby, "The Clinton Parameters," n.d., http://www.peacelobby.org/ clinton_parameters.htm

10. Cited in Joel Greenberg, "Unapologetic, Sharon Rejects Blame for Igniting Violence," *New York Times,* October 5, 2000, http://www.nytimes .com/2000/10/05/world/unapologetic-sharon-rejects-blame-for-igniting-violence.html

11. International Court of Justice, "Legal Consequences of the Construction of a Wall in the Occupied Palestinian Territory," July 9, 2004, http://www.icj-cij.org/docket/index .php?pr=71&p1=3&p2=1&case=131&p3=6

12. Sharon suffered a stroke in 2006 and was replaced as prime minister by Ehud Olmert, heading a coalition led by the newly established centrist Kadima Party.

13. OPT: Geneva Initiative—Draft Permanent Status Agreement, October 12, 2003, http://reliefweb.int/ report/israel/opt-geneva-initiative-draft-permanent-status-agreement

14. "The Covenant of the Islamic Resistance Movement," August 18, 1988, The Avalon Project, Yale Law School, http://avalon.law .yale.edu/20th_century/hamas.asp

15. Cited in "Miserable and Weak Again," *The Economist,* November 16, 2013, 53, http:// www.economist.com/news/middle-east-and-africa/21589927-palestinians-coastal-enclave-abandoned-once-more-every-way-miserable

16. Cited in Jodi Rudoren and Ben Hubbard, "Despite Gains, Hamas Sees a Fight for Its Existence and Presses Ahead," *New York Times,* July 27, 2014, http://www.nytimes.com/2014/07/28/world/ middleeast/despite-gains-hamas-sees-a-fight-for-its-existence-and-presses-ahead.html

17. Barak Mendelsohn, "The Near Enemy," *Foreign Affairs*, July 14, 2014, http://www .foreignaffairs.com/articles/141633/barak-mendelsohn/the-near-enemy

18. Cited in David D. Kirkpatrick, "Arab Leaders, Viewing Hamas as Worse Than Israel, Stay Silent," *New York Times,* July 30, 2014, http:// www.nytimes.com/2014/07/31/world/middleeast/ fighting-political-islam-arab-states-find-themselves-allied-with-israel.html

19. Cited in Kareem Fahim, "Palestinians Find Show of Support Lacking from Arab Leaders amid Offensive," *New York Times,* July 19, 2014, http://www.nytimes. com/2014/07/20/world/middleeast/palestinians-find-show-of-support-lacking-from-arab-nations-amid-offensive.html?_r=0

20. Cited in Jodi Rudoren, "Cease-Fire Extended, but Not on Hamas's Terms," *New York Times,* August 26, 2014, http://www.nytimes.com/2014/08/27/world/middleeast/israel-gaza-strip-conflict.html

21. Cited in Mark Landler, "Gaza War Strains Relations between U.S. and Israel," *New York Times,* August 4, 2014, http://www.nytimes.com/2014/08/05/world/middleeast/gaza-is-straining-us-ties-to-israel.html

22. Cited in Jay Solomon, "U.S. Moves against Hezbollah 'Cartel,'" *Wall Street Journal,* April 23, 2013, http://online.wsj.com/article/SB10001424127887323735604578441251544900808.html

23. Cited in Jo Becker, "Beirut Bank Seen as a Hub of Hezbollah's Financing," *New York Times,* December 13, 2011, http://www.nytimes.com/2011/12/14/world/middleeast/beirut-bank-seen-as-a-hub-of-hezbollahs-financing.html?pagewanted=all

24. Human Rights Watch, "Why They Died" 19:5(E), September 2007, 4, http://www.hrw.org/sites/default/files/reports/lebanon0907.pdf

25. Cited in Jodi Rudoren, "To a Philosopher-General in Israel, Peace Is the Time to Prepare for War," *New York Times,* November 15, 2013, http://www.nytimes.com/2013/11/16/world/middleeast/to-a-philosopher-general-in-israel-peace-is-the-time-to-prepare-for-war.html

26. Cited in Jodi Rudoren, "U.S. Backing of Russian Plan Leaves a Wary Israel Focusing on Self-Reliance," *New York Times,* September 11, 2013, http://www.nytimes.com/2013/09/12/world/middleeast/us-backing-of-russian-plan-leaves-a-wary-israel-focusing-on-self-reliance.html

27. Cited in Scott Lasensky, "Underwriting Peace in the Middle East: U.S. Foreign Policy and the Limits of Economic Inducements," *Middle East Review of International Affairs (MERIA)* 6; 1 (March 2002), 5, http://www.gloria center.org/2002/03/lasensky-2002-03-07

28. Pew Research Global Attitudes Project, "Despite Their Wide Differences, Many Israelis and Palestinians Want Bigger Role for Obama in Resolving Conflict," May 9, 2013, http://www.pewglobal.org/2013/05/09/despite-their-wide-differences-many-israelis-and-palestinians-want-bigger-role-for-obama-in-resolving-conflict

29. Cited in Jodi Rudoren, "Tension Builds in Israeli Coalition at a Critical Junction in Peace Talks," *New York Times,* January 29, 2014, http://www.nytimes.com/2014/01/30/world/middleeast/israel.html

30. Cited in Michael R. Gordon and Jodi Rudoren, "Kerry Achieves Deal to Revive Mideast Talks," *New York Times,* July 19, 2013, http://www.nytimes.com/2013/07/20/world/middleeast/kerry-extends-stay-in-mideast-to-push-for-talks.html?pagewanted=all

31. Cited in Michael R. Gordon and Isabel Kershner, "Israel and Palestinians Set to Resume Peace Talks, U.S. Announces," *New York Times,* July 28, 2013, http://www.nytimes.com/2013/07/29/world/middleeast/israel-agrees-to-prisoner-release-clearing-way-for-talks.html

32. Cited in Jodi Rudoren, "Israeli Decree on West Bank Settlements Will Harm Peace Talks, Palestinians Say," *New York Times,* August 4, 2013, http://www.nytimes.com/2013/08/05/world/middleeast/palestinians-assail-israeli-settlement-decree.html

33. Cited in Isabel Kershner, "Timing of Israeli Housing Plans May Be Part of a Political Calculation," *New York Times,* August 12, 2013, http://www.nytimes.com/2013/08/13/world/middleeast/israel-names-palestinian-prisoners-to-be-released.html.

34. Cited in Yolande Knell, "Reconsidering the Two-State Solution," BBC News, March 21, 2013, http://www.bbc.co.uk/news/world-middle-east-21850739

35. Cited in Jodi Rudoren, "New Apartments Will Complicate Jerusalem Issue," *New York Times,* March 16, 2013, http://www.nytimes.com/2013/03/17/world/middleeast/in-jerusalem-jewish-apartments-in-arab-neighborhoods-complicate-issue.html?pagewanted=all

36. Cited in Michael R. Gordon and Jodi Rudoren, "Kerry Brushes Aside Israeli Official's Reported Criticisms of Peace Effort," *New York Times,* January 14, 2014, http://www.nytimes.com/2014/01/15/world/middleeast/israeli-ministers-reported-comments-deriding-peace-effort-draw-us-rebuke.html

37. Cited in "Netanyahu Says Abbas Must Abandon Unity Deal with Hamas," BBC News, April 24, 2014, http://www.bbc.com/news/world-middle-east-27142594

38. Cited in Jodi Rudoren, "Collapse of Peace Talks Gives Israel an Easy Exit, but Also Carries Risks," *New York Times,* April 25, 2014, http://www.nytimes.com/2014/04/26/world/middleeast/

collapse-of-peace-talks-leaves-israel-in-precarious-position.html?hp

39. Cited in Jodi Rudoren and Isabel Kershner, "Arc of a Failed Deal: How Nine Months of Mideast Talks Ended in Disarray," *New York Times,* April 28, 2014, http://www.nytimes.com/2014/04/29/world/middleeast/arc-of-a-failed-deal-how-nine-months-of-mideast-talks-ended-in-dissarray.html

40. Cited in Isabel Kershner, "Israel Says It Is 'Deeply Disappointed' by Kerry's Remarks on Peace Talks," *New York Times*, April 9, 2014, http://www.nytimes.com/2014/04/10/world/middleeast/middle-east-peace-effort.html

41. Cited in Michael R. Gordon, "Kerry Expresses Regret after Apartheid Remark," *New York Times,* April 28, 2014, http://www.nytimes.com/2014/04/29/world/middleeast/kerry-apologizes-for-remark-that-israel-risks-apartheid.html

42. Cited in ibid.

43. Cited in Nicholas Casey, "As Mideast Hopes Dim, Some Urge Scaling Back of Lofty Goals," *Wall Street Journal,* April 7, 2014, http://www.wsj.com/articles/SB100014240527023048190045794876177074184 6

44. Cited in "Contra Mundum," *The Economist,* May 23, 2015, 39, http://www.economist.com/news/middle-east-and-africa/21651865-israels-new-government-running-out-friends-abroad-contra-mundum

45. Cited in Jodi Rudoren, "Israel 'Troubled' by U.S. Plan to Work with Palestinian Unity Government," *New York Times,* June 3, 2014, http://www.nytimes.com/2014/06/04/world/middleeast/israel-troubled-by-us-plan-to-work-with-palestinian-unity-government.html

46. Cited in Mark Landler, "Hamas Looms over Latest Israel–U.S. Dispute," *New York Times,* June 4, 2014, http://www.nytimes.com/2014/06/05/world/middleeast/hamas-looms-over-latest-israel-us-dispute.html?_r=0

47. Cited in Jodi Rudoren, "Israel Condemns Plan in Washington to Work with New Palestinian Alliance," *New York Times*, June 3, 2014, http://www.nytimes.com/2014/06/04/world/middleeast/israel-troubled-by-us-plan-to-work-with-palestinian-unity-government.html

48. "Managing the Situation or Drifting Towards Disaster," *The Economist*, November 28, 2015, 43–44.

49. Cited in Mark Landler, "A 'Battered' Mideast Envoy Steps Down, but Keeps a Bag Packed," *New York Times*, July 3, 2014, http://www.nytimes.com/2014/07/04/world/middleeast/martin-indyk-mideast-peace-talks.html

50. Cited in Somini Sengupta, "Palestinian Leader Urges U.N. to Back a Deadline to End Israeli Occupation," *New York Times,* September 26, 2014, http://www.nytimes.com/2014/09/27/world/middleeast/un-general-assembly-abbas-israel.html?_r=0

51. Cited in Jodi Rudoren, "Palestinians Set to Seek Redress in a World Court," *New York Times,* December 31, 2014, http://www.nytimes.com/2015/01/01/world/middleeast/palestinians-to-join-international-criminal-court-defying-israeli-us-warnings.html?_r=0

52. Cited in Isabel Kershner, "Israel Warns against Partial Agreement with Iran," *New York Times,* October 15, 2013, http://www.nytimes.com/2013/10/16/world/middleeast/israel-warns-against-partial-agreement-with-iran.htm

53. Cited in "Taking Wing," *The Economist,* August 10, 2013, 44.

54. "Text: Obama's Speech in Cairo," *New York Times,* June 4, 2009, http://www.nytimes.com/2009/06/04/us/politics/04obama.text.html?pagewanted=all

55. Cited in "A Peace Process That Is Going Nowhere," *The Economist*, April 12, 2014, 39.

56. Cited in Peter Baker and Jodi Rudoren, "Obama and Netanyahu: A Story of Slights and Crossed Signals," *New York Times,* November 8, 2015, http://www.nytimes.com/2015/11/09/us/politics/obama-and-netanyahu-a-story-of-slights-and-crossed-signals.html

CHAPTER 11

1. Cited in "The Masochism Tango," *The Economist,* December 15, 2012, 49, http://www.economist.com/news/middle-east-and-africa/21568391-president-barack-obama-would-avoid-entanglement-middle-east-he

2. "Text of Obama's Speech in Israel," *Wall Street Journal*, March 21, 2013, http://blogs.wsj.com/washwire/2013/03/21/text-of-obamas-speech-in-israel

3. Cited in Clyde Haberman, "West Bank Massacre: The Overview; Rabin Urges Palestinians to Put Aside Anger and Talk," *New York Times*, March 1, 1994, http://www.nytimes.com/1994/03/01/world/west-bank-massacre-overview-rabin-urges-palestinians-put-aside-anger-talk.html?pagewanted=all

4. "The Arab Peace Initiative, 2002," http://www.al-bab.com/arab/docs/league/peace02.htm

5. Thomas L. Friedman, "A Wonderful Country," *New York Times*, February 1, 2014, http://www.nytimes.com/2014/02/02/opinion/sunday/friedman-a-wonderful-country.html

6. Cited in Jodi Rudoren, "Palestinian Leader Seeks NATO Forces in Future State," *New York Times*, February 2, 2014, http://www.nytimes.com/2014/02/03/world/middleeast/palestinian-leader-seeks-nato-force-in-future-state.html

7. Cited in "Haniyeh Calls for Formation of Palestinian State on 1967 Lines," *Haaretz*, December 19, 2006, http://www.haaretz.com/news/haniyeh-calls-for-formation-of-palestinian-state-on-1967-lines-1.207641

8. Cited in Jodi Rudoren, "Netanyahu's History on Palestinian Statehood," *New York Times*, March 20, 2015, http://www.nytimes.com/interactive/2015/03/20/world/middleeast/netanyahu-two-state solution.html

9. Cited in Hussein Ibish, "Bibi's First War," *Foreign Affairs*, July 10, 2014, http://www.foreignaffairs.com/articles/141041/hussein-ibish/bibis-first-war

10. Cited in Rudoren, "Netanyahu's History on Palestinian Statehood."

11. Cited in Julie Hirschfeld Davis, "Obama Says He Told Netanyahu That Talk before Election Hurt the Peace Process," *New York Times*, March 21, 2015, http://www.nytimes.com/2015/03/22/world/middleeast/obama-says-he-told-netanyahu-that-campaign-talk-hurt-the-peace-process.html

12. Cited in Jodi Rudoren, "Sticking Point in Peace Talks: Recognition of a Jewish State," *New York Times*, January 1, 2014, http://www.nytimes.com/2014/01/02/world/middleeast/sticking-point-in-peace-talks-recognition-of-a-jewish-state.html

13. Cited In "Could the Peace Dove Fly Again?" *The Economist*, May 11, 2013, 41, http://www.economist.com/news/middle-east-and-africa/21577374-more-flexible-arab-league-trying-bring-wider-array-mediators-together?zid=312&ah=da4ed4425e74339883d473adf5773841

14. Cited in Jodi Rudoren, "Trying to Revive Mideast Peace Talks, Kerry Finds a Conflicted Israel," *New York Times*, June 18, 2013, http://www.nytimes.com/2013/06/18/world/middleeast/trying-to-revive-mideast-peace-talks-kerry-finds-a-conflicted-israel.html?pagewanted=all

15. Cited in ibid.

16. Cited in Arnold Wesker, "My Brother the Quarryman," *The Guardian*, May 28, 2004, http://www.theguardian.com/books/2004/may/29/highereducation.israelandthepalestinians

17. Cited in The Associated Press, "Kerry's 'One State' Comments Cause Consternation in Israel," *New York Times*, December 7, 2015, http://www.nytimes.com/aponline/2015/12/06/world/middleeast/ap-ml-israel-one-state.html

18. "Text of Obama's Speech in Israel," *Wall Street Journal*, March 21, 2013, http://blogs.wsj.com/washwire/2013/03/21/text-of-obamas-speech-in-Israel

19. Cited in Ethan Bronner, "What Mideast Crisis? Israelis Have Moved On," *New York Times*, May 25, 2013, http://www.nytimes.com/2013/05/26/sunday-review/what-mideast-crisis-israelis-have-moved on.html

20. Cited in Jodi Rudoren, "Pushing Peace on the Palestinians," *New York Times*, November 19, 2013, http://www.nytimes.com/2013/11/20/world/middleeast/pushing-peace-on-the-palestinians.html

21. Cited in Jodi Rudoren, "Israeli Move over Housing Poses a Threat to Peace Talks," *New York Times*, November 12, 2013, http://www.nytimes.com/2013/11/13/world/middleeast/netanyahu-halts-some-settlement-plans-but-others-to-proceed.html

22. Cited in ibid.

23. "Text: Obama's Speech in Cairo," *New York Times,* June 4, 2009, http://www.nytimes .com/2009/06/04/us/politics/04obama.text .html?pagewanted=all

24. "Text of Obama's Speech in Israel."

25. "Letter from President Bush to Prime Minister Sharon," The White House, April 14, 2004, http:// georgewbush-whitehouse.archives.gov/news/ releases/2004/04/20040414-3.html

26. Cited in Roger Cohen, "Zero Dark Zero," *New York Times,* February 28, 2013, http://www .nytimes.com/2013/03/01/opinion/global/zero-dark-zero.html

27. Cited in Adiv Sterman, "'Abbas Was Ready to Compromise on Right of Return,'" *Times of Israel,* March 11, 2013, http://www.timesofisrael.com/ abbas-was-willing-to-compromise-on-right-of-return

28. Cited in Harriet Sherwood, "Mahmoud Abbas Outrages Palestinian Refugees by Waiving his Right to Return," The Guardian, November 4, 2012, http:// www.theguardian.com/world/2012/nov/04/mahmoud-abbas-palestinian-territories

29. Jim Zanotti, "U.S. Foreign Aid to the Palestinians," Congressional Research Service, January 18, 2013, http://www.fas.org/sgp/crs/mideast/ RS22967.pdf

30. Cited in Arthur Neslen, "Gaza: A Gas for Blair?" *The Guardian,* July 26, 2007, http://www .theguardian.com/commentisfree/2007/jul/26/ gazaagasforblair

31. See Jihan Abdalla, "Israel Denies Palestinians Equal Water Access," Al-Monitor, April 8, 2013, http:// www.al-monitor.com/pulse/originals/2013/04/ westbank-water-restrictions-israel.html; and Amira Hass, "Two Pipes for Two Peoples: The Politics of Water in the West Bank," *Haaretz,* September 23, 2012, http://www.haaretz.com/news/features/two-pipes-for-two-peoples-the-politics-of-water-in-the-west-bank-1.466250

32. Cited in Jodi Rudoren, "Region Boiling, Israel Takes Up Castle Strategy," *New York Times,* January 18, 2014, http://www.nytimes. com/2014/01/19/world/middleeast/region-boiling-israel-takes-up-castle-strategy.html

33. Natan Sachs, "Why Israel Waits," *Foreign Affairs* 94:6 (November/December 2015), 74.

34. Ariel Ilan Roth, "Why Israel Is So Afraid," *Foreign Affairs*, January 14, 2014, http://www .foreignaffairs.com/articles/140648/ariel-ilan-roth/ why-israel-is-so-afraid

35. Dennis R. Ross, "To Achieve Mideast Peace, Suspend Disbelief," *New York Times,* March 2, 2013, http://www.nytimes.com/ interactive/2013/03/03/opinion/sunday/opinion-israel-palestine-mideast-peace.html

36. "Text of Obama's Speech in Israel."

37. Cited in Michael R. Gordon and Jodi Rudoren, "Kerry, Invoking Mandela, Says Peace in Mideast Is Possible," *New York Times,* December 6, 2013, http://www.nytimes.com/2013/12/07/world/ middleeast/kerry-invoking-mandela-says-peace-in-mideast-is-possible.html

CHAPTER 12

1. Stephen Kinzer, *All the Shah's Men* (Hoboken, NJ: Wiley, 2008), 25.

2. Margaret MacMillan, *Paris, 1919* (London, UK: Macmillan, 2001), 387–388.

3. Andrew Dugan, "Fewer in U.S. Support Iraq Withdrawal Decision Now vs. 2011," *Gallup Politics,* June 25, 2014, http://www .gallup.com/poll/171923/fewer-support-iraq-withdrawal-decision-2011.aspx

4. "Wide Support for Striking ISIS, but Weak Approval for Obama," *Washington Post*–ABC News poll, *Washington Post,* September 9, 2014, http://www .washingtonpost.com/page/2010-2019/ WashingtonPost/2014/09/09/National-Politics/ Polling/release_361.xml

5. Quoted in Jon Meacham, *Destiny and Power: The American Odyssey of George Herbert Walker Bush* (New York: Random House, 2015), cited in Claire Phipps, "'Iron-Ass' Cheney and 'Arrogant' Rumsfeld Damaged America, Says George Bush Sr.," *The Guardian,* November 5, 2015, http://www .theguardian.com/us-news/2015/nov/05/george-bush-senior-iron-ass-cheney-arrogant-rumsfeld-damaged-america

6. Cited in Ronald W. Ferrier, *The History of the British Petroleum Company,* vol. 1 (Cambridge, UK: Cambridge University Press, 1981), 41.

7. Cited in Daniel Yergin, *The Prize: The Epic Quest for Oil, Money, and Power* (New York: Free Press, 2008), 140.

8. John T. McNay, ed., *The Memoirs of Ambassador Henry F. Grady: From the Great War to the Cold War* (Columbia, MO: University of Missouri Press, 2009), 164, 175.

9. Cited in H. Paul Jeffers, *Command of Honor* (London, UK: Penguin Books, 2008), 294.

10. Mark J. Gasiorowski, "The 1953 *Coup D'état* in Iran," *International Journal of Middle East Studies* 19:3 (August 1987), 261, 279.

11. Cited in Dan Merica and Jason Hanna, "In Declassified Document, CIA Acknowledges Role in '53 Iran Coup," CNN, August 19, 2013, http://www.cnn.com/2013/08/19/politics/cia-iran-1953-coup

12. Madeleine K. Albright, "Remarks before the American–Iranian Council," Federation of American Scientists, March 17, 2000, http://www.fas.org/news/iran/2000/000317.htm

13. Roham Alvandi, *Nixon, Kissinger, and the Shah* (New York: Oxford University Press, 2014), 29.

14. Ibid., 50.

15. Laura Secor, "From Shah to Supreme Leader," *Foreign Affairs* (January/February 2014), http://www.foreignaffairs.com/articles/140356/laura-secor/from-shah-to-supreme-leader

16. Cited in Douglas Little, *American Orientalism: The United States and the Middle East since 1945* (Chapel Hill, NC: University of North Carolina Press, 2008), 226.

17. Said Amir Arjomand, "The Causes and Significance of the Iranian Revolution," *State, Culture, and Society* 1:3 (Spring 1985), 44.

18. Cited in William J. Daugherty, "Jimmy Carter and the 1979 Decision to Admit the Shah into the United States," *American Diplomacy*, April 2003, http://www.unc.edu/depts/diplomat/archives_roll/2003_01-03/dauherty_shah/dauherty_shah.html

19. "The Iranian Hostage Crisis, Part II," *Moments in U.S. Diplomatic History* (Arlington, VA: Association for Diplomatic Study and Training, n.d.), http://adst.org/2012/11/the-iran-hostage-crisis-part-ii

20. Kinzer, *All the Shah's Men*, 203.

CHAPTER 13

1. UN Security Council, Resolution 677, November 28, 1990, http://www.un.org/en/ga/search/view_doc.asp?symbol=S/RES/678(1990)

2. George Bush and Brent Scowcroft, *A World Transformed* (New York: Knopf, 1998), 487.

3. U.S. Department of Defense, "Defense Casualty Analysis System," https://www.dmdc.osd.mil/dcas/pages/report_gulf_storm.xhtml (accessed February 3, 2014).

4. Ali A. Allawi, *The Occupation of Iraq: Winning the War, Losing the Peace* (New Haven: Yale University Press, 2007), 63.

5. UN Special Commission (UNSCOM), "Chronology of Main Events," December 1999, http://www.un.org/Depts/unscom/Chronology/chronologyframe.htm

6. UN Security Council, Resolution 1441, November 8, 2002, http://www.un.org/depts/unmovic/documents/1441.pdf

7. Cited in "Iraq War Illegal, Says Annan," BBC News, September 16, 2004, http://news.bbc.co.uk/2/hi/middle_east/3661134.stm

8. Phebe Marr, *The Modern History of Iraq* (Boulder, CO: Westview Press, 2012), 287.

9. Cited in Michael R. Gordon and Eric Schmitt, "Senators Warn Obama before Iraq Leader's Visit," *New York Times*, October 29, 2013, http://www.nytimes.com/2013/10/30/world/middleeast/senators-warn-obama-before-iraq-leaders-visit.html

10. Cited in Michael R. Gordon and Eric Schmitt, "As Security Deteriorates at Home, Iraqi Leader Arrives in U.S. Seeking Aid," *New York Times*, October 31, 2013, http://www.nytimes.com/2013/11/01/world/middleeast/iraqi-leader-on-fighting-terrorism.html

11. Cited in Robert F. Worth, "Redrawn Lines Seen as No Cure in Iraq Conflict," *New York Times*, June 26, 2014, http://www.nytimes.com/2014/06/27/world/middleeast/redrawn-lines-seen-as-no-cure-in-iraq-conflict.html

12. Cited in Alissa J. Rubin and Rod Nordland, "Sunnis and Kurds on Sidelines of Iraqi Leader's Military Plans," *New York Times*, June 16, 2014, http://www.nytimes.com/2014/06/17/world/middleeast/

sunnis-and-kurds-on-sidelines-of-iraq-leaders-military-plans.html

13. "Fragile States Index 2015," Fund for Peace, June 17, 2015, http://fsi.fundforpeace.org

14. Kenneth Katzman, "Iraq: Politics, Governance, and Human Rights," Summary, Congressional Research Service, June 3, 2013, http://www.fas.org/sgp/crs/mideast/RS21968.pdf

15. Cited in Daniel Schorn, "Bush Talks about His Biggest Fear," CBS News, February 11, 2009, http://www.cbsnews.com/2100-500923_162-1980081.html

16. "Transcript of Interview with Vice President Dick Cheney on *Meet the Press*," September 8, 2002, https://www.mtholyoke.edu/acad/intrel/bush/meet.htm

17. "President Bush, Colombia President Uribe Discuss Terrorism," The White House, September 25, 2002, http://www.hsdl.org/?view&did=476019

18. Peter Canellos and Bryan Bender, "Questions Grow over Iraq Links to Qaeda," *Boston Globe,* August 3, 2003, A1.

19. Cited in R. Jeffrey Smith, "Hussein's Prewar Ties to Al-Qaeda Discounted," *Washington Post,* April 6, 2007, http://www.washingtonpost.com/wp-dyn/content/article/2007/04/05/AR2007040502263.html

20. "The 9/11 Commission Report," 334–335, http://www.leadingtowar.com/claims_sources/911%20fullreport.pdf

21. Paul R. Pillar, "Intelligence, Policy, and the War in Iraq," *Foreign Affairs* 85:2 (March/April 2006), 18.

22. Cited in Kim Sengupta, "Occupation Made World Less Safe, Pro-War Institute Says," *The Independent*, May 26, 2004, http://www.independent.co.uk/news/world/middle-east/occupation-made-world-less-safe-prowar-institute-says-6169169.html

23. Cited in Dana Priest, "Iraq New Terror Breeding Ground," *Washington Post,* January 14, 2005, http://www.washingtonpost.com/wp-dyn/articles/A7460-2005Jan13.html

24. Cited in "The Unquenchable Fire," *The Economist,* September 28, 2013, 21.

25. Cited in Michael R. Gordon and Eric Schmitt, "Iran Secretly Sending Drones and Supplies into Iraq, U.S. Officials Say," *New York Times*, June 25, 2014, http://www.nytimes.com/2014/06/26/world/middleeast/iran-iraq.html

26. Cited in Michael R. Gordon, "Kerry Criticizes Iran and Russia for Shipping Arms to Syria," *New York Times,* March 4, 2013, http://www.nytimes.com/2013/03/05/world/middleeast/syria-russia-iran-arms.html

27. Cited in Farnaz Fassihi, "Iran Said to Send Troops to Bolster Syria," *Wall Street Journal,* August 28, 2012, A8.

28. Cited in Michael R. Gordon, Eric Schmitt, and Tim Arango, "Flow of Arms to Syria through Iraq Persists, to U.S. Dismay," *New York Times,* December 1, 2012, http://www.nytimes.com/2012/12/02/world/middleeast/us-is-stumbling-in-effort-to-cut-syria-arms-flow.html

29. Cited in Julian E. Barnes, "Iraq Blames Violence on Civil War Next Door," *Wall Street Journal,* November 1, 2013, A11.

30. Cited in Robert F. Worth, "Yemen, Hailed as Model, Struggles for Stability," *New York Times,* February 18, 2013, http://www.nytimes.com/2013/02/19/world/middleeast/yemen-hailed-as-a-model-struggles-for-stability.html

31. Cited in Neil MacFarquhar, "Yemen Making Strides in Transition to Democracy after Arab Spring," *New York Times,* May 25, 2013, http://www.nytimes.com/2013/05/26/world/asia/yemen-makes-strides-in-transition-to-democracy.html

32. Cited in Rod Nordland and Eric Schmitt, "Experts See Signs of Moderation Despite Houthis' Harsh Slogans," *New York Times,* January 24, 2015, http://www.nytimes.com/2015/01/25/world/middleeast/experts-see-signs-of-moderation-despite-houthis-harsh-slogans.html

33. Cited in Ben Hubbard and Robert F. Worth, "Angry over Syrian War, Saudis Fault U.S. Policy," *New York Times,* October 25, 2013, http://www.nytimes.com/2013/10/26/world/middleeast/saudis-faulting-american-policy-on-middle-east.html

34. Cited in Damien Cave, "Iran Envoy Casts Syria as Part of Wider Conflict," *New York Times,* August 7,

2012, http://www.nytimes.com/2012/08/08/world/middleeast/fighting-grows-more-intense-in-aleppo-syria.html

35. Cited in "Who Is Supplying Weapons to the Warring Sides in Syria?" BBC News, June 14, 2013, http://www.bbc.co.uk/news/world-middle-east-22906965

36. Cited in C. J. Chivers and Eric Schmitt, "Arms Airlift to Syria Rebels Expands, with Aid from C.I.A.," New York Times, March 24, 2013, http://www.nytimes.com/2013/03/25/world/middleeast/arms-airlift-to-syrian-rebels-expands-with-cia-aid.html

37. Cited in Steve Erlanger, "Saudi Prince Criticizes Obama Administration, Citing Indecision in Mideast," New York Times, December 15, 2013, w.nytimes.com/2013/12/16/world/middleeast/saudi-prince-accuses-obama-of-indecision-on-middle-east.html

38. Cited in Michael R. Gordon, "Criticism of United States' Mideast Policy Increasingly Comes from Allies," New York Times, October 23, 2013, http://www.nytimes.com/2013/10/24/world/middleeast/kerry-reassures-Israel-on-iran-but-divisions-remain.html

39. Christopher Davidson, "The Arab Sunset," Foreign Affairs, October 10, 2013, http://www.foreignaffairs.com/articles/140096/christopher-davidson/the-arab-sunset

40. Russell Gold and Daniel Gilbert, "U.S. Rises to No. 1 Energy Producer," Wall Street Journal, October 3, 2013, A1, A8.

41. Cited in "Analysis: Awash in Oil, U.S. Reshapes Mideast Role 40 Years after OPEC Embargo," Reuters, October 17, 2013, http://www.reuters.com/article/2013/10/17/us-usa-energy-geopolitics-analysis-idUSBRE99G14P20131017

42. Mark Thompson, "U.S. to Become Biggest Oil Producer—IEA," CNNMoney, November 12, 2012, http://money.cnn.com/2012/11/12/news/economy/us-oil-production-energy/index.html

43. Cited in Matthew L. Wald, "Shale's Effect on Oil Supply Is Not Expected to Last," New York Times, November 12, 2013, http://www.nytimes.com/2013/11/13/business/energy-environment/shales-effect-on-oil-supply-is-not-expected-to-last.htm

44. Cited in Clifford Krauss, "Texas Refinery Is Saudi Foothold in U.S. Market," New York Times, April 4, 2013, http://www.nytimes.com/2013/04/05/business/texas-refinery-is-saudi-foothold-in-us-market.html

45. William Burr, "A Brief History of U.S.–Iranian Nuclear Negotiations," Bulletin of the Atomic Scientists 65:21 (January 2009), 24–25.

46. Greg Bruno, "Iran's Nuclear Program," Council on Foreign Relations Backgrounder, March 10, 2010, http://www.cfr.org/iran/irans-nuclear-program/p16811

47. Cited in Scott Peterson, "NPT 101: Is Iran Violating the Nuclear Treaty?" Christian Science Monitor, May 4, 2010, http://www.csmonitor.com/World/Middle-East/2010/0504/NPT-101-Is-Iran-violating-the-nuclear-treaty. Emphasis in original.

48. "UN Nuclear Agency IAEA: Iran 'Studying Nuclear Weapons'," BBC News, November 8, 2011, http://www.bbc.co.uk/news/world-middle-east-15643460

49. Cited in Rick Gladstone, "Iran's New President Preaches Tolerance in First UN Appearance," New York Times, September 24, 2013, http://www.nytimes.com/2013/09/25/world/middleeast/irans-new-president-in-first-un-appearance-preaches-tolerance-says-his-country-is-no-threat.html

50. Cited in ibid.

51. Cited in Rick Gladstone and Thomas Erdbrink, "Temporary Deal with Iran Takes Effect," New York Times, January 20, 2014, http://www.nytimes.com/2014/01/21/world/middleeast/iran.html

52. Cited in Tom Cohen, "5 Reasons Diverse Critics Oppose Iran Nuclear Deal," CNN.com, November 25, 2013, http://www.cnn.com/2013/11/25/politics/iran-deal-opponents-5-things/

53. Cited in Holly Yan and Josh Levs, "Iran Nuclear Deal: One Agreement, Wildly Different Reactions," CNN.com, November 24, 2013, http://www.cnn.com/2013/11/24/world/iran-deal-reaction

54. Akbar Ganji, "Who Is Ali Khamenei? The Worldview of Iran's Supreme Leader," Foreign Affairs 92:5 (September/October 2013), 37.

55. David E. Sanger and William J. Broad, "Atomic Labs across the U.S. Race to Stop Iran," New York

Times, April 21, 2015, http://www
.nytimes.com/2015/04/22/us/in-atomic-labs-
across-us-a-race-to-stop-iran.html

56. Cited in Michael R. Gordon and David E. Sanger,
"Iran Agrees to Detailed Nuclear Outline, First Step
toward a Wider Deal," *New York Times,* April 2,
2015, http://www.nytimes.com/2015/04/03/world/
middleeast/iran-nuclear-talks.html

57. Cited in Peter Baker, "A Foreign Policy Gamble by
Obama at a Moment of Truth," *New York Times,*
April 2, 2015, http://www.nytimes.com/2015/04/03/
world/middleeast/a-foreign-policy-gamble-by-
obama-at-a-moment-of-truth.html

58. Cited in ibid.

59. Thomas Erdbrink and David E. Sanger, "Iran's
Supreme Leader Rules out Broad Nuclear
Inspections," *New York Times,* May 20, 2015, http://
www.nytimes.com/2015/05/21/world/middleeast/
iran-nuclear-talks-inspections.html

60. Thomas Erdbrink and David E. Sanger, "Iran's
Supreme Leader, Khamenei, Seems to Pull Back
on Nuclear Talks," *New York Times,* June 23,
2015, http://www.nytimes.com/2015/06/24/world/
middleeast/irans-supreme-leader-stiffens-his-
position-on-nuclear-talks
.html?ref=world

61. "The Iran Nuclear Accord: Making the World a Bit
Safer," *The Economist*, July 18, 2015, http://www
.economist.com/news/briefing/21657820-
imperfect-deal-better-alternatives-making-world-
bit-safer

62. Kelsey Davenport and Daryl G. Kimball, "An
Effective, Verifiable Nuclear Deal with Iran," Arms
Control Association, Iran Nuclear Policy Brief,
http://www.armscontrol.org/files/ACA_Iran_Deal_
fnl4_Updated_July_2015.pdf

63. "P5+1 Nations and Iran Reach Historic Nuclear
Deal," Arms Control Association, July 14, 2015,
http://us10.campaign-archive2.
com/?u=94d82a9d1fc1a60
f0138613f1&id=ba4273f1a0&e=6fc14e143a

64. Peter Van Buren, "It's Not a Nuclear-Armed Iran That
Israel and Saudi Arabia Really Fear," *The Nation*,
July 28, 2015, http://www.thenation.com/article/
its-not-a-nuclear-armed-iran-that-israel-and-saudi-
arabia-really-fear

65. Howard LaFranchi, "Iran Deal: The Ultimate Test
of Obama's 'Hard-Nosed Diplomacy?'" *Christian
Science Monitor,* July 15, 2015, http://www
.csmonitor.com/USA/Foreign-Policy/2015/0715/
Iran-deal-the-ultimate-test-of-Obama-s-hard-
nosed-diplomacy

66. Holly Yan and Josh Levs, "Iran Nuclear Deal: One
Agreement, Wildly Different Reactions," CNN.com,
November 24, 2013, http://www
.cnn.com/2013/11/24/world/iran-deal-reaction

67. Cited in David E. Sanger, "Saudi Arabia Promises to
Match Iran in Nuclear Capability," *New York Times,*
May 13, 2015, http://www.nytimes
.com/2015/05/14/world/middleeast/saudi-arabia-
promises-to-match-iran-in-nuclear-capability.html

68. Cited in Mark Landler, "Israel's U.S. Envoy Shares
Thoughts as He Prepares for a New Chapter," *New
York Times,* July 18, 2013, http://www.nytimes
.com/2013/07/19/world/middleeast/israeli-envoy-
shares-thoughts-as-he-prepares-for-a-new-chapter.
html?pagewanted=all

69. Cited in Jodi Rudoren, "Netanyahu Scoffs at
Iranian Greetings," *New York Times,* September 7,
2013, http://www.nytimes.com/2013/09/08/world/
middleeast/netanyahu-scoffs-at-iranian-greetings
.html

70. Cited in Jodi Rudoren, "Netanyahu Dismisses
Iranian President's Remarks," *New York Times,*
September 20, 2013, http://www.nytimes
.com/2013/09/21/world/middleeast/prime-minister-
netanyahu-on-iranian-president-rouhani.html

71. Cited in Jodi Rudoren, "As the New Iranian Leader
Gets a Warm Reception, Israel Calls for Caution,"
New York Times, September 24, 2013, http://www
.nytimes.com/2013/09/25/world/middleeast/israel-
continues-to-sound-alarm-on-iranian-overture.
html?pagewanted=all

72. Cited in Jodi Rudoren, "Israelis See Ticking
Clock, and Alternate Approaches, on Iran and
Palestinians," *New York Times,* November 25,
2013, http://www.nytimes.com/2013/11/26/world/
middleeast/israelis-see-ticking-clock-and-alternate-
approaches-on-iran-and-palestinians.html

73. Cited in Jodi Rudoren, "Israeli Leaders Denounce
Geneva Accord," *New York Times,* November 24,
2013, http://www.nytimes.com/2013/11/25/world/
middleeast/israeli-leaders-decry-iran-accord.html

74. Cited in "Israel's Netanyahu Says Iran Closer to Nuclear 'Red Line,'" Reuters, July 14, 2013, http://www.reuters.com/article/2013/07/14/us-nuclear-israel-iran-idUSBRE96D08H20130714

75. Cited in David E. Sanger and Jodi Rudoren, "Split on Accord on Iran Strains U.S.–Israel Ties," *New York Times,* November 18, 2013, http://www.nytimes.com/2013/11/19/world/middleeast/split-on-accord-on-iran-strains-us-israel-ties.html

76. "Text of Obama's Speech in Israel," March 21, 2013, http://blogs.wsj.com/washwire/2013/03/21/text-of-obamas-speech-in-israel

77. Cited in Thom Shanker and Isabel Kershner, "Hagel, in Israel, Presses U.S. Agenda on Deterring Iran," *New York Times,* April 21, 2013, http://www.nytimes.com/2013/04/22/world/middleeast/hagel-in-israel-presses-us-agenda-in-iran.html

78. Cited in Mark Landler, "Discussing Iran, Obama and Netanyahu Display Unity," *New York Times,* September 30, 2013, http://www.nytimes.com/2013/10/01/us/politics/tensions-over-iran-seem-to-ebb-between-netanyahu-and-obama.html

79. Cited in Rudoren, "Israeli Leaders Denounce Geneva Accord."

80. Cited in Jodi Rudoren, "On Iran, Netanyahu Can Only Fume," *New York Times,* November 8, 2013, http://www.nytimes.com/2013/11/09/world/middleeast/on-iran-netanyahu-can-only-fume.html

81. Cited in Michael R. Gordon and Isabel Kershner, "In the Wake of Syria Deal, Kerry Emphasizes Iran," *New York Times,* September 15, 2013, http://www.nytimes.com/2013/09/16/world/middleeast/kerry-seeks-allies-support-on-syria-and-1st-stop-is-Israel.html

82. Cited in "Obama Says Iran Nuclear Row 'Larger' Than Syrian Crisis," BBC News, September 15, 2013, http://www.bbc.co.uk/news/world-middle-east-24102723

83. Cited in David E. Sanger, "Quick Turn of Fortunes as Diplomatic Options Open Up with Syria and Iran," *New York Times,* September 19, 2013, http://www.nytimes.com/2013/09/20/us/politics/on-mideast-heads-spin-over-shift-in-diplomacy.html

84. Cited in Gordon and Sanger, "Iran Agrees to Detailed Nuclear Outline, First Step toward a Wider Deal."

85. "The Iran Nuclear Accord: Making the World a Bit Safer," *The Economist,* July 18, 2015, http://www.economist.com/news/briefing/21657820-imperfect-deal-better-alternatives-making-world-bit-safer

86. Ben Caspit, "Netanyahu Rejects U.S. Offer of Military Support: IDF Says Not So Fast," Al-Monitor's Israel Pulse, July 17, 2015, http://www.al-monitor.com/pulse/originals/2015/07/qassem-suleimani-iran-nuclear-agreement-security-package.html

87. Ibid.

CHAPTER 14

1. Cited in Helene Cooper, "Obama Cites Limits of U.S. Role in Libya," *New York Times,* March 28, 2011, http://www.nytimes.com/2011/03/29/world/africa/29proxy.html

2. Sarah Dutton, Jennifer De Pinto, Anthony Salvanto, and Fred Backus, "Do Americans Want to Send Ground Troops to Fight ISIS?" CBS News, February 19, 2015, http://www.cbsnews.com/news/do-americans-want-to-send-ground-troops-to-fight-isis

3. Minxin Pei and Sara Kasper, "Lessons from the Past: The American Record on Nation Building," *Policy Brief* 24, Carnegie Endowment for International Peace, May 2003, http://carnegieendowment.org/files/Policybrief24.pdf

4. Cited in Thomas Erdbrink, "As Sunni Militants Threaten Its Allies in Baghdad, Iran Weighs Options," *New York Times,* June 12, 2014, http://www.nytimes.com/2014/06/13/world/middleeast/as-sunni-militants-threaten-its-allies-in-baghdad-iran-weighs-options.html

5. Cited in David D. Kirkpatrick, "As U.S. and Iran Seek Nuclear Deal, Saudi Arabia Makes Its Own Moves," *New York Times,* March 30, 2015, http://www.nytimes.com/2015/03/31/world/middleeast/saudis-make-own-moves-as-us-and-iran-talk.html

6. Cited in Michael R. Gordon, "Kerry Meets Saudi King to Smooth Relations," *New York Times,* November 4, 2013, http://www.nytimes.com/2013/11/05/world/middleeast/kerry-meets-saudi-king-to-smooth-relations.html

7. "U.S. Imports of Crude Oil and Petroleum Products," U.S. Energy Information Administration, http://www.eia.gov/dnav/pet/hist/LeafHandler.ashx?n=PET&s=MTTIMUS1&f=M

8. See Summer Said and Benoit Faucon, "Saudi Prince Warns of Shale-Oil Threat," *Wall Street Journal,* July 30, 2013, A6.

9. Cited in Brad Plummer, "China Is Using Up Oil Faster Than We Can Produce It," *Washington Post,* April 29, 2013, http://www.washingtonpost.com/blogs/wonkblog/wp/2013/04/29/china-is-using-oil-faster-than-we-can-produce-it

10. "How Much Petroleum Does the United States Import and from Where?" U.S. Energy Information Administration, September 14, 2015, http://www.eia.gov/tools/faqs/faq.cfm?id=727&t=6 (accessed September 21, 2015).

11. Cited in Rick Gladstone and Thomas Erdbrink, "Tensions in Iran after Nuclear Deal Grow in Hostility," *New York Times,* November 15, 2015, http://www.nytimes.com/2015/11/16/world/middleeast/tensions-in-iran-after-nuclear-deal-grow-in-hostility.html

12. Cited in David E. Sanger and Nicole Perlroth, "Iranian Hackers Attack State Dept. via Social Media Accounts," *New York Times,* November 24, 2015, http://www.nytimes.com/2015/11/25/world/middleeast/iran-hackers-cyberespionage-state-department-social-media.html

13. Kenneth Waltz, "Why Iran Should Get the Bomb," *Foreign Affairs* 91:4 (July/August 2012), http://www.foreignaffairs.com/articles/137731/kenneth-n-waltz/why-iran-should-get-the-bomb

14. Michael Mandelbaum, "How to Prevent an Iranian Bomb," *Foreign Affairs* 94:6 (November/December 2015), 22, 23.

15. Cyrus Amir-Mokri and Hamid Biglari, "A Windfall for Iran?" *Foreign Affairs,* 94:6 (November/December 2015), 25–32.

16. Cited in David E. Sanger, "For Netanyahu and Obama, Difference Over Iran Widened into Chasm," *New York Times,* March 3, 2015, http://www.nytimes.com/2015/03/04/us/politics/obama-netanyahu-iran-dispute.html

17. Cited in Jodi Rudoren, "Israel and Others in Mideast View Overtures of U.S. and Iran with Suspicion," *New York Times,* September 29, 2013, http://www.nytimes.com/2013/09/29/world/middleeast/israel-and-others-in-mideast-view-overtures-of-us-and-iran-with-suspicion.html?pagewanted=all

18. Cited in Jay Solomon and Carol E. Lee, "Strains with Israel over Iran Snarl U.S. Goals in Mideast," *Wall Street Journal,* November 18, 2013, A11.

19. Thomas L. Friedman, "What about US?" *New York Times,* November 12, 2013, http://www.nytimes.com/2013/11/13/opinion/friedman-what-about-us.html

20. Cited in Jodi Rudoren, "Netanyahu Dismisses Iranian President's Remarks," *New York Times,* September 20, 2013, http://www.nytimes.com/2013/09/21/world/middleeast/prime-minister-netanyahu-on-iranian-president-rouhani.html

21. Cited in Thomas L. Friedman, "Obama Makes His Case on Iran Nuclear Deal," *New York Times,* July 14, 2015, http://www.nytimes.com/2015/07/15/opinion/thomas-friedman-obama-makes-his-case-on-iran-nuclear-deal.html

22. Ibid.

23. Cited in Barak Ravid, *Haaretz,* March 5, 2012, http://www.haaretz.com/print-edition/news/pm-welcomes-obama-s-recognition-of-israel-s-right-to-defend-itself-by-itself-1.416486

24. Cited in Adam Entous and Julian E. Barnes, "Pentagon Bulks Up 'Bunker Buster' Bomb to Combat Iran," *Wall Street Journal,* May 2, 2013, http://online.wsj.com/article/SB10001424127887324582004578459170138890756.html/

25. Trita Parsi, "Pushing Peace," *Foreign Affairs,* October 1, 2013, http://www.foreignaffairs.com/articles/139981/trita-parsi/pushing-peace

CHAPTER 15

1. See Ilan Goldenberg and Melissa G. Dalton, "Bridging the Gulf," *Foreign Affairs* 94:6 (November/December 2015), 59–66.

2. See Kareem Fahim, "As Conflicts Flare Up, Leaders Fan Sectarian Flames in Middle East," *New York Times,* October 17, 2015, http://www.nytimes.com/2015/10/18/world/middleeast/as-conflicts-flare-up-leaders-fan-sectarian-flames-in-middle-east.html

3. Warren G. Harding, "Return to Normalcy," May 14, 1920, TeachingAmericanHistory.org, http://teachingamericanhistory.org/library/document/return-to-normalcy

4. "X" (George F. Kennan), "The Sources of Soviet Conduct," *Foreign Affairs* 25:4 (July 1947), http://www.foreignaffairs.com/articles/23331/x/the-sources-of-soviet-conduct

5. Robert Kagan, "Superpowers Don't Get to Retire," *New Republic,* May 26, 2014, 11, http://www.newrepublic.com/article/117859/allure-normalcy-what-america-still-owes-world

6. G. John Ikenberry, "The Illusion of Geopolitics," *Foreign Affairs* 93:3 (May/June 2014), 84, 89.

7. Robert Kagan, *The World America Made* (New York: Vintage Books, 2012).

8. William C. Martel, "America's Grand Strategy Disaster," *The National Interest,* June 9, 2014, http://commentators.com/americas-grand-strategy-disaster-the-national-interest

9. Randall L. Schweller, "The Age of Entropy," *Foreign Affairs,* June 16, 2014, http://www.foreignaffairs.com/articles/141568/randall-l-schweller/the-age-of-entropy

10. Kagan, "Superpowers Don't Get to Retire," 21.

11. John Mueller, "Iraq Syndrome Redux," *Foreign Affairs,* June 18, 2014, http://www.foreignaffairs.com/articles/141578/john-mueller/iraq-syndrome-redux

12. Kagan, "Superpowers Don't Get to Retire," 26.

13. Steven Simon and Jonathan Stevenson, "The End of Pax Americana," *Foreign Affairs* 94:6 (November/December 2015), 2.

14. Ibid.

15. Michael Mandelbaum, "How to Prevent an Iranian Bomb," *Foreign Affairs* 94:6 (November/December 2015), 20.

16. Cited in Robert Kagan, "The September 12 Paradigm," *Foreign Affairs* 87:5 (September/October 2008), 29.

17. Ibid., 30, 36.

18. Ali Khedery, "Iraq in Pieces," *Foreign Affairs* 94:6 (November/December 2015), 33.

19. Ibid., 39.

20. Cited in "The War on Terror, Part Two," *The Economist,* May 31, 2014, 23.

21. Cited in ibid.

22. Cited in Peter Baker, "Rebutting Critics, Obama Seeks Higher Bar for Military Action," *New York Times,* May 28, 2014, http://www.nytimes.com/2014/05/29/us/politics/rebutting-critics-obama-seeks-higher-bar-for-military-action.html

23. Cited in ibid.

24. Daniel Byman, "Beyond Counterterrorism," *Foreign Affairs* 94:6 (November/December 2015), 17.

25. Cited in Michael R. Gordon, "U.S. Begins Military Talks with Russia on Syria," *New York Times,* September 18, 2015, http://www.nytimes.com/2015/09/19/world/europe/us-to-begin-military-talks-with-russia-on-syria.html

26. Cited in Peter Baker, "Crises Cascade and Converge, Testing Obama," *New York Times,* July 22, 2014, http://www.nytimes.com/2014/07/23/world/crises-cascade-and-converge-testing-obama.html

27. Cited in Thomas L. Friedman, "Obama on the World," *New York Times,* August 8, 2014, http://www.nytimes.com/2014/08/09/opinion/president-obama-thomas-l-friedman-iraq-and-world-affairs.html

28. Cited in Mark Landler, "A Rift in Worldviews Is Exposed as Clinton Faults Obama on Policy," *New York Times,* August 11, 2014, http://www.nytimes.com/2014/08/12/world/middleeast/attacking-obama-policy-hillary-clinton-exposes-different-worldviews.html

29. "In Russia's Defeat He Trusts," *The Economist,* November 20, 2015, 23. See also James Fallows, "Obama the Analyst," *The Atlantic,* December 6, 2015, http://www.theatlantic.com/politics/archive/2015/12/obama-the-analyst/419049/

30. Richard N. Haass, "The Unraveling," *Foreign Affairs* 93:6 (November/December 2014), 70.

31. Simon and Stevenson, "The End of Pax Americana," 9.

32. "Remarks by the President at the Acceptance of the Nobel Peace Prize," The White House, December 10, 2009, http://www.whitehouse

.gov/the-press-office/remarks-president-acceptance-nobel-peace-prize

33. Cited in Mark Landler, "Ending Asia Trip, Obama Defends His Foreign Policy," *New York Times,* April 28, 2014, http://www.nytimes.com/2014/04/29/world/obama-defends-foreign-policy-against-critics.html

34. Cited in David E. Sanger, "Global Crises Put Obama's Strategy of Caution to the Test," *New York Times,* March 16, 2014, http://www.nytimes

.com/2014/03/17/world/obamas-policy-is-put-to-the-test-as-crises-challenge-caution.html

35. Kagan, *The World America Made,* 94.

36. Cited in Peter Baker, "As World Boils, Fingers Point Obama's Way," *New York Times,* August 15, 2014, http://www.nytimes.com/2014/08/16/world/middleeast/as-world-boils-fingers-point-obamas-way.html

37. Haass, "The Unraveling," 73–74.

Index

About the Authors

Richard W. Mansbach (BA Swarthmore College, DPhil Oxford University) is a former Marshall Scholar and three-time Fulbright Scholar. He has authored, coauthored, or edited seventeen books and numerous articles and book chapters largely concerning theory in global politics and foreign policy. His scholarship has extended our understanding of global politics beyond the traditional notion of territorial states interacting in an anarchic system to encompass a wide variety of actors complexly related across a variety of issues. Increasingly, his work has moved from the dominant role of "states" in international relations theory to encompass a changing cast of actors in a globalizing world and toward the concept of "identity" and the role of psychological, as opposed to geographic, distance in determining loyalties and behavior. His scholarship focuses on the critical role of history and norms in understanding change and continuity in global politics and in the movement from pre-international to international, and ultimately, post-international politics in a globalizing world. Among his books, several are routinely used in major graduate programs, notably: *The Web of World Politics; In Search of Theory: Toward a New Paradigm for Global Politics; The Elusive Quest: Theory and International Politics; Polities: Authority, Identities, and Change; The Elusive Quest Continues: Theory and Global Politics; Remapping Global Politics;* and *Globalization: The Return of Borders to a Borderless World?* In addition, Professor Mansbach was the coeditor of the field's flagship journal *International Studies.* He has also served as department chair at Rutgers University (New Brunswick) and at Iowa State University. He is coauthor, with Kirsten L. Taylor, of *Contemporary American Foreign Policy: Influences, Challenges, and Opportunities.*

Kirsten L. Taylor (BA University of Pittsburgh, PhD McGill University) is associate professor and department chair of government and international studies at Berry College, a private liberal arts college in Northwest Georgia. Her scholarship focuses on the development and transformation of international institutions and norms, with particular emphases on security and environmental institutions. She also has published pedagogical scholarship focusing on teaching with simulations. Her articles have appeared in *International Studies Perspectives, Canadian Journal of Political Science,* and *Comparative Strategy.* Professor Taylor also is coauthor of a textbook, *Introduction to Global Politics,* with Richard W. Mansbach. She is coauthor, with Robert W. Mansbach, of *Contemporary American Foreign Policy.*

SAGE was founded in 1965 by Sara Miller McCune to support the dissemination of usable knowledge by publishing innovative and high-quality research and teaching content. Today, we publish over 900 journals, including those of more than 400 learned societies, more than 800 new books per year, and a growing range of library products including archives, data, case studies, reports, and video. SAGE remains majority-owned by our founder, and after Sara's lifetime will become owned by a charitable trust that secures our continued independence.

Los Angeles | London | New Delhi | Singapore | Washington DC | Melbourne

CQ Press, an imprint of SAGE, is the leading publisher of books, periodicals, and electronic products on American government and international affairs. CQ Press consistently ranks among the top commercial publishers in terms of quality, as evidenced by the numerous awards its products have won over the years. CQ Press owes its existence to Nelson Poynter, former publisher of the *St. Petersburg Times,* and his wife Henrietta, with whom he founded *Congressional Quarterly* in 1945. Poynter established CQ with the mission of promoting democracy through education and in 1975 founded the Modern Media Institute, renamed The Poynter Institute for Media Studies after his death. The Poynter Institute (*www.poynter.org*) is a nonprofit organization dedicated to training journalists and media leaders.

In 2008, CQ Press was acquired by SAGE, a leading international publisher of journals, books, and electronic media for academic, educational, and professional markets. Since 1965, SAGE has helped inform and educate a global community of scholars, practitioners, researchers, and students spanning a wide range of subject areas, including business, humanities, social sciences, and science, technology, and medicine. A privately owned corporation, SAGE has offices in Los Angeles, London, New Delhi, and Singapore, in addition to the Washington DC office of CQ Press.